Marina Owners Workshop Manual

by J H Haynes
Member of the Guild of Motoring Writers

and B L Chalmers - Hunt
TEng(CEI), AMIMI, AMIRTE, AMVBRA

Models covered

UK
   All models Marina Mk 1 & 2. 1798 cc

USA
   Austin Marina Sedan & GT Coupe. 1798 cc (110 cu in)

ISBN 0 85696 489 1

HAYNES PUBLISHING GROUP
SPARKFORD YEOVIL SOMERSET BA22 7JJ ENGLAND
distributed in the USA by
HAYNES PUBLICATIONS INC
861 LAWRENCE DRIVE
NEWBURY PARK
CALIFORNIA 91320
USA

Acknowledgements

Thanks are due to the British Leyland Motor Corporation (Austin/Morris Division) for technical information; to Castrol Limited for lubrication details; to Terry Kimpton Esq. and to the Champion Sparking Plug Company Limited for the provision of spark plug photographs. The bodywork repair photographs used in this manual were provided by Lloyds Industries Limited, who supply 'Turtle Wax', Holts 'Dupli-Color' and a range of other Holts products.

About this manual

Its aims

The aim of this manual is to help you get the best value from your vehicle. It can do so in several ways. It can help you decide what work must be done (even should you choose to get it done by a garage), provide information on routine maintenance and servicing, and give a logical course of action and diagnosis when random faults occur. However, it is hoped that you will use the manual to its full purpose by tackling the work yourself. On simpler jobs it may even be quicker than booking the vehicle into a garage, and going there twice, to leave and collect it. Perhaps most important, a lot of money can be saved by avoiding the costs a garage must charge to cover its labour and overheads.

The manual has drawings and descriptions to show the function of the various components so that their layout can be understood. Then the tasks are described and photographed in a step-by-step sequence so that even a novice can do the work.

Its arrangement

The manual is divided into thirteen Chapters. The Chapters are each divided into Sections, numbered with single figures, eg 5; and the Sections into paragraphs (or sub-sections), with decimal numbers following on from the Section they are in, eg 5.1, 5.2, 5.3 etc.

it is freely illustrated, especially in those parts where there is a detailed sequence of operations to be carried out. There are two forms of illustrations: figures and photographs. The figures are numbered in sequence with decimal numbers, according to their position in the Chapter: eg Fig 6.4 is the 4th drawing/illustration in Chapter 6. Photographs are numbered (either individually or in related groups) the same as the Section or sub-section of the text where the operation they show is described.

There is an alphabetical index at the back of the manual as well as a contents list at the front.

References to the 'left' or 'right' of the vehicle are in the sense of a person in the driver's seat facing forwards.

Unless otherwise stated, nuts and bolts are removed by turning anti-clockwise, and tightened by turning clockwise.

Vehicle manufacturers continually make changes to specifications and recommendations, and these when notified are incorporated into our manuals at the earliest opportunity.

Whilst every care is taken to ensure that the information in this manual is correct no liability can be accepted by the authors or publishers for loss, damage or injury caused by any errors in, or omissions from, the information given.

Introduction to the Marina

There are two approaches to building a car. A conventional design can be used, and from it can be expected the reliability and dependability that must come from the thorough development of a well proven layout. The unconventional car should give some startling advantages, but in return some penalties must be accepted. In the British Leyland Motor Corporation the ordinary mass produced cars are made by the Austin-Morris Group. Their unconventional cars such as the Mini, the Maxi, and more recently the Allegro, have transverse engines driving the front wheels, and unusual suspension, such as hydrolastic and hydragas. These cars are renowned for their road holding and the large space inside with small overall dimensions. The conventional car is usually cheaper to build and to repair. Its different layout suits some owners who do not take to the transverse engined ones. The Marina is aimed at this large market. The dealer and agency loyalty in the United Kingdom was built originally when Austin and Morris were separate, and rivals. Whilst the Maxi and Allegro use the Austin agency, on the home market the Marina was launched as a Morris.

In the USA local British Leyland arrangements call for the Marina to be an Austin. So the Morris Marina is the home version, and the Austin the North American one.

The Morris Marina is available with three body styles and two

engines, only the larger of which is dealt with in this manual. There is the four door Saloon, the two door Coupe, and the five door Estate. There is the ordinary 1.8 engine with one carburettor, and the 1.8 TC with twin carburettors. The TC and the Estate have a brake servo, and the super de luxe trim. The ordinary Coupe and Saloon may be had in a de luxe trim.

In late 1975 the Mk 2 version became available in the same body styles as the Mk 1 but with various cosmetic changes.

The Austin Marina is available in the four door and two door bodies. The two door is the Coupe GT. Only one engine is fitted, and this is a version of the 1.8 engine with single carburettor, and all the necessary equipment to meet the emissions regulations of the USA. It has the brake servo.

Either a manual four-speed gearbox, or Borg Warner 35 automatic transmission can be fitted. The engine at the front drives a live rear axle mounted on semi-elliptic leaf springs.

At the front the suspension is by longitudinal torsion bars.

The Marina 1.8 engine is basically the same as that which is used in the MGB.

The Marina is simple and straightforward to work on. All the major components have been in use in earlier models so have long development behind them to give reliability.

Contents

	Page
Acknowledgements	2
About this manual	2
Introduction to the Marina	2
Buying spare parts and vehicle identification numbers	5
Safety first!	6
Routine maintenance	7
Recommended lubricants and fluids	10
Tools and working facilities	11
Chapter 1 Engine	13
Chapter 2 Cooling system	55
Chapter 3 Fuel system and carburation	61
Chapter 4 Ignition system	75
Chapter 5 Clutch	84
Chapter 6 Gearbox and automatic transmission	91
Chapter 7 Propeller shaft	113
Chapter 8 Rear axle	117
Chapter 9 Braking system	125
Chapter 10 Electrical system	137
Chapter 11 Suspension and steering	155
Chapter 12 Bodywork and underframe	173
Chapter 13 Supplement: Revisions and information on later models	188
Fault Diagnosis	254
Use of English	258
Conversion factors	259
Index	260

Morris Marina TC Coupe

Morris Marina TC Saloon

Morris Marina Estate

Buying spare parts
and vehicle identification numbers

Buying spare parts

Spare parts are available from many sources, for example: Leyland garages, other garages and accessory shops, and motor factors. Our advice regarding spare parts is as follows:

Officially appointed Leyland garages - This is the best source of parts which are peculiar to your car and are otherwise not generally available (eg complete cylinder heads, internal gearbox components, badges, interior trim etc). It is also the only place at which you should buy parts if your car is still under warranty; non-Leyland components may invalidate the warranty. To be sure of obtaining the correct parts it will always be necessary to give the storeman your car's engine and chassis number, and if possible to take the old part along for positive identification. Remember that many parts are available on a factory exchange scheme - any parts returned should always be clean! It obviously makes good sense to go to the specialists on your car for this type of part for they are best equipped to supply you.

Other garages and accessory shops - These are often very good places to buy material and components needed for the maintenance of your car (eg oil filters, spark plugs, bulbs, fan belts, oils and greases, touch-up paint, filler paste etc). They also sell general accessories, usually have convenient opening hours, charge lower prices and can often be found not far from home.

Motor factors - Good factors will stock all of the more important components which wear out relatively quickly (eg clutch components, pistons, valves, exhaust systems, brake cylinders/pipes/hoses/seals/shoes and pads etc). Motor factors will often provide new or reconditioned components on a part exchange basis - this can save a considerable amount of money.

Vehicle identification numbers

The *car and body numbers* are located on two plates fixed to the left-hand bonnet lock platform.

The *engine number* is affixed to the cylinder block on its right-hand side.

The *gearbox number* is stamped on the right-hand side.

The *rear axle number* is stamped on the outside face of the differential casing joint flange.

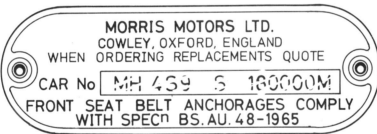

H.10441

Car number analysis
A typical Marina 1.8 car number could be MH2S9T 103101

Prefix number			
	MH 2S 9–10	.... 1.8	2 door Coupe
	MH 4S 9–10	.... 1.8	4 door Saloon
	MH 2S 9T–10	.... 1.8	TC 2 door Coupe
	MH 4S 9T–10	.... 1.8	TC 4 door Saloon
	MH 5W9–10	.... 1.8	Estate

M — Morris. H — 'B' series engine. 2S/4S — 2 or 4 door
9 — Model series 10 .... — serial number

M — BLMC internal reference suffix

Engine number 18V ....10..... 1.8 'B' series engine

(Analysis of the engine number is much more complex because of the options available. Check with a BLMC parts list for clarification).
The engine cylinder block should have '1800' embossed on it.

Safety First!

Professional motor mechanics are trained in safe working procedures. However enthusiastic you may be about getting on with the job in hand, do take the time to ensure that your safety is not put at risk. A moment's lack of attention can result in an accident, as can failure to observe certain elementary precautions.

There will always be new ways of having accidents, and the following points do not pretend to be a comprehensive list of all dangers; they are intended rather to make you aware of the risks and to encourage a safety-conscious approach to all work you carry out on your vehicle.

Essential DOs and DONTs

DON'T rely on a single jack when working underneath the vehicle. Always use reliable additional means of support, such as axle stands, securely placed under a part of the vehicle that you know will not give way.

DON'T attempt to loosen or tighten high-torque nuts (e.g. wheel hub nuts) while the vehicle is on a jack; it may be pulled off.

DON'T start the engine without first ascertaining that the transmission is in neutral (or 'Park' where applicable) and the parking brake applied.

DON'T suddenly remove the filler cap from a hot cooling system — cover it with a cloth and release the pressure gradually first, or you may get scalded by escaping coolant.

DON'T attempt to drain oil until you are sure it has cooled sufficiently to avoid scalding you.

DON'T grasp any part of the engine, exhaust or catalytic converter without first ascertaining that it is sufficiently cool to avoid burning you.

DON'T syphon toxic liquids such as fuel, brake fluid or anti-freeze by mouth, or allow them to remain on your skin.

DON'T inhale brake lining dust — it is injurious to health.

DON'T allow any spilt oil or grease to remain on the floor — wipe it up straight away, before someone slips on it.

DON'T use ill-fitting spanners or other tools which may slip and cause injury.

DON'T attempt to lift a heavy component which may be beyond your capability — get assistance.

DON'T rush to finish a job, or take unverified short cuts.

DON'T allow children or animals in or around an unattended vehicle.

DO wear protection when using power tools such as drill, sander, bench grinder etc, and when working under the vehicle.

DO use a barrier cream on your hands prior to undertaking dirty jobs — it will protect your skin from infection as well as making the dirt easier to remove afterwards; but make sure your hands aren't left slippery.

DO keep loose clothing (cuffs, tie etc) and long hair well out of the way of moving mechanical parts.

DO remove rings, wristwatch etc, before working on the vehicle — especially the electrical system.

DO ensure that any lifting tackle used has a safe working load rating adequate for the job.

DO keep your work area tidy — it is only too easy to fall over articles left lying around.

DO get someone to check periodically that all is well, when working alone on the vehicle.

DO carry out work in a logical sequence and check that everything is correctly assembled and tightened afterwards.

DO remember that your vehicle's safety affects that of yourself and others. If in doubt on any point, get specialist advice.

IF, in spite of following these precautions, you are unfortunate enough to injure yourself, seek medical attention as soon as possible.

Fire

Remember at all times that petrol (gasoline) is highly flammable. Never smoke, or have any kind of naked flame around, when working on the vehicle. But the risk does not end there — a spark caused by an electrical short-circuit, by two metal surfaces contacting each other, or even by static electricity built up in your body under certain conditions, can ignite petrol vapour, which in a confined space is highly explosive.

Always disconnect the battery earth (ground) terminal before working on any part of the fuel system, and never risk spilling fuel on to a hot engine or exhaust.

It is recommended that a fire extinguisher of a type suitable for fuel and electrical fires is kept handy in the garage or work-place at all times. Never try to extinguish a fuel or electrical fire with water.

Fumes

Certain fumes are highly toxic and can quickly cause unconsciousness and even death if inhaled to any extent. Petrol (gasoline) vapour comes into this category, as do the vapours from certain solvents such as trichloroethylene. Any draining or pouring of such volatile fluids should be done in a well ventilated area.

When using cleaning fluids and solvents, read the instructions carefully. Never use materials from unmarked containers — they may give off poisonous vapours.

Never run the engine of a motor vehicle in an enclosed space such as a garage. Exhaust fumes contain carbon monoxide which is extremely poisonous; if you need to run the engine, always do so in the open air or at least have the rear of the vehicle outside the workplace.

If you are fortunate enough to have the use of an inspection pit, never drain or pour petrol, and never run the engine, while the vehicle is standing over it; the fumes, being heavier than air, will concentrate in the pit with possible lethal results.

The battery

Never cause a spark, or allow a naked light, near the vehicle's battery. It will normally be giving off a certain amount of hydrogen gas, which is highly explosive.

Always disconnect the battery earth (ground) terminal before working on the fuel or electrical systems.

If possible, loosen the filler plugs or cover when charging the battery from an external source. Do not charge at an excessive rate or the battery may burst.

Take care when topping up and when carrying the battery. The acid electrolyte, even when diluted, is very corrosive and should not be allowed to contact the eyes or skin.

If you ever need to prepare electrolyte yourself, always add the acid slowly to the water, and never the other way round. Protect against splashes by wearing rubber gloves and goggles.

Mains electricity

When using an electric power tool, inspection light etc which works from the mains, always ensure that the appliance is correctly connected to its plug and that, where necessary, it is properly earthed (grounded). Do not use such appliances in damp conditions and, again, beware of creating a spark or applying excessive heat in the vicinity of fuel or fuel vapour.

Ignition HT voltage

A severe electric shock can result from touching certain parts of the ignition system, such as the HT leads, when the engine is running or being cranked, particularly if components are damp or the insulation is defective. Where an electronic ignition system is fitted, the HT voltage is much higher and could prove fatal.

Routine maintenance

Maintenance should be regarded as essential for ensuring safety and desirable for the purpose of obtaining economy and performance from the car. By far the largest element of the maintenance routine is visual examination.

The maintenance instructions listed are those recommended by the manufacturer. They are supplemented by additional maintenance tasks which, from practical experience, need to be carried out.

The additional tasks are indicated by an asterisk and are primarily of a preventative nature — they will assist in eliminating the unexpected failure of a component.

Weekly, before a long journey, or every 250 miles (400 km)

1 Remove the dipstick and check the engine oil level which should be up to the 'MAX' mark. Top up the oil in the sump with Castrol GTX. On no account allow the oil to fall below the 'MIN' mark on the dipstick. The distance between the 'MAX' and 'MIN' marks corresponds to the approximately 1.5 pints (0.85 litre).

2 Check the battery electrolyte level and top up as necessary with distilled water. Make sure that the top of the battery is always kept clean and free of moisture. See Chapter 10.

3 Inspect the level of water in the translucent plastic reservoir. This should be maintained at the required level mark by adding soft water, such as rain water, via the cap. If the reservoir is empty, remove the radiator filler plug, completely fill the radiator and replace the filler plug. Remove the reservoir screwed cap and half fill the reservoir. Refit the cap. Check for leaks. See Chapter 4.

4 Check the tyre pressure with an accurate gauge and adjust as necessary. Make sure that the tyre walls and treads are free of damage. Remember that the tyre tread should have a minimum of 1 millimetre depth across three quarters of the total width of the tread.

5 Refill the windscreen washer container with soft water. Add an anti-freezing solution satchet in cold weather to prevent freezing (do not use ordinary anti-freeze). Check that the jets operate correctly.

6 Remove the wheel trims and check all wheel nuts for tightness but take care not to overtighten.

Every 6000 miles (10000 km) or 6 months

Complete the service items in the weekly service check as applicable, plus:

1 Run the engine until it is hot and then place a container of 8 pints (4.55 litres) under the engine sump drain plug located on the right hand side at the rear of the sump. Remove the drain plug and its copper sealing washer. Allow the oil to drain out for 10 minutes. Whilst this is being done unscrew the old oil filter cartridge located on the right hand side of the engine and discard. Smear the rubber seal on a new cartridge with a little oil and refit it to the filter head. Screw it on and tighten hand tight only. Clean the oil filler cap in paraffin and wipe dry. Check the drain plug copper sealing washer and if damaged fit a new one. Refit the drain plug and sealing washer. Refill the engine with 6.375 pints (3.8 litres) of Castrol GTX and clean off any oil which may have been spilt over the engine or its components. Run the engine and check the oil level.

The interval between oil changes should be reduced in very hot or dusty conditions or during cool weather with much slow or stop/start driving.

2 Wipe the top of the carburettor suction chamber and unscrew and withdraw the oil cap. Top up the dashpot with fresh Castrol GTX to raise the level to ½ inch (13mm) above the top of the hollow piston rod. Push the damper assembly back into position and screw the cap firmly into position.

3 Check the carburettor adjustment as described in Chapter 3.

4 Carefully examine the cooling and heater systems for signs of leaks. Make sure that all hose clips are tight and that none of the hoses have cracked or perished. Do not attempt to repair a leaking hose, always fit new. Generally inspect the exterior of the engine for signs of water leaks or stains. The method of repair will depend on its location. This check is particularly important before filling the cooling system with anti-freeze as it has a greater searching action than pure water and is bound to find any weak spots.

5 The fan belt adjustment must be tight enough to drive the alternator without overloading the bearings, including the water pump bearings too. The method of adjusting the fan belt is described in Chapter 2. It is correct when it can be pressed in ½ inch (13mm) under moderate hand pressure at the mid point of its longest run from the alternator to the crankshaft pulley.

6 Lubricate the accelerator control linkage cable and pedal fulcrum with a little engine oil.

7 Inspect the steering rack rubber boots for signs of leaking which, if evident, must be rectified as described in Chapter 11.

8 Lubricate the two nipples on each of the front swivel pins with several strokes of the grease gun filled with Castrol LM Grease.

9 Inspect all steering ball joints for signs of wear, leaking rubber boots and securing nuts for tightness. If a ball joint rubber boot has failed the whole assembly should be renewed. See Chapter 11.

10 Check the front wheel alignment. For this special equipment is necessary therefore leave this to the local BLMC garage. See Chapter 11.

H/3312

COOLANT RESERVOIR

1 Pressure cap   2 Reservoir   3 Level mark

11 Wipe the top of the brake and clutch master cylinder and unscrew the caps. Check the level of hydraulic fluid in the reservoirs and top up, if necessary to the marks on the exterior of the reservoir with the recommended fluid. Make sure the cap breather vent is clean and then refit the cap. Take care not to spill any hydraulic fluid on the paintwork as it acts as a solvent.

12 Check the adjustment of the handbrake and footbrake. If travel is excessive refer to Chapter 9 and check the footbrake adjustment and then the handbrake if its travel is still excessive.

13 Refer to Chapter 9 and inspect the brake linings and pads for wear and the front discs and rear drums for scoring.

14 Carefully examine all brake hydraulic pipes and unions for signs of leakage. Check flexible hoses are not in contact with any body or mechanical component when the steering is turned through both locks.

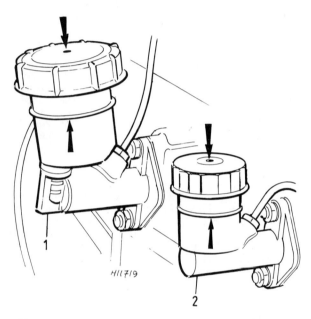

H11719

BRAKE AND CLUTCH MASTER CYLINDER RESERVOIRS

1 Brake master cylinder reservoir

2 Clutch master cylinder reservoir

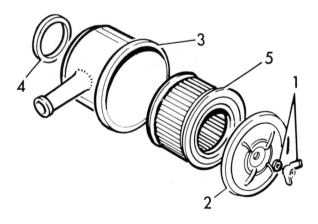

AIR CLEANER COMPONENTS

1 Wing nut and washer   4 Sealing ring
2 Cover   5 Renewable filter element
3 Air cleaner body

15 Lubricate the nipple on the handbrake cable using a grease gun filled with Castrol LM Grease.

16 Lubricate all moving parts of the handbrake system with Castrol GTX.

17 From cars numbered 43892 to 45000 and 48101 and any cars prior to that if fitted with a grease nipple on the propeller shaft front universal joint lubricate the nipple with 3 to 4 strokes of the grease gun filler with Castrol LM Grease.

18 Refer to Chapter 4 and remove the spark plugs. Clean, adjust, if necessary, and replace.

19 Refer to Chapter 4, and clean and adjust the distributor contact breaker points.

20 Spring back the two clips and remove the distributor cap. Lift off the rotor arm. Apply a few drops of thin oil over the screw in the centre of the cam spindle and on the moving contact breaker pivot. Apply a smear of grease to the cam surface. Remove any excess oil or grease with a clean rag. Apply a few drops of oil through the hole in the contact breaker base plate to lubricate the automatic timing control.

21 Refer to Chapter 4, and check the ignition timing. Adjust if necessary.

22 Wipe the area around the gearbox level/filler plug. Unscrew the plug and check the level of oil which should be up to the bottom of the threads. Top up if necessary using Castrol Hypoy and refit the plug. Wipe away any spilled oil.

23 Wipe the area around the rear axle level/filler plug. Unscrew the plug and check the level of oil which should be up to the bottom of the threads. Top up if necessary using Castrol Hypoy and refit the plug. Wipe away any spilled oil.

24 Automatic transmission: With the vehicle standing on level ground, apply the handbrake and move the selector to the 'P' position. Start the engine and allow to run at idle speed for a minimum of 2 minutes. With the engine still running withdraw the dipstick from the filler tube to be found at the rear of the engine compartment. Wipe the dipstick and quickly replace and withdraw the dipstick again. Check the level of oil and top up if necessary with Castrol TQF. Take great care not to overfill.

25 Generally check the operation of all lights and electrical equipment. Renew any blown bulbs with bulbs of the same wattage rating and rectify any electrical equipment fault. See Chapter 10.

26 Check the battery electrolyte specific gravity as described in Chapter 10. Clean the battery terminals and smear them with vaseline (petroleum jelly) to prevent corrosion.

27 Check the alignment of the headlights and adjust if necessary. See Chapter 10.

28 Apply a few drops of engine oil to the dynamo rear bearing (where applicable).

29 Check the condition of the windscreen wiper blades and fit new if the blade end has frayed, softened or perished. They should be renewed every 12 months.

Generally check the exhaust system for signs of leaks. Apply a little Holts Silencer Seal or Gum Gum to small blow holes. If badly corroded the system must be renewed. Check all exhaust mountings for tightness.

Carefully examine all clutch and fuel lines and unions for signs of leakage and flexible hoses for signs of perishing. Check the tightness of all unions and renew any faulty lines or hoses.

Lubricate all door, bonnet and boot lid locks, hinges and controls with Castrol Everyman.

Inspect the seat belts for damage to the webbing. Check that all seat and seat belt mountings are tight.

Make sure that the rear view mirror is firm in its mounting and is not crazed or cracked.

Wash the bodywork and chromium fittings and clean out the interior of the car. Wax polish the bodywork including all chromium and bright metal trim. Force wax polish into any joints in the bodywork to prevent rust formation.

If it is wished change over the tyres to equalise wear.

Balance the wheels to eliminate any vibration especially from the steering. This must be done on specialist equipment.

Lubricate the washer around the wiper spindles with several drops of glycerine.

Every 12,000 miles (20,000 km) or 12 months

Complete the service items in the 6000 mile service check as applicable plus:
1 To fit a new air cleaner element, unscrew the wing nut and lift away the cover, body and element which should be discarded. Wipe out the container and fit a new element. Replace the cover. Make sure that the sealing ring between the air cleaner body and carburettor is not damaged or perished. Refit the air cleaner to the carburettor and secure with the fibre washer and nut. During warm weather position the air cleaner intake away from the exhaust manifold or during cold weather move the air intake colse to the exhaust manifold.
On TC models undo and remove the air manifold securing nuts and bolts, and lift away. Also remove the support securing bolt, spring and plain washers. To gain access to the filter element undo and remove the wing nut and fibre washer. Refitting is the reverse sequence to removal.
2 Remove the oil filler cap and filter assembly on the top of the rocker cover and fit a new one.
3 Refer to Chapter 1, and check the valve rocker clearances. Adjust as necessary.
4 Refer to Chapter 11, and adjust the front wheel bearing end float.
5 Inspect the ignition HT leads for cracks or deterioration. Replace as necessary.
6* Examine the dynamo brushes, replace them if worn and clean the commutator. See Chapter 13.

Every 24,000 miles (40,000 km) or 18 months

Complete the service items in the 6000 and 12,000 mile service check as applicable plus:
1* Examine the hub bearings for wear and replace as necessary. See Chapter 11.
2* Check the tightness of the battery earth lead on the body.
3* Renew the condenser in the distributor. See Chapter 4.
4* Remove the starter motor, examine the brushes and replace as necessary. Clean the commutator and starter drive. See Chapter 10.
5* Test the cylinder compressions, and if necessary remove the cylinder head, decarbonise, grind in the valves and fit new valve springs. See Chapter 1 and Chapter 13.
6 Completely drain the brake hydraulic fluid from the system. All seals and flexible hoses throughout the braking system should be examined and preferably renewed. The working surfaces of the master cylinder, wheel and caliper cylinders should be inspected for signs of wear or scoring and new parts fitted as necessary. Refill the hydraulic system with recommended brake fluid. See Chapter 9.
7 Remove alternator. Clean slip rings. Check bushes. Fit a new drive belt.

Every 36,000 miles (60,000 km) or 3 years

Complete the service items in the 6000 and 12000 mile service as applicable plus:
1 If a brake servo unit is fitted, pull back the filter dust cover and withdraw the end cap. The filter is located in the servo unit housing where the pushrod passes through from the brake pedal. Cut off the old filter element. Cut through the new filter in a diagonal manner to the centre hole and fit it over the pushrod and into the housing. Replace the end cap and dust cover.

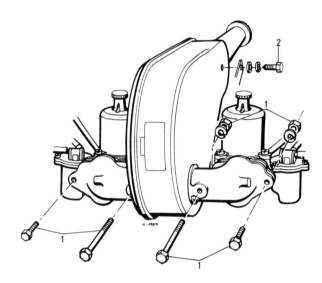

AIR CLEANER ASSEMBLY (TC MODELS ONLY)
1 Air manifold attachments
2 Support securing bolt, spring and plain washer

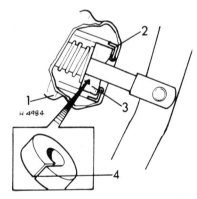

BRAKE SERVO UNIT AIR FILTER

1 Dust cover   3 Filter
2 End cap   4 Position of cut

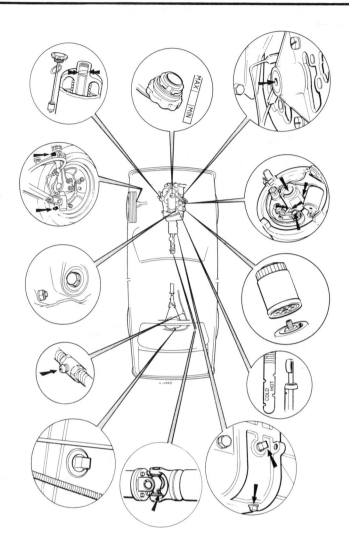

Recommended lubricants and fluids

Component	Lubrication Specification	Castrol product
Engine	Multigrade. To API SE Spec.	**Castrol GTX**
Gearbox (manual)	High quality EP90 gear oil to MIL-L-2105B and API Service GL	**Castrol Hypoy B90**
Automatic transmission	High quality ATF BLMC type F	**Castrol TQF**
Rear axle	High quality EP90 gear oil	**Castrol Hypoy B90**
Grease points	Multi-purpose high melting point lithium based grease	**Castrol LM Grease**
Cooling system	Antifreeze solution complying with BS 3151 or 3152	**Castrol Anti-freeze**
Brake and clutch systems	Hydraulic brake fluid exceeding SAE Spec J1703f	**Castrol Girling Universal Brake and Clutch Fluid**

Note: *The above are general recommendations only. Different operating territories require different lubricants and therefore, if in doubt, consult the driver's handbook or the nearest Leyland dealer.*

Tools and working facilities

Introduction

A selection of good tools is a fundamental requirement for anyone contemplating the maintenance and repair of a motor vehicle. For the owner who does not possess any, their purchase will prove a considerable expense, offsetting some of the savings made by doing-it-yourself. However, provided that the tools purchased are of good quality, they will last for many years and prove an extremely worthwhile investment.

To help the average owner to decide which tools are needed to carry out the various tasks detailed in this manual, we have compiled three lists of tools under the following headings: *Maintenance and minor repair, Repair and overhaul,* and *Special.* The newcomer to practical mechanics should start off with the *Maintenance and minor repair* tool kit and confine himself to the simpler jobs around the vehicle. Then, as his confidence and experience grows, he can undertake more difficult tasks, buying extra tools as, and when, they are needed. In this way, a *Maintenance and minor repair* tool kit can be built-up into a *Repair and overhaul* tool kit over a considerable period of time without any major cash outlays. The experienced do-it-yourselfer will have a tool kit good enough for most repairs and overhaul procedures and will add tools from the *Special* category when he feels the expense is justified by the amount of use these tools will be put to.

It is obviously not possible to cover the subject of tools fully here. For those who wish to learn more about tools and their use there is a book entitled *How to Choose and Use Car Tools* available from the publishers of this manual.

Maintenance and minor repair tool kit

The tools given in this list should be considered as a minimum requirement if routine maintenance, servicing and minor repair operations are to be undertaken. We recommend the purchase of combination spanners (ring one end, open-ended the other); although more expensive than open-ended ones, they do give the advantages of both types of spanner.

> *Combination spanners - 7/16, ½, 9/16, 5/8, ¾, 13/16, 15/16 in AF*
> *Adjustable spanner - 9 inch*
> *Engine sump/gearbox/rear axle drain plug key (where applicable)*
> *Spark plug spanner (with rubber insert)*
> *Spark plug gap adjustment tool*
> *Set of feeler gauges*
> *Brake bleed nipple spanner*
> *Screwdriver - 4 in long x ¼ in dia (flat blade)*
> *Screwdriver - 4 in long x ¼ in dia. (cross blade)*
> *Combination pliers - 6 inch*
> *Hacksaw - junior*
> *Tyre pump*
> *Tyre pressure gauge*
> *Grease gun*
> *Oil can*
> *Fine emery cloth (1 sheet)*
> *Wire brush (small)*
> *Funnel (medium size)*

Repair and overhaul tool kit

These tools are virtually essential for anyone undertaking any major repairs to a motor vehicle, and are additional to those given in the *Maintenance and minor repair* list. Included in this list is a comprehensive set of sockets. Although these are expensive they will be found invaluable as they are so versatile - particularly if various drives are included in the set. We recommend the ½ in square-drive type, as this can be used with most proprietary torque wrenches. If you cannot afford a socket set, even bought piecemeal, then inexpensive tubular box spanners are a useful alternative.

The tools in this list will occasionally need to be supplemented by tools from the *Special* list.

> *Sockets (or box spanners) to cover range in previous list*
> *Reversible ratchet drive (for use with sockets)*
> *Extension piece, 10 inch (for use with sockets)*
> *Universal joint (for use with sockets)*
> *Torque wrench (for use with sockets)*
> *'Mole' wrench - 8 inch*
> *Ball pein hammer*
> *Soft-faced hammer, plastic or rubber*
> *Screwdriver - 6 in long x 5/16 in dia (flat blade)*
> *Screwdriver - 2 in long x 5/16 in square (flat blade)*
> *Screwdriver - 1½ in long x ¼ in dia (cross blade)*
> *Screwdriver - 3 in long x 1/8 in dia (electricians)*
> *Pliers - electricians side cutters*
> *Pliers - needle nosed*
> *Pliers - circlip (internal and external)*
> *Cold chisel - ½ inch*
> *Scriber*
> *Scraper*
> *Centre punch*
> *Pin punch*
> *Hacksaw*
> *Valve grinding tool*
> *Steel rule/straight-edge*
> *Allen keys*
> *Selection of files*
> *Wire brush (large)*
> *Axle stands*
> *Jack (strong scissor or hydraulic type)*

Special tools

The tools in this list are those which are not used regularly, are expensive to buy, or which need to be used in accordance with their manufacturers' instructions. Unless relatively difficult mechanical jobs are undertaken frequently, it will not be economical to buy many of these tools. Where this is the case, you could consider clubbing together with friends (or joining a motorists' club) to make a joint purchase, or borrowing the tools against a deposit from a local garage or tool hire specialist.

The following list contains only those tools and instruments freely available to the public, and not those special tools produced by the vehicle manufacturer specifically for its dealer network. You will find occasional references to these manufacturers' special tools in the text of this manual. Generally, an alternative method of doing the job without the vehicle manufacturer's special tool is given. However, sometimes, there is no alternative to using them. Where this is the case and the relevant tool cannot be bought or borrowed, you will have to entrust the work to a franchised garage.

> *Valve spring compressor*
> *Piston ring compressor*
> *Balljoint separator*
> *Universal hub/bearing puller*
> *Impact screwdriver*
> *Micrometer and/or vernier gauge*
> *Carburettor flow balancing device*
> *Dial gauge*
> *Stroboscopic timing light*
> *Dwell angle meter/tachometer*
> *Universal electrical multi-meter*
> *Cylinder compression gauge*
> *Lifting tackle*
> *Trolley jack*
> *Light with extension lead*

Buying tools

For practically all tools, a tool factor is the best source since he will have a very comprehensive range compared with the average garage or accessory shop. Having said that, accessory shops often offer excellent quality tools at discount prices, so it pays to shop around.

Remember, you don't have to buy the most expensive items on the shelf, but it is always advisable to steer clear of the very cheap tools. There are plenty of good tools around at reasonable prices, so ask the proprietor or manager of the shop for advice before making a purchase.

Care and maintenance of tools

Having purchased a reasonable tool kit, it is necessary to keep the tools in a clean serviceable condition. After use, always wipe off any dirt, grease and metal particles using a clean, dry cloth, before putting the tools away. Never leave them lying around after they have been used. A simple tool rack on the garage or workshop wall, for items such as screwdrivers and pliers, is a good idea. Store all normal spanners and sockets in a metal box. Any measuring instruments, gauges, meters, etc, must be carefully stored where they cannot be damaged or become rusty.

Take a little care when tools are used. Hammer heads inevitably become marked and screwdrivers lose the keen edge on their blades from time-to-time. A little timely attention with emery cloth or a file will soon restore items like this to a good serviceable finish.

Working facilities

Not to be forgotten when discussing tools, is the workshop itself. If anything more than routine maintenance is to be carried out, some form of suitable working area becomes essential.

It is appreciated that many an owner mechanic is forced by circumstances to remove an engine or similar item without the benefit of a garage or workshop. Having done this, any repairs should always be done under the cover of a roof.

Wherever possible, any dismantling should be done on a clean flat workbench or table at a suitable working height.

Any workbench needs a vice: one with a jaw opening of 4 in (100 mm) is suitable for most jobs. As mentioned previously, some clean, dry storage space is also required for tools, as well as the lubricants, cleaning fluids, touch-up paints and so on which become necessary.

Another item which may be required, and which has a much more general usage, is an electric drill with a chuck capacity of at least 5/16 in (8 mm). This, together with a good range of twist drills, is virtually essential for fitting accessories such as wing mirrors and reversing lights.

Last, but not least, always keep a supply of old newspapers and clean, lint-free rags available, and try to keep any working area as clean as possible.

Spanner jaw gap comparison table

Jaw gap (in)	Spanner size
0.250	$\frac{1}{4}$ in AF
0.276	7 mm
0.313	$\frac{5}{16}$ in AF
0.315	8 mm
0.344	$\frac{11}{32}$ in AF; $\frac{1}{8}$ in Whitworth
0.354	9 mm
0.375	$\frac{3}{8}$ in AF
0.394	10 mm
0.433	11 mm
0.438	$\frac{7}{16}$ in AF
0.445	$\frac{3}{16}$ in Whitworth; $\frac{1}{4}$ in BSF
0.472	12 mm
0.500	$\frac{1}{2}$ in AF
0.512	13 mm
0.525	$\frac{1}{4}$ in Whitworth; $\frac{5}{16}$ in BSF
0.551	14 mm
0.563	$\frac{9}{16}$ in AF
0.591	15 mm
0.600	$\frac{5}{16}$ in Whitworth; $\frac{3}{8}$ in BSF
0.625	$\frac{5}{8}$ in AF
0.630	16 mm
0.669	17 mm
0.686	$\frac{11}{16}$ in AF
0.709	18 mm
0.710	$\frac{3}{8}$ in Whitworth, $\frac{7}{16}$ in BSF
0.748	19 mm
0.750	$\frac{3}{4}$ in AF
0.813	$\frac{13}{16}$ in AF
0.820	$\frac{7}{16}$ in Whitworth; $\frac{1}{2}$ in BSF
0.866	22 mm
0.875	$\frac{7}{8}$ in AF
0.920	$\frac{1}{2}$ in Whitworth; $\frac{9}{16}$ in BSF
0.938	$\frac{15}{16}$ in AF
0.945	24 mm
1.000	1 in AF
1.010	$\frac{9}{16}$ in Whitworth; $\frac{5}{8}$ in BSF
1.024	26 mm
1.063	$1\frac{1}{16}$ in AF; 27 mm
1.100	$\frac{5}{8}$ in Whitworth; $\frac{11}{16}$ in BSF
1.125	$1\frac{1}{8}$ in AF
1.181	30 mm
1.200	$\frac{11}{16}$ in Whitworth; $\frac{3}{4}$ in BSF
1.250	$1\frac{1}{4}$ in AF
1.260	32 mm
1.300	$\frac{3}{4}$ in Whitworth; $\frac{7}{8}$ in BSF
1.313	$1\frac{5}{16}$ in AF
1.390	$\frac{13}{16}$ in Whitworth; $\frac{15}{16}$ in BSF
1.417	36 mm
1.438	$1\frac{7}{16}$ in AF
1.480	$\frac{7}{8}$ in Whitworth; 1 in BSF
1.500	$1\frac{1}{2}$ in AF
1.575	40 mm; $\frac{15}{16}$ in Whitworth
1.614	41 mm
1.625	$1\frac{5}{8}$ in AF
1.670	1 in Whitworth; $1\frac{1}{8}$ in BSF
1.688	$1\frac{11}{16}$ in AF
1.811	46 mm
1.813	$1\frac{13}{16}$ in AF
1.860	$1\frac{1}{8}$ in Whitworth; $1\frac{1}{4}$ in BSF
1.875	$1\frac{7}{8}$ in AF
1.969	50 mm

A Haltrac hoist and gantry in use during a typical engine removal sequence

Chapter 1 Engine

For modifications, and information applicable to later models, see Supplement at end of manual

Contents

General description 1
Major operations with engine in place 2
Major operations with engine removed 3
Methods of engine removal... 4
Engine removal with gearbox (from underside).. 5
Engine removal less gearbox 6
Engine removal (through engine compartment).. 7
Separating the engine from the gearbox 8
Dismantling the engine - general 9
Removing ancillary engine components 10
Cylinder head removal - engine in car.. 11
Cylinder head removal - engine on bench 12
Valve removal 13
Valve guide - removal 14
Rocker assembly - dismantling 15
Timing cover, tensioner, gears and chain - removal.. 16
Camshaft - removal 17
Distributor drive - removal 18
Sump, piston, connecting rod and big end bearing - removal ... 19
Gudgeon pin - removal 20
Piston ring - removal... 21
Flywheel and engine backplate - removal 22
Crankshaft and main bearings - removal 23
Lubrication system - description 24
Oil filter - removal and replacement 25
Oil pressure relief valve - removal and replacement.. 26
Oil pump - removal and dismantling 27
Timing chain tensioner - removal and dismantling... 28
Engine - examination and renovation - general 29
Crankshaft - examination and renovation 30
Big end and main bearings - examination and renovation 31
Cylinder bores - examination and renovation 32
Pistons and piston rings - examination and renovation 33

Camshaft and camshaft bearings - examination and renovation 34
Valves and seats - examination and renovation 35
Timing gears and chain - examination and renovation 36
Rockers and rocker shaft - examination and renovation 37
Tappets - examination and renovation 38
Flywheel starter ring gear - examination and renovation 39
Oil pump - examination and renovation 40
Cylinder head and bore - decarbonisation 41
Valve guides - examination and renovation 42
Engine - reassembly - general 43
Crankshaft - replacement 44
Piston and connecting rod - reassembly 45
Piston ring - replacement 46
Piston replacement 47
Connecting rod to crankshaft - reassembly 48
Camshaft - replacement 49
Oil pump and drive shaft - replacement 50
Timing gears, chain tensioner, cover - replacement... 51
Engine backplate - refitting 52
Sump - refitting 53
Oil pressure relief valve and switch - replacement 54
Flywheel and clutch - refitting 55
Water and fuel pump - refitting... 56
Valve and spring - reassembly 57
Rocker shaft - reassembly 58
Tappet replacement 59
Cylinder head - replacement 60
Rocker arm valve - adjustment 61
Distributor and distributor drive - replacement 62
Final assembly... 63
Engine replacement 64
Engine - initial start up after overhaul or major repair 65
Fault diagnosis... 66

Specifications

Manufacturers type number	18V
Number of cylinders...	4
Bore...	3.160 in (80.26 mm)
Stroke	3.5 in (88.9 mm)
Capacity	109.7 in^3 (1798 cm^3)
Firing order	1 3 4 2
Valve operation	Overhead by pushrod
Compression ratio: High (HC)	9.0 : 1
Low (LC)	8.0 : 1 (single carburettor models only)
Cranking pressure: HC	190 lb/in^2 (13.4 kg/cm^2)
LC	170 lb/in^2 (12 kg/cm^2)
Oversize bores	+ 0.010 in (+ 0.254 mm)
	+ 0.020 in (+ 0.508 mm)
	+ 0.030 in (+ 0.762 mm)
	+ 0.040 in (+ 1.016 mm)
Torque HC..	98.5 lb.f.ft at 2000 rpm
LC	95 lb.f.ft at 2000 rpm

Crankshaft

Main journal diameter	2.1265 to 2.127 in (54.01 to 54.02 mm)
Minimum regrind diameter...	2.0865 in (52.997 mm)

Crankpin journal diameter ... ...   1.8759 to 1.8764 in (47.648 to 47.661 mm)
Minimum regrind diameter... ... ...   1.836 in (46.634 mm)
Crankshaft end thrust ... ...   Taken on thrust washers at centre main bearing
Crankshaft endlfoat ... ...   0.002 to 0.003 in (0.051 to 0.076 mm)

Main bearings
Number and type   ... ...   5, thin wall type
Material   ... ...   Steel backed copper - lead or reticular tin
Length: front, centre, rear ... ...   1.125 in (28.5 mm)
        intermediate   ... ...   0.875 in (22.22 mm)
Diametrical clearance ... ...   0.001 to 0.0027 in (0.025 to 0.068 mm)
Undersizes: ... ...   0.010 in (0.254 mm)
        0.020 in (0.508 mm)
        0.030 in (0.762 mm)
        0.040 in (1.016 mm)

Connecting rods
Type   ... ...   Horizontal, split big end
Length between centres... ... ...   6.5 in (165.1 mm)

Big end bearings
Type and material   ... ...   Steel backed copper lead or VP3
Length ... ...   0.775 to 0.785 in (19.68 to 19.94 mm)
Diametrical clearances ... ...   0.0015 to 0.0032 in (0.038 to 0.081 mm)
Endfloat on crankpin (nominal) ... ...   0.008 to 0.012 in (0.20 to 0.30 mm)
Undersizes: ... ...   0.010 (0.254 mm)
        0.020 (0.508 mm)
        0.030 (0.762 mm)
        0.040 (1.016 mm)

Gudgeon pin
Type   ... ...   Pressed in connecting rod
Fit in piston ... ...   Hand push fit at 16°C (60°F)
Outer diameter ... ...   0.8124 to 0.8127 in (20.608 to 20.615 mm)

Pistons
Type   ... ...   Aluminium, solid skirt
Clearance of skirt in cylinder:
        Top ... ...   0.0021 to 0.0037 in (0.0535 to 0.0936 mm)
        Bottom ... ...   0.0018 to 0.0024 in (0.045 to 0.061   mm)
Number of rings ... ...   4 (3 compression, 1 oil control)
Width of ring grooves:
Top and second ... ...   0.064 to 0.065 in (1.625 to 1.65 mm)
Oil control ... ...   1.578 to 1.588 in (40.01 to 40.03 mm)
Gudgeon pin bore ... ...   0.8128 to 0.813 in (20.610 to 20.617 mm)

Piston rings
Compression:
Type: Top ... ...   Plain, sintered alloy
       Second and third.. ... ...   Tapered, sintered alloy
Width: Top, second ... ...   0.0615 to 0.0625 in (1.562 to 1.587 mm)
Fitted gap: Top ... ...   0.012 to 0.017 in (0.304 to 0.431 mm)
Ring to groove clearance:
       Top, second and third ... ...   0.0015 to 0.0035 in (0.038 to 0.088 mm)
Oil control: Type ... ...   Slotted scraper
       Width ... ...   0.1552 to 0.1562 in (3.94 to 3.96 mm)
       Fitted gap.. ... ...   0.015 to 0.045 in (0.381 to 1.147 mm)
       Ring to groove clearance ... ...   0.0016 to 0.0036 in (0.04 to 0.09 mm)

Camshaft
Journal diameters: Front ... ...   1.78875 to 1.78925 in (45.424 to 45.483 mm)
        Centre .. ..   1.72875 to 1.72925 in (43.910 to 43.923 mm)
        Rear ... ...   1.62275 to 1.62325 in (41.218 to 41.230 mm)
Bearing liner inside diameter (finished) :
        Front ... ...   1.79025 to 1.79075 in (45.472 to 45.485 mm)
        Centre .. ..   1.73025 to 1.73075 in (43.948 to 43.961 mm)
        Rear ... ...   1.62425 to 1.62475 in (41.256 to 41.269 mm)
Bearings - type: ... ...   White metal lined, steel backed
Diametrical clearance ... ...   0.001 to 0.002 in (0.0254 to 0.0508 mm)
End thrust... ... ...   Taken on locating plate
Endfloat ... ...   0.003 to 0.007 in (0.076 to 0.178 mm)
Drive ... ...   Chain and sprocket from crankshaft
Timing chain ... ...   0.375 in (9.52 mm) pitches x 52 pitches

Tappets

Type	Bucket with radiused base
Outside diameter...	0.812 in (20.64 mm)
Length	1.495 to 1.505 in (37.977 to 38.227 mm)

Rocker gear

Rocker shaft:	Length	14.032 in (355.6 mm)
	Diameter	0.624 to 0.625 in (15.85 to 15.87 mm)
Rocker arm:		
	Bore	0.7485 to 0.7495 in (19.01 to 19.26 mm)
	Bush internal diameter (finished)..	0.6255 to 0.626 in (15.8 to 15.9 mm)

Valves

Seat angle:	Inlet	45.5°
	Exhaust	45.5°
Head diameter:		
	Inlet	1.625 to 1.630 in (41.27 to 41.40 mm)
	Exhaust	1.343 to 1.348 in (34.11 to 34.23 mm)
Stem diameter:		
	Inlet	0.3422 to 0.3427 in (8.692 to 8.704 mm)
	Exhaust	0.3417 to 0.3422 in (8.66 to 8.692 mm)
Stem to guide clearance:		
	Inlet	0.0015 to 0.0025 in (0.0381 to 0.063 mm)
	Exhaust	0.002 to 0.003 in (0.051 to 0.076 mm)
Valve lift:	Inlet and Exhaust	0.360 in (9.14 mm)

Valve guides

Length:	Inlet	1.875 in (47.63 mm)
	Exhaust	2.203 in (55.95 mm)
Outside diameter: Inlet and Exhaust...		0.5635 to 0.5640 in (14.30 to 14.32 mm)
Inside diameter: Inlet and Exhaust		0.3442 to 0.3447 in (8.743 to 8.755 mm)
Fitted height above head:		
	Inlet	0.75 in (19.05 mm)
	Exhaust	0.625 in (15.87 mm)
Interference fit in head:		
	Inlet and Exhaust	0.0005 to 0.00175 in (0.012 to 0.044 mm)

Valve springs

Free length	1.92 in (48.77 mm) approx.
Fitted length	1.44 in (36.58 mm)
Load at fitted length..	82 lb (37 kg)
Load at top of lift	142 lb (64 kg)
Number of working coils	4.5

Valve timing - timing marks ... ... Dimples in camshaft and crankshaft wheels

Rocker clearance:		
	Running (cold)	0.013 in (0.33 mm)
	Timing..	0.020 in (0.51 mm)
Inlet valve:		
	Opens	5° BTDC
	Closes	45° ABDC
Exhaust valve:		
	Opens...	40° BBDC
	Closes...	10° ATDC

Lubrication

System		Wet sump, pressure fed
Pressure:	Running	50 to 70 lb/in^2 (3.5 to 4.9 kg/cm^2)
	Idling	15 to 25 lb/in^2 (1.0 to 1.8 kg/cm^2)
Oil pump		Hobourn - Eaton rotor type
Capacity		3.25 gallons (14.8 litres) per minute at 1000 rpm
Oil filter		Full flow: disposable cartridge type
By-pass valve opens		8 to 12 lb/in^2 (0.56 to 0.84 kg/cm^2)
Oil pressure relief valve		70 lb/in^2 (4.9 kg/cm^2)
Relief valve spring:		
	Free length	3 in (76 mm)
	Fitted length	2.156 in (54.77 mm)
	Load at fitted length	15.5 to 16.5 lb (7.0 to 7.4 kg)
Sump capacity		6.375 pints (3.8 litres)

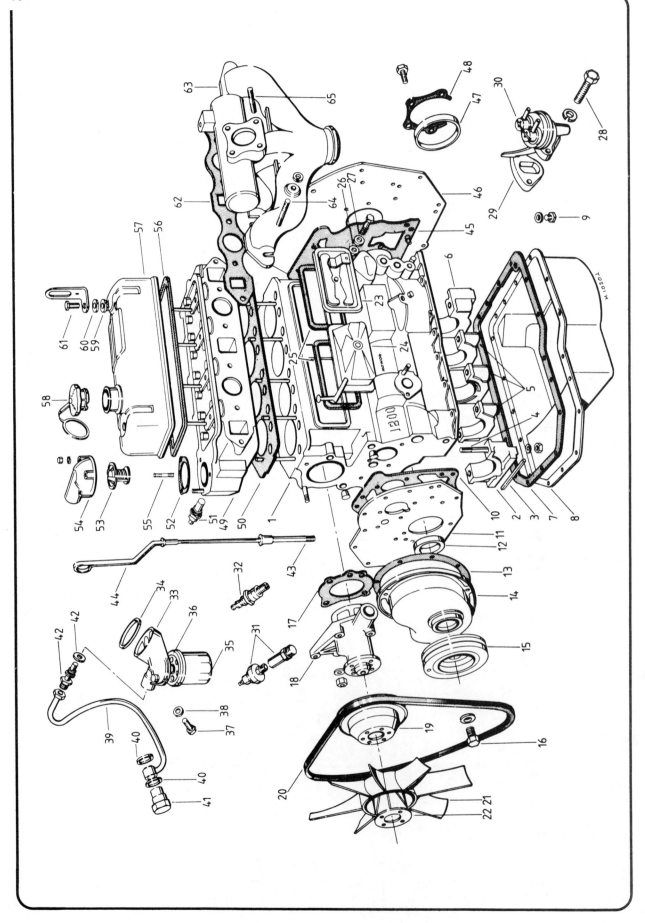

Torque wrench settings

	lb.f.ft	kg.f.m.
Main bearing cap nuts	70	9.7
Big end bearing cap nuts	33	4.6
Gearbox adaptor plate bolts	30	4.15
Crankshaft rear oil seal retainer bolts	25	3.5
Flywheel securing bolts...	40	5.5
Oil pump cover bolts	10	1.38
Oil pump securing bolts	14	1.9
Sump securing bolts...	6	0.8
Cylinder head nuts	45 to 50	6.2 to 6.9
Rocker shaft bracket nuts	25	3.4
Cylinder side cover	3 to 4	0.41 to 0.55
Timing cover — ¼ in bolts	6	0.83
5/16 in bolts	14	1.94
Water pump retaining bolts..	17	2.35
Water outlet elbow	8	1.11
Manifold to cylinder head	15	2.07
Rocker cover fixing bolts	4	0.55
Crankshaft pulley nut	70 to 80	9.68 to 11.06
Camshaft nut	60 to 70	8.30 to 9.68
Distributor clamp bolt	2.5	0.35
Heater outlet adaptor	6 to 8	0.83 to 1.11
Oil release valve dome nut	40 to 45	5.53 to 6.22
Water pump pulley bolts	18	2.49
Thermal transmitter...	16	2.21

FIG.1.1. ENGINE EXTERNAL COMPONENTS

1 Cylinder block
2 Front main bearing cap
3 Cap joint
4 Fixing stud
5 Main bearing caps
6 Rear main bearing cap
7 Sump gasket
8 Sump
9 Sump drain plug
10 Front mounting plate gasket
11 Front mounting plate
12 Oil seal
13 Timing cover gasket
14 Timing cover
15 Crankshaft pulley
16 Pulley bolt
17 Water pump gasket
18 Water pump
19 Pulley
20 Fan belt
21 Fan
22 Lockwasher
23 Cylinder side cover
24 Oil separator
25 Rear cover gaskets
26 Rubber seal
27 Cup washer
28 Petrol pump fixing bolt
29 Distance piece
30 Petrol pump
31 Oil pressure switch
32 Sparking plug
33 Oil filter head (inverted on early models)
34 Oil filter head seal
35 Oil filter cartridge
36 Oil filter cartridge seal
37 Oil filter head bolt
38 Bolt sealing washer
39 Lubrication pipe
40 Sealing washers
41 Banjo bolt
42 Adaptor and seal
43 Dipstick guide tube
44 Dipstick
45 Gasket
46 Engine backplate
47 Oil seal
48 Oil seal retainer
49 Cylinder head
50 Cylinder head gasket
51 Thermal transmitter
52 Thermostat housing gasket
53 Thermostat
54 Water outlet
55 Fixing stud
56 Rocker cover gasket
57 Rocker cover
58 Oil filler cap
59 Rubber seal
60 Cup washer
61 Rocker cover fixing
62 Manifold gasket
63 Manifold
64 Manifold fixing stud
65 Carburettor fixing stud

H.0212

FIG.1.2. ENGINE INTERNAL COMPONENTS

1 Crankshaft
2 Main bearing
3 Thrust washer - upper
4 Thrust washer - lower
5 Main bearing
6 Oil restrictor
7 Key for gear
8 Crankshaft dowel
9 Gear packing washer
10 Timing gear
11 Oil thrower
12 Connecting rod
13 Big end bearing
14 Big end bearing cap
15 Big end bearing cap bolt
16 Big end nuts
17 Gudgeon pin
18 Piston
19 Compression ring - top
20 Compression ring - 2nd
21 Scraper ring
22 Camshaft

23 Camshaft bearing - front
24 Camshaft bearing - centre
25 Camshaft bearing - rear
26 Camshaft locking plate
27 Timing gear
28 Timing gear key
29 Camshaft nut
30 Lock washer
31 Timing chain
32 Slipper head & cylinder
33 Spring
34 Tensioner body,plate & gasket
35 Plug for body
36 Lock washer for plug
37 Lock washer
38 Exhaust valve guide
39 Inlet valve guide
40 Exhaust valve
41 Inlet valve
42 Valve spring collar
43 Valve spring
44 Oil seal

45 Spring cup
46 Valve cotter
47 Valve rocker shaft
48 Plain plug
49 Screwed plug
50 Bracket with tapped hole
51 Plain bracket
52 Spring
53 Valve rocker
54 Bush
55 Adjusting screw
56 Adjusting screw locknut
57 Locking screw
58 Locking plate
59 Spring washer
60 Wahser for rocker shaft
61 Pushrod
62 Tappet
63 Crankshaft spigot bush
64 Flywheel
65 Starter ring
66 Dowel for clutch

67 Lock washer
68 Distributor drive shaft
69 Oil pump body
70 Oil pump cover
71 Oil pump rotors
72 Oil pump gasket
73 Oil pump drive spindle
74 Oil pump strainer
75 Pump cover to body dowel
76 Oil pump cover to strainer screw
77 Oil pump cover screw - short
78 Oil pump cover screw - long
79 Oil pressure relief valve
80 Spring for relief valve
81 Oil pressure relief valve washer
82 Oil pressure cap nut

1 General description

The 1798 cc engine is a four cylinder overhead valve type fitted with either single or twin SU carburettors.

Two valves per cylinder are mounted vertically in the cast iron cylinder head and run in pressed in valve guides. They are operated by rocker arms and pushrods from the camshaft which is located at the base of the cylinder bores in the left hand side of the engine.

The cylinder head has all five inlet and exhaust ports on the left hand side. Cylinders 1 and 2 have a siamised inlet port as have cylinders 3 and 4. Cylinders 1 and 4 have individual exhaust ports and cylinders 2 and 3 share a siamised exhaust port.

The cylinder block and upper half of the crankcase are cast together and a pressed steel oil sump is bolted to the underside. Attached to the rear of the engine backplate is the clutch bell-housing and gearbox.

The dished crown pistons are made from anodised aluminium and they have a solid skirt. Two or three compression and one oil control ring are fitted to each piston depending on type of pistons fitted.

At the front of the engine is a double row chain driving the camshaft via the camshaft and crankshaft sprockets. The chain is tensioned by a spring loaded slipper type tensioner which automatically adjusts for chain stretch. The camshaft is supported by three steel backed white metal bearings. If these are replaced it is necessary to ream the bearings in position.

The overhead valves are operated by means of rocker arms mounted on the rocker shaft running along the top of the cylinder head. The rocker arms are activated by pushrods and tappets which in turn rise and fall in accordance with the lobes on the camshaft. The valves are held closed by single springs.

The static and dynamically balanced forged steel crankshaft is supported by five renewable main bearings. Crankshaft end float is controlled by tour semi-circular thrust washers two of which are located on either side of the centre bearing.

The centrifugal water pump and radiator cooling fan are driven, together with the alternator, from the crankshaft pulley wheel by a rubber/fabric 'fan' belt. The distributor is mounted towards the rear of the right hand side of the cylinder block and advances and retards the ignition timing by mechanical and vacuum means. The distributor is driven at half crankshaft speed by a short shaft and skew gear from a skew gear on the camshaft. The oil pump is mounted inside the crankcase and driven from the camshaft by a short drive spindle.

Attached to the rear of the crankshaft by six bolts and two dowels is the flywheel which carries the diaphragm spring clutch. Mounted on the circumference of the flywheel is the starter ring gear into which the starter motor drive engages when starting the engine.

2 Major operations with engine in place

The following major operations can be carried out to the engine with it in place in the car:
1 Removal and replacement of the cylinder head assembly.
2 Removal and replacement of the sump.
3 Removal and replacement of the big end bearings.
4 Removal and replacement of the pistons and connecting rods.
5 Removal and replacement of the timing chain and gears.
6 Removal and replacement of the camshaft.
7 Removal and replacement of the oil pump.

3 Major operations with engine removed

The following major operations must be carried out with the engine out of the car and on a bench or floor.
1 Removal and replacement of the main bearings.
2 Removal and replacement of the crankshaft.
3 Removal and replacement of the flywheel.

4 Methods of engine removal

The engine can be removed either attached to the gearbox or disconnected from it, by itself. Both methods are described.

It is easier if a hydraulic type trolley jack is used in conjunction with two pairs of axle stands so that the car can be raised sufficiently to allow easy access underneath the car. Overhead lifting tackle will be necessary in both cases.

Because of the weight consideration and the very steep angle to which the engine must be tilted, the do-it-yourself motorist without the use of a pit or ramp should remove the gearbox first. A third method can be used and this is to detach the engine and gearbox from its mountings and lower the unit onto the floor. The front of the car can then be lifted up and the power unit drawn forwards. Using this method (possibly removing the cylinder head as well) can eliminate the need for an overhead hoist and may be of use in a confined space.

Note: Cars fitted with automatic transmission necessitating engine and transmission removal should have the transmission removed first as described in Chapter 6, Section 9, and then followed by the engine. This is because of the size and weight of the transmission.

FIG.1.3. SUMMARY OF ITEMS TO BE DETACHED — ENGINE REMOVAL WITH GEARBOX

1 Carburettor attachments
2 Heater and vacuum hoses
3 Engine mounting nuts, bolts and spring washers
4 Gear change lever
5 Gearbox mounting
6 Speedometer cable
7 Front exhaust pipe mounting
8 Exhaust downpipe to manifold clamp
9 Starter motor cables
10 Electrical leads
11 Air cleaner
12 Propeller shaft flange
13 Nut and bolt
14 Mating marks
15 Fuel pipe connection to pump
16 Clutch pipe bracket
17 Clutch pipe to master cylinder union
18 Heater hose to side of cylinder head
19 Engine lifting bracket

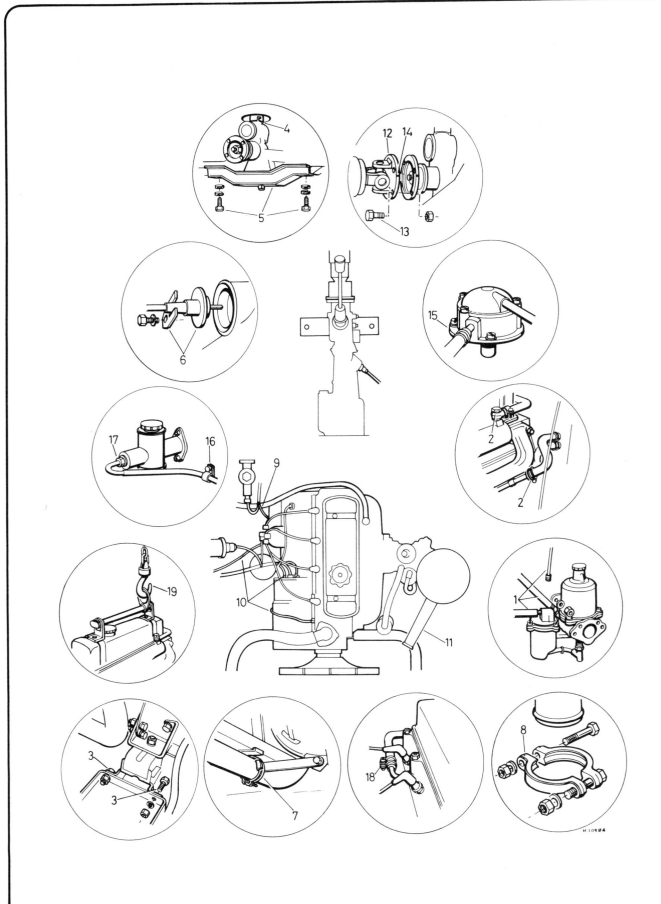

5 Engine removal with gearbox

1 Practical experience has proved that the complete unit can be removed easily in about three hours or less by the following sequence of operations.

2 With the help of an assistant take the weight of the bonnet and undo and remove the four bolts, spring and plain washers (photo). Carefully lift the bonnet up, releasing the prop, and then over the front of the car. Store in a safe place where it will not be scratched (photo).

3 Remove the expansion tank cap and radiator filler plug. Slacken the bottom hose clip and remove the hose from the radiator. Place a container under the hose to catch the coolant especially if anti-freeze is in use (photo).

4 Undo and remove the cylinder block drain plug located towards the rear right hand side of the cylinder block (photo).

5 Disconnect the negative and then the positive battery terminals and tuck the leads to the rear of the battery.

6 Slacken the radiator top hose clip at the thermostat elbow and pull off the hose.

7 Slacken the radiator heater hose at the union to the metal pipe located beneath the exhaust manifold. Pull off the hose (photo). Also remove the hose from the pipe located on the right hand side of the cylinder head.

8 Unwind the expansion tank hose clip at the radiator end and pull off the hose (photo).

9 Slacken the second heater hose clip at the bottom hose and pull off this hose (photo).

10 It will be found easier to work in the engine compartment if the bonnet support is removed. Using a screwdriver ease the clip from the support and unhook the support from its bracket on the front panel (photo).

11 Undo and remove the two bolts, plain and spring washers securing the top radiator supports to the front panel (photo).

12 Undo and remove the two bolts, plain and spring washers that secure the top radiator support brackets to the side panels.

13 Lift away the two top support brackets, carefully detaching the rubber insert from the mounting peg on the radiator.

14 The radiator may now be lifted upwards and away from the car (photo).

15 This photo shows the rubber insert in one of the two lower radiator mounting brackets.

16 Now make sure the total working floor area is clean and dry.

17 Slacken the accelerator cable to linkage clamp bolt and withdraw the accelerator inner cable.

18 Using two open ended spanners slacken the choke control cable nut and withdraw the inner cable.

19 Carefully release the two cables from the outer cable support bracket and withdraw the cables.

20 Detach the accelerator linkage control spring from its lower attachment.

21 Slacken the clip that secures the breather hose to the carburettor and carefully detach the hose.

22 Carefully pull the fuel hose from the union on the carburettor float chamber. Plug the end with a pencil to stop dirt ingress.

23 Slacken the clip that secures the fuel tank feed pipe to the fuel pump. Pull off the hose and plug the end with a pencil (photo).

24 Single carburettor: Undo and remove the wing nut and fibre washer securing the air cleaner body to the carburettor (photo). Lift away the air cleaner lid, element and body.

25 TC: Undo and remove the four nuts and bolts that secure the air cleaner to the carburettors. Lift away the air cleaner assembly.

26 Undo and remove the nuts and spring washers that secure the carburettor(s) to the inlet manifold studs. Ease the carburettor(s) away from the inlet manifold (photos).

27 Lift the metal shield away from the inlet manifold.

28 Undo and remove the four bolts and washers that secure the fan to the water pump hub (photo).

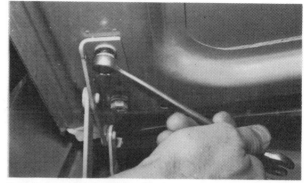
5.2A Bonnet hinge securing bolts

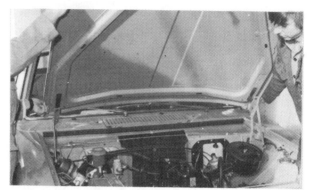
5.2B Lifting away bonnet

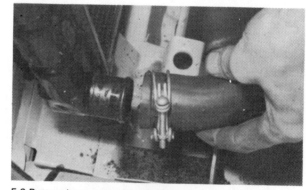
5.3 Bottom hose removal from radiator

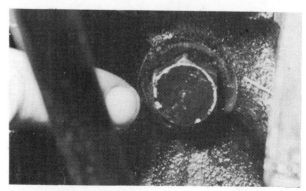
5.4 Cylinder block drain plug

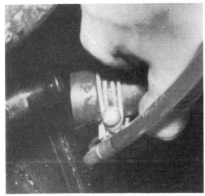

5.7 Heater hose detachment from metal transfer pipe

5.8 Expansion tank hose removal

5.9 Bottom hose connection to metal transfer pipe

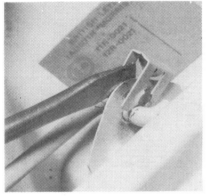

5.10 Bonnet support clip removal

5.11 Radiator top support detachment from front panel

5.14 Lifting away radiator

5.15 Radiator lower mounting rubber insert

5.23 Releasing fuel line from pump

5.24 Air cleaner retaining wing nut removal

5.26A Carburettor securing nuts and spring washers removal

5.26B Lifting away carburettor assembly

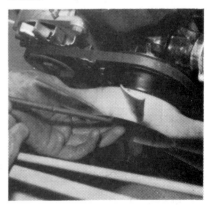

5.28 Removal of fan assembly retaining bolts and washers

29 Lift the metal plate and fan from the front of the water pump (photo).

30 Undo and remove the two exhaust manifold to downpipe clamp nuts and lift away the two halves of the clamp.

31 Slacken the hose clip to the inlet manifold union and ease off the vacuum hose.

32 Undo and remove the nuts and washers that secure the manifold assembly to the side of the cylinder head. Lift away the manifold assembly and recover the gasket.

33 Slacken the clip that attaches the downpipe to the gearbox mounted bracket. Unhook the clip (photo).

34 Undo and remove the nut, bolt and spring washer that secures the exhaust mounting bracket to the gearbox (photo). Lift away the bracket. Tie the exhaust downpipe to the left hand wing inner valance.

35 Working under the car, undo and remove the one bolt and plain washer that secures the braided earth cable to the body (photo).

36 Spring back the alternator terminal block securing clip and detach the terminal block (photo).

37 Mark the spark plug HT cable to ensure refitting in the correct order and disconnect from the spark plugs.

38 Release the HT cable from the centre of the ignition coil, spring back the two clips securing the distributor cap to the distributor body and lift away the distributor cap and HT leads (photo).

39 Disconnect the LT wiring to the distributor and ignition coil and the wiring to oil pressure switch and thermal transmitter (photo).

40 Make a note of the cable connections to the rear of the starter motor solenoid and detach the cables (photo).

41 Working under the car undo and remove the one bolt and spring washer securing the speedometer cable retainer to the gearbox extension housing (photo).

42 Lift away the retainer and withdraw the speedometer cable. Tuck the end of the cable back out of the way so it is not damaged during subsequent operations.

43 Wipe the area around the top of the clutch master cylinder reservoir. Unscrew the cap and place a thin piece of polythene over the top of the reservoir. Replace the cap. This will stop hydraulic fluid syphoning out during subsequent operations.

44 Wipe the area around the clutch slave cylinder hydraulic pipe union and unscrew the union. Wrap a rag around the end of the pipe and tuck back out of the way of the engine (photo).

45 Mark the gearbox and propeller shaft mating flanges so that they may be refitted in their original positions. Undo and remove the four self locking nuts and bolts (photo).

46 Place a piece of wood in the manner shown in this photograph so that the propeller shaft is supported (photo).

47 Using a garage hydraulic jack support the weight of the gearbox and then undo and remove the two bolts, spring and plain washers securing the gearbox mounting bracket to the underside of the body (photo).

48 Undo and remove the one bolt and spring washer securing the mounting bracket to the underside of the gearbox. Lift away the mounting.

49 Unscrew and remove the self tapping screws securing each carpet finisher to the door sill. Lift away the finisher and carpeting so exposing the gear change lever rubber moulding retaining plate (photos).

50 Undo and remove the six self tapping screws securing the gear change lever rubber moulding retaining plate to the floor panel (photo).

51 Slide the plate and moulding and foam sleeve up the gear change lever (photo). Note that sealer is used under the rubber moulding flange.

52 Turn the gear change lever retaining cup in an anti-clockwise direction so releasing the bayonet fixing (photo).

53 Ease the gear change lever up, at the same time being prepared to depress the plunger and spring in the fulcrum ball (photo).

54 Recover the plunger and spring from the fulcrum ball.

55 Place a rope sling or chain around the engine and support its

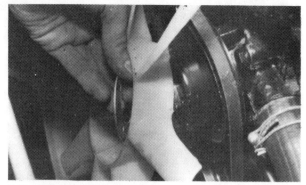
5.29 Lifting away metal plate and fan

5.33 Slackening exhaust downpipe to bracket clip

5.34 Detaching exhaust downpipe bracket from clutch bellhousing

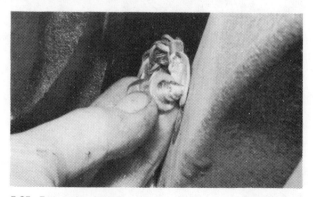
5.35 Removal of bolt securing earth cable to body

5.36 Detaching terminal block from rear of alternator

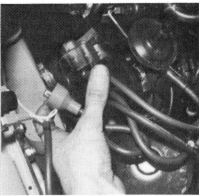
5.38 Removing distributor cap and HT leads

5.39A Detaching cable from oil pressure switch

5.39B Thermal transmitter located in side of cylinder head

5.40 Electric cable connections at rear of starter motor solenoid

5.41 Speedometer cable retainer removal

5.44 Clutch hydraulic pipe detached from slave cylinder

5.45 Propeller shaft detachment from drive flange

5.46 Propeller shaft supported by length of wood

5.47 Gearbox mounting bracket detachment from body

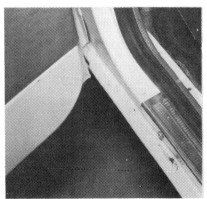
5.49A Front carpet finisher

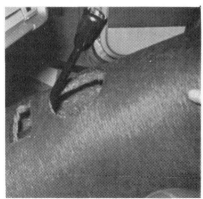
5.49B Front carpet removal

5.50 Removal of rubber moulding self tapping screws

5.51 Sliding moulding and sleeve up gear change lever

5.52 Releasing gear change lever retaining cup

5.53 Plunger and spring located in gear change lever fulcrum ball

5.56 Engine mounting release

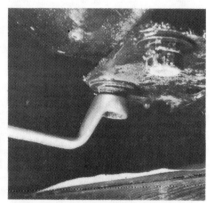

5.57 Sump extension bracket detachment from clutch bellhousing

weight using an overhead hoist. Make sure that there is no possibility of these slipping when the unit is being removed as it has to be lifted out at rather a steep angle.

56 Undo and remove the two nuts, bolts and spring washers securing the engine mounting to the main body member brackets (photo).

57 If the gearbox is to be separated from the engine when away from the vehicle undo and remove the two bolts and spring washers securing the sump extension bracket to the underside of the clutch bellhousing (photo).

58 Check that no controls, cables or pipes have been left connected to the engine or gearbox and that they are safely tucked to one side where they will not be caught as the unit is being removed.

59 Lower the jack supporting the weight of the gearbox and commence raising the engine. Continue lifting the engine until the rear of the sump is clear of the front cross member. The rear of the gearbox can now be lifted by hand over this cross member as either the car is pushed rearwards or the hoist is drawn away from the engine compartment.

60 Lower the unit to the ground. To complete the job, clear out any loose nuts and bolts and tools from the engine compartment and place them where they will not be lost.

6 Engine removal less gearbox

1 If it is necessary to remove only the engine leaving the

gearbox in position, the following sequence will enable the engine to be removed.

2 Follow the instructions given in Section 5, paragraphs 2 - 40 inclusive.

3 Using a garage hydraulic jack support the weight of the gearbox.

4 Undo and remove the two nuts, bolts and spring washers that secure the starter motor to the engine backplate and gearbox bell housing and lift away the starter motor.

5 Place a rope sling or chains around the engine and support its weight using an overhead hoist.

6 Undo and remove the remaining nuts, bolts and spring washers that secure the engine back plate to the gearbox bell housing.

7 Undo and remove the two nuts, bolts and spring washers securing the engine mounting to the main body member brackets.

8 Check that no controls, cables or pipes have been left connected to the engine and that they are safely tucked to one side where they will not be caught as the unit is being removed.

9 Raise the engine slightly to enable the engine mounting to clear their mounting brackets and move it forwards until the clutch is clear of the first motion shaft.

10 Continue lifting the unit, taking care not to damage the front valance and grille. Draw it forwards or push the car rearwards and lower to the ground.

11 To complete the job clear out any loose nuts, and bolts and tools from the engine compartment and place them where they will not be lost.

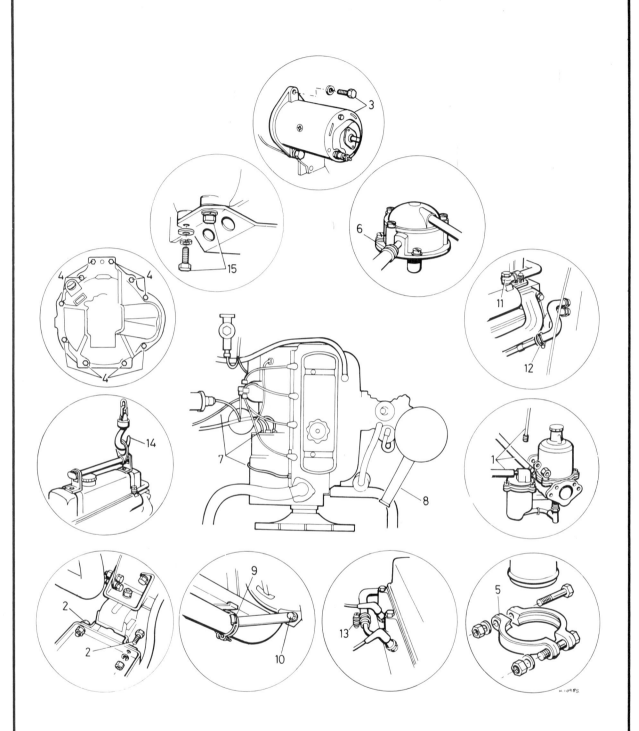

FIG.1.4. SUMMARY OF ITEMS TO BE DETACHED — ENGINE REMOVAL LESS GEARBOX

1 Carburettor attachments
2 Engine mounting nuts, bolts and spring washers
3 Starter motor
4 Clutch bellhousing to engine backplate attachments
5 Exhaust downpipe to manifold clamp
6 Fuel pipe connection pump
7 Electrical leads
8 Air cleaner
9 Front exhaust pipe mounting
10 Mounting bracket attachment
11 Servo unit pipe at inlet manifold
12 Heater hose
13 Heater hose
14 Engine lift bracket
15 Sump bracket to clutch bellhousing bolts, spring and plain washers

7 Engine removal with gearbox (from underside)

1 Follow the instructions given in Section 5, paragraphs 2 — 58 inclusive.
2 Remove the nuts, bolts and spring washers that secure the body mounted engine brackets and completely remove the brackets (photo).
3 Place some wood on the floor of at least the complete length of the engine and gearbox.
4 Carefully lower the complete power unit through the engine compartment until it is resting on the previously placed wood (photo).
5 Release the rope or chains from the engine and transfer these to the two brackets on the inner faces at the front of the longitudinal members (photo).
6 Lift up the front of the body to a sufficient height to clear the front valance and support the body on firmly based axle stands (photo).
7 The complete power unit may now be slid forwards and from under the car (photo).
8 To complete the job clear out any loose nuts and bolts and tools from the engine compartment and place them where they will not be lost.

8 Separating the engine from the gearbox

1 With the engine and gearbox on the floor undo and remove the one remaining nut, bolt and spring washer securing the starter motor to the engine backplate and gearbox bell housing. Lift away the starter motor (photo).
2 Undo and remove the two bolts and spring washers securing the sump extension bracket to the underside of the clutch bell housing if they are still in place.
3 Undo and remove the remaining nuts, bolts and spring washers securing the clutch bell housing to the engine backplate.
4 Carefully draw the gearbox rearwards, detaching it from the dowels located at the top rear of the engine cylinder block. It is important that the weight of the gearbox is not allowed to hang on the first motion shaft as it can easily be bent (photo).

9 Dismantling the engine - general

1 It is best to mount the engine on a dismantling stand, but if one is not available, stand the engine on a strong bench, to be at a comfortable working height. It can be dismantled on the floor but it is not easy.
2 During the dismantling process greatest care should be taken to keep the exposed parts free from dirt. As an aid to achieving this, thoroughly clean down the outside of the engine, removing all traces of oil and congealed dirt.
3 Use paraffin or Gunk. The latter compound will make the job much easier for, after the solvent has been applied and allowed to stand for a time, a vigorous jet of water will wash off the solvent with all the grease and dirt. If the dirt is thick and deeply embedded, work the solvent into it with a wire brush.
4 Finally wipe down the exterior of the engine with a rag and only then, when it is quite clean, should the dismantling process begin. As the engine is stripped, clean each part in a bath of paraffin or Gunk.
5 Never immerse parts with oilways (for example the crankshaft), in paraffin but to clean wipe down carefully with a petrol dampened cloth. Oilways can be cleaned out with nylon pipe cleaners. If an air line is available, all parts can be blown dry and the oilways blown through as an added precaution.
6 Re-use of old engine gaskets is false economy and will lead to oil and water leaks, if nothing worse. Always use new gaskets throughout.
7 Do not throw the old gasket away, for it sometimes happens that an immediate replacement cannot be found and the old gasket is then very useful as a template. Hang up the old gaskets as they are removed.

8 To strip the engine it is best to work from the top down. The underside of the crankcase when supported on wood blocks acts as a firm base. When the stage is reached, where the crankshaft and connecting rods have to be removed, the engine can be turned on its side and all other work carried out with it in this position.
9 Whenever possible, replace nuts, bolts and washers finger tight from wherever they were removed. This helps avoid loss and muddle later. If they cannot be replaced lay them out in such a fashion that it is clear from whence they came.

10 Removing the ancillary engine components

Before basic engine dismantling begins it is necessary to strip it of ancillary components as follows:
    Alternator
    Distributor
    Thermostat
    Oil filter cartridge
    Inlet and exhaust manifold and carburettor
    Water pump
It is possible to strip all these items with the engine in the car if it is merely the individual items that require attention. Presuming the engine is to be out of the car and on the bench and that the item mentioned is still on the engine, follow the procedure described below:
1 Slacken off the alternator retaining bolts and nuts and remove the unit together with its adjustment link.
2 To remove the distributor first disconnect the vacuum advance/retard pipe from the side of the distributor. Undo and remove the two screws with spring and plain washers that secure the distributor clamp flange to the cylinder block. Lift away the distributor and clamp flange.
3 Remove the thermostat cover by undoing and removing the three nuts and spring washers which hold it in position. Lift away the cover and gasket, followed by the thermostat itself.
4 Remove the oil filter cartridge by simply unscrewing it from the oil filter head on the side of the cylinder block.
5 Undo and remove the six nuts and washers that secure the inlet and exhaust manifold assembly to the side of the cylinder head. If the carburettor is still mounted on the inlet manifold release it from the petrol feed pipe from the pump. Lift off the manifold assembly and recover the gasket.
6 Remove the mechanical fuel pump by unscrewing the two retaining nuts and spring washers which hold it to the block. Release it from the petrol feed pipe to the carburettor float chamber and lift away the fuel pump.
7 Undo and remove the retaining bolts and lift away the water pump and gasket.
    The engine is now stripped of ancillary components and is ready for major dismantling to begin.

FIG 1.5 ENGINE FRONT MOUNTING (LEFT), GEARBOX BRACKET (RIGHT)

7.2 Engine mountings removed

7.4A Lowering engine onto wood

7.4B Engine and gearbox resting on wood

7.5 Lifting front of body

7.6 Body at sufficient height to pull power unit forwards

7.7 Pulling power unit away from body

8.1 Removal of starter motor securing bolts

8.4A Drawing gearbox rearwards from engine

8.4B Dowel located at top of clutch bellhousing

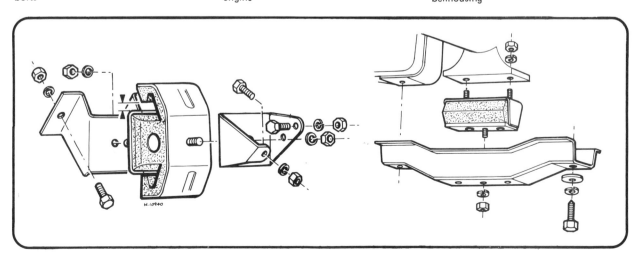

11 Cylinder head removal - engine in car

1   Drain the cooling system as described in Chapter 2.
2   For safety reasons disconnect the negative and then the positive battery terminals and tuck the leads to the rear of the battery (photo).
3   Pull off the feed pipe from the carburettor float chamber union and plug the end of the pipe with a pencil (photo).
4   Slacken the hose clip and remove the breather hose from the carburettor body (photo).
5   Pull the distributor vacuum advance/retard hose union from the carburettor body (photo).
6   Slacken the accelerator cable to linkage securing nut (photo).
7   Press in the two accelerator cable retainer ears on the underside of the support bracket and pull the cable through the bracket (photo).
8   Slacken the nut securing the choke control cable to the choke lever and pull the complete cable through its location on the side of the carburettor (photo).
9   Slacken the top hose to thermostat housing securing clip and pull off the hose (photo).
10 Detach the Lucar terminal from the thermal transmitter located beneath the thermostat housing (photo).
11 Mark the spark plug HT leads to ensure correct refitting and detach the leads from the spark plugs (photo).
12 Slacken the clip securing the heater hose to the angled pipe on the left hand side of the cylinder head. Pull the hose from the pipe (photo).
13 Slacken the clip securing the vacuum servo unit hose to the union on the rear branch of the inlet manifold. Pull off the hose and tuck back on the bulkhead (photo).
14 Undo and remove the two rocker cover securing bolts together with the spacer, plain washer and seal (photo).
15 Lift away the rocker cover and its gasket (photo).
16 Undo and remove the two nuts, plain washers and bolts that secure the clamp around the exhaust downpipe to manifold joint (photo). Lift away the clamp halves.
17 Undo and remove the three nuts and spring washers securing the thermostat cover to the top of the cylinder head (photo). Lift the cover from the three studs and recover the gasket.
18 The thermostat may now be lifted out from its location in the cylinder head (photo).
19 Slacken the eight nuts securing the rocker shaft pedestals to the cylinder head in a progressive manner. Remove the nuts and spring washers (photo).
20 Recover the locking washer from Number 1 pedestal (photo).
21 Lift the rocker shaft assembly from the top of the cylinder head (photo).
22 Remove the push rods, keeping them in the relative order in which they were removed. The easiest way for this is to push them through a sheet of thin card in the correct sequence (photo).
23 Look for any shims located on the rocker shaft retaining studs and carefully lift from the studs (photo).
24 Slacken the remaining cylinder head nuts in a progressive manner in the order shown in Fig 1.6. Lift away the nuts and washers.
25 The cylinder head can now be removed by lifting upwards. If the head is jammed, try to rock it to break the seal. Under no circumstances try to prise it apart from the block with a screwdriver or cold chisel as damage may be done to the faces of the head and block. If the head will not free readily, turn the engine over using the starter motor as the compression in the cylinders will often break the cylinder head joint. If this fails to work, strike the head sharply with a plastic head or wooden hammer, or with a metal hammer onto a piece of wood on the side of the head. Under no circumstances hit the head directly with a metal hammer as this may cause the iron casting to fracture. Several sharp taps with a hammer at the same time pulling upwards should free the head. Lift the head off and place to one side (photo).
26 Recover the old cylinder head gasket (photo).

11.2 Battery earth terminal detachment

11.3 Fuel feed pipe detached from carburettor float chamber

11.4 Breather hose detached from carburettor body

11.5 Vacuum hose detached from carburettor body

11.6 Accelerator linkage detachment

11.7 Detaching accelerator cable from support bracket

11.8 Choke control cable detached from linkage

11.9 Radiator top hose detachment from thermostat housing

11.10 Detaching cable from thermal transmitter

11.11 Detaching HT cables from spark plugs

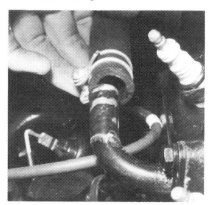
11.12 Removal of hose from pipe on side of cylinder head

11.13 Vacuum hose detachment from inlet manifold

11.14 Rocker cover securing bolt removal

11.15 Lifting away rocker cover

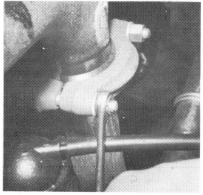
11.16 Removal of exhaust manifold to downpipe clamp

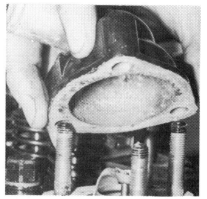
11.17A Lifting away thermostat cover

11.18 Thermostat removal from cylinder head

11.19 Removal of rocker shaft pedestal securing nut and spring washer

11.20 Lifting away special shaped washer

11.21 Lifting rocker shaft assembly from cylinder head

11.22 Removal of pushrods

11.23 Special shims located under rocker shaft pedestal

11.25 Lifting away cylinder head

11.26 Cylinder head gasket removal

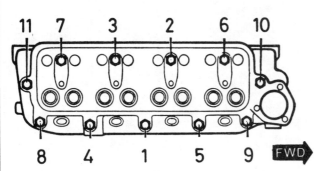

FIG 1.6 CYLINDER HEAD NUT SLACKENING SEQUENCE

12 Cylinder head removal - engine on bench

The sequence for removal of the cylinder head with the engine on the bench is basically identical to the latter operations for removal with the engine in the car. Refer to Section 11 and follow the instructions given in paragraphs 14, 15 and 17 to 26.

13 Valve removal

1 The valves are easily removed from the cylinder head by the following method; Compress each spring in turn with a universal valve spring compressor until the two halves of the collets can be removed. Release the compressor and lift away the spring top cup, the spring, oil seal, lower cup and the valve. (Fig 1.7).
2 If, when the valve spring compressor is screwed down, the valve spring top cup refuses to free and expose the split collet, do not continue to screw down on the compressor as there is a likelihood of damaging it.
3 Gently tap the top of the tool directly over the cup with a light hammer. This should free the cup. To avoid the compressor jumping off the valve retaining cup when it is tapped, hold the compressor firmly in position with one hand.
4 It is essential that the valves are kept in their correct sequence unless they are so badly worn that they are to be renewed. If they are going to be re-used place them in a sheet of card having eight holes numbered 1 to 8 corresponding with the relative positions the valves were in when fitted. Also keep the valve springs, cups etc., in this same correct order.

14 Valve guide - removal

Valve guide removal is a simple task but it is not recommended that you should do this because their replacement is too difficult to do accurately. It is far better to leave their removal and insertion to a BLMC garage (see also Section 42).

15 Rocker assembly - dismantling

1 To dismantle the rocker assembly, release the rocker shaft locating screw from Number 4 pedestal, remove the split pin, flat and spring washers from each end of the shaft and slide from the shaft the pedestals, rocker arms and rocker spacing springs. (Fig 1.8).
2 From the end of the shaft undo the plug which gives access to the inside of the rocker which can now be cleaned of sludge etc. Ensure the rocker arm lubricating holes are clear.

16 Timing cover, tensioner, gears and chain - removal

The timing cover, gears and chain can be removed with the engine in the car provided that the radiator and fan belt are removed first. The procedure for removing the timing cover, tensioner, gears and chain is otherwise the same irrespective of whether the engine is in the car or on the bench. Note that the timing chain may be either a duplex or single row type.
1 Bend back the locking tab of the crankshaft pulley locking washer under the crankshaft pulley retaining bolt.
2 Using a large socket undo and remove the bolt and lock washer. **Note:** If the engine is in the car it will be necessary to remove the starter motor and lock the flywheel ring gear with a large screwdriver to prevent the crankshaft turning.
3 Placing two large screwdrivers or tyre levers behind the crankshaft pulley wheel at 180° to each other carefully lever off the pulley. It is preferable to use a proper extractor if this is available but the large screwdrivers or tyre levers are quite

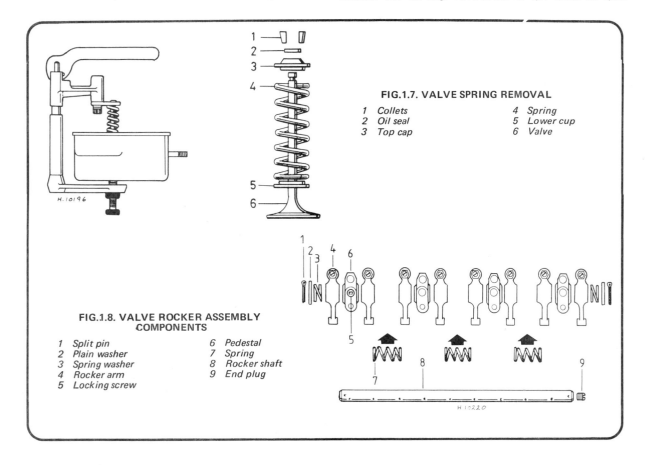

FIG.1.7. VALVE SPRING REMOVAL

1	Collets	4	Spring
2	Oil seal	5	Lower cup
3	Top cap	6	Valve

FIG.1.8. VALVE ROCKER ASSEMBLY COMPONENTS

1	Split pin	6	Pedestal
2	Plain washer	7	Spring
3	Spring washer	8	Rocker shaft
4	Rocker arm	9	End plug
5	Locking screw		

suitable providing care is taken not to damage the pulley flange.

4   Remove the woodruff key from the crankshaft nose with a pair of pliers and note how the groove in the pulley is designed to fit over it. Place the woodruff key in a glass jar for it is a very small part and can easily become lost.

5   Unscrew the bolts holding the timing cover to the block. NOTE that three different sizes of bolt are used, and that each bolt makes use of a large flat washer as well as a spring washer.

6   Pull off the timing cover and its gasket.

7   With the timing cover off, take off the oil thrower noting which way round it is fitted.

8   Where applicable take the bottom plug from the chain tensioner, fit a 1/8 inch Allen key in the cylinder and turn the key clockwise until the slipper head is pulled right back and locked behind the limit head. If the tensioner has no plug it is preferable to remove the tensioner at this stage (paragraph 10), but take care that the slipper head does not fly out under spring tension.

9   Bend back the locking tab on the washer under the camshaft retaining nut and unscrew the nut. Lift away the nut and lock-washer. Ease each timing gear forwards a little at a time by levering behind each gearwheel in turn with two large screwdrivers or tyre levers at 180° to each other. If the gear wheels are locked solid then it will be necessary to use a proper gearwheel and pulley extractor, and if one is available this should be used anyway in preference to levers. With both gearwheels safely off, remove the woodruff keys from the crankshaft and camshaft with a pair of pliers and place them in a jar for safe keeping.

Note the number of very thin packing washers behind the crankshaft gearwheel and remove them very carefully.

10 To remove the tensioner knock back the tabs on the joint lockwasher and undo the two bolts which hold the tensioner and its backplate to the engine.

17 Camshaft - removal

The camshaft can be removed with the engine on the bench or in the car. In either case it will first be necessary to remove the fanbelt and fan, timing cover, gears and chain, distributor drive, rocker shaft assembly and pushrods. If the engine is in the car, also remove the radiator and front grille, then proceed as follows.

1   Undo and remove the single retaining bolt securing each of the two cylinder block side covers. Lift off the covers with their gaskets to provide access to the tappets.

2   Lift out each of the eight tappets and keep them in the correct order as fitted in the engine.

3   Undo and remove the three bolts and spring washers securing the camshaft locating plate to the block. Lift off the locating plate.

4   The camshaft can now be withdrawn. If the engine is in the car it may be necessary to release the engine mountings and lower the engine slightly on a jack to allow the camshaft to clear the grille aperture. Take great care to ensure that the camshaft bearings are not damaged as the camshaft is withdrawn.

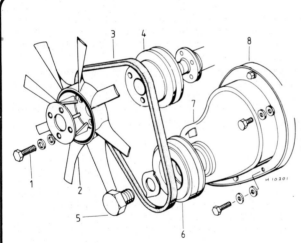

FIG.1.9. TIMING COVER REMOVAL

1   Fan and pulley securing bolt, spring and plain washer
2   Fan
3   Fan belt
4   Fan pulley
5   Crankshaft pulley securing bolt and lock washer
6   Crankshaft pulley
7   Timing cover
8   Gasket

FIG.1.10. TENSIONER

TIMING GEARS AND CHAIN (single row type illustrated)

1   Oil thrower
2   Crankshaft gearwheel
3   Camshaft gearwheel
4   Timing chain
5   Camshaft gearwheel retaining nut and washer
6   Tensioner

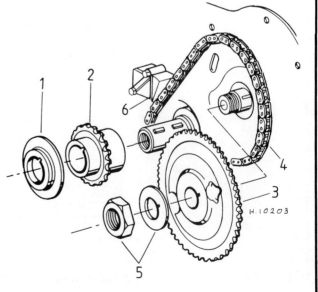

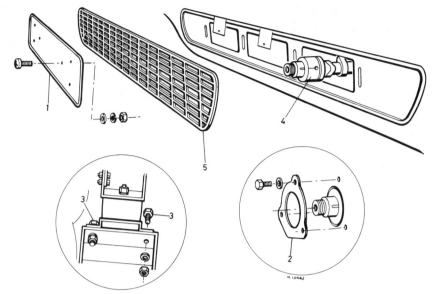

FIG.1.11. CAMSHAFT REMOVAL

1 *Number plate*
2 *Camshaft locking plate*
3 *Engine mounting securing nut bolt and spring washer*
4 *Camshaft*
5 *Front lower grille*

18 Distributor drive - removal

To remove the distributor drive with the sump still in position it is first necessary to remove one of the tappet cover retaining bolts. With the distributor and the distributor clamp plate already removed, this is achieved as follows:

1 Unscrew the single retaining bolt and spring washer to release the distributor housing.
2 Turn the crankshaft until No 1 piston is positioned at either 90° before or after the TDC position so that the pistons are halfway up the bores.
3 With the distributor housing removed, if the sump is still in position, screw into the end of the distributor drive shaft a 5/16 UNF bolt. A tappet cover bolt is ideal for this purpose. The drive shaft can then be lifted out, the shaft being turned slightly in the process to free the shaft skew gear from the camshaft skew gear.
4 If the sump has already been removed then it is a simple matter to push the driveshaft out from inside the crankcase.

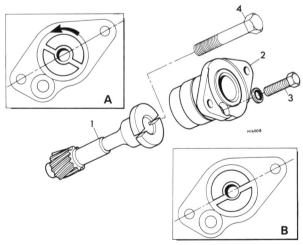

FIG. 1.12. DISTRIBUTOR DRIVESHAFT COMPONENTS

Inset A shows the position of the slot ready for fitting
Inset B shows the shaft correctly installed

1 *Driveshaft*
2 *Housing*
3 *Retaining screw*
4 *$\frac{5}{16}$ in UNF bolt (for removal and refitting of driveshaft)*

19 Sump, piston, connecting rod and big end bearing - removal

The sump, pistons and connecting rods can be removed with the engine still in the car or with the engine on the bench. Proceed with the appropriate methods in either case for removing the cylinder head. The pistons and connecting rods are drawn up out of the top of the cylinder bores.

1 Undo and remove the two bolts, spring and plain washers securing the sump connecting plate to the gearbox bellhousing if the engine is still in the car.
2 Undo and remove the bolts and spring washers holding the sump in position. Lift away the sump and gasket (photo).
3 To gain access to all big-end bearings it is now necessary to remove the oil pump and strainer.
4 Undo and remove the three bolts and spring washers that secure the strainer to the oil pump cover. Lift away the strainer (photo).
5 Undo and remove the three nuts and spring washers that secure the oil pump body to the studs. Carefully withdraw the oil pump (photo).
6 Undo and remove the big end cap retaining nuts using a socket and remove the big end caps one at a time, taking care to keep them in the right order and the correct way round (photo). Ensure that the shell bearings are also kept with their correct connecting rods and caps unless they are to be renewed.

Normally the numbers 1 to 4 are stamped on adjacent sides of the big end caps and connecting rods, indicating which cap fits on which rod and which way round the cap fits. If no numbers or lines can be found then scratch mating marks across the joint from the rod to the cap with a sharp screwdriver; One line for connecting rod Number 1, two for connecting rod number 2 and so on. This will ensure there is no confusion later as it is most important that the caps go back in the position on the connecting rods from which they were removed.

7 If the big end caps are difficult to remove they may be gently tapped with a soft hammer.
8 To remove the shell bearings press the bearing opposite the groove in both connecting rod and the connecting rod cap, and the bearing shell will slide out easily.
9 Withdraw the pistons and connecting rods upwards and ensure they are kept in the correct order, for replacement in the same bore. Refit the connecting rod caps and bearings to the rods if the bearings do not require renewal to minimise the risk of getting the caps and rods muddled.

19.2 Removal of sump securing bolts

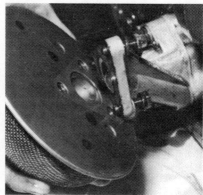

19.4 Oil pump strainer removal

19.5 Lifting away oil pump from mounting studs

19.6 Big end cap retaining nut removal

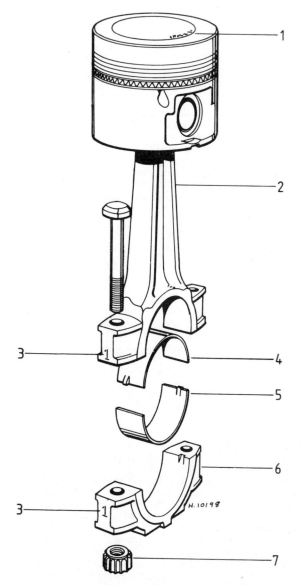

FIG.1.13. PISTON AND CONNECTING ROD ASSEMBLY WITH PRESS FIT GUDGEON PIN

1 Piston - note identification
   marks
2 Connecting rod
3 Identification mark

4 Upper shell bearing half
5 Lower shell bearing half
6 End cap
7 Multi sided nut

20 Gudgeon pin - removal

A press type gudgeon pin is now used and requires a special BLMC tool No. 18 G1150 with adaptor 18 G1150C to remove and replace the pin. This tool is shown in Fig 1.14 and must be used in the following manner:

1 Securely hold the hexagonal body in a firm vice and screw back the large nut until it is flush with the end of the main centre screw. Well lubricate the screw and large nut as they have to withstand high loading. Now push the centre screw in until the nut just touches the thrust race.

2 Fit the adaptors number 18 G1150C onto the main centre screw with the piston ring cut-a-way positioned uppermost. Then slide the parallel sleeve with the groove end first onto the centre screw.

3 Fit the piston with the 'FRONT' or 'A' mark on towards the adaptor on the centre screw. This is important because the gudgeon pin bore is offset and irreparable damage will result in fitting the wrong way round. Next fit the remover/replacer bush on the centre screw with the flange end towards the gudgeon pin.

4 Screw the stop nut onto the main centre screw and adjust it until approximately 0.032 inch (0.8 mm) end play ('A' in Fig 1.14 exists, and lock the stop nut securely with the lock screws. Now check that the remover/replacer bush and parallel sleeve are positioned correctly in the bore on both sides of the piston. Also check that the curved face of the adaptor is clean and slide the piston onto the tool, so it fits into the curved face of the adaptor with the piston rings over the cut-a-way.

5 Screw the large nut up to the thrust race and holding the lock screw turn the large nut with a ring spanner or long socket until the piston pin is withdrawn from the piston.

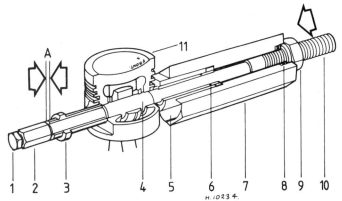

1 Lock screw
2 Stop nut
3 Flange away from gudgeon
   pin remover/replacer bush
4 Gudgeon pin
5 Piston support
   adaptor
6 Groove in sleeve away

        from gudgeon pin
7 Service tool body
8 Thrust race
9 Large nut
10 Centre screw
11 Piston
A See text

FIG.1.14. GUDGEON PIN REMOVAL USING BLMC TOOL 18G 1150 AND ADAPTORS 18G 1150C

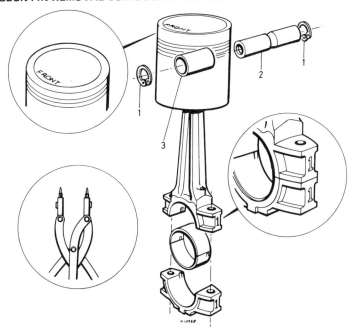

FIG.1.15. EARLIER TYPE FULLY FLOATING GUDGEON PIN

1 Circlip   2 Gudgeon pin   3 Little end bush

6 Some earlier models were fitted with fully floating gudgeon pins and circlips. See Fig 1.15.

21 Piston ring removal

1 To remove the piston rings, slide them carefully over the top of the piston, taking care not to scratch the aluminium alloy of the piston. Never slide them off the bottom of the piston skirt. It is very easy to break piston rings if they are pulled off roughly so this operation should be done with extreme caution. It is helpful to use an old 0.020 inch feeler gauge to facilitate their removal.
2 Lift one end of the piston ring to be removed out of its groove and insert the end of the feeler gauge under it.
3 Turn the feeler gauge slowly round the piston and as the ring comes out of its groove it rests on the land above. It can then be eased off the piston with the feeler gauge stopping it from slipping into any empty grooves if it is any but the top piston ring that is being removed.

22 Flywheel and engine backplate - removal

Having removed the clutch (see Chapter 5) the flywheel and engine backplate can be removed. It is only possible for this complete operation to be carried out with the engine out of the car.
1 Bend back the lockwasher tabs and then undo and remove the six bolts securing the flywheel to the end of the crankshaft. Lift away the shaped lock washer and the flywheel.
2 Some difficulty may be experienced in removing the bolts by rotation of the crankshaft every time pressure is put on the spanner. The only answer is to lock the crankshaft in position whilst the bolts are removed with a wooden wedge placed between the crankshaft and the side of the block inside the crankcase.
3 The engine backplate is held in position by a number of bolts and spring washers of varying size. Release the bolts noting where the different size bolts fit and place them together to avoid their becoming lost. Lift away the backplate from the block complete with the paper gasket.

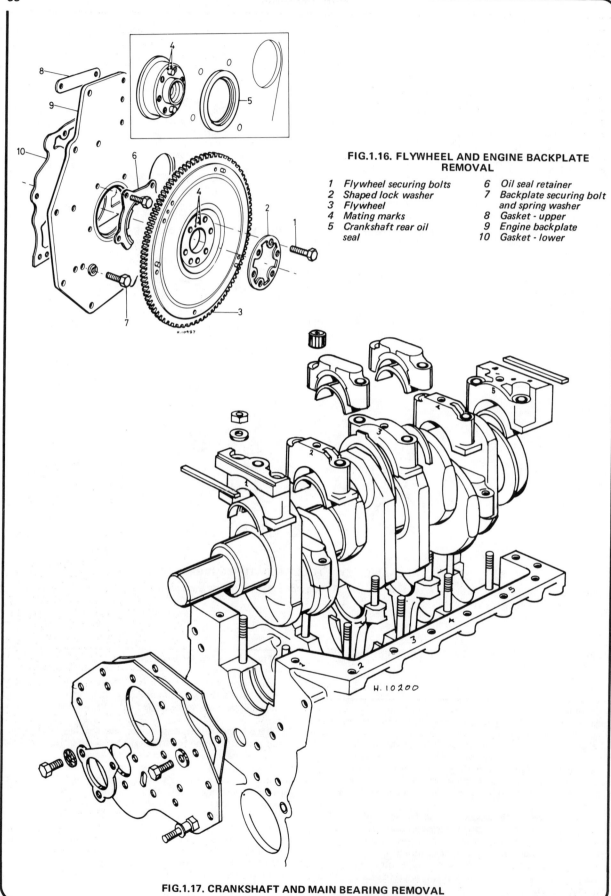

FIG.1.16. FLYWHEEL AND ENGINE BACKPLATE REMOVAL

1	Flywheel securing bolts	6	Oil seal retainer
2	Shaped lock washer	7	Backplate securing bolt and spring washer
3	Flywheel	8	Gasket - upper
4	Mating marks	9	Engine backplate
5	Crankshaft rear oil seal	10	Gasket - lower

FIG.1.17. CRANKSHAFT AND MAIN BEARING REMOVAL

23 Crankshaft and main bearings - removal

Drain the engine oil, remove the timing gears and remove the sump, oil pump, big end bearings, flywheel and engine backplate as already described. Removal can only be attempted with the engine on the bench.

1 Undo and remove the ten nuts securing the main bearing caps to the cylinder block. Then undo and remove the two bolts and spring washers which hold the front main bearing cap against the engine front plate. It will be beneficial if the front plate is completely removed, so remove the remaining securing bolts and spring washers and lift away together with the paper gasket.

2 Make sure that the main bearing caps are numbered 1 to 5 on the front faces and also have the word 'FRONT' towards the front. If not, make identifying marks as necessary.

3 Remove the main bearing caps and the bottom half of each bearing shell, taking care to keep the bearing shells in the right caps if they are to be re-used.

4 When removing the centre bearing cap, note the bottom semi-circular halves of the thrust washers, one half lying on either side of the main bearing. Lay them with the centre bearing along the correct side.

5 Carefully lift out the crankshaft and recover the bearing shell and thrust washer upper halves from their locations in the crankcase.

24 Lubrication system - description

A force feed system of lubrication is fitted with oil circulated around the engine from the sump below the cylinder block. The level of engine oil in the sump is indicated by the dipstick which is fitted on the right hand side of the engine. The optimum level is indicated by the maximum mark. The level of oil in the sump, ideally, should neither be above or below this line. Oil is replenished via the filler cap towards the front of the rocker cover.

The eccentric rotor type oil pump is bolted within the left hand side of the crankcase and is driven by a short shaft from the skew gear on the camshaft.

The pump is of the non-draining variety to allow rapid pressure build up when starting from cold. Oil is drawn from the sump through a gauze screen in the oil strainer, this being shown in Fig 1.20 and is sucked up the pick up and drawn into the oil pump. From the oil pump it is forced under pressure along a gallery on the right hand side of the engine, and through drillings to the big end, main and camshaft bearings. A small hole in each connecting rod allows a jet of oil to lubricate the cylinder wall with each revolution.

From the camshaft front bearing, oil is fed through drilled passages in the cylinder block and head to the front rocker pedestal where it enters the hollow rocker shaft. Holes drilled in the shaft allow for the lubrication of the rocker arms and the valve stems and push rod ends. This oil is at a reduced pressure to the oil delivered to the crankshaft bearings. Oil from the front camshaft bearing lubricates the timing gears and the timing chain. Oil returns to the sump by various passages, the tappets being lubricated by oil returning via the push rod drillings in the block.

A full flow cartridge type filter is fitted and oil passes through this filter before it reaches the main oil gallery. The oil is passed directly from the oil pump to the filter.

25 Oil filter - removal and replacement

1 The external oil filter is of the disposable cartridge type and is located on the right hand side of the engine.

2 Before removing the cartridge place an absorbent cloth around the base to catch the oil released from the cartridge when it has been unscrewed.

3 To renew the oil filter unscrew the old cartridge from the filter head and discard it. Smear the seal on the new filter with a little oil and position it on the filter head. Screw it on and tighten with the hands only. Do not attempt to tighten with a spanner or strap wrench.

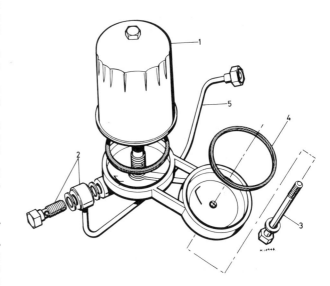

FIG.1.18. OIL FILTER ASSEMBLY

1 Filter cartridge
2 Supply pipe union to filter head
3 Filter head securing bolt
4 'O' ring
5 Supply pipe

26 Oil pressure relief valve - removal and replacement

To prevent excessive oil pressure - which might result when the engine oil is thick and cold - an oil pressure relief valve is built into the left hand side of the engine at the rear. The relief valve is identified externally by a large 9/16 inch domed hexagon nut.

1 To dismantle the valve unscrew the domed nut and remove it complete with sealing washer. The relief spring and valve can then be easily extracted.

2 In position the valve fits over the opposite end of the relief valve spring resting in the dome of the hexagon nut, and bears against a machined seating in the block. When the oil pressure exceeds 70 lb/sq in (4.92 kg cm2), the valve is forced off its seat and the oil by-passes it and returns via a drilling directly into the sump.

3 Check the tension of the spring by measuring its length. If it is shorter than 3 in (76 mm) it should be replaced with a new spring.

4 Examine the valve for signs of pitting which, if evident, it should be carefully lapped using cutting paste. Remove all traces of paste when a good seating has been obtained.

5 Reassembly of the relief valve is the reverse sequence to removal.

27 Oil pump - removal and dismantling

1 With the sump removed undo and remove the three bolts and spring washers that secure the oil strainer to the pump housing. Lift away the oil strainer (Fig 1.20).

2 Undo and remove the nuts and spring washers from the three studs which hold the oil pump to the underside of the crankcase. Lift away the pump and its driveshaft. Recover the pump gasket.

3 Unscrew and remove the three bolts and spring washers that secure the pump cover to the pump body. Carefully pull the cover from the two dowels which hold it in its correct position on the housing (Fig 1.21).

4 Pull out from the pump body the outer rotor and the inner rotor together with pump shaft.

28 Timing chain tensioner - removal and dismantling

1 Remove the cover from the timing gears as described in Section 16 and lock the rubber tensioner in the fully retracted position by removing the bottom plug from the tensioner body and fitting a 1/8 inch Allen key in the cylinder. Turn the key clockwise until the slipper head is pulled right back and locked behind the limit head.

2 Knock back the tabs of the joint lockwasher and undo the two bolts which hold the tensioner and its backplate to the engine.

3 Pull the rubber slipper together with the spring and plunger from the tensioner body. Fit the Allen key to its socket in the cylinder, and holding the slipper and plunger firmly, turn the key clockwise to free the cylinder and spring from the plunger (Fig 1.22).

29 Engine - examination and renovation - general

With the engine stripped and all parts thoroughly cleaned, every component should be examined for wear. The following items should be checked and, where necessary, renewed or renovated as described later.

30 Crankshaft - examination and renovation

Examine the crankpin and main journal surfaces for signs of scoring or scratches and check the ovality of the crankpins at different positions with a micrometer. If more than 0.001 inch

(0.0254 mm) out of round, the crankpins will have to be reground. It will also have to be reground if there are any scores or scratches present. Also check the journals in the same fashion. BMC 'B' series engine centre main bearing are prone to failure. This is not always immediately apparent, but slight vibration in an otherwise normally smooth engine and a very slight drop in oil pressure under normal conditions are clues. If the centre main bearing is suspected of failure it should be investigated immediately, by dropping the sump and removing the centre main bearing cap. Failure to do this will result in badly scored centre main journal. If it is necessary to regrind the crankshaft and fit new bearings, an engineering works will be able to decide how much metal to grind off and be able to supply the correct undersize shells to fit.

31 Big end and main bearings - examination and renovation

1 Big end bearing failure is usually accompanied by a noisy knocking from the crankcase and a slight drop in oil pressure. Main bearing failure is accompanied by vibration which can be quite severe as the engine speed rises and falls, and a drop in oil pressure.

2 Bearings which have not broken up, but are badly worn will give rise to low oil pressure and some vibration. Inspect the big ends, main bearings and thrust washers for signs of general wear, scoring, pitting and scratches. The bearings should be a matt grey in colour. With lead indium bearings, should a trace of copper in colour be noticed the bearings are badly worn, for the lead bearing has worn away to expose the indium underlay. Renew the bearings if they are in this condition or if there is any sign of scoring or pitting.

3 The undersizes available are designed to correspond with regrind sizes 0.010 in bearings are correct for a crankshaft reground 0.010 in undersize. The bearings are in fact slightly more than the stated undersize as running clearances have been allowed for during their manufacture.

4 Very long engine life can sometimes be achieved by changing big end bearings at 30,000 miles and main bearings at 50,000 miles, irrespective of bearing wear. Normally, crankshaft wear is infinitesimal and regular changes of bearings may ensure mileages of between 100,000 and 120,000 miles before crankshaft regrinding becomes necessary. Crankshafts normally have to be reground because of scoring due to bearing failure.

5 Once dismantled only refit new bearing shells. It is false economy to replace old bearings even if they have run for only an hour!

32 Cylinder bores - examination and renovation

1 The cylinder bores must be examined for taper, ovality, scoring and scratches. Start by carefully examining the top of the bores, if they are worn fractionally a very slight ridge will be found on the thrust side. This marks the top of the piston travel. You will have a good indication of the bore wear prior to dismantling the engine, or removing the cylinder head. Excessive oil consumption accompanied by blue smoke from the exhaust is a sure sign of worn cylinder bores and piston rings.

2 Measure the diameter of the bore just under the ridge with a micrometer and compare it with the diameter at the bottom of the bore, which is not subject to such wear. If the difference between the two measurements is more than 0.006 inch (0.1524mm) then it will be necessary to fit a 'ring set' or to have the cylinders rebored and fit oversize pistons and rings. If no micrometer is available remove the rings from one piston and place the piston in each bore in turn about ¾ inch (19mm) below the top of the bore. If an 0.010 inch (0.254mm) feeler gauge can be slid between the piston and the cylinder wall on the thrust side of the bore then remedial action must be taken. Oversize pistons are available in the following sizes:

+ 0.010 inch (0.254mm)   + 0.030 inch (0.762mm)
+ 0.020 inch (0.508mm)   + 0.040 inch (1.016mm)

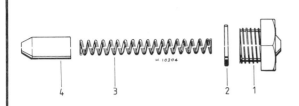

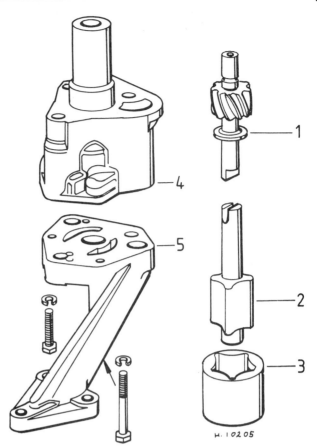

FIG.1.19. OIL PRESSURE RELIEF VALVE

1 Domed nut   3 Valve spring
2 Sealing washer   4 Valve

FIG.1.21. OIL PUMP COMPONENTS

1 Pump shaft   4 Pump body
2 Inner rotor   5 Pump cover
3 Outer rotor

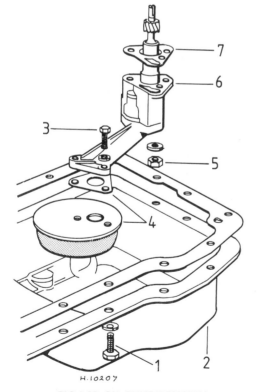

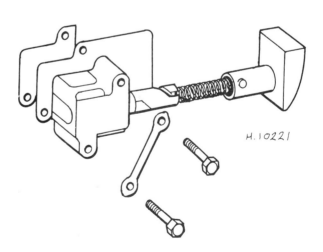

FIG.1.20. OIL PUMP REMOVAL

1 Sump securing bolt and spring washer
2 Sump
3 Oil strainer securing bolt and spring washer
4 Oil strainer and gasket
5 Oil pump securing nut and spring washer
6 Oil pump
7 Gasket

FIG.1.22. TIMING CHAIN TENSIONER COMPONENTS

3 These are accurately machined to just below these measurements so as to provide correct running clearances in bores bored out to the exact oversize dimensions.

4 If the bores are slightly worn but not so badly worn as to justify reboring them, special oil control rings can be fitted to the existing pistons which will restore compression and stop the engine burning oil. Several different types are available and the manufacturers instructions concerning their fitting must be followed closely.

33 Pistons and piston rings - examination and renovation

1 If the old pistons are to be refitted carefully remove the piston rings and then thoroughly clean them. Take particular care to clean out the piston ring grooves. Do not scratch the aluminium in any way. If new rings are to be fitted to the old pistons, then the top ring should be of the stepped type so as to clear the ridge left above the previous top ring. If a normal but oversize new ring is fitted it will hit the ridge and break, because the new ring will not have worn in the same way as the old.

2 Before fitting the rings on the pistons each should be inserted approximately 3 inches (76mm) down the cylinder bore and the gap measureed with a feeler gauge as shown in Fig.1.23. This should be between the limits given in the specifications at the beginning of this Chapter. It is essential that the gap is measured at the bottom of the ring travel, for if it is measured at the top of a worn bore and gives a perfect fit, it could easily seize at the bottom. If the ring gap is too small rub down the ends of the ring with a very fine file until the gap is correct when fitted. To keep the rings square in the bore for measurement, line each one up in turn with an old piston in the bore upside down, and use the piston to push the ring down about 3 inches (76mm). Remove the piston and measure the piston ring gap.

3 When fitting new pistons and rings to a rebored engine the ring gap can be measured at the top of the bore as the bore will now not taper. It is not necessary to measure the side clearance in the piston ring grooves with rings fitted, as the groove dimensions are accurately machined during manufacture. When fitting new oil control rings to the pistons it may be necessary to have the grooves widened by machining to accept the new undersize rings. In this instance the manufacturer will make this quite clear and will supply the address to which the pistons must be sent for machining.

4 When new pistons are fitted, take great care to fit the exact size best suited to the particular bore of your engine. BLMC go one stage further than merely specifying one size piston for all standard bores. Because of very slight differences in cylinder machining during production it is necessary to select just the right piston for the bore. A range of different sizes are available either from the piston manufacturer or from the local BLMC stores.

5 Examination of the cylinder block face will show adjacent to each bore a small diamond shaped box with a number stamped in the metal. Careful examination of the piston crown will show a matching diamond and number. These are the standard piston sizes and will be the same for all bores. If the standard pistons are to be refitted or standard low compression pistons changed to standard high compression pistons, then it is essential that only pistons with the same number in the diamond are used. With larger pistons, the amount of oversize is stamped in an elipse on the piston crown.

6 On engines with tapered second and third compression rings, the top narrow side of the ring is marked with a 'T'. Always fit this side uppermost and carefully examine all rings for this mark before fitting.

34 Camshaft and camshaft bearings - examination and renovation

1 Carefully examine the camshaft bearings for wear. If the bearings are obviously worn or pitted or the metal underlay just showing through, then they must be renewed. This is an operation for your local BLMC garage or local engineering works as it demands the use of specialised equipment. The bearings are removed using a special drift after which the new bearings are pressed in, care being taken that the oil drilling in the bearings line up with those in the block. With another special tool the bearings are then reamed in position.

2 The camshaft itself should show no sign of wear but, if very slight, scoring marks can be removed by gently rubbing down with very fine emery cloth or an oil stone. The greatest care must be taken to keep the cam profiles smooth.

35 Valves and seats - examination and renovation

1 Examine the heads of the valves for pitting or burning, especially the heads of the exhaust valves. The valve seatings should be examined at the same time. If the pitting on the valves is very slight the marks can be removed by grinding the seats and valves together with coarse, and then fine, valve grinding paste. Where bad pitting has occured to the valve seats it will be necessary to recut them and fit new valves. If the valve seats are so worn that they cannot be recut then it will be necessary to fit new valve seat inserts. These latter two jobs should be entrusted to a BLMC garage or engineering works. In practice it is very seldom that the seats are so badly worn that they require renewal. Normally it is the valve that is too badly worn, and you can easily purchase a new set of valves and match them to the seats by valve grinding.

2 Valve grinding is easily carried out. Place the cylinder head upside down on a bench with a block of wood at each end to give clearance for the valve stems. Alternatively place the head at 45° to a wall with the combustion chambers facing away from the wall.

3 Smear a trace of coarse carborundum paste on the seat face and apply a suction grinding tool to the valve head as shown in Fig.1.24. With a semi-rotary action, grind the valve head to its seat, lifting the valve occasionally to redistribute the grinding paste. When a dull matt even surface finish is produced on both the valve seat and the valve, then wipe off the paste and repeat the process with fine carborundum paste, lifting and turning the valve to redistribute the paste as before. A light spring placed under the valve head will greatly ease this operation. When a smooth unbroken ring of light grey matt finish is produced, on both valve and valve seat faces, the grinding operation is complete.

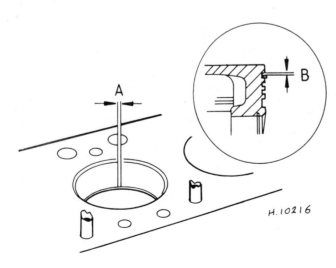

H.10216

FIG.1.23. PISTON RING MEASUREMENT

A End gap   *B Clearance in piston*

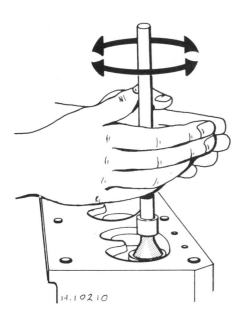

FIG.1.24. VALVE GRINDING USING HAND SUCTION TOOL. LIFT VALVE OFF SEAT OCCASIONALLY TO SPREAD GRINDING PASTE EVENLY OVER SEAT AND VALVE FACE

4   Scrape away all carbon from the valve head and the valve stem. Carefully clean away every trace of grinding compound, taking great care to leave none in the ports or in the valve guides. Clean the valves and valve seats with a paraffin soaked rag then wipe with clean rag. (If an air line is available blow clean).

36 Timing gear and chain - examination and renovation

1   Examine the teeth on both the crankshaft gear wheel and the camshaft gear wheel for wear. Each tooth forms an inverted 'V' with the gear wheel periphery and if worn, the side of each tooth under tension will be slightly concave in shape when compared with the other side of the tooth ie: one side of the inverted 'V' will be concave when compared with the other. If any sign of wear is present the gear wheels must be renewed.
2   Examine the links of the chain for side slackness and renew the chain if any slackness is noticeable when compared with a new chain. It is a sensible precaution to renew the chain every 30,000 miles (48,000 km) and at a lesser mileage if the engine is stripped down for a major overhaul. The actual rollers on a very badly worn chain may be slightly grooved.

37 Rockers and rocker shaft - examination and renovation

1   Remove the threaded plug with a screwdriver from the end of the rocker shaft and thoroughly clean out the shaft. As it acts as the oil passages for the valve gear, clean out these passages and make sure they are quite clear. Check the shaft for straightness by rolling it on a flat surface. It is most unlikely that it will deviate from normal, but, if it does, you must purchase a new shaft. The surface of the shaft should be free from any worn ridges caused by the rocker arms. If any wear is present, renew the rocker shaft. Wear is likely to have occured only if the rocker shaft oil holes have become blocked.
2   Check the rocker arms for wear of the rocker bushes, at the rocker arm face which bears on the valve stem, and of the adjusting ball ended screws. Wear in the rocker arm bush can be checked by gripping the rocker arm tip and holding the rockerarm in place on the shaft, noting if there is any lateral rocker arm shake. If any shake is present, and the arm is very loose on the shaft, remedial action must be taken. It is recommended that if a forged type of rocker arm is fitted it be taken to your local BLMC garage or engineering works to have the old bush drawn out and a new bush fitted. The correct placement of the bush is shown in Fig.1.25.
     If a pressed steel rocker arm is fitted, rebushing must not be undertaken but a new rocker arm obtained.
3   Check the tip of the rocker arm where it bears on the valve head, for cracking or serious wear on the case hardening. If none is present the rocker arm may be refitted, check the pushrods for straightness by rolling them on a flat surface. If bent they must be renewed.

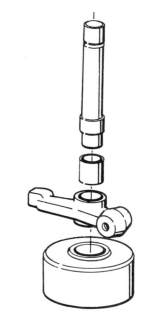

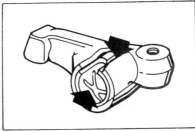

FIG.1.25. ROCKER BUSH REMOVAL AND CORRECT REPLACEMENT

38 Tappets - examination and renovation

Examine the bearing surface of the tappets which run on the camshaft. Any indentation in this surface or any cracks indicate serious wear and the tappets must be renewed. Thoroughly clean them out, removing all traces of sludge. It is most unlikely that the sides of the tappets will be worn, but if they are a loose fit in their bores and can be readily rocked, they should be discarded and new tappets fitted. It is unusual to find worn tappets, and any wear present is likely to occur through excessively high mileages.

39 Flywheel starter ring gear - examination and renovation

1 If the teeth on the flywheel starter ring gear are badly worn, or if some are missing, then it will be necessary to remove the ring. This is achieved by splitting the old ring using a hacksaw and cold chisel. Care must be taken not to damage the flywheel during this process.
2 To fit a new ring gear, it will be necessary to heat it gently and evenly with an oxy-acetyline flame until a temperature of approximately 350°C is reached. (This is indicated by a grey/brown surface colour). With the ring gear at this temperature, fit it to the flywheel with the front of the teeth facing the clutch fitting end of the flywheel. The ring gear should be either pressed or lightly tapped onto its register and left to cool naturally when the contraction of the metal on cooling will ensure that it is a secure and permanent fit. Great care must be taken not to overheat the ring gear, for if this happens the temper of the ring gear will be lost.
3 An alternative method is to use a high temperature oven to heat the ring.
4 Because of the need of oxy-acetylene equipment or a special oven it is not practical for refitment to take place at home. Take the flywheel and new starter ring to an engineering works willing to do the job.

40 Oil pump - examination and renovation

1 Thoroughly clean all the component parts in paraffin and then check the rotor end float and lobe clearances in the following manner:
2 Position the rotors in the pump and place the straight edge of a steel rule across the joint face of the pump. Measure the gap between the bottom of the straight edge and the top of the rotors with a feeler gauge as shown in Fig.1.26. If the measurement exceeds 0.005 inch (0.127mm) then check the lobe clearances as described in the following paragraph. If the lobe clearances are correct then remove the dowels from the joint face of the pump body and lap joint the inner face on a sheet of plate glass.
3 Measure the gaps between the peaks of the lobes and the peaks in the pump body with a feeler gauge, and if the gap exceeds 0.010 inch (0.254mm) then fit a replacement pump. This measurement is shown in Fig.1.26.

41 Cylinder head and bore - decarbonisation

1 This operation can be carried out with the engine either in or out of the car. With the cylinder head off, carefully remove with a wire brush and blunt, plastic scraper, all traces of carbon deposits from the combustion spaces and the ports. The valve stems and valve guides should also be freed from any carbon deposits. Wash the combustion spaces and ports down with paraffin and scrape the cylinder head surface free of any foreign matter with the side of a steel rule or similar article. Take care not to scratch the surfaces.
2 Clean the pistons and top of the cylinder bores. If the pistons are still in the cylinder bores then it is essential that great care is

taken to ensure that no carbon gets into the bores for this will scratch the cylinder walls or cause damage to the piston and rings. To stop it happening first turn the crankshaft so that two of the pistons are at TDC. Place a clean non-fluffy rag into the other two bores or seal them off with paper and masking tape. The waterways and pushrod holes should be covered with a small piece of masking tape to prevent particles of carbon entering the cooling system and damaging the water pump, or entering the lubrication system and causing damage to a bearing surface.
3 There are two schools of thought as to how much carbon ought to be removed from the piston crown. One is that a ring of carbon should be left around the edge of the piston and on the cylinder bore wall as an aid to keep oil consumption low. Although this is probably true for engines with worn bores, on fresh engines, however, the tendency is to remove all traces of carbon.
4 If all traces of carbon are to be removed, press a little grease into the gap between the cylinder walls and the two pistons which are to be worked upon. With a blunt scraper carefully scrape away all carbon from the piston crown, taking care not to scratch the aluminium. Also scrape away the carbon from the surrounding lip of the cylinder wall. When all carbon has been removed, scrape away the grease which will now be contaminated with carbon particles, taking care not to press any into the bores. To assist prevention of carbon build up the piston crown can be polished with a metal polish such as Brasso. Remove the rags or masking tape from the other two cylinders and turn the crankshaft so that the two pistons which were at the bottom are now at the top. Place non-fluffy rag into the other two bores or seal them off with paper and masking tape. Do not forget the water ways and oilways as well. Proceed as previously described.
5 If a ring of carbon is going to be left round the pistonthen this can be helped by inserting an old piston ring in the top of the bore to rest on the piston and ensure that carbon is not accidently removed. Check that there are no particles of carbon in the cylinder bores. Decarbonising is now complete.

42 Valve guides - examination and renovation

Examine the valve guides internally for wear. If the valves are a very loose fit in the guides and there is the slightest suspicion of lateral rocking, then new guides will have to be fitted, their correct location being shown in Fig.1.27. Try to compare them internally by visual inspection with a new guide as well.

43 Engine - reassembly -general

1 To ensure maximum life with minimum trouble from a rebuilt engine, not only must every part be correctly assembled but everything must be spotlessly clean, all the oilways must be clear, locking washers and spring washers must always be fitted where needed and all bearings and other working surfaces must be thoroughly lubricated during assembly. Before assembly begins renew any bolts or studs the threads of which are in any way damaged, and whenever possible use new spring washers.
2 Apart from your normal tools, a supply of non fluffy rag, an oil can filled with engine oil (an empty washing up liquid plastic bottle thoroughly cleaned and washed out, will do), a supply of new spring washers, a set of new gaskets and a torque wrench should be collected together

44 Crankshaft - replacement

Ensure that the crankcase is thoroughly clean and that all the oilways are clear. A thin twist drill is useful for cleaning them out. If possible blow them out with compressed air. Treat the crankshaft in the same fashion and then inject engine oil into the crankshaft oilways.

Commence work on rebuilding the engine by replacing the crankshaft and main bearings.

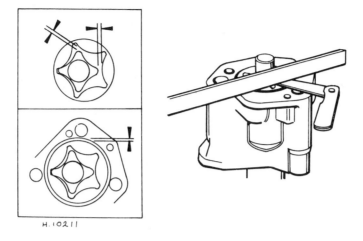

FIG.1.26. OIL PUMP WEAR CHECK

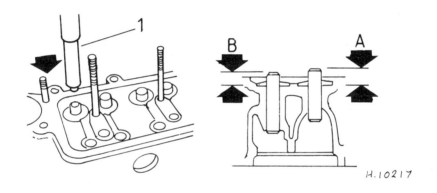

FIG.1.27. CORRECT FITTING DIMENSIONS OF VALVE GUIDE ABOVE MACHINED FACE OF VALVE SPRING SEAT

1   Shaped drift   A   (Inlet) 0.75 in. (19.05 mm)   B   (Exhaust) 0.625 in. (15.87 mm)

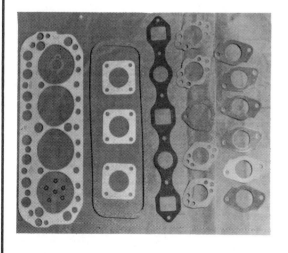
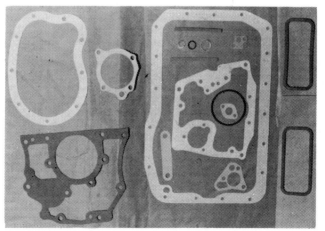

FIG.1.28. GASKET SETS

Left — cylinder head and manifolds   Right — sump and cylinder block

1   Fit the five upper halves of the main bearing shells to their location in the crankcase, after wiping the location clean.

2   Note that on the back of each bearing is a tab which engages in locating grooves in either the crankcase or the main bearing cap housings (Fig.1.17).

3   If new bearings are being fitted, carefully clean away all traces of the protective grease with which they are coated.

4   With the five upper bearing shells securely in place, wipe the lower bearing cap housings and fit the five lower shell bearings to their caps ensuring that the right shell goes into the right cap if the old bearings are being refitted.

5   Wipe the recesses either side of the centre main bearing which locate the upper halves of the thrust washers.

6   Generously lubricate the crankshaft journals and the upper and lower main bearing shells and carefully lower the crankshaft into position. Make sure that it is the right way round.

7   Introduce the upper halves of the thrust washers (the halves without tabs) into their grooves either side of the centre main bearing, rotating the crankshaft in the direction towards the main bearing tab (so that the main bearing shells do not slide out). At the same time feed the thrust washers into the locations with their oil grooves outwards away from the bearing.

8   Fit the main bearing caps in position ensuring that they locate properly. The mating surfaces must be spotlessly clean or the caps will not seat correctly.

9   When replacing the centre main bearing cap ensure that the thrust washers, generously lubricated, are fitted with their oil grooves facing outwards and the locating tab of each washer is in the slot in the bearing cap

10 Replace the main bearing cap nuts and screw them up finger tight.

11 Test the crankshaft for freedom of rotation. Should it be very stiff to turn or possess high spots a most careful inspection must be made, preferably by a skilled mechanic with a micrometer to trace the cause of the trouble. It is very seldom that any trouble of this nature will be experienced when fitting the crankshaft.

12 Tighten the main bearing nuts using a torque wrench set to 70 lb ft (9.7 kg m) and recheck the crankshaft for freedom of rotation.

13 Using a screwdriver between one crankshaft web and a main bearing cap, lever the crankshaft forwards and check the end float using feeler gauges. This should be 0.002 - 0.003 inch (0.051 - 0.076mm). If excessive new thrust washers or slightly oversize ones must be fitted.

14 During removal of the crankshaft gear wheel it should have been noted that there were shims behind the gear wheel. Replace the shims and then the inner Woodruff key.

---

45 Piston and connecting rod - reassembly

If the same pistons are being used, then they must be mated to the same connecting rod with the same gudgeon pin. If new pistons are being fitted it does not matter which connecting rod they are used with, but the gudgeon pins are not to be interchanged. See paragraph 8 for fully floating types. As the gudgeon pin is a press fit a special BLMC tool 18G 1150 with adaptors 18G 1150C is required to fit the gudgeon pin as shown in Fig.1.30 and should be used as follows:

1   Unscrew the large nut and withdraw the centre screw from the body a few inches. Well lubricate the screw thread and correctly locate the piston support adaptor.

2   Carefully slide the parallel sleeve with the groove end last onto the centre screw up as far as the shoulder. Lubricate the gudgeon pin and its bores in the connecting rod and piston with a graphited oil.

3   Fit the connecting rod and piston, side marked 'Front' or 'A' to the tool with the connecting rod entered on the sleeve up to the groove. Fit the gudgeon pin into the piston bore up to the connecting rod. Next fit the remover/replacer bush flange end towards the gudgeon pin.

4   Screw the stop nut onto the centre screw and adjust the nut to give a 0.032 inch (0.8 mm) end play. 'A' as shown in Fig. 1.30.

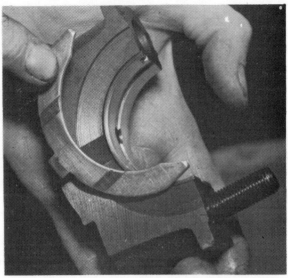

FIG.1.29. CRANKSHAFT THRUST WASHER FITMENT

Lock the nut securely with the lock screw. Ensure that the curved face of the adaptor is clean and slide the piston on the tool so that it fits into the curved face of the adaptor with the piston rings over the adaptor cut away.

5   Screw the large nut up the thrust race. Adjust the torque wrench to a setting of 16 lb ft (2.2kg m) if of the 'click' type which will represent the minimum load for an acceptable fit. Use the torque wrench previously set on the large nut, and a ring spanner on the lock screw. Pull the gudgeon pin into the piston until the flange of the remover/replacer bush is 0.04 inch (1.0 mm) from the piston skirt. It is critically important that the flange is NOT allowed to contact the piston. Finally withdraw the BLMC service tool.

6   Should the torque wrench not 'click' or reach 16 lb ft (2.2kg m) throughout the pull, the fit of the gudgeon pin in the connecting rod is not within limits; the parts must be renewed.

7   Ensure that the piston pivots freely on the gudgeon pin and is free to slide sideways. Should stiffness exist wash the assembly in paraffin, lubricate the gudgeon pin with graphited oil and recheck. Again if stiffness exists dismantle the assembly and check for signs of ingrained dirt or damage.

8   On early type fully floating gudgeon pins make sure the little end bush in the connecting rod is lined up through the oilway orifice. Then heat the piston in boiling water and push the gudgeon pin through the piston, little end bush and out into the other side of the piston. Use circlip pliers to fit in the circlips at each end of the gudgeon pin. Be gentle at all times — use no force. See Fig.1.31.

46 Piston ring - replacement

1   Check that the piston ring grooves and oilways are thoroughly clean and unblocked. Piston rings must always be fitted over the head of the piston and never from the bottom Fig. 1.32.

2   Refitment is the exact opposite procedure to removal, see Section 21.

3   Set all ring gaps 90° to each other.

4   An alternative method is to fit the rings by holding them slightly open with the thumbs and both your index fingers. This method requires a steady hand and great care for it is easy to open the ring too much and break it.

5   The special oil control ring requires a special fitting procedure. First fit the bottom rail of the oil control ring to the piston and position it below the bottom groove. Refit the oil control expander into the bottom groove and move the bottom oil control ring rail up into the bottom groove. Fit the top oil control rail into the bottom groove.

6   Ensure the ends of the expander are butting without overlapping as shown in the inset in Fig. 1.32.

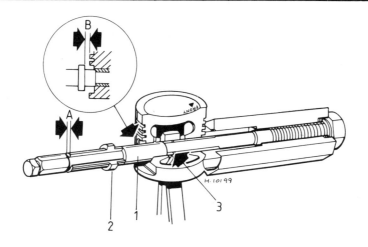

FIG.1.30. GUDGEON PIN REFITTING USING BLMC SERVICE TOOL 18G 1150 AND ADAPTORS 1150C

1　Gudgeon pin   2　Place flange towards gudgeon pin remover/replacer bush   3　Groove in sleeve towards gudgeon pin
　　　　　　　　　　　　　A　0.032 in. (0.8mm)
　　　　　　　　　　　　　B　0.04　in. (1 mm)

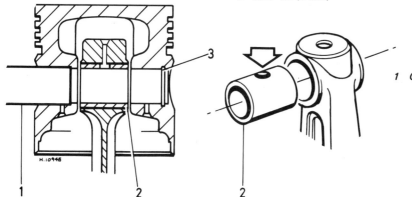

1　Gudgeon pin   2　Little end bush
　　　　　　3　Circlip

FIG.1.31. GUDGEON PIN AND LITTLE END BUSH ASSEMBLY (FULLY FLOATING TYPE)

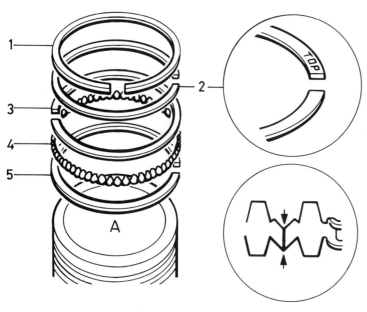

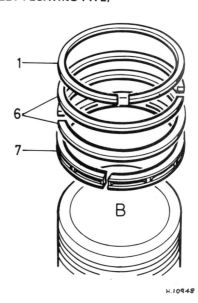

FIG.1.32. PISTON RING ASSEMBLIES

A　Pressed fit gudgeon pin   2　Tapered compression ring   4　Oil control expander   6　Internal stepped
B　Fully floating gudgeon pin   3　Top oil control ring   5　Bottom oil control ring   compression ring
1　Plain compression ring   rail   rail   7　Plain oil control ring

47 Piston - replacement

Fit pistons complete with connecting rods, to the cylinder bores as follows:

1   Wipe the cylinder bores clean with clean non fluffy rag.

2   The pistons, complete with connecting rods, must be fitted to their bores from above. As each piston is inserted into the bore ensure that it is the correct piston/connecting rod assembly for that particular bore and that the front of the piston is towards the front of the bore assuming that the connecting rod is fitted correctly ie., towards the front of the engine. Lubricate the piston well with clean engine oil.

3   Check that the piston ring gaps are 90° to each other.

4   The piston will slide into the bore only as far as the oil control ring and then it will be necessary to compress the piston rings into a clamp. The piston ring compressor should be fitted to the piston before it is inserted into the bore. If a proper piston ring clamp is not available then a suitable jubilee clip will do. Guide the piston into the bore until it reaches the ring compressor (Fig.1.33). Gently tap the piston into the cylinder bore with a wooden or plastic hammer.

48 Connecting rod to crankshaft - reassembly

1   Wipe the connecting rod half of the big end bearing location and the underside of the shell bearing clean, (as for the main bearing shells) and fit the shell bearing in position with its locating torque engaged with the corresponding groove in the connecting rod. Always fit new shells.

2   Generously lubricate the crankpin journals with engine oil and turn the crankshaft so that the crankpin is in the most advantageous position for the connecting rod to be drawn onto it.

3   Fit the bearing shell to the connecting rod cap in the same way as with the connecting rod itself.

4   Generously lubricate the shell bearing and offer up the connecting rod bearing cap to the connecting rod. Fit the connecting rod cap retaining nuts. It will be observed that these are special twelve sided nuts.

5   Tighten the retaining nuts to a torque wrench setting of 33 lb ft (4.6 kg m).

49 Camshaft - replacement

1   Fit the engine front plate with a new gasket between the cylinder block and plate and tighten the retaining bolts and spring washers.

2   Wipe the camshaft bearings and generously lubricate them with engine oil.

3   Temporarily refit the camshaft gear wheel and locating plate and secure with the retaining nut. Using feeler gauges check the end float, which should not exceed 0.003 to 0.007 inch (0.07 to 0.18mm). If this maximum limit is exceeded obtain a new locating plate.

4   Remove the camshaft gear wheel retaining nut, gear wheel and locating plate.

5   Insert the camshaft into the crankcase gently, taking care not to damage the camshaft bearings with the sharp edges of the cams. Take care, the camshaft lobe edges are sharp.

50 Oil pump and drive shaft - replacement

Invert the cylinder block and insert the oil pump drive shaft and its thrust washer (if fitted), the latter being placed on the oil pump side of the gear teeth. Fit a new oil pump to crankcase gasket over the three studs followed by the oil pump. Ensure that the shaft dog correctly engages with the drive gear dog. Fit spring washers on the studs followed by the three nuts. Tighten to a torque wrench setting of 15 lb ft (1.9kg m).

51 Timing gears, chain tensioner, cover - replacement

1   Before reassembly begins check that the shim washers are in place on the crankshaft nose. If new gear wheels are being fitted it may be necessary to fit additional washers as detailed in paragraph 7. These washers ensure that the crankshaft gearwheel lines up correctly with the camshaft gearwheel (Fig.1.34).

2   Replace the woodruff keys in their respective slots in the crankshaft and camshaft and ensure that they are fully seated. If their edges are burred they must be cleaned with a fine file.

3   Lay the camshaft gearwheels on a clean surface so that the two timing dots are adjacent to each other. Slip the timing chain over them and pull the gearwheels back into mesh with the chain so that the timing dots, although further apart, are still adjacent to each other as shown in Fig.1.35.

FIG.1.33. PISTON FITMENT WITH CLAMP

FIG.1.34. SHIM WASHERS ON CRANKSHAFT

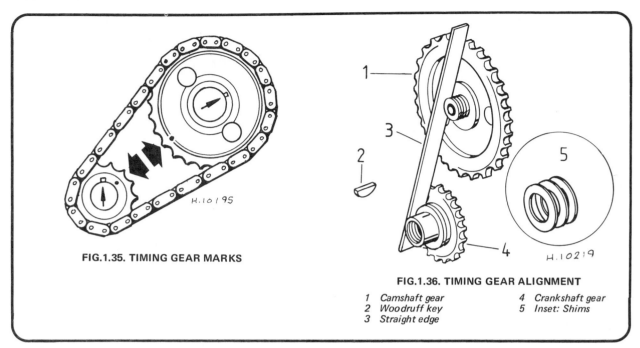

FIG.1.35. TIMING GEAR MARKS

FIG.1.36. TIMING GEAR ALIGNMENT

1	Camshaft gear	4	Crankshaft gear
2	Woodruff key	5	Inset: Shims
3	Straight edge		

4   Rotate the crankshaft so that the woodruff key is at top dead centre. The engine should be in the upright position.

5   Rotate the camshaft so that when viewed from the front the woodruff key is at two o'clock position.

6   Fit the timing chain and gearwheel assembly onto the camshaft and crankshaft keeping the timing marks adjacent. If the camshaft and crankshaft have been positioned accurately, it will be found that the keyways on the gearwheels will match the position of the keys, although it may be necessary to rotate the camshaft a fraction to ensure accurate lining up of the camshaft gear wheel.

7   Press the gearwheels into position on the crankshaft and camshaft as far as they will go. NOTE: If new gearwheels are being fitted they should be checked for alignment before being finally fitted to the engine. Place the gearwheels in position without the timing chain and place the straight edge of a steel rule from the side of the camshaft gear teeth to the crankshaft gearwheel and measure the gap between the steel rule and the gearwheel. Fit shims equal to the measured gap to the front of the crankshaft, behind the gearwheel (Fig. 1.36).

8   Next assemble the timing chain tensioner by inserting one end of the spring into the plunger and fit the other end of the spring into the cylinder.

9   Compress the spring until the cylinder enters the plunger bore and ensure the peg in the plunger engages the helical slot. insert and turn the Allen key clockwise until the end of the cylinder is below the peg and the spring is held compressed.

10 Fit the backplate and secure the assembly to the cylinder block with the two bolts. Turn the tabs of the lockwasher shown in Fig.1.10.

11 With the timing chain in position, the tensioner can now be relaxed. Insert the Allen key and turn it clockwise so the sliper head moves forward under spring pressure against the chain. Do not under any circumstances turn the key anti-clockwise or force the slipper head into the chain. Replace the bottom plug and lock with a tab washer.

12 Replace the oil thrower so that the letter 'F' is on its front face ie., this face must be furthest from the engine.

13 Fit the locking washer to the camshaft gearwheel with its locating tab in the gearwheel keyway is shown.

14 Screw on the camshaft gearwheel retaining nut and tighten securely.

15 Bend up the locking tab of the locking washer to securely hold the camshaft retaining nut.

16 Generously oil the chain and gearwheels.

17 Ensure the interior of the timing cover and the timing cover flange is clean and generously lubricate the oil seal in the timing cover. Then with a new gasket in position, fit the timing cover to the block using the pulley to centralise the cover.

18 Screw in the timing cover retaining bolts with the flat washer next to the cover flange and under the spring washer. The ¼ inch bolts should be tightened with a torque spanner to 6 lb ft (0.83kg m) and the 5/16 inch bolts to 14 lb ft (1.94kg m).

19 Fit the crankshaft pulley to the nose of the crankshaft ensuring that the keyway engages with the woodruff key.

20 Fit the crankshaft retaining bolt locking washer in position and screw on the crankshaft pulley retaining nut. Tighten to a torque of 70 lb ft (9.69kg m) and bend over the locking washer.

52 Engine backplate - refitting

1   Wipe the rear face of the cylinder block and smear a little grease onto a new gasket. Carefully fit the gasket to the cylinder block.

2   Carefully refit the backplate, locating the dowel at the top of the cylinder block in the centre hole at the top of the backplate and the second dowel at the bottom left hand side of the cylinder block.

3   Refit the backplate to the cylinder block securing bolts and spring washers and tighten fully.

53 Sump refitting

1   After the sump has been thoroughly cleaned, scrape all traces of the old sump gasket from the sump flange, and fit new main bearing cap oil seals. Should the oil seal material stand out more than 1/16 inch (1.587mm) above the sump flange it must be cut back to this figure.

2   Thoroughly clean and scrape the crankcase to sump flange. Apply grease to the crankcase to sump flange and carefully fit new gasket halves to the flange.

3   Carefully fit the sump to the underside of the crankcase.

4   Refit the sump retaining bolts, shaped washers and spring washers.

5   Tighten the sump bolts to a torque wrench setting of 6 lb ft (0.8kg m).

54 Oil pressure relief valve and switch - replacement

1   Assemble the valve components in the order of, valve, spring
and domed nut with new washers.
2   Carefully insert the assembly into its location at the rear of
the cylinder block. Tighten the domed nut fully.
3   Locate the oil pressure switch in its drilling in the side of the
cylinder block just above the oil pressure relief valve and tighten
firmly using an open ended spanner (photo).

55 Flywheel and clutch - refitting

1   Clean the mating faces of the crankshaft and flywheel and fit
the flywheel to the dowel in the end of the crankshaft flange.
2   Replace the six flywheel securing bolts and circular washer
and tighten these bolts to a torque wrench setting of 40 lb ft
(5.5kg m). It will be necessary to lock the flywheel using a
screwdriver through the sump bracket and the end engaged in
the starter ring teeth.
3   Bend up the lockwasher tabs.
4   Refit the clutch disc and pressure plate assembly and lightly
secure the position with the six bolts and spring washers (photo).
5   If a first motion shaft is available use this to line up the
clutch disc with the crankshaft spigot bearing. As an alternative
use a suitable piece of wood as a dowel (photo).
6   Firmly tighten the clutch securing bolts in a diagonal manner
(photo). The flywheel may be locked using the screwdriver as
described in paragraph 2.

56 Water and fuel pump - refitting

1   Make sure the mating faces of the water pump and cylinder
block are free of old gasket or jointing compound.
2   Smear a little grease onto the water pump and place on a new
gasket.
3   Fit the water pump to the cylinder block mating it to the
dowels in the cylinder block face.
4   Refit and tighten the securing bolts and spring washers.
5   Clean the mating faces of the crankcase and fuel pump and
fit a new set of gasket to the spacer. Slide the spacer and gaskets
over the studs.
6   Refit the fuel pump and secure with the two nuts and spring
washers.

57 Valve and spring - reassembly

    To refit the valves and the valve springs to the cylinder head,
proceed as follows:
1   Rest the cylinder head on its side, or if the manifold studs are
fitted, with the gasket surface downwards.
2   Fit each valve and valve spring in turn, wiping down and
lubricating each valve stem as it is inserted onto the same valve
guide from which it was removed.
3   As each valve is inserted slip the oil control rubber ring into
place just under the bottom of the cotter groove (use a new
rubber ring if at all possible).
4   Move the cylinder head towards the edge of the work bench
if it is facing downwards and slide it partially over the edge of
the bench so as to fit the bottom half of the valve spring
compressor to the valve head.
5   Slip the valve springs and cap over the valve stem.
6   With the base of the valve compressor on the valve head,
compress the valve spring until the cotters can be slipped into
place in the cotter grooves. Gently release the compressor.
7   Repeat this procedure until all eight valves and valve springs
are fitted.

54.3 Oil pressure switch

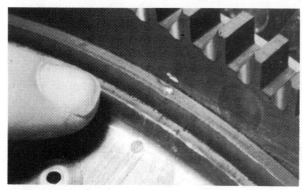

55.4 Clutch mating marks

55.5 Clutch disc centralisation

55.6 Tightening clutch securing bolts

58 Rocker shaft - reassembly

1   To reassemble the rocker shaft fit the split pin, flat washer, and spring washer at the rear end of the shaft and then slide on the rocker arms, rocker shaft pedestals, and spacing springs in the same order in which they were removed (Fig.1.8), and slip the locating plate into place. Finally, fit to the front of the shaft the spring washer, plain washer and split pin, in that order.

59 Tappet - replacement

Generously lubricate the tappets internally and externally and insert them in the bores from which they were removed through the tappet chest.

60 Cylinder head - replacement

1   After checking that both the cylinder block and cylinder head mating faces are perfectly clean, generously lubricate each cylinder with engine oil. Always use a new cylinder head gasket. The old gasket will be compressed and incapable of giving a good seal.
2   Never smear grease or gasket cement either side of the gasket, for pressure leaks may blow through it.
3   The cylinder head gasket is marked FRONT and should be fitted in position according to the markings (photo).
4   Carefully lower the gasket into position ensuring that the stud threads do not damage the side of the holes through which they pass (photo).
5   The cylinder head may now be lowered over the studs until it rests on the cylinder head gasket (photo).
6   With the cylinder head in position fit the pushrods in the same order in which they were removed. Ensure that they locate properly in the stems of the tappets.
7   Refit the two tappet covers with new cork gaskets and tighten the two securing bolts and washers.
8   The rocker shaft assembly can now be lowered over its eight locating studs. Take care that the rocker arms are the right way round (photo). Lubricate the ball ends, and insert the rocker arm ball ends into the pushrod cups. NOTE: Failure to replace the ball ends in the cups can result in the ball ends seating on the edge of a pushrod or outside it when the head and rocker assembly is pulled down tight.
9   Fit the lock plate to the fourth pedestal.
10 Fit the four rocker pedestal nuts and washers, and then the four cylinder heads stud nuts and washers which also hold down the rocker pedestals. Pull the nuts down evenly, but without tightening them right up.
11 Fit the remaining nuts and washers to the cylinder head studs.
12 When all are in position tighten the rocker pedestal nuts to a torque wrench setting of 25 lb ft (3.4 kg m) and the cylinder head nuts to a torque wrench setting of 45 - 50 lb ft (6.2 - 6.9 kg m). The correct order is shown in Fig.1.6.

61 Rocker arm/valve - adjustment

1   The valve adjustments should be made with the engine cold. The importance of correct rocker/valve stem clearances cannot be overstressed as they vitally affect the performance.
2   If the clearances are set too wide, the efficiency of the engine is reduced as the valves open late and close earlier then was intended. If the clearances are set too close there is a danger that the stem and pushrods upon expansion when hot will not allow the valves to close properly which will cause burning of the valve head and possible warping.
3   If the engine is in the car, to get at the rockers, it is merely necessary to remove the two holding down dome nuts from the cover, and then to lift the rocker cover and gasket away.

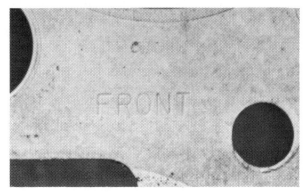
60.3 Cylinder head gasket fitting position

60.4 Fitting new cylinder head gasket

60.5 Lowering cylinder head into position

60.12 Tightening cylinder head securing nuts

4 It is important that the clearance is set when the tappet of the valve being adjusted is on the heel of the cam (ie. opposite the peak). This can be done by carrying out the adjustments in the following order, which also avoids turning the crankshaft more than necessary.

Valve fully open	Check and adjust
Valve Number 8	Valve number 1
Valve Number 6	Valve number 3
Valve Number 4	Valve number 5
Valve Number 7	Valve number 2
Valve Number 1	Valve number 8
Valve Number 3	Valve number 6
Valve Number 5	Valve number 4
Valve Number 2	Valve number 7

5 The correct valve clearance is given in the Specifications at the beginning of this chapter. It is obtained by slackening the hexagonal locknut with a spanner while holding the ball pin against rotation with a screwdriver as shown in Fig.1.37. Then, still pressing down with the screwdriver, insert feeler gauge of the required thickness between the valve stem and head of the rocker arm and adjust the ball pin until the feeler gauge will just move in and out without nipping. Then still holding the ball pin in the correct position, tighten the locknut (photo).

6 An alternative method is to set the gaps with the engine running at idle speed. Although this method may be faster, more practice is needed and it is no more reliable.

7 Refit the rocker cover and gasket, and secure with the dome nuts and washers.

62 Distributor and distributor drive - replacement

It is important to set the distributor drive correctly otherwise the ignition timing will be totally incorrect. It is easy to set the distributor drive in apparently the right position, but in fact exactly 180° out, by omitting to select the correct cylinder which must not only be at TDC but must also be on its firing stroke with both valves closed. The distributor drive should therefore not be fitted until the cylinder head is in position and the valves can be observed. Alternatively, if the timing cover has not been replaced, the distributor drive can be replaced when the dots on the timing wheels are adjacent to each other.

1 The distributor drive shaft can only be fitted with the pistons half way up or down their bores. Turn the crankshaft so that the pistons are in this position (90° before or after TDC).

2 Screw a 5/16 inch UNF bolt about 3½ inches (90mm) long into the threaded hole in the top end of the shaft and fit the shaft to the engine.

3 Rotate the crankshaft so that No. 1 piston is at TDC and on its firing stroke (the dots in the timing gears will be adjacent to each other). When No 1 piston is at TDC the inlet valve on No 4 cylinder is just opening and the exhaust valve closing (photo).

4 With the pistons in the engine at TDC it will not be possible to remove the drive shaft, but it is possible to lift it sufficiently to bring it out of mesh with the drive gear on the camshaft. The drive shaft can then be turned to the correct timing position.

5 When the groove on the crankshaft pulley wheel is in line with the TDC pointer on the timing gear cover, then No 1 and No 4 piston are at TDC 'check that the No 4 cylinder valves are just rocking to ensure correct stroke for No1 cylinder.

6 Position the drive shaft so that the slot is just below the horizontal, and the larger of the two segments (one on each side of the slot) is at the top. As the gear on the shaft engages with the skew gear on the camshaft the drive gear will turn anti-clockwise until the top of the slot is adjacent to the 2 o'clock position. See Fig.1.12.

7 Remove the bolt from the drive shaft.

8 Replace the distributor housing and lock it in position with

61.5A Adjustment of rocker arm/valve clearance

61.5B Checking clearance with feeler gauge

62.3 Timing marks on pulley and cover

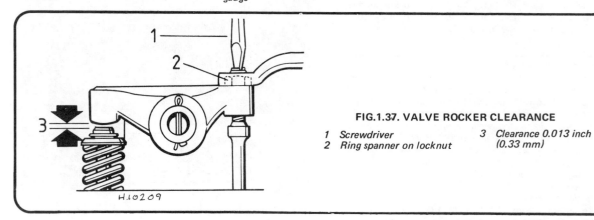

FIG.1.37. VALVE ROCKER CLEARANCE

1 Screwdriver
2 Ring spanner on locknut
3 Clearance 0.013 inch (0.33 mm)

H.10209

the single bolt and spring washer. It is important that the correct bolt is used so that the head does not protrude above the face of the housing.

9 The distributor can now be replaced and the two securing bolts and spring washers which hold the distributor clamping plate to the distributor housing tightened. If the clamp bolt on the clamping plate was not previously loosened and the distributor body was not turned in the clamping plate, then the ignition timing will be as previously set. If the clamping bolt has been loosened, then it will be necessary to retime the ignition as described in Chapter 4.

63 Final assembly

1 Refit the rocker cover, using a new cork gasket and secure in position with the two domed nuts.

2 Fit the two tappet cover plates, using new gaskets and tighten the tappet chest bolts to a torque wrench setting of 2 lb ft (0.3kg m). Do not exceed this figure or the covers will distort and leak oil.

3 Fit a new manifold gasket over the studs taking care not to rip it as it passes over the stud threads.

4 Replace the manifold and secure in position with the six nuts, spring and large plain washers.

5 Insert the thermostat into its housing making sure the word 'FRONT' marked on the flange is towards the front of the engine.

6 Fit a new gasket taking care not to rip the gasket as it passes over the threads of the three studs. Then refit the thermostat housing cover and secure with the three nuts and spring washers.

7 If the dip stick guide tube was removed this should next be inserted into its drilling in the side of the crankcase.

8 Fit a new oil filter canister (see Section 25).

9 It should be noted that in all cases it is best to reassemble the engine as far as possible before refitting it to the car. This means that alternator, fan belt and other minor attachments should be replaced at this stage.

64 Engine replacement

Although the engine or engine and gearbox can be replaced by one man and a suitable hoist, it is easier if two are present. Generally replacement is the reverse sequence to removal. In addition however:

1 Ensure all the loose leads, cables etc., are tucked out of the way. It is easy to trap one and cause much additional work after the engine is replaced.

2 Refit the following:

a) Mounting nuts, bolts and washers.
b) Propeller shaft coupling.

c) Reconnect the clutch pipe to the slave cylinder and bleed the system (see Chapter 5).
d) Speedometer cable.
e) Gear change lever and surround.
f) Carpets.
g) Oil pressure switch cable.
h) Water temperature indicator sender unit cable.
i) Wire to coil, distributor and alternator.
j) Carburettor controls and air cleaner.
k) Exhaust manifold to down pipe.
l) Earth and starter motor cables.
m) Radiator and hoses.
n) Heater hoses.
o) Engine closed circuit breather hoses.
p) Vacuum advance and retard pipe.
q) Battery (if removed).
r) Fuel lines to carburettor(s) and pump.
s) Bonnet.

3 Finally check that the drain taps are closed and refill the cooling system with water and the engine with Castrol GTX.

65 Engine - initial start up after overhaul and major repair

Make sure that the battery is fully charged and that all lubricants, coolants and fuel are replenished.

If the fuel system has been dismantled, it will require several revolutions of the engine on the starter motor to pump petrol to the carburettor(s).

As soon as the engine fires and runs, keep it going at a fast tickover only (no faster) and bring it up to normal working temperatures.

As the engine warms up, there will be odd smells and some smoke from parts getting hot and burning off oil deposits. Look for water or oil leaks which will be obvious if serious. Check also the clamp connection of the exhaust pipe to the manifold as these do not always 'find' their exact gas tight position until the warmth and vibration have acted on them, and it is almost certain that they will need tightening further. This should be done of course, with the engine cold.

When the engine running temperature has been reached, adjust the idling speed as described in Chapter 3.

Stop the engine and wait a few minutes to see if any lubricant or coolant drips out.

Road test the car to check that the timing is correct and giving the necessary smoothness and power. Do not race the engine. If new bearings and/or pistons and rings have been fitted, it should be treated as a new engine and run in at reduced revolutions for 500 miles (800 km). After this mileage, it is good practice to change the engine oil and filter, and to check the tightness of the cylinder head nuts. Adjust the valve clearances also if necessary.

Symptom	Reason/s	Remedy
Engine will not turn over when starter switch is operated	Flat battery Bad battery connections Bad connections at solenoid switch and/or starter motor	Check that battery is fully charged and that all connections are clean and tight.
	Starter motor jammed	Rock car back and forth with a gear engaged. If ineffective remove starter (not automatic).
	Defective solenoid	Remove and check solenoid.
	Starter motor defective	Remove starter and overhaul.
Engine turns over normally but fails to fire and run	No spark at plugs	Check ignition system according to procedures given in Chapter 4.
	No fuel reaching engine	Check fuel system according to procedures given in Chapter 3.
	Too much fuel reaching the engine (flooding)	Check fuel system if necessary as described in Chapter 3.
Engine starts but runs unevenly and misfires	Ignition and/or fuel system faults	Check the ignition and fuel systems as though the engine had failed to start.
	Incorrect valve clearances	Check and reset clearances.
	Burnt out valves	Remove cylinder head and examine and overhaul as necessary.
Lack of power	Ignition and/or fuel system faults	Check the ignition and fuel systems for correct ignition timing and carburettor settings.
	Incorrect valve clearances	Check and reset the clearances.
	Burnt out valves	Remove cylinder head and examine and overhaul as necessary.
	Worn out piston or cylinder bores	Remove cylinder head and examine pistons and cylinder bores. Overhaul as necessary.
Excessive oil consumption	Oil leaks from crankshaft oil seal, rocker cover gasket, drain plug gasket, sump plug washer	Identify source of leak and repair as appropriate.
	Worn piston rings or cylinder bores resulting in oil being burnt by engine Smoky exhaust is an indication	Fit new rings or rebore cylinders and fit new pistons, depending on degree of wear.
	Worn valve guides and/or defective valve stem seals	Remove cylinder head and recondition valve guides and valves and seals as necessary.
Excessive mechanical noise from engine	Wrong valve to rocker clearances	Adjust valve clearances.
	Worn crankshaft bearings Worn cylinders (piston slap)	Inspect and overhaul where necessary.
Unusual vibration	Misfiring on one or more cylinders	Check ignition system.
	Loose mounting bolts	Check tightness of bolts and condition of flexible mountings.

NOTE: When investigating starting and uneven running faults do not be tempted into snap diagnosis. Start from the beginning of the check procedure and follow it through. It will take less time in the long run. Poor performance from an engine in terms of power and economy is not normally diagnosed quickly. In any event the ignition and fuel systems must be checked first before assuming any further investigation needs to be made.

Chapter 2 Cooling system

For modifications, and information applicable to later models, see Supplement at end of manual

Contents

General description   1
Cooling system - draining   2
Cooling system - flushing   3
Cooling system - filling   4
Radiator - removal, and refitting   5
Radiator - inspection and cleaning   6
Thermostat - removal, testing and replacement   7
Water pump - removal and refitting   8

Water pump - dismantling and overhaul   9
Fan belt - removal and replacement   10
Fan belt - adjustment   11
Expansion tank   12
Temperature gauge thermal transmitter   13
Anti-freeze mixture   14
Fault diagnosis   15

Specifications

Type	... ...	Pressurised system with expansion tank

Thermostat type ... ...   Wax
     Thermostat settings: Standard ... ...   82° C (180° F)
                     Hot climate ... ...   74° C (165° F)
                     Cold climate ... ...   88° C (190° F)
     Blow off pressure of expansion tank cap ... ...   15 lb in^2 (1.05 kg cm^2)

Fan belt tension ... ...   0.5 in (13mm) deflection on longest run.
Water pump ... ...   Centrifugal type
     Bearing spindle diameter ... ...   0.6262 - 0.6267 in (15.901 - 15.918mm)
     Impeller bore ... ...   0.6244 - 0.6252 in (15.860 - 15.880mm)
     Pulley hub bore ... ...   0.6239 - 0.6247 in (15.847 - 15.867mm)
     Bearing assembly diameter ... ...   1.1813 - 1.1818 in (30.005 - 30.017mm)
     Body bore ... ...   1.1807 - 1.1811 in (29.99 - 30.00mm)
Cooling system capacity (with heater) ... ...   9 pints (5.1 litres)

TORQUE WRENCH SETTINGS

	lb ft	kg m
Water pump retaining bolts	17	2.35
Water outlet elbow	8	1.11
Water pump pulley set screws	18	2.49
Thermal transmitter	16	2.21

1 General description

The engine cooling water is circulated by a thermo-syphon, water pump assisted system, and the coolant is pressurised. This is primarily to prevent premature boiling in adverse conditions and to allow the engine to operate at its most efficient running temperature; this being just under the boiling point of water. The overflow pipe from the radiator is connected to an expansion chamber which makes topping up virtually unnecessary. The coolant expands when hot, and instead of being forced down an overflow pipe and lost, it flows into the expansion chamber. As the engine cools the coolant contracts and because of the pressure differential flows back into the radiator.

The cap on the expansion chamber is set to a pressure of 15 lb in^2 (1.05 kg cm^2) which increases the boiling point of the coolant to 230°F. If the water temperature exceeds this figure and the water boils, the pressure in the system forces the internal valve of the cap off its seat thus exposing the expansion tank overflow pipe down which the steam from the boiling water escapes and so relieves the pressure. It is therefore important to check that the expansion chamber cap is in good condition and that the spring behind the sealing washers has not weakened. Check that the rubber seal has not perished and its seating in the neck is clean to ensure a good seal. A special tool which enables a cap to be pressure tested is available at some garages.

The cooling system comprises the radiator, top and bottom hoses, heater hoses, the impeller water pump (mounted on the front of the engine it carries the fan blades and is driven by the fan belt) and, the thermostat.

The system functions as follows: Cold water from the radiator circulates up the lower radiator hose to the water pump where it is pushed round the water passages in the cylinder block, helping to keep the cylinder bores and pistons cool.

The water then travels up into the cylinder head and circulates round the combustion spaces and valve seats absorbing more heat. Then, when the engine is at its normal operating temperature, the water travels out of the cylinder head, past the now open thermostat into the upper radiator hose and so into the radiator. The water passes along the radiator from one side to the other where it is rapidly cooled by the rush of cold air through the horizontal radiator core. The water now cool reaches the bottom hose when the cycle is repeated.

When the engine is cold the thermostat (a valve which opens and closes according to water temperature) maintains the circulation of the same water in the engine by returning it via the by-pass hose to the cylinder block. Only when the correct minimum operating temperature has been reached, as shown in the specifications, does the thermostat begin to open allowing water to return to the radiator.

2 Cooling system - draining

1   If the engine is cold, remove the pressure cap from the expansion tank. If the engine is hot, turn the cap **very slowly** to release the pressure in the system. Use a rag over the cap to protect your hands from escaping steam. If the engine is hot and the cap is released suddenly, the drop in pressure can result in the coolant boiling.

2   If the coolant is to be re-used, drain it into a clean container of suitable capacity.

3   Undo and remove the filler plug located on the top left-hand side of the radiator.

4   Slacken the bottom hose clip, detach the hose and allow the coolant to drain from the radiator.

5   Now undo and remove the cylinder block drain plug located at the rear of the right-hand side of the engine behind the distributor.

6   When the coolant has finished draining out of the cylinder block, probe the orifice with a short piece of wire to dislodge any particles of rust or sediment which may be causing a blockage thus preventing complete draining.

3 Cooling system - flushing

1   Generally even with proper use, the cooling system will gradually lose its efficiency as the radiator becomes choked with rust scale, deposits from water and other sediment. To clean the system out, remove the radiator filler plug, cylinder block plug and bottom hose and leave a hose running in the radiator filler plug hole for fifteen minutes.

2   Reconnect the bottom hose, refit the cylinder block plug and refill the cooling system as described in Section 4, adding a proprietary cleaning compound. Run the engine for fifteen minutes. All sediment and sludge should now have been loosened and may be removed by then draining the system and refilling again.

3   In very bad cases the radiator should be reverse flushed. This can be done with the radiator in position, the cylinder block plug is left in position and hose placed in the bottom hose union of the radiator. Water under pressure is forced through the orifice and out of the filler plug hole.

4   The hose is then removed and placed in the filler plug hole and the radiator washed out in the usual manner.

4 Cooling system - filling

1   Fit the cylinder block drain plug and if the bottom hose has been removed it should be reconnected.

2   Fill the system slowly to ensure that no air locks develop. Check that the valve to the heater unit is open, otherwise an air lock may form in the heater. The best type of water to use in the cooling system is rain water.

3   Fill up the radiator to the level of the filler plug and top up the level of coolant in the expansion tank to the level indicated. Refit the radiator filler plug and expansion tank cap.

4   Start the engine and run at a fast idle speed for 30 seconds.

5   Stop the engine and top up the radiator through the filler plug and refit the plug.

6   Run the engine until it has reached its normal operating temperature. Stop the engine and allow to cool.

7   Top up the expansion tank to the level marked.

5 Radiator - removal and refitting

1   Drain the cooling system as described in Section 2.

2   Slacken the clip securing the expansion tank hose to the radiator. Carefully ease the hose from the union pipe on the radiator.

3   Slacken the clips securing the radiator top and bottom hoses to the radiator inlet pipes and carefully ease the two hoses from these pipes.

4   Undo and remove the screws with spring and plain washers securing the two top radiator mounting brackets to the front panel. Lift away these two brackets.

5   The radiator may now be lifted up from its lower mountings and away from the front of the car.

6   Refitting the radiator is the reverse sequence to removal. Refill the cooling system as described in Section 4. Carefully check to ensure that all hose joints are water tight.

6 Radiator - inspection and cleaning

1   With the radiator out of the car, any leaks can be soldered up or repaired with a compound such as Cataloy. Clean out the inside of the radiator by flushing as described in Section 3.

2   When the radiator is out of the car, it is advantageous to turn it upside down for reverse flushing. Clean the exterior of the radiator by hosing down the radiator matrix with a strong jet of water to clean away road dirt, dead flies etc.

3   Inspect the radiator hoses for cracks, internal and external perishing and damage caused by overtightening of the hose clips. Replace the hoses as necessary. Examine the radiator hose clips and renew them if they are rusted or distorted. The drain plugs and washers should be renewed if leaking.

7 Thermostat - removal, testing and replacement

1   To remove the thermostat, partially drain the cooling system (usually 4 pints, 2.27 litres is enough), loosen the upper radiator hose at the thermostat end and ease it off the elbow. Unscrew the three nuts and lift away the washers from the thermostat housing. Lift away the thermostat elbow from the studs followed by the paper joint and finally the thermostat itself.

2   Test the thermostat for correct functioning by suspending it together with a thermometer on a string in a container of cold water. Heat the water and note the temperature at which the thermostat begins to open. This should be 82ºC (180ºF) for a standard thermostat. It is advantageous in winter to fit a thermostat that does not open until 88ºC (190ºF). Discard the thermostat if it opens too early. Continue heating the water until the thermostat is fully open. Then let it cool down naturally. If the thermostat does not fully open in boiling water, or does not close down as the water cools, then it must be discarded and a new one fitted. If the thermostat is stuck open when cold this will be apparent when removing it from the housing.

3   Refitting the thermostat is the reverse procedure to removal. Always ensure that the cylinder head and thermostat housing elbow faces are clean and flat. If the thermostat elbow is badly corroded and eaten away, fit a new elbow. A new paper joint must always be used.

4   If a new winter thermostat is fitted, provided the summer one is functioning correctly it can be placed on one side and refitted in the spring. Thermostats should last for two to three years, at least, between renewal.

8 Water pump - removal and refitting

1   For safety reasons disconnect the battery.

2   Refer to Section 5 and remove the radiator.

3   Refer to Chapter 13 and remove the alternator.

4   Undo and remove the four bolts and spring washers securing the fan blades to the pulley hub. Lift away the circular metal plate, fan blades and pulley.

5   Slacken the clip securing the bottom hose to the water pump and carefully ease off the hose.

6   Undo and remove the four bolts and spring washers which hold the pump to the front of the cylinder block. Note these bolts are of different lengths and must be refitted in their original positions.

7   Lift away the pump and recover the paper gasket.

8   Refitting is the reverse sequence to removal but the following additional points should be noted:

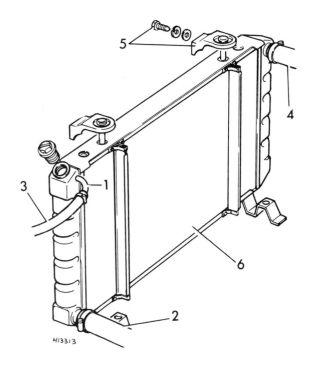

H13313

FIG.2.1 RADIATOR ASSEMBLY

1	Outlet elbow	4	Top hose
2	Bottom hose	5	Securing screws and bracket
3	Expansion tank hose	6	Radiator

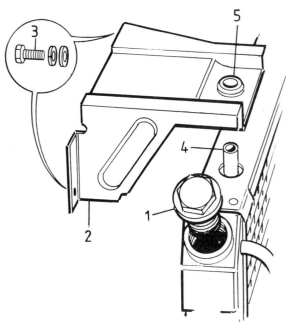

FIG.2.2 RADIATOR UPPER MOUNTING

1	Radiator filler plug		spring and plain washer
2	Mounting bracket	4	Radiator location dowel
3	Bracket securing bolt,	5	Rubber grommet

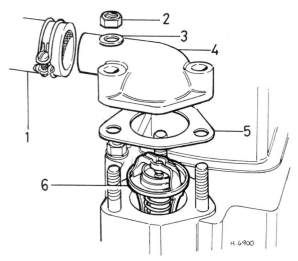

H.6900

FIG.2.3 THERMOSTAT HOUSING

1	Radiator top hose	4	Thermostat housing
2	Nut	5	Gasket
3	Plain washer	6	Thermostat

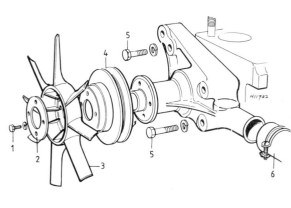

H11732

FIG.2.4 WATER PUMP ATTACHMENTS

1	Fan securing bolts	5	Water pump retaining bolts
2	Packing bolts	6	Bottom hose
3	Fan		
4	Pulley		

a) Clean the mating faces of the water pump body and cylinder block to ensure a good water-tight joint.
b) Always use a new paper gasket.
c) Adjust the fan belt tension as described in Section 11.

9 Water pump - dismantling and overhaul

If the water pump starts to leak, showing signs of excessive movement of the spindle, or is noisy during operation the pump can be dismantled and overhauled. Make sure that individual parts are available, perhaps a better alternative would be to fit a service exchange reconditioned pump.

1 Using a suitable universal puller or a press carefully press the bearing spindle out of the pulley hub.
2 Support the water pump body and carefully tap out the bearing assembly complete with impeller and seal.
3 Next press out the bearing spindle from the impeller and finally remove the water seal from the bearing spindle. Dismantling is now complete.
4 Thoroughly inspect all parts for wear or damage. Replace any faulty parts.
5 To reassemble first press the bearing assembly into the pump body until the dimensions are reached. (See Fig 2.6).
6 Support the bearing spindle and press the pulley hub onto the spindle until dimension B is reached. Again see Fig 2.6.
7 Fit the water seal into the pump body, suitably supporting the bearing spindle. Smear the impeller face, which abuts with

the water seal, with silicone grease, then press the impeller onto the spindle to obtain the dimension 'C' in Fig 2.6.
8 Should it be observed during reassembly that the interference fit of either the hub or impeller on the bearing spindle has been lost the hub and/or impeller must be renewed.

10 Fan belt - removal and replacement

If the fan belt is worn or has over stretched it should be renewed. The most usual reason for replacement is that the belt has broken in service. It is therefore recommended that a spare belt is always carried in the car. Replacement is a reversal of the removal procedure, but if replacement is due to breakage:
1 Loosen the alternator pivot and slotted link bolts and move the alternator towards the engine.
2 Carefully fit the belt over the crankshaft, water pump and alternator pulleys.
3 Adjust the belt as described in Section 11 and tighten the alternator mounting bolts, NOTE: after fitting a new belt it will require adjustment 250 miles (400 km) later.

11 Fan belt - adjustment

1 It is important to keep the fan belt correctly adjusted and should be checked every 6,000 miles (9,600 km) or 6 months. If the belt is loose it will slip, wear rapidly and cause the alternator and water pump to malfunction. If the belt is too

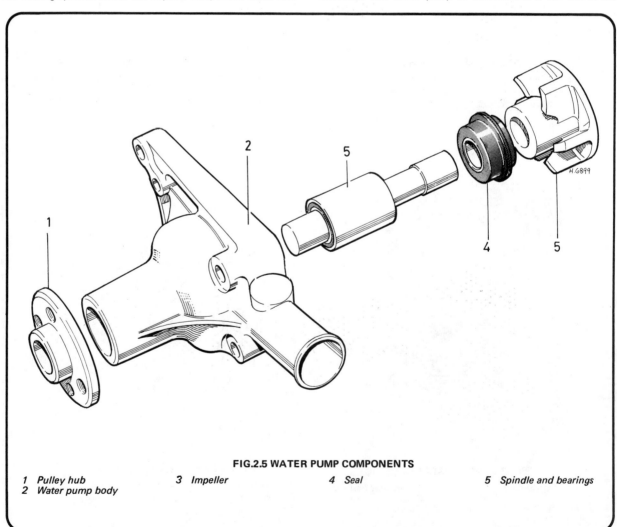

FIG.2.5 WATER PUMP COMPONENTS

1 *Pulley hub*
2 *Water pump body*

3 *Impeller*

4 *Seal*

5 *Spindle and bearings*

tight the alternator and water pump bearings will wear rapidly and cause premature failure.

2 The fan belt tension is correct when there is 0.5 inch (13 mm) of lateral movement at the mid point position between the alternator pulley and the crankshaft pulley.

3 To adjust the fan belt, slacken the securing bolts and move the alternator in or out until the correct tension is obtained. It is easier if the alternator bolts are only slackened a little so it requires some effort to move the unit. In this way the tension of the belt can be arrived at more quickly than by making frequent adjustments. If difficulty is experienced in moving the unit away from the engine a tyre lever placed behind the unit and resting against the block gives a good control so that it can be held in position whilst the securing bolts are tightened. Be careful of the alternator cover - it is fragile.

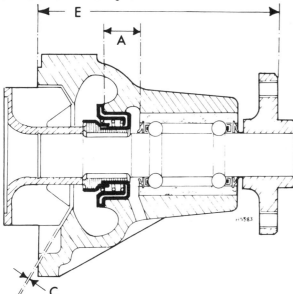

FIG.2.6 WATER PUMP REASSEMBLY DIMENSIONS

A 0.533 to 0.543 inch (13.54 to 13.79 mm)
E 3.244 to 3.264 inch (82.4 to 82.9 mm)
C 0.20 to 0.30 inch (0.508 to 0.762 mm)

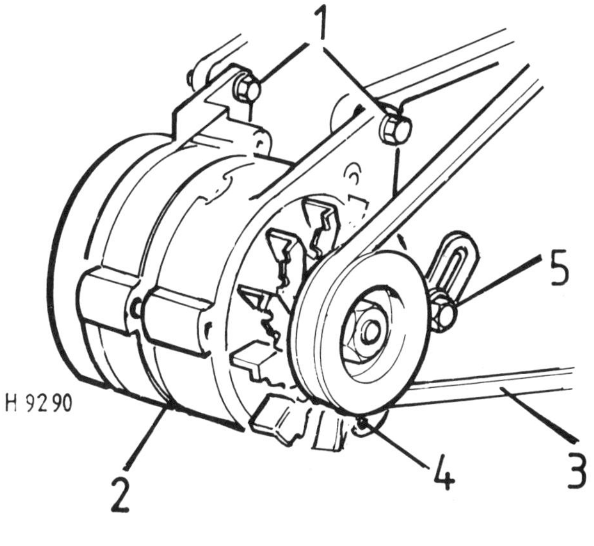

FIG.2.7 FAN BELT ADJUSTMENT

1 Upper mounting bolts   4 Adjustment link pivot bolt
2 Alternator   5 Adjustment link securing nut
3 Fan belt

12 Expansion tank

1 The radiator coolant expansion tank is mounted on the left hand inner wing panel and does not require any maintenance. It is important that the expansion tank pressure filler cap is not removed whilst the engine is hot.

2 Should it be found necessary to remove the expansion tank, disconnect the radiator to expansion tank hose connection at the radiator union having first slackened the clip. Remove the bracket screws and carefully lift away the tank and its hose.

3 Refitting is the reverse sequence to removal. Add either water or anti-freeze solution until it is up to the level mark.

13 Temperature gauge thermal transmitter

1 The thermal transmitter is placed in the cylinder head just below the thermostat and is held in position by a special gland nut to ensure a water tight joint. It is connected to the gauge located on the instrument panel by a cable on the main ignition feed circuit and a special bi-metal voltage stabilizer.

2 To remove the thermal transmitter, partially drain the cooling system (usually 4 pints 2.27 litres is enough). Unscrew the transmitter gland nut from the side of the cylinder head. Withdraw the thermal transmitter. Refitting is the reverse procedure to removal.

3 For information on removing and refitting the gauge refer to Chapter 10.

14 Anti-freeze mixture

1 Prior to anticipated freezing conditions, it is essential that some anti-freeze, (Castrol anti-freeze) is added to the cooling system.

2 If Castrol anti-freeze is not available, any anti-freeze which conforms with specification BS 3151 and BS 3152 can be used. Never use an anti-freeze with an alcohol base as evaporation is too high.

3 Castrol Anti-freeze with an anti corrosion additive can be left

FIG.2.8 EXPANSION TANK ASSEMBLY

1 Pressure cap   2 Expansion tank
          3 Coolant level

in the cooling system for up to two years, but after six months it is advisable to have the specific gravity of the coolant checked at your local garage and thereafter, every three months.
4   Listed below are the amounts of anti-freeze which should be added to ensure adequate protection down to the temperature given.

Amount of anti-freeze	Protection to
33.1/3% mixture	
3 pints (1.7 litres)	-19ºC (-2ºF)
50% mixture	
4½ pints (2.5 litres)	-36ºC (-33ºF)

15 Fault Diagnosis

Cause	Trouble	Remedy
Heat generated in cylinder not being successfully disposed of by radiator	Insufficient water in cooling system	Top up radiator.
	Fan belt slipping (Accompanied by a shrieking noise on rapid engine acceleration)	Tighten fan belt to recommended tension or replace if worn.
	Radiator core blocked or radiator grill restricted	Reverse flush radiator, remove obstructions.
	Bottom water hose collapsed, impeding flow	Remove and fit new hose.
	Thermostat not opening properly	Remove and fit new thermostat.
	Ignition advance and retard incorrectly set (Accompanied by loss of power and perhaps, misfiring)	Check and reset ignition timing.
	Carburettor incorrectly adjusted (mixture too weak)	Tune carburettor.
	Exhaust system partially blocked	Check exhaust pipe for constrictive dents and blockages.
	Oil level in sump too low	Top up sump to full mark on dipstick.
	Blown cylinder head gasket (Water/steam being forced down the radiator overflow pipe under pressure)	Remove cylinder head, fit new gasket.
	Engine not yet run-in	Run-in slowly and carefully.
	Brakes binding	Check and adjust brakes if necessary.
Too much heat being dispersed by radiator	Thermostat jammed open	Remove and renew thermostat.
	Incorrect grade of thermostat fitted allowing premature opening of valve	Remove and replace with new thermostat which opens at a higher temperature.
	Thermostat missing	Check and fit correct thermostat.
Leaks in system	Loose clips on water hoses	Check and tighten clips if necessary.
	Top or bottom water hoses perished and leaking	Check and replace any faulty hoses.
	Radiator core leaking	Remove radiator and repair.
	Thermostat gasket leaking	Inspect and renew gasket.
	Pressure cap spring worn or seal ineffective	Renew pressure cap.
	Blown cylinder head gasket (Pressure in system forcing water/steam down overflow pipe)	Remove cylinder head and fit new gasket.
	Cylinder wall or head cracked	Dismantle engine, dispatch to engineering works for repair.

Chapter 3 Fuel system and carburation

For modifications, and information applicable to later models, see Supplement at end of manual

Contents

General description 1	Carburettor - jet centring 15
Fuel pump - general description 2	Carburettor - float chamber fuel level adjustment 16
Fuel pump - removal and replacement 3	Carburettor - needle replacement 17
Fuel pump - dismantling, inspection and reassembly 4	Carburettor (single) - adjustment and tuning.. 18
Fuel pump - testing 5	Carburettor (twin) - adjustment and tuning 19
Carburettor - description 6	Carburettor (twin) - linkage adjustment 20
Carburettor (single) - removal and replacement.. 7	Throttle cable - removal and refitting... 21
Carburettor (twin) - removal and replacement 8	Choke cable - removal and refitting 22
Carburettor - dismantling and reassembly 9	Throttle pedal - removal and refitting... 23
Carburettor - examination and repair 10	Fuel tank - removal and refitting 24
Carburettor - piston sticking 11	Fuel tank - cleaning 25
Carburettor - float needle sticking.. 12	Fuel tank sender unit - removal and refitting 26
Carburettor - float chamber flooding... 13	Fault diagnosis 27
Carburettor - water or dirt in carburettor 14	

Specifications

Air cleaner

Type	Paper element

Carburettor 1.8

Make and type	Single SU HS6
Piston spring	Yellow
Jet size	0.10 in (2.54 mm)
Standard needle	BAQ

Carburettor 1.8 TC

Make and type	Twin SU HS4
Piston spring	Red
Jet size	0.090 in (2.29 mm)
Standard needle	AAS

Fuel pump

Make and type	SU mechanical AUF 707
Suction (minimum)	6 inches (152 mm) Hg.
Pressure (minimum)	3 lb.f/in^2 (0.21 kg.f.cm^2)F

Fuel tank

Type	Flat tank under rear floor vented by breather pipes
Capacity	11.5 gallons

Torque wrench setting

	lb.f.ft.	kg.f.m.
Manifold to cylinder head	15	2.07

1 General description

The fuel system comprises a fuel tank at the rear of the car, a mechanical fuel pump located on the left hand side of the crankcase and a single or twin horizontally mounted SU carburettor/s. A renewable paper element air cleaner is fitted which must be renewed at the recommended mileages. Operation of the individual components is described elsewhere in this chapter.

2 Fuel pump - general description

The mechanically operated fuel pump is located on the left hand side of the crankcase and is operated by a separate lobe on the camshaft.

As the camshaft rotates the rocker lever is actuated, one end of which is connected to the diaphragm operating rod. When the rocker arm is moved by the cam lobe the diaphragm, via a rocker arm, moves downwards causing fuel to be drawn in through the filter, past the inlet valve flap and into the diaphragm chamber. As the cam lobe moves round, the diaphragm moves upwards under the action of the spring, and fuel flows via the large outlet valve to the carburettor float chamber.

When the float chamber has the requisite amount of fuel in it, the needle valve in the top delivery line closes and holds the diaphragm down against the action of the diaphragm spring until the needle valve in the float chamber opens to admit more fuel.

3 Fuel pump - removal and replacement

1 Remove the fuel inlet and outlet connections from the fuel pump and plug ends of the pipes to stop loss of fuel or dirt ingress.
2 Unscrew and remove the two pump mounting flange nuts and washers. Carefully slide the pump off the two studs followed by the insulating block assembly and gasket.
3 Refitting is the reverse sequence to removal. Inspect the gaskets on either side of the insulating block and if damaged obtain and fit new ones.

4 Fuel pump - dismantling, inspection and reassembly

1 Thoroughly clean the outside of the pump in paraffin and dry. To ensure correct reassembly mark the cover and upper and lower body flanges (Fig.3.1).
2 Remove the three cover retaining screws, lift away the cover followed by the sealing ring and fuel filter (photo).
3 Remove the three remaining screws holding the upper body to the lower body. Separate the two halves taking care not to damage the diaphragm (photo).
4 As the combined inlet and outlet valve is a press fit into the body, very carefully remove the valve taking care not to damage the very fine edge of the inlet valve.
5 Lift away the insert from the outlet cover.
6 With the diaphragm and rocker held down against the action of the diaphragm spring, tap out the rocker lever pivot pin using a parallel pin punch. Lift out the rocker lever and spring (photo).
7 Lift out the diaphragm and spring having first well lubricated the lower seal to avoid damage as the spindle stirrup is drawn through. Unless the seal is damaged it should be left in position as a special extractor is required for removal.
8 Carefully wash the filter gauze in petrol and clean all traces of sediment from the upper body. Inspect the diaphragm for signs of distortion, cracking or perishing and fit a new one if suspect.
9 Inspect the fine edge and lips of the combined inlet and outlet valve and also check that it is a firm fit in the upper body. Finally inspect the outlet cover for signs of corrosion, pitting or distortion and obtain a new part if necessary.
10 To reassemble first check that there are no sharp edges on the diaphragm spindle and stirrup and well lubricate the oil seals. Insert the stirrup and spindle into the spring and then through the oil seal and position the stirrup ready for rocker lever engagement (photo).
11 Fit the combined inlet/outlet valve ensuring that the groove registers in the housing correctly. Check that the fine edge of the inlet valve contacts its seating correctly and evenly.
12 Match up the screw holes in the lower body and holes in the diaphragm and depress the rocker lever until the diaphragm lies flat, fit the upper body and hold in place by the three short screws, but do not tighten fully yet (photo).
13 Refit the filter, outlet cover insert, new sealing washer and outlet cover suitably positioned by aligning the previously made marks. Replace the three long screws and then tighten all screws firmly in a diagonal pattern.
14 Insert the rocker lever and spring into the lower body and retain in position using the rocker lever pivot pin.

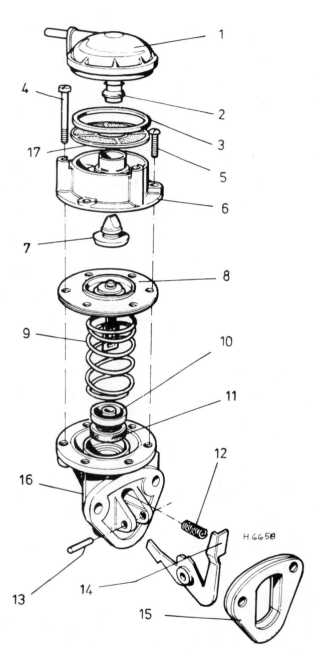

H.6658

FIG 3.1 FUEL PUMP COMPONENT PARTS

1	Top cover	10	Crankcase seal cup
2	Outlet tube	11	Crankcase seal
3	Sealing ring	12	Rocker lever return spring
4	Screw	13	Rocker lever pivot pin
5	Screw	14	Rocker lever
6	Upper body	15	Insulating block
7	Inlet/outlet valve	16	Lower body
8	Diaphragm assembly	17	Filter
9	Diaphragm spring		

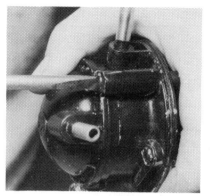
4.2A. Hold the pump firmly

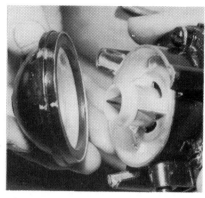
4.2B. Ease off the top cover

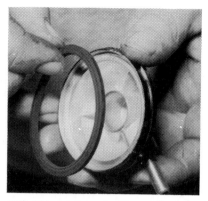
4.2C. Pick out the seal with your finger

4.3A. Undo evenly all round

4.3B. Pull the two halves apart

4.4. Be careful at this stage

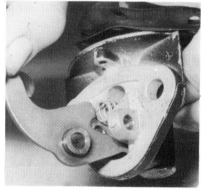
4.6A. Watch the little spring

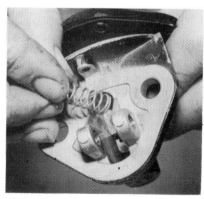
4.6B. Pull out the little spring now

4.7A. Hold this spring whilst extracting the diaphragm

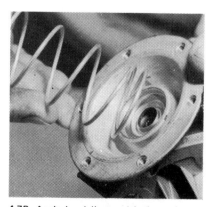
4.7B. Again be delicate with the spring

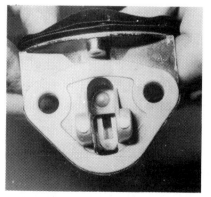
4.10. Press firmly but accurately with both hands

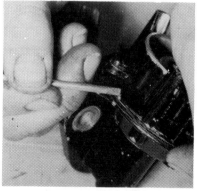
4.12. Line up the covers with the marks

5 Fuel pump - testing

If the pump is suspect or has been overhauled it may be dry tested by holding a finger over the inlet union and operating the rocker lever through three complete strokes. When the finger is released a suction noise should be heard. Next hold a finger over the outlet nozzle and press the rocker arm fully. The pressure generated should hold for a minimum of fifteen seconds.

6 Carburettor - description

1 The variable choke SU carburettor as shown in Fig.3.2 is relatively simple instrument, and is basically the same irrespective of its size and type. It differs from most other carburettors in that instead of having a number of various sized fixed jets for different conditions, only one variable jet is fitted to deal with all possible conditions.

2 Air passing rapidly through the carburettor draws petrol from the jet so forming the petrol/air mixture. The amount of petrol drawn from the jet depends on the position of the tapered carburettor needle, which moves up and down the jet orifice according to the engine load and throttle opening, thus effectively altering the size of jet so that exactly the right amount of fuel is metered for the prevailing conditions.

3 The position of the tapered needle in the jet is determined by engine vacuum. The shank of the needle is held at its top end in a piston which slides up and down the dashpot in response to the degree of manifold vacuum.

4 With the throttle fully open, the full effect of inlet manifold vacuum is felt by the piston which has an air bleed into the choke tube on the outside of the throttle. This causes the piston to rise fully, bringing the needle with it. With the accelerator partially closed, only slight inlet manifold vacuum is felt by the piston (although of course, on the engine side of the throttle the vacuum is greater), and the piston only rises a little, blocking most of the jet orifice with the metering needle.

5 To prevent the piston fluttering and giving a richer mixture when the accelerator pedal is suddenly depressed, an oil damper, and light spring are fitted inside the dashpot.

6 The only portion of the piston assembly to come into contact with the piston chamber or dashpot is the actual piston rod. All other parts of the piston assembly, including the lower choke portion, have sufficient clearance to prevent any direct metal to metal contact which is essential if the carburettor is to function correctly.

7 The correct level of the petrol in the carburettor is determined by the level of the float chamber. When the level is correct the float rises and, by means of a lever resting on top of it, closes the needle valve in the cover of the float chamber. This closes off the supply of fuel from the pump. When the level in the float chamber drops, as fuel is used in the carburettor, the float drops. As it does, the float needle is unseated so allowing more fuel to enter the float chamber and restore the correct level.

7 Carburettor (single) - removal and replacement

1 Unscrew the wing nut securing the air cleaner assembly and lift away the wing nut, fibre washer and air cleaner assembly.

2 Ease the fuel feed pipe from the union on the float chamber cover. Plug the end to prevent dirt ingress (Fig.3.3).

3 Slacken the clip and ease off the engine breather pipe from the union on the carburettor body. Pull off the vacuum advance suction pipe.

4 Slacken the locknut and undo the nut locking accelerator cable to the control arm on the side of the carburettor body. Detach the accelerator cable.

5 Slacken the bolt securing the choke control cable to the operating linkage and detach the choke cable.

6 Undo and remove the four nuts and washers securing the carburettor body to the manifold studs. Lift away the

FIG 3.2 SU CARBURETTOR COMPONENT PARTS

1 Carburettor body
2 Piston lifting pin
3 Spring
4 Sealing washer
5 Plain washer
6 Circlip
7 Piston chamber
8 Piston chamber screw
9 Piston
10 Spring
11 Needle
12 Needle spring
13 Needle support guide
14 Needle support guide locking screw
15 Piston damper
16 Identification tag
17 Throttle adjusting screw
18 Spring
19 Gaskets
20 Distance piece
21 Float chamber and spacer
22 Float chamber gasket
23 Float
24 Float hinge pin
25 Needle and seat
26 Float chamber lid
27 Baffle plate
28 Float chamber lid screw
29 Spring washer
30 Float chamber securing bolt
31 Spring washer
32 Plain washer
33 Throttle spindle
34 Throttle disc
35 Throttle disc securing screw
36 Throttle spindle washer
37 Throttle return lever
38 Progressive throttle (snail cam)
39 Fast idle screw and spring
40 Throttle spindle nut lockwasher
41 Throttle spindle nut
42 Jet assembly
43 Jet flexible pipe sleeve nut
44 Washer
45 Gland
46 Ferrule
47 Jet bearing
48 Jet locating nut
49 Spring
50 Jet adjusting nut
51 Pick-up lever
52 Pick-up lever link
53 Retaining ring
54 Pivot bolt
55 Pivot bolt tube — inner
56 Pivot bolt tube — outer
57 Distance washer
58 Cam lever
59 Cam lever spring
60 Pick-up lever spring
61 Suction chamber piston guide
62 Guide securing screw
63 Throttle lever
64 Rod link and pick-up lever
65 Spring clip
66 Capstat jet assembly (later models)
67 Plastic shrouds (carburettors with sealed adjustment)
68 Aluminium plug (carburettors with sealed adjustment)

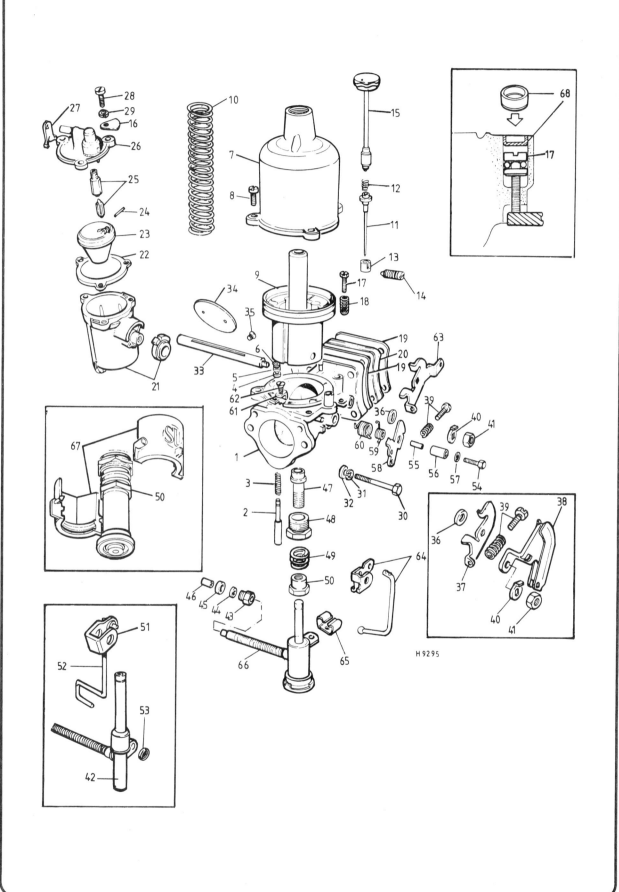

H 9295

carburettor complete with abutment bracket and linkage.
7 Recover the insulator block and gaskets.
8 Refitting the carburettor is the reverse sequence to removal. Always fit new gaskets to the inlet manifold flange and one each side of the insulator block. Refer to Section 22, and adjust the choke control cable and to Section 21 for detail of the throttle cable adjustment.

8 Carburettor (twin) - removal and replacement

1 Undo and remove the four nuts and bolts that secure the air cleaner air manifolds to the carburettors. Lift away the air cleaner and air manifold assembly.
2 Ease the fuel feed pipe from the union on the front carburettor float chamber cover. Plug the end to prevent dirt ingress (Fig.3.4).
3 Detach the engine breather hose at the Y junction.
4 Detach the vacuum advance suction pipe from the carburettor body.
5 Slacken and then remove the nut and washer that secures the accelerator cable clamp.
6 Disconnect the choke control cable from the operating linkage.
7 Disconnect the three throttle return springs from the heat shield.
8 Undo and remove the four nuts and washers securing the carburettor body to the manifold studs. Lift away the carburettors.
9 Recover the insulator block and gaskets.
10 Refitting the carburettors is the reverse sequence to removal. Always fit new gaskets to manifold flanges and insulator blocks.
11 Refer to Section 22 and adjust the choke control cable and to Section 21 for details of the throttle cable adjustment.

9 Carburettor - dismantling and reassembly

1 Unscrew the piston damper and lift away from the chamber and piston assembly. Recover the fibre washer (Fig.3.2).
2 Using a screwdriver or small file, scratch identification marks on the suction chambers and carburettor body so that they may be fitted together again in their original position. Remove the three suction chamber retaining screws and lift the suction chamber from the carburettor body leaving the piston in situ.
3 Lift the piston spring from the piston, noting which way round it is fitted, and remove the piston. Invert it and allow the oil in the damper bore to drain out. Place the piston in a safe place so that the needle will not be touched or the piston roll onto the floor. It is recommended that the piston be placed on the neck of a narrow jar with the needle inside, so acting as a stand.
4 Mark the position of the float chamber lid relative to the body, and unscrew the three screws holding the float chamber lid to the float chamber body. Remove the lid and withdraw the pin thereby releasing the float and float lever, using a spanner or socket remove the needle valve assembly.
5 Release the pick up lever return spring from its retaining lug.
6 Support the plastic moulded base of the jet and remove the screw retaining the jet pick up link and link bracket.
7 Carefully unscrew the flexible jet tube sleeve nut from the float chamber and lift away the jet assembly from the underside of the carburettor body. Note the gland, washer and ferrule at the end of the jet tube.
8 Undo and remove the jet adjustment nut and spring. Also unscrew the jet locknut and lift away together with the brass washer and jet bearing.
9 Unscrew and remove the lever pivot bolt and spacer. Detach the lever assembly and return springs noting the pivot bolt tubes, skid washer and the locations of the cam and pick up springs.
10 Close the throttle and lightly mark the relative position of the throttle disc and carburettor flange.

11 Unscrew the disc retaining screws, open the throttle and ease the disc from its slot in the throttle spindle.
12 Bend back the tabs of the lock washer securing the spindle nut. Undo and remove the nut and detach the lever arm, washer and throttle spindle.
13 Should it be necessary to remove the piston lifting pin, push it upwards and remove the securing clip. Lift away the pin and spring.
14 Reassembly is a straight reversal of the dismantling sequence. It will however be necessary to centre the jet as described in Section 15 during reassembly.

10 Carburettor - examination and repair

The SU carburettor generally speaking is most reliable but even so it may develop one of several faults which may not be readily apparent unless a careful inspection is carried out. The common faults the carburettor is prone to are:
1 Piston sticking
2 Float needle sticking
3 Float chamber flooding
4 Water and dirt in the carburettor
In addition, the following parts are susceptible to wear after high mileages and as they vitally affect the economy of the engine they should be checked and renewed where necessary, every 24,000 miles (38,000 km).
a) The carburettor needle: If this has been incorrectly fitted at some time so that it is not centrally located in the jet orifice, then the metering needle will have a tiny ridge worn on it. If a ridge can be seen then the needle must be renewed. SU carburettor needles are made to very fine tolerances and should a ridge be apparent, no attempt should be made to rub the needle down with fine emery paper. If it is wished to clean the needle, it can be polished lightly with metal polish.
b) The carburettor jet: If the needle is worn it is likely that the rim of the jet will be damaged where the needle has been striking it. It should be renewed, otherwise fuel consumption will suffer. The jet can also be badly worn or ridged on the outside from where it has been sliding up and down between the jet bearing every time the choke has been pulled out. Removal and renewal is the only answer.
c) Check the edges of the throttle and choke tube for wear. Renew if worn.
d) The washers fitted to the base of the jet and under the float chamber lid may leak after a time and can cause a great deal of fuel wastage. It is wisest to renew them automatically when the carburettor is stripped down.
e) After high mileages the float chamber needle and seat are bound to be ridged. They are not an expensive item to replace and must be renewed as a set. They should never be renewed separately.

11 Carburettor - piston sticking

1 The hardened piston rod which slides in the centre guide tube in the middle of the dashpot is the only part of the piston assembly (which comprises the jet needle, suction disc and piston choke) which should make contact with the dashpot. The piston rim and choke periphery are machined to very fine tolerances so that they will not touch the dashpot or the choke tube walls.
2 After high mileage wear in the centre guide tube may allow the piston to touch the dashpot wall. This condition is known as sticking.
3 If piston sticking is suspected and it is wished to test for this condition, rotate the piston about the centre guide tube at the same time as sliding it up and down inside the dashpot wall then that portion of the wall must be polished with a metal polish until the clearance exists. In extreme cases fine emery cloth can be used.
    Great care should be taken to remove only the minimum amount of metal to provide the clearance, as too large a gap will

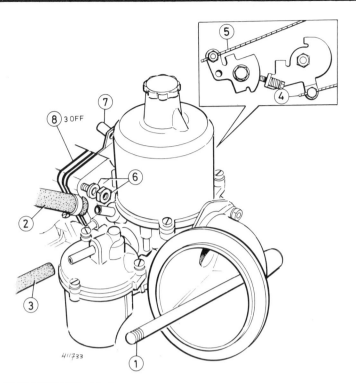

FIG 3.3 SU CARBURETTOR ATTACHMENTS - Single

1 Air cleaner attachment	3 Fuel pipe from pump	5 Choke cable clamp bolt	7 Abutment bracket and linkage
2 Engine breather pipe	4 Accelerator cable	6 Securing nut and plain washer	8 Joint washers

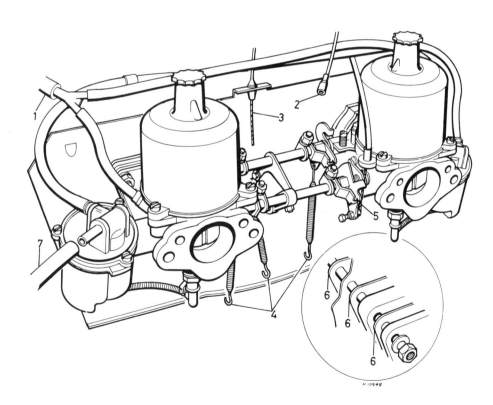

FIG 3.4 SU CARBURETTOR ATTACHMENTS - TWIN

1 Engine breather hose	3 Accelerator cable	5 Choke control cable	7 Fuel feed pipe
2 Vacuum advance suction pipe	4 Throttle return springs	6 Gaskets	

cause air leakage and upset the function of the carburettor. Clean down the walls of the dashpot and the piston rim and ensure that there is no oil on them. A trace of oil may be judiciously applied to the piston rod.

4 If the piston is sticking, under no circumstances try to clear it by trying to alter the tension of the light return spring.

12 Carburettor - float needle sticking

1 If the float needle sticks, the carburettor will soon run dry and the engine will stop, despite there being fuel in the tank.

The easiest way to check a suspected sticking float needle is to remove the inlet pipe at the carburettor and turn the engine over on the starter motor by pressing on the solenoid rubber button (manual gearbox) or operating the ignition/starter switch (automatic transmission). In the latter case remove the white lead on the ignition coil so that the engine does not start. If fuel spurts from the end of the pipe (direct it towards the ground, into a wad of cloth or into a jar) then the fault is almost certain to be a sticking float needle.

2 Remove the float chamber, dismantle the valve and clean the housing and float chamber out thoroughly.

13 Carburettor - float chamber flooding

If fuel emerges from the small breather hole in the cover of the float chamber or runs down the side, this is known as flooding. It is caused by the float chamber needle not seating properly in its housing, normally this is because a piece of dirt or foreign matter is jammed between the needle and needle housing. Alternatively the float may have developed a leak or be maladjusted so that it is holding open the float chamber needle valve even though the chamber is full of petrol. Remove the float chamber cover, clean the needle assembly, check the setting of the float as described later in this chapter and shake the float to verify if any petrol has leaked into it.

14 Carburettor - water or dirt in carburettor

1 Because of the size of the jet orifice, water or dirt in the carburettor is normally cleared. If dirt in the carburettor is suspected, lift the piston assembly and flood the float chamber. The normal level of the fuel should be about 1/16 inch (1.588mm) below the top of the jet, so that on flooding the carburettor the fuel should flow out of the jet hole.

2 If little or no petrol appears, start the engine (the jet is never completely blocked) and with the throttle butterfly fully open blank off the air intake. This will cause a partial vacuum in the choke tube and help suck out any foreign matter from the jet tube. Release the throttle as soon as the engine speed alters considerably. Repeat this procedure several times, stop the engine and then check the carburettor as described in the first paragraph of this section.

3 If this failed to do the trick then there is no alternative but to remove and blow out the jet.

15 Carburettor - jet centering

1 This operation is always necessary if the carburettor has been dismantled, but to check if this is necessary on a carburettor in service, first screw up the jet adjusting nut as far as it will go without forcing it, and lift the piston and then let it fall under its own weight. It should fall onto the bridge making a soft metallic click. Now repeat the above procedure but this time with the adjusting nut screwed right down. If the soft metallic click is not audible in either of the two tests proceed as follows.

2 Disconnect the jet link from the bottom of the jet, and the nylon flexible tube from the underside of the float chamber. Gently slide the jet and the nylon tube from the underside of the carburettor body. Next unscrew the jet adjusting nut and lift away the nut and the locking spring. Refit the adjusting nut without the locking spring and screw it up as far as possible without forcing. Replace the jet and tube but there is no need to reconnect the tube.

3 Slacken the jet locking nut so that it may be rotated with the fingers only. Unscrew the piston damper and lift away the damper. Gently press the piston down onto the bridge and tighten the locknut. Lift the piston using the lifting pin and check that it is able to fall freely under its own weight. Now lower the adjusting nut and check once again. If this time there is a difference in the two metallic clicks, repeat the centering procedure until the sound is the same for both tests.

4 Gently remove the jet and unscrew the adjusting nut. Refit the locking spring and jet adjusting nut. Top up the damper with oil, if necessary, and replace the damper. Connect the nylon flexible tube to the underside of the float chamber and finally reconnect the jet link.

16 Carburettor - float chamber fuel level adjustment

1 It is essential that the fuel level in the float chamber is always correct otherwise excessive fuel consumption may occur. Carburettors fitted to later models have non adjustable floats.

2 With the carburettor fitted to the engine and the float chamber full of petrol remove the piston and dashpot assembly (early models only).

3 Check that the level of fuel in the jet is about 1/16 inch (1.588mm) below the top of the jet. If it is above or below this level it may be adjusted by removing the needle and seat from the underside of the float chamber lid and either add or remove washers so raising or lowering the relative position of the needle valve.

17 Carburettor - needle replacement

1 Should it be necessary to fit a new needle, first remove the piston and suction chamber assembly, marking the chamber for correct reassembly in its original position.

2 Slacken the needle clamping screw and withdraw the needle, guide and spring from the underside of the piston (Fig.3.5).

3 To refit the needle assembly fit the spring and guide to the needle and insert the assembly into the piston making sure that the guide is fitted flush with the face of the piston and the flat on the guide positioned adjacent to the needle guide locking screw. Screw in the guide locking screw.

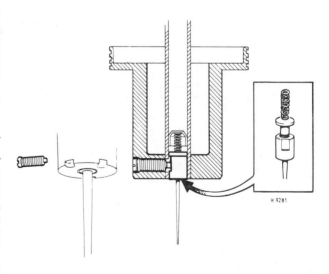

FIG 3.5 NEEDLE LOCATION IN PISTON

18 Carburettor (single) - adjustment and tuning

1   To adjust and tune a single SU carburettor proceed in the following manner. Check the colour of the exhaust at idling speed with the choke fully in. If the exhaust tends to be black and the tail pipe interior is also black, it is a fair indication that the mixture is too rich. If the exhaust is colourless and the deposit in the exhaust pipe is very light grey it is likely that the mixture is too weak. This condition may also be accompanied by intermittent misfiring, while too rich a mixture will be associated with 'hunting'. Ideally the exhaust should be colourless with a medium grey pipe deposit.

2   The exhaust pipe deposit should only be checked after a good run of at least 20 miles. Idling in city traffic and stop/start motoring is bound to produce excessive dark exhaust pipe deposits.

3   Once the engine has reached its normal operating temperature, detach the carburettor air cleaner.

4   Only two adjustments are provided on the SU carburettor. Idling speed is governed by the throttle adjusting screw and the mixture strength by the jet adjusting nut. The SU carburettor is correctly adjusted for the whole of its engine revolution range when the idling mixture strength is correct.

5   To adjust the mixture set the engine to run at about 1000 rpm by screwing in the throttle adjusting screw.

6   Check the mixture strength by lifting the piston of the carburettor approximately 1/32 inch (0.79mm) with the piston lifting pin so as to disturb the air flow as little as possible. If:

a) The speed of the engine increases appreciably the mixture is too rich.

b) The engine speed immediately decreases, the mixture is too weak.

c) The engine speed increases very slightly, the mixture is correct. To enrich the mixture rotate the adjusting nut which is at the bottom of the underside of the carburettor in a clockwise direction, ie, downwards. Only turn the adjusting nut a flat at a time and check the mixture strenth between each turn. It is likely that there will be a slight increase or decrese in rpm after the mixture adjustment has been made so the throttle idling screw should be turned so that the engine idles at 650 rpm.

19 Carburettor (twin) - adjusting and tuning

1   Allow the engine to reach normal operating temperature and then remove the air cleaner assembly. Read paragraphs 1 and 2 of Section 18 as this information is also applicable to twin carburettor installations.

2   With twin carburettors, not only must the carburettors be individually set to ensure correct mixture, but also the air passing through each instrument must be the same throughout the entire engine speed range. This can be adjusted much more accurately if a vacuum synchronizing device is used. However, if this is not available, it is possible to obtain fairly accurate synchronization by listening to the hiss made by the air flowing into the intake of each carburettor. A rubber tube held to the ear is useful for this purpose.

3   Begin the adjustment by slackening the two throttle spindle interconnecting clamps (Fig 3.7).

4   With the engine running at idling speed listen to the hiss from each carburettor intake and, if a difference in intensity is noticed between them, adjust the throttle adjusting screws until the hiss intensity is the same. With the vacuum synchronizing device, all that is necessary is to place the instrument over the intake of each carburettor in turn and adjust the throttle adjusting screws until the reading on the gauge is identical for both carburettors.

5   Once the carburettors have been synchronized, any adjustments to the engine idling speed should be made by turning both throttle adjusting screws by equal amounts in the desired direction.

6   With the carburettors synchronized, the mixture strength in each instrument can be adjusted as described in Section 18, paragraphs 5 and 6.

7   With the carburettor adjustments and tuning complete, adjust the linkage as described in Section 20.

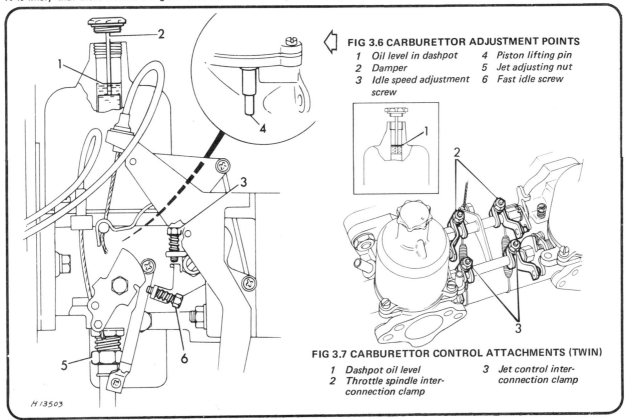

FIG 3.6 CARBURETTOR ADJUSTMENT POINTS

1 Oil level in dashpot	4 Piston lifting pin
2 Damper	5 Jet adjusting nut
3 Idle speed adjustment screw	6 Fast idle screw

FIG 3.7 CARBURETTOR CONTROL ATTACHMENTS (TWIN)

1 Dashpot oil level	3 Jet control interconnection clamp
2 Throttle spindle interconnection clamp	

H 13503

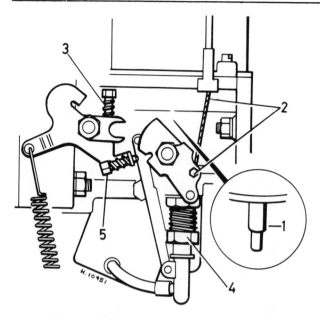

FIG 3.8 CARBURETTOR ADJUSTMENT POINTS (TWIN)

1 Piston lifting pin   3 Throttle adjusting screw
2 Choke control cable   4 Jet adjustment nut
  attachment   5 Fast idle screw

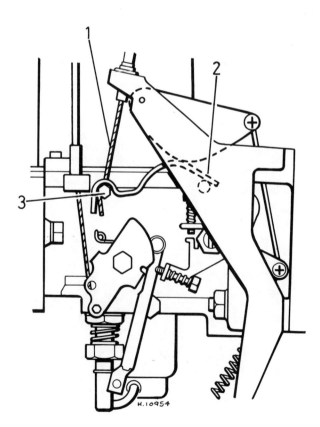

FIG 3.10 THROTTLE CABLE ADJUSTMENT

1 Inner cable   3 Trunnion
2 Cam operating lever

20 Carburettor (twin) - linkage adjustment

1 Set the throttle interconnection clamping levers so that the actuating pins rest on the lower arm of the forks (See Fig. 3.9).
2 Insert a 0.020 inch (0.5 mm) feeler gauge between the throttle shaft operating lever and the choke control interconnecting rod 'A'.
3 Tighten the throttle interconnecting clamping lever bolts, ensuring that there is approximately 0.031 inch (0.79 mm) end float on the interconnecting rod. Remove the feeler gauge.
4 An equal clearance of 0.012 inch (0.31 mm) 'B' should now exist between each lever pin and the bottom of the fork on both carburettors.
5 Reposition the choke control interconnecting rod with approximately 0.031 inch (0.79 mm) end clearance and tighten the clamp bolts.
6 Run the engine at 1000 to 1100 rpm and check the carburettor balance.
7 Reconnect the choke cable and pull out the control approximately 0.5 inch (13 mm) until the linkage is just about to move the jet. Start the engine and adjust the fast idle screws to give an engine speed of 1000 to 1100 rpm when hot.

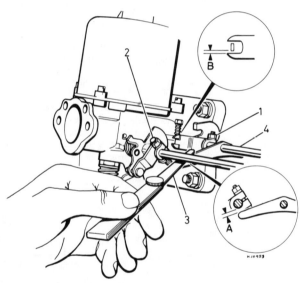

FIG 3.9 CARBURETTOR LINKAGE ADJUSTMENT (TWIN)

1 Throttle spindle clamp   3 Feeler gauge 0.020 in (0.5
2 Jet control clamp   mm)
                                  4 Choke control connecting
                                     rod

21 Throttle cable - removal and refitting

Single carburettor models
1 Using two thin open ended spanners unscrew the cable trunnion screw.
2 Press in the plastic retainers located on the underside of the abutment bracket and carefully ease the cable through the bracket.
3 Detach the inner cable from the accelerator pedal and withdraw the cable into the engine compartment.
4 Refitting is the reverse sequence to removal but it is now necessary to adjust the effective length of the inner cable.
5 Pull down on the inner cable until all free movement of the throttle pedal is eliminated.
6 Hold the cable in this position and raise the cam operating lever until it just contacts the cam (Fig 3.10).

7 Move the trunnion up the cable until it contacts the operating lever, and tighten the trunnion screw.

8 Depress the throttle pedal and make sure that the cable has 1/16 inch (1.6mm) free movement before the cam operating lever begins to move.

Twin carburettor models

9 Follow the procedure given in paragraphs 1 to 5 then insert a 0.020 in (0.5 mm) feeler gauge between the throttle shaft operating lever and the choke control interconnection rod.

10 Ensure that the trunnion components are positioned as shown in Fig 3.11. Feed the cable through the trunnion, fit the brass or copper washer, then fit and tighten the nut.

11 Remove the feeler gauge and check for smooth throttle operation.

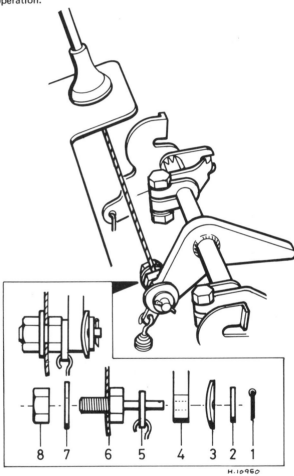

FIG 3.11 THROTTLE CABLE ADJUSTMENT (TWIN)

1 Split pin
2 Plain washer
3 Curved washer
4 Throttle shaft operating lever
5 Spring anchor tag
6 Throttle cable
7 Brass or copper washer
8 Nut

---

22 Choke cable - removal and refitting

1 Using two thin open ended spanners slacken the cable trunnion screw (Fig 3.12).

2 Working behind the switch panel unscrew the large nut and shakeproof washer securing the control to the switch panel.

3 Carefully draw the cable through the body grommet and switch panel.

4 Refitting is the reverse sequence to removal but it is now necessary to adjust the effective length of the inner cable.

5 Set the position of the trunnion to give a free movement on the cable of 0.0625 inch (1.6mm) before the cam lever begins to move (Fig 3.13).

6 Pull out the control approximately 0.5 inch (13mm) until the linkage is just about to move the jet.

7 Start the engine and adjust the carburettor fast idle screw to give an engine speed of 1000 to 1100 rpm.

8 Push the control knob fully in and check that there is a small gap between the end of the fast idle screw and the cam.

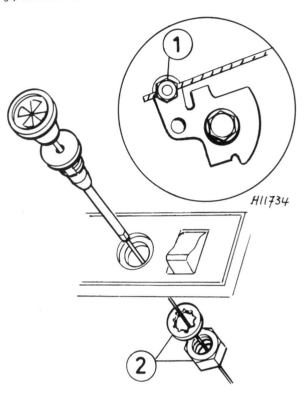

FIG 3.12 CHOKE CABLE REMOVAL

1 Trunnion screw
2 Cable securing nut and shakeproof washer

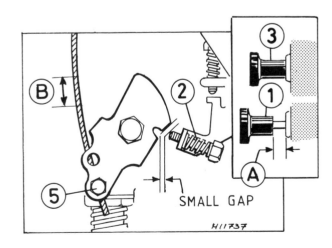

FIG 3.13 CHOKE CABLE ADJUSTMENT

1 Choke control knob (out)
2 Fast idle screw
3 Choke control knob (in)
A 0.5 inch (13 mm)
B 0.0625 inch (1.6mm)
5 Choke cable clamp bolt

23 Throttle pedal - removal and refitting

1　Refer to Fig. 3.14 and detach the throttle cable from the end of the pedal.
2　Undo and remove the two nuts and spring washers securing the pedal bracket to the bulkhead panel. Lift the pedal assembly from the mounting studs.
3　Refitting the throttle pedal is the reverse sequence to removal.

24 Fuel tank - removal and refitting

1　For safety reasons, disconnect the battery.
2　Chock the front wheels, raise the rear of the car and support on axle stands located under the rear axle.
3　Unscrew the fuel tank drain plug and drain the contents of the fuel tank into a container of suitable capacity (Fig 3.15).
4　Detach the cable terminal from the fuel tank sender unit.
5　Using a pair of pliers open the clips securing the hoses and vent pipes and ease off the pipes.
6　Release the vent pipe adjacent to the filler cap.
7　Undo and remove the four bolts, spring and shaped washers securing the tank to the brackets welded to the underside of the body. Lift away the fuel tank.
8　Refitting the fuel tank is the reverse sequence to removal.

25 Fuel tank - cleaning

With time it is likely that sediment will collect in the bottom of the fuel tank condensation, resulting in rust and other impurities is sometimes found in the fuel tank of a car more than three or four years old.

With the tank removed it should be vigorously flushed out and then turned upside down and, if facilities are available, steam cleaned.

26 Fuel tank sender unit - removal and refitting

1　For safety reasons disconnect the battery.
2　Disconnect the fuel gauge sender unit cable.
3　Detach the main fuel pipe from the sender unit by squeezing the ears of the clip with a pair of pliers and pulling off the cable.
4　Using two crossed screwdrivers, remove the fuel gauge tank unit by turning through approximately 30° and lift away from the tank. Take great care not to bend the float wire.
5　If the sender unit is suspect, check the circuit, gauge and sender unit as described in Chapter 10.
6　Refitting is the reverse sequence to removal. Always fit a new sealing washer located between the fuel gauge tank unit and the tank itself.

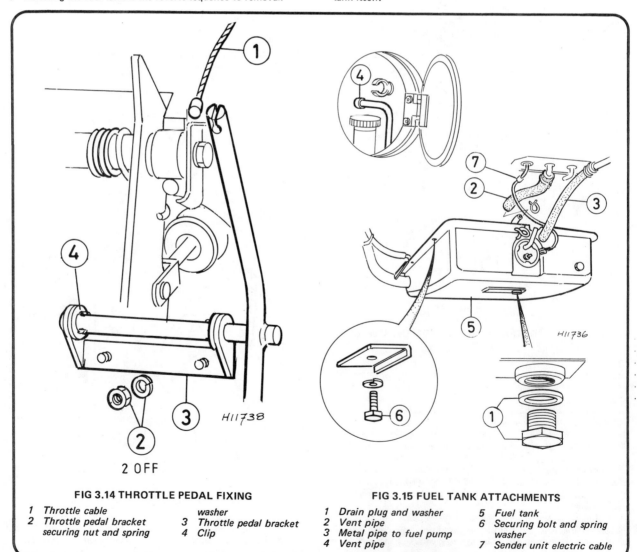

FIG 3.14 THROTTLE PEDAL FIXING

1　Throttle cable
2　Throttle pedal bracket
　　securing nut and spring
　　washer
3　Throttle pedal bracket
4　Clip

FIG 3.15 FUEL TANK ATTACHMENTS

1　Drain plug and washer
2　Vent pipe
3　Metal pipe to fuel pump
4　Vent pipe
5　Fuel tank
6　Securing bolt and spring
　　washer
7　Sender unit electric cable

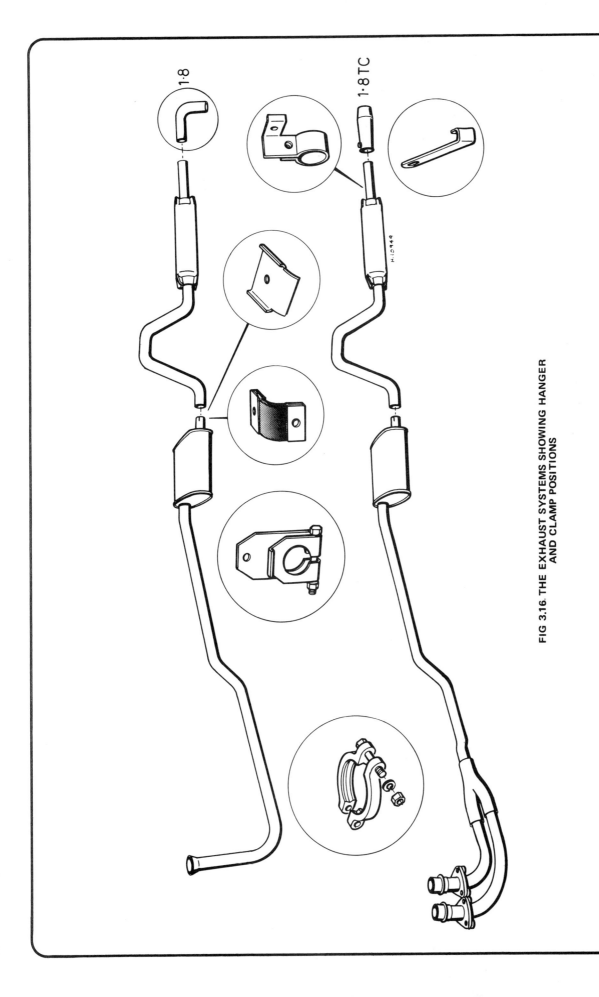

FIG 3.16. THE EXHAUST SYSTEMS SHOWING HANGER AND CLAMP POSITIONS

27 Fault diagnosis

Unsatisfactory engine performance and excessive fuel consumption are not necessarily the fault of the fuel system or carburettor. In fact they more commonly occur as a result of ignition faults. Before acting on the fuel system it is necessary to check the ignition system first. Even though a fault may lie in the fuel system it will be difficult to trace unless the ignition is correct.

The table below therefore, assumes that the ignition system is in order.

Symptom	Reason/s	Remedy
Smell of petrol when engine is stopped	Leaking fuel lines or unions	Repair or renew as necessary.
	Leaking fuel tank	Fill fuel tank to capacity and examine carefully at seams, unions and filler pipe connections. Repair as necessary.
Smell of petrol when engine is idling	Leaking fuel line unions between pump and carburettor	Check line and unions and tighten or repair.
	Overflow of fuel from float chamber due to wrong level setting or ineffective needle valve or punctured float	Check fuel level setting and condition of float and needle valve and renew if necessary.
Excessive fuel consumption for reasons not covered by leaks or float chamber faults	Worn needle	Renew needles.
	Sticking needle	Check correct movement of needle body.
Difficult starting, uneven running, lack of power, cutting out	One or more blockages	Dismantle and clean out float chamber and body.
	Float chamber fuel level too low or needle sticking	Dismantle and check fuel level and needle.
	Fuel pump not delivering sufficient fuel	Check pump delivery and clean or repair as required.
	Intake manifold gaskets leaking, or manifold fractured	Check tightness of mounting nuts and inspect manifold.
Fast idle; erratic	Air leak	Check manifold, brake servo, crankcase ventilator

Chapter 4 Ignition system

For modifications, and information applicable to later models, see Supplement at end of manual

Contents

General description 1
Contact breaker points - adjustment 2
Contact breaker points - removal and replacement 3
Condenser - removal, testing and replacement 4
Distributor - lubrication 5
Distributor - removal and replacement 6
Distributor - dismantling 7

Distributor - inspection and repair 8
Distributor - reassembly 9
Ignition - timing 10
Spark plugs and leads 11
Ignition system - fault symptoms 12
Fault diagnosis - engine fails to start 13
Fault diagnosis - engine misfires 14

Specifications

Spark plugs	Champion N - 9Y
Size	14 mm
Gap	0.024 - 0.026 in (0.625 - 0.660 mm)
Firing order	1 3 4 2
Ignition coil	
1.8	Lucas 11C12 or Delco Remy 7992100 v
1.8TC	Lucas 16C6
Primary resistance at 20°C (68°F)	1.43 to 1.58 ohms
Consumption:	
Ignition on	4.5 to 5 amps at 13.5 volts
at 2000 rpm	1 amp
Distributor	Lucas 25 D 4
Serial No. 1.8 HC	41234
1.8 LC	41260
1.8 TC	41032
Direction of rotation	anti clockwise
Dwell angle	60° ± 3°
Contact breaker gap	0.014 - 0.016 in (0.35 - 0.40 mm)
Condenser capacity	0.18 - 0.24 m.fd.
Static ignition timing	
1.8 SC	HC = 10° BTDC; LC = 9° BTDC
1.8 TC	7° BTDC
Dynamic ignition timing	
Centrifugal advance	
1.8 HC	28° - 32° at 6000 rpm
	26° - 30° at 4800 rpm
	20° - 24° at 3600 rpm
	10° - 14° at 2200 rpm
	2° - 6° at 1200 rpm
	no advance below 300 rpm
1.8 LC	28° - 32° at 2500 rpm
	20° - 24° at 1700 rpm
	14° - 18° at 1200 rpm
	2° - 6° at 600 rpm
	no advance below 600 rpm
1.8 TC	28° - 32° at 5400 rpm
	24° - 28° at 4200 rpm
	18° - 22° at 2300 rpm
	12° - 16° at 1800 rpm
	1° - 5° at 800 rpm
	No advance below 300 rpm
Vacuum advance:	
1.8 HC	
Starts	4 in (101.6 mm) HG
Finishes	12 in (304.8 mm) HG

1.8 LC		
Starts	... ...	6 in (152 mm) HG
Finishes	... ...	13 in (329.12 mm) HG
1.8 TC		
Starts	... ...	3 in (76.2 mm) HG
Finishes	... ...	8 in (203.2 mm) HG

TORQUE WRENCH SETTINGS

	lb ft	kg m
Distributor clamp bolt	2.5	0.35
Distributor flange retaining screws	8 - 10	1.1 - 1.4
Spark plug	30	4.1

1 General description

In order that the engine may run correctly it is necessary for an electrical spark to ignite the fuel/air mixture in the combustion chamber at exactly the right moment in relation to engine speed and load. The ignition system is based on suplying low tension voltage from the battery to the ignition coil, where it is converted into high tension voltage. The high tension voltage is powerful enough to jump the spark plug gap in the cylinders many times a second under high compression pressure, providing that the ignition system is in good working order and that all adjustments are correct.

The ignition system comprises two individual circuits known as the low tension and high tension circuits.

The low tension circuit (sometir , known as the primary circuit) comprises the battery, lead to control box, lead to the ignition switch, to the low tension or primary coil windings (terminal SW) and the lead from the low tension coil windings (terminal CB) to the contact breaker points and condenser in the distributor.

The high tension (secondary circuit) comprises the high tension or secondary coil windings, the heavily insulated ignition lead from the centre of the coil to the centre of the distributor cap, the rotor arm, the spark plug leads and the spark plugs.

The complete ignition system operation is as follows: Low tension voltage from the battery is changed within the ignition coil to high tension voltage by the opening and closing of the contact breaker points in the low tension circuit. High tension voltage is then fed via the carbon brush in the centre of the distributor cap to the rotor arm of the distributor. The rotor arm revolves inside the distributor cap and each time it comes into line with one of the four metal segments in the cap, these being connected to the spark plug leads, the opening and closing of the contact breaker points causes the high tension voltage to build up, jump the gap from the rotor arm to the appropriate metal segment and so, via the spark plug lead, to the spark plug where it finally jumps the gap between the two spark plug electrodes, one being connected to the earth system.

The ignition timing is advanced and retarded automatically to ensure the spark occurs at just the right instant for the particular load at the prevailing engine speed.

The ignition advance is controlled by a mechanical and vacuum operated system. The mechanical governor mechanism comprises two lead weights which move out under centrifugal force from the central distributor shaft as the engine speed rises. As they move outwards they rotate the cams relative to the distributor shaft, and so advance the spark. The weights are held in position by two springs, and it is the tension of the springs which is largely responsible for correct spark advancement.

When fitted the vacuum control comprises a diaphragm, one side of which is connected via a small bore tube to the carburettor, and the other side to the contact breaker plate. Depression in the induction manifold and carburettor, which varies with engine speed and throttle opening, causes the diaphragm to move, so moving the contact breaker plate and advancing or retarding the spark. A fine degree of control is achieved by a spring in the vacuum assembly.

2 Contact breaker points - adjustment

1 To adjust the contact breaker points so that the correct gap is obtained, first release the two clips securing the distributor cap to the distributor body, and lift away the cap. Clean the inside and outside of the cap with a dry cloth. It is unlikely that the four segments will be badly burned or scored, but if they are the cap must be renewed. If only a small deposit is on the segments it may be scraped away using a small screwdriver.

2 Push in the carbon brush, located in the top of the cap, several times to ensure that it moves freely. The brush should protrude at least ¼ inch (6.35 mm).

3 Gently prise the contact breaker points open to examine the condition of their faces. If they are rough, pitted or dirty it will be necessary to remove them for resurfacing, or for replacement points to be fitted.

4 Presuming the points are satisfactory, or that they have been cleaned and replaced, measure the gap between the points by turning the engine over until the contact breaker arm is on the peak of one of the four cam lobes. A 0.014 - 0.016 in (0.36 - 0.40 mm) feeler gauge should now just fit between the points.

5 If the gap varies from this amount, slacken the contact plate securing screw and adjust the contact gap by inserting a screwdriver in the notched hole at the end of the plate, turning clockwise to decrease, and anti- clockwise to increase the gap. Tighten the securing screw and recheck the gap again.

6 Replace the rotor arm and distributor cap and clip the spring blade retainers into position.

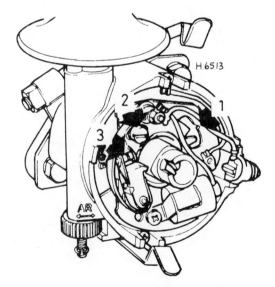

FIG.4.1. CONTACT BREAKER POINTS

1   Screwdriver slot for adjustment   2   Contact plate securing screw
3   Contact breaker points

3 Contact breaker points - removal and replacement

1 If the contact breaker points are burned, pitted or badly worn, they must be removed and replaced.

2 To remove the points, unscrew the terminal nut and remove it together with the top insulating bush and both leads from the stud. Lift off the contact breaker arm and remove the large fibre washer from the terminal pin.

3 The adjustable contact breaker plate is removed by unscrewing one holding down screw and removing it, complete with spring and flat washer.

4 Later type contact breaker points - Undo the nut securing the terminals to the contact breaker point assembly (Photo).

5 Lift the terminals from the threaded stud on the base plate assembly (photo).

6 Undo and remove the bolt and plain washer securing the contact breaker point assembly to the baseplate assembly (Photo).

7 Lift away the contact breaker point assembly (Photo).

8 To replace the points, first position the adjustable contact breaker plate, and secure it with its screw, spring and flat washer. Fit the fibre washer to the terminal pin and fit the contact breaker arm over it. Insert the flanged nylon bush with the condenser lead immediately under its head, and the low tension lead under that, over the terminal pin. Fit the steel washer and screw on the securing nut.

9 Later type contact breaker points. Place the contact breaker points assembly on the baseplate assembly and lightly secure with the bolt and plain washer.

10 Refit the terminal to the threaded stud and secure with the nut.

11 The points are now reassembled and the gap should be set as detailed in the previous section.

4 Condenser - removal, testing and replacement

1 The purpose of the condenser (capacitor) is to ensure that when the contact breaker points open there is no sparking across them which would waste voltage and cause wear.

2 The condenser is fitted in parallel with the contact breaker points. If it develops a short circuit, it will cause ignition failure, as the points will be prevented from interrupting the low tension circuit.

3 If the engine becomes very difficult to start, or begins to miss after several miles running, and the breaker points show signs of excessive burning, then the condition of the condenser must be suspect. A further test can be made by separating the points by hand with the ignition switched on. If this is accompanied by a flash it is indicative that the condenser has failed.

4 Without special test equipment, the only sure way to diagnose condenser trouble is to replace a suspected unit with a new one and note if there is any improvement. They are not expensive.

5 To remove the condenser from the distributor, remove the distributor cap and the rotor arm. Unscrew the contact breaker arm terminal nut, remove the nut, and flanged nylon bush. Undo and remove the condenser securing screw and lift away the condenser.

6 Replacement of the condenser is simply a reversal of the removal process. Take particular care that the condenser lead does not short circuit against any portion of the breaker plate.

5 Distributor - lubrication

1 It is important that the distributor cam is lubricated with petroleum jelly or grease at the specified mileages, and that the breaker arm, governor weights and cam spindle are lubricated with oil once every 6,000 miles (10,000 km).

2 Great care should be taken not to use too much lubricant, as any excess that might find its way onto the contact breaker points could cause burning and misfiring.

3.4 Try to use the correct 'distributor' spanner

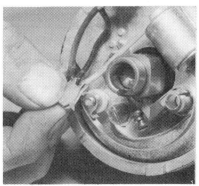

3.5 Release carefully

3.6 Use the right sized screwdriver - not too small

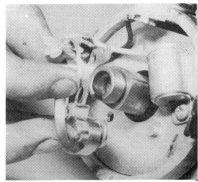

3.7 Use the thumb and two fingers

3   To gain access to the cam spindle, lift away the rotor arm.
    Drop no more than two drops of engine oil onto the screw
head. This will run down the spindle when the engine is hot and
lubricate the bearings. No more than ONE drop of oil should be
applied to the pivot bush.

6 Distributor - removal and replacement

1   For safety reasons disconnect the battery.
2   Release the clips securing the distributor cap to the body and
lift away the distributor cap.
3   Slowly turn the crankshaft until the groove in the crankshaft
pulley lines up with the static ignition point on the timing
indicator, and at the same time the rotor arm is pointing to the
distributor cap segment which is connected to No 1 spark plug.
4   Disconnect the low tension lead from the terminal on the
side of the distributor.
5   Detach the vacuum pipe from the distributor vacuum
advance unit.
6   Undo and remove the two screws, spring and plain washers
securing the distributor clamp plate to the cylinder block.
The distributor may now be lifted up together with the clamp
plate still attached.
7   If it is not wished to disturb the ignition timing, then under
no circumstances should the clamp pinch bolt, which secures
the distributor in its relative position in the clamp, be loosened.
Providing the distributor is removed without the clamp being
loosened from the distributor, and the engine is not turned, the
ignition timing will not be lost.
8   Replacement is a reversal of the above sequence. If the engine
has been turned, it will be necessary to retime the ignition. This
will also be necessary if the clamp pinch bolt has been loosened.
Tighten the flange retaining screws to a torque wrench setting of
8 - 10 lb ft (1.1 - 1.4 kg m).

7 Distributor - dismantling

1   With the distributor removed from the car and on the bench,
if the distributor cap is still in position, ease back the clips
and lift it away. Lift off the rotor arm. If it is very tight lever it
off gently with a screwdriver (Photo).
2   Remove the contact breaker points as described in Section 3.
3   Remove the condenser securing screw from the contact plate
by releasing its securing screw (Photo).
4   Release the vacuum unit flexible link from its mounting pin
on the moving contact plate.
5   Unscrew and remove the two screws and washers which hold
the contact breaker plate and base plate to the distributor body.
Note the earth lead which is secured by one of the two screws.
Remember to replace this lead on reassembly (photo).
6   Lift away the contact breaker plate and base plate. Hold the
contact breaker plate and turn the base plate in a clockwise
direction to separate the two halves.
7   Note the position of the slot in the rotor arm drive in relation
to the offset drive dog at the opposite end of the distributor. It
is essential that this is reassembled correctly as otherwise the
timing may be 180° out.
8   Unscrew the cam spindle retaining screw which is located in
the centre of the rotor arm drive shaft cam. Lift away the screw
(photo).
9   Detach the two return springs from their posts, and separate
the cam plate. Lift away the two control weights.
10 To remove the vacuum unit spring off the small circlip
securing the advance adjustment knurled nut which should then
be unscrewed. With the micrometer adjusting nut removed,
release the spring and the micrometer adjusting nut lock spring
clip. This is the clip that is responsible for the 'clicks' when the
micrometer adjuster nut is turned and it is small and easily lost,
as is the circlip, so put them in a safe place. Do not forget to
replace the lock spring clip on reassembly.
11 It is necessary to remove the distributor drive shaft or spindle
only if it is thought to be excessively worn. With a thin parallel

pin punch drive out the retaining pin from the driving tongue
collar on the bottom end of the distributor drive shaft. The shaft
can then be removed. Recover the thrust washers.
12 The distributor is now ready for inspection.

8 Distributor - inspection and repair

1   Thoroughly wash all mechanical parts in paraffin and wipe
dry using a clean non-fluffy rag.
2   Check the contact breaker points as described in Section 3.
Check the distributor cap for signs of tracking, indicated by a
thin black line between the segments. Replace the cap if evident.
3   If the metal portion of the rotor arm is badly burned or
loose, renew the arm. If slightly burnt, clean the arm with a
fine file. Check that the carbon brush moves freely in the centre
of the distributor cover.
4   Examine the fit of the contact breaker plate on the base plate
and also check the breaker arm pivot for looseness, or wear, and
obtain new as necessary.
5   Examine the centrifugal weights and pivot pins for wear, and
renew the weights or cam assembly if a degree of wear is found.
6   Examine the shaft and fit of the cam assembly on the shaft.
If the clearance is excesive compare the items with new units
and renew either, or both, if they show excessive wear.
7   If the shaft is a loose fit in the distributor bush and can be
seen to be worn, it will be necessary to fit a new shaft and bush.
    Renewal of the bush consists of drifting out the old bush and
fitting a new one. NOTE: Before inserting a new bush it should
be stood in engine oil for 24 hours or two hours in hot oil at
100°C (212°F).
8   If possible examine the length of the centrifugal weight
springs and compare them with new springs. If they have
stretched they should be renewed.

9 Distributor - reassembly

1   Reassembly is a straight forward reversal of the dismantling
process. Note in addition:
2   Lubricate the centrifugal weights and other parts of the
mechanical advance mechanism, the distributor shaft, and the
portion of the shaft on which the cam bears with Castrol GTX
oil during reassembly. Do not oil excessively but ensure that
these parts are adequately lubricated.
3   On reassembling the cam driving pins with the centrifugal
weights check that they are in the correct position so that when
viewed from above, the rotor arm should be at the 6 o'clock
position, and the small offset on the driving dog must be on the
right.
4   Check the action of the weights in the fully advanced and
fully retarded positions and ensure they are not binding.
5   Tighten the micrometer adjusting nut to the middle position
of the timing scale.
6   Finally set the contact breaker points as described in Section
2.

10 Ignition - timing

1   If the clamp plate pinch bolt has been loosened on the distributor and the static timing lost, or if for any other reason
it is wished to set the ignition and timing proceed as follows:
2   Refer to Section 2 and check the contact breaker points.
Reset as necessary.
3   If necessary, assemble the clamp plate to the distributor - but
do not tighten the pinch bolt fully.
4   Remove the rocker cover from the engine. Then, using a
suitable spanner or socket on the crankshaft pulley bolt, turn the
crankshaft until the cut-out in the pulley is in the correct
position, relative to the timing cover pointers, to give the required setting (see Fig. 4.4). Both valves for number one cylinder
should now be closed. This means that the two valve springs will
be uncompressed and that there will be noticeable play between

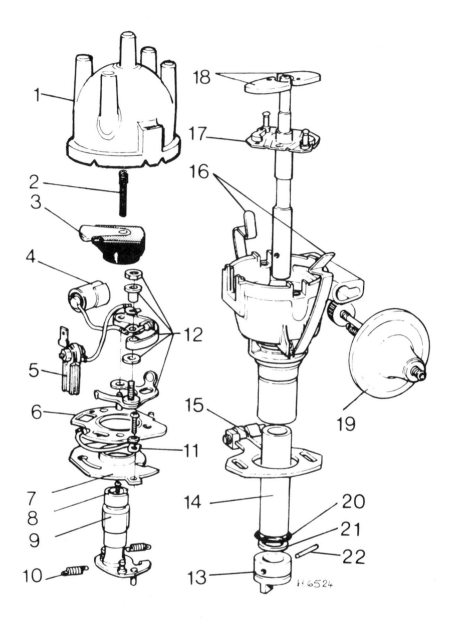

FIG.4.2. DISTRIBUTOR COMPONENT PARTS

1	Distributor cap	12	Contact breaker points
2	Brush and spring	13	Driving dog
3	Rotor arm	14	Bush
4	Condenser	15	Clamp plate
5	Terminal and lead	16	Cap retaining clips
6	Moving baseplate	17	Shaft and action plate
7	Fixed baseplate	18	Bob weights
8	Cam screw	19	Vacuum unit
9	Cam	20	O-ring oil seal
10	Advance spring	21	Thrust washer
11	Earth lead	22	Taper pin

7.1 Be firm but not careless

7.3 Use a Phillips screwdriver

7.5 Do not burr the screw

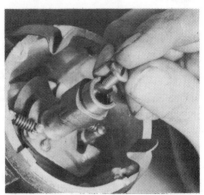
7.8 The screw can be held with a little grease to a screwdriver bit

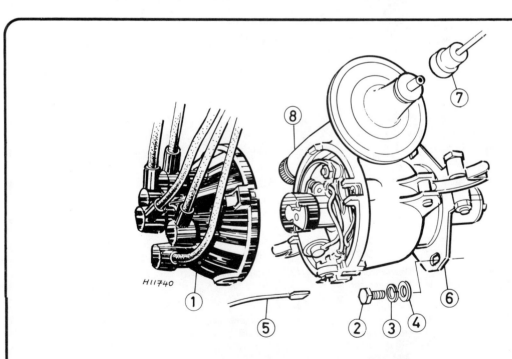

FIG.4.3. DISTRIBUTOR ATTACHMENT POINTS

1 Distributor cap	5 LT lead
2 Bolt	6 Clamp
3 Spring washer	7 Vacuum pipe
4 Plain washer	8 Distributor body

H11740

Measuring plug gap. A feeler gauge of the correct size (see ignition system specifications) should have a slight 'drag' when slid between the electrodes. Adjust gap if necessary

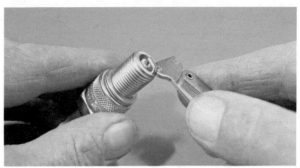

Adjusting plug gap. The plug gap is adjusted by bending the earth electrode inwards, or outwards, as necessary until the correct clearance is obtained. Note the use of the correct tool

Normal. Grey-brown deposits, lightly coated core nose. Gap increasing by around 0.001 in (0.025 mm) per 1000 miles (1600 km). Plugs ideally suited to engine, and engine in good condition

Carbon fouling. Dry, black, sooty deposits. Will cause weak spark and eventually misfire. Fault: over-rich fuel mixture. Check: carburettor mixture settings, float level and jet sizes; choke operation and cleanliness of air filter. Plugs can be re-used after cleaning

Oil fouling. Wet, oily deposits. Will cause weak spark and eventually misfire. Fault: worn bores/piston rings or valve guides; sometimes occurs (temporarily) during running-in period. Plugs can be re-used after thorough cleaning

Overheating. Electrodes have glazed appearance, core nose very white – few deposits. Fault: plug overheating. Check: plug value, ignition timing, fuel octane rating (too low) and fuel mixture (too weak). Discard plugs and cure fault immediately

Electrode damage. Electrodes burned away; core nose has burned, glazed appearance. Fault: pre-ignition. Check: as for 'Overheating' but may be more severe. Discard plugs and remedy fault before piston or valve damage occurs

Split core nose (may appear initially as a crack). Damage is self-evident, but cracks will only show after cleaning. Fault: pre-ignition or wrong gap-setting technique. Check: ignition timing, cooling system, fuel octane rating (too low) and fuel mixture (too weak). Discard plugs, rectify fault immediately

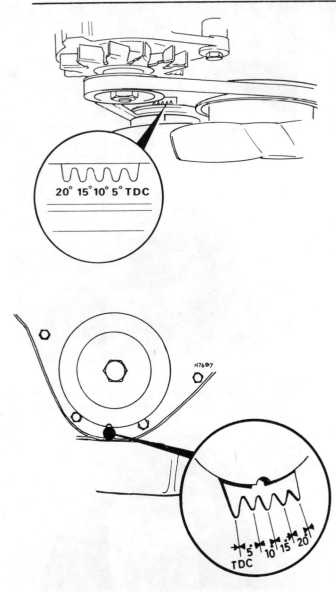

FIG 4.4 ALTERNATIVE TIMING POINTERS USED ON MARINA MODELS

Degrees shown are btdc

necessary, the distributor body can be rotated slightly to align the segment and rotor.

6   Remove the rotor arm. Bearing in mind that the distributor shaft turns anti-clockwise, the heel of the contact breaker should now be just in front of the distributor cam lobe which will open the points. Rotate the distributor body to achieve this, if necessary. In this position the contact breaker points should be closed - if they are not, rotate the distributor body slightly anti-clockwise until they are.

7   Grip the top of the distributor shaft and turn it lightly in a clockwise direction to take up any play in the advance/retard mechanism. While doing this carefully rotate the distributor body in a clockwise direction until the contact breaker points just begin to open. Tighten the distributor clamp pinch bolt. If it is found difficult to determine exactly when the points begin to open, use the following method. Disconnect the low-tension lead from the distributor. Reconnect the lead with a low wattage bulb fitted in series and switch on the ignition. When the light goes out the points have just opened.

8   Ignition timing is now complete. Refit the distributor cap and leads, then replace the rocker cover. If necessary, fine adjustment can be made to the ignition timing using the vernier adjuster (where fitted). The handbook supplied with your car will tell you how this is accomplished.

9   If it was not found possible to align the rotor arm correctly, one of two things is wrong. Either the distributor driveshaft has been incorrectly refitted, in which case it must be removed and replaced as described in Chapter 1, or the distributor has been dismantled and the distributor cam spindle refitted 180⁰ out. To rectify, it will be necessary to partially dismantle the distributor, lift the cam spindle pins from the centrifugal weight holes and turn the cam spindle through 180⁰. Refit the pins into the weights and reassemble.

11 Spark plugs and HT leads

1   The correct functioning of the spark plugs is vital for the proper running and efficient operation of the engine.

2   At intervals of 6,000 miles (10,000 km) the plugs should be removed, examined, cleaned, and if worn excessively, renewed. The condition of the spark plug can also tell much about the general condition of the engine.

3   If the insulator nose of the spark plug is clean and white, with no deposits, this is indicative of a weak mixture, or too hot a plug (a hot plug transfers heat away from the electrode slowly - a cold plug transfers heat away quickly).

4   If the insulator nose is covered with hard black looking deposits, then this is indicative that the mixture is too rich. Should the plug be black and oily then it is likely that the engine is fairly worn, as well as the mixture being too rich.

5   If the insulator nose is covered with light tan to greyish brown deposits, then the mixture is correct, and it is likely that the engine is in good condition.

6   If there are any traces of long brown tapering stains on the outside of the white portion of the plug, then the plug will have to be renewed, as this shows that there is a faulty joint between the plug body and the insulator, and compression is being allowed to leak away.

7   Plugs should be cleaned by a sand blasting machine, which will free them from carbon more than by cleaning by hand. The machine will also test the condition of the plugs under compression. Any plug that fails to spark at the recommended pressure should be renewed.

8   The spark plug gap is of considerable importance, as, if it is too large or too small the size of the spark and its efficiency will be seriously impaired. The spark plug gap should be set to 0.025 inch (0.6425 mm).

9   To set it, measure the gap with a feeler gauge, and then bend open, or close, the outer plug electrode until the correct gap is achieved. The centre electrode should never be bent as this may crack the insulation and cause plug failure, if nothing worse.

the two rocker arms and the valves. If this is not the case, continue to rotate the crankshaft in a clockwise direction until you have both the correct timing setting and both valves for number 1 cylinder closed. Should you accidentally go slightly past the correct setting do not turn the engine backwards to regain it. Instead, continue to turn the crankshaft in a clockwise direction until the correct setting is again reached. **The crankshaft must not be turned again until ignition timing is completed.**

5   Now is the time to refit the distributor (where necessary). If a vernier adjuster is fitted, set this to its central position. Rotate the clamp about the distributor body until the clamp and body are approximately in the relative position shown in Fig. 4.3. Offer up the distributor to the engine and align the clamp plate holes over the holes in the block. Rotate the distributor shaft, via the rotor arm, until the distributor dog engages and the distributor clamp goes fully home against the cylinder block. If the distributor cap were fitted the rotor arm should be pointing to the segment which leads to number 1 cylinder spark plug. If

10 When replacing the plugs, remember to use new washers and replace the leads from the distributor cap in the correct firing order which is 1, 3, 4, 2. No.1 cylinder being the one nearest the fan.

11 The plug leads require no maintenance other than being kept clean and wiped over regularly. At intervals of 6,000 miles (10,000 km), however, pull each lead off the plug in turn and remove them from the distributor cap. Water can seep down these joints giving rise to a white corrosive deposit which must be carefully removed from the end of each cable.

12 Ignition system - fault symptoms

There are two general symptoms of ignition faults. Either the engine will not fire, or the engine is difficult to start and misfires. If it is a regular misfire, i.e. the engine is only running on two or three cylinders, the fault is almost sure to be in the high tension circuit. If the misfiring is intermittent, the fault could be in either the high or low tension circuits. If the engine stops suddenly, or will not start at all, it is likely that the fault is in the low tension circuit. Loss of power and overheating, apart from faulty carburettor settings, are normally due to faults in the distributor, or incorrect ignition timing.

13 Fault diagnosis - engine fails to start

1 If the engine fails to start and it was running normally when it was last used, first check that there is fuel in the petrol tank. If the engine turns over normally on the starter motor and the battery is evidently well charged, then the fault may be in either the high or low tension circuits. First check th e HT circuit. NOTE - If the battery is known to be fully charged, the ignition comes on, and the starter motor fails to turn the engine, CHECK THE TIGHTNESS OF THE LEADS ON THE BATTERY TERMINALS and also the secureness of the earth lead to the CONNECTION TO THE BODY. It is quite common for the leads to have worked loose, even if they look and feel secure. If one of the battery terminal posts gets very hot when trying to operate the starter motor this is a sure indication of a faulty connection to that terminal.

2 One of the commonest reasons for bad starting is wet or damp spark plug leads and distributor. Remove the distributor cap. If condensation is visible, internally dry the cap with a rag and also wipe over the leads. Replace the cap.

3 If the engine still fails to start, check that current is reaching the plugs by disconnecting each plug lead in turn at the spark plug ends and holding the end of the cable about 3/16 inch (4.7 mm) away from the cylinder block. Spin the engine on the starter motor by pressing the rubber button on the starter motor solenoid switch (under the bonnet) for manual gearbox models. For automatic transmission models a second person should operate the ignition/starter switch.

4 Sparking between the end of the cable and the block should be fairly strong with a regular blue spark (hold the lead with rubber to avoid electric shocks). If current is reaching the spark plugs, then remove them and clean and regap them to 0.024 - 0.026 inch (0.625 - 0.660 mm). The engine should now start.

5 Spin the engine as before, when a rapid succession of blue sparks between the end of the lead and the block indicate that the coil is in order, and that either the distributor cap is cracked, the carbon brush is stuck or worn, the rotor arm is faulty, or the contact points are burnt, pitted or dirty. If the points are in bad shape, clean and reset them as described in Section 2.

6 If there are no sparks from the end of the lead from the coil, then check the connections of the lead to the coil and distributor cap, and if they are in order, check out the low tension circuit starting with the battery.

7 Switch on the ignition and turn the crankshaft so that the contact breaker points have fully opened. Then, with either a 20 volt voltmeter or bulb and length of wire, check that current from the battery is reaching the starter solenoid switch. No read-

ing indicates that there is a fault in the cable to the switch or in the connections at the switch or at the battery terminals. Alternatively, the battery earth lead may not be properly earthed to the body.

8 If in order, then check that current is reaching the ignition switch by connecting the voltmeter to the ignition switch input terminal (the one connected to the brown cable) and earth. No reading indicates a break in the wire or a faulty connection at the switch terminals or wiring to the control box (where fitted).

9 If the correct reading (approx 12 volts) is obtained check the output terminal on the ignition switch (the one with the white cable) no reading means that the ignition switch is broken. Replace with a new unit and start the car.

10 If current is reaching the ignition switch output terminal, then check the A3 terminal on the fuse unit with the voltmeter. No reading indicates a break in the wire or loose connections between the ignition and the A3 terminal. Even if the A3 - A4 fuse is broken, current should still be reaching the coil as it does not pass through the fuse. Remedy and the car should now start.

11 Check the switch terminal on the coil (it is marked + and the lead from the switch is connected to it). No reading indicates loose connections or a broken wire from the A3 terminal on the fuse unit. If this proves to be a fault, remedy and re-start the car.

12 Check the contact breaker terminal on the coil (it is marked — or CB and the lead to the distributor is connected to it). If no reading is recorded on the voltmeter then the coil is broken and must be replaced. The car should start when a new coil has been fitted.

13 If a reading is obtained at the — terminal then check the wire from the coil for loose connections etc. The final check on the low tension circuit is across the contact breaker points. No reading indicates a broken condenser, which when replaced will enable the car to finally start.

14 Fault diagnosis - engine misfires

1 If the engine misfires regularly, run it at a fast idling speed, and short out each of the spark plugs in turn by placing an insulated screwdriver across the plug terminal to the cylinder block.

2 No difference in engine running will be noticed when the plug in the defective cylinder is short circuited. Short circuiting the working plugs will accentuate the misfire.

3 Remove the plug lead from the end of the defective plug and hold it about 3/16 in (4.76 mm) away from the block. Restart the engine. If sparking is fairly strong and regular the fault must lie in the spark plug.

4 The plug may be loose, the insulation may be cracked or the electrodes may have burnt away giving too wide a gap for the spark to jump across. Worse still, the earth electrode may have broken off. Either renew the plug, or clean it, reset the gap and then test it.

5 If there is no spark at the end of the plug lead, or if it is weak and intermittent, check the ignition lead from the distributor to the plug. If the insulation is cracked or damaged, renew the lead. Check the connections at the distributor cap.

6 If there is still no spark, examine the distributor cap carefully for signs of tracking. This can be recognised by a very thin black line running between two or more segments, or between a segment and some other part of the distributor. These lines are paths which now conduct electricity across the cap thus letting it run to earth. The only answer is to fit a new distributor cap.

7 Apart from the ignition timing being incorrect, other causes of misfiring have already been dealt with under the section dealing with failure of the engine to start.

8 If the ignition timing is too far retarded, it should be noted that the engine will tend to overheat, and there will be quite a noticeable drop in power. If the engine is overheating and power is down, and the ignition is correct, then the carburettor should be checked, as it is likely that this is where the fault lies. See Chapter 3 for details.

Chapter 5 Clutch

For modifications, and information applicable to later models, see Supplement at end of manual

Contents

General description   1
Clutch system - bleeding   2
Clutch pedal - removal and replacement   3
Clutch - removal and replacement   4
Clutch - inspection   5
Clutch flexible hose - removal and replacement   6
Clutch master cylinder - removal and refitting   7
Clutch master cylinder - dismantling, examination and re-
assembly   8

Clutch slave cylinder - removal and replacement   9
Clutch slave cylinder dismantling, examination and reassembly 10
Clutch release bearing assembly - removal, overhaul and re-
fitting   11
Fault diagnosis and cure   12
Clutch squeal   13
Clutch slip   14
Clutch spin   15
Clutch judder   16

Specifications

Type	Borg and Beck or Laycock, diaphragm spring
Drive plate diameter	8 inch (203mm)
Number of damper springs	6
Damper spring colour	3 dark green/light green, 1 dark green/lavender, 1 dark green/white, 1 dark green/orange
Facing materials (identification colour)	H26 Wound yarn green/red
	WR7 Wound yarn white
	RYZ Wound yarn blue
	DSW8 Wound asbestos red
Master cylinder bore	0.625 in (15.8750mm)
Slave cylinder bore	0.875 in (22.2mm)

1 General description

The Marina 1.8 models are fitted with an 8 inch (203 mm) diameter diaphragm spring clutch operated hydraulically by a master and slave cylinder.

The clutch comprises a steel cover which is bolted and dowelled to the rear face of the flywheel and contains the pressure plate and clutch disc or driven plate.

The pressure plate, diaphragm spring, and release plate are all attached to the clutch assembly cover.

The clutch disc is free to slide along the splined first motion shaft and is held in position between the flywheel and pressure plate by the pressure of the diaphragm spring.

Friction lining material is riveted to the clutch disc which has a spring cushioned hub to absorb transmission shocks and to help ensure a smooth take off.

The clutch is actuated hydraulically. The pendant clutch pedal is connected to the clutch master cylinder and hydraulic fluid reservoir by a short pushrod. The master cylinder and hydraulic reservoir are mounted on the engine side of the bulkhead in front of the driver.

Depressing the clutch pedal moves the piston in the master cylinder forwards so forcing hydraulic fluid through the clutch hydraulic pipe to the slave cylinder.

The piston in the slave cylinder moves forward on the entry of the fluid and actuates the clutch release arm by means of a short push rod. The opposite end of the release arm is forked and is located behind the release bearing.

As this pivoted clutch release arm moves backwards it bears against the release bearing pushing it forwards to bear against the release plate, so moving the centre of the diaphragm spring inwards. The spring is sandwiched between two annular rings which act as fulcrum points. The centre of the spring is pushed out, so moving the pressure plate backwards and disengaging the pressure plate from the clutch disc.

When the clutch pedal is released, the diaphragm spring forces the pressure plate into contact with the high friction linings on the clutch disc and at the same time pushes the clutch disc a fraction of an inch forwards on its splines so engaging the clutch disc with the flywheel. The clutch disc is now firmly sandwiched between the pressure plate and the flywheel so the drive is taken up.

As the friction linings on the clutch disc wear the pressure plate automatically moves closer to the disc to compensate. There is therefore no need to periodically adjust the clutch.

2 Clutch system - bleeding

1 Gather together a clean jam jar, a length of rubber tubing which fits tightly over the bleed nipple on the slave cylinder, a tin of hydraulic brake fluid and someone to help.

2 Check that the master cylinder is full. If it is not, fill it and cover the bottom two inches of the jar with hydraulic fluid.

3 Remove the rubber dust cap from the bleed nipple (if fitted) on the slave cylinder, and with a suitable spanner open the bleed nipple approximately three quarters of a turn.

4 Place one end of the tube securely over the nipple and insert the other end in the jam jar so that the tube orifice is below the level of the fluid.

5 The assistant should now depress the pedal and hold it down at the end of its stroke. Close the bleed screw and allow the pedal to return to its normal position.

6 Continue this series of operations until clear hydraulic fluid without any traces of air bubbles emerges from the end of the tubing. Make sure that the reservoir is checked frequently to ensure that the hydraulic fluid does not drop too far thus letting air into the system.

7 When no more air bubbles appear, tighten the bleed nipple on the downstroke.

8 Replace the rubber dust cap (if fitted) over the bleed nipple. Allow the hydraulic fluid in the jar to stand for at least 24 hours before reusing it to allow all the minute air bubbles to escape.

3 Clutch pedal - removal and replacement

1 Refer to Chapter 12 and remove the parcel shelf.

2 Straighten the ears and extract the split pin that retains the master cylinder operating rod yoke to pedal clevis pin. Lift away the plain washer and withdraw the clevis pin.

3 Straighten the ears and extract the split pin from the clutch pedal end of the pedal pivot shaft. Lift away the plain washer.

4 Carefully release the pedal return spring from the pedal and slide the pedal from the end of the shaft.

5 Inspect the pedal bush for signs of wear which if evident, either the old bush should be drifted out and a new one fitted, or a new pedal assembly obtained.

6 Refitting is the reverse sequence to removal. Lubricate the pedal bush and shaft and also the spring coils to prevent squeaking.

4 Clutch - removal and refitting

1 Remove the gearbox as described in Chapter 6, Section 2.

2 With a scriber or file mark the relative position of the clutch cover and flywheel to ensure correct refitting if the original parts are to be used.

3 Remove the clutch assembly by unscrewing the six bolts holding the cover to the rear face of the flywheel. Unscrew the

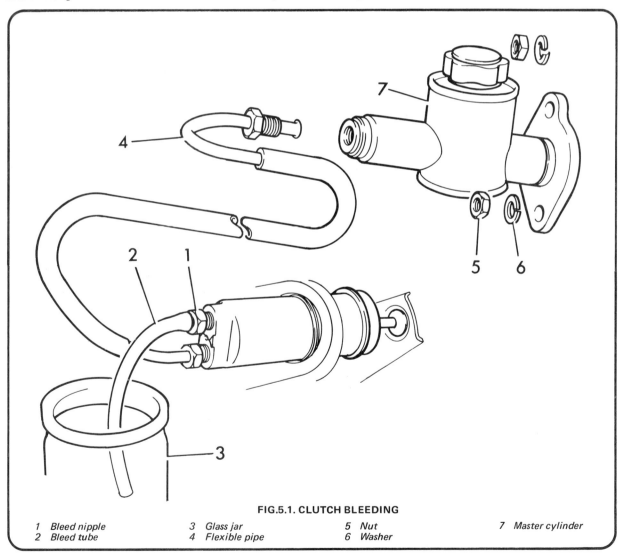

FIG.5.1. CLUTCH BLEEDING

| 1 | Bleed nipple | 3 | Glass jar | 5 | Nut | 7 | Master cylinder |
| 2 | Bleed tube | 4 | Flexible pipe | 6 | Washer | | |

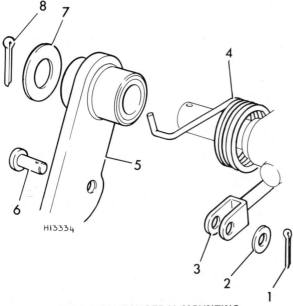

FIG.5.2. CLUTCH PEDAL MOUNTING

1 Split pin	5 Clutch pedal
2 Plain washer	6 Clevis pin
3 Pushrod	7 Plain washer
4 Spring	8 Split pin

bolts diagonally half a turn at a time to prevent distortion of the cover flange, also to prevent an accident caused by the cover flange binding on the dowels and suddenly flying off.

4 With the bolts and spring washers removed, lift the clutch assembly off the locating dowels. The driven plate or clutch disc will fall out at this stage, as it is not attached to either the clutch cover assembly or the flywheel. Carefully make a note of which way round it is fitted.

5 It is important that no oil or grease gets on the clutch disc friction linings, or the pressure plate and flywheel faces. It is advisable to handle the parts with clean hands and to wipe down the pressure plate and flywheel faces with a clean dry rag before inspection or refitting commences.

6 To refit the clutch place the clutch disc against the flywheel with the clutch spring housing facing outwards away from the flywheel. On no account should the clutch disc be replaced the wrong way round as it will be found quite impossible to operate the clutch with the friction disc incorrectly fitted.

7 Replace the clutch cover assembly loosely on the dowels. Replace the six bolts and spring washers and tighten them finger tight so that the clutch disc is gripped but can still be moved.

8 The clutch disc must now be centralised so that when the engine and gearbox are mated, the gearbox input shaft splines will pass through the splines in the centre of the hub.

9 Centralisation can be carried out quite easily by inserting a round bar or long screwdriver through the hole in the centre of the clutch, so that the end of the bar rests in the small hole in the end of the crankshaft containing the input shaft bearing bush. Moving the bar sideways or up and down will move the clutch disc in whichever direction is necessary to achieve centralisation.

10 Centralisation is easily judged by removing the bar and viewing the driven plate hub in relation to the hole in the centre of the diaphragm spring. When the hub appears exactly in the centre of the diaphragm spring hole all is correct. Alternatively, if an old input shaft can be borrowed this will eliminate all the guesswork as it will fit the bush and centre of the clutch hub exactly, obviating the need for visual alignment.

11 Tighten the clutch bolt firmly in a diagonal sequence to ensure that the cover plate is pulled down evenly, and without

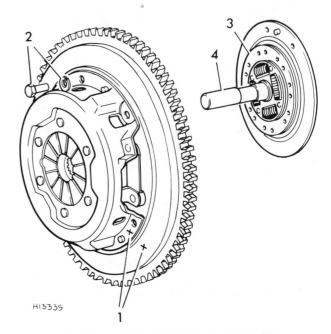

FIG.5.3. CLUTCH MOUNTED ON FLYWHEEL

1 Alignment marks	3 Clutch drive plate
2 Securing bolt and spring washer	4 Aligning tool

distortion of the flange.

12 Mate the engine and gearbox, bleed the slave cylinder if the pipe was disconnected and check the clutch for correct operation.

5 Clutch inspection

1 In the normal course of events clutch dismantling and reassembly is the term used for simply fitting a new clutch pressure plate and friction disc. Under no circumstances should the diaphragm spring clutch unit be dismantled. If a fault develops in the pressure plate assembly an exchange replacement unit must be fitted.

2 If a new clutch disc is being fitted it is false economy not to renew the release bearing at the same time. This will preclude having to replace it at a later date when wear on the clutch linings is very small.

3 Examine the clutch disc friction linings for wear or loose rivets and the disc for rim distortion, cracks and worn splines.

4 It is always best to renew the clutch driven plate as an assembly to preclude further trouble, but, if it is wished to merely renew the linings, the rivets should be drilled out, and not knocked out with a centre punch. The manufacturers do not advise that the linings only are renewed and personal experience dictates that it is far more satisfactory to renew the driven plate complete than to try to economise by fitting only new friction linings.

5 Check the machined faces of the flywheel and the pressure plate. If either is badly grooved it should be machined until smooth, or replaced with a new item. If the pressure plate is cracked or split it must be renewed.

6 Examine the hub splines for wear and also make sure that the centre hub is not loose.

6 Clutch flexible hose - removal and replacement

1 Wipe the slave cylinder end of the translucent hose to prevent dirt ingress. Obtain a clean and dry glass jam jar and have it ready to catch the hydraulic fluid during the next operation.
2 Carefully unscrew the union at the slave cylinder end and drain the fluid into the jar.
3 Unscrew the union at the master cylinder end.
4 Where applicable, remove the screw which secures the hose clip to the body, then remove the hose.
5 Refitting is the reverse of the removal procedure but ensure that the screw threads are clean.
6 It will be necessary to bleed the clutch hydraulic system as described in Section 2 of this Chapter.

7 Clutch master cylinder - removal and refitting

1 Drain the fluid from the clutch master reservoir by attaching a rubber tube to the slave cylinder bleed nipple. Undo the nipple by approximately three quarters of a turn and then pump the fluid out into a suitable container by means of operating the clutch pedal. Note that the pedal must be held in against the floor at the completion of each stroke and the bleed nipple tightened before the pedal is allowed to return. When the pedal

has returned to its normal position loosen the bleed nipple and repeat the process, until the clutch master cylinder is empty.
2 Place a rag under the master cylinder to catch any hydraulic fluid that may be spilt. Unscrew the union nut from the end of the metal pipe where it enters the clutch master cylinder and gently pull the pipe clear.
3 Straighten the ears and extract the split pin from the operating fork clevis pin on the pedal.
4 Unscrew and remove the two nuts and spring washers securing the master cylinder and lift away. Take care not to allow any hydraulic fluid to come into contact with the paintwork as it acts as a solvent.
5 Refitting the master cylinder is the reverse sequence to removal. Bleed the system as described in Section 2 of this Chapter.

8 Clutch master cylinder - dismantling, examination and re-assembly

1 Ease back the rubber dust cover from the push rod end.
2 Using a pair of circlip pliers release the circlip retaining the push rod assembly. Lift away the push rod complete with rubber boot and plain washer.
3 By shaking hard, the piston with its seal, dished washer, second seal, and spring retainer may be removed from the cylinder bore.

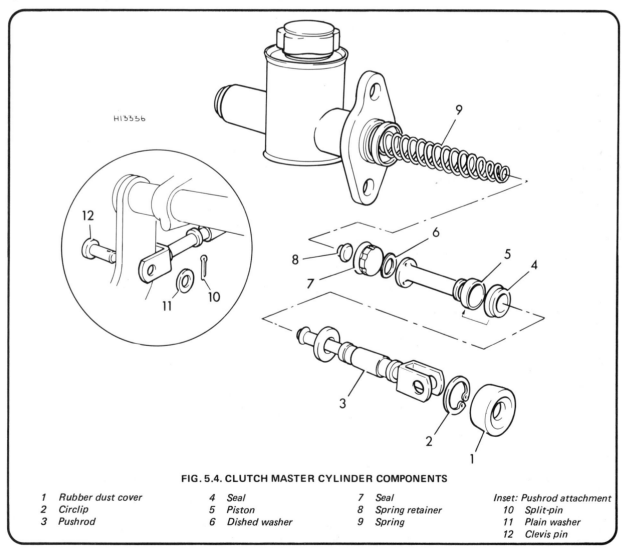

FIG. 5.4. CLUTCH MASTER CYLINDER COMPONENTS

1	Rubber dust cover	4	Seal	7	Seal
2	Circlip	5	Piston	8	Spring retainer
3	Pushrod	6	Dished washer	9	Spring

Inset: Pushrod attachment
10 Split-pin
11 Plain washer
12 Clevis pin

4 Lift away the long spring noting which way round it is fitted.
5 If they prove stubborn carefully use a foot pump air jet on the hydraulic pipe connection and this should move the internal parts, but do take care as they will fly out. We recommend placing a pad over the push rod end to catch the parts.
6 Carefully ease the secondary cup seal from the piston noting which way round it is fitted.
7 Thoroughly clean the parts in brake fluid or methylated spirits. After drying the items inspect the seals for signs of distortion, swelling, splitting or hardening although it is recommended new rubber parts are always fitted after dismantling as a matter of course.
8 Inspect the bore and piston for signs of deep scoring marks which, if evident, means a new cylinder should be fitted. Make sure the by pass ports are clear by poking gently with a piece of thin wire.
9 As the parts are refitted to the cylinder bore make sure that they are thoroughly wetted with clean hydraulic fluid.
10 Refit the secondary cup seal onto the piston making sure it is the correct way round.
11 Insert the spring with its retainer into the master cylinder bore.
12 Next refit the main cup seal with its flat end facing towards the open end of the bore.
13 Replace the wavy washer and carefully insert the piston into the bore. The small end of the piston should be towards the wavy washer. Make sure that the lip of the seal does not roll over as it enters the bore.
14 Smear a little rubber grease onto the ball end of the push rod and refit the push rod assembly. Slide down the plain washer and secure in position with the circlip.
15 Pack the rubber dust cover with rubber grease and place over the end of the master cylinder.

9 Clutch slave cylinder - removal and replacement

1 Wipe the top of the master cylinder reservoir and unscrew the cap. Place a piece of polythene sheet over the top of the reservoir and replace the cap. This will stop hydraulic fluid syphoning out during subsequent operations.
2 Wipe the area around the hydraulic pipe on the slave cylinder and disconnect the metal pipe from the slave cylinder.
3 Turn the slave cylinder until the flat on the shoulder faces

the clutch housing.
4 Using a piece of metal bar or a large screwdriver carefully draw the clutch release lever rearwards until it is possible to lift out the slave cylinder. It will be found helpful to push the operating rod into the slave cylinder to clear the operating lever, then remove the rod and slave cylinder.
5 Refitting the slave cylinder is the reverse sequence to removal. It is very important that the bleed nipple is uppermost, otherwise it will be impossible to bleed all air from the system.
6 Bleed the clutch hydraulic system as described in Section 2.

10 Clutch slave cylinder - dismantling, examination and reassembly

1 Clean the outside of the slave cylinder before dismantling.
2 Pull off the rubber dust cover and by shaking hard, the piston, seal, filler and spring should come out of the cylinder bore.
3 If they prove stubborn carefully use a foot pump air jet on the hydraulic hose connection and this should remove the internal parts, but do take care as they will fly out. We recommend placing a pad over the dust cover end to catch the parts.
4 Wash all internal parts with either brake fluid or methylated spirits and dry using a non fluffy rag.
5 Inspect the bore and piston for signs of deep scoring which, if evident, means a new cylinder should be fitted.
6 Carefully examine the rubber components for signs of swelling, distortion, splitting, hardening or other wear although it is recommended new rubber parts are always fitted after dismantling.
7 All parts should be reassembled wetted with clean hydraulic fluid.
8 Refit the spring, large end first into the cylinder bore.
9 Replace the cup filler into the bore.
10 Fit a new cup seal and replace the piston making sure that both are fitted the correct way round.
11 Apply a little rubber grease to both ends of the push rod and also pack the dust cover.
12 Fit the dust cover over the end of the slave cylinder engaging the lips over the groove in the body.
13 Fit the push rod to the slave cylinder by pushing through the hole in the dust cover.

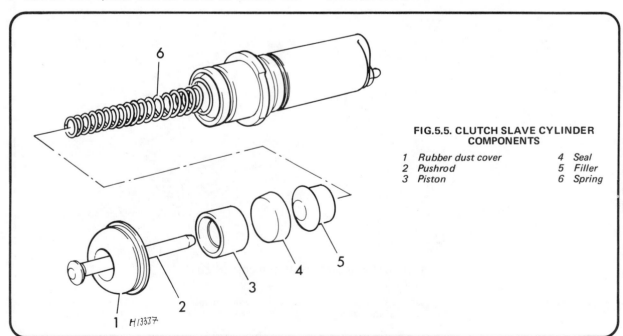

FIG.5.5. CLUTCH SLAVE CYLINDER COMPONENTS

1 Rubber dust cover	4 Seal
2 Pushrod	5 Filler
3 Piston	6 Spring

H13337

11 Clutch release bearing assembly - removal and overhaul and refitting

1 To gain access it is necessary to remove the gearbox as described in Chapter 6.
2 Detach the operating lever from the release bearing and slide off the bearing assembly.
3 If the bearing is worn or shows signs of overheating it may be removed using a large bench vice or a press and suitable packing.
4 When refitting a new bearing always apply the load to the inner race.
5 Fit the release bearing onto the gearbox first motion shaft front end cover.
6 Engage the pivots of the operating lever into the groove in the release bearing and at the same time engage the lever retaining spring clip with the fulcrum pin in the gearbox housing.
7 Press the operating lever fully into position.
8 Replacement of the gearbox is now the reverse sequence to removal.

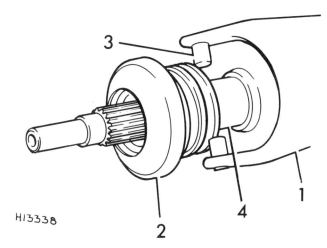

H13338

FIG.5.6. CLUTCH RELEASE ASSEMBLY

1 *Operating lever*
2 *Release bearing*
3 *Operating lever dowels*
4 *First motion shaft front end cover*

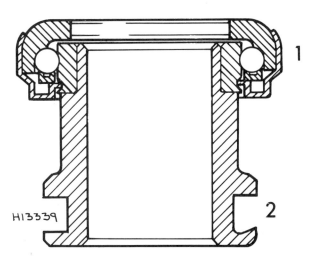

H13339

FIG.5.7. CROSS SECTION THROUGH CLUTCH RELEASE BEARING

1 *Bearing assembly*
2 *Bearing carrier*

12 Fault diagnosis and remedy

There are four main faults in which the clutch and release mechanism are prone. They may occur by themselves, or in conjunction with any of the other faults. They are clutch squeal, slip, spin and judder.

13 Clutch squeal

1 If on taking up the drive or when changing gear, the clutch squeals, this is indicative of a badly worn clutch release bearing.
2 As well as regular wear due to normal use, wear of the clutch release bearing is much accentuated if the clutch is ridden or held down for long periods in gear, with the engine running. To minimise wear of this component the car should always be taken out of gear at traffic lights and for similar hold ups.
3 The clutch release bearing is not an expensive item, but difficult to get at.

14 Clutch slip

1 Clutch slip is a self evident condition which occurs when the clutch friction plate is badly worn, oil or grease have got onto the flywheel or pressure plate faces, or the pressure plate itself is faulty.
2 The reason for clutch slip is that due to one of the faults above, there is either insufficient pressure from the pressure plate, or insufficient friction from the friction plate to ensure solid drive.
3 If small amounts of oil get onto the clutch, they will be burnt off under the heat of the clutch engagement, and in the process, gradually darken the linings. Excessive oil on the clutch will burn off leaving a carbon deposit which can cause quite bad slip, or fierceness, spin and judder.
4 If clutch slip is suspected, and confirmation of this condition is required, there are several tests which can be made.
5 With the engine in second or third gear and pulling lightly sudden depression of the accelerator pedal may cause the engine to increase its speed without any increase in road speed. Easing off on the accelerator will then give a definite drop in engine speed without the car slowing.
6 In extreme cases of clutch slip the engine will race under normal acceleration conditions.
7 If slip is due to oil or grease on the linings a temporary cure can sometimes be effected by squirting carbon tetrachloride into the clutch. The permanent cure is, of course, to renew the clutch driven plate and trace and rectify the oil leak.

15 Clutch spin

1 Clutch spin is a condition which occurs when there is a leak in the clutch hydraulic actuating mechanism, there is an obstruction in the clutch either in the first motion shaft or in the operating lever itself, or the oil may have partially burnt off the clutch lining and have left a resinous deposit which is causing the clutch disc to stick to the pressure plate or flywheel.
2 The reason for clutch spin is that due to any, or a combination of, the faults just listed, the clutch pressure plate is not completely freeing from the centre plate even with the clutch pedal fully depressed.
3 If clutch spin is suspected, the condition can be confirmed by extreme difficulty in engaging first gear from rest, difficulty in changing gear, and very sudden take up of the clutch drive at the fully depressed end of the clutch pedal travel as the clutch is released.
4 Check the clutch master cylinder and slave cylinder and the connecting hydraulic pipe for leaks. Fluid in one of the rubber dust covers fitted over the end of either the master or slave cylinder is a sure sign of a leaking piston seal.

5 If these points are checked and found to be in order then the fault lies internally in the clutch, and it will be necessary to remove the clutch for examination.

16 Clutch judder

1 Clutch judder is a self evident condition which occurs when the gearbox or engine mountings are loose or too flexible, when there is oil in the face of the clutch friction plate or when the clutch pressure plate has been incorrectly adjusted.

2 The reason for clutch judder is that due to one of the faults just listed, the clutch pressure plate is not freeing smoothly from the friction disc, and is snatching.

3 Clutch judder normally occurs when the clutch pedal is released in first or reverse gears, and the whole car shudders as it moves backwards or forwards.

Chapter 6 Gearbox and automatic transmission

For modifications, and information applicable to later models, see Supplement at end of manual

Contents

General description	1
Gearbox - removal and replacement	2
Gearbox - dismantling	3
Gearbox - examination and renovation	4
Input shaft - dismantling and reassembly..	5
Mainshaft - dismantling and reassembly	6
Gearbox - reassembly	7
Manual gearbox fault diagnosis	8

Automatic transmission - general description	9
Automatic transmission fluid level...	10
Automatic transmission - removal and replacement..	11
Torque converter - removal and replacement..	12
Starter inhibitor/reverse light switch - check and adjustment	13
Down shift cable - adjustment	14
Selector linkage - adjustment	15
Automatic transmission - fault diagnosis	16

Specifications

Manual gearbox	4 forward speeds, 1 reverse. Synchromesh fitted to all forward speeds

Gearbox ratios:

Fourth (top)	1.000 : 1
Third	1.307 : 1
Second	1.916 : 1
First	3.111 : 1
Reverse	3.422 : 1

Overall ratios:

Fourth (top)	3.636 : 1
Third	4.751 : 1
Second	7.003 : 1
First	11.313 : 1
Reverse	12.444 : 1

Road speed per 1000 rpm in top gear	18.1 mph (29.2 kph)
2nd and 3rd gear endfloat on bushes	0.002 − 0.006 in (0.050 − 0.152 mm)
Endfloat of bushes on shaft	0.004 − 0.006 in (0.101 − 0.152 mm)
Washer sizes available:	
Colour code - Plain	0.152 − 0.154 in (3.860 − 3.911 mm)
Green..	0.156 − 0.158 in (3.962 − 4.013 mm)
Blue	0.161 − 0.163 in (4.089 − 4.140 mm)
Orange	0.165 − 0.167 in (4.191 − 4.241 mm)
Yellow	0.169 − 0.171 in (4.293 − 4.343 mm)
Laygear needle roller retaining rings:	
Fitted depth - inner	0.840 − 0.850 in (21.336 − 21.590 mm)
outer...	0.010 − 0.015 in (0.254 − 0.381 mm)
Centre bearing to circlip endfloat	0.000 − 0.002 in (0.000 − 0.050 mm)
Washer sizes available:	
Colour code - Plain	0.119 − 0.121 in (3.022 − 3.073 mm)
Green..	0.122 − 0.124 in (3.123 − 3.173 mm)
Blue	0.125 − 0.127 in (3.198 − 3.248 mm)
Orange	0.128 − 0.130 in (3.273 − 3.323 mm)
Reverse idler gear bush - fitted depth..	Flush to 0.010 in (0.254 mm) below gear face

Automatic transmission	Borg Warner model 35
Shift speeds	
('D' selected with accelerator in kickdown position)	
Upshift	
1 − 2	36 − 43 mph (58 − 69 kph)
2 − 3	61 − 67 mph (98 − 108 kph)
Downshift	
3 − 2	56 − 63 mph (90 − 101 kph)
2 − 1 or 3 − 1	29 − 38 mph (47 − 61 kph)

Ratios:
    First   ... ...   2.39 : 1
    Second... ... ...   1.45 : 1
    Third   ... ...   1 : 1
    Reverse .. ..   2.09 : 1

Capacities
    Manual gearbox   ... ...   1½ pints (0.85 litres)
    Automatic transmission
                       Oil pan only...   5   pints (3   litres)
                       With torque converter... ... ...   9.5 pints (5.4 litres)
                       With torque converter and oil cooler   ...   11 pints (6.2 litres)

Torque wrench settings

Manual gearbox	lb.f.ft	kg.f.m
Flywheel housing retaining bolts	28 — 30	3.9 — 4.1
Rear extension to gearbox bolts	18 — 20	2.4 — 2.7
Drive flange nuts...	90 — 100	12.4 — 13.8

Automatic transmission		
Drive flange nut	55 — 60	7.6 — 8.3
Drive plate to crankshaft	50	6.9
Converter to drive plate bolts	25 — 30	3.4 — 4.1
Oil pan to gearbox bolts	9 — 12	1.2 — 1.6
Drain plug	8 — 10	1.1 — 1.4
Starter inhibitor switch locknut	4 — 6	0.5 — 0.8

1 General description

The manual gearbox fitted contains four forward and one reverse gear. Synchromesh is fitted to all four forward gears.

The gear change lever is mounted on the extension housing and operates the selector mechanism in the gearbox by a long shaft. When the gear change lever is moved sideways the shaft is rotated so that the pins in the gearbox end of the shaft locate in the appropriate selector fork. Forward or rearward movement of the gear change lever moves the selector fork which in turn moves the synchromesh unit outer sleeve until the gear is firmly engaged. When reverse gear is selected, a pin on the selector shaft engages with a lever and this in turn moves the reverse idler gear into mesh with the laygear reverse gear and mainshaft. The direction of rotation of the mainshaft is thereby reverse.

The gearbox input shaft is splined and it is onto these splines that the clutch driven plate is located. The gearbox end of the input shaft is in constant mesh with the laygear cluster, and the gears formed on the laygear are in constant mesh with the gears on the mainshaft with the exception of the reverse gear. The gears on the mainshaft are able to rotate freely which means that when the neutral position is selected the mainshaft does not rotate.

When the gear change lever moves the synchromesh unit outer sleeve via the selector fork, the synchromesh cup first moves and friction caused by the conical surfaces meeting takes up initial rotational movement until the mainshaft and gear are both rotating at the same speed. This condition achieved, the sleeve is able to slide over the dog teeth of the selected gear thereby giving a firm drive. The synchromesh unit inner hub is splined to the mainshaft and because the outer sleeve is splined to the inner hub engine torque is passed to the mainshaft and propeller shaft.

2 Gearbox - removal and replacement

1 The gearbox can be removed in unit with the engine as described in Chapter 1. An alternative method is to separate the gearbox bellhousing from the engine end plate, lower the gearbox and remove from under the car, leaving the engine in position. Use this method if only clutch and/or gearbox repairs are to be made.

2 Disconnect the battery, raise the car and put on axle stands if a ramp is not available. The higher the car is off the ground the easier it will be to work underneath.

3 Undo the gearbox drain plug and drain the oil into a clean container. When all oil has drained out replace the drain plug.

4 Undo and remove the nuts and plain washers that secure the exhaust manifold to downpipe clamp(s).

5 Refer to Chapter 3 and remove the carburettor(s).

6 Wipe the top of the clutch master cylinder and unscrew the cap. Place a piece of thin polythene sheet over the filler neck and refit the cap. This is to stop clutch hydraulic fluid syphoning out during subsequent operations.

7 Undo the union nut that secures the clutch hydraulic pipe to the end of the slave cylinder. Unscrew the hydraulic pipe clip securing screw and tie back the hydraulic pipe.

8 Unscrew and remove the self tapping screws securing each carpet finisher to the door sill. Lift away the finisher and carpeting so exposing the gear change lever rubber moulding retaining plate.

9 Undo and remove the self tapping screws securing the gear change lever rubber moulding retaining plate to the floor panel. Lift away the plate. Then slide the rubber moulding and foam sleeve up the gear change lever. Note that sealer is used under the rubber moulding flange.

10 Turn the gear change lever retaining cup in an anti clockwise direction so releasing the bayonet fixing. Ease the gear change lever up, at the same time being prepared to depress the plunger and spring in the fulcrum ball. Recover the plunger and spring from the fulcrum ball.

11 With a scriber or file mark the gearbox and propeller shaft drive flanges to ensure correct refitting. Then undo and remove the four locknuts and bolts that secure the gearbox and propeller shaft drive flange. Using string or wire tie the propeller shaft to the torsion bar.

12 Undo and remove the bolt and spring washer that secures the speedometer drive cable retaining clip on the side of the gearbox extension. Lift away the clip and carefully withdraw the speedometer cable.

13 Make a note of the electric cable connections to the starter motor, detach the cables and undo and remove the two bolts and spring washers securing the starter motor. Carefully lift away the starter motor.

14 On single carburettor models slacken the clip screw and then undo and remove the nut, spring washer and bolt from the exhaust steady bracket.

15 Using a hoist or jack support the weight of the engine and gearbox. If a jack is being used place it under the rear of the sump with a piece of wood between jack and sump.

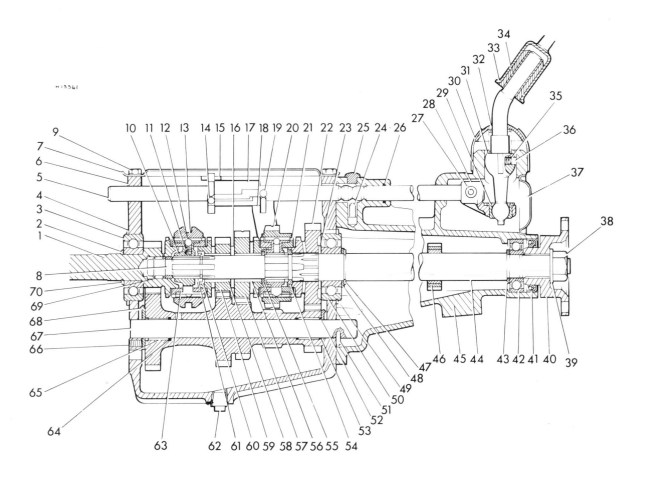

FIG 6.1 THE MANUAL GEARBOX - CROSS SECTION

1	1st motion shaft	18	Reverse operating lever	35	Anti-rattle spring	53	Rear thrust washer

1   1st motion shaft
2   Circlip
3   Front ball-bearing
4   Snap ring
5   Gear selector shaft
6   Gearbox case
7   Top cover
8   Spacer
9   Top cover bolt
10 3rd and 4th speed
    synchromesh hub
11 Spring
12 Ball
13 3rd and 4th speed
    operating sleeve
14 Selector shaft pin
15 Interlock spool plate
16 Selective washer
17 Interlock spool

18 Reverse operating lever
19 Selector shaft roll pin
20 Mainshaft reverse gear
    and 1st/2nd operating
    sleeve
21 Synchromesh cup
22 1st speed gear
23 Thrust washer
24 Detent plunger
25 Plug
26 O-ring
27 Yoke pin
28 Gear lever yoke
29 Seat
30 Dust cover
31 Lower gear lever
32 Seal
33 Upper gear lever
34 Bush

35 Anti-rattle spring
36 Anti-rattle plunger
37 End cover
38 Self-locking nut
39 Flange washer
40 Flange and stone-guard
    assembly
41 Seal
42 End ball-bearing
43 Thrust washer
44 Mainshaft
45 Gearbox rear extension
46 Speedometer wheel
47 Circlip
48 Selective washer
49 Snap ring
50 Centre ball-bearing
51 Layshaft dowel
52 Retaining ring

53 Rear thrust washer
54 Split collar
55 Thrust washer
56 Gear bush
57 3rd speed gear
58 Gear bush
59 2nd speed gear
60 Thrust washer
61 Circlip
62 Drain plug
63 Synchromesh cup
64 Retaining ring
65 Needle roller bearing
66 Laygear preload springs
    (later models only)
67 Layshaft
68 Thrust washer
69 Needle roller bearing
70 Circlip backing washer

16 Undo and remove the two bolts, plain and spring washers that secure the sump connecting plate to the underside of the gearbox bellhousing.

17 Undo and remove the two bolts, flat and spring washers that secure the gearbox rear cross member to the underside of the body frame.

18 Undo and remove the nut and spring washer that secures the rear cross member to the rear mounting.

19 Undo and remove the seven bolts and spring washers securing the bellhousing to the engine end plate.

20 Disconnect the power unit braided earthing strap.

21 Make sure the weight of the gearbox is not allowed to be taken solely on the first motion shaft as it bends easily.

22 Lower the rear of the engine until there is sufficient clearance between the top of the bellhousing and underside of the body and carefully draw the gearbox rearwards. Lift away the gearbox from the underside of the car.

23 Refitting the gearbox is the reverse sequence to removal. Do not forget to refill the gearbox if the oil has been previously drained. It will be necessary to bleed the clutch hydraulic system as described in Chapter 5.

94

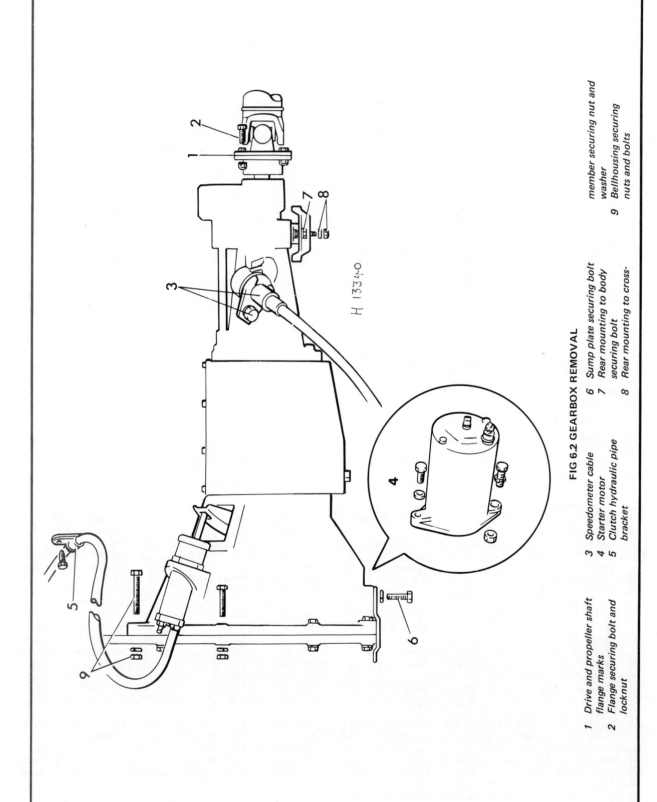

H 13340

FIG 6.2 GEARBOX REMOVAL

1 Drive and propeller shaft flange marks
2 Flange securing bolt and locknut
3 Speedometer cable
4 Starter motor
5 Clutch hydraulic pipe bracket
6 Sump plate securing bolt
7 Rear mounting to body securing bolt
8 Rear mounting to cross-member securing nut and washer
9 Bellhousing securing nuts and bolts

3 Gearbox - dismantling

1 Before commencing work, clean the exterior of the gearbox thoroughly using a solvent such as paraffin or 'Gunk'. After the solvent has been applied and allowed to stand for a time, a vigorous jet of water will wash off the solvent together with all oil and dirt. Finally wipe down the exterior of the unit with a dry non fluffy rag.

2 NOTE: All numbers in brackets refer to Fig.6.3 unless stated otherwise.

3 Detach the operating lever from the release bearing and slide off the bearing assembly.

4 Undo and remove the five bolts securing the clutch bell-housing to the gearbox casing. Note that the lowermost bolt has a plain copper washer whereas the remaining bolts have spring washers.

5 Lift away the bellhousing. Recover the paper gasket from the front of the gearbox casing.

6 Undo and remove the nine bolts and spring washers securing the top cover to the main casing.

7 Lift away the cover and paper gasket. The main casing has been modified on later cars — the top extension and main casing are now one casting. If the gearbox is of the earlier type comprising two parts temperarily replace two of the bolts to hold the two parts together.

8 Note which way up the interlock spool is fitted and lift it from the top of the main casing.

9 Undo and remove the one bolt and spring washer securing the reverse lift plate (14) to the rear extension. Lift away the lift plate.

10 Using a screwdriver carefully remove the rear extension end cover (12).

11 With a mole wrench hold the drive flange (86) and using a socket wrench undo and remove the locking nut (88) and plain washer (87).

12 Tap the drive flange (86) from the end of the mainshaft (83).

13 Lift out the speedometer drive pinion and housing assembly (24 - 27) from the rear extension.

14 Make a special note of the location of the selector shaft pegs and interlock spool (16) so that there will be no mistakes on reassembly.

15 Using a suitable diameter parallel pin punch carefully remove the roll pin (17) from the bellhousing end of the selector shaft (20).

16 Undo and remove the eight bolts and spring washers securing the rear extension (11) to the gearbox casing (1).

17 Draw the rear extension rearwards whilst at the same time feeding the interlock spool (16) from the selector shaft (20).

18 With the rear extension (11) and selector shaft (20) away from the gearbox casing lift out the interlock spool (16).

19 Recover the paper gasket (7) from the rear face of the gearbox casing (1).

20 If oil was leaking from the end of the rear extension or the bearing (85) requires renewal, the oil seal must be removed and discarded. It must never be refitted but always renewed. Ease it out with a screwdriver noting which way round the lip is fitted.

21 To remove the bearing obtain a long metal drift and tap it out working from inside the rear extension. Note which way round the bearing is fitted as indicated by the lettering.

22 Slide the washer from over the end of the mainshaft.

23 Make a special note of the location of the speedometer drive gear (77) on the mainshaft, if necessary by taking a measurement.

24 Using a tapered but blunt drift drive the speedometer drive gear from the mainshaft. Beware because it is very tight and it can break.

25 Using a suitable diameter drift tap out the selector fork shaft (45) towards the front of the gearbox casing.

26 Note the location of the two forward gear selector forks (43, 44) and lift these from the synchromesh sleeve (54, 68).

27 Using a suitable diameter drift tap out the layshaft (93) working from the front of the gearbox casing. This is because there is a layshaft restraining pin (94) at the rear to stop it

rotating.

28 Using a small drift placed on the bearing outer track tap out the gearbox input shaft (81). If necessary recover the caged needle roller bearing (82), from the end of the mainshaft.

29 The mainshaft may now be drifted rearwards slightly sufficiently to move the bearing and locating circlip (73). Using a screwdriver between the circlip (74) and casing ease the bearing out of its bore and from its locating shoulder on the mainshaft. Lift away the bearing from the end of the mainshaft.

30 The complete mainshaft may now be lifted away through the top of the gearbox main casing.

31 Unscrew the dowel bolt (38) that locks the reverse idler shaft (39) to the gearbox casing. Lift away the bolt and spring washer.

32 Using a small drift tap the reverse idler shaft rearwards noting the hole in the shaft into which the dowel bolt locates.

33 Note which way round the reverse idler is fitted and lift it from the casing.

34 Lift out the laygear cluster noting which way round it is fitted.

35 Recover the two thrust washers noting that the tags locate in grooves in the gearbox casing.

4 Gearbox - examination

1 The gearbox has been stripped, presumably, because of wear or malfunction, possibly excessive noise, ineffective synchromesh or failure to stay in a selected gear. The cause of most gearbox ailments is failure of the ball bearings on the input or mainshaft and wear on the synchro rings, both the cone surfaces and dogs. The nose of the mainshaft which runs in the needle roller bearing in the input shaft is also subject to wear. This can prove very expensive as the mainshaft would need replacement and this represents about 20% of the total cost of a new gearbox.

2 Examine the teeth of all gears for signs of uneven or excessive wear and, of course, chipping. If a gear on the mainshaft requires replacement check that the corresponding laygear is not equally damaged. If it is the whole laygear may need replacing also.

3 All gears should be a good running fit on the shaft with no signs of rocking. The hubs should not be a sloppy fit on the splines.

4 Selector forks should be examined for signs of wear or ridging on the faces which are in contact with the operating sleeve.

5 Check for wear on the selector rod and interlock spool.

6 The ball bearings may not be obviously worn but if one has gone to the trouble of dismantling the gearbox it would be short sighted not to renew them. The same applies to the four synchronizer rings although for these the mainshaft has to be completely dismantled for the new ones to be fitted.

7 The input shaft bearing retainer is fitted with an oil seal and this should be renewed if there are any signs that oil has leaked past it into the clutch housing or, of course, if it is obviously damaged. The rear extension has an oil seal at the rear as well as a ball bearing race. If either have worn or oil has leaked past the seal the parts should be renewed.

8 Before finally deciding to dismantle the mainshaft and replace parts it is advisable to make enquiries regarding the availability of parts and their cost. It may still be worth considering an exchange gearbox even at this stage. You should reassemble it before exchange.

H15342

FIG 6.3 GEARBOX COMPONENTS

1 Gearbox case
2 Oil filler/level plug
3 'O' ring
4 Gaskets
5 Top cover
6 Top cover bolt
7 Gasket
8 Plug
9 Detent plunger
10 Detent spring
11 Rear extension
12 End cover
13 Reverse light switch
    set screw
14 Reverse lift plate
15 Oil seal
16 Interlock spool
17 Selector shaft roll pin
18 Reverse operating lever pin
19 Reverse operating lever
20 Gear selector shaft
21 Magnet
22 Interlock spool plate
23 Retaining clip
24 Seal
25 Housing
26 'O' ring
27 Speedometer pinion
28 Gear lever yoke
29 Seat
30 Spring
31 Anti-rattle plunger
32 Lower gear change lever
33 Upper gear change lever
34 Dust cover
35 Retaining cup
36 Knob
37 Drain plug
38 Reverse idler spindle
    locating screw
39 Reverse idler spindle
40 Reverse idler gear bush
41 Reverse idler gear
42 Reverse idler distance piece
43 3rd/4th speed selector forks
44 1st/2nd speed selector
    forks
45 Selector fork shaft
46 Circlip
47 Backing washer
48 Snap-ring
49 Ball bearing
50 Synchromesh cup
51 Ball
52 Spring
53 3rd/4th speed synchromesh
    hub
54 3rd/4th speed operating
    sleeve
55 Synchromesh cup
56 Mainshaft circlip
57 3rd speed gear thrust
    washer
58 3rd speed gear
59 Gear bush
60 Selector washer
61 Gear bush
62 2nd speed gear
63 Thrust washer
64 Synchromesh cup
65 Ball
66 Spring
67 1st/2nd speed synchro
    hub
68 Mainshaft reverse gear
69 Synchromesh cup
70 Split collar
71 1st speed gear
72 Thrust washer
73 Mainshaft centre bearing
74 Snap-ring
75 Selective washer
76 Circlip
77 Speedometer wheel
78 Oil flinger
79 Front thrust washer
80 Bearing outer retaining
    ring
81 1st motion shaft (input
    shaft)
82 Needle-roller bearing
83 Mainshaft
84 Washer
85 Ball bearing
86 Drive flange
87 Washer
88 Self-locking nut
89 Laygear gear cluster
90 Bearing retaining inner
    ring
91 Needle rollers
92 Rear thrust washer
93 Layshaft
94 Layshaft dowel
95 Laygear preload springs
    (later models only)

5 Input shaft - dismantling and reassembly

1 Place the input shaft in a vice, splined end upwards, and with a pair of circlip pliers, remove the circlip which retains the ball bearing in place. Lift away the spacer.

2 With the bearing resting on the top of open jaws of the vice and splined end upwards, tap the shaft through the bearing with a soft faced hammer. Note that the offset circlip groove in the outer track of the bearing is towards the front of the input shaft.

3 Lift away the oil flinger.

4 Remove the oil caged needle roller bearing from the centre of the rear of the input shaft if it is still in place.

5 Remove the circlip from the old bearing outer track and transfer it to the new bearing.

6 Replace the oil flinger and with the aid of a block of wood and vice tap the bearing into place. Make sure it is the right way round.

7 Finally refit the spacer and bearing retaining circlip.

6 Mainshaft - dismantling and reassembly

1 The component parts of the mainshaft are shown in Fig.6.4.

2 Lift the 3rd and 4th gear synchromesh hub and operating sleeve assembly from the end of the mainshaft.

3 Remove the 3rd gear synchromesh cup.

4 Using a small screwdriver ease the 3rd gear retaining circlip from its groove in the mainshaft. Lift away the circlip.

5 Lift away the 3rd gear thrust washer.

6 Slide the 3rd gear and bush from the mainshaft followed by the thrust washer. Note this is a selective thrust washer.

7 Slide the 2nd gear and bush from the mainshaft followed by the grooved washer. Note which way round it is fitted.

8 Detach the 2nd gear synchromesh cup from inside the 2nd and 1st gear synchromesh hub and lift away.

9 Slide the 2nd and 1st gear synchromesh hub and reverse gear sleeve assembly from the mainshaft. Recover the 1st gear synchromesh cup.

10 Using a small electricians screwdriver lift out the two split collars from their groove in the mainshaft.

11 Slide the 1st gear mainshaft washer from the mainshaft and follow this with the 1st gear and its bush.

12 The mainshaft is now completely dismantled.

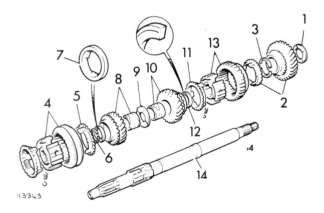

43343

FIG 6.4 MAINSHAFT ASSEMBLY

1 Thrust washer
2 1st speed gear and
   synchro cup
3 Split collar
4 3rd and 4th speed
   synchro unit
5 Synchro cup
6 Mainshaft circlip
7 3rd speed gear

   thrust washer
8 3rd speed gear and
   bush
9 Selective washer
10 2nd speed gear and bush
11 Synchromesh cup
12 Thrust washer
13 1st/2nd speed synchro unit
14 Mainshaft

13 Before reassembling refer to Fig.6.5 and measure the end float of the 2nd and 3rd gears on their respective bushes. The end float should be within the limits quoted in the specifications. Obtain a new bush if necessary to achieve the correct end float.

14 Temporarily refit the 2nd gear washer, oil grooved face away from the mainshaft shoulder, to the mainshaft. Assemble to the mainshaft the 3rd gear bush, selective washer 2nd gear bush, 3rd gear thrust washer with its oil grooved face to the bush, and fit the 3rd gear mainshaft circlip. Measure the end float of the bushes on the mainshaft which should be within the limits quoted in the specifications. Obtain a new selective washer to obtain the correct end float. Remove the parts from the mainshaft.

15 To reassemble first slide the bush into the 1st gear hub (photo).

16 Insert the washer into the coned end of the 1st gear (photo).

17 Slide the 1st gear onto the mainshaft followed by the larger washer (photo).

18 Fit the two halves of the split collar into the groove in the mainshaft and push the 1st gear hard up against the collar (photo).

19 Fit the synchromesh cup onto the cone of the 1st gear (photo).

20 Slide the 1st and 2nd gear synchromesh hub and reverse gear sleeve on the mainshaft and engage it with the synchromesh cup (photo).

21 Fit the 2nd gear synchromesh cup to the synchromesh hub (photo).

22 Fit the 2nd gear washer onto the end of the mainshaft splines so that the oil grooved face is towards the front of the mainshaft (photo).

23 Slide the 2nd gear bush onto the mainshaft (photo).

24 Fit the 2nd gear onto the bush on the mainshaft and engage the taper with the internal taper of the synchromesh cup (photo).

25 Fit the 2nd and 3rd gear selective washer (photo).

26 Slide the 3rd gear bush onto the mainshaft (photo).

27 Fit the 3rd gear onto the bush on the mainshaft, the cone facing the front of the mainshaft (photo).

28 Slide the 3rd gear thrust washer onto the mainshaft splines (photo).

29 Ease the 3rd gear retaining circlip into its groove in the mainshaft. Make quite sure it is fully seated (photo).

30 Fit the 3rd gear synchromesh cup onto the cone of the 3rd gear (photo).

31 Finally slide the 3rd and 4th gear synchromesh hub and operating sleeve assembly and engage it with the synchrmesh cup (photo).

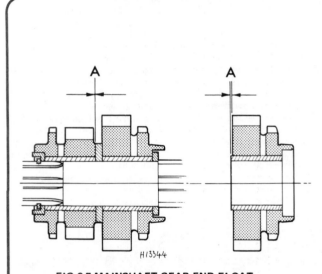

FIG 6.5 MAINSHAFT GEAR END FLOAT

*A = 0.002 to 0.006 inch
(0.050 to 0.152 mm)*

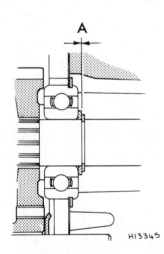

FIG 6.6 SELECTIVE WASHER THICKNESS 'A'

6.15 Sliding bush into 1st gear hub

6.16 Fitting washer into coned end of 1st gear

6.17 Fitting 1st gear and large washer onto mainshaft

6.18 Inserting split collar into groove

6.19 Synchromesh cup for 1st gear

6.20 Fitting synchromesh hub and reverse gear sleeve

6.21 2nd gear synchromesh cup placement on synchromesh hub

6.22 The oil grooves face must face towards front of mainshaft

6.23 Sliding 2nd gear bush onto mainshaft

6.24 Fitting 2nd gear onto bush

6.25 2nd and 3rd gear selective washer

6.26 Sliding 3rd gear bush onto mainshaft

6.27 Fitting 3rd gear onto bush

6.28 Sliding 3rd gear thrust washer onto mainshaft

6.29 The circlip must be correctly located in its groove

6.30 Fitting 3rd gear synchromesh cup onto synchromesh hub

6.31 Sliding 3rd and 4th gear synchro-mesh hub assembly onto mainshaft

7 Gearbox - reassembly

1 Place the magnet in the base of the gearbox. On later produced gearboxes the magnet is cast into the gearbox casing (photo).

2 Position the laygear needle bearing roller bearing inner retainers into the laygear bore. Apply Castrol LM Grease to the ends of the laygear and replace the needle rollers. Retain in position with the outer retainers (photo).

3 Make up a piece of tube the same diameter as the layshaft and the length of the laygear plus thrust washers and slide the tube into the laygear. This will retain the needle rollers in position. Apply grease to the thrust washers and fit to the ends of the laygear. The tags must face outwards (photo).

4 Carefully lower the laygear into the bottom of the gearbox casing (photo).

5 Fit the reverse gear operating lever to the operating lever pivot. Hold the reverse idler in its approximate fitted position and slide in the idler shaft, drilled end first (photo).

6 Carefully line up the drilled hole in the idler shaft and gearbox casing and replace the dowel bolt and spring washer (photo).

7 The assembled mainshaft may now be fitted into the gearbox casing (photo).

8 Ease the mainshaft bearing up the mainshaft, circlip offset on the outer track towards the rear (photo).

9 Place a metal lever in the position shown in this photo so supporting the mainshaft spigot (photo).

10 Using a suitable diameter tube carefully drift the mainshaft bearing into position in the rear casing (photo).

11 Fit the 3rd gear synchromesh cup onto the end of the input shaft.

12 Lubricate the needle roller bearing and fit into the end of the input shaft (photo).

13 Fit the input shaft to the front of the gearbox casing, taking care to engage the synchromesh cup with the synchromesh hub (photo).

14 Tap the input bearing until the circlip is hard up against the front gearbox casing. Check that the mainshaft bearing outer track circlip is hard up against the rear casing. Refit the washer and circlip.

15 Invert the gearbox. Fit the pin into the drilled hole in the layshaft and carefully insert the layshaft from the rear of the main casing. This will push out the previously inserted tube. The pin must be to the rear of the main casing (photo).

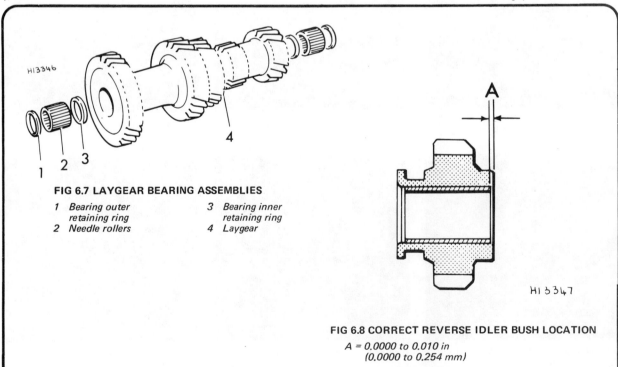

HI3346

FIG 6.7 LAYGEAR BEARING ASSEMBLIES

1 Bearing outer retaining ring
2 Needle rollers
3 Bearing inner retaining ring
4 Laygear

HI3347

FIG 6.8 CORRECT REVERSE IDLER BUSH LOCATION

A = 0.0000 to 0.010 in
(0.0000 to 0.254 mm)

7.1 Location of magnet

7.2 Inserting needle bearing rollers

7.3 Thrust washer with tag facing outwards

7.4 Lowering laygear into gearbox
casing

7.5 Sliding idler shaft into position

7.6 Special dowel bolt with shaped end

7.7 Fitting mainshaft into gearbox
casing

7.8 Sliding bearing up mainshaft

7.9 Supporting mainshaft spigot

7.10 Drifting bearing into position

7.12 Inserting the needle roller bearing
into input shaft

7.13 Fitting input shaft

16 Line up the layshaft pin with the groove in the rear face and push the layshaft fully home (photo).

17 Fit the 3rd and 4th gear selector fork to the synchromesh sleeve (photo).

18 Fit the 1st and 2nd gear selector fork to the synchromesh sleeve (photo).

19 Slide the selector fork shaft from the front through the two selector forks and into the rear of the main casing (photo).

20 Fit a new gasket to the rear face of the main casing and retain in position with a little grease (photo).

21 Place the speedometer drive gear onto the mainshaft and using a tube drive the gear into its previously noted position (photo).

22 Slide the washer up the mainshaft to the speedometer drive gear (photo).

23 Place the rear extension bearing into its bore, letters facing outwards (photo).

24 Tap the bearing into position using a suitable diameter socket (photo).

25 Fit a new rear extension oil seal and tap into position with the previously used socket. The lip must face inwards (photo).

26 Slide the interlock spool onto the selector shaft making sure it is the correct way round as shown. This is to give an idea of the final fitted position. Remove the interlock spool again (photo).

27 Place the interlock spool on the selector forks with the flanges correctly engaged (photo).

28 Offer up the gearbox rear extension to the rear of the main casing, at the same time feeding the selector shaft through the interlock spool. It will be necessary to rotate the selector shaft to obtain correct engagement (photo).

29 Secure the rear extension with the eight bolts and spring washers (photo).

30 Refit the spring pin into the end of the selector shaft ensuring the ends are equidistant from the shaft (photo).

31 This photo shows the interlock spool and selector shaft correctly aligned with the pegs engaged (photo).

32 Insert the speedometer driven gear and housing into the rear extension (photo).

33 Fit the drive flange onto the mainshaft splines (photo).

34 Hold the drive flange and tighten the retaining nut and washer fully (photo).

35 Replace the reverse lift plate and secure with the bolt and spring washer (photo).

36 Refit the rear extension end cover and tap into position with the end of the lip flush with the end of the casing (photo).

37 Replace the interlock spool plate in the same position as was noted before removal (photo).

38 Fit a new gasket to the top of the gearbox casing and replace the top cover (photo).

39 Secure the top cover with the nine bolt and spring washers which should be progressively tightened in a diagonal manner (photo).

40 Fit a new O ring to the input shaft retainer and refit the retainer (photo).

41 Fit a new gearbox casing front face gasket and retain in position with a little grease (photo).

42 Move the gearbox to the end of the bench and offer up the clutch bellhousing (photo).

43 Replace the five bolts securing the bellhousing to the main casing. Note four bolts have spring washers and the fifth (lowermost) has a copper washer (photo).

44 Slide the clutch release bearing assembly onto its guide at the same time engaging the release lever (photo).

45 If the gearbox was removed in unit with the engine it may now be reattached. Secure in position with the retaining nuts, bolts and spring washers (photo).

46 Refill the gearbox with 1½ pints (0.85 litres) Castrol Hypoy B (photo).

7.15 The pin must be to the rear of the gearbox casing

7.16 Lining up pin with groove

7.17 Fitting 3rd and 4th gear selector fork to synchromesh sleeve

7.18 Fitting 1st and 2nd gear selector fork to synchromesh sleeve

7.19 Inserting selector fork shaft through selector forks

7.20 Fitting new gasket to gearbox casing rear face

7.21 Drift speedometer drive gear up to previously made mark

7.22 Slide washer up mainshaft to speedometer drive gear

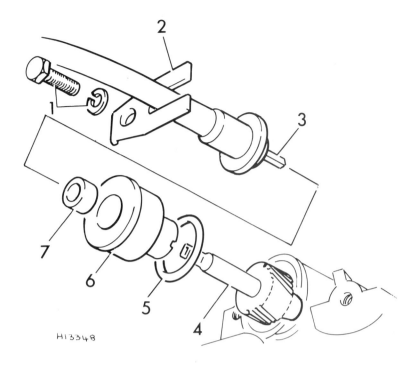

H13348

FIG 6.9 SPEEDOMETER DRIVE ASSEMBLY

1 Bolt and spring washer   5 'O' ring
2 Retaining clip   6 Housing
3 Inner cable   7 Seal
4 Speedometer pinion

7.23 The bearing code letters must face outwards

7.24 Using socket and hammer to tap bearing into position

7.25 Fitting rear extension oil seal with lip facing inwards

7.26 Trial fitting of interlock spool

7.27 Fitting interlock spool to selector forks

7.28 Rotate the selector shaft to obtain correct engagement

7.29 Tightening rear extension securing bolts in a progressive manner

7.30 Refitting spring pin to end of selector shaft

7.31 Interlock spool and selector shaft aligned with pegs engaged

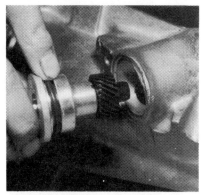
7.32 Insert speedometer driven gear assembly into rear extension

7.33 Offering up the flange to mainshaft

7.34 Tightening flange retaining nut

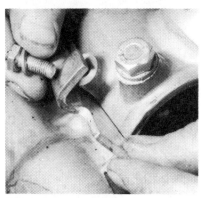
7.35 Refitting reverse lift plate

7.36 The lip must be flush with end of casing

7.37 Refitting interlock spool plate

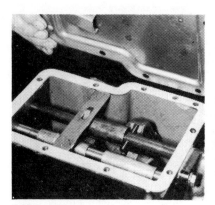
7.38 Positioning top cover on new gasket

7.39 Securing top cover to gearbox casing

7.40 Fitting new 'O' ring to input shaft retainer

7.41 Fit a new gasket to gearbox casing front face

7.42 Positioning clutch bellhousing

7.43 This bolt requires a copper washer

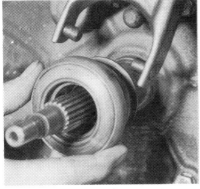

7.44 Sliding clutch release bearing assembly onto its guide

7.45 Clutch bellhousing upper flange bolts replacement

7.46. Use a funnel if possible - flexitops will work

8 Manual gearbox - fault diagnosis

Symptom	Reason/s	Remedy
WEAK OR INEFFECTIVE SYNCHROMESH		
General wear	Synchronising cones worn, split or damaged	Dismantle and overhaul gearbox. Fit new gear wheels and synchronising cones
	Synchromesh dogs worn, or damaged	Dismantle and overhaul gearbox. Fit new synchromesh unit.
JUMPS OUT OF GEAR		
General wear or damage	Broken gearchange fork rod spring	Dismantle and replace spring.
	Gearbox coupling dogs badly worn	Dismantle gearbox. Fit new coupling dogs.
	Selector fork rod groove badly worn	Fit new selector fork rod.
EXCESSIVE NOISE		
Lack of maintenance	Incorrect grade of oil in gearbox or oil level too low	Drain, refill, or top up gearbox with correct grade of oil.
	Bush or needle roller bearings worn or damaged	Dismantle and overhaul gearbox. Renew bearings.
	Gearteeth excessively worn or damaged	Dismantle and overhaul gearbox. Renew gear wheels.
	Laygear thrust washers worn allowing excessive end play	Dismantle and overhaul gearbox. Renew thrust washers.
EXCESSIVE DIFFICULTY IN ENGAGING GEAR		
Clutch not fully disengaging	Clutch fault	Refer to Chapter 5.

9 Automatic transmission - general description

Borg-Warner automatic transmission is fitted.

The automatic transmission system comprises two main components: a three-element hydrokinetic torque converter coupling capable of torque multiplication at an infinitely variable ratio between 2:1 and 1:1 and a torque speed responsive and hydraulically operated epicyclic gearbox comprising a planetary gear set providing three forward ratios and reverse ratio.

Due to the complexity of the automatic transmission unit, if performance is not up to standard, or overhaul is necessary, it is imperative that this is undertaken by BLMC main agents who will have special equipment for accurate fault diagnosis and rectification.

The content of the following sections is therefore solely general and servicing information.

10 Automatic transmission - fluid level

It is important that the transmission fluid is manufactured to the correct specification, use Castrol TQF. The capacity of the unit is approximately 9½ pints (5.4 litres) - with oil cooler 11 pints (6.2 litres), when dry, but for a drain and refill, which is not actually necessary except during repairs, the capacity will be approximately 5 pints (3 litres) as the converter cannot be completely drained. The location of the dipstick is shown in Fig. 6.10. Full information on checking the oil level will be found in the Routine maintenance section at the beginning of this manual.

11 Automatic transmission - removal and replacement

1 Any suspected faults must be referred to the main agent before unit removal as with this type of transmission its fault must be confirmed using special equipment before it is removed from the car.
2 As the automatic transmission is relatively heavy it is best if the car is raised from the ground on ramps but it is possible to remove the unit if the car is placed on high axle stands.
3 Disconnect the battery.
4 Disconnect the downshift cable from the throttle linkage at the side of the carburettor.
5 Remove the dipstick from its guide tube.

6 Detach the exhaust downpipe from the manifold. Release the support clip from the support bracket.
7 Undo the bolt securing the engine earth cable to the torque converter housing.
8 Place a clean container of 8 pints (4.55 litres) capacity under the sump drain plug, remove the drain plug and allow to drain Replace the drain plug.
9 Release the spire nut securing the manual selector rod to the gearbox lever. Draw the selector rod from the lever.
10 Make a note of the electric cable connections to the starter inhibitor and reverse lamp switch. Detach the cable terminals.
11 Undo the dipstick filler tube union nut whilst the adaptor is held to stop if moving.
12 If an oil cooler is fitted wipe the area around the two union nuts and undo the nuts. Plug the ends to stop dirt ingress.
13 With a scriber or file mark the propeller shaft and gearbox flanges so that they may be refitted in their original positions.
14 Undo and remove the four locknuts and bolts that secure the two flanges together.
15 Lift the front end of the propeller shaft away from the rear of the gearbox and tie to the torsion bar with string or wire.
16 Undo and remove the speedometer cable clamp bolt and spring washer on the gearbox extension. Lift away the clamp and withdraw the inner cable.
17 Using a hoist take the weight of the complete power unit or alternatively a hydraulic jack to take the weight under the torque converter housing.
18 Undo and remove the two bolts, spring and plain washers that secure the rear mounting cross member to the underside of the body.
19 Carefully lower the gearbox so as to give access to the top,
20 Using a second jack support the weight of the gearbox.
21 Undo and remove the six bolts and spring washers that secure the gearbox to the torque converter housing.
22 Very carefully draw the gearbox rearwards until it is clear of the torque converter and then lift away from the underside of the car. It is very important that the weight of the gearbox is not allowed to hang on the input shaft.
23 Refitting is the reverse sequence to removal but in addition:
24 Carefully align the converter and front pump driving dogs and slots in the horizontal plane.
25 Carefully align and then locate the input shaft and drive dogs.
26 Tighten the six gearbox securing bolts to a torque wrench setting of 8 to 13 lb ft (1.1 to 1.8 kg cm).
27 Refill the gearbox with Castrol TQF and check the fluid level as described in Section 10.

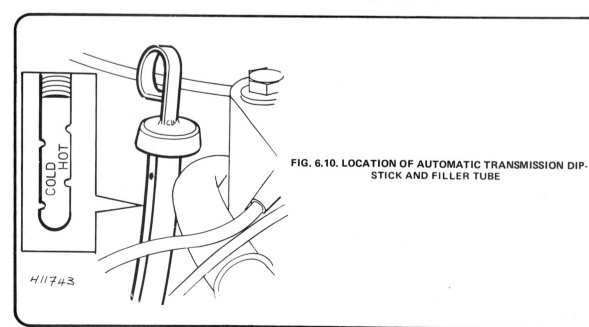

COLD
HOT

H11743

FIG. 6.10. LOCATION OF AUTOMATIC TRANSMISSION DIP-STICK AND FILLER TUBE

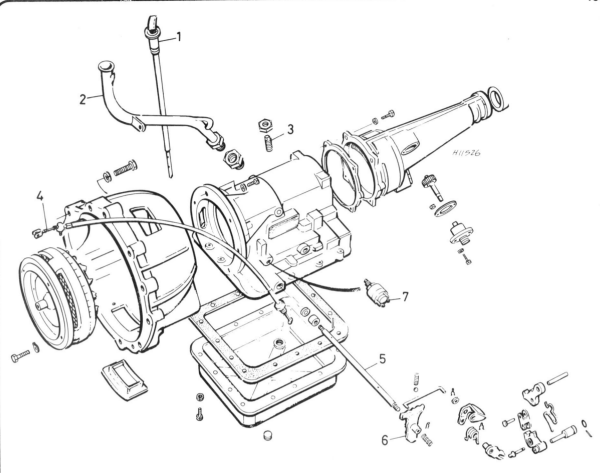

FIG. 6.11. MAIN COMPONENTS OF EXTERNAL CASING WITH TORQUE CONVERTER

1	Dipstick	3	Rear band adjuster	5	Manual control shaft	7	Reverse light starter
2	Tube	4	Downshift cable	6	Manual detent pawl		inhibitor switch

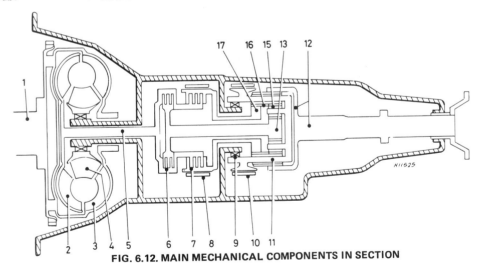

FIG. 6.12. MAIN MECHANICAL COMPONENTS IN SECTION

1	Engine crankshaft	6	Front clutch	11	Planet pinion carrier		
2	Turbine	7	Rear clutch	12	Ring gear and output shaft	15	Short planet pinion
3	Impeller	8	Front brake band			16	Long planet pinion
4	Stator	9	Unidirectional clutch	13	Forward sun gear and shaft	17	Reverse sun gear
5	Input shaft	10	Rear brake band				

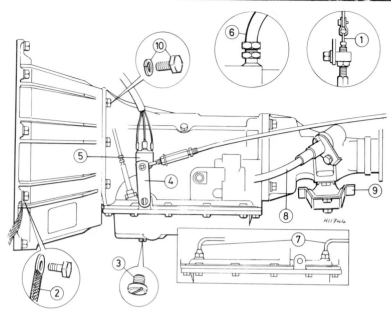

FIG.6.13. AUTOMATIC TRANSMISSION GEARBOX REMOVAL.
SUMMARY OF ITEMS TO BE DISCONNECTED

1 *Downshift cable*	4 *Manual selector rod*	6 *Dipstick tube*	9 *Rear mounting*
2 *Earth cable*	5 *Starter inhibitor and*	7 *Oil cooler pipes*	10 *Bolts and spring*
3 *Drain plug*	*reverse light switch*	8 *Speedometer cable*	*washers*

12. Torque converter - removal and replacement

1   Refer to Section 11 and remove the transmission.
2   Undo and remove the starter motor electric cable terminal secuirng nut and washers. Detach the cable. Pre engaged starter motor, detach the cable terminals from the solenoid.
8   Undo and remove the two starter motor securing nut and spring washer and bolt and spring washer. Lift away the starter motor.
4   Undo and remove the two bolts and spring washers securing the engine sump connecting plate to the torque converter housing.
5   Support the weight of the engine and then undo and remove the bolts and spring washers that secure the torque converter housing to the gearbox mounting plate.
6   Lower the rear of the engine until it is possible to lift away the torque converter housing.
7   With a scriber mark the relative positions of the drive plate and torque converter if these are to be refitted. This will ensure

they are replaced in their original positions.
8   Working through the aperture in the mounting plate, turn the converter, unlock the tab washers and then progressively slacken the four bolts.
9   Support the torque converter and completely remove the bolts and lock washers. Lift away the torque converter. Be perpared to mop up oil that will issue from the torque converter as it cannot be drained completely.
10 Refitting the torque converter is the reverse sequence to removal but in addition:
11 Position the torque converter onto the drive plate aligning up the previously made marks if original parts are being refitted. Refit the four bolts with new tab washers and tighten in a progressive manner to a final torque wrench setting of 25 to 30 lb ft (3.4 to 4.1 Kg fm). Bend over the lock tabs.
12 Check that the dowel is in position and then place the converter housing in position on the mounting plate aligning the dowel hole. Refit the bolts and spring washers and tighten in a progressive manner to a torque wrench setting of 8 to 13 lb ft. (1.1 to 1.8 Kg fm).

FIG.6.14. TORQUE CONVERTER REMOVAL

1 *Sump connecting plate*	3 *Alignment marks*
securing bolt	4 *Securing plate*
2 *Housing retaining*	5 *Housing*
bolts	6 *Torque converter*

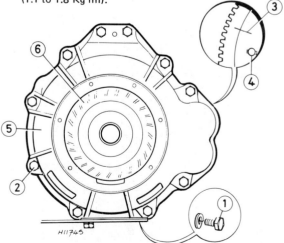

13. Starter inhibitor/reverse light switch - check and adjustment

1 Firmly chock all wheels and apply the handbrake.
2 Make a note of the electrical cable connections to the switch and then detach the terminals. Starter terminals (narrow) white/red. Reverse terminals (wide) green/green and brown.
3 Connect a test lamp and battery across the starter terminals (Fig.6.15) - these are the narrow ones - and select positions P R N D 2 1 in order. The test light should only come on in the P and N positions.
3 Connect the test lamp and battery across the reverse light terminals - these are the wide ones - and select ' 1 2 D N R P' in order. The test light should only come on in the R position.
4 If adjustment is necessary leave the test light connected to the reverse terminals. If the light is out slacken the switch locknut using a cranked spanner. Do not grip the switch body.
5 Unscrew the switch slowly until the test light comes on. Screw the switch in until the light just goes out and mark the relative positions of the switch and case.
6 Connect the test light to the starter terminals and the light should be off. Slowly screw in the switch until the test light comes on (approximately three quarters of a turn) and mark the position of the switch relative to the previous made mark on the case. Remove the test light.
7 Turn the switch until it is mid way between the two marks and retighten the locknut.
8 Reconnect the cables to the switch.
9 Check that the starter motor only operates in the P and N position of the selector and that the reverse light only comes on in the R position.
10 If the switch is to be renewed always apply a little liquid sealer to the threads of the new switch to stop any possibility of oil leaks from this point.

14. Downshift cable - adjustment

Before the cable is adjusted it is necessary to confirm that it is the cable that is malajusted and not some other fault. Generally if difficulty is experienced in obtaining 2:1 downshift in the 'kick-down' position at just below 31 mph it is an indication that the outer cable is too short. If there is a bumpy or delayed shift at low throttle opening it is an indication the outer cable is too long.

During production of the car the adjustment is set by a crimped stop on the carburettor end of the inner cable and it is unusual for this setting to change except at high mileages when the inner cable can stretch. To adjust proceed as follows:—
1 Apply the handbrake firmly and chock the front wheels.
2 Run the engine until it reaches normal operating temperature. Adjust the engine idle speed to approximately 700—750 rpm with the selector in the 'D' position.
3 Stop the engine and with an open spanner slacken the locknut (4), Fig.6.16, and adjust the outer cable control to the stop (2), should the stop have been moved or be loose it will be necessary to remove the transmission sump pan.
4 Reset the engine idle to normal speed with the selector in the 'N' position. Stop the engine.
5 Wipe the area around the drain plug and sump. Place a clean container of at least 8 pints capacity under the pan drain plug. Undo the plug and allow the oil to drain into the container.
6 Undo and remove the fifteen sump pan retaining bolts and spring washers. Take care not to damage the joint between the transmission casing and sump pan.
7 Refer to Fig.6.16 and check that the position of the downshift cam is in the idling position as shown in the illustration.
8 Adjust the length of the outer cable so as to remove all the slack from the inner cable.
9 Again refer to Fig.6.16 and check the position of the downshift cam with the throttle pedal in the 'kickdown' position as shown in the illustration.
10 Refit the sump pan joint, sump pan and retaining bolts with spring washers. Tighten the bolts in a diagonal pattern.
11 Refill the transmission with correct grade transmission fluid.

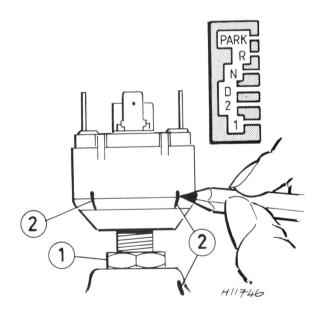

FIG 6.15 STARTER INHIBITOR/REVERSE LIGHT SWITCH

1 Locknut   2 Pencil mark

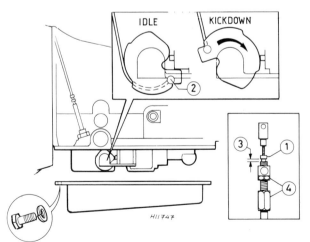

FIG 6.16 DOWNSHIFT CABLE ADJUSTMENT

1 Nipple   3 Clearance
2 Cable located in cam   4 Adjuster/locknut

15. Selector linkage - adjustment

1   Apply the handbrake firmly.

2   Move the selector handle to the 'N' position and adjust its position slightly to ensure that it is under the control of the control valve detent.

3   Move the selector handle to the 'P' position and release the handbrake. Rock the car to and fro and the pawl should hold the vehicle. If either of the two above conditions do not exist the selector rod must be reset.

4   Refer to Fig.6.17 and disconnect the selector rod from the manual lever.

5   Move the manual lever fully forwards as far as it will go and then move it back by three detents (clicks) to the neutral position.

6   Hold the selector in the 'N' position and the end of the selector rod should enter the hole in the manual lever.

7   If necessary adjust the length of the selector rod with the turnbuckle until the selector rod end will enter the hole.

8   Reconnect the selector rod and tighten the turnbuckle locknuts.

9   Carefully move the selector handle into all positions to make sure that the control valve detent is not over-ridden.

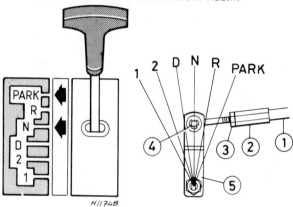

H11748

FIG.6.17. SELECTOR LINKAGE ADJUSTMENT

1   Selector rod
2   Turnbuckle
3   Locknut
4   Spire nut
5   Manual lever

16. Automatic transmission - fault diagnosis

Stall test procedure

The function of a stall test is to determine that the torque converter and gearbox are operating satisfactorily.

1   Check the condition of the engine. An engine which is not developing full power will affect the stall test readings.

2   Allow the engine and transmission to reach correct working temperatures.

3   Connect a tachometer to the vehicle.

4   Chock the wheels and apply the handbrake and footbrake.

5   Select L or R and depress the throttle to the 'kickdown' position. Note the reading on the tachometer which should be 1800 rpm. If the reading is below 1000 rpm suspect the converter for stator slip. If the reading is down to 1200 rpm the engine is not developing full power. If the reading is in excess of 2000 rpm, suspect the gearbox for brake band or clutch slip.

NOTE: Do not carry out a stall test for a longer period than 10 seconds, otherwise the transmission will overheat.

Converter diagnosis

Inability to start on steep gradients, combined with poor acceleration from rest and low stall speed (1000 rpm), indicates that the converter stator uni-directional clutch is slipping. This condition permits the stator to rotate in an opposite direction to the impeller and turbine, and torque multiplication cannot occur.

Poor acceleration in third gear above 30 mph and reduced maximum speed, indicates that the stator uni-directional clutch has seized. The stator will not rotate with the turbine and impeller and the 'fluid flywheel' phase cannot occur. This condition will also be indicated by excessive overheating of the transmission although the stall speed will be correct.

Road test procedure

Road testing procedure is given with a diagnosis and rectification plan. It is not expected that the DIY owner will be able to undertake much rectification work should it be necessary but it will enable him to understand the working a little better.

Selector position	Ratio	D 3	D,2 2	D,2 1	1 1	R
Applied	Front clutch	*	*	*	*	
	Rear clutch	*				*
	One-way clutch			*		
	Front band		*			
	Rear band				*	*
Driven	Forward sun	*	*	*	*	
	Reverse sun	*				*
Held	Planet carrier			*	*	*
	Reverse sun		*			

ROAD TEST	FAULT DIAGNOSIS	RECTIFICATION
		See the chart overleaf
1. Check that the starter will operate only with the selector lever in 'P' and 'N' and that the reverse lights (when fitted) operate only in 'R'	Starter will not operate in 'P' or 'N' Starter operates in all selector positions	19 20
2. Apply the hand and foot brakes and with the engine idling select 'N−D', 'N−2', 'N−I' and 'N−R'. Gearbox engagement should be felt in each position	Excessive bump on engagement of 'D', '2', 'I' or 'R'	4, 3

3. Check the stall speed in 'I' and 'R'.
 	
Do not stall for more than 10 seconds
	High stall speed:
	  a With slip and squawk in 'L'
	  b With slip and squawk in 'R'
	Low stall speed: more than 600 rpm below normal
	Low stall speed: less than 600 rpm below normal
		
		1, 2, 3, 13a, c, f, 11
		1, 2, 3, 13a, c, f, e, 12
		
		21
		
		23

4. Transmission at normal temperature, select 'D'; Release the brakes and accelerate with minimum throttle. Check for 1−2 and 2−3 shifts. Confirm that third gear has been obtained by selecting '2' when a 3−2 shift should be felt NOTE: A feature of this transmission is that a slight increase in throttle depression between 15 and 30 mph (25 and 48 kmph) may produce a 3−2 down-shift (part throttle down-shift)	No drive in 'D' '2' or 'I' No drive in 'D', drive in 'I' No drive in 'D', '2', 'I' or 'R' Delayed or no 1−2 shift Slip on 1−2 shift Delayed or no 2−3 shift (if normal drive in 'R', omit 12) Slip or engine run-up on 2−3 shift Bumpy gear-shifts Drag in 'D' and '2' Drag or binding on 2−3 shift	1, 2, 3, 13a, 11, 16 1, 2, 3, 16 1, 2, 3, 13a, 11, 16, 17 3, 14, 13a, 5, 6 2, 3, 5, 6, 7, 13c, f 3, 14, 13,g, h, c, d, 5, 6, 12 2, 3, 5, 13a, c, 12 3 8 5, 6
5. From a standing start, accelerate using 'kick-down'. Check for 1−2 and 2−3 shifts	Slip and squawk or judder on full throttle take-off in 'D' Loss of performance and overheating in third gear Other possible faults are as given in test No. 4	1, 2, 3, 13a, c, 11 21 Continue as in test 4

6. a. At 40 mph (65 kmph) in top gear release the accelerator and select '2'. Check for 3−2 shift and engine braking.
    Check for 2−1 roll out
b. At 15 mph (25 kmph) in second gear release the accelerator and select 'I'.
    Check for 2−1 shift
	No 3−2 down-shift or engine braking
	
	No 2−1 down-shift and engine braking
		1, 5, 6, 7, 12
		
		8, 9, 10

7. a. At 40 mph (65 kmph) in top gear, depress the accelerator to kick-down, when the gearbox should down-shift to second gear b. At 20 mph (30 kmph) in second gear, depress the accelerator to kick-down when the gearbox should down-shift to first gear	Transmission will not down-shift Transmission will not down-shift	3, 13f, g, 14 3, 13f, g, 14
8. a. Stop, engage 'I' and accelerate to 20 mph (30 kmph). Check for clutch slip or break-away noise (squawk) and that no up-shift occurs b. Stop, engage 'R' and reverse the vehicle using full throttle if possible. Check for clutch or break-away noise (squawk)	Slip, squawk or judder on take-off in 'L' Transmission up-shifts Slip, squawk or judder on take-off in 'R' As above, with engine braking available in 'I' Slip but no judder on take-off in 'R'. No engine braking available in 'I' Drag in 'R' No drive in 'R', no engine braking in 'I' As above, with engine braking in 'I'	1, 2, 3, 13, 11 1 1, 2, 3, 13b, c, e, f, g,12 1, 2, 3 1, 2, 3, 8, 9, 10 5 1, 2, 3, 8, 13e,f,g, 9, 10, 12 1, 2, 3, 13e, 12
9. Stop the vehicle facing downhill, apply the brakes and select 'P'. Release the brakes and check that the pawl holds. Re-apply the brakes before disengaging 'P' Repeat facing uphill	Parking pawl inoperative Miscellaneous: Screech or whine increasing with engine speed Grinding or grating noise from gearbox Knocking noise from torque converter area At high speeds in 'D' transmission downshifts to second ratio and immediately upshifts back to third ratio	1, 15 17 18 22 12

RECTIFICATION CHART

1. Recheck fluid level
2. Check manual linkage adjustment
3. Check adjustment of down-shift valve cable
4. Reduce engine idle speed
5. Check adjustment of front band
6. Check front servo seals and fit of tubes
7. Check front band for wear
8. Check adjustment of rear band
9. Check rear servo seal and fit of tubes
10. Check rear band for wear
11. Examine front clutch, check ball valve and seals, also forward sun gear shaft sealing rings. Verify that cup plug in driven shaft is not leaking or dislodged.
12. Examine rear clutch, check ball valve and seals. Verify that rear clutch spring seat inner lip is not proud. Check fit of tubes.
13. Strip valve bodies and clean, checking:
    a. Primary regulator valve sticking
    b. Secondary regulator valve sticking
    c. Throttle valve sticking
    d. Modulator valve sticking
    e. Servo orifice control valve sticking
    f. 1 to 2 shift valve sticking
    g. 2 to 3 shift valve sticking
    h. 2 to 3 shift valve plunder sticking
14. Strip governor valve and clean
15. Examine parking pawl, gear, and internal linkage
16. Examine one-way clutch
17. Strip and examine pump and drive tangs
18. Strip and examine gear train
19. Adjust starter inhibitor switch inwards
20. Adjust starter inhibitor switch outwards
21. Replace torque converter
22. Examine torque converter drive plate for cracks or fracture
23. Check engine performance

Chapter 7 Propeller shaft

Contents

General description 1
Propeller shaft - front - removal and replacement 2
Propeller shaft - rear - removal and replacement 3
Universal joints - inspection and repair 4

Universal joints - renewal 5
Centre bearing - removal and replacement 6
Sliding joint - dismantling, overhaul and reassembly 7

Specifications

Split in two halves (front and rear), tubular with centre bearing

Diameter : Front	3 in (76.2 mm)	
Rear	2 in (50.8 mm)	
Universal joints	Hardy Spicer with roller bearings	

TORQUE WRENCH SETTING	lb ft	kg m
Centre bearing mounting bolts	22	3.0
Differential flange retaining bolt nuts	28	3.8
Gearbox flange retaining bolt nuts	22	3.0

1 General description

Drive is transmitted from the gearbox to the rear axle by means of a finely balanced Hardy Spicer tubular propeller shaft split into two halves and supported at the centre of a rubber mounted bearing.

Fitted to the front, centre and rear of the propeller shaft assembly are universal joints which allow for vertical movement of the rear axle and slight movement of the complete power unit on its rubber mountings. Each universal joint comprises a four legged centre spider, four needle roller bearings and two yokes.

Fore and aft movement of the rear axle is absorbed by a sliding spline at the rear of the propeller shaft assembly. This is splined and mates with a sleeve and yoke assembly. When assembled a dust cap, steel washer, and cork washer seal the end of the sleeve and sliding joint.

The yoke flange of the front universal joint is fitted to the gearbox mainshaft flange with four bolts, spring washers and nuts, and the yoke flange on the rear universal joint is secured to the pinion flange on the rear axle in the same way.

2 Propeller shaft - front - removal and replacement

1 Jack up the rear of the car and support on firmly based axle stands. Alternatively position the rear of the car on a ramp. Chock the front wheels.
2 The propeller shaft is carefully balanced to fine limits and it is important that it is replaced in exactly the same position prior to its removal. Scratch marks on the gearbox, differential pinion and propeller shaft drive flanges for correct re-alignment when refitting.
3 Support the weight of the front propeller shaft. Undo and remove the four gearbox end flange nuts and bolts.
4 Support the weight of the rear propeller shaft. Undo and remove the four axle end flange nuts and bolts.
5 Undo and remove the two bolts, spring and plain washers

that retain the centre bearing mounting to the body brackets.
6 Lift away the propeller shaft assembly from the underside of the car.
7 To separate the two halves of the propeller shaft assembly, first bend back the locking washer tab and undo and remove the retaining bolt. Lift away the 'C' washer and tab washer.
8 Draw the front propeller shaft away from the rear propeller shaft universal joint splines.
9 Reconnection and refitting the two propeller shaft halves is the reverse sequence to removal but the following additional points should be noted.
a) Ensure that the mating marks scratched on the propeller shaft, gearbox and differential pinion flanges are lined up.
b) Tighten the centre bearing mounting bolts to a torque wrench setting of 22 lb ft (3.0 kg m).
c) Tighten the front and rear flange retaining nuts to a torque wrench setting of 28 lb ft (3.8 kg m).

3 Propeller shaft - rear - removal and replacement

The sequence for removing the rear propeller shaft is the same as for removing the front propeller shaft in that the complete assembly must be removed first and then the two halves parted. See Section 2.

4 Universal joints - inspection and repair

1 Wear in the needle roller bearings is characterised by vibration in the transmission, 'clonks' on taking up the drive, and in extreme cases of lack of lubrication, metallic squeaking, and ultimately grating and shrieking sounds as the bearings break up.
2 It is easy to check if the needle roller bearings are worn with the propeller shaft in position, by trying to turn the shaft with one hand, and the other hand holding the rear axle flange when the rear universal is being checked, and the front half coupling when the front universal joint is being checked. Any movement

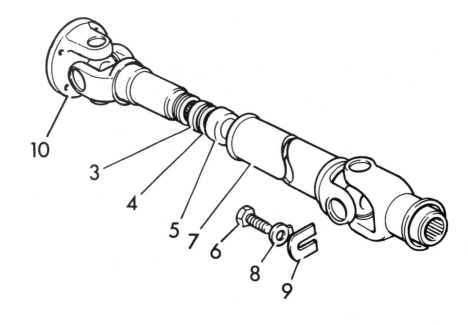

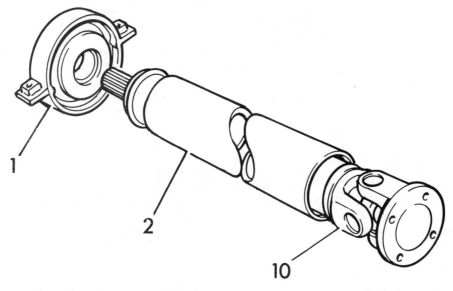

H13356

FIG.7.1. FRONT AND REAR PROPELLER SHAFTS

1	Centre bearing mounting	6	Retaining bolt
2	Front shaft	7	Rear shaft
3	Seal	8	Tab washer
4	Seal retainer	9	'C' washer
5	Screw cap	10	Universal joints

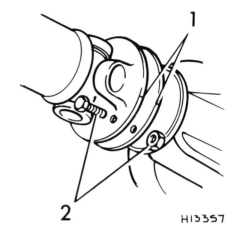

FIG.7.2. PROPELLER SHAFT ATTACHMENTS

1 Front/rear propeller shaft   2 Securing bolt and
   and gearbox/rear axle flanges   self locknut

H13357

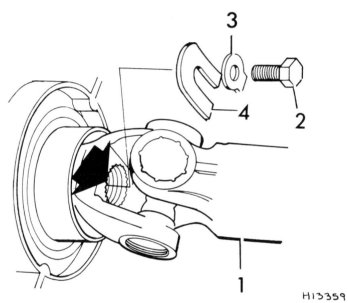

H13359

**FIG.7.3. REAR PROPELLER SHAFT TO
CENTRE BEARING ATTACHMENT**

1 Rear propeller shaft   3 Lockwasher
2 Bolt   4 'C' washer

FIG.7.4. CENTRE BEARING ATTACHMENT

1 Bolt   3 Plain washer
2 Spring washer   4 Centre bearing assembly

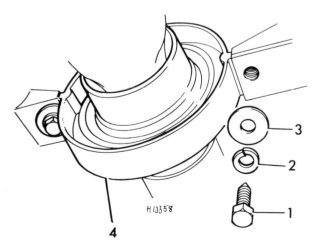

H13358

between the propeller shaft and the front, centre or rear half couplings is indicative of considerable wear. Check also by trying to lift the shaft and noticing any movement in the splines.

3 Test the propeller shaft for wear, and if worn it will be necessary to purchase a new rear half coupling, or if the yokes are badly worn, an exchange half propeller shaft. It is not possible to fit oversize bearings and journals to the trunnion bearing holes, even on the type where the joints can be renewed.

5 Universal joints - renewal

1 Some models are fitted with universal joints which are staked in position. Where this type of joint is used, it is not possible to renew them so an exchange shaft must be obtained.

2 Where the universal joints are retained by circlips, clean away all traces of dirt then mark the yokes so that they can be refitted in the same relative positions.

3 Remove the grease nipple (front joint only), then remove the circlips using long-nosed pliers or a suitable screwdriver. If difficult to remove, apply some penetrating oil and tap the bearing housing away from the circlip to alleviate the pressure.

4 It should be possible to drive out the bearings, but if they will not move by this method mount the assembly in a vice and press them out using a socket on one bearing housing and another socket on the yoke to allow the opposite housing to slide out.

5 Repeat this operation as necessary for the other bearings then remove the spider from the yoke. On front joints where a grease nipple is fitted, some leverage may be required.

6 Clean the yokes carefully then fit new oil seals to the new spider. Pack each bearing housing with a lithium based grease (eg; Castrol LM grease), place the spider in the yoke and press in the bearing. Ensure that the needle rollers are not dislodged.

7 Ensure that the oil seals register over the bearing housing lips then fit the circlips.

8 On the front joint, fit the grease nipple and apply 3 strokes from a grease gun containing a lithium based grease.

6 Centre bearing - removal and replacement

1 Refer to Section 2 and remove the propeller shaft assembly. Separate the two halves.

2 Using a universal puller and suitable thrust block (a suitable size bolt will do) draw the centre bearing from the end of the front propeller shaft.

3 To fit a new bearing simply drift it into position using a piece of suitable diameter metal tube.

4 Reconnect and refit the propeller shaft assembly, this being the reverse sequence to removal.

7 Sliding joint - dismantling, overhaul and reassembly

1 Refer to Section 2 and remove the propeller shaft assembly.

2 Unscrew the dust cap from the sleeve and then slide the sleeve from the shaft. Take off the steel washer and the cork washer.

3 With the sleeve separated from the shaft assembly the splines can be inspected. If worn it will be necessary to purchase a new sleeve assembly, or propeller shaft rear section.

4 To reassemble, fit the dust cap, steel washer, and a new cork gasket over the splined part of the propeller shaft.

5 Grease the splines and then line up the arrow on the sleeve assembly with the arrow on the splined portion of the propeller shaft, and push the sleeve over the splines. Fit the washers to the sleeve and screw up the dust cap.

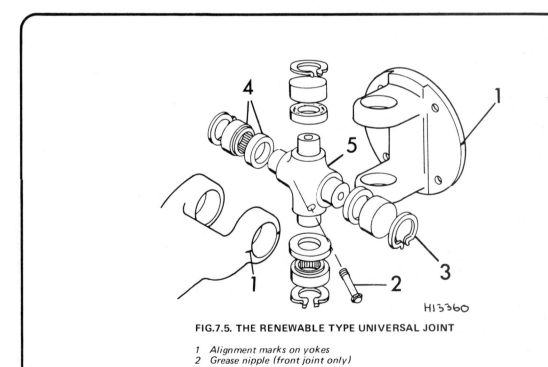

H13360

FIG.7.5. THE RENEWABLE TYPE UNIVERSAL JOINT

1 Alignment marks on yokes
2 Grease nipple (front joint only)
3 Circlip
4 Needle roller bearing (complete with seal)
5 Spider

Chapter 8 Rear axle

For modifications, and information applicable to later models, see Supplement at end of manual

Contents

General description   1
Rear axle - removal and replacement   2
Axle shaft, bearing and oil seal - removal and replacement ...   3
Pinion oil seal - removal and replacement   4

Differential assembly - removal and replacement   5
Differential unit - dismantling, inspection, reassembly and
adjustment   6

Specifications

Type	Hypoid - semi floating
Ratio	3.636:1 (11/40)
Distance of bearing from threaded end of axle shaft	2.84 in (72.14mm)
Differential bearing shims	0.003 in (0.076mm)
	0.005 in (0.127mm)
	0.010 in (0.254mm)
	0.020 in (0.508mm)
Differential case - maximum stretch	0.008 in (0.20 mm)
Differential pinion gears thrust washer range	8 in 0.002 in (0.05mm) increments
Thrust washer range	0.027 in (0.685mm) - 0.043 in (1.092mm)
Crown wheel runout (max)	0.003 in (0.076mm)
Crown wheel optimum setting	0.005 in (0.127mm)
Pinion bearing pre-load	15 to 18 lb ft (0.17 - 0.21 kg m)
Pinion head washer sizes:	
Standard	0.077 in (1.956mm)
Alternative	0.075 in (1.905mm) - 0.096 in (2.438mm) in a range of 21 increments
Pinion bearing shims	0.003 in (0.76mm)
	0.005 in (0.127mm)
	0.010 in (0.254mm)
	0.030 in (0.762mm)
Lubricant capacity	1.25 pints (0.71 litres)

TORQUE WRENCH SETTINGS

	lb ft	kg m
Backplate securing nuts	18	2.5
Axle shaft nut	85	11.7
Differential case to axle retaining nuts	20	2.7
Pinion bearing pre-load	15 - 18	0.17 - 0.21
Drive flange nut	90	12.4
Axle to spring 'U' bolt nuts	14	1.9
Propeller shaft flange retaining nuts	28	3.8

1 General description

The rear axle is of the semi floating type and is held in place by semi-elliptic springs. These springs provide the necessary lateral and longitudinal location of the axle. The rear axle incorporates a hypoid crownwheel and pinion, and a two pinion differential. All repairs can be carried out to the component parts of the rear axle without removing the axle casing from the car.

The crownwheel and pinion together with the differential gears are mounted on the differential unit which is bolted to the front face of the banjo type axle casing.

Adjustments are provided for the crownwheel and pinion backlash, pinion depth of mesh, pinion shaft bearing pre-load, and backlash between the differential gears. All these adjustments may be made by varying the thickness of the various shims and thrust washers.

The axle half shafts are easily withdrawn and are splined at their inner ends to fit into the splines in the differential wheels. The inner wheel bearing races are mounted on the outer ends of the axle casing and are secured by nuts and lock washers. The rear bearing outer races are located in the hubs.

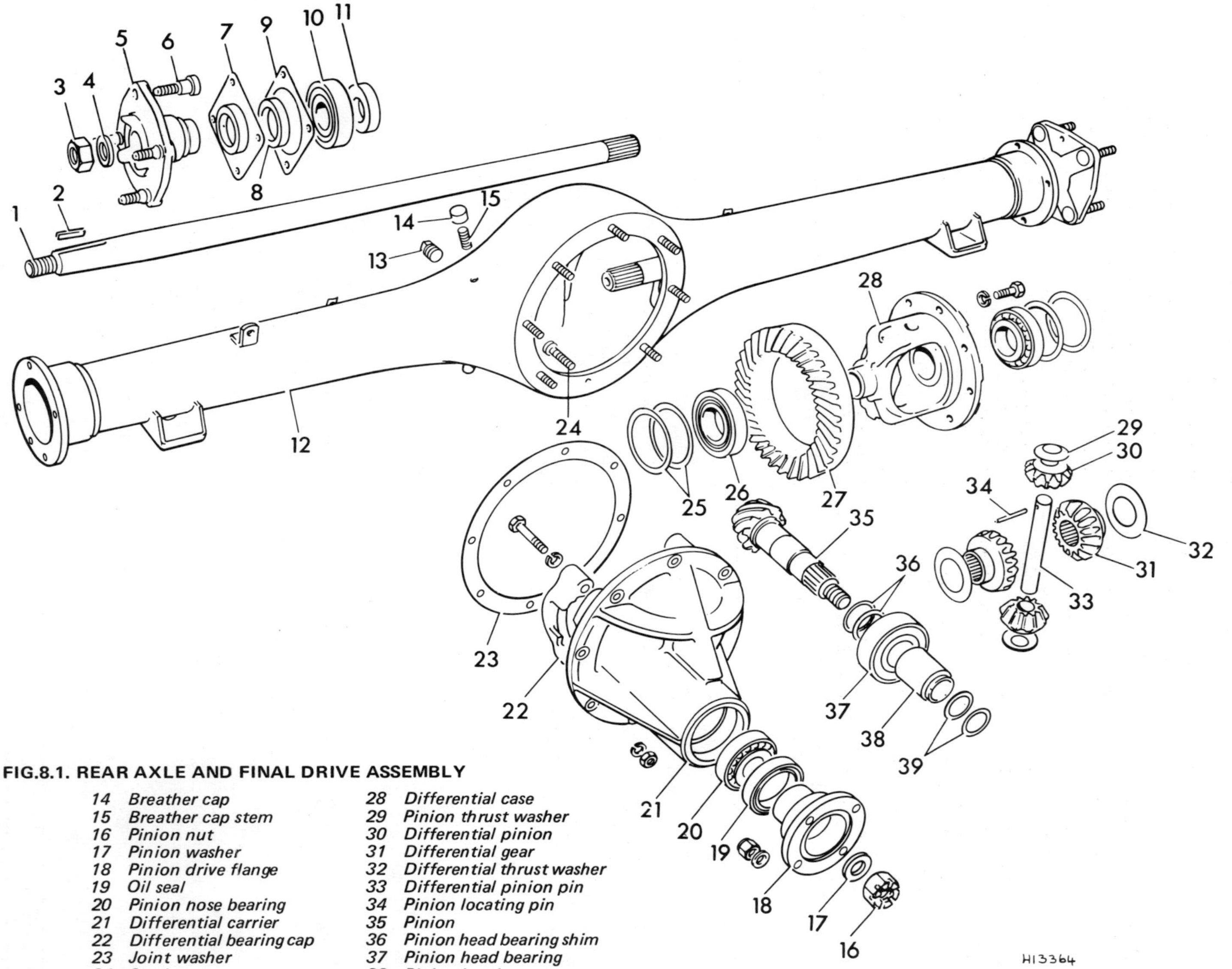

H13364

FIG.8.1. REAR AXLE AND FINAL DRIVE ASSEMBLY

1 Axle shaft
2 Axle shaft key
3 Axle shaft nut
4 Axle shaft washer
5 Rear hub
6 Wheel stud
7 Oil seal housing
8 Oil seal
9 Joint washer
10 Rear hub bearing
11 Rear hub oil seal
12 Rear axle case
13 Filler plug
14 Breather cap
15 Breather cap stem
16 Pinion nut
17 Pinion washer
18 Pinion drive flange
19 Oil seal
20 Pinion nose bearing
21 Differential carrier
22 Differential bearing cap
23 Joint washer
24 Stud
25 Differential bearing shim
26 Differential bearing assy.
27 Crownwheel
28 Differential case
29 Pinion thrust washer
30 Differential pinion
31 Differential gear
32 Differential thrust washer
33 Differential pinion pin
34 Pinion locating pin
35 Pinion
36 Pinion head bearing shim
37 Pinion head bearing
38 Pinion bearing spacer
39 Pinion nose bearing
   shim

2 Rear axle - removal and replacement

1 Chock the front wheels, jack up the rear of the car and place on firmly based axle stands located under the body and forward of the rear axle.

2 With a scriber or file mark the pinion and propeller shaft drive flanges so that they may be refitted in their original positions.

3 Undo and remove the four nuts and bolts that secure the rear propeller shaft flange to the pinion flange. Lower the propeller shaft.

4 Remove the wheel trims, undo and remove the wheel nuts and lift away the road wheels.

5 Wipe the top of the brake master cylinder reservoir, unscrew the cap and place a piece of thin polythene sheet over the top of the reservoir. Refit the cap. This will prevent hydraulic fluid syphoning out during subsequent operations.

6 Wipe the area around the union nut on the brake feed pipe at the axle bracket. Unscrew the union nut.

7 Undo and remove the locknut and washer from the flexible hose.

8 Detach the flexible hose from its support bracket.

9 Extract the split pins locking the brake lever clevis pins. Lift away the plain washers and withdraw the clevis pins.

10 Undo and remove the nut and spring washer that secures the

compensating lever pin to the axle case suport bracket. Lift away the compensating lever assembly.

11 Undo and remove the bolt and spring washer that secures the hand brake cable clip to the axle casing.

12 Using axle stands or other suitable means support the weight of the rear axle.

13 Undo and remove the eight 'U' bolt locknuts.

14 Detach the shock absorber mounting brackets and move back to one side. If necessary tie back with string or wire.

15 Detach the lower mounting plates and rubber pads.

16 Lift away the 'U' bolts and rubber bump stops.

17 The rear axle may now be lifted over the rear springs, and drawn away from one side of the car. Make a special note of the location of the spring packing wedge, upper locating plates and rubber pad.

18 Refitting the rear axle is the reverse sequence to removeal. The following additional points should be noted:

a) Make sure that the spring packing wedges are refitted in their original positions.

b) Inspect the rubber mounting pads and if they show signs of deterioration fit new ones.

c) Tighten the 'U' bolt nuts to a torque wrench setting of 14 lb ft (1.9 kg m).

d) It will be necessary to bleed the brake bydraulic system. See Chapter 9.

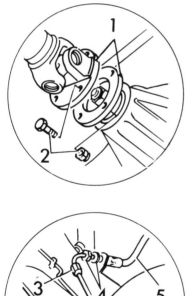
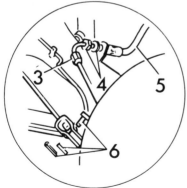
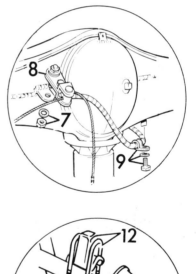
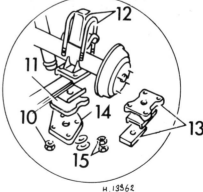

FIG.8.2. REAR AXLE ATTACHMENT POINTS FOR AXLE REMOVAL

1 Propeller shaft and pinion drive flange mating marks
2 Bolt and self locking nut
3 Brake hydraulic pipe union nut
4 Brake hydraulic flexible hose locknut and washer
5 Brake hydraulic flexible hose
6 Handbrake cable clevis pin, plain washer and split pin
7 Compensating lever nut and spring washer
8 Compensator
9 Cable mounting bracket bolt and spring washer
10 'U' bolt locknuts
11 Rubber pad
12 'U' bolts and rubber bump stops
13 Spring packing wedge upper locating plate rubber pad
14 Shock absorber mounting plate
15 Shock absorber retaining nut and locknut

3 Axle shaft, bearing and oil seal - removal and replacement

1   Chock the front wheels, jack up the rear of the car and place on firmly based axle stands. Remove the rear wheel.
2   Undo and remove the axle shaft nut and plain washer.
3   Undo and remove the two screws that secure the brake drum to the hub flange. Lift away the brake drum.
4   Should it be tight to remove, back off the brake adjusters and using a soft faced hammer tap outwards on the circumference of the brake drum.
5   Using a heavy duty puller and suitable thrust block over the end of the axle shaft draw off the rear hub from the axle shaft.
6   Extract the split pin from the handbrake lever clevis pin at the rear of the brake backplate. Lift away the plain washer and withdraw the clevis pin so separating the handbrake cable yoke from the handbrake lever.
7   Wipe the top of the brake master cylinder reservoir, unscrew the cap and place a piece of thin polythene sheet over the top of the reservoir. Refit the cap. This will prevent hydraulic fluid syphoning out during subsequent operations.
8   Wipe the area of the brake pipe union/s at the rear of the wheel cylinder and unscrew the union/s from the wheel cylinder.
9   Undo and remove the four nuts, spring washers and bolts that secure the brake backplate to the axle casing.
10 Make a note of the fitted position of the dry lip relative to the brake wheel cylinder and remove the oil catcher.
11 The brake backplate assembly may now be lifted away.
12 Remove the rear hub oil seal and retainer assembly; the seal should be renewed if it is worn or has any signs of leaking. To remove the old seal carefully ease it out using a screwdriver. Once removed an oil seal must never be refitted.
13 Place a clean container under the end of the axle banjo to catch any oil that will issue from the end.
14 Using a screwdriver or a pair of pliers remove the axle shaft key and put it in a safe place where it will not be lost.

15 Using either an impact slide hammer or, if not available, mole grips on the end of the axle shaft (with the nut refitted), draw the axle shaft from the casing.
16 The inner oil seal may be removed by using a piece of metal bar shaped in the form of a hook. Pull on the seal and draw it from inside the axle casing.
17 If required the bearing may be removed from the axle shaft by placing the bearing on the top of the jaws of the vice and driving the axle shaft through using a soft faced hammer on the end of the axle shaft nut.
18 Refitting the oil seal, bearing and axle shaft is the reverse sequence to removal but the following additional points should be noted:
a) Pack the bearing with a lithium based grease. Lubricate the new oil seal with a little Castrol GTX.
b) When refitting the oil seal the lip must face inwards.
c) Using a suitable diameter tube drift the bearing onto the axle shaft until the distance of the bearing to the threaded end of the axle shaft is 2.84 inches (72.14 mm).
d) Always use a new rear hub joint washer.
e) The backplate securing nuts should be tightened to a torque wrench setting of 18 lb ft (2.5 kg m).
f) To ensure positive locking of the axle shaft nut always apply a little Loctite CV to the axle shaft thread.
g) Tighten the axle shaft nut to a torque wrench setting of 85 lb ft (11.7 kg m).
h) Top up the rear axle oil level.
i) Bleed the brake hydraulic system as described in Chapter 9.

4 Pinion oil seal - removal and replacement

1   Chock the front wheels, jack up the rear of the car and support on firmly based axle stands.
2   With a scriber or file mark the propeller shaft and pinion flanges so that they may be refitted correctly in their original positions.

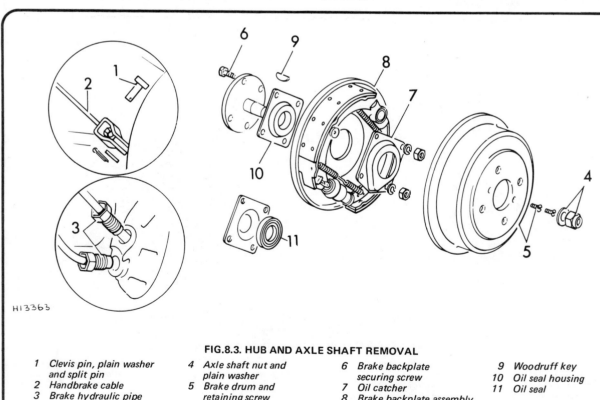

H13363

FIG.8.3. HUB AND AXLE SHAFT REMOVAL

1 Clevis pin, plain washer and split pin	4 Axle shaft nut and plain washer	6 Brake backplate securing screw	9 Woodruff key
2 Handbrake cable	5 Brake drum and retaining screw	7 Oil catcher	10 Oil seal housing
3 Brake hydraulic pipe		8 Brake backplate assembly	11 Oil seal

3   Undo and remove the four nuts, bolts and spring washers that secure the pinion flange to the propeller shaft flange. Lower the propeller shaft to the floor.

4   Apply the handbrake really firmly. Using a pair of pliers extract the flange nut locking split pin.

5   With a socket wrench undo the flange nut. Lift away the nut and plain washer. (See Fig. 8.1).

6   Place a container under the pinion end of the rear axle to catch any oil that seeps out.

7   Using a universal puller and suitable thrust block draw the pinion flange from the pinion

8   The old oil seal may now be prised out using a screwdriver or thin piece of metal bar with a small hook on one end.

9   Refitting the new oil seal is the reverse sequence to removal, but the following additional points should be noted:

a)   Soak the new oil seal in Castrol GTX for 1 hour prior to fitting.

b)   Fit the new seal with the lip facing inwards using a tubular drift.

c)   Tighten the driving flange nut to a torque wrench setting of 90 lb ft (12 kg m). Lock with a new split pin.

d)   Top up the rear axle oil level as necessary.

5   Differential assembly - removal and replacement

1   If it is wished to overhaul the differential carrier assembly or to exchange it for a Factory reconditioned unit first remove the axle shafts as described in Section 3.

2   Mark the propeller shaft and pinion flanges to ensure their replacement in the same relative positon.

3   Undo and remove the four nuts and bolts from the flanges. Separate the two parts and lower the propeller shaft to the ground.

4   Place a container under the differential unit assembly to catch oil that will drain out during subsequent operations.

5   Undo and remove the eight nuts and spring washers that secure the differential unit assembly to the axle casing.

6   Draw the assembly forwards from over the studs on the axle casing. Lift away from under the car. Remove the paper joint washer.

7   Refitting the differential assembly is the reverse sequence to removal. The following additional points should be noted:

a)   Always use a new joint washer and make sure the mating faces are clean, then apply a non-setting jointing compound.

b)   Tighten the differential retaining nuts to a torque wrench setting of 22 lb ft (3.18 kg m).

c)   Refill the axle with 1.25 pints (0.71 litres) of Castrol Hypoy B.

6   Differential unit - dismantling, inspection, reassembly and adjustment

Make sure before attempting to dismantle the differential that it is both necessary and economic. A special tool is needed and whilst not difficult some critical measurements have to be taken. It may well be cheaper to exchange the final drive assembly as a complete unit at the outset.

1   Obtain a special tool called an axle stretcher before commencing to dismantle the unit. It has a BLMC part number of 18G131C with adaptor plates 18G131E.

2   Hold the differential unit vertically in a vice and then using a scriber or dot punch mark the bearing caps and adjacent side of the differential carrier so that the bearing caps are refitted to their original positions.

3   Undo and remove the four bolts and spring washers securing the end caps.

4   Assemble the axle housing stretcher adaptor plates on the differential unit casing. Next fit the stretcher to the adaptor plates.

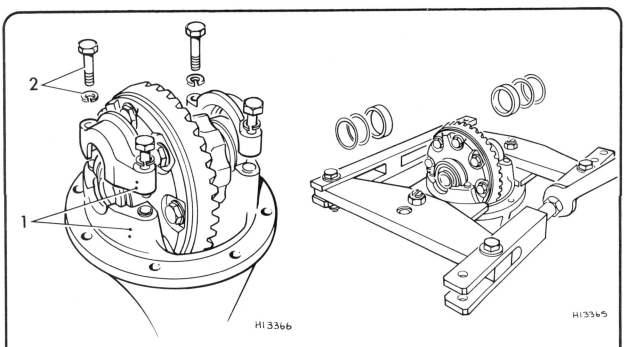

H13366   H13365

FIG.8.4. DIFFERENTIAL BEARING CAP REMOVAL   **FIG.8.5. USE OF SPECIAL TOOL TO STRETCH AXLE CASING**

1   Bearing cap identification marks   *2   Bearing cap securing bolt and spring washer*

5 The differential unit case should now be stretched by tightening the nut three or four flats until the differential carrier can be levered out and the bearing shims and caps removed. IMPORTANT: To avoid damage to the case do not attempt to spread any more than is necessary. To assist each flat on the nut is numbered to give a check on the amount turned. The maximum stretch is 0.008 inch (0.20 mm). When removing the differential carrier do not lever against the spreader.

6 Mark the relative positions of the crownwheel and differential carrier to ensure correct refitting.

8 Undo and remove the eight bolts and spring washers securing the crownwheel to the differential carrier.

9 Separate the crownwheel from the differential carrier. If a little tight, tap with a soft faced hammer.

10 Using a parallel pin punch carefully drive out the differential pinion pin locking peg.

11 With a suitable diameter soft metal drift remove the differential pinion pin.

12 Rotate the differential gear wheels until the differential pinions are opposite the openings in the differential gear case, remove the differential pinions and their selective thrust washers. Keep the pinions and respective thrust washers together.

13 Remove the differential gear wheels and their thrust washers.

14 Transfer the differential unit casing from its position in the vice and hold the drive flange firmly in the jaws.

15 Extract the drive flange nut split pin and using a socket undo and remove the drive flange nut and washer.

16 Using a universal puller and suitable thrust block remove the drive flange from the pinion.

17 The pinion may next be removed. To do this carefully drive out using a hard wood block and hammer.

18 Remove the pinion bearing shims and spacer.

19 If the pinion bearings are to be renewed the inner bearings should be drawn off the pinion using a universal puller with long legs.

20 Lift the pinion head washer away from behind the pinion head.

21 Using a tapered soft metal drift carefully drift out the pinion outer bearing cup, bearing and oil seal. Also remove the pinion inner bearing cup.

22 Dismantling is now complete. Thoroughly wash all parts in paraffin and wipe dry using a clean non fluffy rag.

23 Lightly lubricate the bearings and reassemble. Test for signs of roughness by rotating the inner and outer tracks. Check the rollers for signs of pitting, wear or excessive looseness in their cage. Inspect the thrust washers for signs of excessive wear. Check for signs of wear on the differential pinion shaft and pinion gears. Any parts that show signs of wear should be renewed.

24 The crownwheel and pinion must only be replaced as a matched pair. The pair number is etched on the outer face of the crownwheel and the forward face of the pinion.

25 If it is found that only one of the differential bearings is worn, both differential bearings must be renewed. Likewise if one pinion bearing is worn, both pinion bearings must be renewed.

26 To reassemble first fit the differential bearing cones to the gear carrier using a piece of tube of suitable diameter.

27 Place the thrust washers behind the two differential gears and then fit them to their bores in the gear carrier. Make sure these gears rotate easily.

28 Place the two pinion gears in mesh with the two differential gears, leaving out the thrust washers and rotate the gear cluster until the pinion pin hole in the carrier is lined up with the pinions. Insert the pinion pin.

29 Press each pinion in turn firmly into mesh with the differential gears. Measure the required thrust washer thickness using feeler gauges so that no backlash exists.

30 Remove the pinion gears, keeping them in their respective positions and select a thrust washer whose thickness is the same as that determined by the feeler gauges. Eight thrust washers are available in 0.002 inch (0.05mm) increments from 0.027 inch to 0.041 inch (0.685 - 1.03mm).

31 Lubricate the thrust washers, pinions and pinion pin and reassemble into the differential carrier. Check that there is no

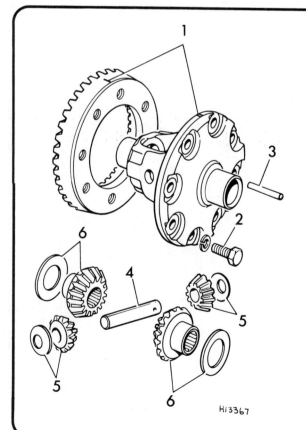

FIG.8.6. DIFFERENTIAL UNIT COMPONENTS

1 Crownwheel and differential carrier mating marks
2 Crownwheel securing bolt and spring washer
3 Locking peg
4 Differential pinion pin
5 Differential pinion thrust washer
6 Differential gearwheel and thrust washer

HI3367

backlash. When this condition exists the gears will be stiff to rotate by hand.

32 Lock the pinion using the locking peg. Secure the peg by peening the metal of the differential carrier.

33 Carefully clean the crownwheel and gear carrier mating faces and fit the crownwheel. Any burrs can be removed with a fine oilstone. If the original parts are being used line up the previously made marks.

34 Secure the crownwheel with the eight bolts and spring washers which should be tightened in a diagonal and progressive manner.

35 Fit the carrier bearing cups to the bearings and place the assembly in the case. Leave out the shims at this stage.

36 Replace the bearing caps in their original positions and tighten the retaining bolts. Using either a dial indicator gauge or feeler gauges check the run out of the crownwheel and carrier. This must not exceed 0.003 inch (0.076mm).

37 If a reading in excess is obtained check for dirt on the crownwheel or carrier mating faces or under the bearing cups.

38 Remove the bearing cups again.

39 If the pinion bearing cups were removed for the fitting of new bearings, these should next be replaced. For this use a tube of suitable diameter and carefully drift them into position. Make sure they are fitted the correct way round with the tapers facing outwards.

40 Fit the spacer behind the pinion head and using a tube of suitable diameter refit the inner bearing again using a piece of metal tube of similar diameter.

41 Lubricate the bearing and fit the pinion to the casing. Slide on the bearing spacer, chamfered end towards the drive flange followed by the shims that were previously removed.

42 Lubricate the outer bearing and then fit to the end of the pinion.

43 Fit the drive flange and nut. Tighten the nut to a torque wrench setting of 90 lb ft (12.4 kg m). Rotate the pinion several times before the nut is fully tightened so that the bearings settle to their running positions.

44 If available use a pull scale and determine the bearing preload by wrapping string round the pinion flange and hooking the

other end onto the pull scale. The reading should be between 15 - 18 lb ft (0.17 - 0.21 kg m). Should the reading be in excess of this amount the shim thickness should be increased and conversely if the reading is too low decrease the shim thickness.

45 Remove the pinion nut, pinion and outer bearing and fit the required thickness shim to the pinion. Four shims are available in sizes from 0.003 - 0.030 inch (0.076 - 0.76mm). For assistance 0.001 inch (0.254mm) thickness shim equals aproximately 4 lb ft (0.04 kg m) pre-load.

46 Soak a new oil seal in Castrol GTX for 1 hour and then fit to the differential case. Replace the drive flange, washer and nut and tighten the nut to a torque wrench setting of 90 lb ft (12.4 kg m).

47 Lock the nut using a new split pin.

48 Place the bearing cups on the differential bearings and fit the differential carrier into the case. Replace the shims in their original positions.

49 Refit the bearing caps in their original positions and tighten the bearing cap bolts with spring washers in a progressive and diagonal manner.

50 Remove the axle spreader.

51 Using a dial indicator gauge or feeler gauges determine the total backlash which should be between 0.004 - 0.006 inch (0.10 - 0.15mm).

52 Should adjustment be necessary remove the shims behind the differential bearings once the caps have been removed and fit differential thickness shims. It should be noted that a movement of 0.002 inch (0.05mm) shim thickness from one differential bearing to the other will vary the backlash by approximately 0.002 inch (0.05mm).

53 Smear a little 'engineers blue' onto the crownwheel teeth and rotate the pinion in a forward and reverse direction several times.

54 The correct tooth marking on the crownwheel is shown in illustration 1, of Fig. 8.8. If the position is different as shown in illustration 2 - 5 inclusive the arrows in the crownwheel and pinion diagrams to the right of the illustrations indicate the course of action to be taken.

55 When the correct tooth marking and backlash is correct the final drive unit may now be refitted.

See over for Fig.8.8. — correct tooth marking

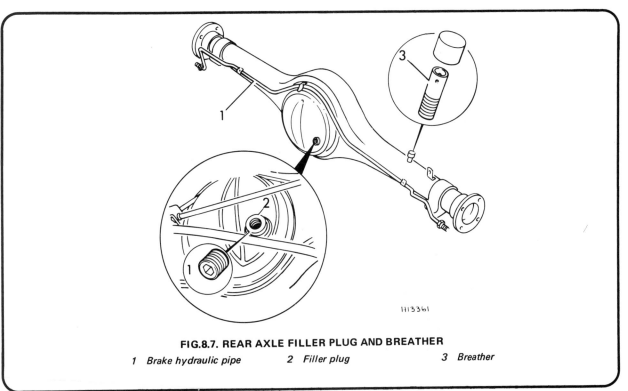

FIG.8.7. REAR AXLE FILLER PLUG AND BREATHER

1 Brake hydraulic pipe   2 Filler plug   3 Breather

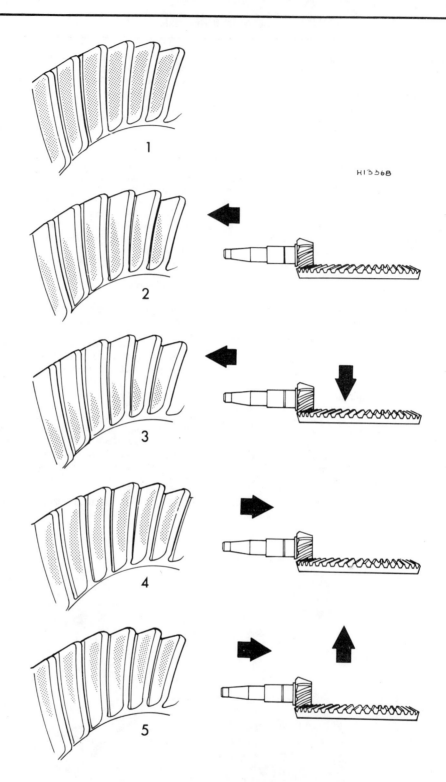

H13368

FIG.8.8. TOOTH MARKING FOR THE CROWNWHEEL

1 Correct tooth contact
2 Heavy contact at tooth toe towards the centre. Move pinion away from crownwheel
3 Heavy contact with toe at tooth flank bottom. Move pinion away from crownwheel and crownwheel from pinion
4 Heavy contact at tooth heel and towards the centre. Move pinion towards crownwheel
5 Heavy contact on heel at tooth face. Move pinion towards crownwheel and crownwheel towards pinion

Chapter 9 Braking system

For modifications, and information applicable to later models, see Supplement at end of manual

Contents

General description	1
Rear drum brake - adjustment (manual adjusters)	2
Bleeding the hydraulic system...	3
Front disc brake caliper pad - removal and refitting	4
Front disc brake caliper - removal and refitting..	5
Front brake disc - removal and refitting...	6
Rear drum brake shoes - inspection, removal and refitting ...	7
Rear drum backplate - removal and refitting	8
Master cylinder - removal and refitting	9
Master cylinder - dismantling and reassembly	10
Rear drum brake wheel cylinder - removal and refitting... ...	11

Rear drum brake wheel cylinder - overhaul	12
Front disc brake caliper - overhaul	13
Handbrake cable - adjustment	14
Handbrake cable - removal and refitting...	15
Handbrake lever assembly - removal and refitting	16
Brake pedal assembly - removal and refitting	17
Brake servo unit - description	18
Brake servo unit - removal and refitting	19
Brake servo unit - air filter renewal	20
Fault diagnosis	21

Specifications

Front - disc

Disc diameter...	9.785 in (248.5 mm)
Disc run-out	0.006 in (0.152 mm)
Total pad area	17.4 in^2 (286.77 cm^2)
Total swept area	182.8 in^1 (2671 cm^2)
Pad lining material (service replacement)	Ferodo 2445
Minimum pad thickness..	1/8 in (3.1 mm)

Rear - drum

Drum diameter	8 in (203.2 mm)
Lining dimensions	8 x 1.5 x 0.1875 in (203.2 x 38.1 x 4.76 mm)
Total swept area	76 in^2 (490.2 cm^2)
Lining material	Ferodo 2626
Wheel cylinder diameter..	0.620 in (15.74 mm)

Master cylinder diameter:

Non servo	0.70 in (17.78 mm)
With servo	0.75 in (19.05 mm)

Servo unit	Girling Supervac

Torque wrench settings

	lb. f. ft.	Kg. f. m.
Bleed screw	4 — 6	0.5 — 0.8
Master cylinder retaining nuts...	15 — 19	1.7 — 2.1
Caliper retaining bolts	50	6.9
Wheel cylinder retaining bolts...	4 — 5	0.55 — 0.7
Backplate securing nuts and bolts...	35 — 42	4.8 — 5.8
Brake disc securing bolts	38 — 45	5.25 — 6.22

1 General description

Disc brakes are fitted to the front and drum brakes to the rear of the Marina 1.8. They are operated by hydraulic pressure created in the master cylinder when the brake pedal is depressed. This pressure is transferred to the respective wheel or caliper cylinders by a system of metal and flexible pipes and hoses.

The metal pipe to the rear brakes is connected to a flexible hose located on the right hand rear suspension. A short metal pipe connects the hose to the bottom union connection, on the rear right hand wheel cylinder. The upper part of the right hand wheel cylinder is connected to the lower part of the left hand wheel cylinder by a metal pipe which is attached to the rear axle casing.

The rear drum brakes are of the internally expanding type whereby the shoes and linings are moved outwards into contact with the rotating brake drum. One wheel cylinder is fitted.

The handbrake operates on the rear brakes only using a system of links and cables.

The front disc brakes are of the conventional fixed caliper design. Each half of the caliper contains a piston which operates in a bore, both being interconnected so that under hydraulic pressure their pistons move towards each other. By this action they clamp the rotating disc between two friction pads to slow rotational movement of the disc. Special seals are fitted between the piston and bore and these seals are able to stretch slightly when the piston moves, to apply the brake. When the hydraulic pressure is released the seals return to their natural shape and draw the pistons back slightly so giving a running clearance between the pads and disc. As the pads wear the piston is able to slide through the seal allowing wear to be taken up.

The front disc brakes are self-adjusting; the rear drum brakes may be either self-adjusting or manually adjusted.

A brake servo unit is fitted as standard on the 1.8 TC and as an optional extra to other 1.8 models. It is fitted between the brake pedal and master cylinder to add pressure on the master cylinder pushrod when the brake pedal is being depressed. This therefore reduces driver foot effort.

2 Rear drum brake - adjustment (manual adjusters)

1 Chock the front wheels, release the handbrake completely, jack up the rear of the car, and support it on firmly based stands.
2 A single adjuster for each side is located on the rear of the backplate near the top (See Fig. 9.4a), and the surrounding area should be cleaned of all dirt and a small amount of engine oil smeared onto the adjuster threads.
3 Turn the adjuster clockwise (as viewed from the centre of the rear axle), preferably with a square adjuster spanner, until the brake drum is locked. Then back off the adjuster until the drum rotates without any signs of binding. About two clicks is normal.
4 Repeat the procedure given in paragraph 3 for the remaining wheel.
5 Finally lower the car to the ground.

3 Bleeding the hydraulic system

Whenever the brake hydraulic system has been overhauled, a part renewed, or the level in the reservoir becomes too low, air will have entered the system, necessitating its bleeding. During the operation, the level of hydraulic fluid in the reservoir should not be allowed to fall below half full, otherwise air will be drawn in again.
1 Obtain a clean and dry glass jar, plastic tubing fifteen inches long and of suitable diameter to fit tightly over the bleed screw, and a supply of Castrol Girling Brake Fluid.
2 Check that on each rear brake backplate the wheel cylinder is free to slide within its locating slot. Ensure that all connections are tight and all bleed screws closed. Chock the wheels and release the handbrake.
3 Fill the master cylinder reservoir and the bottom inch of the jar with hydraulic fluid. Take extreme care that no fluid is allowed to come into contact with the paintwork as it acts as a solvent and it will damage the finish.
4 Remove the rubber dust cap (if fitted) from the end of the bleed screw on the front disc brake caliper which is furthest away from the master cylinder. Connect one end of the bleed tube to the bleed screw and insert the other end of the bleed tube in the jar containing 1 inch of hydraulic fluid.
5 Use a suitable open ended spanner and unscrew the bleed screw about half a turn.
6 An assistant should now pump the brake pedal by first depressing it one full stroke followed by three short but rapid strokes and allowing the pedal to return of its own accord. Check the fluid level in the reservoir. Carefully watch the flow of fluid into the glass jar and, when air bubbles cease to emerge with the fluid, during the next down stroke, tighten the bleed screw. Remove the plastic bleed tube and tighten the bleed screw, preferably to a torque wrench setting of 4 - 6 lb ft (0.5 - 0.8 kg m). Replace the rubber dust cap.
7 Repeat operation in paragraphs 4 - 6 for the second front brake.
8 The rear brakes should be bled in the same manner as the front, except that each brake pedal stroke should be slow with a pause of three or four seconds between each stroke.
9 Sometimes it may be found that the bleeding operation for one or more cylinders is taking a considerable time. The cause is probably due to air being drawn past the bleed screw threads when the screw is lose. To counteract this condition, it is recommended that at the end of each downward stroke the bleed screw be tightened to stop air being drawn past the threads.
10 If after the bleed operation has been completed, the brake pedal operation still feels spongy, this is an indication that there is still air in the system, or that the master cylinder is faulty.
11 Check and top up the reservoir fluid level with fresh hydraulic fluid. Never reuse old brake fluid.

4 Front disc brake caliper pad - removal and refitting

1 Chock the rear wheels, apply the handbrake, jack up the

front of the car and support on firmly based axle stands. Remove the road wheel.
2 Extract the two pad retaining pin spring clips and withdraw the two retaining pins (Fig.9.1).
3 Lift away the brake pads and anti squeak shims noting which way round the shims are fitted.
4 Inspect the thickness of the lining material and, if it is less than 1/8 inch (3.1 mm) the pads must be renewed.
5 If new pads are being fitted always use those manufactured to the recommended specifications given at the beginning of this Chapter.
6 To refit the pads, it is first necessary to extract a little brake fluid from the system. To do this, fit a plastic bleed tube to the bleed screw and immerse the free end in 1 inch of hydraulic fluid in a jar. Slacken off the bleed screw one complete turn and press

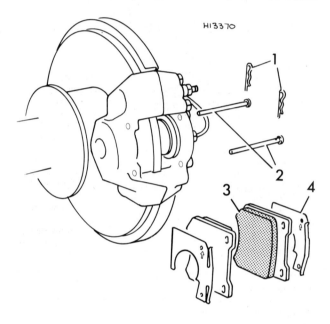

FIG.9.1. FRONT DISC BRAKE PAD REMOVAL

1 Spring clip	*3 Pad*
2 Retaining pin	*4 Anti-squeak shim*

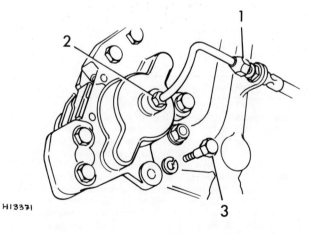

FIG.9.2. FRONT DISC BRAKE CALIPER ATTACHMENTS

1 Metal pipe union nut	*3 Securing bolt and spring*
2 Metal pipe union	*washer*

back the pistons into their bores. Tighten the bleed screw and remove the bleed tube.

7 Wipe the exposed end of the pistons and in the recesses of the caliper free of dust or road dirt.

8 Refitting the pads is now the reverse sequence to removal but the following points should be noted:

a) The anti-squeak shims are fitted with the arrows pointing upwards.

b) If it is suspected that air has entered through the system during the operating described in paragraph 6, the system must be bled as described in Section 3.

9 Wipe the top of the hydraulic fluid reservoir and remove the cap. Top up and depress the brake pedal several times to settle the pads. Recheck the hydraulic fluid level.

5 Front disc brake caliper - removal and refitting

1 Apply the handbrake, chock the rear wheels, jack up the front of the car and support on firmly based stands. Remove the road wheel.

2 Wipe the top of the master cylinder reservoir, unscrew the cap and place a piece of thin polythene sheet over the top. Refit the cap. This is to stop hydraulic fluid syphoning out during subsequent operations.

3 Wipe the area around the caliper flexible hose to metal pipe union and the metal pipe to caliper connection. Unscrew the union nuts and lift away the metal pipe (Fig.9.2).

4 Undo and remove the two bolts and spring washers securing the caliper to the steering swivel. Lift the caliper from the disc.

5 Refitting the caliper is the reverse sequence to removal but the following additional points should be noted:

a) The two caliper securing bolts should be tightened to a torque wrench setting of 50 lbft (6.9 kgm).

b) Bleed the brake hydraulic system as described in Section 3.

c) Depress the brake pedal several times to reset the pads in their correct operating position.

6 Front brake disc - removal and refitting

1 Chock the rear wheels, apply the handbrake, jack up the front of the car and support on firmly based axle stands. Remove the road wheel.

2 Refer to Section 5 of this chapter and remove the caliper assembly.

3 Using a wide blade screwdriver ease off the hub grease cap.

4 Straighten the hub nut retainer locking split pin ears and extract the split pin. Remove the nut retainer and then undo and remove the nut splined washer.

5 Withdraw the complete front hub assembly from the spindle.

6 To separate the disc from the hub first mark the relative position of the hub and disc. Undo and remove the four bolts securing the hub to the disc and separate the two parts.

7 Should the disc surfaces be grooved and a new disc not obtainable, it is permissible to have the two faces ground by an engineering works. Score marks are not serious provided that they are concentric but not excessively deep. It is however, far better to fit a disc rather than to re-grind the original one.

8 To refit the disc to the hub make sure that the mating faces are very clean and then line up the previously made alignment marks if the original parts are to be used. Secure with the four bolts which should be tightened in a progressive and diagonal manner to a final torque wrench setting of 38 - 45 lb ft (5.25 - 6.22 kg m).

9 Refitting is now the reverse sequence to removal but the following additional points should be noted:

a) Before refitting the caliper check the disc runout at a 4.75 inch (120.7mm) radius of the disc. The runout must not exceed 0.006 inch (0.152mm). If necessary remove the disc and check for dirt on the mating faces. Should these be clean reposition the disc on the hub.

b) The hub bearing end float must be adjusted as described in Chapter 11.

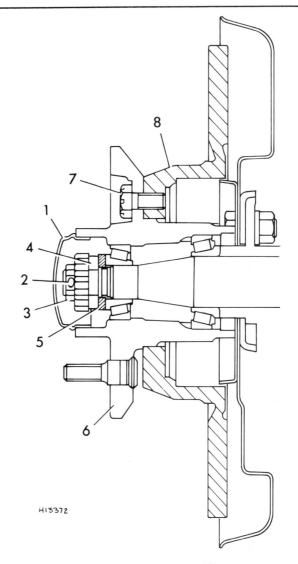

H13372

FIG.9.3. FRONT BRAKE DISC

1	Grease cap	5	Splined washer
2	Split pin	6	Hub
3	Nut retainer	7	Disc securing bolt
4	Nut	8	Disc

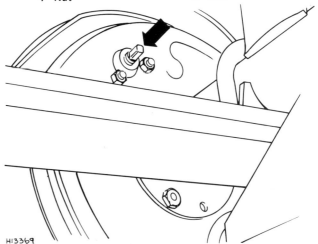

H13369

FIG. 9.4a LOCATION OF REAR BRAKE ADJUSTER (ARROWED)

7 Rear drum brake shoes - inspection, removal and refitting

After high mileages, it will be necessary to fit replacement shoes with new linings. Refitting new brake linings to shoes is not considered economic, or possible, without the use of special equipment. However, if the services of a local garage or workshop having brake re-lining equipment are available there is no reason why the original shoes should not be successfully relined. Ensure that the correct specification linings are fitted to the shoes.

1 Chock the front wheels, jack up the rear of the car and place on firmly based axle stands. Remove the road wheel.
2 Undo and remove the two brake drum retaining screws and carefully pull off the brake drum. If it is tight it may be tapped outwards using a soft faced hammer.
3 The brake linings should be renewed if they are so worn that the rivet heads are flush with the surface of the lining. If bonded linings are fitted, they must be renewed when the lining material has worn down to 1/16 inch (1.6 mm) at its thinnest point.
4 Using a pair of pliers release the steady springs and pins from the shoes by rotating through 90°. Lift away the steady spring, pin and cup washers from each brake shoe web (Fig.9.4b or 9.4c).
5 With a screwdriver ease the trailing shoe from its backplate anchor post (automatic adjusters) or adjuster link (manual adjusters) and the wheel cylinder adjuster slot.
6 Lift away the brake shoes complete with return springs. It will be necessary to ease the leading shoe from the handbrake operating lever.
7 Detach the pull-off springs, and remove the retaining spring and support plate from the leading shoe.
8 On automatic adjustment versions, remove the adjuster from the wheel cylinder and slacken the adjuster ratchet back.
9 If the shoes are to be left off for a while, do not depress the brake pedal otherwise the pistons will be ejected from the cylinders causing unnecessary work. Retain the pistons with strong elastic bands.
10 Thoroughly clean all traces of dust from the shoes, backplate and drum using a stiff brush. Do not use compressed air as it blows up dust which must not be inhaled as it is of an asbestos

nature. Brake dust can cause judder or squeal and, therefore it is important to clean away all traces.
11 Check that each piston is free in its cylinder, the rubber dust covers are undamaged and in position and that there are no hydraulic fluid leaks.
12 Check that the wheel cylinder is free to move in its slot in the backplate.
13 Prior to reassembly, smear a trace of Castrol PH Brake Grease to the ends of the brake shoes, steady platforms anchor posts and the thread of the adjuster. Do not allow any grease to come into contact with the linings or rubber parts. Refit the shoes in the reverse sequence to removal. The two pull off springs should preferably be renewed every time new shoes are fitted, and must be refitted in their original web holes (see Fig.9.4b or 9.4c).
14 Replace the brake drum and secure with the two retaining screws.
15 Refit the road wheel and lower the car to the ground. Operate the handbrake several times so as to set the automatic adjuster, or adjust the brakes (as appropriate). Road test to ensure that the brakes operate correctly.

8 Rear drum backplate - removal and refitting

For full information refer to Chapter 8, Section 3 which described removal of the axle shaft and hub assembly.

9 Master cylinder - removal and refitting

Standard model
1 Apply the handbrake and chock the front wheels. Drain the fluid from the master cylinder reservoir and master cylinder by attaching a plastic bleed tube to one of the front brake bleed screws. Undo the screw one turn and then pump the fluid out into a clean glass container by means of the brake pedal. Hold the brake pedal against the floor at the end of each stroke and tighten the bleed nipple. When the pedal has returned to its normal position, loosen the bleed nipple and repeat the process until the master cylinder reservoir is empty.
2 Wipe the area around the hydraulic pipe union on the master cylinder. Undo the union nut and lift out the hydraulic pipe (Fig.9.5).
3 Undo and remove the nuts and spring washers securing the master cylinder to the pedal bracket.
4 Straighten the ears on the split pin retaining the push rod to brake pedal clevis pin, extract the split pin, lift away the plain washer and withdraw the clevis pin.
5 Lift away the master cylinder taking care not to allow any hydraulic fluid to drip onto the paintwork.
6 To refit the master cylinder position the push rod in line with the top hole in the brake pedal. Insert the clevis pin, replace the plain washer and lock with a new split pin. It is important that the master cylinder pushrod is connected to the TOP HOLE of the two holes in the brake pedal lever.
7 Replace the two nuts and spring washers that secure the master cylinder to the pedal bracket. Tighten to a torque wrench setting of 15.5 to 19.5 lb ft (2.1 to 2.7 kg m).
8 Reconnect the hydraulic pipe to the master cylinder union. Slide down the union nut and very carefully start the threads. It is easy to cross thread. Tighten the union fully.
9 Refer to Section 3 and bleed the brake hydraulic system.

Servo model
1 Drain the hydraulic fluid from the reservoir and master cylinder as described in paragraph 1 in the previous sub section.
2 Wipe the area around the hydraulic pipe union on the master cylinder. Undo the union nut and lift out the hydraulic pipe.
3 Undo and remove the two nuts and spring washers that secure the master cylinder to the servo unit.
4 Lift away the master cylinder taking care not to allow any hydraulic fluid to drip onto the paintwork.
5 Refitting is the reverse sequence to removal. Refer to paragraphs 8 and 9 in the previous sub-section for additional information.

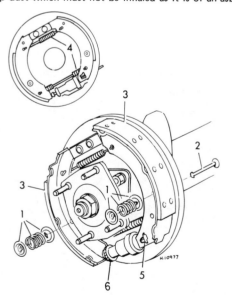

FIG.9.4b. REAR DRUM BRAKE ASSEMBLY (AUTOMATIC ADJUSTMENT TYPE)

1 *Cup washers and spring*
2 *Steady pin*
3 *Brake shoe*
4 *Brake shoe pull-off springs*
5 *Shoe retaining spring and support plate*
6 *Automatic adjuster ratchet wheel*

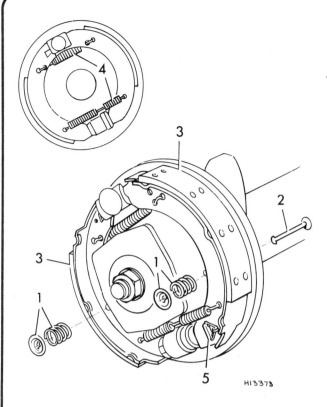

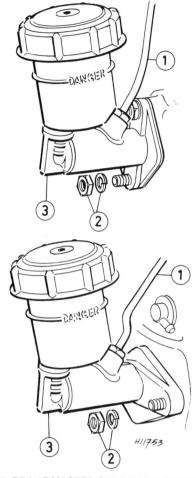

FIG.9.4c REAR DRUM BRAKE ASSEMBLY
(MANUAL ADJUSTMENT TYPE)

1 Cup washer and spring	4 Brake shoe pull-off springs
2 Steady pin	5 Shoe retaining spring and
3 Brake shoe	support plate

H13373

FIG.9.5. BRAKE MASTER CYLINDER ATTACHMENTS:
NON-SERVO; TOP. SERVO; BOTTOM

1 Hydraulic pipe	3 Master cylinder
2 Securing nut and spring washer	

H11753

FIG. 9.6. BRAKE MASTER CYLINDER
COMPONENT PARTS

1 Rubber boot
2 Circlip
3 Pushrod and dished washer
4 Piston assembly
5 Piston
6 Thimble
7 Piston seal
8 Spring
9 Valve
10 Valve spacer
11 Curved washer
12 Valve seal

Inset: Section through whole master cylinder
plus valve assembly

1 Seal
2 Dished washer
3 Valve spacer

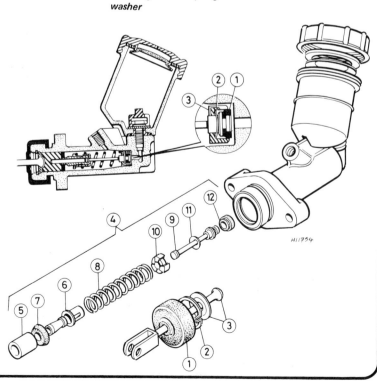

H11754

10 Master cylinder - dismantling and reassembly

If a replacement master cylinder is to be fitted, it will be necessary to lubricate the seals before fitting to the car as they have a protective coating when originally assembled. Remove the blanking plug from the hydraulic pipe union seating. Ease back and remove the plunger dust cover. Inject clean hydraulic fluid into the master cylinder and operate the piston several times so the fluid will spread over all the internal working surfaces.

If the master cylinder is to be dismantled after removal, proceed as follows:

1 Ease back the dust cover from the end of the master cylinder body. Using a pair of pointed pliers contract and lift out the circlip. Withdraw the pushrod and dished washer (Fig.9.6).
2 Carefully withdraw the complete piston assembly from the master cylinder bore. If this is difficult apply a low air pressure jet to the hydraulic pipe outlet connection.
3 With a small screwdriver lift the thimble leaf and separate the piston from the thimble.
4 Using the fingers remove the piston seal from the piston.
5 Compress the spring and remove the valve stem through the elongated hole in the thimble.
6 Lift away the thimble from the spring.
7 Remove the valve spacer and curved washer from the valve stem.
8 Carefully remove the valve seal from the valve head.
9 Thoroughly wash all parts in clean hydraulic fluid or methylated spirits.
10 Examine the bore of the cylinder carefully for any signs of scores or ridges. If this is found to be smooth all over, new seals can be fitted. If there is any doubt of the condition of the bore, then a new master cylinder must be fitted.
11 If examination of the seals shows them to be apparently oversize or swollen, or very loose on the piston or valve suspect oil contamination in the system. Ordinary lubricating oil will swell these rubber seals, and if one is found to be swollen it is reasonable to assume that all seals in the braking system will need attention.
12 All components should be assembled wet by dipping in clean brake fluid.
13 Fit the valve seal to the valve head so that the smallest diameter is on the valve head.
14 Fit the curved washer to the shoulder of the valve stem so that the domed side is to the shoulder.
15 Fit the valve spacer with the legs of the spacer towards the curved washer.
16 Locate the spring centrally on the valve spacer and insert the thimble into the spring.
17 Carefully push the end of the thimble so as to compress the spring against the valve spacer and insert the valve stem through the elongated hole of the thimble. Locate the valve stem in the centre of the thimble.
18 Fit the seal to the piston with the flat surface of the seal against the piston.
19 Insert the small end of the piston into the thimble until the thimble leaf engages under the shoulder of the piston.
20 Carefully insert the piston assembly into the master cylinder bore making sure the seal is not rolled or nipped as it enters the bore.
21 Fit the pushrod with the dished washer into the cylinder bore and retain in position with the circlip. Make sure the circlip is fully seated into its locating groove. Smear the pushrod and master cylinder bore of the dust cover with Girling Rubber Grease and refit the dust cover.
22 The master cylinder is now ready for refitting to the car.

11 Rear drum brake wheel cylinder - removal and refitting

1 If hydraulic fluid is leaking from the brake wheel cylinder, it will be necessary to dismantle it and replace the seal. Should brake fluid be found running down the side of the wheel or if it is noted that a pool of liquid forms alongside one wheel and the level in the master cylinder has dropped, it is indicative of seal failure.
2 Remove the brake drum and brake shoes as described in Section 7.
3 Wipe the top of the brake master cylinder reservoir and unscrew the cap. Place a piece of thin polythene sheet over the top of the reservoir and replace the cap.
4 Using an open ended spanner, carefully unscrew the hydraulic pipe connection union to the rear of the wheel cylinder. Note that the feed pipe from the left hand and right hand wheel cylinder locates in the lower opening (Fig.9.7).
5 Again using an open ended spanner undo and remove the bridge feed pipe from the right hand wheel cylinder.
6 Extract the split pin and lift away the washer and clevis pin that connects the handbrake cable yoke to the wheel cylinder operating lever.
7 Ease off the rubber boot from the rear of the wheel cylinder
8 Using a screwdriver carefully draw off the retaining plate and spring plate from the rear of the wheel cylinder.
9 The wheel cylinder may now be lifted away from the brake backplate. Detach the handbrake lever from the wheel cylinder.
10 To refit the wheel cylinder first smear the backplate where the wheel cylinder slides with a little Castrol PH Grease. Refit the handbrake lever on the wheel cylinder ensuring that it is the correct way round. The spindles of the lever must engage in the recess on the cylinder arms.
11 Slide the spring plate between the wheel cylinder and backplate. The retaining plate may now be inserted between the spring plate and wheel cylinder taking care the pips of the spring plate engage in the holes of the retaining plate.
12 Replace the rubber boot and reconnect the handbrake cable yoke to the handbrake lever. Insert the clevis pin, head upwards, and plain washer. Lock with a new split pin.
13 Refitting the brake shoes and drum is the reverse sequence to removal. Adjust the brakes as described in Section 2 (if manually adjusted) and finally bleed the hydraulic system following the instructions in Section 3.

12 Rear drum brake wheel cylinder - overhaul

1 Ease off the rubber dust cover protecting the open end of the cylinder bore (Fig.9.8).
2 Withdraw the piston from the wheel cylinder body.
3 Using fingers carefully remove the piston seal from the piston noting which way round it is fitted. (Do not use a screwdriver as this could scratch the piston).
4 Inspect the inside of the cylinder for score marks caused by impurities in the hydraulic fluid. If any are found the cylinder will require renewal. NOTE: If the wheel cylinder is to be renewed always ensure that the replacement is exactly similar to the one removed.
5 If the cylinder is sound, thoroughly clean it out with fresh hydraulic fluid.
6 The old rubber seal will probably be swollen and visibly worn so it must be discarded. Smear the new rubber seal with hydraulic fluid and fit it to the piston so that the small diameter is towards the piston.
7 Carefully insert the piston and seal into the bore making sure the fine edge lip does not roll or become trapped.
8 Refit the dust cover engaging the lip with the groove in the outer surface of the wheel cylinder body.

13 Front disc brake caliper - overhaul

1 Extract the two pad retaining pin spring clips and withdraw the two retaining pins (Fig.9.9).
2 Lift away the brake pads and anti-squeak shims noting which way round the shims are fitted.
3 Temporarily reconnect the caliper to the hydraulic system and support its weight. Do not allow the caliper to hang on the flexible hose, but support its weight. Using a small G clamp hold

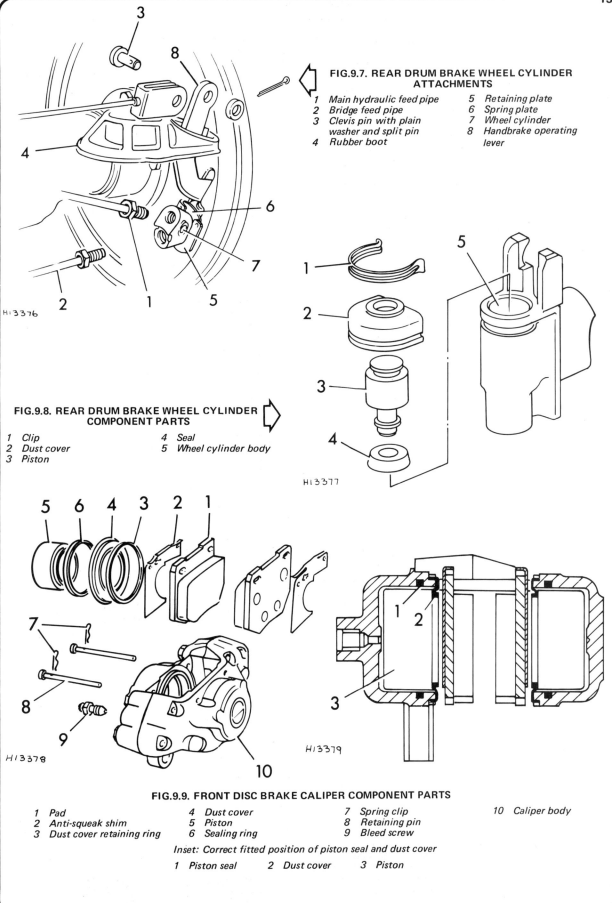

FIG.9.7. REAR DRUM BRAKE WHEEL CYLINDER ATTACHMENTS

1	Main hydraulic feed pipe	5	Retaining plate
2	Bridge feed pipe	6	Spring plate
3	Clevis pin with plain washer and split pin	7	Wheel cylinder
4	Rubber boot	8	Handbrake operating lever

H13376

FIG.9.8. REAR DRUM BRAKE WHEEL CYLINDER COMPONENT PARTS

1	Clip	4	Seal
2	Dust cover	5	Wheel cylinder body
3	Piston		

H13377

H13378

H13379

FIG.9.9. FRONT DISC BRAKE CALIPER COMPONENT PARTS

1	Pad	4	Dust cover	7	Spring clip	10 Caliper body
2	Anti-squeak shim	5	Piston	8	Retaining pin	
3	Dust cover retaining ring	6	Sealing ring	9	Bleed screw	

Inset: Correct fitted position of piston seal and dust cover

1 Piston seal   2 Dust cover   3 Piston

the piston in the mounting half of the caliper. Carefully depress the footbrake pedal with the bleed nipple open so as to bleed the system, and then close the nipple. Depress the footbrake again and this will push the piston in the rim half of the caliper outwards. Release the dust cover retaining ring and the cover. Depress the footbrake again until the piston has been ejected sufficiently to continue removal by hand. It is advisable to have a container or tray available to catch any hydraulic fluid once the piston is removed.

4 Using a tapered wooden rod or an old plastic knitting needle, carefully extract the fluid seal from its bore in the caliper half.

5 Remove the G clamp from the mounting half piston. Temporarily refit the rim half piston and repeat the operations in paragraphs 3 and 4 of this section.

6 Thoroughly clean the internal parts of the caliper using only clean hydraulic fluid or methylated spirits. Any other fluid cleaner will damage the internal seals, between the two halves of the caliper. DO NOT SEPARATE THE TWO HALVES OF THE CALIPER.

7 Inspect the caliper bores and pistons for signs of scoring which if evident a new assembly should be fitted.

8 To reassemble the caliper, first wet a new fluid seal with Castrol Girling Brake Fluid and carefully insert it into its groove in the rim half of the caliper seating, ensuring that it is correctly fitted. Refit the dust cover into its special groove in the cylinder.

9 Release the bleed screw in the caliper one complete turn. Coat the side of the piston with hydraulic fluid and with it positioned squarely in the top of the cylinder bore, ease the piston in until approximately 5/16 inch (7.94mm) is left protruding. Engage the outer lip of the dust cover in the piston groove and push the piston into the cylinder as far as it will go. Fit the dust cover retaining ring.

10 Repeat the operations in paragraphs 8 and 9 for the mounting half of the caliper.

11 Fit the pads and anti-squeak shims into the caliper and retain in position with the two pins and spring clips.

12 The caliper is now ready for refitting.

14 Handbrake cable - adjustment

1 Refer to Section 6 and adjust the rear brakes.

2 Chock the front wheels and completely release the handbrake. Pull up the handbrake four clicks on the ratchet.

3 Jack up the rear of the car and support on firmly based stands.

4 Check the cable adjustments by attempting to rotate the rear wheels. If this is possible the cable may be adjusted as described in the subsequent paragraphs.

5 Refer to Fig.9.10 and slacken the adjuster locknut.

6 Turn the adjustment nut clockwise whilst the outer cable is held with an open ended spanner until the correct adjustment is obtained. Retighten the locknut.

7 Release the handbrake and check that the rear wheels can be rotated freely.

8 Lower the rear of the car to the ground.

15 Handbrake cable - removal and refitting

1 Slacken the two adjustment nuts securing the cable to its support bracket.

2 Straighten the ears, extract the split pin locking the clevis pin retaining the inner cable yoke to the handbrake lever. Lift away the plain washer and withdraw the clevis pin (Fig.9.11).

3 Repeat the previous paragraphs sequence for the clevis pin on both rear wheel cylinder operating levers.

4 Undo and remove the bolt and spring washer that secures the handbrake cable clip to the axle casing.

5 Undo and remove the trunnion retaining nut and spring washer.

6 Slacken the nut securing the compensating levers to the bracket.

7 Slacken the nut securing the cables to the compensating lever and remove the cables.

8 Refitting the cables is the reverse sequence to removal. It will be necessary to adjust the handbrake as described in Section 13 of this chapter.

16 Handbrake lever assembly - removal and refitting

1 Draw back the floor covering from around the handbrake lever. Undo and remove the four self tapping screws retaining the handbrake lever gaiter to the floor panel.

2 Straighten the ears and extract the split pin retaining the handbrake cable to lever clevis pin. Lift away the plain washer and withdraw the clevis pin.

3 Slide the gaiter up the handbrake. Undo and remove the two nuts, spring washers and bolts that secure the handbrake lever assembly to its mounting bracket. Lift away the handbrake lever assembly.

4 Refitting the handbrake lever assembly is the reverse sequence to removal. Lubricate all pivots with Castrol GTX.

17 Brake pedal assembly - removal and refitting

1 Refer to Chapter 12 and remove the complete instrument panel and the front parcel tray.

2 Refer to Chapter 3 and remove the throttle pedal.

3 Refer to Chapter 5 and remove the clutch master cylinder.

4 Wipe the top of the brake master cylinder and remove the cap. Place a piece of thin piece of polythene over the top of the reservoir and refit the cap. This is to prevent the hydraulic fluid syphoning out during subsequent operations.

5 Disconnect the brake master cylinder fluid pipe from the four way connector on the bulkhead.

6 Slacken the clip and detach the vacuum hose from the servo unit connector if a brake servo unit is fitted.

7 Make a note of the cable connections on the ignition coil. Detach the cables and remove the ignition coil.

8 Undo and remove the nuts, bolts, spring and plain washers securing the pedal housing assembly to the bulkhead (Fig.9.12).

9 Partially withdraw the pedal assembly and disconnect the electrical connections at the stop light switch.

10 Carefully pull the throttle and speedometer cable through their grommets in the pedal assembly.

11 The pedal and housing assembly may now be lifted away from inside the car.

12 Detach the return spring from the brake and clutch pedals (Fig.9.13).

13 Undo and remove the locknut and plain washer retaining the brake pedal pivot pin. Lift away the throttle pedal stop noting which way round it is fitted.

14 Withdraw the clutch pedal complete with pivot pin and finally remove the brake pedal.

15 Refitting the pedal assembly is the reverse sequence to removal. Lubricate all pivots with Castrol GTX.

18 Brake servo unit - description

A vacuum servo unit can be fitted into the brake hydraulic circuit in series with the master cylinder, to provide power assistance to the driver when the brake pedal is depressed.

The unit operates by vacuum obtained from the induction manifold and comprises basically a booster diaphragm and a non-return valve.

The servo unit and hydraulic master cylinder are connected together so that the servo unit piston rod acts as the master cylinder pushrod. The driver's braking effort is transmitted through another pushrod to the servo unit piston and its built in control system. The servo unit piston does not fit tightly into the cylinder, but has a strong diaphragm to keep its edges in constant contact with the cylinder wall so assuring an air tight seal between the two parts. The forward chamber is held under

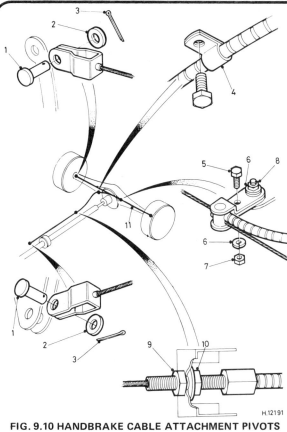

H.12191

H/3383

FIG. 9.10 HANDBRAKE CABLE ATTACHMENT PIVOTS

1 Clevis pin	7 Retaining nut
2 Plain washer	8 Trunnion retaining nut
3 Split pin	9 Locknut
4 Handbrake cable pin	10 Adjustment nut
5 Retaining bolt	11 Rear cable
6 Spring washer	

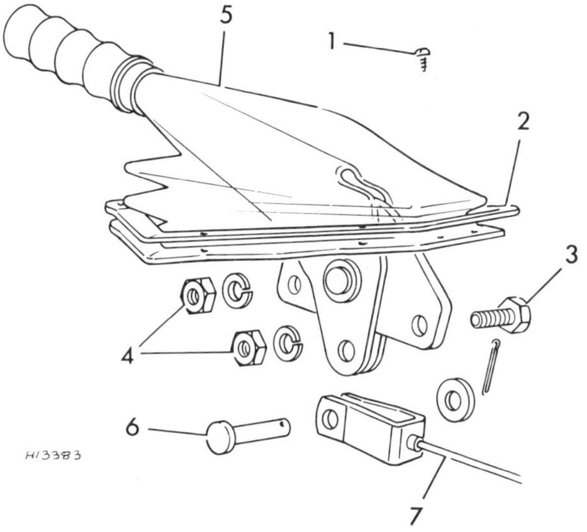

FIG.9.11. HANDBRAKE LEVER ATTACHMENTS

1 Self-tapping screw	5 Handbrake lever
2 Gaiter and metal plate	6 Clevis pin with plain
3 Mounting bolt	washer and split pin
4 Nut and spring washer	7 Handbrake cable

H11757

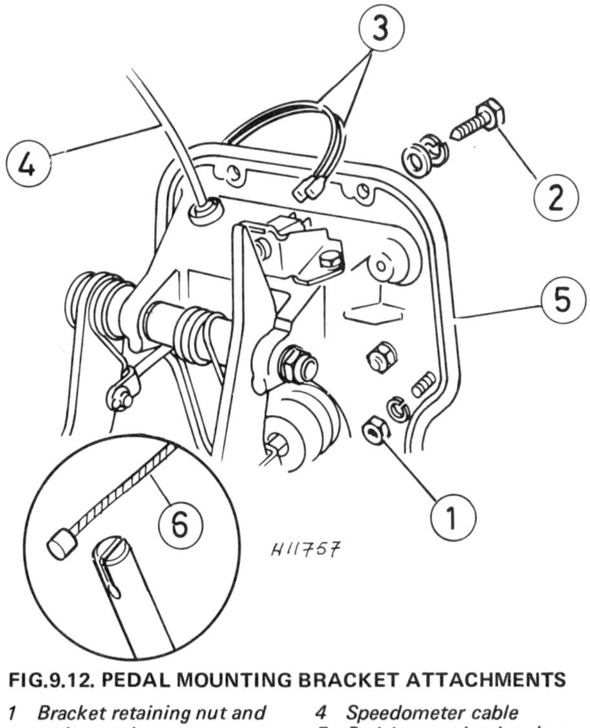

FIG.9.12. PEDAL MOUNTING BRACKET ATTACHMENTS

1 Bracket retaining nut and spring washer	4 Speedometer cable
2 Bracket retaining bolt with spring and plain washer	5 Pedal mounting bracket
3 Stop light cables	6 Inset: Throttle cable attachment to pedal

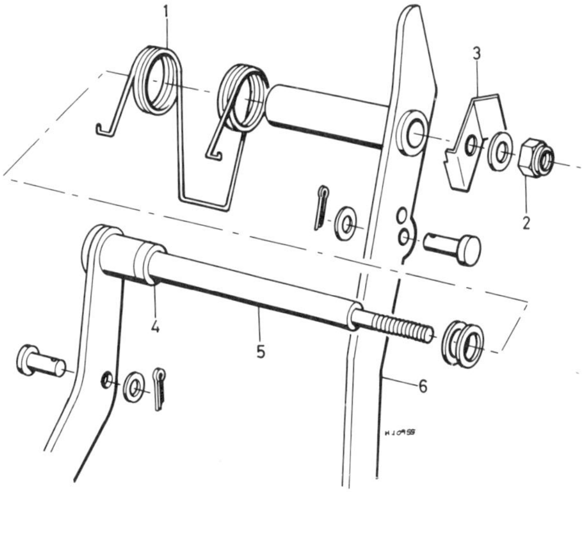

FIG.9.13. BRAKE AND CLUTCH PEDAL COMPONENTS

1 Return spring	4 Clutch pedal
2 Locknut and plain washer	5 Pivot pin
3 Throttle pedal stop	6 Brake pedal

vacuum conditions created in the inlet manifold of the engine and, during periods when the brake pedal is not in use, the controls open a passage to the rear chamber so placing it under vacuum. When the brake pedal is depressed, the vacuum passage to the rear chamber is cut off and the chamber opened to atmospheric pressure. The consequent rush of air pushes the servo piston forward in the vacuum chamber and operates the main pushrod to the master cylinder. The controls are designed so that assistance is given under all conditions and, when the brakes are not required, vacuum in the rear chamber is established when the brake pedal is released. Air from the atmosphere entering the rear chamber is passed through a small air filter.

19 Brake servo unit - removal and refitting

1 Refer to Section 8 and remove the brake master cylinder.
2 Slacken the hose clip and detach the vacuum hose from the servo connector.
3 Refer to Chapter 12 and remove the front parcel tray.
4 Detach the throttle cable from the throttle pedal (Fig.9.14).
5 Undo and remove the two nuts and spring washers that secure the throttle pedal bracket. Lift away the throttle pedal and bracket.

6 Straighten the ears of the split pin retaining the servo to brake pedal push rod clevis pin. Extract the split pin, lift away the plain washer and withdraw the clevis pin.
7 Undo and remove the four nuts and spring washers that secure the servo unit to the mounting bracket. Lift away the servo unit.
8 Refitting the servo unit is the reverse sequence to removal. It is important that the servo operating rod is attached to the BOTTOM hole of the two holes in the brake pedal lever. Bleed the brake hydraulic system as described in Section 3.

20 Brake servo unit - air filter renewal

Under normal operating conditions the vacuum servo unit is very reliable and does not require overhaul except possibly at very high mileages. In this case it is far better to obtain a service exchange unit, rather than repair the original.

However, the air filter may be renewed and fitting details are given. This will not however, repair any fault.
1 Pull back the dust cover (Fig.9.14) and slide up the push rod.
2 Using a screwdriver ease out the end cap and then with a pair of scissors cut off the old air filter.
3 Make a diagonal cut through the new air filter element and fit over the pushrod. Hold in position and refit the end cap.
4 Reposition the dust cover on the servo unit body.

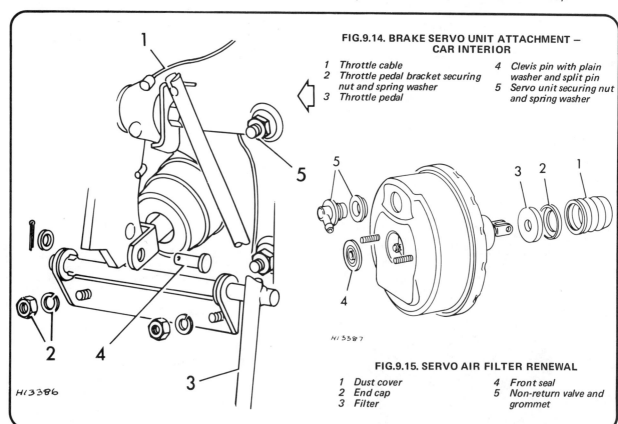

FIG.9.14. BRAKE SERVO UNIT ATTACHMENT — CAR INTERIOR

1 Throttle cable
2 Throttle pedal bracket securing nut and spring washer
3 Throttle pedal
4 Clevis pin with plain washer and split pin
5 Servo unit securing nut and spring washer

H13386

FIG.9.15. SERVO AIR FILTER RENEWAL

1 Dust cover
2 End cap
3 Filter
4 Front seal
5 Non-return valve and grommet

H13387

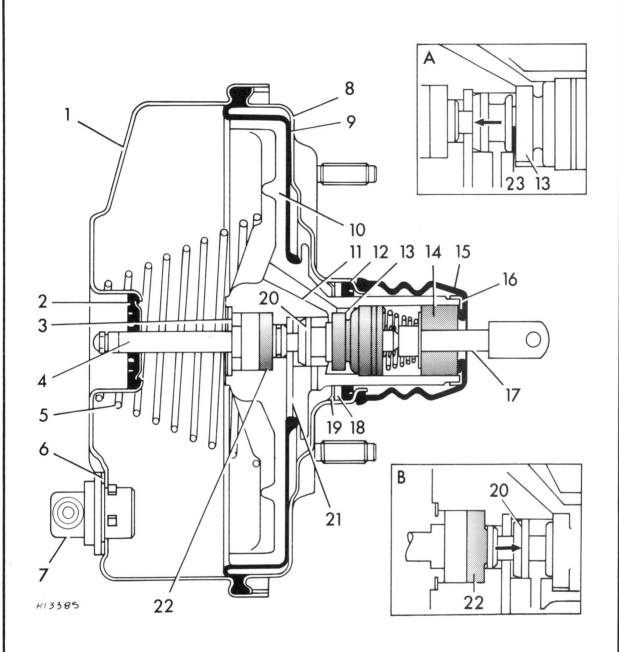

HI3385

FIG.9.16. GIRLING SUPERVAC SERVO UNIT – IN SECTION

1	Front shell	7	Non-return valve	13	Control valve	18	Bearing
2	Seal and plate assembly	8	Rear shell	14	Filter	19	Retainer
3	Retainer (sprag washer)	9	Diaphragm	15	Dust cover	20	Control piston
4	Pushrod (hydraulic)	10	Diaphragm plate	16	End cap	21	Valve retaining plate
5	Diaphragm return spring	11	Vacuum port	17	Valve operating rod	22	Reaction disc
6	'O' ring	12	Seal		assembly	23	Atmospheric port

Insets: A Control valve closed, control piston moved forward - atmospheric port open.
       B Pressure from diaphragm plate causes reation disc to extrude, presses back control piston and closes atmospheric port.

Symptom	Reason/s	Remedy
PEDAL TRAVELS ALMOST TO FLOORBOARDS BEFORE BRAKES OPERATE		
Leaks and air bubbles in hydraulic system	Brake fluid level too low	Top up master cylinder reservoir. Check for leaks.
	Wheel cylinder or caliper leaking	Dismantle wheel cylinder or caliper, clean fit new rubbers and bleed brakes.
	Master cylinder leaking (bubbles in master cylinder fluid)	Dismantle master cylinder, clean, and fit new rubbers. Bleed brakes.
	Brake flexible hose leaking	Examine and fit new hose if old hose leaking Bleed brakes.
	Brake line fractured	Replace with new brake pipe. Bleed brakes.
	Brake system unions loose	Check all unions in brake system and tighten as necessary. Bleed brakes.
Normal wear	Linings over 75% worn	Fit replacement shoes and brake linings.
BRAKE PEDAL FEELS SPRINGY		
Brake lining renewal	New linings not yet bedded-in	Use brakes gently until springy pedal feeling leaves.
	Brake drums or discs badly worn and weak or cracked	Fit new brake drums or discs.
	Master cylinder securing nuts loose	Tighten master cylinder securing nuts. Ensure spring washers are fitted.
BRAKE PEDAL FEELS SPONGY AND SOGGY		
Leaks or bubbles in hydraulic system	Wheel cylinder or caliper leaking	Dismantle wheel cylinder or caliper, clean, fit new rubbers, and bleed brakes.
	Master cylinder leaking (bubbles in master cylinder reservoir)	Dismantle master cylinder, clean, and fit new rubbers and bleed brakes. Replace cylinder if internal walls scored.
	Brake pipe line or flexible hose leaking	Fit new pipe line or hose.
	Unions in brake system loose	Examine for leaks, tighten as necessary.
BRAKES UNEVEN & PULLING TO ONE SIDE		
Oil or grease leaks	Linings and brake drums or discs contaminated with oil, grease, or hydraulic fluid	Ascertain and rectify source of leak, clean brake drums, fit new linings.
	Tyre pressures unequal	Check and inflate as necessary.
	Brake backplate caliper or disc loose	Tighten backplate caliper or disc securing nuts and bolts.
	Brake shoes or pads fitted incorrectly	Remove and fit shoes or pads correct way round.
	Different type of linings fitted at each wheel	Fit the linings specified all round.
	Anchorages for front or rear suspension loose	Tighten front and rear suspension pick-up points including spring locations.
	Brake drums or discs badly worn, cracked or distorted	Fit new brake drums or discs.
BRAKES TEND TO BIND, DRAG, OR LOCK-ON		
Incorrect adjustment	Brake shoes adjusted too tightly	Slacken off rear brake shoe adjusters two clicks.
	Handbrake cable over-tightened	Slacken off handbrake cable adjustment.
Wear or dirt in hydraulic system or incorrect fluid	Reservoir vent hole in cap blocked with dirt	Clean and blow through hole.
	Master cylinder by-pass port restricted - brakes seize in 'on' position	Dismantle, clean, and overhaul master cylinder. Bleed brakes.
	Wheel cylinder seizes in 'on' position	Dismantle, clean and overhaul wheel cylinder. Bleed brakes.
Mechanical wear	Drum brake shoe pull-off springs broken, stretched or loose	Examine springs and replace if worn or loose.
Incorrect brake assembly	Drum brake shoe pull-off springs fitted wrong way round, omitted, or wrong type used	Examine, and rectify as appropriate.

Chapter 10 Electrical system

For modifications, and information applicable to later models, see Supplement at end of manual

Contents

General description	1
Battery - removal and replacement	2
Battery - maintenance and inspection	3
Battery - electrolyte replenishment	4
Battery - charging	5
Alternator - general description	6
Alternator - routine maintenance	7
Starter motor - general description	8
Starter motor (M418G) - testing on engine	9
Starter motor (M418G) - removal and replacement	10
Starter motor (M418G) - dismantling and reassembly...	11
Starter motor (2M100 pre-engaged) - testing on engine ...	12
Starter motor (2M100 pre-engaged) - removal and replacement	13
Starter motor (2M100 pre-engaged) - dismantling and reassembly	14
Starter motor solenoid - removal and replacement	15
Flasher unit and circuit - fault tracing and rectification	16
Windscreen wiper arms - removal and replacement..	17
Windscreen wiper mechanism - fault diagnosis and rectification	18
Windscreen wiper blades - changing wiping arc...	19
Windscreen wiper motor - removal and replacement	20
Windscreen wiper motor - dismantling, inspection and reassembly	21
Wheelboxes and drive cable tubes - removal and replacement...	22
Horns - fault tracing and rectification..	23
Headlight units - removal and replacement	24
Headlight beam - adjustment	25
Side and front flasher bulbs - removal and replacement	26
Stop, tail and rear flasher bulbs - removal and replacement.. ...	27
Number plate light bulbs - removal and replacement	28
Panel illumination lamp bulbs - removal and replacement.. ...	29
Ignition, starter, steering lock switch - removal and replacement	30
Headlight dip/flasher, horn direction indicator switch - removal and replacement	31
Lighting switch - removal and replacement	32
Heater fan switch - removal and replacement	33
Stop light switch - removal and replacement..	34
Instrument panel printed circuit - removal and replacement...	35
Gauge units - removal and replacement	36
Speedometer - removal and replacement...	37
Speedometer cable - removal and replacement	38
Voltage stabilizer - removal and replacement	39
Instrument operation - testing	40
Fuses	41
Fault diagnosis	42

Specifications

12 volt negative earth type

Battery ... ...
Lucas A9, A11, A13
Exide 6VTP7 — BR, 6VTP9 — BR, 6VTPZ11 — BR

Capacity at 20 hr rate/maximum fast charge time

A9	40 amp : 1½ hours
A11...	50 amp : 1½ hours
A13...	60 amp : 1 hour
6VTP7 — BR	30 amp : 1½ hours
6VTP9 — BR	40 amp : 1½ hours
6VTPZ11 — BR	50 amp : 1½ hours

Alternator ... ...
Lucas 16ACR, 17ACR or 18ACR

Output at 14 volts and 6,000 rpm ... ...
34 amps (16ACR), 36 amps (17ACR), 45 amps (18ACR)

Maximum permissible rotor speed ... ...
12,500 rpm

Stator phases ... ...
3

Rotor poles ... ...
12

Rotor winding resistance at 20°C (68°F):

Alternator type	Resistance	Winding identification colour
16ACR	4.3 ohms ± 5%	Pink
16ACR	3.3 ohms ± 5%	Purple
17ACR	4.2 ohms ± 5%	Pink
17ACR	3.2 ohms ± 5%	Green
18ACR	3.2 ohms ± 5%	Green

Brush length (new) ... ...
0.5 inch (12.6 mm)

Brush spring tension ... ...
7 to 10 oz.f. (198 to 283 gm.f.) with brush face flush with brush box

Control unit ... ...
Integral with alternator

Starter motor ... ...
Lucas M418G inertia or 2M100 pre-engaged

	M418G	2M100
Lock torque	17 lb.f.ft. (2.35 kg.fm) with 420 amp load	14.4 lb.f.ft. (2.02 kg.f.m.) with 463 amp load
Torque at 1000 rpm	8 lb.f.ft. (1.11 kg.f m) with 320 amp load	7.3 lb.f.ft. (1.02 kg.f.m.) with 300 amp load
Light running current	45 amp at 7,400-8,500 rpm	40 amp at 6,000 rpm

Brush spring tension...	36 oz.f. (1.02 kg.f.)	36 oz.f. (1.02 kg.f.)
Brush length minimum	0.313 inch (7.938 mm)	0.375 inch (9.5 mm)
Solenoid pre-engaged type:		
Closing coil resistance	–	0.25 to 0.27 ohms
Holding coil resistance	–	0.76 to 0.80 ohms

Wiper motor	Lucas 14W (two speed)
Armature endfloat	0.004 to 0.008 inch (0.1 to 0.21 mm)
Light running current: normal speed	1.5 amp
high speed	2.0 amp
Light running speed:	
normal speed	46 to 52 rpm
high speed	60 to 70 rpm

Replacement bulb	Watts	Part Number
Headlamp	60/45	GLU 101
Sidelamp	6	GLB 9?9
Front flasher	21	GLB 382
Stop, tail lamp	6/21	GLB 380
Rear flasher	21	GLB 382
Number plate	5	GLB 501
Interior...	6	GLB 254
Panel and warning	2.2	37H 2139
Reverse lamp (when fitted)		BFS 272
Luggage compartment lamp (when fitted)		GLB 254
Automatic transmission selector (when fitted)...		88–625625

1 General description

The electrical system is of the 12 volt type and the major components comprise, a 12 volt battery of which the negative terminal is earthed, a Lucas alternator which is fitted to the front right hand side of the engine and is driven from the pulley on the front of the crankshaft, and a starter motor which is mounted on the rear right hand side of the engine.

The battery supplies a steady amount of current for the ignition, lighting and other electrical circuits, and provides a reserve of electricity when the current consumed by the electrical equipment exceeds that being produced by the alternator.

The battery is charged by a Lucas 16 ACR alternator and information will be found in Section 6.

When fitting electrical accesories to cars with a negative earth system it is important, if they contain silicone diodes or transistors, that they are connected correctly, otherwise serious damage may result to the component concerned. Items such as radios, tape recorders, electronic tachometer, automatic dipping, parking lamp and anti-dazzle mirrors should all be checked for correct polarity.

It is important that the battery negative lead is always disconnected if the battery is to be boost charged or if any body and most mechanical repairs are to be carried out, using electric arc welding equipment. Serious damage can be caused to the more delicate instruments, specially those containing semi-conductors. It is equally important to ensure that neither battery lead is disconnected while the engine is running, and that the battery terminals are not, inadvertently connected with the polarity reversed.

2 Battery - removal and replacement

1 The battery is in a special carrier fitted on the right hand wing valance of the engine compartment. It should be removed once every three months for cleaning and testing. Disconnect the negative and then the positive leads from the battery terminals by slackening the clamp retaining nuts and bolts or by unscrewing the retaining screws if terminal caps are fitted instead of clamps.

2 Unscrew the clamp bar retaining nuts, and lower the clamp bar to the side of the battery. Carefully lift the battery from its carrier. Hold the battery vertical to ensure that none of the electrolyte is spilled.

3 Replacement is a direct reversal of this procedure. NOTE: Replace the positive lead before the negative lead and smear the terminals with petroleum jelly (vaseline) to prevent corrosion. NEVER use an ordinary grease as applied to other parts of the car.

3 Battery - maintenance and inspection

1 Normal weekly battery maintenance consists of checking the electrolyte level of cells to ensure that the separators are covered by ¼ inch of electroyte. If the level has fallen, top up the battery using distilled water only. Do not overfill. If the battery is overfilled or any electrolyte spilled, immediately wipe away excess as electrolyte attacks and corrodes any metal it comes into contact with very rapidly.

2 If the battery is of the Lucas 'Pacemaker' design a special topping up procedure is necessary as follows:

a) The electrolyte levels are visible through the translucent battery case or may be checked by fully raising the vent cover and tilting to one side. The electrolyte level in each cell must be kept such that the separator plates are just covered. To avoid flooding the battery must not be topped up within half an hour of it having been charged from any source other than from the generating system fitted to the car.

b) To top up the levels in each cell, raise the vent cover and pour distilled water into the trough until all the rectangular filling slots are full of distilled water and the bottom of the trough is just covered. Wipe the cover seating grooves dry and press the cover firmly into position. The correct quantity of distilled water will automatically be distributed to each cell.

c) The vent must be kept closed at all times except when being topped up.

3 If the battery has the Auto-fill device fitted, a special topping up sequence is required. The white balls in the Auto-fill battery are part of the automatic topping up device which ensures correct electrolyte level. The vent chamber should remain in position at all times except when topping up or taking specific gravity readings. If the electrolyte level in any of the cells is below the bottom of the filling tube top up as follows:

a) Lift off the vent chamber cover.

b) With the battery level, pour distilled water into the trough until all the filling tubes and trough are full.

c) Immediately replace the cover to allow the water in the

trough and tubes to flow into the cells. Each cell will automatically receive the correct amount of water.

4 As well as keeping the terminals clean and covered with petroleum jelly, the top of the battery, and especially the top of the cells, should be kept clean and dry. This helps to prevent corrosion and ensures that the battery does not become partially discharged by leakage through dampness and dirt.

5 Inspect the battery securing nuts, battery clamp plate, tray and battery leads for corrosion (white fluffy deposits on the metal which are brittle to touch). If any corrosion is found, clean off the deposit with ammonia and paint over the clean metal with an anti-rust, anti-acid paint.

6 At the same time inspect the battery case for cracks. If a crack is found, clean and plug it with one of the proprietary compounds marked by such firms as Holts for this purpose. If leakage through the crack has been excessive then it will be necessary to refill the appropriate cell with fresh electrolyte as described later. Cracks are frequently caused at the top of the battery case by pouring in distilled water in the middle of winter AFTER instead of BEFORE a run. This gives the water no chance to mix with the electrolyte and so the former freezes and splits the battery case.

7 If topping up becomes excessive and the case has been inspected for cracks that could cause leakage, but none are found, the battery is being overcharged and the alternator output should be checked.

8 With the battery on the bench at the three monthly interval check, measure the specific gravity with a hydrometer to determine the state of charge and condition of the electrolyte. There should be very little variation between the different cells and, if a variation in excess of 0.025 is present, it will be due to either:

a) Loss of electrolyte from the battery at some time caused by spillage or a leak, resulting in a drop in the specific gravity of the electrolyte when the deficiency was replaced with distilled water instead of fresh electrolyte.

b) An internal short circuit caused by buckling of the plates or similar malady pointing to the likelihood of total battery failure in the near future.

9 The specific gravity of the electrolyte for fully charged conditions at the electrolyte temperature indicated, is listed in Table A. The specific gravity of a fully discharged battery at different temperatures of the electrolyte is given in Table B.

TABLE A

Specific gravity - battery fully charged

1.268 at 100°F or 38°C electrolyte temperature
1.272 at 90°F or 32°C electrolyte temperature
1.276 at 80°F or 27°C electrolyte temperature
1.280 at 70°F or 21°C electrolyte temperature
1.284 at 60°F or 16°C electrolyte temperature
1.288 at 50°F or 10°C electrolyte temperature
1.292 at 40°F or 4°C electrolyte temperature
1.296 at 30°F or -1.5°C electrolyte temperature

TABLE B

Specific gravity - battery fully discharged

1.098 at 100°F or 38°C electrolyte temperature
1.102 at 90°F or 32°C electrolyte temperature
1.106 at 80°F or 27°C electrolyte temperature
1.110 at 70°F or 21°C electrolyte temperature
1.114 at 60°F or 16°C electrolyte temperature
1.118 at 50°F or 10°C electrolyte temperature
1.122 at 40°F or 4°C electrolyte temperature
1.126 at 30°F or -1.5°C electrolyte temperature

4 Battery - electrolyte replenishment

1 If the battery is in a fully charged state and one of the cells maintains a specific gravity reading which is 0.025 or lower than the others and a check of each cell has been made with a voltage meter to check for short circuits (a four to seven second test should give a steady reading of between 1.2 and 1.8 volts), then it is likely that electrolyte has been lost from the cell with the low reading at some time.

2 Top up the cell with a solution of 1 part sulphuric acid to 2.5 parts of water. If the cell is already fully topped up draw some electrolyte out of it with a pipette. The total capacity of each cell is approximately 1/3 pint.

3 When mixing the sulphuric acid and water NEVER ADD WATER TO SULPHURIC ACID — always pour the acid slowly onto the water in a glass container. IF WATER IS ADDED TO SULPHURIC ACID IT WILL EXPLODE.

4 Continue to top up the cell with the freshly made electrolyte and to recharge the battery and check the hydrometer readings.

5 Battery charging

1 In winter time when a heavy demand is placed on the battery, such as when starting from cold, and much electrical equipment is continually in use, it is a good idea to occasionally have the battery fully charged from an external source at a rate of 3.5 to 4 amps.

2 Continue to charge the battery at this rate until no further rise in specific gravity is noted over a four hour period.

3 Alternatively, a trickle charger, charging at the rate of 1.5 amps can be safely used overnight.

4 Special rapid 'boost' charges which are claimed to restore the power of the battery in 1 to 2 hours are most dangerous unless they are thermostatically controlled as they can cause serious damage to the battery plates through overheating.

5 While charging the battery note that the temperature of the electrolyte should never exceed 100°F.

6 Alternator - general description

A Lucas alternator is fitted as standard to many models covered by this manual. The main advantage of the alternator lies in its ability to provide a high charge at low revolutions. Driving slowly in heavy traffic with a dynamo invariably means no charge is reaching the battery. In similar conditions even with the wipers, heater, lights and perhaps radio switched on, the alternator will ensure a charge reaches the battery.

An important feature of the alternator is a built in output control regulator, based on 'thick film' hybrid integrated micro-circuit technique, which results in this alternator being a self contained generating and control unit.

The system provides for direct connection of a charge light, and eliminates the need for a field switching relay and warning light control unit, necessary with former systems.

The alternator is of the rotating field ventilated design and comprises pricipally a laminated stator on which is wound a star connected 3 phase output winding, a twelve pole rotor carrying the field windings - each end of the rotor shaft runs in ball race bearings which are lubricated for life, natural finish aluminium dicast end brackets, incorporating the mounting lugs, a rectifier pack for converting the AC output of the machine to DC for battery charging, and an output control regulator.

The rotor is belt driven from the engine through a pulley keyed to the rotor shaft. A pressed steel fan adjacent to the pulley draws cooling air through the machine. This fan forms an integral part of the alternator specification. It has been designed to provide adequate air flow with a minimum of noise, and to withstand the high stresses associated with maximum speed. Rotation is clockwise viewed on the drive end. Maximum continuous rotor speed is 12500 rpm.

Rectification of alternator output is achieved by six silicone diodes housed in a rectifier pack and connected as a 3 phase full wave bridge. The rectifier pack is attached to the outer face of the slip ring end bracket and contains also three 'field' diodes. At normal operating speeds, rectified current from the stator output windings flows through these diodes to provide self excitation of the rotor field, via brushes bearing on face type slip rings.

The slip rings are carried on a small diameter moulded drum attached to the rotor shaft outboard of the rotor shaft axle, while the outer ring has a mean diameter of ¾ inch. By keeping the mean diameter of the slip rings to a minimum, relative speeds between brushes and rings, and hence wear, are also minimal. The slip rings are connected to the rotor field winding by wires carried in grooves in the rotor shaft.

The brush gear is housed in a moulding screwed to the outside of the slip ring end bracket. This moulding thus encloses the slip ring and brush gear assembly, and together with the shielded bearing, protects the assembly against the entry of dust and moisture.

The regulator is set during manufacture and requires no further attention. Briefly the 'thick film' regulator comprises resistors and conductors screen printed onto a 1 inch square aluminium substrate. Mounted on the substrate are Lucas semi-conductors consisting of three transistors, a voltage reference diode and a field recirculation diode, and two capacitors. The internal connections between these components and the substrate are made by Lucas patented connectors. The whole assembly is 1/16 inch thick and is housed in a recess in an aluminium heat sink, which is attached to the slip ring end bracket. Complete hermetic sealing is achieved by a silicone rubber encapsulent to provide environmental protection.

Electrical connections to external circuits are brought out to Lucar connector blades, these being grouped to accept a moulded connector socket which ensure correct connections.

7 Alternator - routine maintenance

1   The equipment has been designed for the minimum amount of maintenance in service, the only items subject to wear being the brushes and bearings.
2   Brushes should be examined after 60,000 miles (100,000 km) and renewed if necessary. This is a job best left to the local BLMC garage or auto-electrical engineering works.
3   The bearings are pre-packed with grease for life, and should not require any further attention.
4   For full information on fan belt adjustment see Chapter 2.

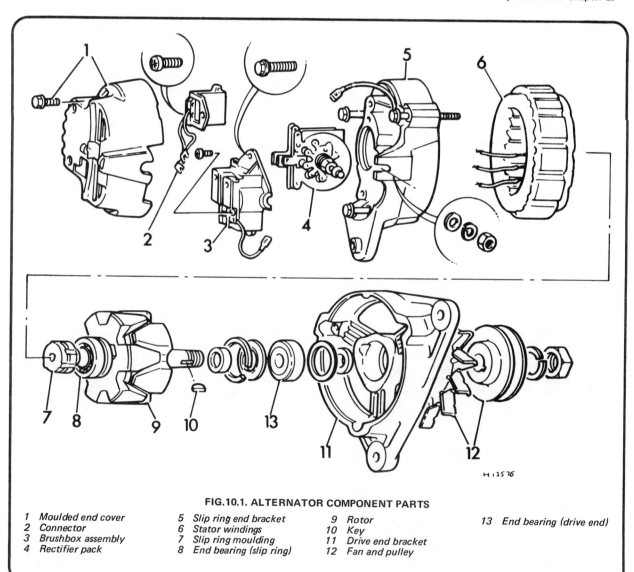

FIG.10.1. ALTERNATOR COMPONENT PARTS

1 Moulded end cover	5 Slip ring end bracket	9 Rotor
2 Connector	6 Stator windings	10 Key
3 Brushbox assembly	7 Slip ring moulding	11 Drive end bracket
4 Rectifier pack	8 End bearing (slip ring)	12 Fan and pulley

13 End bearing (drive end)

8 Starter motor - general description

One of two types of starter motor have been fitted to the 1.8 Marina models., an inertia or pre-engaged type.

Both starter motors are interchangeable and engage with a common flywheel starter ring gear. The relay for the inertia starter motor is mounted next to the ignition coil whereas the pre-engaged type has the solenoid switch on the top of the motor.

The principle of operation of the inertia type starter motor is as follows: When the ignition switch is turned, current flows from the battery to the starter motor solenoid switch which causes it to become energized. Its internal plunger moves inwards and closes an internal switch so allowing full starting current to flow from the battery to the starter motor. This creates a powerful magnetic field to be induced into the field coils which causes the armature to rotate.

Mounted on helical spines is the drive pinion which, because of the sudden rotation of the armature, is thrown forwards along the armature shaft and so into engagement with the flywheel ring gear. The engine crankshaft will then be rotated until the engine starts to operate on its own and, at this point, the drive pinion is thrown out of mesh with the flywheel ring gear.

The method of engagement on the pre-engaged starter differs considerably in that the drive pinion is brought into mesh with the starter ring gear before the main starter current is applied.

When the ignition is switched on, current flows from the battery to the solenoid which is mounted on the top of the starter motor body. The plunger in the solenoid moves inwards so causing a centrally pivoted lever to move in such a manner that the forked end pushes the drive pinion into mesh with the starter ring gear. When the solenoid plunger reaches the end of its travel, it closes an internal contact and full starting current flows to the starter field coils. The armature is then able to rotate the crankshaft so starting the engine.

A special one way clutch is fitted to the starter drive pinion so that when the engine just fires and starts to operate on its own, it does not drive the starter motor.

9 Starter motor (M418G) - testing on engine

1 If the starter motor fails to operate, then check the condition of the battery by turning on the headlamps. If they glow brightly for several seconds and then gradually dim, the battery is in an uncharged condition.
2 If the headlamps glow brightly and it is obvious that the battery is in good condition then check the tightness of the battery wiring connections (and in particular the earth lead from the battery terminal to its connection on the body frame).Check the tightness of the connections at the solenoid switch and at the starter motor. Check the wiring with a voltmeter for breaks or shorts due to failure of insulation.
3 If the wiring is in order then check that the starter motor switch is operating. To do this, press the rubber covered button in the centre of the solenoid switch located next to the ignition coil, if it is working the starter motor will be heard to 'click' as it tries to rotate. Alternatively check it with a voltmeter.
4 If the battery is fully charged, with wiring in order, and the switch working but the starter motor fails to operate then it will have to be removed from the car for examination. Before this is done, however, ensure that the starter pinion has not jammed in mesh with the flywheel. Check by turning the square end of the armature shaft with a spanner. This will free the pinion if it is stuck in engagement with the flywheel teeth.

10 Starter motor (M418G) - removal and replacement

1 Disconnect the negative and then the positive terminals from the battery. Also disconnect the starter motor cable from the terminal on the starter motor end cover.
2 Undo and remove the bolt and spring washer and the nut and spring washer that secure the starter motor to the engine back-plate.
3 Lift the starter motor away by manipulating the drive gear out from the ring gear area and then from the engine compartment.

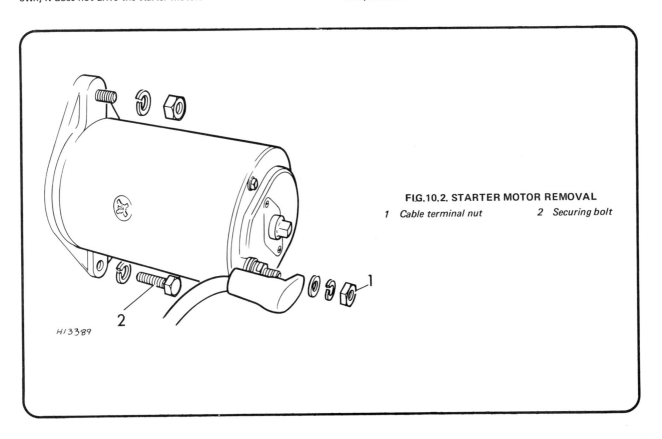

FIG.10.2. STARTER MOTOR REMOVAL
1   Cable terminal nut   2   Securing bolt

4 Refitting is the reverse sequence to removal. Make sure that the starter motor cable, when secured in position by its terminal retaining nut does not touch any part of the body or power unit which could damage the insulation.

11 Starter motor (M418G) - dismantling and reassembly

Such is the reliability of starter motors generally and the difficulty in undertaking an effective repair without special equipment any dismantling and overhaul work is best left to an auto electrician. However, the drive gear can be dismantled from this type of starter motor easily if this, solely, is at fault. An exploded component illustration, Fig.10.3, is given to show just how a starter motor would dismantle.

1 To dismantle the starter motor drive, first use a press or large valve spring compressor to push the retainer clear of the circlip which can then be removed. Lift away the retainer and main spring.

2 Slide off the remaining parts with a rotary action of the armature shaft.

3 It is most important that the drive gear is completely free from oil, grease and dirt. With the drive gear removed, clean all parts thoroughly in paraffin. Under no circumstances oil the drive components. Lubrication of the drive components could easily cause the pinion to stick.

4 Reassembly of the starter motor drive is the reverse sequence to dismantling. Use a press or the large valve spring compressor to compress the spring and retainer sufficiently to allow a new circlip to be fitted to its groove on the shaft.

FIG. 10.3. M418G STARTER MOTOR COMPONENT PARTS

1	Drive assembly	19	Drive end bracket
2	Circlip	20	Bush — driving end
3	Anchor platofront	21	Commutator end bracket
4	Main spring	22	Bush — commutator end
5	Drive head sleeve	23	Shaft cap
6	Retaining pin*	24	Terminal nuts and washers
7	Thrust washer (fibre)	25	Terminal post
8	Anchor plate — rear	26	Through-bolt
9	Screwed sleeve	27	Brush tension spring
10	Retaining ring*	28	Brush
11	Control nut	29	Field coils
12	Cushioning spring	30	Armature*
13	Thrust washer — control nut	31	Cover band
14	Locating collar	32	Armature**
15	Circlip	33	Drive head sleeve**
16	Anti-drift spring	34	Spiral pin**
17	Pinion and barrel	35	Waved circlip**
18	Woodruff key	36	Cover band seal**

  * For starter motors Serial No 25555
 ** For starter motors Serial No 25598

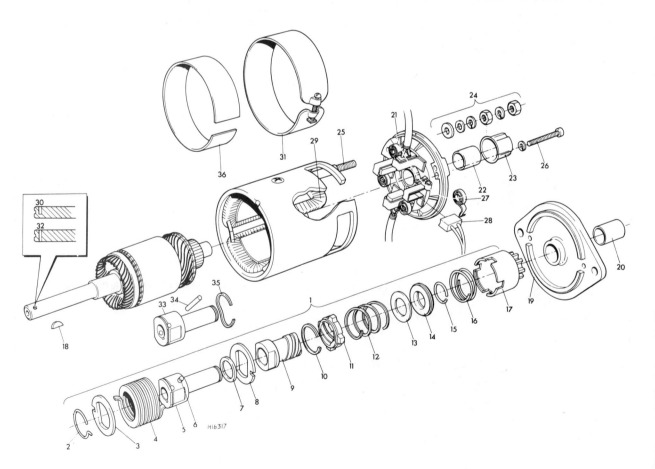

12 Starter motor (2M100 pre-engaged) - testing on engine

The testing procedure is basically similar to the inertia engagement type as described in Section 9. However, note the following instructions before finally deciding to remove the starter motor.

Ensure that the pinion gear has not jammed in mesh with the flywheels due either to a broken solenoid spring or dirty pinion gear splines. To release the pinion, engage a low gear and, with the ignition switched off, rock the car backwards and forwards which should release the pinion from mesh with the ring gear. If the pinion still remains jammed the starter motor must be removed for further examination.

13 Starter motor (2M100 - pre-engaged) - removal and replacement

1 Disconnect the positive and then the negative terminals from the battery.
2 Make a note of the electrical connections at the rear of the solenoid and disconnect the top heavy duty cable. Also release the two Lucar terminals from the rear of the solenoid. There is no need to undo the lower heavy duty cable at the rear of the solenoid.
3 Undo and remove the bolt and spring washer, and nut and spring washer which hold the starter motor in place and lift away upwards.

4 Replacement is a straightforward reversal of the removal sequence. Check that the electtrical cable connections are clean and firmly attached to their respective terminals.

14 Starter motor (2M100 - pre-engaged) - dismantling and reassembly

See Section 11 concerning the difficulty in effective repairs on the inertia starter motor. The pre-engaged is of similar complexity and should be left totally in the hands of an auto electrician.

Again an exploded component illustration is given, Fig.10.4 to show how this type of starter motor would dismantle.

15 Starter motor solenoid - removal and replacement

1 For safety reasons disconnect the battery.
2 Carefully ease back the rubber cover to gain access to the terminals (see Fig.10.3).
3 Make a note of the Lucar terminal connections and detach these connections.
4 Undo and remove the heavy duty cable terminal connection nuts and spring washers. Detach the two terminal connectors.
5 Undo and remove the two retaining screws and lift away the solenoid.
6 Refitting is the reverse sequence to removal.

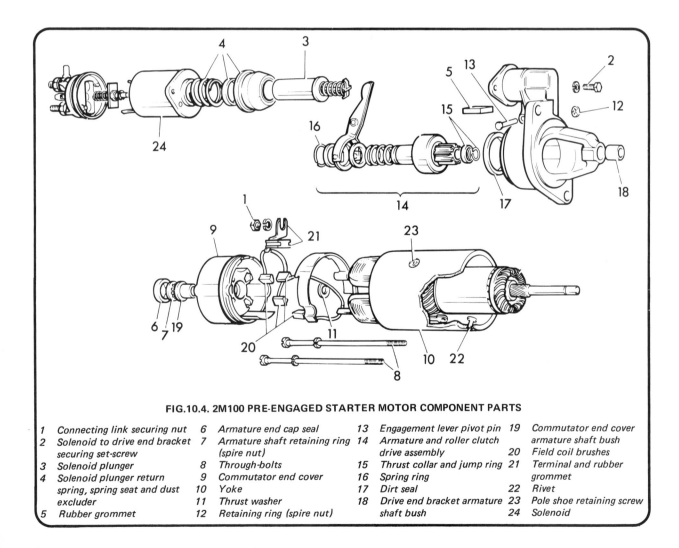

FIG.10.4. 2M100 PRE-ENGAGED STARTER MOTOR COMPONENT PARTS

1	Connecting link securing nut	6	Armature end cap seal	13	Engagement lever pivot pin
2	Solenoid to drive end bracket securing set-screw	7	Armature shaft retaining ring (spire nut)	14	Armature and roller clutch drive assembly
3	Solenoid plunger	8	Through-bolts	15	Thrust collar and jump ring
4	Solenoid plunger return spring, spring seat and dust excluder	9	Commutator end cover	16	Spring ring
		10	Yoke	17	Dirt seal
5	Rubber grommet	11	Thrust washer	18	Drive end bracket armature shaft bush
		12	Retaining ring (spire nut)		

19	Commutator end cover armature shaft bush
20	Field coil brushes
21	Terminal and rubber grommet
22	Rivet
23	Pole shoe retaining screw
24	Solenoid

16 Flasher unit and circuit - fault tracing and rectification

The flasher unit located as shown in Fig.10.5 is enclosed in a small metal container and is operated only when the ignition is on by the composite switch mounted on the right hand side of the steering column.

If the flasher unit fails to operate, or works either very slowly or very rapidly, check out the flasher indicator circuit as described below, before assuming there is a fault in the unit itself.

1   Examine the direction indicator bulbs front and rear for broken filaments.

2   If the external flashers are working but the internal flasher warning lights on one or both sides have ceased to function, check the filaments and replace as necessary.

3   With the aid of the wiring diagram check all the flasher circuit connections if a flasher bulb is sound but does not work.

4   In the event of total indicator failure check fuse A3 - A4.

5   With the ignition switched on, check that current is reaching the flasher unit by connecting a voltmeter between the 'plus' or 'B' terminal and earth. If this test is positive, connect the 'plus' or 'B' terminal and the 'L' terminal and operate the flasher switch. If the flasher bulb lights up the flasher unit itself is defective and must be replaced as it is not possible to dismantle and repair it.

6   To remove the flasher unit first disconnect the battery. Make a note of the electrical cable terminal positions and detach the two terminal connections. The unit may now be pulled out from its holder.

7   Refitting the flasher unit is the reverse sequence to removal.

17 Windscreen wiper arms - removal and replacement

1   Before removing a wiper arm, turn the windscreen wiper switch on and off to ensure the arms are in their normal parked position with the blades parallel with the bottom of the windscreen.

2   To remove the arm, pivot the arm back and pull the wiper arm head off the splined drive, at the same time easing back the clip with a screwdriver.

3   When replacing an arm, place it so it is in the correct relative parked position and then press the arm head onto the splined drive until the retaining clip clicks into place.

18 Windscreen wiper mechanism - fault diagnosis and rectification

Should the windscreen wipers fail, or work very slowly then check the terminals for loose connections, and make sure the insulation of the external wiring is not broken or cracked. If this is in order, then check the current the motor is taking by connecting up an ammeter in the circuit and turning on the wiper switch. Consumption should be 1.5 amps for normal speed or 2 amps for high speeds.

If no current is passing, check the A3 - A4 fuse. If the fuse has blown, replace it after having checked the wiring to the motor and other electrical circuits serviced by this fuse for short circuits. Further information will be found in Section 40. If the fuse is in good condition, check the wiper switch. Should the wiper take a very high current, check the wiper blades for freedom of movement. If this is satisfactory check the wiper motor and drive cable for signs of damage. Measure the end float which should be between 0.002 - 0.008 inch (0.051 - 0.203mm). The end float is set by the thrust screw. Check that excessive friction in the cable connecting tubes, caused by too small a curvature, is not the cause of the high current consumption.

If the motor takes a very low current, ensure that the battery is fully charged. Check the brush gear after removing the commutator yoke assembly, and ensure that the brushes are free to move. If necessary, renew the tension springs. If the brushes are very worn they should be replaced with new ones. The armature may be checked by substitution.

19 Windscreen wiper blades - changing wiping arc

If it is wished to change the area through which the wiper blades move, this is simply done by removing each arm in turn from each splined drive, and then replacing it on the drive in a slightly different position.

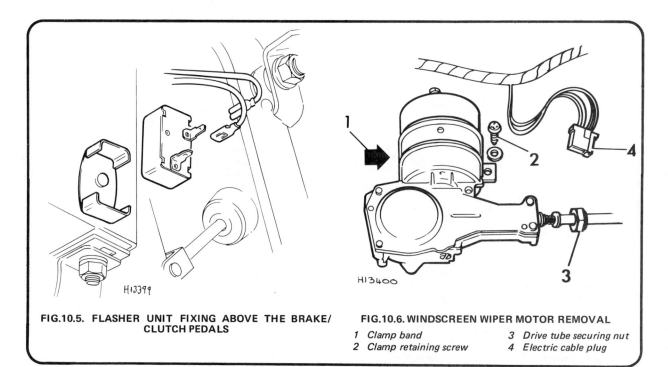

FIG.10.5. FLASHER UNIT FIXING ABOVE THE BRAKE/ CLUTCH PEDALS

FIG.10.6. WINDSCREEN WIPER MOTOR REMOVAL

1   Clamp band   3   Drive tube securing nut
2   Clamp retaining screw   4   Electric cable plug

20 Windscreen wiper motor - removal and replacement

1   Refer to Section 17 and remove the wiper arms and blades.
2   Undo and remove the screw and plain washer that secures the wiper motor clamp to the body valance. Release the clamp and rubber moulding by pressing the clamp band into the release slot (Fig.10.6).
3   Undo the wiper drive tube securing nut and slide the nut down the tube.
4   Next disconnect the electrical cable plug from the motor socket.
5   Lift the motor clear of the body valance whilst at the same time pulling the inner cable from the tube.
6   Refitting the wiper motor and inner cable is the reverse sequence to removal. Take care in feeding the inner cable through the outer tube and engaging the inner cable with each wiper wheelbox spindle. Lubricate the inner cable with Castrol LM Grease.

21 Windscreen wiper motor - dismantling, inspection and reassembly

The only repair which can be effectively undertaken by the do it yourself mechanic to a wiper motor is brush replacement. Anything more serious than this will mean either exchanging the complete motor or having a repair done by an auto electrician. Spare part availability is really the problem. Brush replacement is described here.
1. Refer to Fig.10.7 and remove the four gearbox cover retaining screws and lift away the cover. Release the circlip and flat washer securing the connecting rod to the crankpin on the shaft and gear. Lift away the connecting rod followed by the second flat washer.
2   Release the circlip and flat washer securing the shaft and gear to the gearbox body.
3   De-burr the gear shaft and lift away the gear making careful note of the location of the dished washer.
4   Scribe a mark on the yoke assembly and gearbox to ensure correct reassembly and unscrew the two yoke bolts from the motor yoke assembly. Part the yoke assembly including armature from the gearbox body. As the yoke assembly has residual magnetism ensure that the yoke is kept well away from metallic dust.
5   Unscrew the two screws securing the brush gear and the terminal and switch assembly and remove both the assemblies.
6   Inspect the brushes for excessive wear. If the main brushes are worn to a limit of 3/16 inch (4.76mm) or the narrow section of the third brush is worn to the full width of the brush fit a new brush gear assembly. Ensure that the three brushes move freely in their boxes.
7   Reassembly at this stage is a straight reversal of disassembly.

22 Wheelboxes and drive cable tubes - removal and replacement

1   Refer to Section 20 and remove the windscreen wiper motor.
2   Refer to Chapter 12 and remove the instrument panel.
3   Refer to Chapter 12 and remove the glovebox.
4   Refer to Section 17 and remove the windscreen wiper arms.
5   Undo and remove the nuts that secure the wheelboxes to the body. Lift away the shaped spacer from each wheelbox (Fig.10.8).

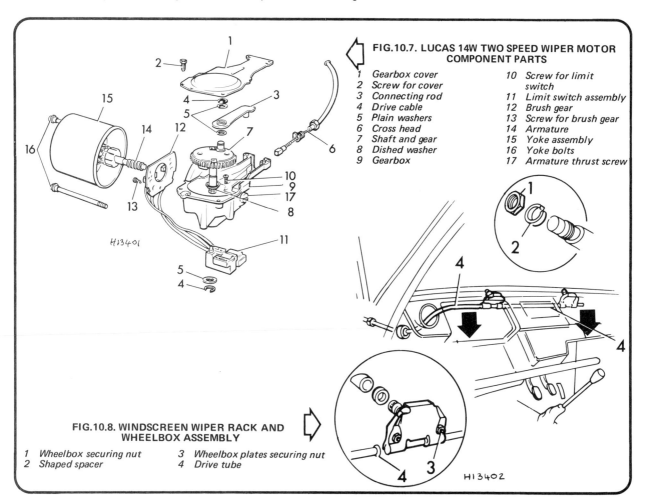

FIG.10.7. LUCAS 14W TWO SPEED WIPER MOTOR COMPONENT PARTS

1 Gearbox cover	10 Screw for limit switch
2 Screw for cover	
3 Connecting rod	11 Limit switch assembly
4 Drive cable	12 Brush gear
5 Plain washers	13 Screw for brush gear
6 Cross head	14 Armature
7 Shaft and gear	15 Yoke assembly
8 Dished washer	16 Yoke bolts
9 Gearbox	17 Armature thrust screw

FIG.10.8. WINDSCREEN WIPER RACK AND WHEELBOX ASSEMBLY

1 Wheelbox securing nut	3 Wheelbox plates securing nut
2 Shaped spacer	4 Drive tube

6 Slacken the two nuts that clamp the two wheelbox plates on the glovebox side. Carefully pull out the drive tube from the wheelbox.
7 Carefully remove the free drive tube and its grommet through the glovebox opening.
8 Lift away the two wheelbox units through the instrument panel opening.
9 Recover the spacer and washer from each wheelbox unit.
10 Refitting the wheelboxes and drive cable tubes is the reverse sequence to removal.

23 Horns - fault tracing and rectification

1 If a horn works badly or fails completely, first check that the wiring leading to it for short circuits and loose connections. Also check that the horn is firmly secured and that there is nothing lying on the horn body.
2 The horn is protected by the A1 - A2 fuse and if this has blown the circuit should be checked for short circuits. Further information will be found in Section 40.
3 The horn should never be dismantled, but it is possible to adjust it. This adjustment is to compensate for wear of the moving parts only and will not affect the tone. To adjust the horn proceed as follows:
a) There is a small adjustment screw on the broad rim of the horn, nearly opposite the two terminals (See Fig.10.9). Do not confuse this with the large screw in the centre.
b) Turn the adjustment screw anti-clockwise until the horn just fails to sound. Then turn the screw a quarter of a turn clockwise which is the optimum setting.
c) It is recommended that if the horn has to be reset in the car, the A1 - A2 fuse should be removed and replaced with a piece of wire, otherwise the fuse will continually blow due to the high current required for the horn in continual operation.
d) Should twin horns be fitted, the horn which is not being adjusted should be disconnected while adjustments of the other takes place.

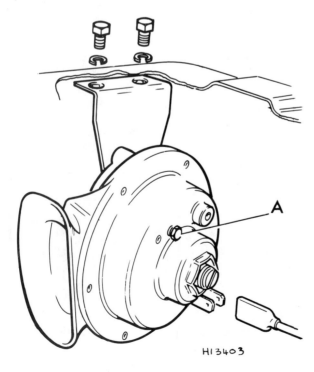

H13403

FIG.10.9. THE HORN

A Adjustment screw

24 Headlight units - removal and replacement

1 Sealed beam (or renewable bulb) light units are fitted.
2 The method of gaining access to the light unit for replacement is identical for all types of light units and bulbs.
3 Undo and remove the four screws that secure the top of the front grille to the body panel.
4 Carefully lift the grille outwards and upwards so releasing it from its locating holes in the body.
5 Undo and remove the three securing screws and lift away the headlamp rim.
6 Sealed beam unit: Disconnect the plug from the rear of the light unit and lift away the light unit.
   Spring clip bulb holder: Disconnect the plug from the bulb holder and release the spring clip from the reflector. Lift away the bulb.
   Cap type bulb holder: Push and turn the cap anti-clockwise. Lift off the cap and withdraw the bulb.
7 Refitting in all cases is the reverse sequence to removal. Where a bulb is fitted make sure that the locating clip or slot in the bulb correctly registers in the reflector.

25 Headlight beam - adjustment

1 The headlights may be adjusted for both vertical and horizontal beam positions by the two screws, these being shown in Fig. 10.10.
2 They should be set so that on full or high beam, the beams are set slightly below parallel with a level road surface. Do not forget that the beam position is affected by how the car is normally loaded for night driving, and set the beams with the car loaded to the position.
3 Although this adjustment can be set approximately at home, it is recommended that this be left to a local garage who will have the necessary equipment to do the job more accurately.

26 Side and front flasher bulbs - removal and replacement

1 Undo and remove the two screws securing the lamp lens to the lamp body and lift away the lenses (Fig.10.11).
2 Either bulb is retained by a bayonet fixing, so to remove a bulb push in slightly and rotate in an anti clockwise direction.
3 Refitting is the reverse sequence to removal. Take care not to tighten the two lens retaining screws as the lenses can be easily cracked.

27 Stop, tail and rear flasher bulbs - removal and replacement

1 Open the boot lid.
2 The bulb holders may now be drawn downwards and rearwards into the luggage compartment (Fig.10.12).
3 Two bulbs are used, the inner one being of the double filament type and are retained in position by a bayonet fixing. To remove a bulb, push in slightly and rotate in an anti clockwise direction.
4 The double filament bulb has offset pins on the bayonet fixing so it is not possible to fit it the wrong way round.
5 Refitting is the reverse sequence to removal.

28 Number plate light bulb - removal and replacement

1 The lenses may be removed by depressing and turning through 90o lift away the lenses (Fig.10.13).
2 Carefully pull on the bulb and it will be released from its holder. It will be noticed that capless bulbs are used.
3 Refitting is the reverse sequence to removal.

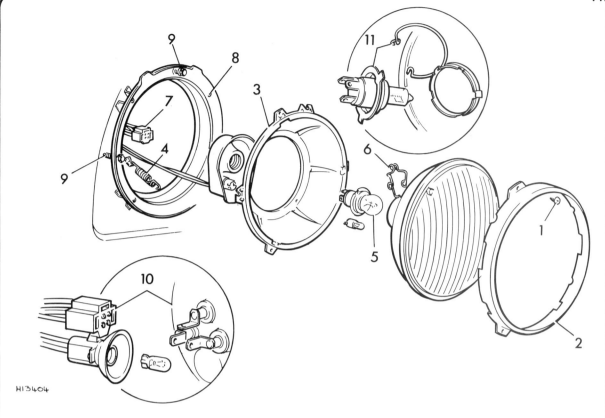

FIG.10.10. HEADLIGHT UNIT COMPONENT PARTS

1	Rim securing screw	4	Inner shell tensioning spring	7	Electrical connector	10	Sealed beam type fitting
2	Rim	5	Bulb	8	Snap rivet	11	Renewable bulb type fitting
3	Inner shell	6	Bulb clip	9	Vertical and horizontal adjustment screws		

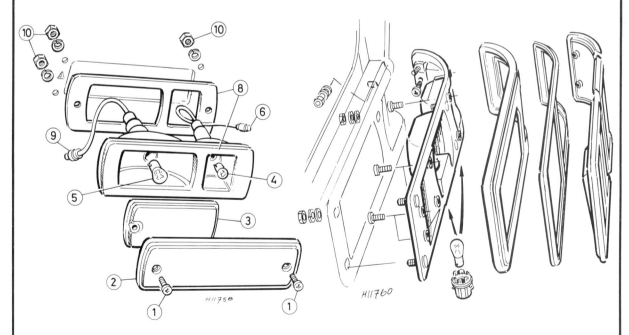

FIG.10.11. SIDE AND FRONT FLASHER ASSEMBLY

1	Lens securing screws	6	Sidelamp connection
2	Lens - plain	7	Light assembly body
3	Lens - coloured	8	Rubber seal
4	Sidelamp bulb	9	Flasher connection
5	Flasher bulb	10	Light assembly retaining nuts

FIG.10.12. STOP, TAIL AND REAR FLASHER ASSEMBLY

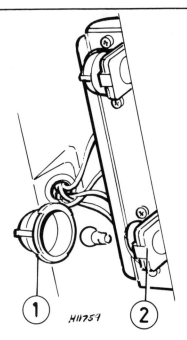

FIG.10.13. REAR NUMBER PLATE LIGHTS

1 Lens   *2 Fixing clip*

29 Panel illumination lamp bulb - removal and replacement

1 Disconnect the battery.
2 Refer to Chapter 12 and remove the instrument panel.
3 Pull out the bulb holder from the rear of the panel giving access to the bulb (Fig.10.14).
4 Carefully pull on the bulb and it will be released from its holder. It will be noticed that capless bulbs are used.
5 Refitting is the reverse sequence to removal.

30 Ignition, starter, steering lock switch - removal and replacement

1 Disconnect the battery.
2 Undo and remove the four screws that secure the switch cowls. Lift the cowls from over the switch stalks.
3 Detach the multi-pin plug from the electrical leads to the switch assembly at the harness socket (Fig.10.15).
4 Undo and remove the one screw that retains the switch assembly in the lock housing.
5 Slide the switch assembly from the lock housing.
6 Refitting is the reverse sequence to removal. Make sure that the locating peg on the switch correctly registers in the groove in the lock housing.

31 Headlight dip/flasher, horn, direction indicator switch - removal and replacement

1 Disconnect the battery and remove the steering column cowl.
2 Refer to Chapter 11 and remove the steering wheel.
3 Detach the multi-pin plug from the electrical leads to the switch assembly at the harness socket located under the facia (Fig.10.16).
4 Slacken the switch clamp tightening screw located on the underside of the switch and ease the switch assembly from the steering column.

FIG.10.16 COMBINATION SWITCH ATTACHMENTS

1 Multi pin plug   *3 Switch assembly*
2 Switch clamp screw

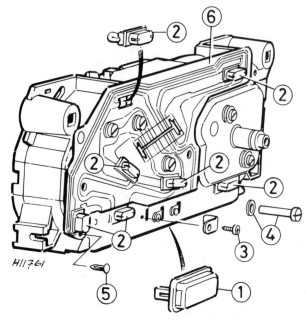

FIG.10.14. REAR VIEW OF INSTRUMENT PANEL

1 Voltage stabilizer   *4 Sleeve screw and washer*
2 Light bulb holders in situ   *5 Plastic retaining peg*
3 Tab connector retaining screw   *6 Printed circuit*

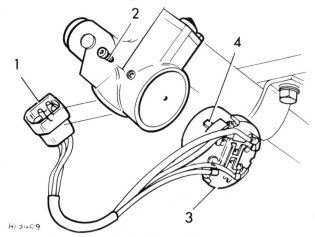

FIG.10.15. COMBINED IGNITION, STARTER AND STEERING LOCK SWITCH

1 Multi pin plug   *3 Switch assembly*
2 Switch assembly retaining screw   *4 Locating peg*

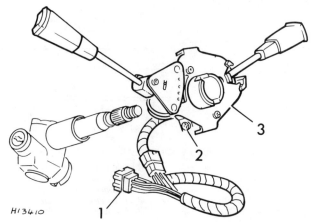

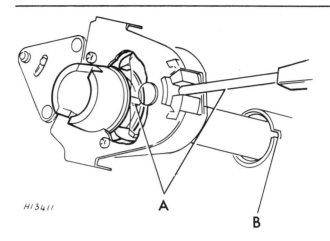

H13411

FIG.10.17. COMBINATION SWITCH ALIGNMENT

5   Refitting the switch assembly is the reverse sequence to removal. Make sure that the lug on the inner diameter of the switch locates in the slot in the outer steering column as shown in 'B' Fig.10.17 and also that the striker dog on the nylon switch centre is in line with and towards the switch stalk 'A'.

32 Lighting switch - removal and replacement

1   Disconnect the battery.
2   Withdraw the choke control as far as possible (manual choke only).
3   Undo and remove the two crosshead screws retaining the finisher, and move the finisher up the choke control knob as far as possible (Fig.10.18).
4   Make a note of the two cable connections at the rear of the switch and detach the two terminals.
5   To remove the switch it is necessary to compress four little clips, two each side of the switch body and then draw the switch forwards from the panel. Although a U shaped tool is desirable to do this it is possible for one person to compress the clips whilst a second person pulls the switch forwards.
6   Refitting the lighting switch is the reverse sequence to removal.

33 Heater fan switch - removal and replacement

1   Disconnect the battery.
2   Carefully pull off the two heater control knobs.
3   Undo and remove the three crosshead screws securing the finisher. Lift away the finisher.
4   Make a note of the two cable connections at the rear of the switch and detach the two terminals.
5   To remove the switch it is necessary to compress four little clips, two each side of the switch body and then draw the switch forwards from the panel. Although a U shaped tool is desirable to do this it is possible for one person to compress the clips whilst a second person pulls the switch forwards.
6   Refitting the heater fan switch is the reverse sequence to removal.

34 Stop light switch - removal and replacement

1   Make a note of the two cable connections at the rear of the switch located on the top of the brake pedal mounting bracket. Detach the two terminals (Fig.10.19).
2   Undo and remove the two bolts and spring washers securing the switch mounting bracket to the brake pedal mounting bracket. Lift away the switch and bracket.

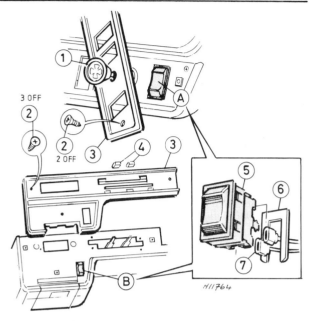

H11764

FIG.10.18. LIGHTING SWITCH (A) AND HEATER FAN SWITCH (B) REMOVAL

1   Choke control
2   Finisher retaining screw
3   Finisher
4   Heater control knob
5   Switch
6   'U' shape metal tool to compress switch clips
7   Switch terminal connectors

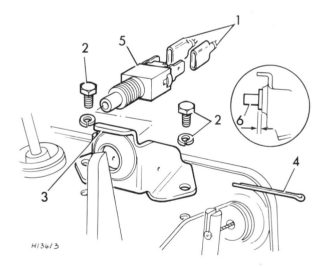

H13413

FIG.10.19. STOP LIGHT SWITCH REMOVAL

1   Switch terminal connections
2   Switch bracket securing screw and spring washer
3   Bracket
4   Split pin
5   Switch
6   Switch adjustment

3   Straighten the ears of the switch locking split pin and withdraw the split pin.
4   The switch may now be unscrewed from its mounting bracket.
5   Refitting the stop light switch is the reverse sequence to removal. It is however, necessary to adjust the position of the switch when refitting to its mounting bracket.
6   Screw the switch into its mounting bracket until one complete thread of the switch housing is visible on the pedal side of the bracket. Lock with a new split pin.

35 Instrument panel printed circuit - removal and replacement

1   Refer to Chapter 12 and remove the instrument panel.
2   Withdraw the voltage stabilizer from the rear of the instrument panel printed circuit.
3   Withdraw the warning light and panel light bulb holders from the speedometer and gauges.
4   Undo and remove the three screws securing the voltage stabiliser tag connectors to the rear of the instrument panel printed circuit. Lift away the tag connector.
5   Undo and remove the four long sleeve screws and shaped washers that secure the gauge units to the rear of the instrument panel.
6   Very carefully ease out the plastic pegs securing the printed circuit to the rear of the instrument panel. Lift away the printed circuit.
7   Refitting the printed circuit is the reverse sequence to removal.

36 Gauge units - removal and replacement

1   This section is applicable for the removal of either the fuel gauge or temperature gauge.
2   Refer to Chapter 12 and remove the instrument panel.
3   Undo and remove the four screws and washers that secure the instrument pack to the instrument panel.
4   Undo and remove the four long sleeve screws and shaped washers that secure the gauge units to the rear of the instrument panel.
5   Spring back the three clips that retain the instrument glass and panel.
6   Undo and remove the three screws that secure the instruments face plate.
7   Lift away the fuel gauge and/or temperature gauge.
8   Refitting the gauge units is the reverse sequence to removal.

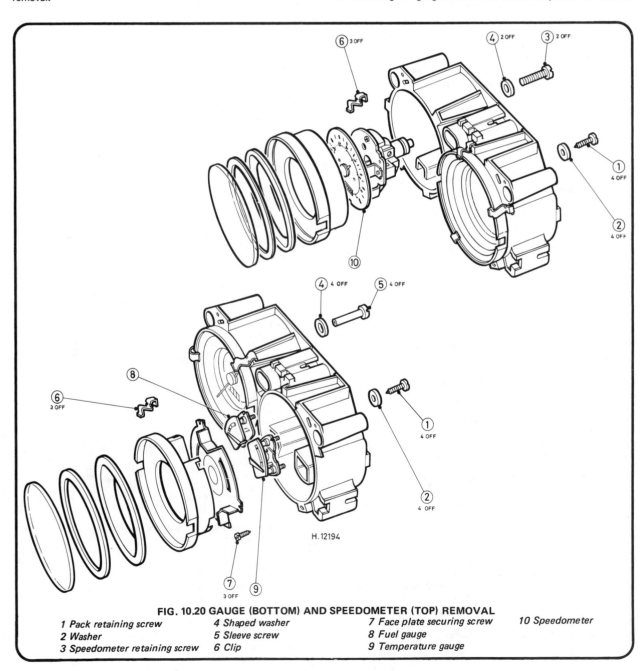

FIG. 10.20 GAUGE (BOTTOM) AND SPEEDOMETER (TOP) REMOVAL

1 Pack retaining screw	4 Shaped washer	7 Face plate securing screw	10 Speedometer
2 Washer	5 Sleeve screw	8 Fuel gauge	
3 Speedometer retaining screw	6 Clip	9 Temperature gauge	

37 Speedometer - removal and replacement

1 Refer to Chapter 12 and remove the instrument panel.
2 Undo and remove the four screws and washers that secure the instrument pack to the instrument panel. Lift away the instrument pack.
3 Undo and remove the two screws that secure the speedometer in position.
4 Spring back the three clips that retain the instrument glass and bezel. Lift away the speedometer head.

38 Speedometer cable - removal and replacement

1 Working under the car, disconnect the speedometer cable from the gearbox by removing the bolt that secures the cable retaining flange. Then withdraw the cable from the drive pinion in the gearbox. Disconnect the battery earth lead.
2 Working from behind the instrument panel, release the speedometer cable from the speedometer head by depressing the cable locking clip and withdrawing the cable from the speedometer head.
3 The inner cable can now be withdrawn from the outer cable.
4 To remove the outer cable, pull it through the brake pedal housing complete with grommet.
5 Replacement is the reverse of the removal procedure. Ensure that the rubber grommet is properly located in the brake pedal housing.

39 Voltage stabilizer - removal and replacement

1 The voltage stabilizer is a push fit into the rear of the instrument panel printed circuit.
2 Before removal, as a safety precaution disconnect the battery.
3 Carefully pull the voltage stabilizer from the rear of the printed circuit.
4 Refitting is the reverse sequence to removal. Note that the terminals of the stabilizer are offset, so it cannot be fitted the wrong way round.

40 Instrument operation - testing

The bi-metal resistance equipment for the fuel and thermal type temperature gauges comprises an indicator head and transmitter with the unit connected to a common voltage stabilizer. This item is fitted because the method of operation of the equipment is voltage sensitive, and a voltage stabilizer is necessary to ensure a constant voltage supply at all times.

Special test equipment is necessary when checking the operation of the stabilizer but should it be found that both the fuel and temperature gauges are both reading inaccurately, it is worth-while removing the stabilizer and tapping it firmly onto a hard surface; in many cases this will provide at the very least a temporary cure.

The gauges can be checked by applying 8 volts dc directly to their terminals; this can be done in-situ by removing the voltage stabilizer and connecting 8 volts (+) to the I socket on the rear of the printed circuit panel and 8 volts (-) to earth. The gauges should give a full scale deflection. If the leads to the thermal transmitter or fuel tank unit are disconnected, the gauges should not give any reading when the ignition is switched on. If these leads are then earthed, both gauges should give a full scale deflection.

41 Fuses

The fuse box is located inside the car behind the facia panel just above the parcel shaft and is attached to the inner body panel on the steering wheel side of the car.

Fuse A1 - A2: This has a 35 amp rating and protects the equipment which operates independant of the ignition switch. These include, interior lamp, horn-push, headlamp flasher and luggage compartment lamp (if fitted). When fitting accessories which are required to operate independantly of the ignition circuit connect to the terminal marked '2'.

Fuse A3 - A4: This has a 35 amp rating and protects the circuits which operate only when the ignition is switched on. These include, flashing direction indicators, windscreen wiper motor, brake stop warning lamps, reverse lamps (when fitted), and heated backlight (when fitted). When fitting accessories which are required to operate only when the ignition is switched on, connect to the terminal marked '4'.

A line fuse located in a cylindrical fuse holder adjacent to the instrument wiring connector near the fuse box protects the rear and number plate light bulbs.

A second line fuse located adjacent to the heater blower motor switch protects the heater blower motor. This fuse is accessible from behind the centre facia panel.

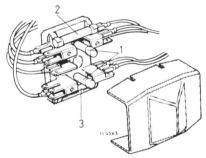

1 Spare fuses   2 35 amp fuse   3 35 amp fuse

42 Fault diagnosis

Symptom	Reason/s	Remedy
STARTER MOTOR FAILS TO TURN ENGINE		
No electricity at starter motor	Battery discharged	Charge battery.
	Battery defective internally	Fit new battery.
	Battery terminal leads loose or earth lead not securely attached to body	Check and tighten leads.
	Loose or broken connections in starter motor circuit	Check all connections and check any that are loose.
	Starter motor switch or solenoid faulty	Test and replace faulty components with new
Electricity at starter motor: faulty motor	Starter motor pinion jammed in mesh with ring gear	Disengage pinion by turning squared end of armature shaft.
	Starter brushes badly worn, sticking, or brush wires loose	Examine brushes, replace as necessary, tighten down brush wires.
	Commutator dirty, worn, or burnt	Clean commutator, recut if badly burnt.
	Starter motor armature faulty	Overhaul starter motor, fit new armature.
	Field coils earthed	Overhaul starter motor.

Symptom	Reason/s	Remedy
STARTER MOTOR TURNS ENGINE VERY SLOWLY		
Electrical defects	Battery in discharged condition	Charge battery.
	Starter brushes badly worn, sticking, or brush wires loose	Examine brushes, replace as necessary, tighten down brush wires.
	Loose wires in starter motor circuit	Check wiring and tighten as necessary.
STARTER MOTOR OPERATES WITHOUT TURNING ENGINE		
Dirt or oil on drive gear	Starter motor pinion sticking on the screwed sleeve	Remove starter motor, clean starter motor drive.
Mechanical damage	Pinion or ring gear teeth broken or worn	Fit new gear ring, and new pinion to starter motor drive.
STARTER MOTOR NOISY OR EXCESSIVELY ROUGH ENGAGEMENT		
Lack of attention or mechanical damage	Pinion or ring gear teeth broken or worn	Fit new ring gear, or new pinion to starter motor drive.
	Starter drive main spring broken	Dismantle and fit new main spring.
	Starter motor retaining bolts loose	Tighten starter motor securing bolts. Fit new spring washer if necessary.
BATTERY WILL NOT HOLD CHARGE FOR MORE THAN A FEW DAYS		
Wear or damage	Battery defective internally	Remove and fit new battery.
	Electrolyte level too low or electrolyte too weak due to leakage	Top up electrolyte level to just above plates.
	Plate separators no longer fully effective	Remove and fit new battery.
	Battery plates severely sulphated	Remove and fit new battery.
	Drive belt slipping	Check belt for wear, replace if necessary, and tighten.
	Battery terminal connections loose or corroded	Check terminals for tightness, and remove all corrosion.
	Short in lighting circuit causing continual battery drain	Trace and rectify.
	Regulator unit not working correctly	Check setting, clean, and replace if defective.
IGNITION LIGHT FAILS TO GO OUT, BATTERY RUNS FLAT IN A FEW DAYS		
Dynamo not charging	Drive belt loose and slipping, or broken	Check, replace, and tighten as necessary.
	Brushes worn, sticking, broken or dirty	Examine, clean, or replace brushes as necessary.
	Brush springs weak or broken	Examine and test. Replace as necessary.
	Commutator dirty, greasy, worn, or burnt	Clean commutator and undercut segment separators.
	Armature badly worn or armature shaft bent	Fit new or reconditioned armature.
Or alternator not charging		Seek professional advice from BLMC garage.
WIPERS		
Wiper motor fails to work	Blown fuse	Check and replace fuse if necessary.
	Wire connections loose, disconnected, or broken	Check wiper wiring. Tighten loose connections.
	Brushes badly worn	Remove and fit new brushes.
	Armature worn or faulty	If electricity at wiper motor remove and overhaul and fit replacement armature.
	Field coils faulty	Purchase reconditioned wiper motor.
Wiper motor works very slow and takes excessive current	Commutator dirty, greasy, or burnt	Clean commutator thoroughly.
	Drive to wheelboxes too bent or unlubricated	Examine drive and straighten out severe curvature. Lubricate.
	Wheelbox spindle binding or damaged	Removal, **overhaul, or fit replacement.**
	Armature bearings dry or unaligned	Replace with new bearings correctly aligned.
	Armature badly worn or faulty	Remove, overhaul, or fit replacement armature.
Wiper motor works slowly and takes little current	Brushes badly worn	Remove and fit new brushes.
	Commutator dirty, greasy, or burnt	Clean commutator thoroughly.
	Armature badly worn or faulty	Remove and overhaul armature or fit replacement.
Wiper motor works but wiper blades remain static	Driving cable rack disengaged or faulty	Examine and if faulty, replace.
	Wheelbox gear and spindle damaged or worn	Examine and if faulty, replace.
	Wiper motor gearbox parts badly worn	Overhaul or fit new gearbox.

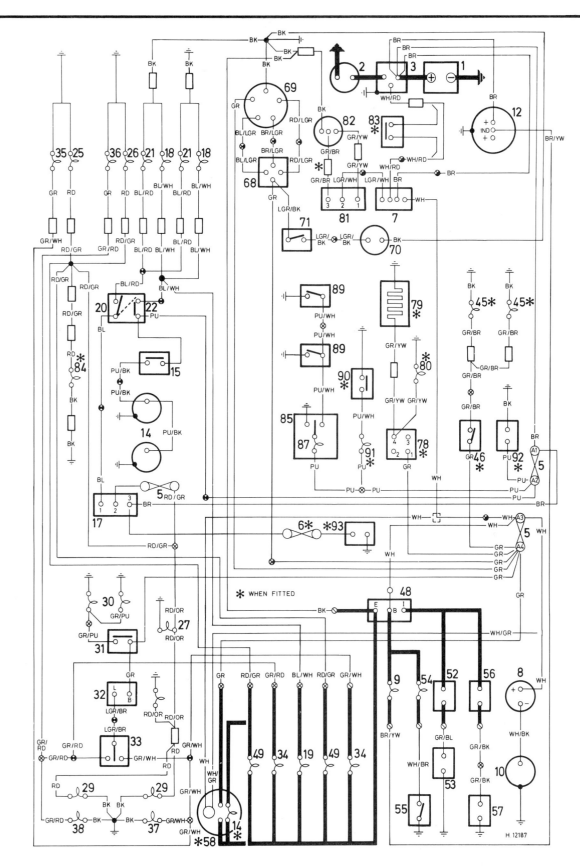

THEORETICAL WIRING DIAGRAM FOR MK I MODELS WITH ALTERNATOR
The coding is given on page 154

Key to wiring diagram on page 242

1 Battery
2 Starter motor
3 Starter motor solenoid
4 Starter motor (pre-engaged)
5 Fuse unit
6 In-line fuse
7 Ignition switch
8 Ignition coil
9 Ignition warning lamp
10 Distributor
11 Dynamo
12 Alternator
13 Control box (A-RB106, B-RB340)
14 Horn(s)
15 Horn switch
16 Ballast resistor (coil)
17 Lighting switch
18 Headlamp main beam
19 Main beam warning lamp
20 Dip switch
21 Headlamp dipped beam
22 Headlamp flasher switch
23 Headlamp (inner - RH)
24 Headlamp (inner - LH)
25 Sidelamp (RH)
26 Sidelamp (LH)
27 Rear lamp (RH)
28 Rear lamp (LH)
29 Number plate lamp(s)
30 Stop lamp(s)
31 Stop lamp switch
32 Indicator unit
33 Indicator switch
34 Indicator warning lamp
35 Indicator (front - RH)
36 Indicator (front - LH)
37 Indicator (rear - RH)
38 Indicator (rear — LH)
39 Indicator repeater unit
40 Indicator repeater lamp (RH)
41 Indicator repeater lamp (LH)
42 Hazard warning lamp
43 Hazard warning switch
44 Hazard warning flasher unit
45 Reversing lamp(s)
46 Reversing lamp(s) switch
47 Reversing lamp(s) and auto inhibitor switch
48 Voltage stabilizer
49 Panel lamp(s)

50 Panel lamp(s) resistor
51 Printed circuit instrument panel
52 Fuel gauge
53 Fuel gauge sender unit
54 Oil pressure warning lamp
55 Oil pressure switch
56 Water temperature gauge
57 Water temperature gauge sender unit
58 Tachometer
59 Clock
60 Split braking test switch
61 Split braking shuttle valve
62 Handbrake switch
63 Handbrake warning lamp
64 Anti-run-on valve
65 Anti-run-on valve relay
66 Mixture control warning lamp switch
67 Mixture control warning lamp switch
68 Wiper switch
69 Wiper motor
70 Screen washer motor
71 Screen washer motor switch
72 Induction heater and thermostat
73 Tailgate switch
74 Tailgate wiper motor
75 Tailgate washer motor (estate)
76 Tailgate wiper/washer switch
77 Screen wiper/washer switch
78 Rear window demist switch
79 Rear window demist unit
80 Rear window demist warning lamp
81 Heater blower motor switch
82 Heater blower motor
83 Automatic gearbox safety switch
84 Automatic gearbox quadrant lamp
85 Interior lamp switch
86 Interior lamp switch (rear)
87 Interior lamp
88 Interior lamp (rear - estate)
89 Door switch
90 Luggage compartment lamp switch
91 Luggage compartment lamp
92 Cigar lighter
93 Radio
94 Glovebox lamp
95 Glovebox lamp switch
96 Bonnet lamp
97 Bonnet switch
98 Panel lamp switch

Colour code

Black BK	Yellow YW
Blue BL	White WH
Brown BR	Light green LGR
Red RD	Orange OR
Green GR	Pink Pl
Grey GY	Purple PU

Chapter 11 Suspension and steering

For modifications, and information applicable to later models, see Supplement at end of manual

Contents

General description 1
Front hub bearings - removal and refitting 2
Front hub bearings - adjustment 3
Lower suspension arm - removal and refitting 4
Front shock absorber - removal and refitting 5
Swivel pin - removal and refitting 6
Swivel pin balljoint - removal and refitting 7
Lower swivel pin link - removal and refitting 8
Eyebolt bush - removal and refitting 9
Torsion bar - removal and refitting 10
Tie rod - removal and refitting 11
Rear hub assembly - removal and refitting 12
Rear road spring - removal and refitting 13
Rear road spring shackles - removal and refitting 14
Bump stop - removal and refitting 15

Rear shock absorber - removal and refitting 16
Steering wheel - removal and refitting 17
Steering column top bush - removal and refitting 18
Steering column lock and ignition starter switch housing -
removal and refitting 19
Steering column universal joint couplings - removal and
refitting 20
Upper steering column - removal and refitting 21
Steering rack and pinion - removal and refitting 22
Steering rack and pinion - dismantling, overhaul and re-
assembly 23
Front wheel alignment 24
Suspension trim height - adjustment 25
Fault diagnosis 26

Specifications

Front suspension ... ... Independant by torsion bar with lever type shock absorbers
   King pin inclination ... ... 7½% positive
   Camber angle ... ... 0⁰ 50' positive
   Castor angle ... ... 2⁰ positive, early produced cars 5⁰
   Hub bearing end float ... ... 0.001 to 0.005 in (0.025 - 0.0127mm)
   Swivel pin link lower bush finished diameter ... ... 0.688 ± 0.0005 in (17.48 ± 0.013mm)
   Trim height:
      Normal ... ... 25 3/8 ± 1/4 inch (644 ± 6.4 mm)
      With new torsion bars ... ... + 5/16 inch (7.94mm)

Rear suspension ... ... Semi elliptic leaf spring with telescopic shock absorbers
   Number of spring leaves 2
   Width of leaves ... ... 2 inches (50.8mm)
   Gauge of leaves ... ... 0.3 to 0.164 in (7.62 - 0.076mm)
   Working load ... ... 270 lb (122.7 kg)

Steering
   Front wheel alignment ... ... 1/16 in (1.6mm) toe in
   Pinion bearing pre-load ... ... 0.001 to 0.003 inch (0.025 to 0.076mm)
   Oil capacity of rack and pinion ... ... 1/3 pint (190 cm³)
   Rack travel ... ... 6.5 in (16.5cm)
   Rack travel - either side of centre ... ... 3.25 in (8.25 cm)
   Pinion rotations, full rack travel ... ... 3.98 turns
   Pinion pre-load ... ... 0.001 -0.003 in (0.025 - 0.76mm)
   Shims available ... ... 0.002 in (0.050mm)
      0.005 in (0.127mm)
      0.010 in (0.1254mm)
      0.060 in (1.524mm)
   Cover gasket thickness ... ... 0.010 in (0.254 mm)
   Yoke clearance ... ... 0.002 - 0.005 in (0.050 - 0.127mm)
   Shims available ... ... 0.002 in (0.050mm)
      0.010 in (0.254mm)
      0.005 in (0.127mm)
   Cover gasket thickness ... ... 0.010 in (0.254mm)
   Ball pin centre dimension (ball pins screwed to tie rod
   equal amount) ... ... 43.7 in (1109.98 mm)

Wheels ... ... 4 stud pressed steel 13 in x 4½

Saloon tyre fitment: Standard	5.20 x 13 cross ply		
: Optional	145 x 13 radial ply		
Tyre pressures	Normal load		Heavy load

	Normal load		Heavy load	
	Front	Rear	Front	Rear
Cross ply tyres	26 lb/sq.in.	28 lb/sq.in.	28 lb/sq.in.	30 lb/sq.in.
	(1.8kg/cm^2)	(2.0kg/cm^2)	(2.0kg/cm^2)	(2.1kg/cm^2)
Radial tyres	24 lb/sq.in.	26 lb/sq.in.	26 lb/sq.in.	28 lb/sq,in.
	(1.6kg/cm^2)	(1.8kg/cm^2)	(1.8kg/cm^2)	(2.0kg/cm^2)

Estate tyre fitment: Standard	155 x 13 radial		
: Optional	165 x 70 radial		
Tyre pressures	Normal load		Heavy load

	Normal load		Heavy load	
	Front	Rear	Front	Rear
	26 lb/sq.in	28 lb/sq.in.	26 lb/sq.in.	32 lb/sq.in.
	(1.8kg/cm^2)	(2.0kg/cm^2)	(1.8kg/cm^2)	2.25kg/cm^2)
Maximum payload	900 lb (408 kg)		

TORQUE WRENCH SETTING

Front suspension	lb ft	kg m
Ball pin retainer locknut	70 - 80	9.6 - 11.0
Eyebolt nut	50 - 54	6.9 - 7.4
Torsion bar reaction lever lockbolt	22	3.0
Reaction pad nut	35 - 40	4.8 - 5.5
Shock absorber retaining nuts	26 - 28	3.5 - 3.8
Tie rod fork nut	48 - 55	6.6 - 7.6
Tie rod to fork	22	3.0
Caliper bracket or dust shield bolts	35 - 42	4.8 - 5.8

Rear suspension		
Upper shackle pin nuts	28	3.9
Spring eye bolt nuts	40	5.5
Spring 'U' bolt nuts	40	5.5
Shock absorber to spring bracket	28	3.9
Shock absorber to body bracket	28	3.9

Steering		
Rack clamp bracket nuts	20 - 22	2.77 - 3.04
Tie rod ball pin nuts	20 - 24	2.77 - 3.3
Flexible joint pinch bolt nut	17 - 20	2.7 - 3.3
Pinion end cover retaining bolts	12 - 15	1.6 - 2.0
Pinion pre load	15 (lb in)	0.17
Rack yoke cover bolts	12 - 15	1.6 - 2.0
Tie rod housing locknut	33 - 37	4.6 - 5.6
Tie rod ball spheres pre load	32 - 52 (lb in)	0.37 - 0.6
Steering column mounting bolts	14 - 18	1.94 - 2.49
Flexible joint coupling bolts	20 - 22	2.77 - 3.04
Steering column lock shear screw	14	1.94
Steering wheel nut	43 - 50	6.1 - 6.9
Tie rod locknuts	35 - 40	4.8 - 5.5

1 General description

The component parts of the right hand side front suspension unit are shown in Fig.11.I. Although the left hand side front suspension is identical in principle some parts are handed and therefore not interchangeable.

Attached to the hub is the road wheel as is also the brake disc, these being retained by countersunk screws or bolts. The hub rotates on two opposed tapered roller bearings mounted on the swivel pin stub axle and is retained on the stub axle by a nut. Also attached to the swivel pin is the disc brake dust shield.

The shock absorber is attached to the body and its arm carries at the outer end the ball joint for the swivel pin top attachment. Its arm therefore acts as an upper suspension wishbone. The bottom end of the steering swivel screws into the lower link which is mounted between the outer ends of the lower arms. This link is mounted on a pivot pin so that the suspension is able to move in a vertical manner. Horizontal movement of the suspension is controlled by a tie rod assembly. The inner ends of the lower arms are free to pivot about an eye bolt and the rear arm is spline attached to the torsion bar. The rear of the torsion bar is attached to the body so that both the body weight and road shocks are taken by the torsion bar.

Rear suspension is by semi elliptic leaf springs, the springs being mounted on rubber bushed shackle pins. Double acting telescopic hydraulic shock absorbers are fitted to absorb road shocks and damp spring oscillations.

A rack and pinion steering is used. The steering wheel is splined to the upper inner column which in turn is connected to the lower column by a flexible coupling. A second flexible coupling connects the lower column to the steering gearbox pinion. The pinion teeth mesh with those machined in the rack so that rotation of the pinion moves the rack from one side of the housing to the other. Located at either end of the rack are tie rods and ball joints which are attached to the suspension swivel pin steering arms.

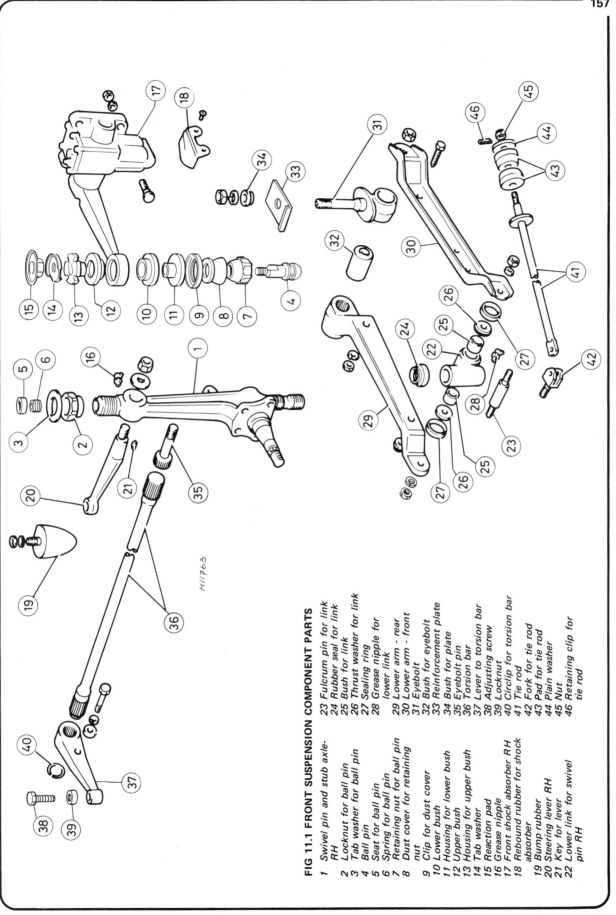

H11763

FIG 11.1 FRONT SUSPENSION COMPONENT PARTS

1 Swivel pin and stub axle-RH
2 Locknut for ball pin
3 Tab washer for ball pin
4 Ball pin
5 Seat for ball pin
6 Spring for ball pin
7 Retaining nut for ball pin
8 Dust cover for retaining nut
9 Clip for dust cover
10 Lower bush
11 Housing for lower bush
12 Upper bush
13 Housing for upper bush
14 Tab washer
15 Reaction pad
16 Grease nipple
17 Front shock absorber RH
18 Rebound rubber for shock absorber
19 Bump rubber
20 Steering lever RH
21 Key for lever
22 Lower link for swivel pin RH

23 Fulcrum pin for link
24 Rubber seal for link
25 Bush for link
26 Thrust washer for link
27 Sealing ring
28 Grease nipple for lower link
29 Lower arm - rear
30 Lower arm - front
31 Eyebolt
32 Bush for eyebolt
33 Reinforcement plate
34 Bush for plate
35 Eyebolt pin
36 Torsion bar
37 Lever to torsion bar
38 Adjusting screw
39 Locknut
40 Circlip for torsion bar
41 Tie rod
42 Fork for tie rod
43 Pad for tie rod
44 Plain washer
45 Nut
46 Retaining clip for tie rod

2 Front hub bearings - removal and refitting

1   Jack up the front of the car and support on firmly based axle stands.

2   Remove the wheel trim and the road wheels.

3   Refer to Chapter 9 and remove the disc brake caliper.

4   Using a wide blade screwdriver carefully ease off the grease cap.

5   Straighten the split pin ears and extract the split pin. Lift away the nut retainer and then undo and remove the hub nut. Withdraw the splined washer. The hub may now be drawn from the axle stub.

6   Remove the outer bearing cone.

7   Using a screwdriver ease out the oil seal noting that the lip is innermost. Lift away the inner bearing cone.

8   If the bearings are to be renewed carefully drift out the bearing cups working from the inside of the hub.

9   Thoroughly wash all parts in paraffin and wipe dry using a non fluffy rag.

10 Inspect the bearings for signs of rusting, pitting or overheating. If evident, a new set of bearings must be fitted.

11 Inspect the oil seal journal face of the stub axle shaft for signs of damage. If evident, either polish with fine emery tape or if very bad a new stub axle will have to be fitted.

12 To reassemble, if new bearings are to be fitted, carefully drift in the new bearing cups using a piece of tube of suitable diameter. Make sure they are fitted the correct way round with the tapers facing outwards.

13 Work some high melting point grease into the inner bearing cone and fit it into the hub.

14 Smear a new oil seal with a little Castrol GTX and fit it with the lip innermost using a tube of suitable diameter. The final fitted position should be flush with the flange of the hub.

15 Fit the hub to the axle stub. Work some high melting point grease into the outer bearing cone and fit it into the hub.

16 Refit the splined washer and nut.

17 It is now necessary to adjust the hub bearing end float and full information will be found in Section 3 of this chapter.

18 Refit the grease cap, road wheel and wheel trim. Lower the front of the car to the ground.

3 Front hub bearings - adjustment

1   Jack up the front of the car and suport on firmly based axle stands.

2   Remove the wheel trim, road wheel and grease cap.

3   Straighten the split pin ears and extract the split pin. Lift away the hub nut retainer.

4   Back off the hub nut and spin the hub. Whilst it is spinning tighten the nut using a torque wrench set to 5 lbf ft (0.69 kgf m).

5   Stop the hub spinning and slacken the nut. Tighten the nut again but this time finger tight only.

6   Position the nut retainer so that the left-hand half of the split pin hole is covered by one of the arms of the retainer.

7   Slacken the nut and retainer until the split pin hole is fully uncovered.

8   Fit a new split pin and lock by opening the ears of the split pin and bending circumferentially around the nut retainer.

9   Fit the grease cap and replace the road wheel and wheel trim.

10 It will be observed that the end float setting achieved can cause a considerable amount of movement when the tyre is 'rocked'. Do not reduce the end float any further provided it has been set correctly as described. The bearings must not on any account be pre-loaded.

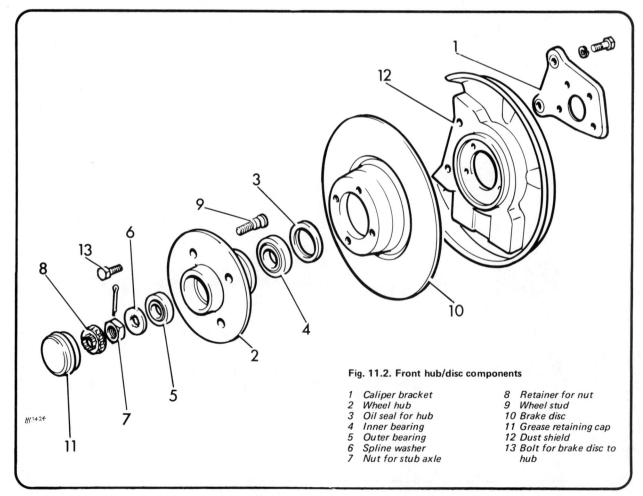

Fig. 11.2. Front hub/disc components

1	Caliper bracket	8	Retainer for nut
2	Wheel hub	9	Wheel stud
3	Oil seal for hub	10	Brake disc
4	Inner bearing	11	Grease retaining cap
5	Outer bearing	12	Dust shield
6	Spline washer	13	Bolt for brake disc to
7	Nut for stub axle		hub

4 Lower suspension arm - removal and refitting

1 Jack up the front of the car and suport on firmly based axle stands. Suitably support the suspension unit under the rear lower arm.

2 Remove the wheel trim and the road wheel.

3 Undo and remove the nut and spring washer from the eye bolt pin.

4 Undo and remove the front nut and spring washer from the swivel lower link pin.

5 Undo and remove the nut, bolt and spring washer retaining the tie rod to the tie rod fork.

6 Undo and remove the nut retaining the tie rod fork to the lower suspension arms. Lift away the fork.

7 Undo the nut, bolt and spring washer that clamps the front and rear lower arms together.

8 The front lower suspension arm may now be lifted away.

9 Refer to Section 10 and remove the torsion bar.

10 Withdraw the eyebolt pin and then undo and remove the rear nut and spring washer from the swivel lower link pin.

11 The rear lower suspension arm may now be lifted away.

12 Refitting the lower suspension arm assembly is the reverse sequence to renewal, but the following additional points should be noted:

    a) Tighten the rod fork nut to a torque wrench setting of 48 - 55 lb ft (6.6 - 7.7 kg m).

    b) Tighten the tie rod to fork nut to a torque wrench setting of 22 lb ft (3.0 kg m).

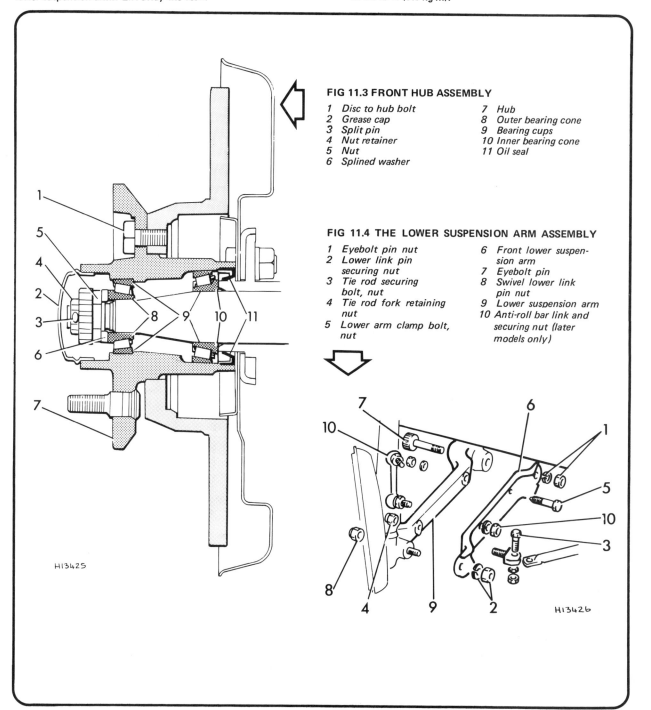

FIG 11.3 FRONT HUB ASSEMBLY

1 Disc to hub bolt	7 Hub
2 Grease cap	8 Outer bearing cone
3 Split pin	9 Bearing cups
4 Nut retainer	10 Inner bearing cone
5 Nut	11 Oil seal
6 Splined washer	

FIG 11.4 THE LOWER SUSPENSION ARM ASSEMBLY

1 Eyebolt pin nut	6 Front lower suspen-sion arm
2 Lower link pin securing nut	7 Eyebolt pin
3 Tie rod securing bolt, nut	8 Swivel lower link pin nut
4 Tie rod fork retaining nut	9 Lower suspension arm
5 Lower arm clamp bolt, nut	10 Anti-roll bar link and securing nut (later models only)

H13425

H13426

5 Shock absorber - removal and refitting

Note: *The torque figure given in paragraph 9 (b) is the true (actual) torque for the reaction pad nut. To obtain this figure a torque wrench has to be used with a special crowfoot adaptor (BL part No 18G1237) and, because the torque is applied to the adaptor rather than the nut, a formula must be used so that the indicated (metered) torque can be related to the true torque. Refer to Fig. 11.5B for the formula.*

If you do not have this crowfoot adaptor, an open-ended spanner can be used, but you should arrange for your BL dealer to check the tightness of the nut after fitting.

1 Jack up the front of the car and support on firmly based axle stands. Suitably support the lower suspension arm.
2 Remove the wheel trim and road wheel.
3 Unlock the reaction pad nut. Using a mole wrench or 'C' spanner hold the upper bush housing and remove the nut (Fig. 11.5).
4 Lift away the lock washer, upper bush housing and upper bush.
5 Raise the shock absorber arm. Undo and remove the four nuts and plain washers that secure the shock absorber to its mounting.
6 Lift away the shock absorber.
7 Test the operation of the shock absorber by topping up the level if necessary and then moving the shock arm up and down. If the action is weak or jerky then either the unit is worn or air has entered the operating cylinders. Move the arm up and down ten times and if the performance has not improved a new shock absorber must be obtained.
8 Inspect the shock absorber arm bushes for wear. If evident, obtain new bushes.
9 Refitting the shock absorber is the reverse sequence to removal, but the following additional points should be noted:
a) Always use a new reaction pad lockwasher.
b) Tighten the reaction pad nut to a torque wrench setting of 35 - 40 lb ft (4.8 - 5.5 kg m) using the crowfoot adaptor number 18G1237.
c) Tighten the shock absorber retaining nuts to a torque wrench setting of 26 - 28 lb ft (3.5 - 3.8 kg m).

6 Swivel pin - removal and refitting

1 Refer to Section 5 and follow the instructions given in paragraphs 1 - 4 inclusive.
2 Raise the shock absorber arm.
3 Wipe the top of the brake master cylinder reservoir. Remove the cap and place a piece of thick polythene over the top. Refit the cap. This is to stop syphoning of fluid during subsequent operations.
4 Wipe the area around the flexible brake hose connection at the body mounted bracket. Hold the flexible hose metal end nut and undo and remove the metal pipe union nut. Undo and remove the flexible hose securing nut and star washer and draw the flexible hose from the bracket.
5 Remove the front half of the lower suspension arm as described in Section 4.
6 Undo and remove the lower link pin rear nut and spring washer. On later models a special overtravel nut is used without a spring washer. Where one of these is used mark the fitted position before removal.
7 The swivel pin assembly may now be lifted away.
8 Refitting the swivel pin assembly is the reverse sequence to removal. If an overtravel nut is used, it must be refitted in the same position (see paragraph 6).

7 Swivel pin ball joint - removal and refitting

Note: *The torque figure given in paragraph 9 is the true (actual) torque for the ball retainer locknut. To obtain this figure a torque wrench has to be used with a special crowfoot adaptor*

(BL part No 18G1192) and, because the torque is applied to the adaptor rather than the nut, a formula must be used so that the indicated (metered) torque can be related to the true torque. Refer to Fig 11.5B for the formula.

If you do not have this crowfoot adaptor, a large open-ended spanner can be used but you should arrange for your BL dealer to check the tightness of the nut after fitting.

1 Refer to Section 5 and follow the instructions given in paragraphs 1 - 4 inclusive.
2 Raise the shock absorber arm.
3 Remove the dust cover and retaining clip.
4 Unlock the tab washer and using an open ended spanner hold the locknut. With a ring spanner undo the ball pin retainer.
5 Lift away the ball pin, ball seat and spring. Finally remove the tab washer and locknut.
6 To reassemble first obtain a new tab washer. Pack the ball pin retainer with Castrol LM Grease.
7 Fit the tab washer and locknut and then replace the ball seat and spring. Refit the ball pin and its retainer.
8 Fully slacken the locknut and tighten the ball retainer until the torque required to produce articulation of the ball pin is 32 - 52 lb in (0.38 - 0.56 kg cm).
9 Hold the ball retainer against rotation and tighten the locknut to a torque wrench setting of 70 - 80 lb ft (9.6 - 11.0 kg m) using the crowfoot adaptor.
10 Lock the retainer and the locknut with the tab washer.
11 Reassembly is now the reverse sequence to removal.

8 Lower swivel pin link - removal and refitting

1 Jack up the front of the car and support on firmly based axle stands. Suitably support the rear lower suspension arm.
2 Remove the wheel trim and road wheel.
3 Refer to Chapter 3 and remove the disc brake caliper.
4 Using a wide blade screwdriver carefully ease off the grease cap.
5 Straighten the split pin ears and extract the split pin. Lift away the nut retainer and then undo and remove the hub nut. Withdraw the splined washer.
6 The hub may now be drawn from the axle stub.
7 Wipe the top of the brake master cylinder reservoir. Remove the cap and place a piece of thin polythene over the top. Refit the cap. This is to stop syphoning of fluid during subsequent operations.
8 Wipe the area around the flexible brake hose connection at the body mounted bracket. Hold the flexible hose metal end nut and undo and remove the metal pipe union nut.
9 Undo and remove the flexible hose securing nut and star washer and draw the flexible hose from the bracket.
10 Undo and remove the four nuts, bolts and spring washers securing the dust shield and caliper bracket to the swivel pin. Lift away the dust shield and caliper bracket.
11 Refer to Section 4 and remove the front half of the lower suspension arm.
12 Undo and remove the remaining nut and spring washer from the lower link pin.
13 Swing the swivel pin forwards and remove the rubber sealing rings and thrust washers from the lower link.
14 Withdraw the lower link pin.
15 Unscrew and remove the lower link from the swivel pin. (Right-hand thread for the right-hand side, left-hand thread for the left-hand side).
16 Thoroughly wash all parts in paraffin and wipe dry using a non fluffy rag.
17 Check for excessive wear across the thrust faces and in the threaded bore. If wear is excessive a new swivel link must be obtained.
18 Check the lower link bushes for wear and if this is evident new bushes should be fitted by a BLMC garage as it has to be ream finished. If an expanding reamer and micrometer are available however the old bushes should be drifted out. Further instructions are given in paragraphs 22 and 23.

19 Inspect the thrust washers for signs of damage or wear which, if evident, new thrust washers must be obtained.

20 Remove the grease nipple and ensure that both it and its hole are free from obstruction.

21 Obtain a new set of rubber sealing rings.

22 If new bushes are to be fitted these should be drifted or pressed in so that the oil groove is located as shown in Fig. 11.7. The bush oil groove blank ends should be towards the outside edge of the link.

23 Using the expanding reamer line ream the new bushes to a finished size of 0.688 in ± 0.0005 in (17.48 mm ± 0.013 mm).

24 Pack the area between the lower link bushes and the swivel pin threads with approximately 2.5 ccs of Duckhams Q5648 grease, or the equivalent.

25 Place the swivel pin link and seal on the swivel pin and screw on the link. Engage the seal on the recessed shoulder of the link and screw the link fully onto the swivel pin.

26 Unscrew the link one complete turn.

27 Reassembly is now the reverse sequence to removal, but the following additional points should be noted:

a) The caliper bracket and dust shield retaining bolts should be tightened to a torque wrench setting of 35 - 42 lb ft (4.8 - 5.8 kg m).

b) Refer to Section 3 and adjust the front hub bearing endfloat.

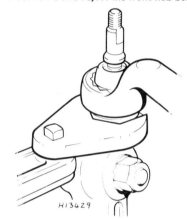

FIG. 11.5A USING THE CROWFOOT ADAPTOR

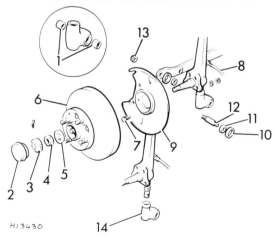

FIG 11.6 LOWER SWIVEL PIN LINK REMOVAL

1 Lower link bushes	8 Brake hydraulic hose
2 Grease cap	9 Disc brake mudshield
3 Nut retainer and split pin	10 Sealing ring
4 Nut	11 Thrust washer
5 Splined washer	12 Lower link pin
6 Hub	13 Link pin securing nut and spring washer
7 Mudshield retaining bolt and spring washer	14 Lower link

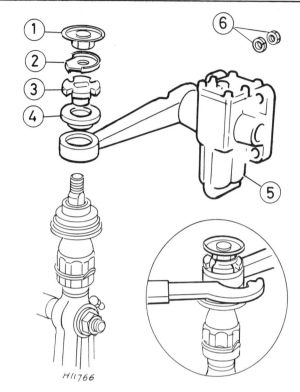

FIG 11.5 FRONT SHOCK ABSORBER REMOVAL

1 Reaction pad nut	4 Upper bush
2 Lockwasher	5 Shock absorber arm
3 Upper bush housing	6 Nut and spring washer

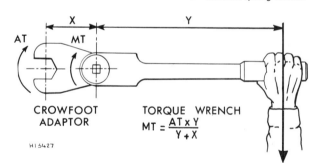

FIG. 11.5B METHOD OF CALCULATING METERED TORQUE WHEN USING SPECIAL CROWFOOT ADAPTOR

$$MT = \frac{AT \times Y}{Y + X}$$

MT = Metered torque   Y = Effective length of torque wrench
AT = Actual torque   X = Effective length of adaptor

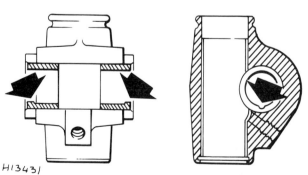

FIG 11.7 CORRECT POSITION OF BUSH OIL GROOVE

9 Eye bolt bush - removal and refitting

1 Refer to Section 10 and remove the torsion bar.
2 Undo and remove the nut and spring washer from the eyebolt
3 Withdraw the eyebolt pin.
4 Draw the suspension assembly clear of the eyebolt.
5 Undo and remove the nut, spring washer and spacer from the eyebolt.
6 Lift away the eyebolt and, if fitted, the reinforcement plate.
7 The bush may be removed with pieces of suitable diameter tube by pressing it out in a bench vice.
8 To fit a new bush lubricate its outer surface with a little soapy water and press it in using the reverse procedure to removal.
9 Refitting the eyebolt is the reverse sequence to removal, but the following additional points should be noted:
a) It is not necessary to fit the reinforcement plate when a later type eyebolt is being used. This is identifiable by having a 2.5 inch (63 mm) elliptical diameter.
b) The eyebolt retaining nut should be tightened to a torque wrench setting of 50 - 54 lb ft (6.9 - 7.4 kg m).

10 Torsion bar - removal and refitting

1 Unscrew and remove the grease nipple from the swivel pin lower link.
2 Place a wooden block 8 inch (200 mm) thick on the floor under the lower suspension arm as near as possible to the disc brake dust shield as shown in Fig.11.9.
3 Jack up the front of the car. Remove the wheel trim and road wheel.
4 Carefully lower the car until the weight of the suspension is placed on the woden block.
5 Unlock the reaction pad nut. Using a mole wrench or 'C' spanner hold the upper bush housing and remove the nut.
6 Remove the upper bush housing and the upper bush.
7 Raise the shock absorber arm clear of the ball pin and lift away the lower bush.
8 Undo and remove the steering track rod ball pin nut.

9 Using a universal ball joint separator release the ball pin from the steering lever.
10 Jack up the front of the car so as to relieve the torsion bar load and yet the lower suspension arm is still just resting on the wooden block.
11 Undo and remove the bolt, spring washer and special washer that secures the torsion bar reaction lever onto the chassis member.
12 Remove tne reaction lever from the chassis member and move the lever forwards along the torsion bar.
13 Release the nut that retains the eybolt through the chassis member and make sure that the suspension lowers itself by ½ inch (12mm).
14 Ease the torsion bar forwards until it clears the shoulder from the chassis housing. Lower the torsion bar and remove it in a rearwards direction.
15 Using a pair of circlip pliers remove the torsion bar circlip.
16 Slide off the reaction lever from the torsion bar.
17 Refitting the torsion bar is the reverse sequence to removal but the following additional points should be noted:
a) Once a torsion bar has been fitted and used on one side of the car it must not under any circumstances be used on the other side. This is because a torsion bar becomes handed once it has been in use. Torsion bars are only interchangeable when new.
b) Do not fit a torsion bar that is corroded or deeply scored as this will affect its reliability and in bad cases cause premature failure.
c) The reaction lever adjustment screw must be set to the midway position of its travel and the locknut tightened before refitting.
d) Tighten the eyebolt nut to a torque wrench setting of 50 - 54 lb ft (6.9 - 7.4 kg m).
e) Tighten the reaction lever to chassis member bolt to 22 lb ft (3.0 kg m).
f) Tighten the track rod ball pin nut to a torque wrench setting of 20 to 24 lb ft (2.7 to 3.3 kg m).
g) Tighten the reaction pad nut to 35 - 40 lb ft (4.8 - 5.5 kg m). (Refer to Section 5).
18 Refer to Section 25 and adjust the front suspension trim height if necessary.

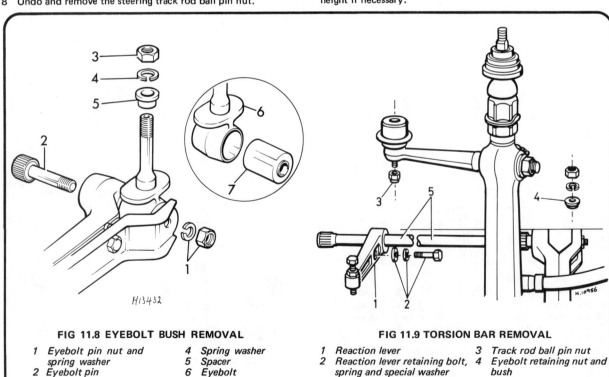

FIG 11.8 EYEBOLT BUSH REMOVAL

1	Eyebolt pin nut and	4	Spring washer
	spring washer	5	Spacer
2	Eyebolt pin	6	Eyebolt
3	Nut	7	Bush

FIG 11.9 TORSION BAR REMOVAL

1	Reaction lever	3	Track rod ball pin nut
2	Reaction lever retaining bolt,	4	Eyebolt retaining nut and
	spring and special washer		bush
		5	Torsion bar

11 Tie rod - removal and refitting

1 Jack up the front of the car and support on firmly based axle stands.
2 Remove the wheel trim and road wheel.
3 Using a pair of pliers remove the tie rod spring clip from the end of the tie rod.
4 Undo and remove the locking nut and large plain washer.
5 Slide off the rubber outer pad.
6 Undo and remove the nut, spring washer and bolt that secures the tie rod to the fork end.
7 Remove the rubber inner pad from the tie rod.
8 Undo and remove the nut that secures the rod fork and lift away the fork from the lower suspension arm.
9 Refitting the tie rod is the reverse sequence to removal but the following additional points should be noted:
a) Inspect the two rubber pads and if they show signs of oil contamination, cracking or perishing obtain and fit a new pair of pads.
b) The tie rod to fork nut should be tightened to a torque wrench setting of 22 lb ft (3.0 kg m).
c) Tighten the rod fork nut to a torque wrench setting of 48 - 55 lb ft (6.6 - 7.6 kg m).

12 Rear hub assembly - removal and refitting

1 Chock the front wheel, jack up the rear of the car and place on firmly based axle stands.
2 Remove the wheel trim and road wheel. Apply the handbrake.
3 Undo and remove the axle shaft nut and washer.
4 Release the handbrake and referring to Chapter 9, back off the brake adjuster. Remove the two countersunk screws that retain the brake drum and pull off the brake drum. If it is tight tap the circumference with a soft faced hammer.
5 Using a heavy duty puller and suitable thrust block pull the hub from the end of the axle shaft.
6 Remove the axle shaft key.
7 Refitting the rear hub assembly is the reverse sequence to removal. The axle shaft nut must be tightened to a torque wrench setting of 85 lb ft (11.7 kg m).

13 Rear road spring - removal and refitting

1 Refer to Section 14 and remove the road spring shackle plate.
2 Jack up the rear of the car and support on firmly based axle stands located under the main longitudinal chassis numbers. Support the weight of the axle on the side which the spring is to be removed.
3 Undo and remove the shock absorber locknut, plain nut and plain washer. Note the location of the lower bush in the shock absorber lower mounting plate and remove the lower bush.
4 Undo and remove the nut, spring washer and bolt that secures the front spring eye to the body mounted brackets.
5 Undo and remove the four nuts from the two 'U' bolts.
6 Carefully lower the spring and its mountings.
7 Remove the shock absorber mounting plate followed by the spring mounting plates and mounting rubbers. Note the fitted location of the spring mounting wedge.
8 Lift away the two 'U' bolts.
9 If the spring bushes are worn or have deteriorated they should be pressed out using suitable diameter tubes and a large bench vice.
10 Should the spring have considerably weakened or failed neccessitating the fitting of a new one, rear springs must be renewed in pairs and not singly as the remaining spring will have settled slightly. Unless the springs have the same performance and characteristics road holding can be adversely affected.
11 Refitting the road spring is the reverse sequence to removal, but the following additional points should be noted:

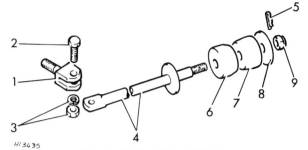

FIG 11.10 TIE ROD REMOVAL

1 Tie rod fork	6 Inner pad
2 Tie rod retaining bolt	7 Outer pad
3 Nut and spring washer	8 Plain washer
4 Tie rod	9 Nut
5 Spring clip	

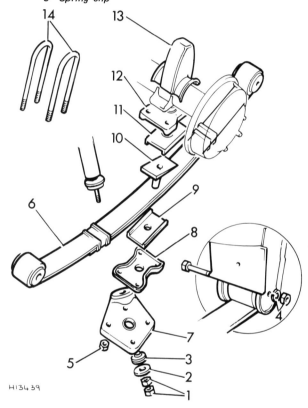

FIG 11.11 REAR SPRING REMOVAL

1 Shock absorber retaining nut and locknut	8 Spring mounting plate (lower)
2 Plain washer	9 Rubber pad
3 Lower bush	10 Wedge
4 Forward spring eyebolt securing nut and spring washer	11 Rubber pad
5 'U' bolt nut	12 Spring mounting plate (upper)
6 Spring assembly	13 Rubber bump stop
7 Shock absorber mounting plate	14 'U' bolts

a) Tighten the upper shackle pin nuts to a torque wrench setting of 28 lb ft (3.9 kg m).
b) Tighten the spring eye bush bolt nuts to a torque wrench setting of 40 lb ft (5.5 kg m).
c) Tighten the 'U' bolt nuts to a torque wrench setting of 14 lb ft (1.9 kg m).
d) Tighten the shock absorber to spring bracket retaining nut to a torque wrench setting of 28 lb ft (3.9 kg m) and then secure by tightening the locknut.

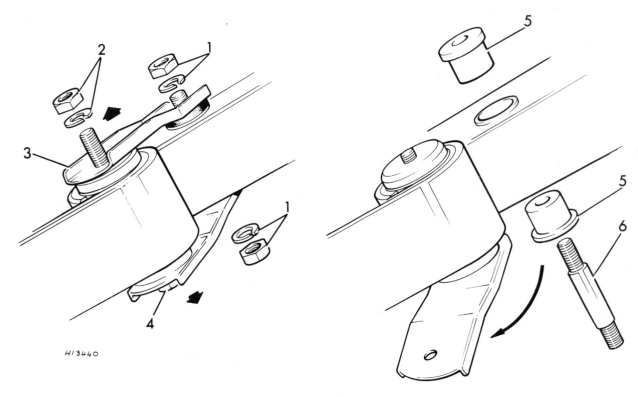

H13440

FIG 11.12 REAR SPRING SHACKLE

1 Upper shackle pin securing nut and spring washer	securing nut and spring washer	4 Shackle bolt
2 Lower spring shackle bolt	3 Inner shackle plate	5 Upper shackle bushes
		6 Upper shackle pin

14 Rear road spring shackles - removal and refitting

1 Chock the front wheels, jack up the rear of the car and place on firmly based axle stands located under the main longitudinal chassis members.

2 Remove the wheel trim and road wheel.

3 Undo and remove the nut and spring washer on each side of the upper shackle pin.

4 Undo and remove the nut and spring washer from the spring bush bolt.

5 Lift away the inner shackle plate.

6 Using a suitable diameter parallel pin punch partially drift out the spring bolt and then release the outer plate from the upper pin (Fig.11.12).

7 Remove the upper shackle pin and lift away the two half bushes.

8 Inspect the bushes for signs of deterioration or oil contamination which, if evident, new bushes should be obtained.

9 Refitting is the reverse sequence to removal, but the following additional points should be noted:

a) Tighten the upper shackle pin nuts to a torque wrench setting of 28 lb ft (3.9 kg m).

b) Tighten the spring eye bush bolt nut to a torque wrench setting of 40 lb ft (5.5 kg m).

15 Bump stop - removal and refitting

1 Chock the front wheels, jack up the rear of the car and place on firmly based axle stands located under the main longitudinal chassis members.

2 Remove the wheel trim and road wheel.

3 Support the weight of the axle on the side to be worked upon.

4 Undo and remove the shock absorber locknut, plain nut, and plain washer. Note the location of the lower bush in the shock absorber mounting bracket and lift away the lower bush.

5 Undo and remove the four 'U' bolt nuts.

6 Lift away the shock absorber mounting plate and spring locating bracket and rubber.

7 Lift away the bump stop and two 'U' bolts.

8 Refitting the bump stop rubber is the reverse sequence to removal but the following additional points should be noted:

a) Check the condition of the spring mounting rubber and if its condition has deteriorated a new mounting rubber should be obtained and fitted.

b) The shock absorber to spring bracket retaining nut should be tightened to a torque wrench setting of 28 lb ft (3.9 kg m).

16 Rear shock absorber - removal and refitting

1 Undo and remove the shock absorber lower locknut and retaining nut.

2 Lift away the plain washer and note the position of the lower bush. Lift away the lower bush.

3 Contract the shock absorber thereby detaching it from the mounting bracket.

4 Note the position of the upper bush and then lift it away followed by the plain washer.

5 Undo and remove the nut, spring washer and bolt that fixes the upper part of the shock absorber to the body bracket. Lift away the shock absorber.

6 To test the shock absorber alternatively compress and extend it throughout its full movement. If the action is jerky or weak, it is an indication that either it is worn or there is air in the hydraulic cylinder. Continue to compress and extend it and if the action does not become more positive a new shock absorber should be obtained. If the shock absorber is showing signs of

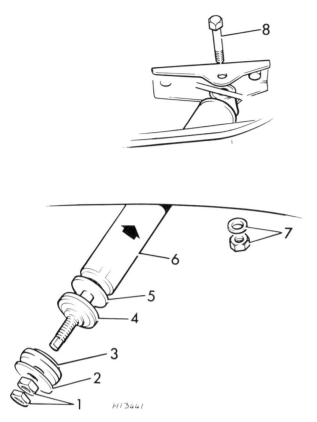

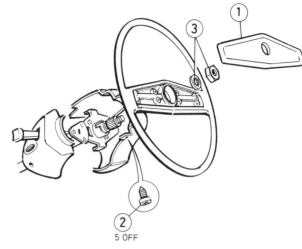

5 OFF

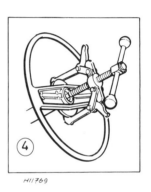

H11769

FIG 11.13 REAR SHOCK ABSORBER REMOVAL

1 Shock absorber retaining nut and locknut	5 Plain washer
2 Plain washer	6 Shock absorber
3 Lower bush	7 Upper mounting bolt securing nut and spring washer
4 Upper bush	8 Upper mounting bolt

FIG 11.14 STEERING WHEEL REMOVAL

1 Safety pad	4 Using a universal puller to remove steering wheel
2 Switch cowl securing screw	
3 Steering wheel securing nut and shakeproof washer	

leaking it should be discarded as it is not possible to overhaul it.
7 Check the bushes and if they show signs of deterioration a new set of bushes should be obtained.
8 Refitting the shock absorber is the reverse sequence to removal but the following additional points should be noted:
a) Tighten the shock absorber to body bracket retaining bolt nut to a torque wrench setting of 28 lb ft (3.9 kg m).
b) The shock absorber to spring bracket should be tightened to a torque wrench setting of 28 lb ft (3.9 kg m), and then locked with the locknut.

17 Steering wheel - removal and refitting

1 Using a knife carefully prise the safety pad from the centre of the steering wheel.
2 Undo and remove the five self tapping screws that secure the switch cowls. Lift away the cowls from over the switch arms.
3 Undo and remove the nut and shakeprof washer that secures the steering wheel to the upper inner column.
4 With a centre punch mark the relative positions of the steering wheel hub and inner column so that they may be refitted in the same position as they were prior to removal.
5 With the palms of the hands behind the spokes and near to the centre hub, thump the steering wheel from the steering inner column splines. If it is very tight it will be necessary to use a

universal puller fitted with long feet and a suitable thrust block.
6 Refitting the steering wheel is the reverse sequence to removal, but the following additional points should be noted:
a) The steering wheel securing nut should be tightened to a torque wrench setting of 43 - 50 lb ft (6.0 - 6.9 kg m).
b) When refitting the safety pad to the centre of the steering wheel the pins at each end of the pad must be located and inserted first. This will make sure that the width between the safety pad and steering wheel is equally spaced on either side of the pad.

18 Steering column top bush - removal and refitting

1 Refer to Section 17 and remove the steering wheel.
2 Slacken the screw that retains the combined switch mechanism and lift the switch mechanism from over the top of the inner column.
3 Using a screwdriver ease the top bush from the inside of the outer column.
4 To refit the top bush first align the slits in the column bush with the depression in the outer column and ensure that the chamfered end of the bush enters the column first.
5 Using a suitable diameter metal drift carefully drive the top bush into position.
6 Refitting the combined switch mechanism and steering wheel is now the reverse sequence to removal.

HI3447

FIG. 11.15. RACK AND PINION STEERING ASSEMBLY

1	Steering wheel
2	Motif pad
3	Nut
4	Shakeproof washer
5	Upper bush
6	Shear bolt
7	Clamp plate
8	Steering lock
9	Upper column (outer)
10	Upper column (inner)
11	Screw
12	Tie-rod end
13	Self-locking nut
14	Clip (small)
15	Rack seal
16	Clip (large)
17	Locknut
18	Ball housing
19	Tie-rod
20	Ball seat
21	Locknut (tie-rod end)
22	Thrust spring
23	Rack
24	Bolt
25	Lower bush
26	Nut
27	Flexible coupling
28	Column (lower)
29	Bolt
30	Pinion oil seal
31	Sealing washer
32	Nut
33	Locating plate
34	Rack bearing
35	Rack bearing screw
36	Sealing rubber
37	Pinion housing
38	Pinion bearing
39	Washer
40	Pinion
41	Pinion bearing
42	Shim
43	Shim – 0.060 in (1.524 mm)
44	Shim gasket – 0.010 in (0.254 mm)
45	End cover
46	Bolt and spring washer
47	Pinch bolt
48	Flexible joint (half)
49	Nut
50	Shouldered bolt
51	Rubber bush
52	Joint plate
53	Support yoke
54	O-ring
55	Shim
56	Thrust spring
57	Joint gasket
58	End cover
59	Bolt and spring washer
60	Pinch bolt
61	Flexible joint (half)
62	Nut
63	Rack mounting rubbers
64	Rack clamps
65	Rack U-bolts

19 Steering column lock and ignition starter switch housing - removal and refitting

1   Refer to Section 17 and remove the steering wheel.
2   Refer to Chapter 12 and remove the lower facia panel.
3   Refer to Chapter 12 and remove the instrument panel.
4   Locate the multi pin terminal connector on the end of the wiring harness to the column lock and ignition starter switch and disconnect the cable connection.
5   Using either a drill or a drill and 'easy out' stud extractor remove the two special shear bolts.
6   Lift away the clamp plate and the steering lock.
7   To refit offer up the steering column lock and ignition switch and clamp plate so that the indent in the top of the column is lined up with the clamp plate grub screw.
8   Lightly tighten the two new shear bolts and the one grub screw.
9   Check the operation of the lock to ensure that it operates correctly.
10 Slowly tighten the two shear bolts until the heads shear at the waisted point. This will normally occur at a torque wrench setting of 14 lb ft (1.94 kg m).
11 Reassembly is now the reverse sequence to removal.

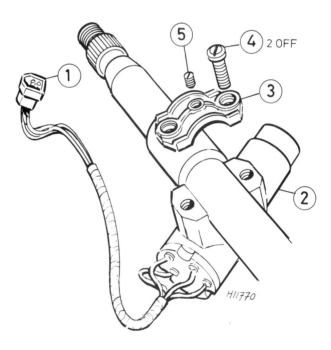

FIG 11.16 STEERING COLUMN LOCK AND IGNITION STARTER SWITCH HOUSING REMOVAL

1	Multi-pin connector	3	Clamp plate
2	Steering lock housing	4	Shear bolts
		5	Grub screw

20 Steering column universal joint coupling - removal and refitting

1   Refer to Section 21 and remove the upper steering column.
2   Undo and remove the pinch bolt and nut that secures the lower column to the rack pinion.
3   Lift away the lower steering column assembly.
4   Undo and remove the pinch bolt and nut that secures the lower column to the flexible joint.
5   Unlock and remove the four shouldered bolts from the flexible joint.
6   Lift away the rubber washers noting that the conical face mates with the countersunk face of the joint plate.
7   Lift away the plain washers from each of the four shouldered bolts.
8   Undo and remove the two nuts and bolts that retain the flexible coupling to the lower steering column.
9   Inspect the flexible couplings for signs of deterioration which if evident a new coupling must be obtained.
10 Refitting the couplings is the reverse sequence to removal. The flexible joint coupling bolts should be tightened to a torque wrench setting of 20 - 22 lb ft (2.77 - 3.04 kg m). If a new coupling has been fitted it will be necessary to break the band that compresses the coupling.

21 Upper steering column - removal and refitting

1   Refer to Section 17 and remove the steering wheel.
2   Refer to Chapter 12, and remove the lower facia panel.
3   Refer to Chapter 12 and remove the instrument panel.
4   Disconnect the multi pin connector on the end of the wiring harness to the switch mechanism at the harness connector.
5   Slacken the screw that retains the combined switch mechanism and lift the switch mechanism from over the top of the inner column.
6   Disconnect the multi pin connector on the end of the wiring harness to the ignition switch at the harness connection.
7   Undo and remove the two nuts and bolts that secure the upper column to the flexible coupling.
8   Undo and remove the two screws, plain and spring washers that secure the column to the upper support bracket.
9   Undo and remove the two locknuts, plain and spring washers that attach the column to the lower support bracket bolts.
10 Lift away the upper steering column.
11 To refit the upper steering column first engage the steering lock.
12 Centralise the steering rack by making sure the front wheels are in the straight ahead position.
13 Refitting is now the reverse sequence to removal but the following additional points should be noted:
a) The steering column mounting bolts should be tightened to a torque wrench setting of 20 - 22 lb ft (2.77 - 3.04 kg m).
b) The flexible joint coupling bolts should be tightened to a torque wrench setting of 20 - 22 lb ft (2.77 - 3.04 kg m).
c) If a new flexible coupling has been fitted it will be necessary to break the band that compresses the coupling. Lift away the band.

22 Steering rack and pinion - removal and refitting

1   Refer to Chapter 12 and remove the lower facia panel.
2   Refer to Chapter 12 and remove the instrument panel.
3   Disconnect the steering column combined switch mechanism and ignition switch connections at the wiring harness multi pin connectors.
4   Undo and remove the two screws, plain and spring washers securing the steering column to the upper support bracket.
5   Undo and remove the two locknuts, plain and spring washers that secure the steering column to the lower support bracket.
6   Undo and remove the pinch bolt and nut securing the flexible

joint to the steering rack pinion.
7   The steering column assembly may now be lifted away.
8   Carefully pull off the two heater rain water vent tubes from the front of the bulkhead.
9   Jack up the front of the car and support with firmly based axle stands located under the two longitudinal chassis members.
10 Undo and remove the nut that secures each tie rod ball pin end. Using a universal ball joint separator detach the tie rod ball pin ends from the steering levers.
11 Undo and remove the two nuts and plain washers securing each rack clamp bracket to the bulkhead. Make a note of the fitted position of the packing strip relative to the body panel. Lift away the packing strip.
12 The clamp brackets and rubber inserts may now be removed. The rubber inserts have slots cut in them to enable them to be removed from the rack tube.
13 The rack assembly may now be lifted from the car through the wheel arch opening.
14 Lift away the pinion seal from over the end of the pinion.
15 Refitting the steering rack and pinion assembly is the reverse sequence to removal, the following additional points should be noted:
a) Check the pinion seal and the two clamp bracket rubber inserts for signs of oil contamination or deterioration. If evident new parts must be obtained.
b) The rack clamp nuts should be tightened to a torque wrench setting of 20 - 22 lb ft (2.77 - 3.04 kg m).
c) The tie rod ball pin nuts should be tightened to a torque wrench setting of 20 - 24 lb ft (2.77 - 3.3 kg m).
d) Tighten the lower flexible joint pinch bolt to a torque wrench setting of 6 - 8 lb ft (0.4 - 0.5 kg m).
16 It will now be necessary to check and reset the front wheel alignment. Further information will be found in Section 24.

23 Steering rack and pinion - dismantling, overhaul and re-assembly

1   Wash the outside of the rack and pinion assembly in paraffin or Gunk and wipe dry with a non fluffy rag.
2   Slacken off the two tie rod end locknuts and unscrew the two tie rod ends as complete assemblies.
3   Unscrew and remove the two locknuts from the ends of the tie rods.
4   Slacken the rack seal clips at either end of the rack assembly body. Remove the clips and two rack seals.
5   Using a small chisel carefully ease out the locknut indent from each of the ball joint housings.
6   Using two mole wrenches or one mole wrench and a soft metal drift hold the locknut and unscrew the ball joint housing from each end of the rack. Lift away the tie rods.
7   Recover the ball cup and spring from each end of the rack.
8   Using a small chisel carefully ease out the locknut indent from the rack. Unscrew the locknuts.
9   Undo and remove the rack bearing pan head retaining screw located in the rack tube end as opposed to the pinion housing.
10 The bearing may now be removed from the rack housing.
11 Undo and remove the two bolts and spring washers that secure the rack yoke cover plate.
12 Lift away the cover plate, shims and joint washer.
13 Recover the rack support yoke from the pinion housing.
14 Remove the 'O' ring and thrust spring from the support yoke.
15 Undo and remove the two bolts and spring washers that secure the pinion end cover plate. Lift away the cover plate, shims and joint washers.
16 Carefully push out the pinion and the lower bearing. Note which way round the bearing is fitted.
17 The steering rack may now be withdrawn from the rack tube. Note which way round the rack is fitted in the rack tube.
18 Using a soft metal drift, tap out the upper pinion bearing and its washer. Note which way round the bearing is fitted.
19 Recover the pinion shaft oil seal from the pinion housing.
20 The steering rack assembly is now fully dismantled. Clean all

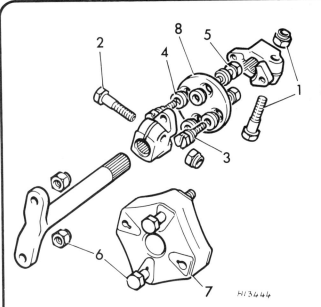

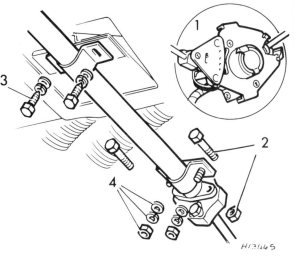

FIG 11.18 UPPER STEERING COLUMN REMOVAL

1 Combination switch
2 Upper column to flexible coupling bolt and locknut
3 Column to upper support

bracket, bolt, plain and spring washer
4 Column to lower support bracket securing nut spring and plain washer

FIG 11.17 STEERING COLUMN UNIVERSAL JOINT COUPLINGS

1 Pinch bolt and locknut (lower)
2 Pinch bolt and locknut (upper)
3 Flexible joint shouldered bolt
4 Conical rubber washers
5 Plain washer and nut
6 Flexible coupling securing locknut and bolt
7 Flexible coupling (upper)
8 Joint plate

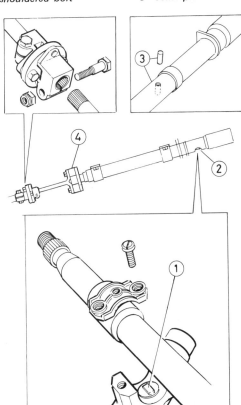

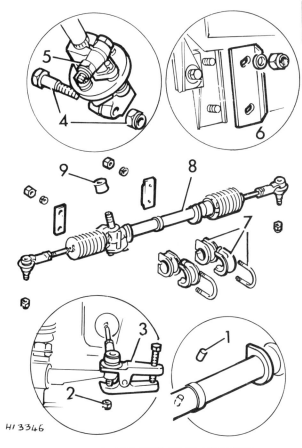

FIG 11.19 UPPER STEERING COLUMN ATTACHMENTS

1 Steering lock engagement sector
2 Slot in column
3 Steering rack central-isation
4 Lower universal coupling

FIG 11.20 STEERING RACK REMOVAL

1 Rubber sealing plug
2 Tie-rod ball-pin nut
3 Balljoint separator tool
4 Lower pinch-bolt and locknut
5 Upper pinch-bolt
6 Rack clamp plate
7 Rack clamps, rubber inserts and U-bolts
8 Rack and pinion assembly
9 Pinion seal

parts in paraffin and wipe dry with a non fluffy rag.

21 Thoroughly inspect the rack and pinion teeth for signs of wear, cracks or damage. Check the ends of the rack for wear especially where it moves in the bushes.

22 Examine the rubber gaiters for signs of cracking, perishing or other damage which if evident new gaiters must be obtained.

23 Inspect the ball ends and housing for wear which if evident new parts will be necessary. Any other parts that show wear or damage must be renewed.

24 To reassemble first fit a new rack bearing into the rack housing so that the flats of the bearing are positioned offset to the bearing retaining screw hole.

25 Using a 0.119 inch (3.00mm) diameter drill located in the retaining screw hole drill through the bearing. Clear away any swarf from the bearing and the housing.

26 Apply some non hardening oil resistant sealing compound to the bush retaining screw and refit the screw.

27 It is very important that the screw does not protrude into the bore of the bearing. Should this condition exist the end of the screw must be filed flat.

28 Fit the pinion washer to the pinion followed by the upper bearing. The thrust face must face towards the pinion washer.

29 Carefully fit the rack into the rack housing the correct way round as noted during dismantling.

30 Insert the pinion into the housing and then centralise the rack relative to the rack housing. Fit a peg into the centre locating hole.

31 Position the pinion making sure the groove in the pinion serrations is facing and also parallel with the rack teeth.

32 Refit the lower bearing with the thrust face facing towards the pinion.

33 Replace the bearing shims and make sure that the bearing shim pack stands proud of the pinion housing. If necessary add new shims to achieve this condition.

34 Refit the pinion housing end cover but without the paper gasket. Secure in position with the two bolts and spring washers. The two bolts should only be tightened sufficiently to nip the end cover.

35 Using feeler gauges measure the gap between the pinion housing and the end cover. Make a note of the measurement.

36 Undo and remove the two pinion housing end cover securing bolts and spring washers. Lift away the end cover.

37 Adjust the number of shims in the end pack so as to obtain a 0.011 to 0.013 inch (0.279 - 0.330 mm) gap. A range of shims is available for this adjustment. Details may be found in the specifications at the beginning of this chapter.

38 It is important that the 0.060 inch (1.524 mm) shim is positioned next to the joint washer. Refit the shim pack, joint washer and end cover.

39 Apply a little non hardening oil resistant sealing compound to the end cover securing bolts. Fit the two bolts and spring washers and tighten to a torque wrench setting of 12 - 15 lb ft (1.6 - 2.0 kg m).

40 Carefully fit a new pinion oil seal.

41 Refit the damper yoke, cover plate gasket and cover plate.

42 Replace the cover bolts and spring washers and gradually tighten these in a progressive manner whilst turning the pinion to and fro through 180o until it is just possible to rotate the pinion between the finger and thumb.

43 Using feeler gauges measure the gap between the cover the the housing.

44 Remove the cover and reassemble this time including the damper spring, a new 'O' ring oil seal and shims to the previous determined measurement plug 0.002 - 0.005 inch (0.05 - 0.13mm).

45 Tighten the bolts that secure the yoke cover to a torque wrench setting of 12 - 15 lb ft (1.6 - 2.0 kg m).

46 Screw a new ball housing locknut onto each end of the rack to the limits of the thread.

47 Insert the two thrust springs into the ends of the rack.

48 Fit each tie rod into its ball housing and locate the ball cup against the thrust spring.

49 Slowly tighten the two ball housings until the tie rod is just nipped.

50 Using a mole wrench and a soft metal drift carefully tighten the locknut onto the ball housing. Again check that the tie rod is still pinched.

51 Next slacken the ball housing back by one eigth of a turn to allow full articulation of the tie rods.

52 Fully tighten the locking ring to the housing. Whilst this is

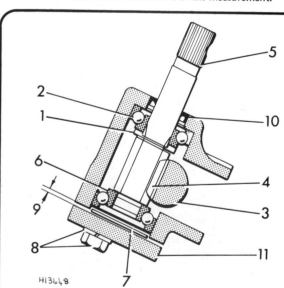

FIG 11.21 PINION END CROSS SECTION

1 Pinion washer	7 Shims
2 Upper bearing	8 Bolt and spring washer
3 Rack	9 Gap measurement
4 Pinion teeth	10 Pinion shaft oil seal
5 Pinion	11 End cover
6 Lower bearing	

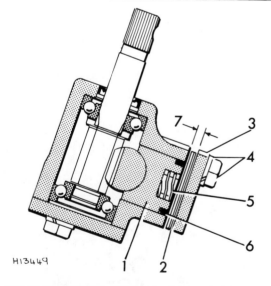

FIG 11.22 DAMPER COVER SHIM THICKNESS

1 Damper yoke	5 Damper spring
2 Shims and gasket	6 'O' ring seal
3 Cover plate	7 Gap measurement
4 Bolt and spring washer	

being done make sure the housing does not turn.

53 Using a centre punch or blunt chisel drive the ball housing edge of the locking ring into the locking slots of the ball housing and opposite into the locking slot of the rack.

54 Replace the two rack rubber seals and secure with the large clips to the housing. Position the two small clips and tighten on the pinion end.

55 Refit the tie rod locknuts and then screw on each tie rod end by an equal amount until the dimension between the two ball pin centres is 43.7 inches (110.9cm). Tighten the locknuts sufficiently to prevent this initial setting being lost during refitting.

56 Using a squirt type oil can insert 1/3 pint (0.19 litre) of recommended grade oil through the pinion seal. Finally position the small seal clip and lightly tighten.

---

24 Front wheel alignment

The front wheels are correctly aligned when they are turning in at the front 1/16 inch (1.6mm). It is important that this measurement is taken on a centre line drawn horizontally and parallel to the ground through the centre line of the hub. The exact point should be in the centre of the sidewall of the tyre and not on the wheel rim which could be distorted and therefore give inaccurate readings.

The adjustment is effected by loosening the locknut on each tie rod ball joint and also slackening the rubber gaiter clip holding it to the tie rod, both tie rods then being turned equally until the adjustment is correct.

This is a job best left to a BLMC garage, as accurate alignment requires the use of special equipment. If the wheels are not in alignment, tyre wear will be heavy and uneven, and the steering be stiff and unresponsive.

---

25 Front suspension trim height - adjustment

Before checking the front trim height of the car it must be prepared by removing the contents of the boot, with the exception of the spare wheel. Ideally there should be two gallons of petrol in the tank. Check and adjust the tyre pressures as necessary. Stand the car on a level surface and measure the vertical distance between the underside of the wheel arch and the floor, this distance being taken through the centre line of the hub.

The height measurement should be 25 3/8 ± 1/4 in (644 ± 6.4 mm) when the vehicle has been in service. However, if new torsion bars are fitted this dimension must be increased by 5/16 in (8 mm) to allow for initial settling.

Coarse adjustment

This is applicable when there is a need to increase the trim height by more than 3/4 in (19 mm) or decrease it by more than 1 1/4 in (32 mm).

1 Refer to Section 5 and follow the instructions given in paragraphs 1 to 4 inclusive.

2 Undo and remove the steering tie rod end ball pin nut. Using a universal ball joint separator, detach the ball pin from the steering lever.

3 Raise the shock absorber arm and then jack up the car so as to relieve the torsion bar load and yet still allow the lower suspension arm to be supported.

4 Mark the relative position of the torsion bar lever and car body with a scriber. Do not mark the torsion bar.

5 Ease the lever forwards out of mesh with the torsion bar splines and reposition it one spline up or down as necessary.

6 Reassembling is now the reverse sequence. It will be necessary to make a final fine adjustment on completion of reassembly.

Fine adjustment

1 Refer to Fig 11.23 and remove the adjustment lever lock bolt, spring washer and spacer.

2 Slacken the adjuster screw locknut and turn the adjuster screw in a clockwise direction to increase the trim height or anti-clockwise to decrease it. Retighten the locknut.

3 Refit the adjustment lever lockbolt.

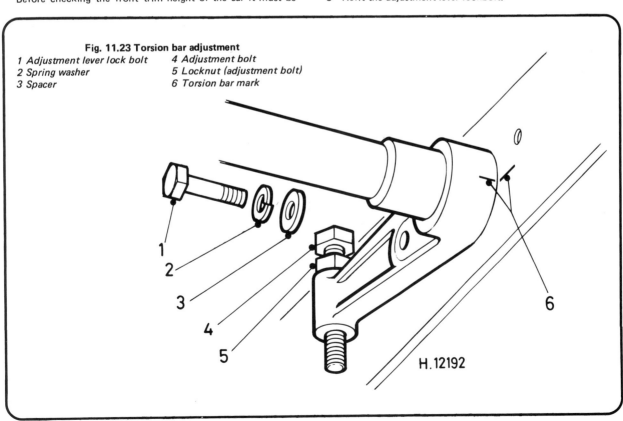

Fig. 11.23 Torsion bar adjustment

1 Adjustment lever lock bolt   4 Adjustment bolt
2 Spring washer   5 Locknut (adjustment bolt)
3 Spacer   6 Torsion bar mark

H.12192

Symptom	Reason/s	Remedy

STEERING FEELS VAGUE, CAR WANDERS AND FLOATS AT SPEED

General wear or damage	Tyre pressures uneven	Check pressures and adjust as necessary.
	Shock absorbers worn	Test, and replace if worn.
	Steering gear ball joints badly worn	Fit new ball joints.
	Suspension geometry incorrect	Check and rectify.
	Steering mechanism free play excessive	Adjust or overhaul steering mechanism.
	Front suspension and rear suspension pick-up points out of alignment or badly worn	Normally caused by poor repair work after a serious accident. Extensive rebuilding necessary.
	Front suspension lacking grease	Check condition and grease or replace worn parts and re-grease.

STIFF AND HEAVY STEERING

Lack of maintenance or accident damage	Tyre pressures too low	Check pressures and inflate tyres.
	No grease in steering ball joints	Replace.
	Front wheel toe-in incorrect	Check and reset toe-in.
	Suspension geometry incorrect	Check and rectify.
	Steering gear incorrectly adjusted too tightly	Check and re-adjust steering gear.
	Steering column badly misaligned	Determine cause and rectify (usually due to bad repair after severe accident damage and difficult to correct).

WHEEL WOBBLE AND VIBRATION

General wear or damage	Wheel nuts loose	Check and tighten as necessary.
	Front wheels and tyres out of balance	Balance wheels and tyres and add weights as necessary.
	Steering ball joints badly worn	Replace steering gear ball joints.
	Hub bearings badly worn	Remove and fit new hub bearings.
	Steering gear free play excessive	Adjust and overhaul steering gear.

Chapter 12 Bodywork and underframe

For modifications, and information applicable to later models, see Supplement at end of manual

Contents

General description	1
Maintenance - body and chassis	2
Maintenance - upholstery and carpets..	3
Body repairs - minor...	4
Body repairs - major...	5
Maintenance - locks and hinges	6
Door rattles - tracing and rectification	7
Door - removal and refitting	8
Door hinge - removal and refitting	9
Door trim panel and capping - removal and refitting	10
Door exterior handle - removal and refitting	11
Door lock adjustment	12
Door remote control handle - removal and refitting	13
Door private lock - removal and refitting	14
Door glass - removal and refitting...	15
Bonnet - removal and refitting...	16
Bonnet lock - removal and refitting	17
Bonnet lock control cable - removal and refitting	18
Boot lid hinge and tailgate - removal and refitting...	19
Boot lid lock - removal and refitting	20
Windscreen and rear window - removal and refitting	21
Parcel tray - removal and refitting	22
Facia panel - removal and refitting	23
Lower facia panel - removal and refitting	24
Glovebox - removal and refitting	25
Bumpers - removal and refitting	26
Radiator grille - removal and refitting..	27
Heater unit - removal and refitting	28
Heater fan and motor - removal and refitting	29
Heater matrix - removal and refitting	30
Windscreen demister duct - removal and refitting	31
Instrument panel - removal and refitting...	32

1 General description

The combined body and underframe is of all welded construction. This makes a very strong and torsionally rigid shell.

The Marina 1.8 is two or four doors, with a fifth rear door on the Estate. The door hinges are securely bolted to both the door and body. The drivers door Is locked from the outside by means of a key and all other doors may be locked from the inside.

The toughened safety glass is fitted to all windows; the windscreen has a specially toughened 'zone' in front of the driver. In the event of the windscreen shattering this 'zone' breaks into much larger pieces than the rest of the screen thus giving the driver much better vision than would otherwise be possible.

The front seats are of the adjustable bucket type whilst the rear seat is a bench seat, without a central arm rest.

For occupant safety all switches and controls are suitably recessed or positioned so that they cannot cause body harm. Provision is made for the fitting of either static or automatic seat belts.

The instruments are contained in two dials located above the steering column. A heater and ventilation system is fitted incorporating a full flow system with outlet ducts at instrument panel level.

2 Maintenance - body and chassis

1 The condition of the bodywork is of considerable importance as it is on this in the main that the second-hand value of the car will mainly depend. It is much more difficult to repair neglected bodywork than to renew mechanical assemblies. The hidden portions of the body, such as the wheel arches, the underframe and the engine compartment are equally important, although obviously not requiring such frequent attention as the immediately visible paintwork.

2 Once a year, or every 12,000 miles, it is advisable to visit a garage equipped to steam clean the body. This will take about 1½ hours. All traces of dirt and oil will be removed and the underside can then be inspected carefully for rust, damaged hydraulic pipes, frayed electrical wiring and similar maladies. The car should be greased on completion of this job.

3 At the same time the engine compartment should be cleaned in a similar manner. If steam cleaning facilities are not available, then brush 'Gunk' or a similar cleaner over the whole of the engine, and engine compartment, with a stiff brush, working it well in where there is an accumulation of oil and dirt. Do not paint the ignition system, and protect it with oily rags when the 'Gunk' is washed off. As the 'Gunk' is washed away it will take with it all traces of oil and dirt, leaving the engine looking clean and bright.

4 The wheel arches should be given particular attention, as under sealing can easily come away here, and stones and dirt thrown up from the road wheels can soon cause the paint to chip and flake, and so allow rust to set in. If rust is found, clean down the bare metal with wet and dry paper. Paint on an anti-corrosive coating such as 'Kurust', or if preferred red lead, and renew the undercoating and top coat.

5 The bodywork should be washed once a week or when dirty. Thoroughly wet the car to soften the dirt, and then wash the car down with a soft sponge and plenty of clean water. If the surplus dirt is not washed off very gently it will in time wear the paint as surely as wet and dry paper. It is best to use a hose if this is available. Give the car a final wash down and then dry with a soft chamois leather to prevent the formation of spots.

6 Spots of tar and grease thrown up from the road can be removed by a rag dampened in petrol.

7 Once every three months, give the bodywork and chromium trim a thoroughly good wax polish. If a chromium cleaner is used to remove rust on any of the cars plated parts, remember that any cleaner also removes part of the chromium so use only when absolutely necessary.

3 Maintenance - upholstery and carpets

1 Remove the carpets or mats, and thoroughly vacuum clean the interior of the car every three months, or more frequently if necessary.
2 Beat out the carpets and vacuum clean them if they are very dirty. If the upholstery is soiled apply an upholstery cleaner with a damp sponge and wipe off with a clean dry cloth.

4 Body repairs - minor

1 Major damage must be repaired by a specialist body repair shop but there is no reason why you cannot successfully beat out, repair, and respray minor damage yourself. The essential items which the owner should gather together to ensure a really professional job are:-
a) A plastic filler such as Holts 'Cataloy'.
b) Paint whose colour matches exactly that of the bodywork, either in a can for application by a spray gun, or in an aerosol can.
c) Fine cutting paste.
d) Medium and fine grade wet and dry paper.
2 Never use a metal hammer to knock out small dents as the blows tend to scratch and distort the metal. Knock out the dent with a mallet or rawhide hammer and press on the underside of the dented surface with a metal dolly or smooth wooden block roughly contoured to the normal shape of the damaged area.
3 After the worst of the damaged area has been knocked out, rub down the dent and surrounding area with medium wet and dry paper and thoroughly clean away all traces of dirt.
4 The plastic filler comprises a paste and hardener which must be thoroughly mixed together. Mix only a small portion at a time as the paste sets hard within five to fifteen minutes depending on the amount of hardener used.
5 Smooth on the filler with a knife or stiff plastic to the shape of the damaged portion and allow to thoroughly dry — a process

which takes about six hours. After the filler has dried it is likely that it will have contracted slightly so spread on a second layer of filler if necessary.
6 Smooth down the filler with fine wet and dry paper wrapped round a suitable block of wood and continue until the whole area is perfectly smooth and it is impossible to feel where the filler joins the rest of the paintwork.
7 Spray on from an aerosol can, or with a spray gun, an anti-rust undercoat, smooth down with wet and dry paper and then spray on two coats of the final finishing using a circular motion.
8 When thoroughly dry polish the whole area with a fine cutting paste to smooth the resprayed areas into the remainder of the wing and to remove the small particles of spray paint which will have settled round the area.
9 This will leave the wing looking perfect with not a trace of the previous dent.

5 Body repairs - major

1 Because the body is built on the monocoque principle and is integral with the underframe, major damage must be repaired by specialists with the necessary welding and hydraulic straightening equipment.
2 If the damage is severe, it is vital that on completion of the repair the chassis is in correct alignment. Less severe damage may also have twisted or distorted the chassis although this may not be visible immediately. It is therefore always best on completion of repair to check for twist and squareness to make sure all is well.
3 To check for twist, position the car on a clean level floor, place a jack under each jacking point, raise the car and take off the wheels. Raise or lower the jacks until the sills are parallel with the ground. Depending where the damage occurred, using an accurate scale, take measurements at the suspension mounting points and if comparable readings are not obtained it is an indication that the body is twisted.

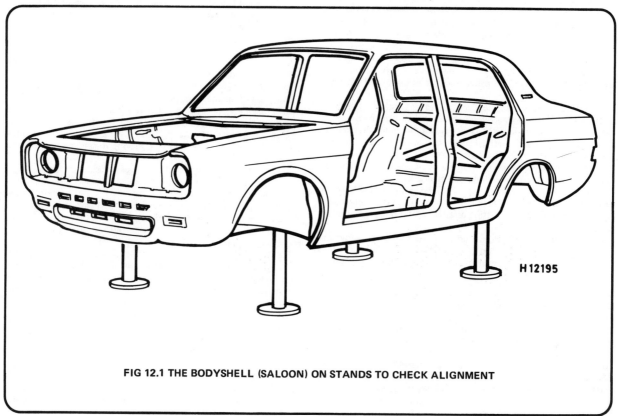

H 12195

FIG 12.1 THE BODYSHELL (SALOON) ON STANDS TO CHECK ALIGNMENT

4 After checking for twist, check for squareness by taking a series of measurements on the floor. Drop a plumb line and bob weight from various mounting points on the underside of the body and mark these points on the floor with chalk. Draw a straight line between each point and measure and mark the middle of each line. A line drawn on the floor starting at the front and finishing at the rear should be quite straight and pass through the centres of the other lines. Diagonal measurements can also be made as a check for squareness.

6 Maintenance - locks and hinges

Once every 6,000 miles (10,000 km) or 6 months the door, bonnet and boot hinges should be oiled with a few drops of engine oil from an oil can. The door striker plates can be given a thin smear of grease to reduce wear and ensure free movement.

7 Door rattles - tracing and rectification

The most common cause of door rattles is a misaligned, loose or worn striker plate but other causes may be:
1) Loose door handles, window winder handles or door hinges.
2) Loose, worn or misaligned door lock components.
3) Loose or worn remote control mechanism.
Or a combination of these.
2 If the striker catch is worn as a result of door rattles renew it and adjust as described later in this Chapter.
3 Should the hinges be badly worn then they must be renewed.

8 Door - removal and refitting

1 Refer to Section 10 and remove the door trim panel.
2 Working inside the door mark the outline of the stiffener plate at each hinge position (Fig.12.2). An assistant should now take the weight of the door.
3 Undo and remove the locknuts and plain washers that secure the door to the hinge.
4 Lift away the stiffener plates and finally the door.
5 Refitting the door is the reverse sequence to removal. Should it be necessary to adjust the position of the door in the aperture leave the locknuts slightly loose and reposition the door by trial and error. Fully tighten the locknuts.

9 Door hinge - removal and refitting

1 Remove the door then refer to Section 22 and remove the front parcel tray.
2 Using a wide blade screwdriver carefully ease back the side trim panel door seal and then the trim panel.
3 If the rear door hinges are to be removed, using a wide blade screwdriver ease back the 'B' post door seals. Undo and remove the carpet finisher retaining screws, slide the front seat forward and ease the trim panel retaining clips from the 'B' post. Hinge the trim panel up at the PVC lining crease. This will give access to the door hinge retaining nuts.
4 Undo and remove the locknuts and plain washers securing each hinge (Fig.12.2). Lift away the stiffener plates and finally the door hinges.
5 Refitting the door hinge is the reverse sequence to removal.

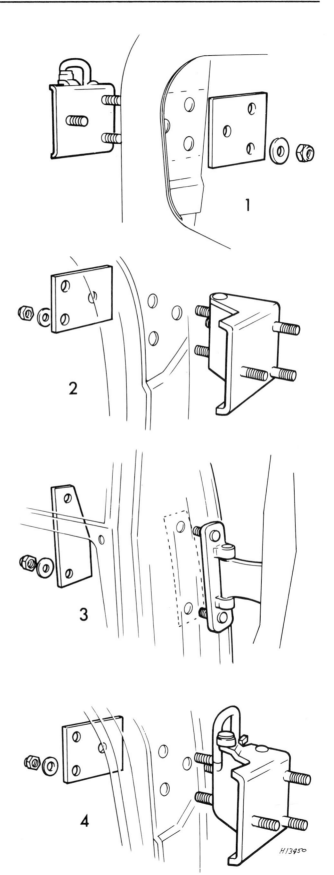

FIG 12.2 FRONT AND REAR DOOR HINGE ASSEMBLIES

1 *Top front door*   3 *Top rear door*
2 *Bottom front door*   4 *Bottom rear door*

10 Door trim panel and capping - removal and refitting

1 Wind the window up fully and note the position of the handle.
2 Undo and remove the screw and spacer that secures the window regulator handle. Lift away the handle (Fig.12.3).
3 Undo and remove the two screws that retain the arm rest. Lift away the arm rest.
4 With a screwdriver carefully slide the upper and lower bezels from the remote control door handle.

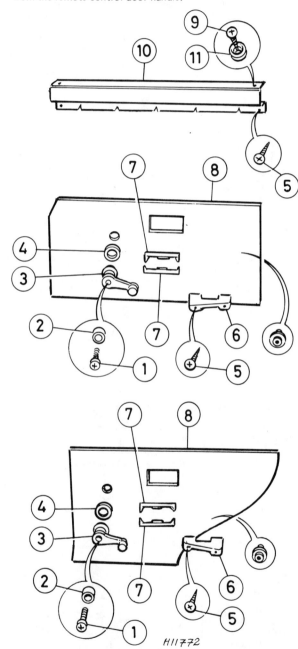

FIG 12.3 DOOR TRIM PANEL AND CAPPING

1 Screw	7 Upper and lower bezel
2 Spacer	8 Trim panel
3 Window regulator handle	9 Screw
4 Bezel	10 Capping
5 Screw	11 Shaped washer
6 Rim rest	

5 With a wide blade screwdriver or knife inserted between the trim panel and door carefully ease the trim panel clips from the door. Lift away the trim panel.
6 Should it be necessary to remove the trim capping, undo and remove the screws and shaped washers and unclip the trim capping from the door.
7 Refitting is the reverse sequence to removal. If the capping has been removed make sure that the door glass seal and wiper strip are correctly positioned.

11 Door exterior handle - removal and refitting

1 It is important to check that if the door lock is not operating correctly that the cause is not due to maladjustment. Full information on this will be found in Section 12.
2 Refer to Section 10 and remove the door trim.
3 Undo and remove the two nuts or screws, plain and shakeproof washers. Lift away the clamp bracket.
4 Front door: Disconnect the private lock control rod clip from the locking bar cross shaft. Carefully unclip and detach the screwed rod at the exterior handle release lever.
5 Rear door only: Disconnect the screwed rod at the cross lever but do not alter the rod adjustment.
6 Lift away the handle assembly.
7 Refitting is the reverse sequence to removal. Lubricate all moving parts with Castrol GTX.

12 Door lock adjustment

Four adjustments may be made to the door locks and it will usually be found that any malfunction of a lock is caused by incorrect adjustment.

Exterior handle
1 Refer to Section 10 and remove the trim panel.
2 Close the door and partially operate the exterior release lever. Check that there is free movement of the lever before the point is reached where the transfer lever and its screwed rod move.
3 Operate the exterior release lever fully and check that the latch disc is released from the door striker before the lever is fully open.
4 To adjust, disconnect the screwed rod and screw in or out to achieve the correct setting.

Remote control
1 Refer to Section 10 and remove the trim panel.
2 Undo and remove the screw and slacken the control retaining screws.
3 Move the remote control assembly towards the latch unit. Retighten the retaining screws and make sure that the operating lever is against its stop 'A' (Fig.12.4 or 12.5).

Safety locking lever
Refer to Section 10 and remove the trim panel.

Front
1 Disconnect the long lock rod from the safety locking lever and then the short rod from the locking bar. Push the locking bar against its stop 'B' and move the safety locking lever to the locked position.
2 Refit the long rod in the safety locking lever and then press in the legs of the clip. Adjust the short rod so as to fit into the rod bush in the locking bar.
3 Release the safety locking lever and make sure that the operating lever is quite free to operate.

Rear
1 Disconnect the long lock rod from the safety locking lever and then the short lock rod from the locking lever.
2 Press the free wheeling operating lever against the stop 'D' and position the safety locking lever in the locked position.

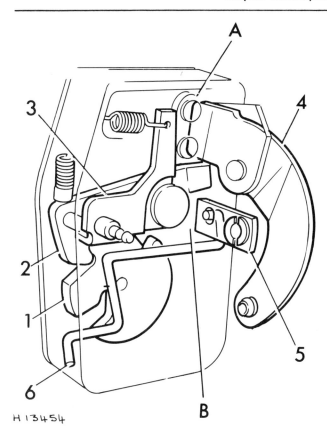

H13454

FIG 12.4 FRONT DOOR LOCK MECHANISM

1 Latch disc	5 Locking bar
2 Latch disc release lever	6 Locking bar cross shaft
3 Cross control lever	Positive stop A
4 Operating lever	Positive stop B

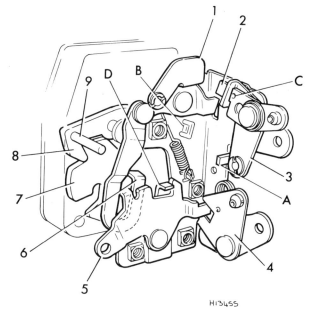

H13455

FIG 12.5 REAR DOOR LOCK MECHANISM

1 Cross lever	7 Latch disc
2 Child safety intermediate	8 Latch disc release lever
lever	9 Striker pin
3 Operating lever	Positive stop B and C
4 Locking lever	Positive stop A
5 Free wheel actuating lever	Positive stop D
6 Operating tab	

3 Reconnect the long lock rod to the safety locking lever. Push in the legs of the clip and adjust the short rod to fit into the rod bush in the locking lever.

4 Release the safety locking lever and ensure that the operating tab aligns with the striker pin of the latch disc release lever.

Door striker

1 It is very important that the latch disc is in the open position. Also do not slam the door whilst any adjustment is being made otherwise damage may result.

2 Slacken the striker plate retaining screws until it is just sufficient to allow the door to close and latch.

3 Push the door inwards or pull it outwards without operating the release lever until the door is level with the body and aperture.

4 Open the door carefully and with a pencil round the striker plate to act as a datum.

5 Place the striker accurately by trial and error until the door can be closed easily without signs of lifting, dropping or rattling.

6 Close the door and make sure that the striker is not positioned too far in by pressing on the door. It should be possible to press the door in slightly as the seals are compressed.

7 Finally tighten the striker plate retaining screws.

---

13 Door remote control handle - removal and refitting

It is important to check that if the door lock is not operating

correctly that the cause is not due to maladjustment. Full information on this will be found in Section 12.

2 Refer to Section 10 and remove the door trim.

3 Undo and remove the three screws, shakeproof and plain washers that secure the remote control.

4 Undo and remove the lock screw.

5 Detach the long remote control lock rod from the safety locking lever.

6 Detach the remote control release rod from the operating lever.

7 Lift away the remote control assembly.

8 Front door only: Undo and remove the screw and plain washer that secures the glass channel. Detach the exterior handle transfer lever from the lifting stud of the cross control lever.

9 Rear door only: Detach the exterior handle screwed rod from the cross lever.

10 Detach the remote control release rod from the operating lever of the disc lock front door or free wheel assembly - rear door.

11 Detach the lock rod clip from the lock bar cross shaft.

12 Front door only: Detach the short lock rod from the locking bar.

13 Rear door only: Detach the short lock rod from the free wheel locking lever.

14 Using a pencil mark the position of the disc latch body on the door. Undo and remove the four screws that secure the disc latch and the free wheel from the rear door.

15 With a pencil mark the position of the door pillar and remove the two screws retaining the striker plate assembly. The striker plate may now be lifted away. The tapped stiffener plate is retained inside the door 'B' post by retaining tags.

16 Refitting the door remote control assembly is the reverse sequence to removal. Lubricate all moving parts with Castrol GTX.

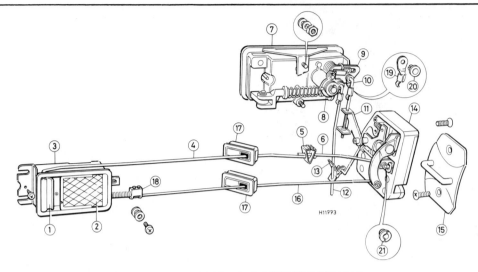

FIG 12.6 FRONT DOOR LOCK COMPONENT PARTS

1 Safety locking lever	7 Outside handle	11 Transfer lever	17 Door rod guide
2 Remote release handle	8 Lock barrel free wheel	12 Lock rod (outside handle)	18 Retaining clip
3 Remote control assembly	lever	13 Lock rod clip	19 Rod clip
4 Remote lock rod-long	9 Outside handle release	14 Disc lock assembly	20 Rod bush
5 Remote lock rod clip	lever	15 Lock striker	21 Rod bush (cross
6 Remote lock rod-short	10 Screwed rod	16 Remote release rod	control lever)

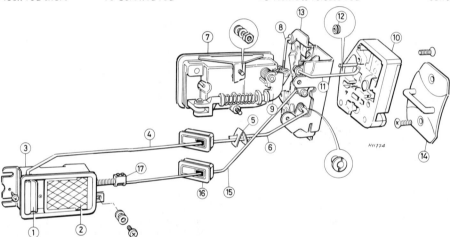

FIG 12.7 REAR DOOR LOCK COMPONENT PARTS

1 Safety locking lever	5 Remote lock rod clip	9 Outside handle release	12 Door grommet
2 Remote release lever	6 Remote lock rod-short	lever	13 Free-wheel assembly
3 Remote control assembly	7 Outside handle	10 Disc lock assembly	14 Lock striker
4 Remote lock rod-long	8 Screwed rod	11 Child safety lever rod	15 Remote release rod
			16 Door rod guide
			17 Retaining clip

14 Door private lock - removal and refitting

1 Refer to Section 11 and remove the door exterior handle.
2 Using a small screwdriver carefully remove the circlip and lift away the spring and special washers (Fig.12.8).
3 The lock barrel may now be removed.
4 Refitting is the reverse sequence to removal.

15 Door glass - removal and refitting

1 Refer to Section 10 and remove the door trim.
2 Lower the window until the glass regulator channel appears in the door inner aperture.
3 Undo and remove the four screws and spring washers that secure the regulator and lift away the regulator (Fig.12.9).

4 Front door: Carefully lower the glass to the bottom of the door.
5 Rear door: Raise the glass fully.
6 If the capping is fitted this should next be removed. Undo and remove the screws and shaped washers. Unclip the trim capping from the door.
7 Using a screwdriver carefully so as not to damage the paint-work spring off the six clips that retain the glass wiper strip. Lift away the wiper strip.
8 Carefully remove the window channel rubber by easing it out of the door glass aperture.
9 Using a drill of suitable diameter remove the 'pop' rivet that retains the top of the centre window channel.
10 Undo and remove the screw and plain washer that retains the bottom of the centre window channel.
11 The window channel may now be removed by turning it through 90° and aligning the narrowest section with the glass

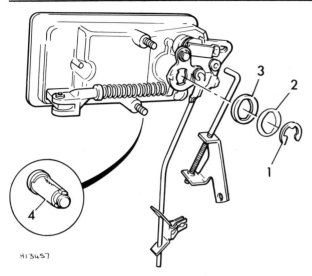

FIG 12.8 DOOR PRIVATE LOCK ASSEMBLY REMOVAL

1 Circlip   *3 Shaped washer*
2 Spring washer   *4 Lock barrel*

aperture in the door.
12 Remove the door fixed or opening quarter light whichever is fitted, and its sealing rubber.
13 The window glass may now be lifted out of the glass aperture.
14 Finally remove the regulator channel and its protective rubber from the glass.
15 Refitting the door glass is the reverse sequence to removal. If a new glass is to be fitted make sure that the regulator channel is refitted centrally on the door glass. Lubricate all moving parts with Castrol GTX.

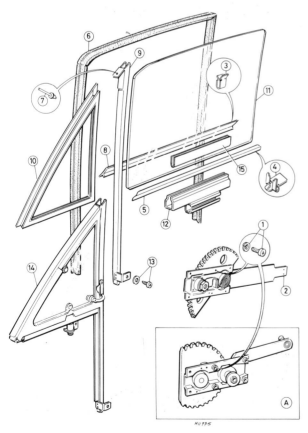

FIG 12.9 DOOR GLASS ASSEMBLY REMOVAL

1 Regulator securing bolt and   *10 Quarter light sealing rubber*
*   spring washer*   *11 Door glass*
2 Regulator   *12 Regulator channel*
3 Clip   *13 Channel securing screw*
4 Clip   *and plain washer*
5 Glass wiper strip   *14 Opening quarter light*
6 Window channel rubber   *assembly*
7 'Pop' rivet   *15 Protective rubber*
8 Glass outer weatherstrip *Inset 'A' shows rear*
9 Window channel   *regulator*

16 Bonnet - removal and refitting

1 Open the bonnet and support on its stay.
2 With a pencil mark the outline of the hinge on the bonnet to assist correct refitting. If the hinge is to be removed also mark the inner panel as well.
3 An assistant should now take the weight of the bonnet. Undo and remove the bonnet to hinge retaining bolts, spring and plain washers at both hinges. Carefully lift away the bonnet over the front of the car (Fig. 12.10).
4 Refitting is the reverse sequence to removal. Alignment in the body may be made by leaving the securing bolts slightly loose and repositioning by trial and error. The securing bolts must not be overtightened as they could damage the outer bonnet panel.

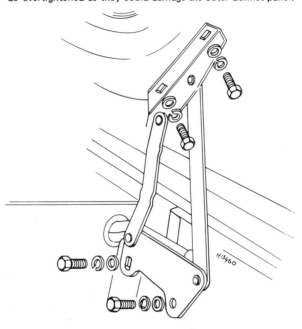

FIG 12.10 BONNET HINGE ASSEMBLY

17 Bonnet lock - removal and refitting

1 Open the bonnet and support it on its stay, then unscrew and remove the two radiator support bracket retaining screws and move the top of the radiator back to gain access to the lock.
2 Slacken the nut and detach the release cable from the trunnion located at the lock lever (Fig. 12.11).
3 Detach the release cable and its clip from the bonnet lock.
4 Undo and remove the three bolts, plain and shakeproof washers securing the bonnet lock. Lift away the bonnet lock.
5 Undo and remove the two bolts, plain and shakeproof washers that secure the locking pin assembly to the underside of the bonnet.

6 Detach the return spring and remove the rivet that secures the safety catch.

7 Refitting is the reverse sequence to removal. It is now necessary to adjust the lock pin assembly until a clearance of 2 inches (50.8 mm) exists ('A' Fig. 12.11) between the thimble and bonnet panel.

8 Carefully lower the bonnet and check the alignment of the pin thimble with the lock hole. If misaligned slacken the fixing bolts and move the assembly slightly. Retighten the fixing bolts.

9 Close the bonnet and check its alignment with the body wing panels. If necessary reposition the lock pin assembly.

10 The bonnet must contact the rubber stops. To adjust the position of the stops, screw in or out as necessary.

11 Lubricate all moving parts and finally check the bonnet release operations.

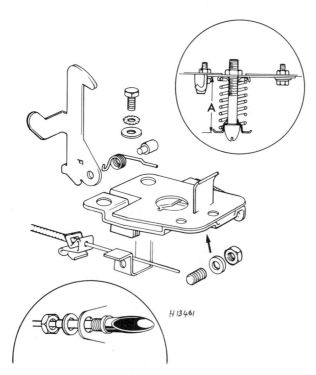

FIG 12.11 BONNET LOCK ASSEMBLY

18 Bonnet lock control cable - removal and refitting

1 Open the bonnet and support on its stay, then unscrew and remove the two radiator support bracket retaining screws and move the top of the radiator back to gain access to the lock.

2 Slacken the nut and detach the release cable from the trunnion located at the lock lever (Fig. 12.11).

3 Detach the release cable and its clip from the bonnet lock.

4 Release the outer control cable from its snap clamp and then unscrew and remove the screw that secures each clip to the wing valance. Lift away the two clips.

5 Undo and remove the nut and shakeproof washer that secures the outer cable to the body side bracket mounted below the facia panel.

6 Carefully withdraw the control cable assembly through the body grommet.

7 Refitting is the reverse sequence to removal. It is however, necessary to adjust the inner cable. Push the release knob in fully and make sure that the lock release lever is not pre-loaded by the release cable.

8 There must be a minimum movement of 0.5 in (12.7 mm) prior to the release of the bonnet. To adjust, slacken the cable

trunnion nut and re-adjust the cable so that the bonnet is released within 0.5 to 2.0 in (12.7 to 50.8 mm) of cable movement.

19 Boot lid hinge and tail gate - removal and refitting

1 Open the lid and using a pencil mark the position of the hinge relative to the luggage compartment lid.

2 Undo and remove the four bolts, spring and plain washers that secure the hinges to the lid. Lift away the lid over the back of the car. For this operation it is desirable to have the assistance of a second person.

3 To remove the hinge undo and remove the two nuts, plain and spring washers that secure each hinge to the body bracket. Lift away the hinge (Fig. 12.12).

4 Refitting is the reverse sequence to removal, but if adjustment is necessary leave the bolts securing the hinge to the lid slack.

5 Close the lid and adjust the position to ensure correct trim spacing. Open the lid and tighten the hinge bolts. Do not over-tighten as they could damage the outer lid panel.

6 The tail gate of the Estate is removed by undoing the hinge bolts or the tailgate itself. Have an assistant hold the tail gate in the open position so that as the bolts are removed it will still remain supported. Do not forget to scribe round the hinges so that they can be refitted in a similar position. Refitting a new tailgate will mean that the exact positioning when closed will have to be adjusted using the same method as for a side door.

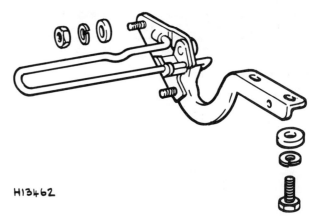

FIG.12.12 BOOT LID HINGE

20 Boot lid lock - removal and refitting

1 Using a pencil mark the outline of the lock catch plate on the lid under the panel.

2 Undo and remove the three bolts, spring and plain washers that secure the lock catch (Fig. 12.13).

3 Slacken the locknut and unscrew the spindle. Lift away the shakeproof washer, spindle striker and spring.

4 Break off the two retaining ears of the barrel housing spring retaining clip using a screwdriver and withdraw the barrel assembly and sealing gasket from outside the lid. A new clip will be necessary during reassembly.

5 Using a pencil mark the outline of the striker on the body panel.

6 Undo and remove the two bolts, spring and plain washers retaining the striker. Lift away the striker.

7 Refitting is the reverse sequence to removal. Lubricate all moving parts with Castrol GTX.

21 Windscreen and rear window glass - removal and refitting

If you are unfortunate enough to have a windscreen shatter, fitting a replacement windscreen is one of the few jobs which the average owner is advised to leave to a professional. For the owner who wishes to do the job himself the following instructions are given:

1 Remove the wiper arms from their spindles using a screwdriver to lift the retaining clip from the spindle end and pull away.

2 Using a screwdriver very carefully prise up the end of the finisher strip and withdraw it from its slot in the rubber moulding (Fig. 12.14).

3 The assistance of a second person should now be enlisted, ready to catch the glass when it is released from its aperture.

4 Working inside the car, commencing at one top corner, press the glass and ease it from its rubber moulding.

5 Remove the rubber moulding from the windscreen aperture.

6 Now is the time to remove all pieces of glass if the screen has shattered. Use a vacuum cleaner to extract as much as possible. Switch on the heater boost motor and adjust the controls to 'Screen defrost' but watch out for flying pieces of glass which might be blown out of the ducting.

7 Carefully inspect the rubber moulding for signs of splitting or deterioration. Clean all traces of sealing compound from the rubber moulding and windscreen aperture flange.

8 To refit the glass, first apply sealer between the rubber and glass.

9 Press a little 'Dum Dum' onto four or five inches of the body flange on either side of each corner.

10 Apply some 'Bostik' mastic sealer to the body flange.

11 With the rubber moulding correctly positioned on the glass it is now necessary to insert a piece of cord about 16 ft long all round the outer channel in the rubber surround which fits over the windscreen aperture flange. The two free ends of the cord should finish at either top or bottom centre and overlap each other by a minimum of 1 ft.

12 Offer the screen up to the aperture and get an assistant to press the rubber surround hard against the body flange. Slowly pull one end of the cord moving round the windscreen so drawing the lip over the windscreen flange on the body. If necessary use a piece of plastic or tapered wood to assist in locating the lip on the windscreen flange.

13 The finisher strip must next be fitted to the moulding and for this a special tool is required. An illustration of this tool is shown in Fig 12.14 and a handyman should be able to make up an equivalent using netting wire and a wooden file handle.

14 Fit the eye of the tool into the groove and feed in the finisher strip.

15 Push the tool around the complete length of the moulding, feeding the finisher into the channel as the eyelet opens it. The back half beds the finisher into the moulding.

16 Clean off traces of sealer using turpentine.

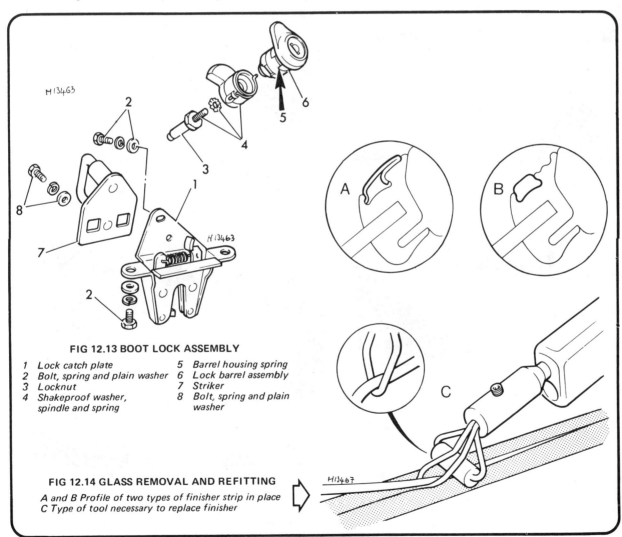

FIG 12.13 BOOT LOCK ASSEMBLY

1 Lock catch plate	5 Barrel housing spring
2 Bolt, spring and plain washer	6 Lock barrel assembly
3 Locknut	7 Striker
4 Shakeproof washer, spindle and spring	8 Bolt, spring and plain washer

FIG 12.14 GLASS REMOVAL AND REFITTING

A and B Profile of two types of finisher strip in place
C Type of tool necessary to replace finisher

This sequence of photographs deals with the repair of the dent and paintwork damage shown in this photo. The procedure will be similar for the repair of a hole. It should be noted that the procedures given here are simplified – more explicit instructions will be found in the text

In the case of a dent the first job – after removing surrounding trim – is to hammer out the dent where access is possible. This will minimise filling. Here, the large dent having been hammered out, the damaged area is being made slightly concave

Now all paint must be removed from the damaged area, by rubbing with coarse abrasive paper. Alternatively, a wire brush or abrasive pad can be used in a power drill. Where the repair area meets good paintwork, the edge of the paintwork should be 'feathered', using a finer grade of abrasive paper

In the case of a hole caused by rusting, all damaged sheet-metal should be cut away before proceeding to this stage. Here, the damaged area is being treated with rust remover and inhibitor before being filled

Mix the body filler according to its manufacturer's instructions. In the case of corrosion damage, it will be necessary to block off any large holes before filling – this can be done with zinc gauze or aluminium tape. Make sure the area is absolutely clean before...

...applying the filler. Filler should be applied with a flexible applicator, as shown, for best results; the wooden spatula being used for confined areas. Apply thin layers of filler at 20-minute intervals, until the surface of the filler is slightly proud of the surrounding bodywork

Initial shaping can be done with a Surform plane or Dreadnought file. Then, using progressively finer grades of wet-and-dry paper, wrapped around a sanding block, and copious amounts of clean water, rub down the filler until really smooth and flat. Again, feather the edges of adjoining paintwork

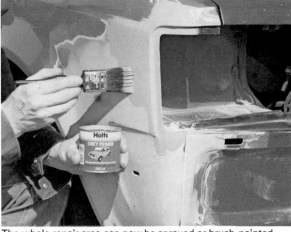

The whole repair area can now be sprayed or brush-painted with primer. If spraying, ensure adjoining areas are protected from over-spray. Note that at least one inch of the surrounding sound paintwork should be coated with primer. Primer has a 'thick' consistency, so will fill small imperfections

Again, using plenty of water, rub down the primer with a fine grade of wet-and-dry paper (400 grade is probably best) until it is really smooth and well blended into the surrounding paintwork. Any remaining imperfections can now be filled by carefully applied knifing stopper paste

When the stopper has hardened, rub down the repair area again before applying the final coat of primer. Before rubbing down this last coat of primer, ensure the repair area is blemish-free — use more stopper if necessary. To ensure that the surface of the primer is really smooth use some finishing compound

The top coat can now be applied. When working out of doors, pick a dry, warm and wind-free day. Ensure surrounding areas are protected from over-spray. Agitate the aerosol thoroughly, then spray the centre of the repair area, working outwards with a circular motion. Apply the paint as several thin coats

After a period of about two weeks, which the paint needs to harden fully, the surface of the repaired area can be 'cut' with a mild cutting compound prior to wax polishing. When carrying out bodywork repairs, remember that the quality of the finished job is proportional to the time and effort expended

22 Parcel tray - removal and refitting

1   Refer to Fig.12.15 and undo and remove the screw and plain washer.

2   Undo and remove the nut, shakeproof washer, bolt and plain washer.

3   Remove the parcel tray from the inside of the car taking care not to damage the headlining or interior trim.

4   Refitting the parcel tray is the reverse sequence to removal.

23 Facia panel - removal and refitting

1   Refer to Section 32 and remove the instrument panel.

2   Refer to Section 25 and remove the glovebox.

3   Refer to Section 24 and remove the lower facia panel.

4   Undo and remove the six nuts, spring and plain washers that secure the facia to the windscreen lower panel (Fig.12.16).

5   Undo and remove the three bolts that secure the facia panel to the lower rail.

6   Undo and remove the four bolts, plain and spring washers that secure the two outer brackets to the lower rail.

7   Undo and remove the two bolts, spring and plain washers that secure the upper steering column bracket.

8   Slacken the two nuts that secure the lower steering column bracket and remove the facia panel from the inside of the car taking care not to damage the headlining or interior trim.

9   Refitting the facia panel is the reverse sequence to removal.

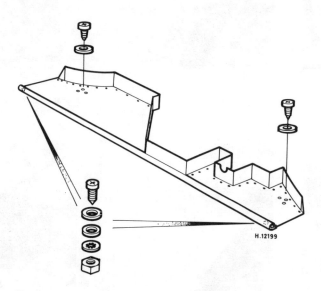

FIG 12.15 PARCEL SHELF ATTACHMENTS

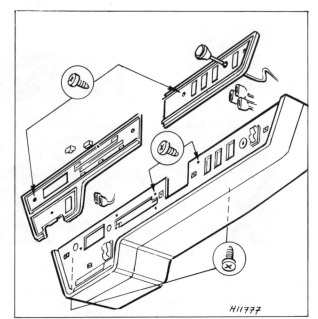

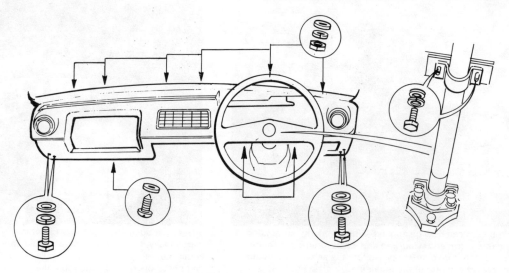

FIG 12.16 FACIA PANEL ASSEMBLY - INSET: LOWER FACIA PANEL ASSEMBLY

24 Lower facia panel - removal and refitting

1 Open the bonnet and slacken the choke control cable clamp at the carburettor. Detach the control cable and pull out the choke control knob and inner cable.
2 Undo and remove the two self tapping screws that secure the right hand switch trim panel. Lift away the panel.
3 Undo and remove the three self tapping screws that secure the left hand switch trim panel. Lift away the panel.
4 Undo and remove the two screws that secure the heater controls.
5 Undo and remove the three screws that retain the facia lower panel.
6 Undo and remove the two self tapping screws that secure the facia lower panel brackets to the upper facia panel.
7 Carefully draw the panel forwards and make a note of the electrical cable connections at the rear of the heater and lighting switches. Detach the cable connectors from the rear of the switches.
8 The choke control outer cable and facia lower panel may now be lifted away from the inside of the car.
9 Refitting is the reverse sequence to removal.

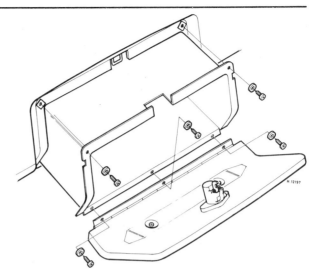

FIG 12.17 GLOVEBOX LID

25 Glovebox - removal and refitting

1 Open the glovebox lid. Undo and remove the three screws that secure the hinge and lower the lid (Fig.12.17).
2 Undo and remove the two screws that retain the glovebox compartment. Lift away the glovebox.
3 Undo and remove the two screws that secure the glovebox lid catch. Lift away the catch and spacer plates.
4 Refitting is the reverse sequence to removal.

26 Bumpers - removal and refitting

Front

1 Refer to Fig.12.18 and undo and remove the bolt, spring and plain washer and mounting rubber from each end of the bumper.
2 Undo and remove the bolts, spring and plain washer that secures each support bracket to the body.
3 Lift away the front bumper assembly.
4 Undo and remove the bolts, spring and plain washers securing each bracket to the bumper.
5 Refitting is the reverse sequence to removal.

Rear

The sequence for removing the rear bumper is basically identical to that for the front bumper with the exception that before the bumper support brackets are released, the electric cables to the number plate light must be disconnected.

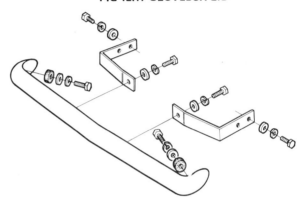

FIG 12.18 BUMPER ASSEMBLIES

Top   Front
Bottom   Rear (with number plate light connection)

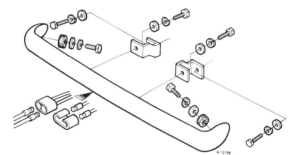

27 Radiator grille - removal and refitting

1 Refer to Fig.12.19 and undo and remove the four self tapping screws and plain washers that secure the case to the body.
2 The grille and case may now be lifted upwards and forwards away from the front of the car.
3 To detach the grille from the case undo and remove the self tapping screws and the plain washers.
4 Refitting is the reverse sequence to removal. Make sure that the rubber inserts are correctly positioned in the body panel cut-out and the locating pegs of the case are located in the centre of the rubber inserts.

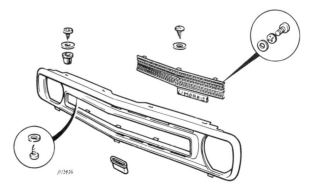

FIG 12.19 RADIATOR GRILLE ASSEMBLY

28 Heater unit - removal and refitting

1   Refer to Section 24 and remove the lower facia panel.
2   Refer to Section 32 and remove the instrument panel.
3   Detach the demister duct tubes from the heater.
4   Refer to Chapter 2, Section 2 and completely drain the cooling system.
5   Slacken the two heater hose clips located at the front of the bulkhead and remove the two hoses (Fig.12.20).
6   Pull off the two plenum chamber drain tubes located at the front of the bulkhead.
7   Undo and remove the nut and spring washer that holds the top of the heater unit to the bulkhead.
8   Undo and remove the two bolts, spring and plain washers that hold the heater side brackets to the bulkhead.
9   Detach the heater motor cable terminals from the wiring harness connector.
10 Place some plastic sheeting on the floor to prevent water damaging the carpeting. Draw the top of the heater unit rearwards to clear the upper fixing stud.
11 Pull the lower section of the heater rearwards until the heater unit is tilted so that it can be removed from under the facia support rail in front of the passengers position. Lift away from inside the car.
12 Refitting is the reverse sequence to removal but there are several additional points to be noted to ensure a satisfactory and watertight job.
13 Undo and remove the three self tapping screws that secure the air intake grille to the bulkhead top panel. Lift away the grille.
14 Place the heater in the car and lift into position engaging the top stud with the hole in the bulkhead. Refit the securing spring washer and nut but leave lose.
15 Working through the air intake grille hole carefully work the seal over the grille housing panel. Always fit a new seal if the condition of the original one is suspect.

29 Heater fan and motor - removal and refitting

1   Refer to Section 28 and remove the heater unit.
2   Undo and remove the heater plenum chamber securing self tapping screws and lift away the plenum chamber (Fig.12.21).
3   Undo and remove the three nuts and plain washers that secure the motor and fan assembly to the heater body. Lift away the motor.
4   If it is necessary to remove the fan, note which way round on the motor spindle it is fitted and remove the spring clip on the fan boss. Lift away the fan.
5   Refitting the heater fan and motor is the reverse sequence to removal. Before fitting a new motor always test it by placing the cable terminals on the battery terminals.

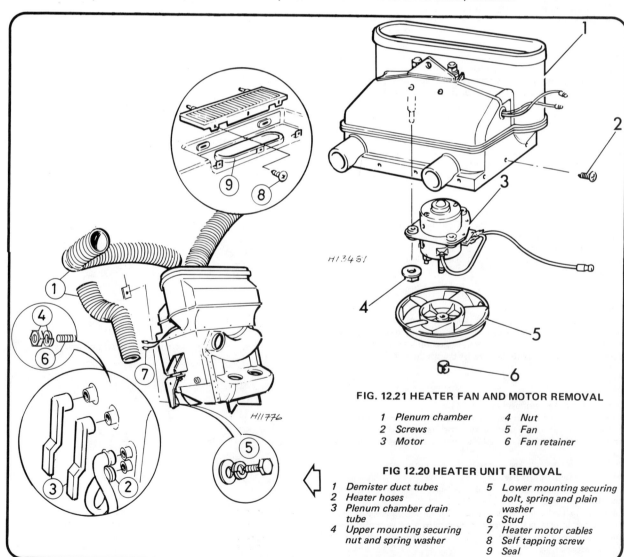

FIG. 12.21 HEATER FAN AND MOTOR REMOVAL

1 Plenum chamber	4 Nut
2 Screws	5 Fan
3 Motor	6 Fan retainer

FIG 12.20 HEATER UNIT REMOVAL

1 Demister duct tubes	5 Lower mounting securing bolt, spring and plain washer
2 Heater hoses	
3 Plenum chamber drain tube	6 Stud
4 Upper mounting securing nut and spring washer	7 Heater motor cables
	8 Self tapping screw
	9 Seal

30 Heater matrix - removal and refitting

1   Refer to Section 28 and remove the heater unit.
2   Carefully remove the packing rubber from the forward end of the heater unit.
3   Undo and remove the screws securing the matrix cover plate to the heater body. Lift away the cover plate.
4   The heater matrix may now be slid out from its location in the heater body.
5   If the matrix is leaking or blocked follow the instructions given in Chapter 2, Section 6.
6   Refitting the heater matrix is the reverse sequence to removal.

31 Windscreen demister duct - removal and refitting

1   Refer to Section 32 and remove the instrument panel.
2   Refer to Section 25 and remove the glovebox.
3   Detach the tubes from the demister duct (Fig. 12.23).
4   Working under the facia undo and remove the two nuts, shakeproof and plain washers that secure the duct in position.
5   Carefully raise the duct finisher to clear the bolts and lift away the duct.
6   Refitting the duct is the reverse sequence to removal.

32 Instrument panel - removal and refitting

1   Undo and remove the four crosshead screws, spring and plain washers that secure the instrument panel to the facia. Note that the two longest screws are located above the instruments (Fig.12. 24).
2   Draw the instrument panel away from the facia panel.
3   Press the release lever on the speedometer cable connector and detach the speedometer cable.
4   Disconnect the electrical multi pin connector from the rear of the instrument panel. Completely lift away the instrument panel.
5   Refitting the instrument panel is the reverse sequence to removal.

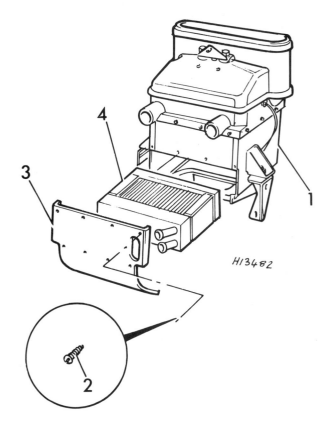

FIG. 12.22 HEATER MATRIX REMOVAL

1   *Heater casing*   3   *Cover plate*
2   *Screw*   4   *Matrix*

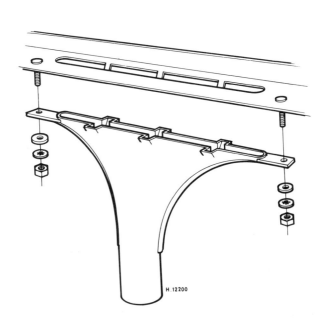

FIG. 12.23 WINDSCREEN DEMISTER DUCT

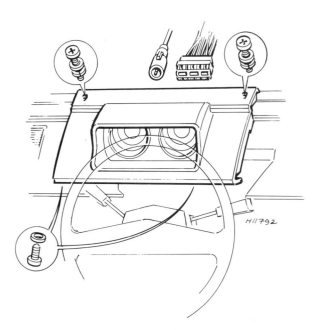

FIG. 12.24 INSTRUMENT PANEL REMOVAL

Chapter 13 Supplement:
Revisions and information on later models

Contents

Introduction 1
Specifications 2
Engine 3
    Engine changes (Marina Mk 2 models)
    Engine removal and repair procedure (Austin
    Marina models)
Cooling system 4
    Radiator — removal and refitting
    Fan belt — removal and refitting (Austin Marina models)
    Air pump drivebelt — adjustment (Austin Marina models)
    Radiator — removal and refitting (Austin Marina models)
    Thermostat — removal and refitting (Austin Marina models)
    Water pump — removal and refitting (Austin Marina models)
Fuel system and carburation 5
    Fuel pump — removal and refitting (Austin Marina models)
    Single SU carburettor — adjustment and tuning
    Twin SU carburettors — adjustment and tuning
    Choke cable — removal and refitting (Marina Mk 2 models)
    Throttle cable — removal and refitting (Marina Mk 2 models)
    Fuel tank — removal and refitting (Marina Mk 2 models)
    Exhaust emission regulations (Austin Marina models)
    Carburettor (SU HIF6) — general description and
    tuning (early Austin Marina models)
    Carburettor (SU HIF6) — dismantling, inspection and
    reassembly
    Carburettor heater (SU HIF6) — general
    Carburettor (Zenith 175 CD 5T) — general description and
    tuning (later Austin Marina models)
    Carburettor (Zenith 175 CD5T) — dismantling, inspection
    and reassembly
    Carburettor hot air intake — general
    Crankcase emission control — general
    Exhaust port air injection (emission control system) —
    general
    Air injection system (emission control system) — servicing
    Fuel line filter (emission control system) — general
    Absorption canister (emission control system) — general
    Anti-run-on valve (emission control system) — general
    Engine compression test
    Emission control systems — fault diagnosis and routine
    maintenance
Ignition system 6
    Contact breaker points — adjustment (Marina Mk 2 and
    Austin Marina models)
    Contact breaker points — removal and refitting (Marina
    Mk 2 and Austin Marina models)
    Condenser — removal and refitting (Marina Mk 2 and
    Austin Marina models)
    Distributor — removal and refitting (Marina Mk 2 and
    Austin Marina models)
    Distributor (43D4 and 45D4) — dismantling
    Distributor (43D4 and 45D4) — inspection and repair
    Distributor (43D4 and 45D4) — reassembly
    Ignition timing (Marina Mk 2 and Austin Marina models)

Clutch 7
    Clutch pedal — removal and refitting (Marina Mk 2 models)
Gearbox and automatic transmission 8
    Manual gearbox — removal and refitting
    Manual gearbox — dismantling and reassembly (Marina
    Mk 2 models)
    Automatic transmission (Marina Mk 2 models) — general
    Automatic transmission (Marina Mk 2 models) — fluid
    level checking
    Transmission sump — draining and refilling
    Automatic transmission — removal and refitting
    Starter inhibitor/reverse light switch — removal and
    refitting
Rear axle 9
    Rear axle — removal and refitting (Marina Mk 2 models)
Braking system 10
    General description
    Dual brake system — bleeding
    Tandem brake master cylinder — removal and refitting
    Tandem brake master cylinder (early type) — dismantling
    and reassembly
    Tandem brake master cylinder (later type) — dismantling
    and reassembly
    Handbrake cable — removal and refitting (Marina Mk 2
    models)
    Handbrake lever assembly — removal and refitting (Marina
    Mk 2 models)

    Centre console — removal and refitting (Marina Mk 2
    GT and HL models)
    Brake pedal assembly — removal and refitting (Marina
    Mk 2 models)
    Brake servo unit — removal and refitting (Marina Mk 2
    models)
    Pressure differential warning actuator valve (early
    type) — removal, overhaul and refitting
    Pressure differential warning actuator valve (self-reset
    type) — removal, overhaul and refitting
    Brake pressure warning switch (early type) — centralisation
    Flexible hose — inspection, removal and refitting
Electrical system 11
    Alternator — removal and refitting
    Alternator — testing the charging circuit in situ
    Alternator — overhaul
    Dynamo — testing in position
    Dynamo — removal and refitting
    Dynamo — dismantling and inspection
    Dynamo — repair and reassembly
    Control box (RB 106/2) — general description
    Control box (RB 106/2) — cut-out and regulator
    contacts maintenance
    Control box (RB 106/2) — voltage regulator adjustment
    Control box (RB 106/2) — cut-out adjustment
    Control box (RB 340) — general description

Control box (RB 340) — cut-out and regulator contacts maintenance
Control box (RB 340) — regulator adjustment
Control box (RB 340) — cut-out adjustment
Starter motor (M35J) — testing, removal and refitting
Starter motor (M35J) — dismantling and reassembly
Starter motor (M35J PE — pre-engaged type) — testing, removal and refitting
Starter motor (M35J PE — pre-engaged type) — dismantling and reassembly
Front flasher repeater lamp bulb — renewal (Austin Marina models)
Reverse lamp bulb — renewal (Marina Mk 2 models)
Tail, stop, and flasher lamp (Estate) — removal and refitting
Rear number plate lamp (Estate) — removal and refitting
Reversing lamp (flush fitting type) — removal and refitting
Reversing lamp (protruding type) — removal and refitting
Long range driving lamps — removal and refitting
Roof lamp (Saloon) — removal and refitting
Roof lamp (Estate) — removal and refitting
Wiper/washer switch — removal and refitting (Marina Mk 2 models)
Lighting switch — removal and refitting (Marina Mk 2 models)
Heater fan switch — removal and refitting (Marina Mk 2 models)
Instrument panel printed circuit — removal and refitting (Marina Mk 2 models)
Gauge units — removal and refitting (Marina Mk 2 models)
Speedometer — removal and refitting (Marina Mk 2 models)
Handbrake warning light switch — removal and refitting
Tachometer — removal and refitting (Marina Mk 2 models)
Tailgate wiper motor, wheelbox and rack tubes (Estate models) — removal and refitting
Seat belt buzzer and timer module — removal and refitting (Austin Marina models)
Headlamp relay — removal and refitting (Austin Marina models)
Starter circuit relay — removal and refitting (Austin Marina models)
Seat switch — removal and refitting (Austin Marina models)

Suspension and steering...   12
General description
Lower suspension arm — removal and refitting (Marina Mk models)
Front shock absorber — removal and refitting (Marina Mk 2 models)
Swivel pin — removal and refitting (Marina Mk 2 models)
Swivel pin balljoint — removal and refitting (Marina Mk 2 models)
Lower swivel pin link — removal and refitting (Marina Mk 2 models)
Torsion bar — removal and refitting (Marina Mk 2 models)
Anti-roll bar (front) — removal and refitting (Marina Mk 2 models)
Rear hub assembly — removal and refitting (all models)

Anti-roll bar (rear) — removal and refitting (Marina Mk 2 models)
Steering wheel — removal and refitting (Marina Mk 2 models)
Steering column lock and ignition starter switch — removal and refitting (Marina Mk 2 and Austin Marina models)
Steering column universal joint coupling — removal and refitting (later Marina Mk 1 and Austin Marina models)
Upper steering column — removal and refitting (Marina Mk 2, Austin Marina, and later Marina Mk 1 models)
Steering rack and pinion — removal and refitting (Marina Mk 2 models)
Front suspension trim height — adjustment (later Marina Mk 1 and all Marina Mk 2 and Austin Marina models)

Bodywork and underframe   13
Door trim panel and capping — removal and refitting (Marina Mk 2 models)
Door exterior handle — removal and refitting (late Marina Mk 1 and Austin Marina models)
Door exterior handle — removal and refitting (Marina Mk 2 models)
Rear quarter trim pad and capping — removal and refitting (Marina Mk 1 models)
Tailgate hinge (Estate models) — removal and refitting
Tailgate lock (Estate models) — removal and refitting
Tailgate lock striker plate (Estate models) — removal and refitting
Tailgate exterior handle and lock (Estate models) — removal and refitting
Bumper — removal and refitting (UK models)
Bumper — removal and refitting (Austin Marina models)
Sump guard — removal and refitting
Tailgate glass and backlight — removal and refitting
Rear parcel tray — removal and refitting
Console assembly — removal and refitting (Marina Mk 1 models)
Facia panel — removal and refitting (Marina Mk 2 models)
Lower facia panel — removal and refitting (Austin Marina models)
Glovebox - removal and refitting (Marina Mk 2 models)
Radiator grille — removal and refitting (Austin Marina models)
Heater unit — removal and refitting (Marina Mk 2 models)
Heater control cables — removal and refitting (Marina Mk 2 models)
Windscreen demister duct — removal and refitting (Marina Mk 2 models)
Instrument panel — removal and refitting (Marina Mk 2 models)
Front seat (type 1) — removal and refitting
Front seat (type 2) — removal and refitting
Rear seat squab and cushion (Saloon) — removal and refitting
Rear seat cushion (Estate) — removal and refitting
Rear seat squab (Estate) — removal and refitting
Rear body side glass (Estate) — removal and refitting
Quarter light — removal and refitting

1 Introduction

This Chapter supplements the first twelve Chapters of this manual and povides coverage of modifications and new procedures incorporated in later versions of the Morris Marina Mk 1 Saloon and Coupe. In addition, information is given on the Morris Marina Estate (introduced in late 1972), the Morris Marina Mk 2 models (introduced in late 1975), and the Austin Marina (USA version). The manufacturer's policy is one of continual refinement of both design and construction, and throughout the seven years of production, this has meant that the

Marina 1.8 has been a very popular model. Its conventional engine and transmission layout, together with the inclusion of several well tried BLMC components in the suspension, make it an ideal car for the home mechanic. Throughout the manual there are relatively few instances where special tools are required and in many cases a substitute procedure will eliminate their use.

The Sections of this Chapter are arranged in the order corresponding to that in which the relevant subjects were covered in Chapters 1 - 12. It is recommended that this Chapter is always referred to before commencing work on any part of the car. If a particular component, procedure or specification is not detailed in this Chapter, it may be assumed that the information in one of the other 12 Chapters is still pertinent.

2　Specifications

Engine (later UK models)
Pistons

Number of rings (all models except early Mk 1 version)	3 (2 compression, 1 oil control)
Gudgeon pin bore	0.8130 to 0.8132 in (21.650 to 21.925 in)

Valves

Head diameter (inlet) — Marina Mk 2 models	1.562 to 1.567 in (39.675 to 39.802 mm)
Stem diameter — Marina Mk 2 models:	
Inlet	0.3429 to 0.3434 in (8.709 to 8.722 mm)
Exhaust	0.3423 to 0.3428 in (8.694 to 8.707 mm)
Stem to guide clearance — Marina Mk 2 models:	
Inlet	0.0008 to 0.0018 in (0.0203 to 0.0457 mm)
Exhaust	0.0014 to 0.0024 in (0.0355 to 0.0609 mm)
Valve timing — Marina Mk 2 GT and HL models:	
Inlet opens	16° BTDC
Inlet closes	56° ABDC
Exhaust opens	51° BBDC
Exhaust closes	21° ATDC

Lubrication

Oil pressure relief valve	60 lbf/in^2 (4.2 kgf/cm^2)
Sump capacity	6.25 pints (3.5 litres)

Engine (Austin Marina)
Type (early) ... ...
18V 659 M

Type (later)

Manual transmission	18V 795 AE
Automatic transmission	18V 850 AE

Torque (SAE net) ... ...
87.8 lbf ft at 2500 rpm

Power (SAE net) ... ...
68.5 BHP at 5000 rpm

Compression ratio ... ...
8.0 : 1

Valves

Seat angle...	45°
Head diameter (inlet)	1.562 to 1.567 in (39.675 to 39.802 mm)
Stem diameter (inlet)	0.3429 to 0.3434 in (8.709 to 8.722 mm)
Stem diameter (exhaust)	0.3423 to 0.3428 in (8.694 to 8.707 mm)
Stem to guide clearance (inlet)...	0.008 to 0.018 in (0.0203 to 0.0457 mm)
Stem to guide clearance (exhaust)	0.0014 to 0.0024 in(0.0355 to 0.0609 mm)
Valve timing:	
Inlet opens	5° BTDC
Inlet closes	45° ABDC
Exhaust opens	51° BBDC
Exhaust closes	21° ATDC

Lubrication

Oil pump feed capacity	3.32 Imp gal (4.0 US gal) (15.14 litres) per minute at 1000 rpm
Sump capacity	0.83 Imp gal (1.0 US gal) (3.78 litres)

Cooling system
Total capacity (including heater) — Austin Marina models ... ...
8.95 Imp pints (10.75 US pints) (5.1 litres)

Fuel system and carburation
Air cleaner (late Marina Mk 1 and all Marina Mk 2 models)

Type	Paper element with warm/cold intake positions

Fuel pump (Marina Mk 2 models)

Make and type	SU mechanical AUF 800

Carburettor — 1.8 (late Marina Mk 1 models)

Standard needle	BAS
Exhaust CO content	3.5 to 4.5%

Carburettor — 1.8 TC (late Marina Mk 1 models)
Standard needle ... ...   ABA
Exhaust CO content ... ...   3 to 4.5%

Carburettor — 1.8 (Marina Mk 2 models)
Standard needle ... ...   BCW
Exhaust CO content ... ...   3 to 4.5%

Carburettor — 1.8 GT and HL (Marina Mk 2 models)
Standard needle ... ...   ACE
Exhaust CO content ... ...   3 to 4.5%

Carburettor (early Austin Marina models)
Make and type ... ...   Single SU HIF 6
Needle ... ...   BBE or BBQ (cold air intake)

Carburettor (late Austin Marina models)
Make and type ... ...   Single Zenith 175CD5T
Choke needle ... ...   K
Fast idle setting ... ...   0.025 in nominal
Exhaust CO content ... ...   5.5% ± 1% (air pump disconnected and injector pipe plugged)

Fuel tank
Capacity (Austin Marina models) ... ...   10.8 Imp gal (13.0 US gallons) (49.2 litres)

Idling Speed
1971 Marina Mk 1 models (1.8 and 1.8 TC) ... ...   800 rpm
1972 — 1975 Marina Mk 1 models (1.8) ... ...   750 rpm
1972 — 1975 Marina Mk 1 models (1.8 TC) ... ...   800 rpm
Marina Mk 2 models (1.8) ... ...   750 rpm
Marina Mk 2 models (1.8 GT and HL) ... ...   800 rpm
Austin Marina models ... ...   850 rpm

Fast idle speed
Marina Mk 1 models (except 1971 1.8 TC) ... ...   1100 to 1200 rpm
Marina Mk 1 models (1971 1.8 TC) ... ...   1000 rpm
Marina Mk 2 models (1.8) ... ...   1300 rpm
Marina Mk 2 models (1.8 GT and HL) ... ...   1500 rpm

Ignition system
Spark plug gap (Marina Mk 2 GT and HL models) ... ...   0.034 to 0.036 in (0.375 to 0.925 mm)

Ignition coil (Marina Mk 2 GT and HL models) ... ...   Lucas 16C6

Distributor (Marina Mk 1 models)
Late 1.8 LC serial number   41389

Distributor (Marina Mk 2 models)
Type ... ...   Lucas 45D4
Serial number:
    HC   41415
    LC   41432
Marina GT and HL models   41410
Dwell angle ... ...   51° ± 5°

Static ignition timing
Marina Mk 2 models (except GT and HL) ... ...   3° BTDC
Marina GT and HL models) ... ...   7° BTDC

Stroboscopic ignition timing at 1000 rpm (vacuum pipe disconnected)
Marina Mk 2 (except GT and HL):
    LC engines ... ...   6° BTDC
    HC engines ... ...   8° BTDC
Marina GT and HL models ... ...   10° BTDC

Spark plug gap (Austin Marina models) ... ...   0.034 to 0.036 in (0.875 to 0.925 mm)

Ignition coil (Austin Marina models) ... ...   Lucas 16C6

Distributor (Austin Marina models)
Type ... ...   Lucas 45D4

Serial number   41599
Dwell angle ... ...   51° ± 5°

Stroboscopic ignition timing (Austin Marina models)
at 1500 rpm ... ...   13° BTDC

Clutch
Master cylinder bore (Marina Mk 2 models) ... ...   0.5 in (12.7 mm)

Gearbox and Automatic transmission
Automatic transmission
Type (Marina Mk 2 models) ... ...   Borg Warner model 65
Fluid capacity (total) ... ...   11.5 Imp pt (6.54 litres) (13.8 US pt)

Rear axle
Torque wrench settings

	lbf ft	kgf m
Backplate securing nuts	18	2.5
Axleshaft nut	110	15.21
Differential case to axle retaining nuts	20	2.7
Axle to spring U-bolt nuts	15 to 18	2.0 to 2.4
Pinion bearing pre-load	15 to 18 lbf in	17 to 21 kgf cm

Braking system
Front disc brake pad specification
Late Marina Mk 1 models:
   Non servo ... ...   DON 227
   Servo ... ...   Ferodo 2430
Austin Marina models (with servo) ... ...   Mintex 108
Service replacement (except Sweden) ... ...   Ferodo 2445

Rear brake shoe lining specification
Late Marina Mk 1 models ... ...   DON 202

Wheel cylinder diameter
Late Marina Mk 1 models ... ...   0.625 in (15.87 mm) with automatic adjuster
Austin Marina models ... ...   0.70 in (17.78 mm)

Torque wrench settings

	lbf ft	kgf m
Backplate securing nuts and bolts	32 to 38	4.43 to 5.26

Electrical system
Alternator maximum permissible rotor speed
(Marina Mk 2 and Austin Marina models) ... ...   15 000 rpm

Alternator (Marina Mk 2 models)
Minimum brush length ... ...   0.3125 in (7.94 mm)
Brush spring tension (flush with box) ... ...   9 to 13 ozf (255 to 268 gmf)

Dynamo
Type ... ...   Lucas C40/1
Max output ... ...   22 ± 1 amps
Cut-in speed ... ...   1585 rpm at 13.5 volts
Field resistance ... ...   6.0 ohms at 20°C (68°F)
Brush spring tension ... ...   20 – 34 ozf (567 – 964 gmf)
Min brush length ... ...   0.3125 in (7.9375 mm)
Pulley ratio ... ...   1.7 : 1

Control unit
Type
   LHD ... ...   Lucas RB 340
   RHD ... ...   Lucas RB 106
Setting at 20°C (68°F):

	RB106	RB340
3000 rpm (dynamo)	16.0 – 16.6 volts	14.5 – 15.5 volts
Cut in voltage	12.7 – 13.3 volts	12.7 – 13.3 volts
Drop off voltage	8.5 – 11.0 volts	9.5 – 11.5 volts

Starter motor
Type M35J

Brush spring tension ... ... 28 oz (0.8 kgf)
Min brush length ... ... 0.375 in (9.5 mm)
Lock torque ... ... 7 lbf ft (0.97 kgf m) with 350 − 375 amps
Torque at 1000 rpm ... ... 4.4 lbf ft (0.61 kgf m) with 260 − 275 amps
Light running current ... ... 65 amps at 8000 − 10 000 rpm

Solenoid
Fitment ... ... Pre-engaged type
Closing coil resistance ... ... 0.21 − 0.25 ohm
Holding coil resistance ... ... 0.9 − 1.1 ohm

Wiper motor
Armature endfloat (Marina Mk 2 models) ... ... 0.002 to 0.008 in (0.051 to 0.20 mm)

Replacement bulbs (Marina Mk 2 models)

	Watts
Halogen sealed beam unit (RH steering)	60/55
Halogen headlamp bulb (LH steering)	60/55
Tungsten sealed beam unit (LH steering)	60/50
Halogen rectangular headlamp	55
Glovebox lamp	6
Engine compartment lamp, clock lamp	5
Heated backlight switch, brake failure lamp, and hazard warning switch	0.75
Sidelamp	5
Reverse lamp (Saloon)	21
Reverse lamp (Estate)	18
Luggage compartment lamp	6
Automatic selector lever lamp	3
Direction indicator repeater lamp	5

Suspension and steering
Front suspension (Marina Mk 2 models)
Type ... ... Independent by torsion bar with lever type shock absorbers and anti-roll bar

Camber angle (except GT and HL) ... ... 0° 46' positive
Camber angle (GT and HL) ... ... 0° 33' positive

Rear suspension (Marina Mk 2 models)
Type ... ... Semi-elliptic leaf spring with telescopic shock absorbers and anti-roll bar

Number of spring leaves:
   Saloon 2
   Estate and heavy duty ... ... 3 or 4
Working load (Estate models) ... ... 320 lb (145 kg)

Steering wheel total travel ... ... 3.7 turns

Wheels (Marine Mk 2 models)
Type ... ... 4 stud pressed steel 4¼ C x 13

Tyres (Marina Mk 2 models)
Size (radial ply) ... ... 155 x 13

Tyre pressures (Marina Mk 2 models):	Front	Rear
Saloon	26 lbf/in^2 (1.8 kgf/cm^2)	28 lbf/in^2 (2.0 kgf/cm^2)
Estate (unladen)	26 lbf/in^2 (1.8 kgf/cm^2)	28 lbf/in^2 (2.0 kgf/cm^2)
Estate (laden)	26 lbf/in^2 (1.8 kgf/cm^2)	32 lbf/in^2 (2.25 kgf/cm^2)

Torque wrench settings

	lbf ft	kgf m
Rear shock absorber to body bracket retaining bolt	45	6.2

Main overall dimensions (Marina Mk 2 models)
Length
Saloon Super ... ... 14 ft 1 in (4.291 m)
Saloon Special and HL ... ... 14 ft 2 in (4.317 m)
Coupe Super, Special, and GT ... ... 13 ft 11 in (4.242 m)
Estate ... ... 14 ft 2 3/32 in (4.320 m)

Width
Saloon models ... ... 5 ft 5 3/16 in (1.655 m)
Coupe models ... ... 5 ft 5 3/64 in (1.652 m)
Estate ... ... 5 ft 5 5/32 in (1.654 m)

Height

Saloon Super, Special, and HL ...	...	...	...	...	...			4 ft 8 39/64 in (1.437 m)
Coupe Super, Special and GT ...	...	...	...	...	...			4 ft 7½ in (1.408 m)
Estate ...	...	...	...	...	...	...	...	4 ft 19/32 in (1.437 m)

Wheelbase

Wheelbase ...	...	...	...	...	...	...	8 ft 0 5/32 in (2.441 m)

Kerbside weight

Saloon (GT and HL) ...	...	...	...	...	...	...		2144 lb (972 kg)
Coupe (GT and HL) ...	...	...	...	...	...	...		2116 lb (959 kg)
Saloon (all other models) ...	...	...	...	...	...			2093 lb (949 kg)
Coupe (all other models) ...	...	...	...	...	...			2065 lb (936 kg)
Estate ...	...	...	...	...	...	...	...	2203 lb (999 kg)

---

3 Engine

Engine changes — Marina Mk 2 models

1 The basic engine components have remained unchanged and there have been relatively few other modifications. Externally, the oil filter has been inverted so that now it is positioned beneath the oil filter head, and the fuel pump has been modified. Internally, the double row timing chain and gears have been replaced by single row components, and the pistons are fitted with three rings (two compression and one oil control) instead of four on the original engine.

Engine removal and repair procedure (Austin Marina models)

2 The basic procedure is identical to that given in Chapter 1 but it will be necessary to integrate the removal and refitting of the components described in Section 5 of this Supplement into the existing procedure.

---

4 Cooling system

Radiator — removal and refitting

1 Late Marina Mk 1 models and all Marina Mk 2 models have a shroud fitted to the front of the radiator and this necessitates a slightly different removal procedure.
2 Refer to Chapter 2, Section 5 and follow the instructions given in paragraphs 1, 2 and 3.
3 Disconnect each side shroud panel from the upper radiator brackets, then unscrew and remove the screws and nuts retaining the brackets to the front panel.
4 Remove the radiator brackets and lift them off the radiator locating pins.
5 Remove the two upper shroud retaining screws and lift the shroud away; the radiator can now be lifted off its lower mountings, followed by the lower shroud.
6 Follow the instructions given in Chapter 2, Section 5, paragraph 6 when refitting the radiator.

Fan belt — removal and refitting (Austin Marina models)

7 It will be necessary first to remove the air pump drivebelt prior to following the instructions given in Chapter 2, Section 10. To do this loosen the air pump pivot and adjustment bolts and swivel the unit downwards as far as it will go; the belt can then be removed.

Air pump drivebelt — adjustment (Austin Marina models)

8 The lower fan belt is adjusted following the procedure given in Chapter 2, Section 11.
9 After fitting the upper air pump drivebelt, the tension must be adjusted to give 0.5 inch (13 mm) lateral movement at a point midway along the belt run; firm thumb pressure will give the required load on the belt.
10 The adjustment procedure is identical to that for the alternator, but care should be exercised not to overtighten the air

pump drivebelt otherwise the water pump bearings will be over-loaded.

Radiator — removal and refitting (Austin Marina models)

11 The radiator filler plug is in the form of an adaptor plug and the expansion tank hose is connected direct to this adaptor. Also the radiator shrouds are of a slightly different design to that on the UK model. However, the removal and refitting procedure is identical to that given in Chapter 2 except for these minor alterations.

Thermostat — removal and refitting (Austin Marina models)

12 Remove the air pump drivebelt as described in paragraph 7.
13 Partially drain the cooling system, loosen the upper radiator hose at the thermostat end and ease it off the housing.
14 Remove the air pump pivot bolt and temporarily support the air pump away from the thermostat housing.
15 Unscrew and remove the gulp valve hose clip retaining screw, then unscrew the three nuts and lift the thermostat housing away, together with the spring washers, and gasket.
16 Testing of the thermostat is identical to the procedure given in Chapter 2, Section 7 and refitting is a direct reversal of the removal procedure. Adjust the air pump drivebelt as described in paragraphs 8 to 10.

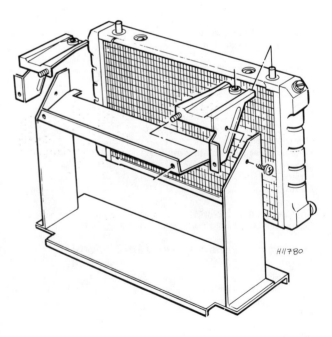

Fig. 13.1 Radiator shroud components as fitted to later Marina models

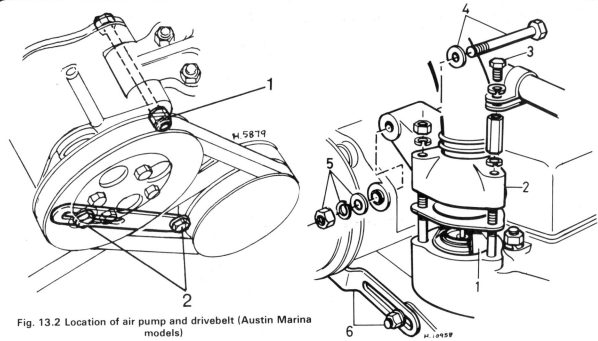

H.5879

Fig. 13.2 Location of air pump and drivebelt (Austin Marina models)

1 Upper pivot bolt
2 Adjustment link bolts

H.10958

Fig. 13.4 Thermostat and housing components (Austin Marina models)

1 Thermostat
2 Housing
3 Retaining bolt
4 Air pump pivot bolt
5 Pivot bolt retaining nut and washers
6 Adjusting link and locking bolt

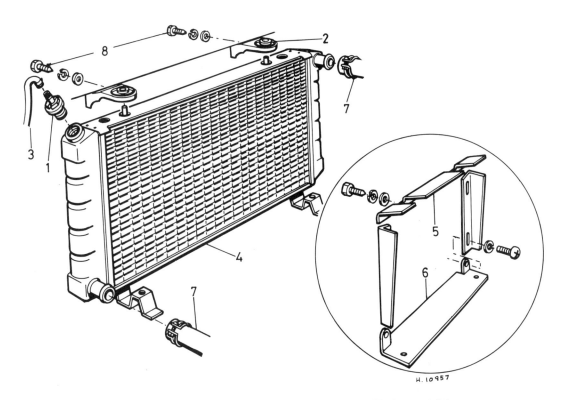

H.10957

Fig. 13.3 Radiator and shroud components (Austin Marina models)

1 Filler plug
2 Upper mounting
3 Expansion tank hose
4 Radiator
5 Upper shroud
6 Lower shroud
7 Hoses
8 Screws

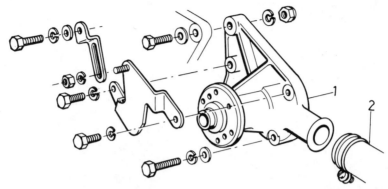

Fig. 13.5 Water pump and air pump support bracket components (Austin Marina models)

1 Water pump   2 Bottom hose   3 Pulley

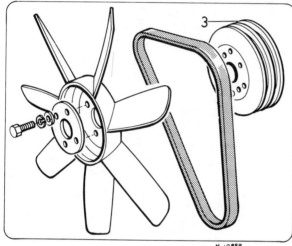

5   Unscrew and remove the earth lead screw and withdraw the fuel pump from the clamp band.
6   Refitting the fuel pump is a reversal of the removal procedure.

Single SU carburettor — adjustment and tuning

7   The procedure given in Chapter 3, Section 18 can be followed but where an engine tachometer and/or exhaust gas analyser is available, the following procedure will apply.
8   On SU Capstat carburettors the idling and/or mixture adjusters are sealed by the manufacturers with black and blue seals; check that the current regulations permit the removal of these seals as only suitably equipped garages are being supplied with the red replacement seals.
9   Remove the piston damper and top-up the oil level using engine oil so that it is 0.5 in (13 mm) above the top of the piston rod. Then refit the piston damper.
10 Remove the air cleaner and check that the piston is free to move up and down with only the resistance of the damper oil retaining it on the upward stroke.
11 Refit the air cleaner and check the throttle linkage for full and free movement.
12 Check that the choke control cable operates correctly and that it has 1/16 in (1.6 mm) of free movement when in its normal 'off' position.
13 Connect up the tachometer and/or exhaust gas analyser in accordance with the manufacturer's instructions.
14 The engine must be at normal operating temperature and tuning should commence after running the engine at 2500 rpm

Water pump — removal and refitting (Austin Marina models)

17 Disconnect the battery negative lead.
18 Remove the radiator as described in paragraph 11.
19 Loosen the alternator and air pump pivot and adjustment bolts and remove the two drivebelts.
20 Unscrew and remove the four fan blade retaining screws and withdraw the metal plate, fan blade and pulley together with the spring and plain washers.
21 Detach the air pump adjusting link and bracket by unscrewing the two upper water pump retaining bolts, then unscrew and remove the alternator pivot bolt from the water pump body.
22 Slacken the clip securing the bottom hose to the water pump and carefully ease off the hose.
23 Unscrew and remove the remaining water pump retaining bolts, noting that these are longer than the upper bolts and therefore must be fitted in their original positions.
24 Follow the procedure given in paragraphs 7 and 8 in Chapter 2, Section 8 and finally adjust the air pump drivebelt as described in paragraphs 8 to 10 inclusive of this Section.

5   Fuel system and carburation

Fuel pump — removal and refitting (Austin Marina models)

1   Disconnect the battery negative terminal.
2   Carefully pull the fuel and air vent pipes from the pump body.
3   Disconnect the electrical supply lead from the lower terminal.
4   Unscrew and remove the bolts, nuts and washers securing the pump clamp to the bracket and then remove the clamp band screw.

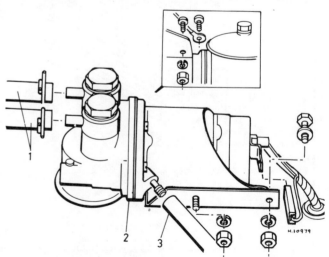

Fig. 13.6 Electric fuel pump fitted to Austin Marina models
1 Fuel feed and supply hoses   2 Pump body
3 Air vent pipe

for a short period. If tuning is not completed within three minutes, run the engine again at 2500 rpm before continuing.

15 First adjust the idling screw until the engine speed is correct as given in the Specifications sections.

16 If the engine will not run smoothly, turn the mixture adjusting nut one flat at a time, up to weaken and down to enrich the mixture until the engine idles at its fastest speed. Then turn the nut up slowly until the speed just starts to decrease.

17 If the idling speed is now incorrect adjust the idling screw as necessary and again carry out the procedure given in paragraph 16.

18 Using the exhaust gas analyser check the CO content percentage is within the specified limits and make minor adjustments to the mixture to achieve the correct reading. If more than half a turn of the mixture nut is needed to correct the CO content, the carburettor must be removed and serviced.

19 Switch off the engine and disconnect the exhaust gas analyser and, where applicable, reseal the adjusters.

20 Now pull the choke out until the linkage nearly moves the jet, start the engine, and adjust the fast idle speed screw to achieve the correct engine speed as given in the Specifications section.

21 Switch off the engine and disconnect the tachometer.

Twin SU carburettors — adjustment and tuning

22 The procedure in Chapter 3, Section 19 may be followed but if a tachometer and/or an exhaust gas analyser is available, use the same method described in paragraphs 7 to 21 inclusive of this Section, but make sure that any adjustments are applied equally to both carburettors.

23 The throttle and choke jet interconnecting levers must be adjusted as described in Chapter 3, Section 20.

Choke cable — removal and refitting (Marina Mk 2 models)

24 Disconnect the battery negative terminal.

25 Detach the choke cable from the carburettor lever and unclip it from the throttle cable.

26 Move the steering wheel ninety degrees to the left from the straight ahead position so that the spokes are vertical, and then remove the cowl retaining screw and withdraw the right-hand steering column cowl.

27 Unscrew and remove the three left-hand cowl retaining screws and remove the left-hand cowl.

28 When fitted, loosen the locknut and unscrew the clamp screw retaining the warning light switch to the choke cable, slide the switch along the cable, and disconnect the electrical leads. Separate the clamp from the switch and remove the switch from the cable.

29 Carefully pull the cable through the body grommet and then unscrew the cable locknut from behind the left-hand cowl.

30 Extract the choke cable from the cowl and recover the lock-washer.

31 Refitting is a reversal of the removal procedure, but note that the large peg on the switch body locates in the hole nearest the control knob.

32 The choke cable must be adjusted to give 0.06 in (2 mm) free movement.

Throttle pedal — removal and refitting (Marina Mk 2 models)

33 Before carrying out the instructions given in Chapter 3, Section 23, disconnect the throttle pedal return spring and retaining clip.

34 Refitting is a reversal of the removal procedure.

Fuel tank — removal and refitting (Marina Mk 2 models)

35 The removal procedure is similar to that described in Chapter 3, Section 24 but the following exceptions and additions should be noted:

  a) *No drain plug is provided, therefore the fuel must be syphoned from the fuel tank.*

  b) *Unscrew and remove the retaining screw and detach the filler neck clamp from the body.*

  c) *Unscrew and remove the retaining screws and withdraw the pipe protective cover.*

36 Refitting is a reversal of the removal procedure but make sure that, on Estate models, the pipe is fitted over the top of the chassis number. On Saloon models it is recommended that a sealing compound is used to prevent water entering the luggage compartment.

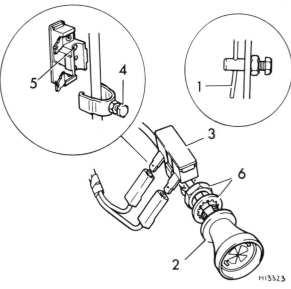

Fig. 13.7 Choke cable removal procedure (Marina Mk 2 models)

1 Choke inner cable   4 Switch clamp screw
2 Choke cable knob   5 Locating peg
3 Warning lamp switch   6 Nut and washer

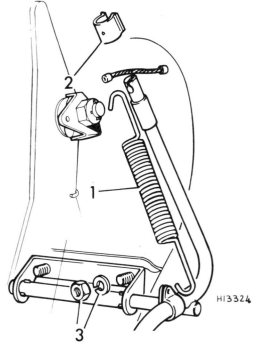

Fig. 13.8 Throttle pedal components (Marina Mk 2 models)

1 Return spring   3 Bracket retaining nut and
2 Retaining clip   washer

Fig. 13.9 Fuel tank components (Marina Mk 2 models)

1	Fuel pipe to tank connection	6	Self-tapping screw
2	Filler neck clamp	7	Cover
3	Clamp screw	8	Sender unit supply lead
4	Clamp screw	9	Hose clip
5	Vent pipe	10	Support plate

Exhaust emission regulations (Austin Marina models)

37 The engine, fuel and ignition systems have been modified as briefly described in the introduction to this Chapter, so that the car will comply with the USA Federal Regulations covering emission of hydrocarbons and carbon monoxide. To achieve this the ignition and fuel systems must be accurately set using special equipment.

38 Information given on servicing emission control equipment will enable the reader to clean and/or overhaul the various components but when completed the car must be taken to the local British Leyland dealer for final adjustments to be made. Failure to do this will probably mean that the car does not comply with the regulations.

Carburettor (SU HIF 6) — general description and tuning (early Austin Marina models)

39 Early Austin Marina models were fitted with an SU HIF 6 carburettor instead of the SU HS6 as described in Chapter 3. These carburettors still work on the same principle as all SU carburettors with dashpots holding pistons to regulate the airflow, and needles to control the fuel flow from the jet. From above, SU HIF 6 carburettors look much the same, but there is no float chamber beside the piston. Instead this is concentric with the jet and gives the bottom of the carburettor a fatter shape. By placing the float chamber centrally it limits fuel level changes when braking, accelerating and cornering.

40 The jet is held in place by a horizontal arm. This is made of a bi-metallic material, so will vary the jet height to give compensation for temperature changes. These would otherwise give mixture variation due to fuel viscosity changes. This jet mounting arm is connected through a pivot to a lever. The lever is moved by a screw in the side of the carburettor body to adjust the mixture. The screw head may be hidden under a seal.

41 The rich mixture needed for cold starting is provided by a special jet. This has a progressive control to allow partial enrichment and is worked by turning a cam lever on the carburettor

side, opposite to that having the mixture control screw. This lever has the cam so that as it is moved to enrich the mixture the cam will push up the fast idle screw to open the throttle. The valve that controls this cold start mixture is a hollow inner core that is rotated within a cylindrical sleeve to bring a hole in it in line with one in the sleeve.

42 An emulsion bypass passage runs from the jet bridge to the throttle. At small throttle openings unevaporated fuel droplets will be drawn along this passage, and will be mixed with this faster travelling air. To match this passage there is a slot cut out of the base of the piston.

43 The HIF 6 has an over-run valve in the throttle disc, and the spring biased needle described in Chapter 3/17.

Carburettor tuning

44 Mixture setting is much the same as described in Chapter 3/18 and the engine response is similar. However there are two differences. Instead of turning the jet adjusting nut on the bottom, the side screw is used, and this moves the jet by means of the bi-metal arm. Before making an adjustment which means undoing any seal, check you will not be breaking any regulation.

45 The initial setting after dismantling is to screw the jet up as far as it will go, then start turning the screw clockwise. Note when the jet starts to move down, and thereafter screw two turns.

46 If the idle throttle setting has been lost, unscrew the throttle stop screw till the throttle is completely shut. Then screw it in again one complete turn. Screw in the fast idle screw until it is close to, but not touching, the cam on the choke mechanism.

47 Remove the air cleaner then start and warm-up the engine.

48 Once the engine is warmed up, the fast idle screw should be adjusted to give 1200 rpm. Push in the choke control, and adjust the throttle stop screw to give the correct idle speed, as given in the Specifications section.

49 Now adjust the mixture. A vacuum gauge can be very useful and is inexpensive. It also allows other engine tests to be made, so is worthwhile. This gauge should be tapped into the inlet manifold. It must have its own tapping and not temporarily use one of the others, as this could upset the carburation and ruin the adjustment. The most accurate setting can be achieved using an exhaust gas analyser, and this may be essential to meet local emission regulations.

50 To weaken the mixture, screw the screw out (anti-clockwise). As the screw is coupled through the bi-metal arm there may be some lag in the movement of the jet. Tap the carburettor body to encourage it to find its new position. Also note where the mixture seems best when screwing in one direction; count the ¼ turns of the screw, going on past the correct position, and then coming back again, still counting the distance the screw has been turned to try and note the correct position. This is half-way between the two positions which make the engine slow down because of mixture being too weak or too rich.

51 The correct setting for the jet can be found from a combination of engine speed, which should be as fast as possible, and if a vacuum gauge is being used the highest steady reading, and listening to the exhaust note. The exhaust note should be smooth. If it is haphazardly irregular accompanied by a burping noise, with the engine still running fairly fast, a weak mixture is indicated. This can be confirmed by lifting the piston about 0.1 in (3 mm) with the lifting device on the side of the carburettor, or a very fine screwdriver; the engine should immediately slow down and will be very liable to stall. If the mixture is too rich the idle speed will tend to be low, accompanied by a rhythmic sound from the exhaust. Lifting the piston about 0.1 (3 mm) will result in the engine speeding up. Readings on a vacuum gauge with a weak mixture will be fairly high, but with fluctuation, whilst for a rich mixture the needle will show a low reading with rhythmic fluctuations. Moving the jet a ¼ turn of the adjusting screw from the correct setting should give an indication of weak or rich mixture. It is best to err in the direction of weakness; when the air cleaner is fitted there is a slight enrichment of the mixture.

52 Finally, having got the mixture correct, recheck that the idle speed is correct.

53 If at times the engine does not seem to respond to adjustment of the mixture correctly, blip the throttle a few times to clear the petrol that will collect in the inlet manifold, and burn soot off the spark plugs.

54 Refit the air cleaner.

55 On the road it might be found that the mixture has been set a trace rich or weak. Richness is apparent by the car idling well when cool, but when hot becoming lumpy and, after a few seconds, slower and more and more uneven. A weak mixture is indicated by a liability to stall when coming down to idling speed; if only slightly weak there will be a slow erratic idle which then steadies and speeds up. If the mixture setting appears to be unsatisfactory try a correction of ¼ turn only at a time, on the jet adjusting screw.

56 It is not practicable to fine tune the carburettors by referring to the colour of the exhaust, as the colour will depend upon the driving conditions immediately before it is examined. But on a long journey, immediately on halting, an indication of whether the mixture is rich or weak can be obtained by the paleness of the tail pipe. This will indicate not that readjustment of the setting of the carburettor jet screw is needed but whether a richer or weaker needle is needed. The carburettor must be set for the correct idle. If not giving the right mixture on the road then a different needle is needed.

Carburettor (SU HIF 6) — dismantling, inspection and reassembly

57 Assuming that you have the carburettor on the workbench, start by cleaning the exterior thoroughly well with paraffin or a degreasing solvent, using a stiff brush where necessary.

58 Undo the cap at the top of the carburettor and withdraw it complete with the small damper piston. Empty the oil from the dashpot.

59 Mark the position of the float chamber cover relative to the body and remove it by unscrewing the four screws holding it down. Empty out any fuel still in the fuel chamber.

60 The float is held to the body by a pivot having a screw head on it. Unscrew and remove the pivot with its sealing washer, remove the float, unscrew the needle valve socket and remove it and the needle.

61 Dismantle the various control linkages, being sure by studying Figs 13.10, 13.11 and 13.13 that you know how they fit together. It is an easy matter to sort this out before you take them apart but much more difficult when they are in bits.

62 Unscrew the nut holding the fast idle cam, having first straightened its tab washer; take off the cam, and the spring which is contained in a small housing behind it. Undo the two screws holding down this housing and pull on the spindle which held the fast idle cam and the whole cold start assembly will come out of the body.

63 Undo the screws holding the throttle disc into its shaft, being careful not to put too much pressure on the shaft in the process (support it with the other hand). Remove the disc and withdraw the throttle shaft.

64 Mark the flanges and remove the top part of the body (suction chamber) and the piston. Be careful of the needle on the end of the piston — a good idea is to stand the piston on a narrow-necked jar with the needle hanging inside it.

65 Unscrew the jet retaining (pivot) screw and remove the bimetal assembly holding the jet.

66 The carburettor is now sufficiently dismantled for inspection to be carried out. One or two adjusting screws and the like have been left in the body, but it is recommended that these are only removed when you are actually ensuring that the various channels are clear. Generally speaking the SU carburettor is very reliable but even so it may develop faults which are not readily apparent unless a careful inspection is carried out, yet may nevertheless affect engine performance. So it is well worthwhile giving the carburettor a good look over when you have got it dismantled.

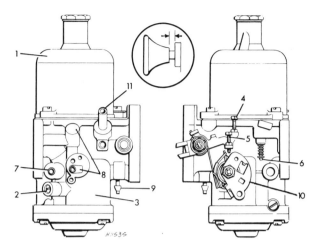

Fig. 13.10 The SU HIF 6 carburettor

1 Dashpot	8 Float chamber vent
2 Jet adjusting screw	9 Ignition vacuum connec-
3 Float chamber	tion (blanked off for some
4 Throttle stop screw	markets)
5 Fast idle screw	10 Cold start cam
6 Piston lifting pin	11 Crankcase fume con-
7 Fuel inlet	nection

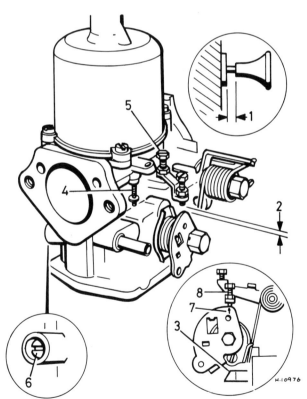

Fig. 13.11 The SU HIF 6 carburettor controls

There should be $\frac{1}{16}$ in movement (1) before the choke control starts moving the carburettor lever. There should be a small clearance (2) between the lever cam when on its stop (3) and the fast idle screw (8). Fine adjustment is done when choke pulled till arrow (7) is lined up with screw. Also shown is the piston lifting pin (4), throttle stop screw (5), and round the other side, the mixture screw (6)

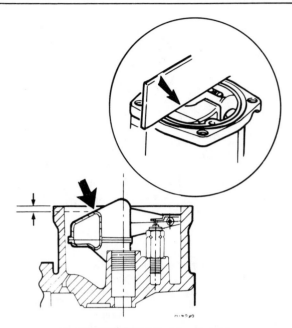

Fig. 13.12 SU HIF 6 float level setting

67 Inspect the carburettor needle for ridging. If this is apparent you will probably find corresponding wear on the inside of the jet. If the needle is ridged, it must be renewed. Do not attempt to rub it down with abrasive paper as carburettor needles are made to very fine tolerances.

68 When installing the needle locate it carefully in the piston. The shoulder should be flush with the piston face and the engraved line should point directly away from the channel in the piston sidewall. Note that this makes the needle incline in the direction of the carburettor air cleaner flange when the piston is fitted.

69 Inspect the jet for wear. Wear inside the jet will accompany wear on the needle. If any wear is apparent on the jet, renew it. It may be unhooked from the bi-metal spring and this may be used again.

70 Inspect the piston and the carburettor body (suction chamber) carefully for signs that these have been in contact. When the carburettor is operating the main piston should not come into contact with the carburettor body. The whole assembly is supported by the rod of the piston which slides in the centre guide tube, this rod being attached to the cap in the top of the carburettor body. It is possible for wear in the centre guide to allow the piston to touch the wall of the body. Check for this by assembling the small piston in the carburettor body and sliding the large one down, rotating it about the centre guide tube at the same time. If contact occurs and the cause is worn parts, renew them. In no circumstances try to correct

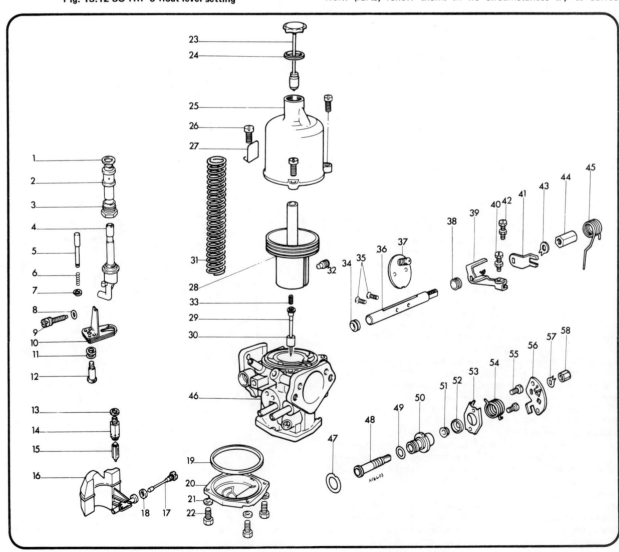

piston sticking by altering the tension of the return spring, although very slight contact with the body may be cured — as a temporary measure — by polishing the offending portion of the body wall with metal polish or extremely fine emery cloth.

71 The fit of the piston in the suction chamber can be checked by plugging the air hole in the body and assembling the piston in the chamber without its return spring, fitting the damper piston without filling the dashpot with oil. If the assembly is now turned upside down the chamber should fall to the bottom in 5-7 seconds. If the time is appreciably less than this, the piston and suction chamber should both be renewed since they are matched to each other.

72 Check for wear on the throttle shaft and bushes through which it passes. Apart from the nuisance of a sticking throttle, excessive wear here can cause air leaks in the induction system adversely affecting engine performance. Worn bushes can be extracted and new bushes fitted if necessary. The cold start device can be dismantled for cleaning, and new parts used where necessary when reassembling.

73 Reassembly is a straightforward reversal of the dismantling process. During reassembly the float level can be checked and adjusted if necessary by inverting the carburettor body so that the needle valve is held shut by the weight of the float. Using a straight edge across the face of the float chamber measure the gap at the point arrowed (Fig 13.12). It should be 0.004 $\pm$ 0.02 in (1.0 $\pm$ 0.5 mm). The arm can be bent carefully, if necessary, to obtain the dimensions.

74 When assembling the jet, position the adjusting screw so that the upper edge of the jet comes level with the bridge. This gives the initial position for jet adjustment.

75 When the carburettor is assembled, the dashpot should be filled with engine oil until it is ½ inch (13 mm) above the top of the hollow piston rod. Check that the piston is operating properly by lifting it with the lifting pin and letting it fall. It should hit the bridge of the carburettor with an audible metallic click. If it does not, perhaps the needle is fouling the jet (it is supposed to touch it lightly). This should not occur with careful assembly; there is no provision for centering the jet but if it is properly assembled this is not necessary.

Carburettor heater (SU HIF 6) — general

76 The carburettor on cars for certain markets has a heater. This is an electrical element connected to the carburettor throat and the dashpot. This improves driveability when cold, particularly on cars with emission control equipment, that otherwise might be temperamental. It can also prevent carburettor icing.

Fig. 13.14 Location of SU HIF 6 carburettor heater (black arrow) and gulp valve (white arrow)

Fig. 13.13 Exploded view of the SU HIF 6 carburettor

1 Jet bearing washer	16 Float	31 Piston spring	46 Body
2 Jet bearing	17 Float pivot	32 Needle retaining screw	47 Cold start seal
3 Jet bearing nut	18 Pivot seal	33 Needle spring	48 Cold start spindle
4 Jet assembly	19 Float chamber cover seal	34 Throttle spindle seal	49 O-ring
5 Lifting pin	20 Float chamber cover	35 Throttle disc screws	50 Cold start body
6 Lifting pin spring	21 Spring washer	36 Throttle spindle	51 Spindle seal
7 Circlip	22 Screw (4)	37 Throttle disc	52 End cover
8 Adjusting screw seal	23 Piston damper	38 Throttle spindle seal	53 Retaining plate
9 Jet adjusting screw	24 Damper washer	39 Throttle actuating lever	54 Cold start spring
10 Bi-metal jet lever	25 Suction chamber	40 Fast idle screw and nut	55 Retaining screw
11 Jet spring	26 Screw (3)	41 Throttle lever	56 Fast idle cam
12 Jet retaining (pivot) screw	27 Identity tag	42 Throttle adjusting screw and nut	57 Tab washer
13 Needle seat washer (if required)	28 Piston	43 Tab washer	58 Nut
14 Float needle seat	29 Jet needle	44 Nut	
15 Float needle	30 Needle guide	45 Throttle spring	

Carburettor (Zenith 175 CD 5T) — general description and tuning (later Austin Marina models)

77 The Zenith carburettor operates on the same principle as the SU HIF 6 although there are a few component differences which are apparent by observing Fig. 13.17. For accurate tuning it is essential to use a tachometer and exhaust gas analyser and it must be stressed that the general engine condition, including ignition timing and valve rocker clearances, will determine whether an accurate carburettor adjustment can be made.

78 First remove the air cleaner and unscrew the air valve damper.

79 Lift the air valve, with the finger, slowly to its uppermost stop, then release it; the valve should return smoothly to the carburettor bridge, finally making an audible 'click'. If the air valve fails to do this, the carburettor should be overhauled before being tuned.

80 Top-up the dashpot oil level if necessary and tighten the damper.

81 Refit the air cleaner and then check that the throttle operates through its full travel.

82 Run the engine until it reaches its normal operating temperature.

83 Disconnect and plug the air manifold hose from the air pump and detach the float chamber vent pipe.

84 Connect the tachometer and exhaust gas analyser in accordance with the manufacturer's instructions and then run the engine at 2500 rpm for half a minute. Tuning should commence immediately but, if it is not completed within three minutes, the engine should be run at 2500 rpm again.

85 Turn the idle adjusting screw until the correct specified idle speed is obtained and then check the CO percentage on the exhaust gas analyser.

86 The fine idle mixture screw should be turned clockwise to enrich and anti-clockwise to weaken but if the correct mixture cannot be obtained, the air valve needle will need adjusting; a special adjustment tool is required for this operation.

87 First turn the fine idle mixture screw fully clockwise, then turn it anti-clockwise 2½ turns.

88 Remove the suction chamber and air valve as described in paragraphs 101 and 102 and check that the needle initial adjustment is correct and that the needle is biased towards the air cleaner intake. If this is correct, refit the suction chamber and air valve and adjust the coarse idle mixture nut clockwise to enrich and anti-clockwise to weaken.

89 If the correct mixture still cannot be obtained first position the coarse idle nut in its mid-range position then remove the suction chamber and air valve again.

90 Fit the special adjustment tool into the dashpot until the outer part engages the air valve and the inner hexagon engages the adjuster plug; to avoid tearing the diaphragm make sure that the outer tool is correctly engaged.

91 Turn the inner tool clockwise to enrich or anti-clockwise to weaken the mixture as required, whilst holding the outer tool stationary.

92 Refit the air valve and suction chamber and adjust the CO percentage again on the fine and coarse adjusters.

93 Remove the plug from the air manifold hose and refit the hose to the air pump.

94 Run the engine at 2500 rpm for half a minute then adjust the idle speed screw to give the correct idle speed.

95 Switch off the engine and finally refit the float chamber vent pipe.

Carburettor (Zenith 175 CD 5T) — dismantling, inspection and reassembly.

96 Assuming that the carburettor is on the workbench, start by cleaning the exterior thoroughly with paraffin or a degreasing solvent.

97 Unscrew the damper cap, then, with the air valve raised, extract the retainer followed by the complete damper.

98 Prise the plug from the bottom of the float chamber and drain the fuel.

99 Unscrew and remove the six screws and withdraw the float chamber from the carburettor together with the gasket.

100 Note the position of the float assembly and carefully pull the spindle from the retaining clips; the needle valve and washer can then be unscrewed and removed.

101 Note the location marks on the top cover, then unscrew and remove the retaining screws and lift the cover off the air valve.

102 Remove the spring followed by the air valve and diaphragm, noting that the diaphragm has a locating tag for correct fitment.

103 If the diaphragm is faulty, unscrew and remove the four retaining screws and remove the ring, nylon spacer, and diaphragm, again noting that the diaphragm has an inner locating tag.

104 Loosen the needle retaining grub screw and insert the special tool in the air valve; turn the tool centre anti-clockwise two or three complete turns. Remove the grub screw and withdraw the needle and housing assembly but do not make any attempt to remove the adjuster as this is a fixed assembly.

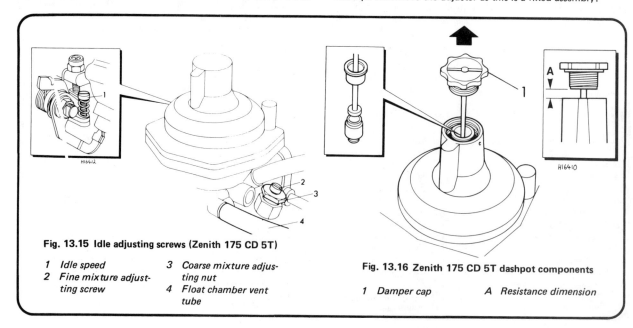

Fig. 13.15 Idle adjusting screws (Zenith 175 CD 5T)

1 Idle speed   3 Coarse mixture adjus-
2 Fine mixture adjust-   ting nut
   ing screw   4 Float chamber vent
                                tube

Fig. 13.16 Zenith 175 CD 5T dashpot components

1 Damper cap   A Resistance dimension

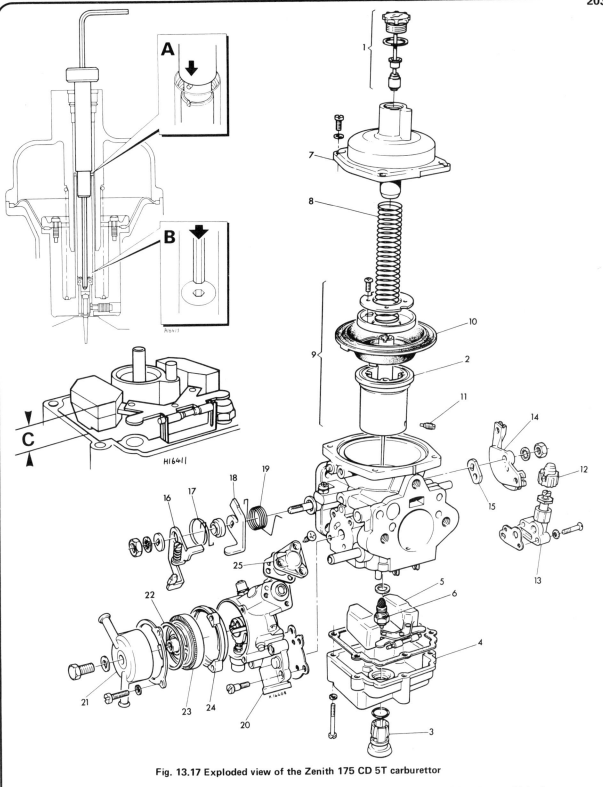

Fig. 13.17 Exploded view of the Zenith 175 CD 5T carburettor

1	Damper assembly	9	Air valve unit
2	Air valve piston	10	Diaphragm
3	Float chamber plug	11	Air valve grub screw
4	Float chamber	12	Idle air regulator cover
5	Float	13	Idle air regulator
6	Needle valve	14	Throttle quadrant
7	Top cover	15	Locating plate
8	Spring	16	Automatic choke operating lever unit

17	Outer spring
18	Inner operating lever
19	Inner spring
20	Automatic choke
21	Water jacket
22	Sealing rim
23	Heat mass
24	Insulator

25	Vacuum kick piston cover
A	Upper part of adjusting tool
B	Lower part of adjusting tool
C	Float level measurement points

105 Unscrew and remove the two retaining screws and remove the idle air regulator and gasket; the adjuster cover can be unclipped from the assembly.

106 Remove the throttle quadrant and plate after unscrewing and removing the retaining nut.

107 Unscrew and remove the automatic choke lever retaining nut and remove the washer, spacer, outer lever, bush, spring, inner lever, and spring in strict order.

108 Unscrew and remove the automatic choke body retaining screws and withdraw the automatic choke and gasket.

109 Note the relative position of the automatic choke cover and unscrew and remove the retaining bolt and washer; detach the cover and sealing ring.

110 Mark the position of the heat mass in relation to the automatic choke body, remove the three screws and withdraw the heat mass and insulator.

111 Mark the relative position of the vacuum piston cover and then remove the screws, cover and gasket.

112 Clean all the carburettor components and then check them for wear and deterioration. In particular check the air valve and float chamber needles for 'ridging' and the diaphragm rubber for splits. If available, use an air line or tyre pump to blow through all the internal parts and passages.

113 Reassembly is a reversal of the dismantling procedure but the following points should be noted:

   a) *The float assembly should be adjusted either by bending the float tabs or altering the thickness of the needle valve washers so that, when the valve is shut, the highest points of the floats are within 0.625 to 0.672 in (15.87 to 17.07 mm) from the float chamber face.*

   b) *The automatic choke mechanism should be checked and adjusted as described in paragraphs 114 to 126 inclusive.*

   c) *The carburettor dashpot should be filled with oil so that resistance is felt when the damper cap is 1/8 in (6 mm) from the top of the dashpot.*

114 With the automatic choke assembled, check that the vacuum kick piston, fast idle cam, and thermostat lever are free to move. Move the cam away from the lever and make sure that it returns and remains there when the lever is rotated (the throttle butterfly must be wedged open for this check).

115 Rotate the idle speed screw until a gap of 3/32 in (2.4 mm) exists between the choke and throttle levers. Rotate the throttle stop screw until a clearance of 0.025 in (0.6 mm) exists between the fast idle pin and the cam; lock the screw after adjusting.

116 Tighten the clamp plate screws to a torque wrench setting of 8 to 10 lbf in (0.09 to 0.12 kgf m).

Carburettor hot air intake — general

117 With some types of air cleaner, the air is drawn in by two possible routes. When cold, the air comes from a shield round the exhaust manifold. When hot it comes in direct from the front of the car. The T-junction where these two intakes join is controlled by a temperature sensitive disc valve. It is advisable to check this valve does move over. If it jams in the hot position driveability when cold will suffer. If jammed in the cold position, engine performance will be reduced.

Crankcase emission control — general

118 All engines now have a control system for removing fumes from the crankcase of the engine, to be burnt in the combustion chamber.

119 Fumes are drawn from the engine at the side tappet chest and led round the front, then to the carburettors, to a tapping close to the dashpot piston, where the depression is a constant value, and so a valve is unnecessary. The air supply to this breathing system comes normally through the oil filler cap in the rocker cover. This has a small hole to restrict the air flow, and a filter to clean it.

120 Systems that have a carburettor fuel evaporative loss control have a normal sealed oil filler cap, and instead draw air from the fuel absorption canister. The air flow from the canister goes to the rocker cover, through a union which incorporates a restrictor hole.

121 The crankcase emission control can be tested as follows. With the engine idling undo the oil filler cap. This will allow an unrestricted flow of air into the engine, so its speed should increase, and weakening of the mixture and its accompanying symptoms will occur.

Exhaust port air injection (emission control system) — general

122 An air injection system is fitted on cars going to North America. This blows air into the exhaust ports to promote burning of any hydrocarbons (unburnt fuel) that come from the cylinders, which would otherwise be released to the atmosphere. An air pump driven by a rubber belt from the engine draws air through an air cleaner and delivers it to an air supply manifold along the cylinder head. Drillings pass through the cylinder head to each exhaust port. A check valve in the air delivery pipe to the manifold prevents blow-back of high pressure exhaust to the air pump, and in the event of failure of the pump stops exhaust gasses passing that way.

123 When slowing down with the engine on the over-run the air pump also supplies air to the inlet manifold through a gulp valve.

124 The pump is a rotary vane type driven by a belt from the water pump pulley. The belt is tensioned by moving the pump away from the cylinder block in a similar manner to a generator when adjusting the fan belt. The air cleaner has a renewable element filter. The pump has a relief valve to allow excessive air pressure to blow off to the atmosphere.

125 The drivebelt tension should allow a total deflection of 0.5 in (12.7 mm) under hand pressure at the midway point of the run of the belt between the pulleys.

Air injection system (emission control system) — servicing

126 The air pump should be tested with the engine running at 1000 rpm.

127 Disconnect the gulp valve air supply hose at the gulp valve and plug it, to prevent any escape of air from the pump. Disconnect the hose from the air supply manifold, and put a pressure gauge on it. The air pump should give a gauge reading of not less than 2.75 lbf in^2 (0.19 kgf/cm^2). A low reading is likely to be due to three causes:

   a) *The air cleaner might be blocked. Fit a new element and recheck.*

   b) *The relief valve might not be seating correctly. Check this by blanking off the valve, and renew it if it is faulty.*

   c) *The pump may need servicing.*

128 To overhaul the pump remove it from the engine and proceed as follows:

   a) *Remove the three port-end cover bolts and take off the cover.*

   b) *Remove the four screws securing the rotor bearing end plate and remove the end plate. Lift out the vanes and take the carbon strips and springs from the rotor.*

   c) *Clean all the components with a lint free cloth.*

   d) *Repack the bearings with 'Esso Andok 260'.*

   e) *Renew worn or damaged vanes.*

   f) *Fit new carbons. Note that the slots which carry the carbon and springs are the deeper ones, and the carbons are fitted with the chamfered edge to the inside.*

   g) *Reassemble in reverse order. The underside of the heads of the screws retaining the rotor bearing end plate must be smeared with a locking compound like 'Loctite'.*

129 Check the relief valve. Speed the engine up until the valve blows off. This should give a gauge reading of between 4.5 and 6.5 lbf/in^2 (0.32 and 0.45 kgf/cm^2). It is difficult to detect when the valve blows off. Do not try to sense this by putting a finger between the valve and the driving pulley. Adhesive tape can be put over the blow-off hole to form an orifice from which the flow of air can be felt.

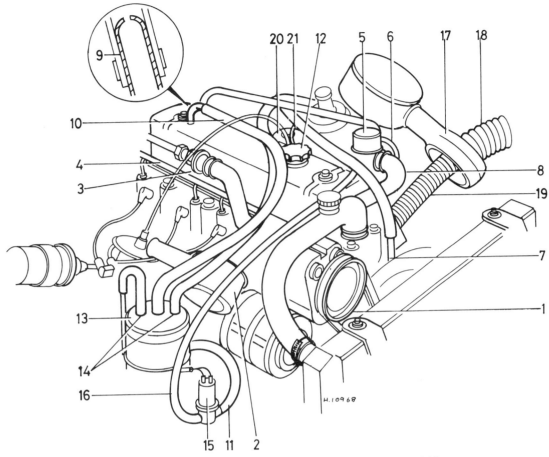

Fig. 13.18 Emission control components (Austin Marina models)

1	Air pump		
2	Air pump air cleaner	trap	canister
3	Check valve	8 Breather pipe	14 Vapour pipes
4	Air manifold	9 Restricted connection	15 Running-on control
5	Gulp valve	10 Purge line	valve
6	Sensing pipe	11 Air vent pipe	16 Running-on control
7	Oil separator/flame	12 Sealed oil filler cap	pipe
		13 Charcoal absorption	17 Air temperature

control valve
18 Cool air duct
19 Warm air duct
20 Exhaust gas recirculation (EGR) valve
21 Exhaust gas recirculation valve hose

130 Check valve: The air supply pipe being already removed from the check valve, remove the valve itself from the air manifold. Hold the air manifold connection to prevent that twisting, and unscrew the check valve. Blow through the valve by mouth, in each direction in turn. Air should only pass through the valve when blown from the side of the air supply hose connection. If air passes in the wrong direction renew the check valve. Do not use compressed air for this test, this is too powerful. When refitting to the air manifold hold the latter's connection to prevent it twisting whilst screwing in and tightening the check valve.

131 Gulp valve: The gulp valve cures sudden enrichment of the mixture following the closing of the throttle after running on full power. The fuel will continue to flow out of the carburettor slightly longer than will the air after the throttle is closed, as it is heavier. The gulp valve is connected to the inlet manifold. It has a valve which will feel the manifold depression on throttle closure. There is a small hole in the disc on the valve which will normally equalise pressure both sides, thus the spring can maintain the valve in the closed position, and so the gulp valve is shut. On sudden closure of the throttle the sharp increase of manifold depression is felt on one side of the valve, and will open it. The small hole will not have time to act. As the valve is open, air from the air pump is allowed to enter the inlet mani-

fold and so weaken the mixture. In a few moments the pressure will become equal on both sides of the valve and it will close it again.

132 To test the gulp valve:

a) *Disconnect the air supply hose from the air pump to the valve.*

b) *Connect a vacuum gauge with a T-connection to the disconnected end of the gulp valve air hose.*

c) *Start the engine and run it at idling speed.*

d) *With a finger close the open connection on the gauge T-piece, and check that a zero gauge reading is shown for at least 15 seconds. As the idle speed is constant the gulp valve should be closed, and so no reading registered on the gauge. Do not increase the engine speed above an idle during this test.*

e) *Now open the throttle, allow the engine to speed up, and then shut it sharply. As the engine speed falls the gauge should register a vacuum. Remove the finger from the end of the pipe to release the vacuum, and then repeat the test a number of times. The gauge should register a vacuum on this method. If it does not, renew the gulp valve.*

133 *Inlet manifold depression limit valve:* There is a small valve in the throttle disc to limit the manifold depression under overrun conditions.

134 To check this, disconnect the gulp valve pipe from the inlet manifold. Connect a vacuum gauge to the union on the inlet manifold. Warm the engine up at fast idle speed until the normal operating temperature is reached. Speed the engine up to 3000 rpm, and then release the throttle quickly. The vacuum gauge reading should immediately rise to between 20.5 and 22 inches (520 and 560 mm) Hg. If the vacuum is greater than this the throttle disc limit valve will not be functioning; a new disc with valve must then be fitted, after which the carburettor requires retuning.

135 *Air manifold and injectors:* To check the air flow:

a) *Disconnect the air manifold from the cylinder head connections.*

b) *Slacken the air supply hose at the check valve, rotate the manifold until the pipes point upwards and retighten the hose clip.*

c) *Run the engine (at idle only) and check that air comes out of all the pipes, and equally from each. Also check that exhaust gases blow from each of the injectors in the cylinder head vacated by the air pipes.*

d) *Be careful not to displace the injectors in the cylinder head as they may be free.*

e) *If an injector is blocked turn the engine over till that exhaust valve is shut. Using a hand drill to ensure a light touch, pass a 1/8 inch drill through the injector bore, taking care not to touch the exhaust valve stem at the other end. Blow out the carbon through the injector before turning the engine over again.*

Fuel line filter (emission control system) — general

136 In markets where the exhaust emission control system is fitted, a fuel line filter is added to ensure that no dirt impedes its operation. The filter should be renewed every 12 000 miles (20 000 km). It is removed by releasing the clip holding it to the exhaust manifold shield and pulling off the flexible pipes. Ensure the replacement item is fitted the right way round. After fitting the new filter run the engine for a few minutes and check for leaks.

Absorption canister (emission control system) — general

137 To prevent fumes being emitted by fuel as it evaporates either from the tank or the carburettor float chamber, their breathers are plumbed in to an absorption canister. This has a charcoal body into which the fuel vapour is absorbed whilst the engine is switched off. When the engine is next run the fuel vapour absorbed is sucked into the engine by the air breathing system, and burned.

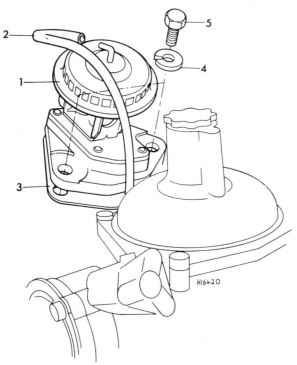

Fig. 13.19 Exhaust gas recirculation (EGR) valve location

1 Valve	4 Spring washer
2 Vacuum hose	5 Bolt
3 Gasket	

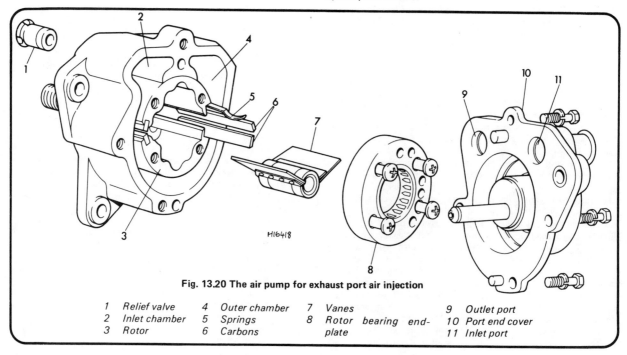

Fig. 13.20 The air pump for exhaust port air injection

1 Relief valve	4 Outer chamber	7 Vanes	9 Outlet port
2 Inlet chamber	5 Springs	8 Rotor bearing end-	10 Port end cover
3 Rotor	6 Carbons	plate	11 Inlet port

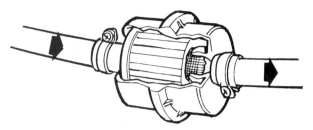

Fig. 13.21 Fuel line filter (emission control system)

138 The air filter, located in the bottom section of the canister, must be renewed every 12 000 miles (20 000 km). This filter protects not only the absorption canister, but also the engine breathing system.

139 The filter is renewed as follows. Disconnect the air vent tube (1) (Fig. 13.22) from the base of the canister. Then disconnect from the top of the two vapour pipes (2) and the purge pipe (3), and finally unscrew the mounting clip nut and bolt (4), taking care to catch the spacer that is in the clamp, and lift away the canister.

140 The air filter may be removed by unscrewing the bottom end cap (5) of the canister which will then expose the filter (6). Lift it out and throw it away. Wipe inside the cap with a non-fluffy rag, and fit a new filter pad, followed by the cap.

141 Remount the canister in the clip, and reconnect the pipes. The purge pipe to the engine valve rocker cover must be fitted to the centre connection on the top of the canister.

142 In time the canister loses its ability to absorb, so at 50 000 miles (80 000 km) the complete canister must be renewed.

Anti-run-on valve (emission control system) — general

143 Using the car on low octane fuel and with the lean mixture required to meet anti-pollution standards makes the engine liable to run-on by self ignition after switching off. This puts great stress on the engine. It will try to run backwards, and there may be blow back through the carburettor.

144 The anti-run-on valve cuts off fuel to the carburettor jet when the ignition is switched off. So although combustion chamber temperature might be so high that running-on would have otherwise occurred, the engine will quickly and smoothly stop.

145 The valve is on the right-hand side of the engine compartment near the absorption canister. A pipe comes to it from the inlet manifold. Another goes to the absorption canister to connect to the line going to the float chamber air vent. The valve is operated by an electric solenoid. This solenoid is activated when the ignition is switched off, but there is still oil pressure in the engine. Immediately after the ignition is switched off the engine will be still turning so there will still be oil pressure. The anti-run-on valve opens, and connects full inlet manifold suction to the carburettor float chamber air space using the air vent piping. This stops fuel flow to the jet so the engine stops. Oil pressure then drops and switches off the valve. The engine is now ready to start again.

Engine compression test

146 Cars used with the lean mixture necessary to meet some countries' regulations, and using fuel with low lead content, are liable to burn the exhaust valve seats. This applies, amongst others, to North America and Germany.

147 If valve burning is detected early it can be easily rectified. Long before it is noticeable to the car it can be detected by a compression test.

148 A special gauge for this, and an assistant, will be needed. The gauges are not very expensive, and will be a useful investment. But if necessary a garage can quickly do this check.

149 Warm up the engine.

150 Remove all the spark plugs.

151 Push the rubber seal of the gauge hard against the spark plug hole in the cylinder head.

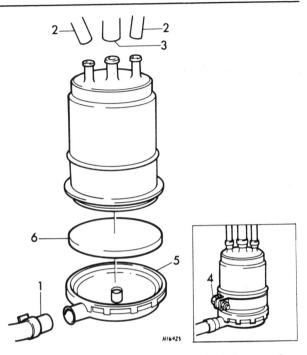

Fig. 13.22 Absorption canister assembly (emission control system)

1 Air intake from anti-run-on valve
2 Vapour pipes from tank and float chamber
3 Purge pipe to engine rocker
box
4 Clamp
5 Screwed bottom cover
6 Renewable filter pad

Fig. 13.23 Anti-run-on valve location (emission control system)

1 Control hose
2 Valve control pipe
3 Air vent pipe
4 Electrical supply leads
5 Removal procedure
6 Valve body

152 Get an assistant to open the throttle wide, and work the starter. The engine should be cranked for about three seconds; long enough to build up a reading on the gauge.

153 Write down the reading.

154 Relieve the pressure in the gauge, and repeat for the other cylinders.

155 If the readings are not all within 5 lbf/in^2 (0.35 kgf/cm^2) of each other do the whole test again. If the second reading for a particular cylinder varies from the first, do that one again to get a better average.

156 If it is definite that there is a variation of more than 5 lbf/in^2 (0.35 kgf/cm^2) between cylinders, then it indicates the valves are not seating properly, and they should be reground.

157 Should this job be necessary early in the life of the car, it does not follow that it will continue to be necessary in the future at the same frequency. If the valves are carefully reground by hand a better seating can be obtained than by machining and these will last longer before further attention is required. See Chapter 1/35.

158 Note that little stress has been laid on the actual gauge readings; it is the difference between the cylinders that is important. The actual reading depends on the accuracy of the gauge, the compression ratio of the engine, and the state of wear in the piston rings. It is assumed that these all wear the same, and none are broken.

Emission control system — fault diagnosis and routine maintenance

159 The addition of emission control adds some new hazards to fault finding. Yet do not always blame this system; the usual conventional faults will most often be the cause of trouble.

160 Erratic running, with poor driveability, if not a conventional defect, is most likely to be the gulp valve.

161 If the engine stops after short periods it may be fuel starvation due to a blockage in the air lines to or from the absorption canister. This can be checked by quickly taking off the fuel filler cap as the engine fails, to listen for an intake of air.

162 If enrichment of the mixture is needed to get a correct exhaust emission reading there is likely to be an air leak to the crankcase, either on the engine itself, or the breather system piping.

163 If the exhaust temperature seems excessive check the air injectors for air throughout.

164 Leaks can often be located by listening with a plastic pipe.

165 There are additions to the routine maintenance tasks scheduled at the beginning of this manual to suit the emission control fitments of certain models.

6000 miles (10 000 km)

166 Check the tension of the air pump drivebelt.

12 000 miles (20 000 km)

167 Renew the air filter element on the air pump.

168 Renew the air filter in the fuel vapour absorption canister. There is no filter in the oil filler cap on cars fitted with absorption canisters. So delete reference to renewing the cap.

169 Renew the fuel line filter.

170 If a low lead fuel is being used, test the cylinder compressions at the end of the car's first 12 000 miles.

18 000 miles (30 000 km)

171 Test the cylinder compressions. If one cylinder varies from the others by more than 5% remove the cylinder head and grind in the valves. Whilst carrying out any decarbonisations, the air injection system should be serviced as described in the 24 000 mile service.

24 000 miles (40 000 km)

172 Service the air injection system as described in paragraphs 126 to 135 inclusive. Check the air pump pressure, and if it is low, dismantle the pump. Remove the valves and check them. Remove the air supply manifold from the head and check its airflow, and that the exhaust port injectors are clear. Renew the air pump drivebelt.

50 000 miles (80 000 km)

173 Renew the complete absorption canister.

---

6 Ignition system

Contact breaker points — adjustment (Marina Mk 2 and Austin Marina models)

1 Follow the procedure given in Chapter 4, Section 2 but to adjust the gap, place a screwdriver in the contact breaker plate slot and lever against the pillar provided in the baseplate; turn it clockwise to decrease and anti-clockwise to increase the gap.

Contact breaker points — removal and refitting (Marina Mk 2 and Austin Marina models)

2 Unscrew and remove the contact plate retaining screw and remove the spring and plain washer.

3 Separate the moving contact spring from the terminal insulated post and detach the terminal plate. The contact set can now be removed completely.

4 Clean the new points with a methylated spirit moistened cloth, then connect the terminal plate to the moving contact spring and position the complete assembly on the baseplate.

5 Refit the retaining screw and washers and then press the moving contact spring onto the insulated post, making sure that it is located between the two shoulders.

6 Finally adjust the gap as described in Chapter 4, and paragraph 1 of this Section.

Condenser — removal and refitting (Marina Mk 2 and Austin Marina models)

7 The procedure is similar to that described in Chapter 4, Section 4, but in this case the terminal plate must be removed from the insulated post and the main supply lead and grommet pulled through the distributor body. The condenser is retained by one screw which also carries the baseplate earth lead.

Distributor — removal and refitting (Marina Mk 2 and Austin Marina models)

8 The procedure is identical to that given in Chapter 4, Section 6, but instead of a distributor mounted supply lead terminal, an in-line connection is fitted which is simply separated. On some Austin Marina models, the vacuum advance unit is not connected to the carburettor.

Distributor (43D4 and 45D4) — dismantling

9 With the distributor removed from the car and on the bench, if the distributor cap is still in position, ease back the clips and lift it away. Lift off the rotor arm. If it is very tight lever it off gently with a screwdriver.

10 Note the relative position of the offset drive dog to the rotor arm lobe. The centre line of the drive dog is parallel with and offset to the centre line of the rotor arm.

11 Lift away the cam oiling pad.

12 Unscrew and remove the two screws securing the vacuum unit. Note that two prongs protrude downwards from the baseplate and straddle one of the retaining screws.

13 Detach the operating arm from the moveable plate and lift away the assembly.

14 Carefully push the grommet and low tension lead through the body towards the inside of the housing.

15 Unscrew and remove the baseplate securing screw.

16 Carefully lever the baseplate from its retaining groove in the body (early type only).

17 Next remove the base and bearing plate assembly.

18 Using a suitable diameter parallel pin punch drive out the parallel pin securing the drive dog to the spindle.

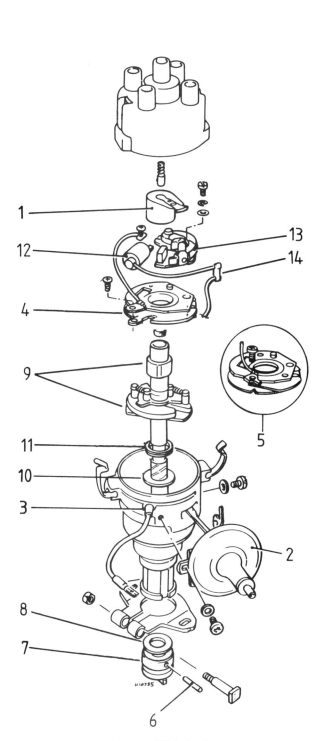

Fig. 13.24 Lucas 45D4 distributor

1	Rotor arm	9	Cam spindle and auto-
2	Vacuum unit		matic advance weights
3	Low tension lead		assembly
4	Baseplate	10	Steel washer
5	Baseplate (early cars)	11	Spacer
6	Retaining pin — drive dog	12	Capacitor
7	Drive dog	13	Contact set
8	Thrust washer	14	Low tension lead
			connector

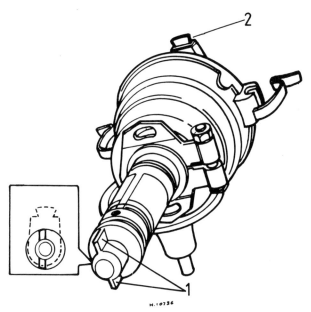

Fig. 13.25 Distributor drive dog position (1) relative to the rotor arm (2)

19 Remove the drive dog and the thrust washer. Note that the raised pips on the washer face towards the drive dog.
20 Remove the centre spindle complete with the automatic advance weights and springs.
21 Lift the steel washer and nylon spacer from the spindle.
22 Push the moving contact spring towards the centre of the distributor and unclip the low tension lead.
23 Unscrew and remove the screw that secures the earth lead tag and capacitor.
24 Unscrew and remove the screw, spring and plain washers that secure the fixed contact. Lift away the contact assembly.

Distributor (43D4 and 45D4) — inspection and repair
25 Thoroughly wash all mechanical parts in petrol and wipe dry with a clean non-fluffy rag.
26 Carefully check the fit of the drive spindle in its bush and spindle cam for wear.
27 The automatic advance mechanism should not be dismantled other than to remove the control springs. If any of the moving parts are excessively worn or are damaged the complete spindle assembly should be renewed. If the spindle bearing is worn allowing excessive side play, the complete distributor must be renewed.
28 Check the spring between the fixed and moveable plates. Operate the plate and examine for freedom of movement and excessive wear. Renew as a complete assembly.
29 Examine the distributor body and cap for cracks and signs of tracking.
30 Examine the pick up brush for wear and freedom of movement in its holder. Renew if necessary.
31 Check the rotor arm for damage, electrode security and burning or tracking. Renew if necessary.

Distributor (43D4 and 45D4) — reassembly
32 Reassembly is a straightforward reversal of the dismantling process. In addition, however, note the following.
33 During reassembly grease the pivots of the weights and springs and the spindle bearing area with a little Rocol MP (Molypad).
34 Grease the outside of the contact breaker hollow pivot post and lightly smear the spindle cam with a little general purpose grease.

35 Apply one or two drops of engine oil to the oiling pad.
36 Make sure the baseplate is pressed against the register in the body of the distributor so that the chamfered edge engages the undercut (early type only).
37 Measure across the centre of the distributor at a right angle to the slot in the baseplate (early type only).
38 Tighten the securing screw and re-measure the distance across the body. Unless the measurement has increased by at least 0.006 inch (0.152 mm) the contact breaker baseplate must be renewed (early type only).
39 Reset the contact breaker points gap to 0.014 – 0.016 inch (0.36 – 0.40 mm).
40 If a new drive spindle has been fitted, tap the drive end of the distributor dog to flatten the pips on the dog washer to ensure the correct degree of endfloat.

Ignition timing (Marina Mk 2 and Austin Marina models)

41 To make an accurate check of the ignition timing it is necessary to use a stroboscopic timing light whereby the timing is checked with the engine running. This is particularly important with the Austin Marina model due to the emission control systems fitted to the engine.
42 If the timing has been completely lost during dismantling, set it first to 5° BTDC using the static method described in Chapter 4 Section 10; this will enable the engine to be started.
43 Disconnect the distributor vacuum pipe (when fitted) and plug the end with a suitable dowel.
44 Connect the timing light to number 1 spark plug lead in accordance with the manufacturer's instructions, and if necessary wipe clean the timing marks on the crankshaft pulley and timing case.
45 Run the engine at the speed given in the Specifications, and shine the timing light onto the timing marks; the notch on the crankshaft pulley should appear opposite the relevant pointer on the timing case. The distributor should be adjusted if necessary by loosening the clamp bolt and rotating the body clockwise to advance and anti-clockwise to retard the timing. Tighten the clamp when the adjustment is completed.
46 On models fitted with a vacuum pipe, check the vacuum advance operation by running the engine at a fast idle speed whilst still watching the timing marks, then reconnect the vacuum pipe to the distributor; the ignition should immediately advance if the vacuum capsule is working correctly.
47 Finally stop the engine and disconnect the timing light.

---

7 Clutch

Clutch pedal – removal and refitting (Marina Mk 2 models)

1 The procedure is similar to that described in Chapter 5 but, instead of removing the parcel shelf, it is only necessary to disconnect and withdraw the supply tube from the face level vent.
2 On reassembly ensure that the supply tube is fully entered into the vent protrusion.

---

8 Gearbox and Automatic transmission

Manual gearbox – removal and refitting

1 On late Marina Mk 1 and all Mk 2 models, there is no need to remove the carburettor(s) when removing the gearbox.
2 A revised procedure for removing the gearbox on all models eliminates the need to remove the gear lever, rubber moulding, and retaining plate from inside the car; paragraphs 8, 9 and 10 in Section 2 of Chapter 6 may therefore be substituted by the following procedure.
3 Move the gear lever to the neutral position and complete the procedure in Chapter 6 prior to lowering the gearbox.

4 Lower the gearbox together with the gear lever until the gear lever retaining cover can be reached from beneath the car, then press down the cover and turn it anti-clockwise to release its bayonet fixing. This will release the gear lever and the remaining removal procedures can then be completed.
5 On Austin Marina models, in addition to the procedure given in Chapter 6, it is necessary to remove the reverse lamp clip and disconnect the reverse lamp leads prior to removing the gearbox.

Manual gearbox – dismantling and reassembly (Marina Mk 2 models)

6 The procedure is similar to that described in Chapter 6 but note that there is an additional ring on the mainshaft and three laygear preload springs are fitted in the front of the gearbox casing.

Automatic transmission (Marina Mk 2 models) – general

7 The Borg Warner model 65 automatic transmission fitted to Marina Mk 2 models is very similar in construction to the model 35 described in Chapter 6. Minor modifications to various components are shown in the accompanying illustrations. But for these the procedures given in Chapter 6 apply equally to both transmission models.
8 Although the downshift cable may be adjusted using the procedure given in Chapter 6 Section 14, it is recommended that it is adjusted using the fluid pressure test method. As specialised equipment is necessary for this method, the work is best entrusted to a BLMC garage.

Automatic transmission (Marina Mk 2 models) – fluid level checking

9 Make sure that the car is on a level surface, then apply the handbrake and move the selector lever to 'P'. Let the engine idle for at least two minutes then, while still idling, pull out the dipstick and wipe it clean with a lint-free cloth or tissue. Insert the dipstick and draw it out again, noting the level.
10 If the engine was started from cold, the level should be up to 'H' mark on the 'cold' scale on the dipstick. If the engine is hot (after at least 30 minutes of running) the level should be up to the 'H' mark of the 'hot' scale. Add fluid of the correct type (NOT Dexron type) down the dipstick/filler tube to bring it up to the correct level. The difference between the 'H' and 'L' marks corresponds to ¾ pint (1.0 US pint) (0.43 litres). Take great care that no dirt enters the transmission when topping up or internal damage will occur.

Transmission sump – draining and refilling

11 Drive the vehicle on to a ramp or have available adequate jacks to provide access to the underside of the car.
12 Select 'P' and apply the handbrake.
13 Raise the ramp or jacks.
14 Models with a drain plug: Wipe around the drain plug and then remove it; drain the contents into a container of at least 11.5 pt (13.8 US pt) (6.54 litre) capacity.
15 Models without a drain plug: Unscrew the dipstick/filler pipe at the union on the lower sidewall of the sump, and allow the oil to drain into a container of at least 11.5 pt (13.8 US pt/ 6.54 litre) capacity. Unscrew the sump bolts, then remove the sump and its gasket.
16 Refitting is a straightforward reverse of the removal procedure, using a new gasket or joint washer as necessary. Add fluid to bring it up to the 'H' mark on the 'cold' scale, then run the engine and select each gear in turn. Now check the fluid level as described in paragraphs 9 and 10.

Automatic transmission – removal and refitting

17 Although the rear mounting is slightly different the removal and refitting procedures are virtually identical to those given in Chapter 6, Section 11. One important point to note is that the transmission is removed complete with converter housing and not separately, leaving the converter housing in position on the

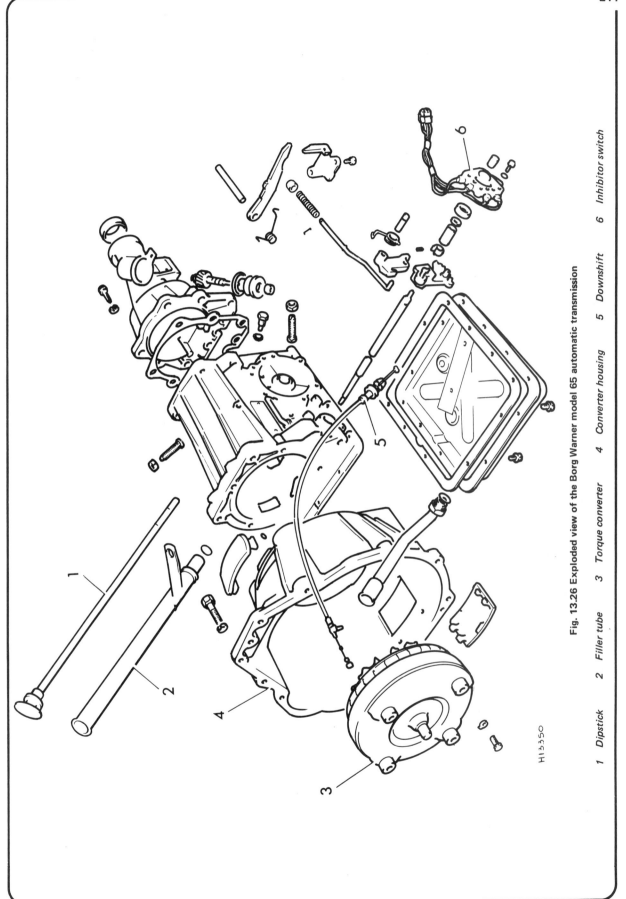

Fig. 13.26 Exploded view of the Borg Warner model 65 automatic transmission

H13350

| 1 Dipstick | 2 Filler tube | 3 Torque converter | 4 Converter housing | 5 Downshift | 6 Inhibitor switch |

engine, as was the case on the earlier model 35 transmissions. It should also be noted that the total fluid capacity is now 11.5 pints (13.8 US pints) (6.54 litres), and that there may be no earth cable attached to the transmission. There is also a rubber stop adjacent to the engine mounting bracket; the locknut on the bolt must be slackened and the rubber stop moved well clear of the engine mounting bracket when the transmission is being removed. Finally, the starter inhibitor/reversing light switch leads should be disconnected at the multiplug connector/s, not individually from the switch itself.

18 When refitting, follow the reverse of the removal procedure, but take note of the following points:

  a) *Align the torque converter and front pump driving dogs and slots horizontally.*
  b) *Carefully align the transmission to locate the input shaft and driving dogs.*
  c) *Make sure that the propeller shaft is correctly aligned when it is refitted (refer to Chapter 7 as necessary).*
  d) *Adjust the rubber stop to obtain 0.020 to 0.060 in (0.5 to 1.5 mm) clearance between the front face of the stop and the rear face of the engine mounting bracket, then tighten the locknut.*
  e) *Refill the transmission up to the 'M' mark on the 'cold' scale, run the engine and then select each gear in turn. Now check the fluid level as described previously.*

Starter inhibitor/reverse light switch — removal and refitting

19 Apply the handbrake and chock the wheels. Raise the car for access to the left-hand side of the transmission. Disconnect the battery earth terminal.
20 Disconnect the electrical wiring at the multiplug connector (there may be two connectors on certain models).
21 Remove the thread protector then remove the single bolt securing the switch to the transmission.
22 Refitting is the reverse sequence to removal. No adjustment is required.

9 Rear axle

Rear axle — removal and refitting (Marina Mk 2 models)

1 Follow the procedure given in Chapter 8 Section 2 but note the following:

  a) *Some models are not fitted with a brake compensating lever assembly and therefore paragraph 10 will not apply.*
  b) *Some models are fitted with a rear anti-roll bar and therefore between paragraphs 14 and 15 carry out the following. Unscrew and remove the anti-roll bar clamp retaining nuts and bolts and detach the clamps.*
  c) *Tighten the U-bolt nuts to a torque wrench setting of 15 to 18 lbf ft (2.0 to 2.4 kgf m).*

10 Braking system

General description

1 All Marina Mk 2 and Austin Marina models are now fitted with a brake servo unit as standard equipment.

Dual brake system — bleeding

2 When a tandem master cylinder is fitted, a slightly different technique for bleeding is required. First attach bleed tubes to both the left-hand front and left-hand rear brakes and bleed both at the same time. Note that the left-hand rear bleed nipple controls the bleeding operation for both rear wheels.
3 Use firm full strokes of the brake pedal and continue bleeding in a similar manner to that described in Chapter 9 until all the air is expelled.

4 Finally bleed the right-hand front brake and top-up the hydraulic fluid level in the reservoir as necessary with fresh hydraulic fluid; never re-use old brake fluid.
5 After completing the bleeding operations, check the operation of the brakes and the brake failure warning system.

Tandem brake master cylinder — removal and refitting

6 Drain the tandem master cylinder and reservoir in a similar manner to that described for the single master cylinder.
7 Using an open ended spanner, unscrew the two hydraulic pipe union nuts on the side of the master cylinder and carefully withdraw the hydraulic pipes.
8 Unscrew and remove the two nuts and spring washers securing the brake master cylinder to the rear of the servo unit and lift away the master cylinder.
9 Extract the master cylinder O-ring seal.
10 Refitting is a reversal of the removal procedure but the following additional points should be noted:

  a) *Renew the master cylinder O-ring seal.*
  b) *Tighten the master cylinder retaining nuts to 15.5 to 19.5 lbf ft (2.1 to 2.7 kgf m).*
  c) *Bleed the hydraulic system as described in paragraph 2 to 5 inclusive of this Section.*

Tandem brake master cylinder (early type) — dismantling and reassembly

11 Refer to the introduction to Chapter 9, Section 9 with regard to replacement master cylinders.
12 Undo and remove the two screws holding the reservoir to the master cylinder body. Lift away the reservoir. Using a suitably sized Allen key, or wrench, unscrew the tipping valve nut and lift away the seal. Using a suitable diameter rod, push the primary plunger down the bore, this operation enabling the tipping valve to be withdrawn.
13 Using a compressed air jet, very carefully applied to the rear outlet pipe connection, blow out all the master cylinder internal components. Alternatively, shake out the parts. Take care that adequate precautions are taken to ensure all parts are caught as they emerge.
14 Separate the primary and secondary plungers from the intermediate spring. Use the fingers to remove the gland seal from the primary plunger.
15 The secondary plunger assembly should be separated by lifting the thimble leaf over the shouldered end of the plunger. Using the fingers, remove the seal from the secondary plunger.
16 Depress the secondary spring, allowing the valve stem to slide through the keyhole in the thimble, thus releasing the tension on the spring.
17 Detach the valve spacer, taking care of the spring washer which will be found located under the valve head.
18 Examine the bore of the cylinder carefully for any signs of scores or ridges. If this is found to be smooth all over new seals can be fitted. If, however, there is any doubt of the condition of the bore, then a new cylinder must be fitted.
19 If examination of the seals shows them to be apparently oversize, or swollen, or very loose on the plungers, suspect oil contamination in the system. Oil will swell these rubber seals and if one is found to be swollen, it is reasonable to assume that all seals in the braking system will need attention.
20 Thoroughly clean all parts in methylated spirits. Ensure that the bypass ports are clear.
21 All components should be assembled wet by dipping in clean brake fluid. Using fingers only, fit new seals to the primary and secondary plungers ensuring that they are the correct way round. Place the dished washer with the dome against the underside of the valve seat. Hold it in position with the valve spacer ensuring that the legs face towards the valve seal.
22 Refit the plunger return spring centrally on the spacer, insert the thimble into the spring and depress until the valve stem engages in the keyhole of the thimble.
23 Insert the reduced end of the plunger into the thimble, until

the thimble engages under the shoulder of the plunger, and press home the thimble leaf. Refit the intermediate spring between the primary and secondary plungers.

24 Check that the master cylinder bore is clean and smear with clean brake fluid. With the complete assembly suitably wetted with brake fluid, carefully insert the assembly into the bore. Ease the lips of the plunger seals carefully into the bore. Push the assembly fully home.

25 Refit the tipping valve assembly, and seal, to the cylinder bore and tighten the securing nut to a torque wrench setting of 35 to 45 lbf ft (4.8 to 6.22 kgf m). Refit the hydraulic fluid reservoir and tighten the two retaining screws.

26 The master cylinder is now ready for refitting to the servo unit. Bleed the complete hydraulic system and road test the car.

Tandem brake master cylinder (later type) — dismantling and reassembly

27 Refer to the introduction to Chapter 9, Section 9 with regard to replacement master cylinders.

28 Unscrew the filler cap, and lever out the plastic baffle and rubber washer.

29 Extract the hairpin retaining clips and withdraw the two fluid reservoir securing pins, then lift the reservoir off the master cylinder.

30 Note the fitted position of the two reservoir seals and then extract them from the master cylinder body.

31 With the master cylinder mounted in a soft-jawed vice, use a suitable diameter rod to push the plunger fully down the cylinder bore and then extract the secondary plunger stop pin.

32 Using a pair of circlip pliers, extract the circlip from the end of the master cylinder bore and then remove the primary plunger assembly; place each item on a clean surface in the exact order of removal noting which way round the seals are fitted.

33 Shake out or alternatively blow out with a tyre pump or air line, the secondary plunger assembly; apply air pressure to the secondary outlet port.

34 Withdraw the two vacuum seals and spacers from the primary plunger tube end, and detach the spring, retainer, seal, and washer from the inner end of the primary plunger.

35 Similarly remove the spring and seals from the secondary plunger, again noting their fitted position.

36 Follow the instructions in paragraphs 18 to 20 inclusive of this Section.

37 All seals should be assembled wet by dipping in clean brake fluid. Using the fingers only, fit new seals to the primary and secondary plungers ensuring that they are the correct way round.

38 Reassembly is a reversal of the dismantling procedure but the following additional points should be noted:

a) *The secondary plunger return spring is larger than the primary plunger return spring.*

b) *The master cylinder bore should be smeared with clean brake fluid before inserting the plunger assemblies.*

c) *The primary plunger, vacuum seals, and spacers should be lubricated at the friction areas shown in Fig. 13.27 using grease supplied with the overhaul kit.*

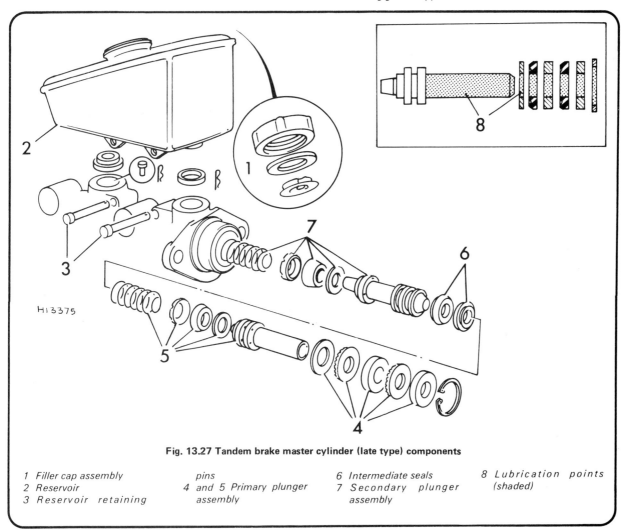

H13375

Fig. 13.27 Tandem brake master cylinder (late type) components

1 Filler cap assembly	pins	6 Intermediate seals	8 Lubrication points
2 Reservoir	4 and 5 Primary plunger	7 Secondary plunger	(shaded)
3 Reservoir retaining	assembly	assembly	

Handbrake cable — removal and refitting (Marina Mk 2 models)

39 Compensating levers are not fitted to Marina Mk 2 handbrake cables and it is therefore not necessary to carry out the procedure given in Chapter 9 Section 14, paragraphs 5, 6 and 7.

Handbrake lever assembly — removal and refitting (Marina Mk 2 models)

40 On GT and HL models only remove the centre console as described in paragraphs 42 to 47 of this Section.
41 The removal and refitting procedure is then identical to that described in Chapter 9, Section 15 except that it may be necessary to make cuts at each corner of the carpet when removing the handbrake lever gaiter retaining screws. If a handbrake switch is fitted it will also be necessary to disconnect the feed cable.

Centre console — removal and refitting (Marina Mk 2 GT and HL models)

42 Unscrew and remove the gear lever knob and the two front console retaining screws. Disconnect the battery negative terminal.
43 Unclip the rear end of the front console member, and disconnect the supply lead and lamp holder from the rear of the clock; the front console member can now be lifted away over the gear lever.
44 Using a screwdriver, prise up the forward edge of the handbrake aperture trim panel and withdraw it over the handbrake lever.
45 Prise the seat belt stalk seal out of the rear of the console and remove the ashtray.
46 Unscrew and remove the five retaining screws and carefully lift the console over the handbrake and gear levers.
47 Refitting the centre console is a reversal of the removal procedure.

Brake pedal assembly — removal and refitting (Marina Mk 2 models)

48 The procedure is identical to that described in Chapter 9, Section 16 except that instead of removing the instrument panel and front parcel tray, it is only necessary to remove the face vent hose.

Brake servo unit — removal and refitting (Marina Mk 2 models)

49 The procedure is identical to that described in Chapter 9, Section 18 except that paragraphs 3 and 4 should be omitted.

Pressure differential warning actuator valve (early type) — removal, overhaul and refitting

50 Wipe the top of the brake hydraulic fluid reservoir and unscrew the cap. Place a piece of polythene over the top and refit the cap. This is to prevent hydraulic fluid syphoning out. For safety reasons disconnect the battery.
51 Detach the cable connector at the top of the pressure differential warning actuator (PDWA) valve switch.
52 Wipe the area around the PDWA valve assembly and, using an open ended spanner, unscrew the union nut securing the rear brake fluid pipe to the valve, followed by the master cylinder to valve rear brake pipe, front brake fluid pipe and finally the master cylinder to valve front brake pipe.
53 Undo the PDWA valve securing bolt and lift away the bolt, spring washer and the valve itself.
54 Wipe down the outside of the valve and then unscrew the switch from the top of the body. Tip the valve upside down and recover the ball bearing located under the switch.
55 Unscrew and remove the small end plug and copper gasket. The gasket should not be re-used but a new one must be obtained.
56 Carefully shake out the large piston assembly.
57 Unscrew and remove the large end plug and copper gasket. The gasket should not be re-used but a new one must be obtained.
58 Carefully shake out the small piston assembly.
59 Using the fingers, or a piece of non-metal tapered rod such as a knitting needle, remove the seals from the pistons.
60 Examine the bore of the valve carefully for any signs of scores, ridges or corrosion. If this is found to be smooth all over, new seals can be fitted. If there is any doubt of the condition of the bore, a new valve must be obtained.
61 If examination of the two seals shows them to be apparently oversize or swollen, or very loose on the pistons, suspect oil contamination in the system. Oil will swell these rubber seals, and if one is found to be swollen, it is reasonable to assume that all seals in the braking system will need attention.
62 Thoroughly clean all parts in methylated spirits.

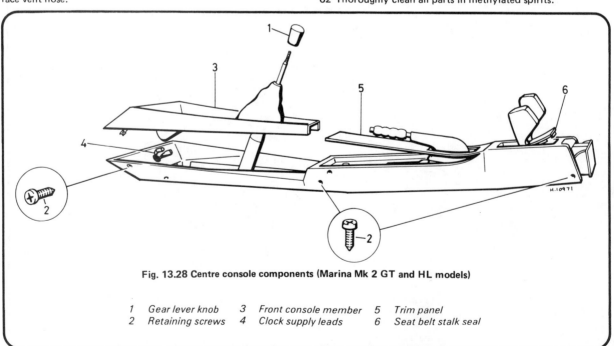

Fig. 13.28 Centre console components (Marina Mk 2 GT and HL models)

1 Gear lever knob	3 Front console member	5 Trim panel
2 Retaining screws	4 Clock supply leads	6 Seat belt stalk seal

63 All parts must be assembled wet by dipping in clean brake fluid. Fit new seals to the pistons with the larger diameter of the seals facing towards the small diameter end of the pistons.

64 Insert the long piston into the bore until the radial groove is opposite the electrical switch aperture. The piston must not be pushed down too far so that the seal passes the switch and ball bearing aperture, otherwise the seal will be damaged and a further new one will have to be fitted.

65 Drop the ball bearing into place and move the piston slightly, if necessary, until the ball bearing is seating in the radial groove. Refit the electric switch and tighten to a torque wrench setting of 2 to 2.5 lbf ft (0.3 to 0.35 kgf m).

66 Screw in the small end plug, fitted with a new copper gasket, and tighten to a torque wrench setting of 16 to 20 lbf ft (2.21 to 2.27 kgf m).

67 Carefully insert the short piston into the bore and finally screw in the large end plug with a new copper gasket. Tighten the end plug to a torque wrench setting of 16 to 20 lbf ft (2.12 to 2.27 kgf m).

68 Refitting is the reverse sequence to removal. It will be necessary to bleed the complete hydraulic system and full information will be found in paragraphs 2 to 5 inclusive of this Section.

Pressure differential warning actuator valve (self-reset type) — removal, overhaul and refitting

69 Disconnect the battery negative terminal and the valve switch supply lead.

70 Follow the procedure given in paragraphs 50, 52 and 53.

71 Wipe down the outside of the valve and then unscrew and remove the switch from the top of the body.

72 Unscrew and remove the end plug and gasket; a new gasket

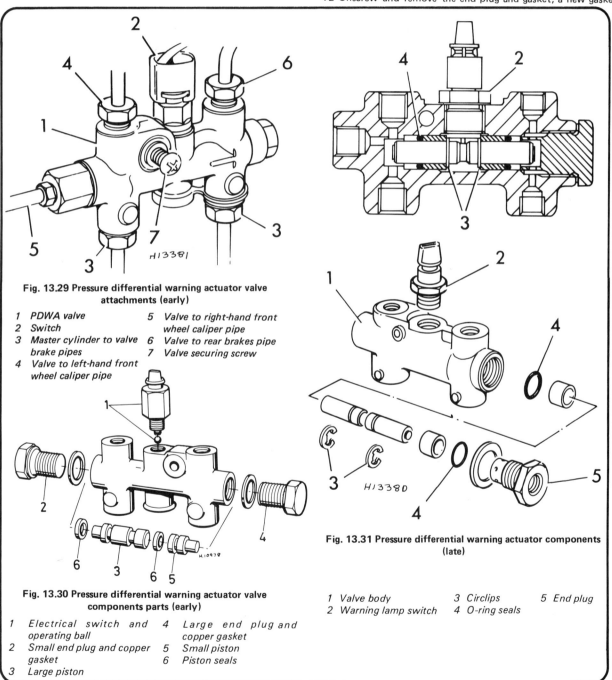

Fig. 13.29 Pressure differential warning actuator valve attachments (early)

1 PDWA valve	5 Valve to right-hand front wheel caliper pipe
2 Switch	
3 Master cylinder to valve brake pipes	6 Valve to rear brakes pipe
4 Valve to left-hand front wheel caliper pipe	7 Valve securing screw

Fig. 13.30 Pressure differential warning actuator valve components parts (early)

1 Electrical switch and operating ball	4 Large end plug and copper gasket
2 Small end plug and copper gasket	5 Small piston
3 Large piston	6 Piston seals

Fig. 13.31 Pressure differential warning actuator components (late)

1 Valve body	3 Circlips	5 End plug
2 Warning lamp switch	4 O-ring seals	

must be fitted on reassembly.

73 Shake or tap out the piston components noting the order in which they are fitted and making sure the sleeve and O-ring are recovered from the bottom of the bore.

74 Carefully prise the C-clips from the piston grooves and discard them together with the O-rings.

75 Follow the procedure given in paragraphs 60, 61 and 62.

76 To reassemble the valve, first fit the piston C-clips into their grooves, and the two sleeves and seals onto the piston, making sure that they slide freely on the piston.

77 Smear some fresh brake fluid on the cylinder bore and the piston assembly, and then insert the piston fully into the bore.

78 Screw in the end plug so that the O-ring enters onto the piston and then remove it and press the O-ring further down the bore until it contacts the sleeve.

79 Fit a new gasket to the end plug then screw it into the valve body and tighten it down to a torque wrench setting of 38 lbf ft (5.2 kgf m).

80 Using a screwdriver through the switch aperture, move the piston to its central position, then screw in the switch and tighten it to a torque wrench setting of 3.5 lbf ft (0.48 kgf m). Make sure that the piston is central otherwise the switch may foul the two sleeves.

81 Refitting is a reversal of the removal procedure but it will be necessary to bleed the complete hydraulic system as described in paragraphs 2 to 5 inclusive of this Section.

Brake pressure warning switch (early type) — centralisation

82 To centralise the switch proceed as follows:

83 Refit the bleed tube to a wheel on the other hydraulic circuit to the one just bled. Then an assistant should apply the brakes and hold them firmly and watch the warning light.

84 Slacken the bleed nipple. The assistant might feel pedal movement as the shuttle moves; the warning light will go out; as soon as it does shut the nipple. If the nipple is tightened too late the valve will move past centre, and the light will come on again. The procedure must then be repeated, but more quickly this time, on a brake on the other hydraulic circuit.

Flexible hose — inspection, removal and refitting

85 Inspect the condition of the flexible hydraulic hoses leading from the brake and clutch metal pipes. If any are swollen, damaged, cut or chafed, they must be renewed.

86 Unscrew the metal pipe union nut from its connection to the flexible hose, and then, holding the hexagon on the hose with a spanner, unscrew the attachment nut and washer.

87 The end of the flexible hose can now be withdrawn from the mounting bracket and will be quite free.

88 Disconnect the flexible hose from the slave or wheel cylinder by unscrewing it, using a spanner.

89 Refitting is the reverse sequence to removal. It will not be necessary to bleed the brake hydraulic system as described in Chapter 9, Section 2 or paragraphs 2 to 5 inclusive of this Section (dual circuit braking system).

Hydraulic pipes and hoses — general

90 Periodically all brake pipes, pipe connections and unions should be carefully examined.

91 First examine for signs of leakage where the pipe unions occur. Then examine the flexible hoses for signs of chafing and fraying and, of course, leakage. This is only a preliminary part of the flexible hose inspection, as exterior condition does not necessarily indicate the interior condition, which will be considered later.

92 The steel pipes must be examined carefully and methodically. They must be cleaned off and examined for any signs of dents, or other damage and rust and corrosion. Rust and corrosion should be scraped off, and if the depth of pitting in the pipes is significant, they will need renewing. This is particularly likely in those areas underneath the body and along the rear axle where the pipes are exposed to full force of road and weather conditions.

93 If any section of pipe is to be taken off, first wipe and then remove the fluid reservoir cap and place a piece of polythene over the reservoir. Refit the cap. This will stop syphoning during subsequent operations.

94 Rigid pipe removal is usually quite straightforward. The unions at each end are undone, the pipe and union pulled out, and the centre sections of the pipe removed from the body clips. The joints may sometimes be very tight. As one can only use an open ended spanner and the unions are not large, burring of the flats is not uncommon when attempting to undo them. For this reason a self-locking grip wrench (mole) is often the only way to remove a stubborn union.

95 Removal of flexible hoses is described in paragraphs 85 to 89.

96 With the flexible hose removed, examine the internal bore. If it is blown through first, it should be possible to see through it. Any specks of rubber which come out, or signs of restriction in the bore, mean that the rubber lining is breaking up and the pipe must be renewed.

97 Rigid pipes which need renewal can usually be purchased at any garage where they have the pipe, unions and special tools to make them up. All they need to know is the total length of the pipe, the type of flare used at each end of the union, and the length and thread of the union.

98 Refitting of the pipe is a straightforward reversal of the removal procedure. If the rigid pipes have been made up it is best to get all the sets (bends) in them before trying to fit them. Also if there are any acute bends, ask your supplier to put these in for you on a special tube bender. Otherwise you may kink the pipe and thereby decrease the bore area and fluid flow.

99 With the pipes refitted, remove the polythene from the reservoir cap and bleed the system as described in Chapter 9, Section 2 or paragraphs 2 to 5 inclusive of this Section (dual circuit braking systems).

11 Electrical system

Alternator — removal and refitting

1 Disconnect the battery negative terminal.

2 Loosen the pivot and adjustment bolts and swivel the alternator towards the engine to facilitate the removal of the fan belt.

3 Disconnect the multi-connector from the alternator end cover.

4 Unscrew and remove the pivot and adjustment bolts and withdraw the alternator from the engine.

5 Refitting is a reversal of the removal procedure but adjust the fan belt as described in Chapter 2.

Alternator — testing the charging circuit in situ

6 Initially ensure that the battery terminals are clean, the battery is fully charged, all cables and terminals are in good condition and that the drivebelt is correctly tensioned.

Battery voltage test

7 Remove the cable connector from the alternator then connect the negative terminal of a voltmeter to a chassis earth point. Switch on the ignition and connect the voltmeter positive lead to each of the alternator cable connectors in turn.

8 If there is no voltage at the 'IND' cable connector, check charge indicator lamp and associated wiring.

9 If there is no voltage at the main charging cable connector, check for continuity between the battery and alternator.

10 If satisfactory at paragraphs 8 and 9, proceed to the alternator test below.

Alternator test

11 Reconnect the alternator cable connector then disconnect the brown eyelet-ended cable at the starter motor solenoid. Connect an ammeter between the solenoid terminal and the brown cable, and a voltmeter across the battery terminals. Run the engine to obtain an alternator speed of 6000 rpm (approx 2500 rpm of the engine).

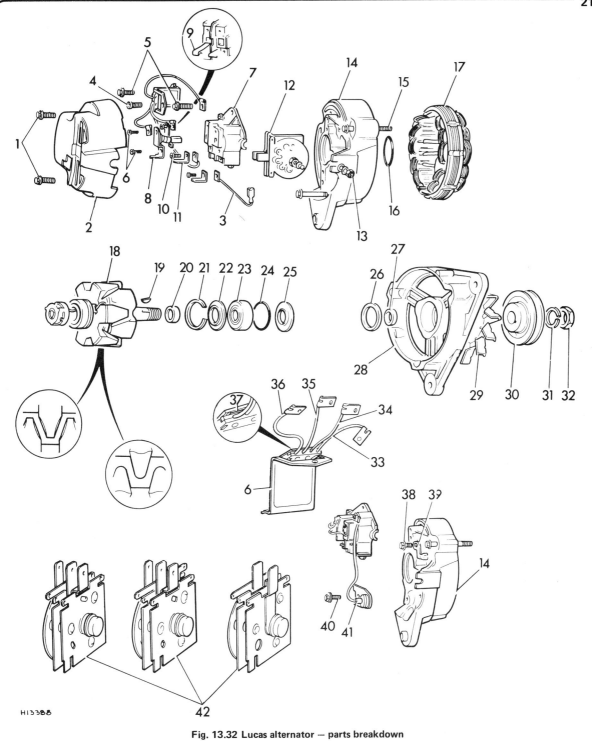

Fig. 13.32 Lucas alternator — parts breakdown

H13388

1	Screw	13	Nut and washers	23	Bearing	34	F green lead
2	End cover	14	Slip ring end bracket	24	O-ring	35	+ yellow lead
3	Lead (typical)	15	Through-bolts	25	Cover plate	36	B+ red lead
4	Screw	16	O-ring	26	Felt washer	37	Copper strip (alternative to item 33)
5	Screws	17	Stator lamination pack	27	Distance piece		
6	Regulator	18	Rotor assembly with	28	Drive end bracket	38	Screw
7	Brush box mounting		bearing and slip ring	29	Fan	39	Earthing link
8	Brush assembly	19	Key	30	Pulley	40	Screw
9	Brush spring	20	Distance piece	31	Spring washer	41	Avalanche diode
10	Screws	21	Circlip	32	Nut	42	Rectifiers (alternative types to item 12)
11	Terminals	22	Cover plate	33	Black earth lead		
12	Rectifier assembly						

12 If there is no current reading, remove and overhaul the alternator.

13 If there is a negative ammeter reading and a voltmeter reading of 13.6 — 14.4 volts (13.6 — 14.6 volts for alternators fitted with 8TRD, 11TR or 14TR regulator units from February 1972), and if the battery is in a low state of charge, a bench test of the alternator should be carried out to check for the specified current. This is not a do-it-yourself task, and must be entrusted to an automotive electrical specialist.

14 If less than 10 amps is registered and a voltage below 13.6 is obtained, the alternator voltage regulator must be renewed.

15 If more than 10 amps is registered and a voltage above 14.4 volts (or 14.6 volts — see paragraph 130) is obtained, the alternator voltage regulator must be renewed.

Alternator — overhaul

Note: Before commencing repair work of any kind on the alternator, it must be appreciated that more harm than good can be done by any person inexperienced with the use of a soldering iron and electrical test equipment in connection with semiconductor devices. Before commencing, read through this Section carefully and ascertain the availability of any spare parts which may be required. If in any doubt about the feasibility of the job, or your own capabilities, it is best to obtain a service exchange unit or contact a recognised automotive electrical specialist.

16 Remove the alternator end cover (2 screws) and make a note of the position and colour of the rectifier spade terminal leads. Remove the leads.

17 Where applicable, remove the surge protection avalanche diode from the end bracket (1 screw).

18 Remove the brush box moulding (2 screws) and the regulator (1 screw) from the end bracket.

19 Where applicable, remove the rectifier earthing link (1 screw).

20 Unsolder the three stator cables from the rectifier using the minimum practicable amount of heat.

21 Remove the rectifier after slackening the nut.

22 Mark the drive-end bracket, stator lamination pack and slip ring end bracket to aid reassembly.

23 Remove the three through-bolts and withdraw the end bracket and lamination pack. Remove the O-ring from inside the end bracket.

24 Remove the nut and washer then withdraw the pulley and fan from the rotor.

25 Press the rotor out of the drive-end bracket bearing and withdraw the distance piece from the rotor.

26 Remove the circlip, bearing, cover plates, O-ring and felt washer from the drive-end bracket.

27 If it is necessary to remove the slip ring end bearing, unsolder the two field connections and withdraw the slip ring and bearing from the rotor shaft. When reassembling this bearing, ensure that the shielded side is towards the slip ring assembly and use only Fry's HT3 solder or equivalent to remake the field connections.

28 Inspect the bearings for roughness of running and wear; if necessary repack with Shell Alvania RA Grease or equivalent.

29 If necessary, clean the slip ring with very fine glass paper.

30 Using a 110 volt AC supply and a 15 watt test lamp between one of the slip rings and one of the rotor lobes, check the field winding insulation.

31 Check the field winding resistance (between the slip rings) against that specified.

32 Check the stator windings for continuity between each lead using a 12 volt DC supply and a 36 watt test lamp.

33 Check the stator winding insulation between the stator lamination pack and any one of the 3 cables, using 110 volts AC and a 15 watt test lamp.

34 Check the 9 diodes between each diode pin and its heat sink for current flow in one direction only, using 12 volts DC and a 1.5 watt test lamp. Renew the rectifier assembly if any diode is faulty.

35 Remove the single screw retaining the regulator to the brush box. Note the fitted position of the coloured leads then remove the screws and terminal strips retaining the brushes.

36 Remove the brushes, noting the leaf spring at the side of the inner brush.

37 Assembly is essentially the reverse of the dismantling procedure, but the following points must be carefully noted.

  a) If a rectifier unit is renewed, the replacement unit must be identical to that which was removed.

  b) Connect the black regulator earth lead to the screw retaining the brushbox assembly to the end bracket. If there is no earth cable, the regulator earths through its case as indicated by a copper strip between the top bracket inner surface and the lead clamp. When fitting this type of regulator, ensure that a good earth exists.

  c) Connect the regulator 'F' terminal green lead under the inner brush retaining plate (on some versions this lead is replaced by a metal connecting strip).

  d) Connect the '+' terminal yellow lead above the outer brush retaining plate, ensuring that the conductor cannot bridge the two brush retaining plates.

  e) If a battery positive (B+) red lead is fitted on the regulator, connect it under the screw retaining the 'B+' spade connector, or to the middle positive heat sink plate side spade connector of the rectifier assembly, as appropriate.

  f) Connect the avalanche diode to the outer heat sink plate side spade connector, or to the screw retaining the outer brush and the yellow regulator lead, as appropriate; an extension link and an additional screw may be provided.

  g) Support the inner track of the bearing when refitting the rotor to the end bracket.

  h) Use only M grade 45/55 tin-lead solder or equivalent when remaking the stator to rectifier connections.

  j) Tighten the pulley nut to 25 lbf ft (3.46 kgf m) torque.

38 After installation of the alternator, check the output, as described in paragraphs 6 to 15 of this Section.

Dynamo — testing in position

39 If, with the engine running, no charge comes from the dynamo, or the charge is very low, first check that the fan belt is in place and is not slipping. Then check that the leads from the control box to the dynamo are firmly attached and that one has not come loose from its terminal.

40 The lead from the 'D' terminal on the dynamo should be connected to the 'D' terminal on the control box, and similarly the 'F' terminals on the dynamo and control box should also be connected together. Check that this is so and that the leads have not been incorrectly fitted.

41 Make sure none of the electrical equipment, such as the lights or radio, is on, and then pull the leads off the dynamo terminals marked 'D' and 'F'. Join the terminals together with a short length of wire.

42 Attach to the centre of this length of wire the positive clip of a 0 — 20 volts voltmeter and run the other clip to earth on the dynamo yoke. Start the engine and allow it to idle at approximately 750 rpm. At this speed the dynamo should give a reading of about 15 volts on the voltmeter. There is no point in raising the engine speed above a fast idle as the reading will then be inaccurate.

43 If no reading is recorded then check the brushes and brush connections. If a very low reading of approximately 1 volt is observed then the field winding may be suspect.

44 If a reading of between 4 to 6 volts is recorded it is likely that the armature winding is at fault.

45 With the Lucas C40-1 windowless yoke dynamo, it must be removed and dismantled before the brushes and commutator can be attended to.

46 If the voltmeter shows a good reading, then with the temporary link still in position, connect both leads from the control

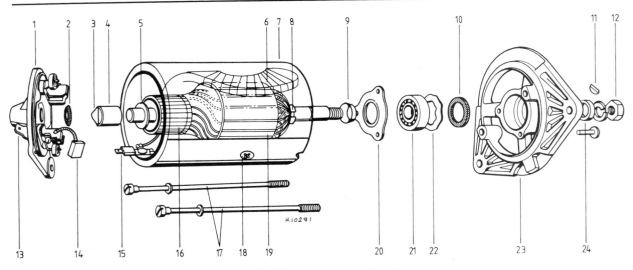

Fig. 13.33 Dynamo component parts

1	Commutator end bracket	7	Yoke	13	Output terminal	19 Armature
2	Felt ring	8	Shaft collar	14	Brush	20 Bearing retaining plate
3	Felt ring retainer	9	Shaft collar retaining cup	15	Field terminal F	21 Ball bearing
4	Bronze bush	10	Felt ring	16	Commutator	22 Corrugated washer
5	Thrust washer	11	Shaft key	17	Through-bolts	23 Driving end bracket
6	Field coils	12	Shaft nut	18	Pole screw	24 Pulley spacer

box to 'D' and 'F' on the dynamo ('D' to 'D' and 'F' to 'F'). Release the lead from the 'D' terminal at the control box end and clip one lead from the voltmeter to the end of the cable, and the other lead to a good earth. With the engine running at the same speed as previously, an identical voltage to that recorded at the dynamo should be noted on the voltmeter. If no voltage is recorded there is a break in the wire. If the voltage is the same as recorded at the dynamo then check the 'F' lead in a similar fashion. If both readings are the same as at the dynamo then it will be necessary to test the control box.

Dynamo — removal and refitting

47 Undo and remove the bolt from the adjustment link.
48 Slacken the two mountings bolts and nuts and push the dynamo towards the engine. Lift the fan belt from the pulley.
49 Remove the mounting nuts and bolts and lift away the dyanamo.
50 Refitting is a reversal of the above procedure. Do not finally tighten the retaining bolts and adjustment link bolt until the fan belt has been tensioned correctly.

Dynamo — dismantling and inspection

51 Mount the dynamo in a vice and unscrew and remove the two through-bolts from the commutator end bracket.
52 Mark the commutator end bracket and the dynamo casing so the end bracket can be refitted in its original position. Pull the end bracket off the armature shaft. Note: Some versions of the dynamo may have a raised pip on the edge of the casing. If so, marking the end bracket and casing is unnecessary. A pip may also be found on the drive end bracket at the opposite end of the casing.
53 Lift the two brush springs and draw the brushes out of the brush holders.
54 Measure the brushes and if worn down to 0.25 in (6.35 mm) or less, unscrew the screws holding the brush leads to the end bracket. Take off the brushes complete with leads.
55 If no locating pip can be found, mark the drive end bracket and the dynamo casing so that the drive end bracket can be refitted in its original position. Then pull the drive end bracket, complete with armature, out of the casing.
56 Check the condition of the ball bearing in the drive end plate by firmly holding the plate and noting if there is visible side movement of the armature shaft in relation to the end plate.

If play is present, the armature assembly must be separated from the end plate. If the bearing is sound there is no need to carry out the work described in the following two paragraphs.
57 Hold the armature in one hand (mount it carefully in a vice if preferred) and undo the nut holding the pulley wheel and fan in place. Pull off the pulley wheel and fan.
58 Next move the Woodruff key from its slot in the armature shaft and also the bearing locating ring.
59 Place the drive end bracket across the open jaws of a vice with the armature downwards and gently tap the armature shaft from the bearing in the endplate with the aid of a suitable drift.
60 Carefully inspect the armature and check it for open or short circuited windings. It is a good indication of an open circuited armature when the commutator segments are burnt. If the armature has short circuited, the commutator segments will be very badly burnt, and the overheated armature windings badly discoloured. If open or short circuits are suspected then test by substituting the suspect armature for a new one.
61 Check the resistance of the field coils. To do this, connect an ohmmeter between the field terminals and the yoke and note the reading on the ohmmeter which should be about 6 ohms. If the ohmmeter reading is infinity this indicates an open circuit in the field winding. If the ohmmeter reading is below 5 ohms this indicates that one of the field coils is faulty and must be renewed.
62 Field coil renewal involves the use of a wheel operated screwdriver, a soldering iron, caulking and riveting. This operation is considered to be beyond the scope of most owners. Therefore, if the field coils are at fault either purchase a reconditioned dynamo, or take the casing to a BLMC garage or electrical engineering works for new field coils to be fitted.
63 Next check the condition of the commutator. If it is dirty and blackened, clean it with a petrol dampened rag. If the commutator is in good condition the surface will be smooth and quite free from pits or burnt areas, and the insulated segments clearly defined.
64 If, after the commutator has been cleaned, pits and burnt spots are still present, wrap a strip of glass paper round the commutator taking great care to move the commutator ¼ of a turn every ten rubs until it is thoroughly clean.
65 In extreme cases of wear, the commutator can be mounted in a lathe and, with the lathe turning at high speed, a very fine cut may be taken off the commutator. Then polish it with glass

paper. If it has worn so that the insulators between the segments are level with the top of the segments, then undercut the insulators. The best tool to use for this purpose is half a hacksaw blade ground to a thickness of the insulator, and with the handle end of the blade covered in insulating tape to make it comfortable to hold.

66 Check the bush bearing in the commutator end bracket for wear by noting if the armature spindle rocks when placed in it. If worn it must be renewed.

67 The bush bearing can be removed by a suitable extractor or by screwing an inch tap four or five times into the bush. The tap, complete with bush, is then pulled out of the end bracket.

68 **Note:** The bush bearing is of the porous bronze type and, before fitting a new one, it is essential that it is allowed to stand in engine oil for at least 24 hours before fitment. In an emergency the bush can be immersed in hot oil (100°C) for 2 hours.

69 Carefully fit the new bush into the end plate, pressing it in until the end of the bearing is flush with the inner side of the endplate. If available, press the bush in with a smooth shouldered mandrel the same diameter as the armature shaft.

Dynamo — repair and reassembly

70 To renew the ball bearing fitted to the drive end bracket, drill out the rivets which hold the bearing retainer plate to the end bracket and lift off the plate.

71 Press out the bearing from the end bracket and remove the corrugated and felt washers from the bearing housing.

72 Thoroughly clean the bearing housing and the new bearing, and pack with high melting point grease.

73 Place the felt washer and corrugated washer in that order in the end bracket bearing housing.

74 Then fit the new bearing.

75 Gently tap the bearing into place with the aid of a suitable drift.

76 Refit the bearing plate and fit three new rivets.

77 Open up the rivets with the aid of a suitable cold chisel.

78 Finally peen over the open end of the rivets with the aid of a ball hammer.

79 Refit the drive end bracket to the armature shaft. Do not try and force the bracket on but, with the aid of a suitable socket abuting the bearing, tap the bearing on gently, so pulling the end bracket down with it.

80 Slide the spacer up the shaft and refit the Woodruff key.

81 Refit the fan and pulley wheel and then fit the spring washer and nut and tighten the latter. The drive end of the dynamo is now fully assembled.

82 If the brushes are little worn and are to be used again then ensure that they are placed in the same holders from which they were removed. When refitting brushes either new or old, check that they move freely in their holders. If either brush sticks, clean with a petrol moistened rag and if still stiff, lightly polish the sides of the brush with a very fine file until the brush moves quite freely in its holder.

83 Tighten the two retaining screws and washers which hold the wire leads to the brushes in place.

84 It is far easier to slip the end plate with brushes over the commutator if the brushes are raised in their holders and held in this position by the pressure of the springs resting against their flanks.

85 Refit the armature to the casing and then the commutator end plate, and screw up the two through bolts.

86 Finally, hook the ends of the two springs off the flanks of the brushes and onto their heads so the brushes are forced down into contact with the armature.

Control box (RB 106/2) — general description

87 The control box comprises the voltage regulator and the cut-out. The voltage regulator controls the output from the dynamo depending on the state of the battery and the demands of the electrical equipment, and ensures that the battery is not over-charged. The cut-out is really an automatic switch and connects the dynamo to the battery when the dynamo is turning fast enough to produce a charge. Similarly it disconnects the battery from the dynamo when the engine is idling or stationary so that the battery does not discharge through the dynamo.

Control box (RB 106/2) — cut-out and regulator contacts maintenance

Note: Disconnect the battery negative terminal before starting the following work.

88 Every 12 000 miles check the cut-out and regulator contacts. If they are dirty or rough or burnt place a piece of fine glass paper (**do not use emery paper or carborundum paper**) between the cut-out contacts, close them manually and draw the glass paper through several times.

89 Clean the regulator contacts in exactly the same way, but use emery or carborundum paper and **not** glass paper. Carefully clean both sets of contacts from all traces of dust with a rag moistened in methylated spirits.

Control box (RB 106/2) — voltage regulator adjustment

90 If the battery is in sound condition, but is not holding its charge, or is being continually over-charged, and the dynamo is in sound condition, then the voltage regulator in the control box must be adjusted.

91 Check the regulator setting by removing and joining together the cables from the control box terminals 'A1' and 'A'. Then connect the negative lead to a 20—volt voltmeter to the 'D' terminal on the dynamo and the positive lead to a good earth. Start the engine and increase its speed until the voltmeter needle flicks and then steadies. This should occur at about 2000 rpm. If the voltage at which the needle steadies is outside the limits listed below, then remove the control box cover and turn the adjusting screw in the illustration clockwise a quarter of a turn at a time to raise the setting, and a similar amount anti-clockwise to lower it.

Air temperature	Open circuit voltage
10°C or 50°F	16.1 to 16.7
20°C or 68°F	16.0 to 16.6
30°C or 86°F	15.9 to 16.5
40°C or 104°F	15.8 to 16.4

92 It is vital that the adjustments be completed within 30 seconds of starting the engine as otherwise the heat from the shunt coil will affect the readings.

Control box (RB 106/2) — cut-out adjustment

93 Check the voltage required to operate the cut-out by connecting a voltmeter between the control box terminals 'D' and 'E'.

94 Remove the control box cover, start the engine and gradually increase its speed until the cut-outs close. This should occur when the reading is between 12.7 and 13.3 volts.

95 If the reading is outside these limits turn the cut-out adjusting screw in the illustration a fraction at a time clockwise to raise the voltage, and anti-clockwise to lower it. To adjust the drop-off voltage bend the fixed contact blade carefully. The adjustment to the cut-out should be completed within 30 seconds of starting the engine as otherwise heat build-up from the shunt coil will affect the readings.

96 If the cut-out fails to work, clean the contacts, and if there is still no response, renew the cut-out and regulator unit.

Control box (RB 340) — general description

97 The control box comprises three units: two separate vibrating armature type single contact regulators and a cut-out relay. One of the regulators is sensitive to change in current and the other to changes in voltage.

98 Adjustments can be made only with a special tool which resembles a screwdriver with a multi-toothed blade. This can be obtained through Lucas agents.

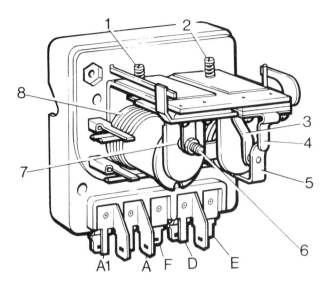

Fig. 13.34 Lucas RB 106/2 control box

1 Regulator adjustment screw	6 Regulator fixed contact
2 Cut-out adjustment screw	screw
3 Fixed contact blade	7 Regulator moving contact
4 Stop arm	8 Regulator series windings
5 Armature tongue and	
moving contact	

99 The regulators control the output from the dynamo depending on the state of the battery and the demands of the electrical equipment and ensure that the battery is not over-charged. The cut-out is really an automatic switch and connects the dynamo to the battery when the dynamo is turning fast enough to produce a charge. Similarly it disconnects the battery from the dynamo when the engine is idling or stationary so that the battery does not discharge through the dynamo.

Control box (RB 340) — cut-out and regulator contacts maintenance
100 Refer to paragraphs 93 to 96 inclusive.

Control box (RB 340) — regulator adjustment
101 If the battery is being under-charged check that the fan belt is not slipping and the dynamo is producing its correct output. Check the battery lead terminals for secureness on their posts. If the battery is being over-charged this points fairly definitely to an incorrectly set regulator.
102 Checking the action of the regulator and cut-out is not difficult but must be completed as quickly as possible (**not** more than 30 seconds for each test), to avoid errors caused by heat of the coils. Essential test equipment comprises a 0–20 volt voltmeter and a moving coil −40 to +40 amp ammeter and an air temperature gauge. Also required is a special adjusting tool obtainable through Lucas agents.
103 The regulator portion of the three bobbin type control box comprises the voltage regulator and the current regulator. The third bobbin at the 'B' terminal end is the cut-out.
104 To test the regulator take off the control box cover and slip a piece of thin card between the cut-out points. Connect the voltmeter between the control box terminal 'D' and a good earth. Start and run the engine at about 3000 rpm when a steady reading on the voltmeter should be given as shown in the table.

Air temperature	Open circuit voltage
10°C or 50°F	14.9 to 15.5

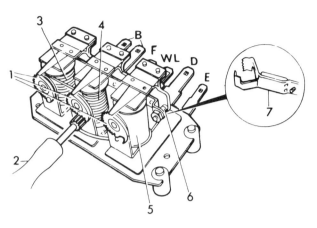

Fig. 13.35 Lucas RB 340 control box

1 Adjusting cams	5 Voltage regulator
2 Lucas setting tool	6 Voltage regulator contacts
3 Cut-out relay	7 Clip
4 Current regulator	

20°C or 68°F	14.7 to 15.3
30°C or 86°F	14.5 to 15.1
40°C or 104°F	14.3 to 14.9

105 If the reading fluctuates by more than 0.3 volts then it is likely that the contact points are dirty. If the reading is steady but incorrect turn the voltage adjustment cam clockwise with the special Lucas tool to increase the settings, and anti-clockwise to lower it.
106 Stop the engine and then restart it, gradually increasing the speed. If the voltage continues to rise with a rise in engine speed this indicates short circuited or fused points or a faulty magnet coil. If this is the case the only remedy is to fit an exchange control box.
107 The dynamo should be able to provide 22 amps at 3000 rpm irrespective of the state of the battery.
108 To test the dynamo output take off the control box cover, and short out the voltage regulator contacts by holding them together with a bulldog clip.
109 Pull off the Lucar connectors from the control box terminals 'B' and connect an ammeter reading to ±40 amps to the two cables just disconnected and to *one* of the 'B' Lucar connectors.
110 Turn on all the lights and other electrical equipment and start the engine. At about 3000 rpm the dynamo should be giving between 21 and 23 amps as recorded on the ammeter. If the ammeter needle flickers it is likely that the contact points are dirty.
111 To increase the current turn the cam on top of the current regulator clockwise, and to lower it, anti-clockwise.

Control box (RB 340) — cut-out adjustment
112 Check the voltage required to operate the cut-out by connecting a voltmeter between the control box terminal 'WL' and a good earth. Remove the control box cover, start the engine and gradually increase its speed until the cut-outs close. This should occur when the reading is between 12.7 to 13.3 volts.
113 If the reading is outside these limits turn the adjusting cam on the cut-out relay a fraction at a time clockwise to raise the voltage cut-in point and anti-clockwise to lower it.
114 To adjust the drop off voltage bend the fixed contact blade carefully. The adjustment to the cut-out should be completed within 30 seconds of starting the engine as otherwise heat build up from the shunt coil will affect the readings.

115 If the cut-out fails to work, clean the contacts and, if there is still no response, renew the cut-out and regulator unit.

Starter motor (M35J) — testing, removal and refitting
116 Refer to Chapter 10, Sections 9 and 10, as the procedure is identical to that of the model M418G starter motor.

Starter motor (M35J) — dismantling and reassembly
117 With the starter motor on the bench, first mark the relative positions of the starter motor body to the two end brackets.
118 Undo and remove the two screws and spring washers securing the drive end bracket to the body. The drive end bracket, complete with armature and drive, may now be drawn forwards from the starter motor body.
119 Lift away the thrust washer from the commutator end of the armature shaft.
120 Undo and remove the two screws securing the commutator end bracket to the starter motor body. The commutator end bracket may now be drawn back about an inch allowing sufficient access so as to disengage the field brushes from the bracket. Once these are free, the end bracket may now be completely removed.
121 With the motor stripped, the brushes and brush gear may be inspected. To check the brush spring tension, fit a new brush into each holder in turn and, using an accurate spring balance,

push the brush on the balance tray until the brush protrudes approximately 0.063 in (1.6 mm) from the holder. Make a note of the reading which should be approximately 28 ounces (0.8 kg). If the spring pressures vary considerably the commutator end bracket must be renewed as a complete assembly.
122 Inspect the brushes for wear and fit a new brush which is nearing the minimum length of 0.375 in (9.53 mm). To renew the end bracket brushes, cut the brush cables from the terminal posts and, with a small file or hacksaw, slot the head of the terminal posts to a sufficient depth to accommodate the new leads. Solder the new brush leads to the posts.
123 To renew the field winding brushes, cut the brush leads approximately 0.25 in (6.35 mm) from the field winding junction and carefully solder the new brush leads to the remaining stumps, making sure that the insulation sleeves provide adequate cover.
124 If the commutator surface is dirty or blackened, clean it with a petrol dampened rag. Carefully examine the commutator for signs of excessive wear, burning or pitting. If evident it may be reconditioned by having it skimmed at the local engineering works or BLMC dealer who possesses a centre lathe. The thickness of the commutator must not be less than 0.8 inch. For minor reconditioning, the commutator may be polished with glass paper. **Do not undercut the mica insulators between the commutator segments.**

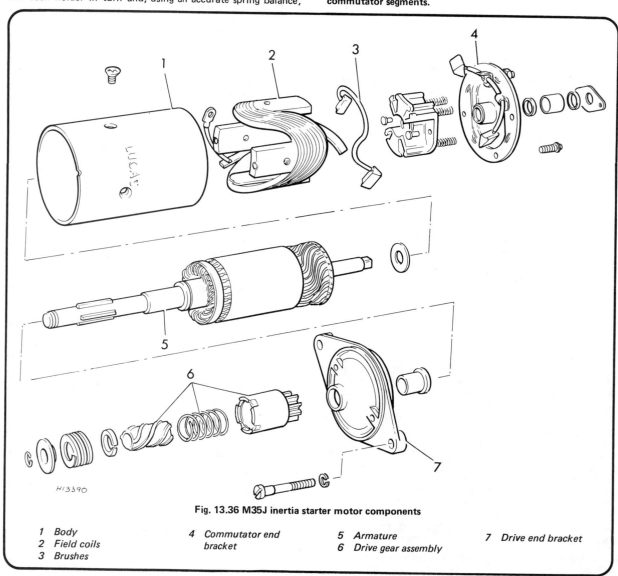

Fig. 13.36 M35J inertia starter motor components

1 *Body*	4 *Commutator end*	5 *Armature*	7 *Drive end bracket*
2 *Field coils*	*bracket*	6 *Drive gear assembly*	
3 *Brushes*			

125 With the starter motor dismantled, test the field coils for open circuit. Connect a 12 volt battery, with a 12 volt bulb in one of the leads, between each of the field brushes and a clean part of the body. The lamp will light if continuity is satisfactory between the brushes, windings and body connection.
126 Renewal of the field coils calls for the use of a wheel operated screwdriver, a soldering iron, caulking and riveting operations and is beyond the scope of the majority of owners. The starter motor body should be taken to an automotive electrical engineering works for new fields coils to be fitted. Alternatively, purchase an exchange Lucas starter motor.
127 Check the condition of the bushes, they should be renewed when they are sufficiently worn to allow visible side movement of the armature shaft.
128 To renew the commutator end bracket bush, drill out the rivets securing the brush box moulding and remove the moulding, bearing seal retaining plate and felt washer seal.
129 Screw in a 0.5 in (12.7 mm) tap and withdraw the bush with the tap.
130 As the bush is of the phosphor bronze type it is essential that it is allowed to stand in engine oil for at least 24 hours before fitment. Alternatively soak in oil at 100°C for 2 hours.
131 Using a suitable diameter drift, drive the new bush into position. Do not ream the bush as its self lubricating properties will be impaired.
132 To remove the drive end bracket bush it will be necessary to remove the drive gear as described in paragraphs 134 and 135.
133 Using a suitable diameter drift remove the old bush and fit a new one as described in paragraphs 130 and 131.
134 To dismantle the starter motor drive, first use a press to push the retainer clear of the circlip which can then be removed. Lift away the retainer and main spring.
135 Slide off the remaining parts with a rotary action of the armature shaft.
136 It is most important that the drive gear is completely free from oil, grease and dirt. With the drive gear removed, clean all parts thoroughly in paraffin. **Under no circumstances oil the**

drive components. Lubrication of the drive components could easily cause the pinion to stick.
137 Reassembly of the starter motor drive is the reverse sequence to dismantling. Use a press to compress the spring and retainer sufficiently to allow a new circlip to be fitted to its groove on the shaft. Remove the drive from the press.
138 Reassembly of the starter motor is the reverse sequence to dismantling.

Starter motor (M35J PE — pre-engaged type) — testing, removal, and refitting
139 Refer to Chapter 10, Section 12 and 13 as the procedure is identical to that for the model 2M100 starter motor.

Starter motor (M35J PE — pre-engaged type) — dismantling and reassembly
140 The complex construction of the pre-engaged starter motor and the need for special equipment dictates that this work is best entrusted to a suitably qualified auto electrician; an exploded component illustration is given to show how this type of starter motor would dismantle.

Front flasher repeater lamp bulb — removal (Austin Marina models)
141 Unscrew and remove the lens retaining screw and detach the lens from the retaining clip.
142 The bulb has a bayonet fitting and is removed by depressing it and turning it anti-clockwise.
143 Refitting the bulb and lens is a reversal of the removal procedure.

Reverse lamp bulb — renewal (Marina Mk 2 models)
144 The reverse lamp bulbs are incorporated into the rear lamp cluster, and bulb renewal follows the identical procedure to that described in Chapter 10, Section 27.

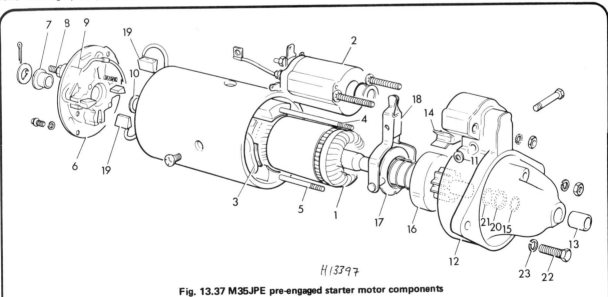

H13397

Fig. 13.37 M35JPE pre-engaged starter motor components

1	Armature	7	Commutator end bracket bush	12	Drive end bracket	18	Lever and pivot assembly
2	Solenoid	8	Field terminal	13	End bracket bush	19	Brush
3	Field coil	9	Terminal insulating bush	14	Grommet	20	Thrust collar
4	Pole piece and long stud	10	Thrust plate	15	Jump ring	21	Shim
5	Pole piece and short stud	11	Pivot pin retaining clip	16	Roller clutch drive	22	Fixing bolt
6	Commutator end bracket			17	Bearing bush	23	Lock washer

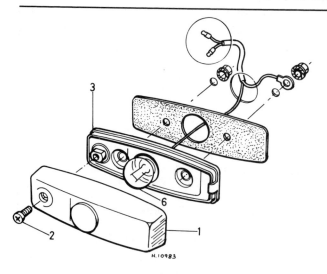

Fig. 13.38 Front flasher repeater lamp components (Austin Marina models)

1 Lens   2 Retaining screw   3 Lamp body   6 Light bulb

Tail, stop and flasher lamp (Estate) — removal and refitting

145 *Right-hand side:* Remove the rear compartment trim pad.
146 *Left-hand side:* Remove the spare wheel cover and spare wheel.
147 Remove the rubber plug located at the side of the light housing in the body.
148 Cover up the opening in the body directly below the rear of the light assembly.
149 Undo and remove the nut, spring and plain washers securing the light assembly to the body.
150 Withdraw the light assembly from the body.
151 Pull out the bulb holders from the rear of the light.
152 To remove the lens, undo and remove the six screws securing the lens to the light body.
153 Lift away the lens noting that the flasher lens laps over the stop and tail light lens and must be removed first.
154 Reassembling and refitting the light assembly is the reverse sequence to removal.

Rear number plate lamp (Estate) — removal and refitting
155 Make a note of all connections and disconnect the wires at the snap connectors located under the body at the rear of the light.
156 Carefully pull the light assembly out from the rear bumper.
157 The bulb is of the capless type and can be simply pulled out of its holder.
158 Refitting the light assembly is the reverse sequence to removal. Note that the cut-out in the lens cover engages over the register of the bulb holder.

Reversing lamp (flush fitting type) — removal and refitting
159 Working inside the luggage compartment, disconnect the harness connector.
160 Undo and remove the two nuts securing the light assembly to the body.
161 Withdraw the light assembly from the body.
162 To remove the bulb undo and remove the two screws securing the light cover to the body. Lift away the light cover.
163 The bulb is of the festoon type and is simply released from the spring blade terminals.
164 Refitting the bulb or light assembly is the reverse sequence to removal.

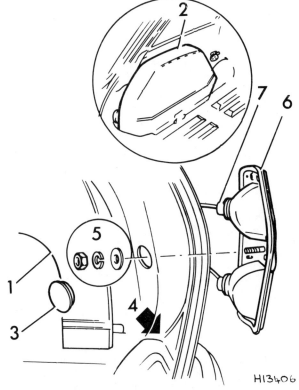

Fig. 13.39 Location of rear lamp cluster (Estate)

1 Trim pad	*5 Nut and washers*
2 Spare wheel cover	*6 Lamp assembly*
3 Rubber plug	*7 Bulb holder*
4 Opening in body	

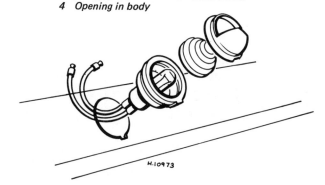

Fig. 13.40 Rear number plate lamp components (Estate)

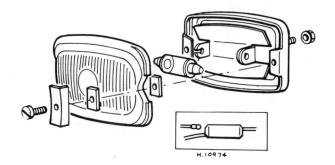

Fig. 13.41 Flush fitting reverse lamp components

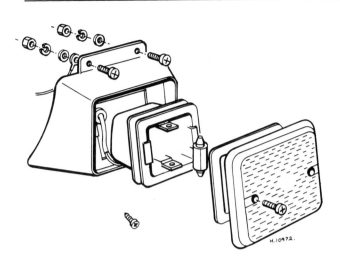

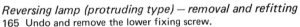

Fig. 13.42 Protruding type reverse lamp components

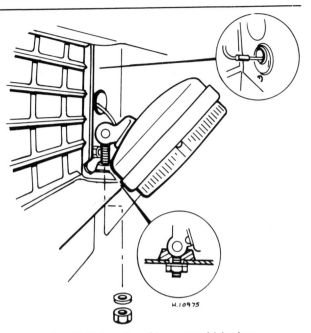

Fig. 13.43 Location of long range driving lamp

Reversing lamp (protruding type) — removal and refitting
165 Undo and remove the lower fixing screw.
166 Working inside the luggage compartment, disconnect the harness connector.
167 Undo and remove the two bolts, plain and spring washers and nuts securing the light assembly to the body.
168 Disconnect the earth lead.
169 Withdraw the reverse light assembly from the body.
170 To remove the bulb, undo and remove the two screws securing the lens and seal to the body. Lift away the lens and seal.
171 The bulb is of the festoon type and is simply released from the spring blade terminals.
172 Refitting the bulb or light assembly is the reverse sequence to removal. Make sure that the earth lead terminal makes good contact with the body.

Long range driving lamps — removal and refitting
173 Open and support the bonnet and remove the battery from its locating tray.
174 Disconnect the lamp supply lead.
175 Unscrew and remove the lamp retaining nut and washer, then ease the bottom of the lamp rearwards and withdraw it through the grille, making sure that the sealing adaptor is retained.
176 Refitting is a reversal of the removal procedure but before finally tightening the retaining nut, make sure that the lamp is positioned in the horizontal plane and facing straight ahead.

Roof lamp (saloon) — removal and refitting
177 Disconnect the battery negative terminal.
178 Squeeze the lens together and detach it from the lamp body.
179 Extract the festoon type bulb and then remove the two lamp body retaining screws.
180 Carefully pull the lamp from the roof, at the same time disconnecting the two supply leads.
181 Refitting is a reversal of the removal procedure.

Roof lamp (Estate) — removal and refitting
182 Squeeze the lens at the top and bottom and detach the lens.
183 Disconnect the battery earth terminal for safety reasons.
184 Carefully push the wire terminals out from the light terminal.
185 Undo and remove the two screws securing the light assembly to the body and lift away the assembly.
186 Refitting the light assembly is the reverse sequence to removal.

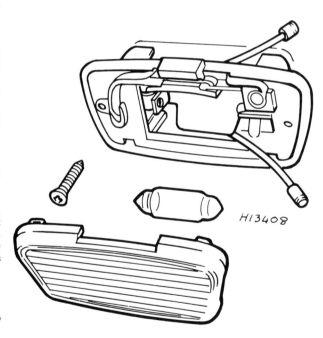

Fig. 13.44 Roof lamp (Saloon) components

Wipe/washer switch — removal and refitting (Marina Mk 2 models)
187 Follow the procedure given in Chapter 10, Section 31 and then extract the two switch retaining rivets.

Lighting switch — removal and refitting (Marina Mk 2 models
188 Disconnect the battery negative terminal.
189 Depress the upper and lower retaining springs on the rear of the switch body and press the switch out from the panel.
190 Disconnect the connector plug from the rear of the switch.
191 Refitting is a reversal of the removal procedure.

Heater fan switch — removal and refitting (Marina Mk 2 models)

192 Disconnect the battery negative terminal.
193 Depress the clips on the rear sides of the switch body and press the switch out from the panel.
194 Note the location of the supply leads, then disconnect them from the switch terminals.
195 Refitting is a reversal of the removal procedure.

Instrument panel printed circuit — removal and refitting (Marina Mk 2 models)

196 On Mk 2 models fitted with a quad instrument panel, in addition to the procedure given in Chapter 10, Section 35, it is also necessary to remove the main beam warning light connection and the four plastic retaining pins, prior to the removal of the printed circuit. Reverse the procedure when refitting.

Gauge units — removal and refitting (Marina Mk 2 models)

197 Disconnect the battery and remove the instrument panel.
198 On quad instrument panels, remove the bulb holders, temperature gauge and printed circuit, and finally the fuel gauge.
199 On other instrument panels, remove the speedometer and instrument lens from its retaining clips followed by the instrument face plate. The coolant and fuel gauge can then be removed.
200 Refitting is a reversal of the removal procedure.

Speedometer — removal and refitting (Marina Mk 2 models)

201 Disconnect the battery negative terminal.
202 Unscrew and remove the two instrument cowl retaining screws and withdraw the cowl.
203 Depress the speedometer cable locking clip and release the cable from the speedometer head.
204 Unscrew and remove the instrument cluster retaining screws and pull the assembly forwards.
205 Note the location of the various leads and bulb holders, then disconnect them and withdraw the instrument cluster.
206 Remove the speedometer and instrument lens from its retaining clips followed by the face plate (where applicable).
207 Unscrew and remove the two speedometer retaining screws and carefully withdraw the speedometer from the cluster.

Handbrake warning light switch — removal and refitting

208 Remove the centre console as described in paragraphs 42 to 47 inclusive of the braking system section of this Supplement.
209 Disconnect the switch supply lead, unscrew and remove the switch retaining screw and remove the switch.
210 Refitting is a reversal of the removal procedure, but to prevent entry of water from beneath the car, it is advisable to coat the gaiter fixing screw holes with a suitable sealing compound.

Tachometer — removal and refitting (Marina Mk 2 models)

211 Remove the instrument cluster as described in paragraphs 201 to 206 inclusive, then unscrew and remove the three tachometer and printed circuit retaining nuts and withdraw the printed circuit.
212 Unscrew and remove the three tachometer retaining screws and withdraw the unit from the cluster.
213 Refitting is a reversal of the removal procedure.

Tailgate wiper motor, wheelbox and rack tubes (Estate models) — removal and refitting

214 Carefully prise the trim pad away from the tailgate interior panel. The removal procedure is then similar to that described in Chapter 10, Sections 18 to 22 inclusive, and refitting is a direct reversal of the removal procedure.

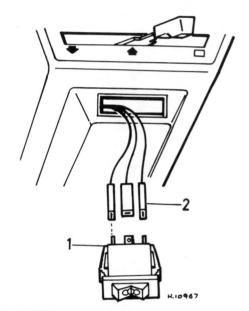

Fig. 13.45 Heater fan switch location (Marina Mk 2 models)

1 Retaining arms   2 Supply leads

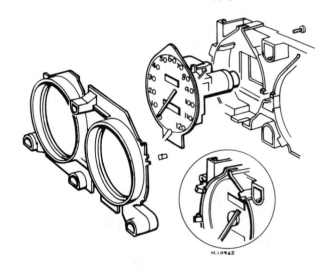

Fig. 13.46 Speedometer components (Marina Mk 2 models)

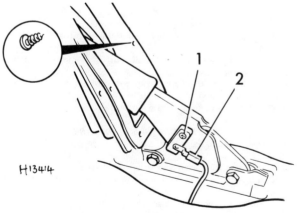

Fig. 13.47 Handbrake warning light switch location

1 Switch   2 Supply lead

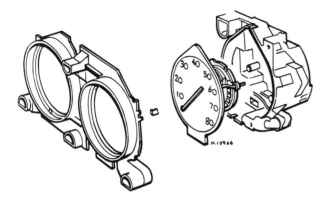

Fig. 13.48 Tachometer components (Marina Mk 2 models)

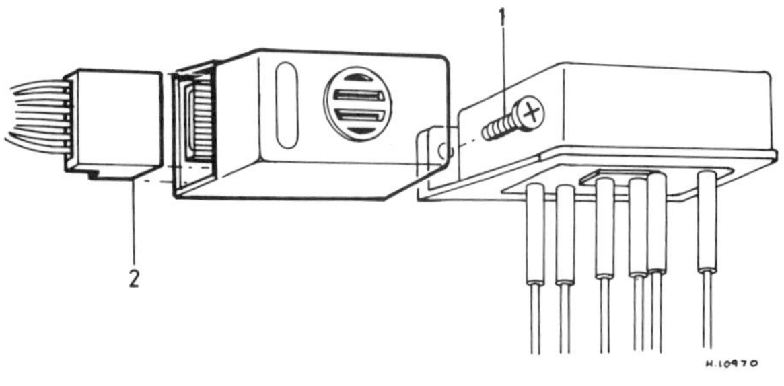

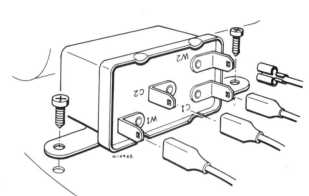

Fig. 13.49 Seat belt buzzer and timer module (Austin Marina
models)

1 Retaining screw   2 Lead connector plug

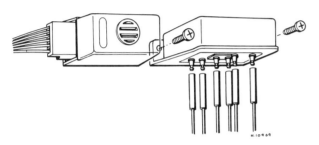

Fig. 13.50 Headlamp relay location (Austin Marina models)

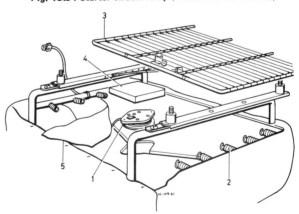

Fig. 13.51 Starter circuit relay (Austin Marina models)

Seat belt buzzer and timer module – removal and refitting (Austin Marina models)
215 Disconnect the battery negative terminal.
216 Unscrew and remove the unit retaining screw and withdraw the unit to expose the wiring connector plug.
217 Depress the retaining clip and pull the connector from the unit.
218 Refitting is a reversal of the removal procedure.

Headlamp relay – removal and refitting (Austin Marina models)
219 The headlamp relay is mounted next to the seat belt buzzer and timer module and the latter must first be removed as described in paragraphs 215 to 218 inclusive.
220 Note the location of the snap connectors on the relay, then carefully remove them.
221 Unscrew and remove the remaining relay retaining screw and lift the relay away from its location. Refitting is a reversal of the removal procedure.

Starter circuit relay – removal and refitting (Austin Marina models)
222 Disconnect the battery negative terminal.
223 Note the location of the four supply leads then detach them from their Lucar terminals.
224 Unscrew and remove the two relay retaining screws and withdraw the unit.
225 Refitting is a reversal of the removal procedure.

Fig. 13.52 Seat switch components (Austin Marina models)

1 Switch   4 Cover pad
2 Retaining spring   5 Protective cover
3 Grid retainer

Seat switch – removal and refitting (Austin Marina models)
226 Remove the front seat as described in the last Section of this Supplement, after disconnecting the switch lead.
227 With the seat upside down, remove the spring case from the springs and remove the pad from the switch.
228 Pull back the cover, with the supply lead and withdraw the switch.
229 Refitting is a reversal of the removal procedure.

Wiring diagrams Pages 240 – 253

12 Suspension and steering

General description

1   Marina Mk 2 models are fitted with front and rear suspension anti-roll bars and it is therefore necessary to incorporate the removal and refitting procedures into the existing Sections of Chapter 11 as follows.

Lower suspension arm — removal and refitting (Marina Mk 2 models)

2   Between paragraphs 2 and 3 of Section 4, Chapter 11, un-screw and remove the two anti-roll bar link retaining nuts and washers and pull the link away from the anti-roll bar and lower suspension arm.

3   Refit the front anti-roll bar link in the reverse order of removal.

Front shock absorber -- removal and refitting (Marina Mk 2 models)

4   The upper attachment of the ball joint ball pin has been modified to eliminate the upper bush and housing.

5   The procedure described in Chapter 11, Section 5 is still applicable, but between paragraphs 4 and 5, free the shock absorber arm from the swivel pin ball joint using a universal ball joint separator tool.

Swivel pin — removal and refitting (Marina Mk 2 models)

6   Free the shock absorber arm as described in paragraph 5 of this Section and remove the anti-roll bar link as described in paragraph 2.

7   Remove the front lower suspension arm as described in Chapter 11, Section 4.

Swivel pin ball joint — removal and refitting (Marina Mk 2 models)

8   The upper attachment of the ball pin to the shock absorber arm has been modified to eliminate the upper bush and housing. The ball pin shank is now a taper fit in the shock absorber arm and is removed using a universal ball joint separator after un-screwing the reaction pad. Apart from that, the procedure is the same as described in Chapter 11, Section 7.

Lower swivel pin link — removal and refitting (Marina Mk 2 models)

9   Refer to paragraphs 2 and 3 of this Section when removing the lower suspension arm.

Torsion bar — removal and refitting (Marina Mk 2 models)

10   The procedure is identical to that given in Chapter 11 but separate the shock absorber arm from the swivel pin ball joint as described in paragraph 5 of this Section and remove the anti-roll bar link as described in paragraph 2 of this Section.

11   When refitting the torsion bar, it should be initially set-up using the following procedure, prior to fitting the reaction lever with the adjusting screw set in the midway section.

12   First measure the height of the eye bolt centre above the floor (dimension A). Then deduct the dimension given in the following table to obtain the dimension C (Fig. 13.54).

Torsion bar diameter	0.75 in (19.05 mm)	0.812 in (20.63 mm)
Settled dimension	8.626 in (219.28 mm)	7.37 in (197.20 mm)
New dimension	8.87 in (225.30 mm)	7.66 in (194.56 mm)

13   Adjust the swivel link pin centre to dimension C, and retain it in this position while the reaction lever is being fitted, making sure that the eye bolt centre to floor dimension is not altered.

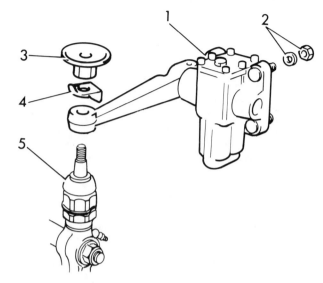

H13428

Fig. 13.53 Front shock absorber components (Marina Mk 2 models)

1   Shock absorber   4   Lockwasher
2   Nut and washer   5   Swivel link
3   Reaction pad nut

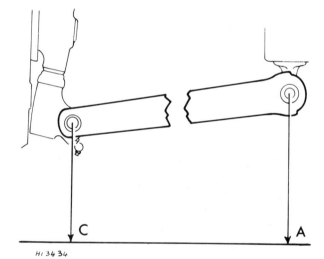

H13434

Fig. 13.54 Torsion bar setting dimensions (Marina Mk 2 models)

Anti-roll bar (front) — removal and refitting (Marina Mk 2 models)

14   Jack up the front of the car and support it on firmly based axle stands.

15   Unscrew and remove the link retaining nuts and spring washers from both ends of the anti-roll bar and detach the link ends.

16   Mark the anti-roll bar mounting carriers 'left' and 'right' so that they can be refitted in their original positions, then unscrew and remove the four retaining screws.

17   Note that the front left-hand face of the anti-roll bar, near the link position, is marked 'L' and then lower the complete bar.

18   Detach the rubbers bushes from the anti-roll bar and unscrew and remove the anti-roll bar links from the lower suspension arms.

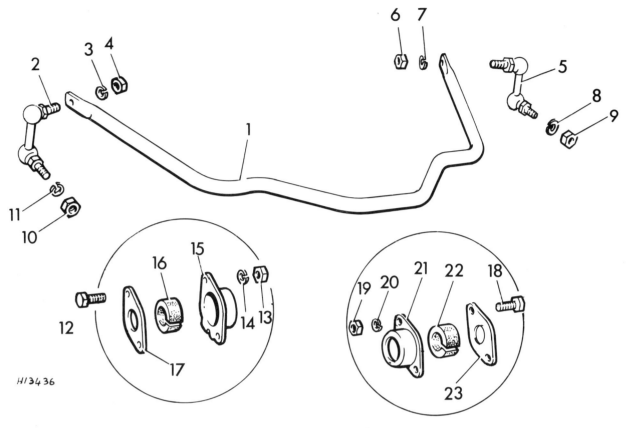

Fig. 13.55 Front anti-roll bar components (Marina Mk 2 models)

1	Front anti-roll bar	7 & 8	Spring washer	14	Spring washer	19	Nut
2	Link (RH)	9 & 10	Nut	15	Bearing carrier (RH)	20	Spring washer
3	Spring washer	11	Spring washer	16	Bearing	21	Bearing carrier (LH)
4	Nut	12	Bolt	17	Bearing retainer	22	Bearing
5	Link (LH)	13	Nut	18	Bolt	23	Bearing retainer
6	Nut					

19 Renew any bushes or links which show any indication of wear or deterioration.

20 Refitting is a reversal of the removal procedure but soak the rubber bushes in soapy water prior to tightening the retaining carriers.

Rear hub assembly — removal and refitting (all models)
21 Removal of the rear hub assembly is identical to that described in Chapter 11, Section 12 but, when refitting the assembly, thoroughly clean the threads of the axleshaft and nut, and apply three drops of a suitable thread locking compound before finally tightening the nut to a torque wrench setting of 105 lbf ft (14.51 kgf m).

Anti-roll bar (rear) — removal and refitting (Marina Mk 2 models)
22 Jack up the rear of the car and support it on firmly based axle stands.
23 Remove the wheel trim road wheels.
24 Unscrew and remove the shock absorber retaining nuts from each lower mounting and push the shock absorber lower cylinders out of their locating holes.
25 Loosen the shock absorber upper mounting nuts and swivel each shock absorber towards the centre of the car.
26 Unscrew and remove the anti-roll bar clamp retaining bolts, and unclip the clamps from the mounting base.
27 The anti-roll bar can now be removed and the rubber moun-

tings eased off the bar. If the end fittings are to be renewed, first mark their location and loosen the locknuts, then unscrew them from the anti-roll bar.

28 Refitting the anti-roll bar is a direct reversal of the removal procedure but the following additional points should be noted:

   a) *Make sure that the end fitting bushes line up with the chassis number bolt holes and adjust them on the anti-roll bar if necessary. It is important not to distort the rubber bushes when inserting the pivot bolt.*
   b) *Tighten the anti-roll bar pivot bolts to 48 to 55 lbf ft (6.6 to 7.6 kgf m) with a torque wrench.*
   c) *Make sure that the anti-roll bar locknuts are tightened securely.*

Steering wheel — removal and refitting (Marina Mk 2 models)
29 Disconnect the battery negative terminal.
30 Prise the safety pad from the steering wheel.
31 Unscrew and remove the steering wheel retaining nut and washer, and mark the relative positions of the steering wheel hub and inner column.
32 With the palms of the hands behind the spokes and near to the centre hub, knock the steering wheel from the inner column splines. If it is tight, it will be necessary to use a universal puller and a suitable thrust block, and the steering column cowl will also need to be removed as follows.

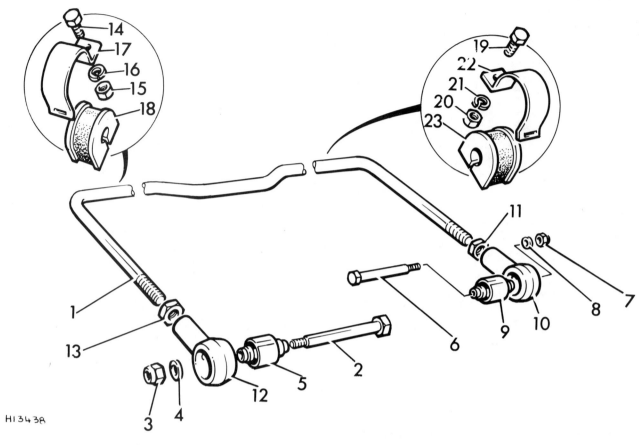

Fig. 13.56 Rear anti-roll bar components (Marina Mk 2 models)

1 Rear anti-roll bar	7 Locknut	13 Locknut	19 Bolt
2 Bolt	8 Washer	14 Bolt	20 Nut
3 Locknut	9 Slotted bush	15 Nut	21 Spring washer
4 Washer	10 End fitting	16 Spring washer	22 Clamp
5 Slotted bush	11 Locknut	17 Clamp	23 Bearing
6 Bolt	12 End fitting	18 Bearing	

33 Disconnect the choke cable at the carburettor.

34 Unscrew and remove the right-hand cowl retaining screw and withdraw the cowl over the switch lever.

35 Unscrew and remove the left-hand cowl retaining screws and withdraw the cowl, at the same time pulling the choke cable through the bulkhead panel, until the cowl is clear of the steering wheel.

36 Refitting the steering wheel follows a reversal of the removal procedure but the following additional points should be noted:

a) *Make sure that the nylon switch centre is positioned correctly.*

b) *The steering wheel securing nut should be tightened to a torque wrench setting of 32 to 37 lbf ft (4.43 to 5.13 kgf m)*

c) *Adjust the choke control cable so that it has 1/16 in (2 mm) free movement.*

Steering column lock and ignition starter switch — removal and refitting (Marina Mk 2 and Austin Marina models)

37 Remove the steering wheel and cowl assembly.

38 Locate the multi-pin connector on the end of the column lock and ignition switch wiring harness and separate the connection. Similarly separate the two connections from the wiper and lighting switches.

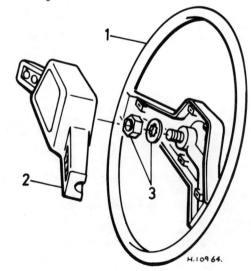

Fig. 13.57 Steering wheel components (Marina Mk 2 models)

1 Steering wheel   2 Safety pad   3 Retaining nut and washer

39 Unscrew and remove the four outer steering column retaining screws and washers and withdraw the outer column through the facia panel.
40 Extract the felt bush from the inner steering column lower mounting.
41 Follow the procedure given in Chapter 11, Section 19, paragraphs 5 to 10 inclusive and then locate the felt bush in the outer column lower end. Refitting is then a reversal of the removal procedure.

Steering column universal joint coupling — removal and refitting (late Marina Mk 1 and Austin Marina models)
42 The removal procedure is similar to that described in Chapter 11, Section 20 except that on Austin Marina models the front parcel tray must first be removed from the car. In addition, on Mk 1 and Austin Marina models, the four flexible joint shouldered bolts are fitted with locking wire which must be broken and removed prior to unscrewing them.
43 The refitting procedure is different in the following respect. First reassemble half the joint and insert and tighten the two hexagon-headed bolts. Then reassemble the remaining half using the two Pozidrive or slotted head bolts. The hexagon type bolts should be tightened to 6 to 9 lbf ft (0.83 to 1.24 kgf m), the alternative type to 8 to 12 lbf ft (1.1 to 1.6 kgf m) using a torque wrench.
44 The remaining refitting procedure is as given in Chapter 11, Section 20.

Upper steering column — removal and refitting (Marina Mk 2, Austin Marina, and late Marina Mk 1 models)
45 Disconnect the battery negative terminal and remove the steering wheel.
46 On later Marina Mk 1 models follow the removal procedure given in Chapter 11, Section 21, paragraphs 2 to 10 inclusive.
47 On Austin Marina models disconnect the cowl illumination lamp lead connectors and detach the steering column cowl. Then follow the procedure given in Chapter 11, Section 21, paragraphs 5 to 9 inclusive and finally withdraw the upper steering column through the facia panel.
48 On Marina Mk 2 models follow the procedure given in Chapter 11, Section 21, paragraphs 1 to 10 inclusive but omit paragraphs 2 and 3.
49 Refitting the upper steering column is similar to the procedure given in Chapter 11, Section 21 but the steering rack should be centralised by removing the rubber bung and inserting a ¼ in (6.35 mm) diameter rod so that it locates in the hole provided in the rack gear, prior to refitting the column; remember to remove the rod after completing the work.
50 The steering column mounting bolts should be tightened to a torque wrench setting of 14 to 18 lbf ft (1.94 to 2.49 kgf m).

Steering rack and pinion — removal and refitting (Marina Mk 2 models)
51 Jack up the front of the car and support it with axle stands placed beneath the front chassis members.
52 Unscrew and remove the steering tie-rod ball pin retaining nuts and, using a suitable universal balljoint separator, disconnect the tie-rods from the steering levers.
53 Unscrew and remove the lower pinch bolt retaining the flexible joint to the rack pinion.
54 Loosen the intermediate shaft pinch bolt and move the joint upwards away from the pinion.
55 Unscrew and remove the rack U-bolt retaining nuts and washers and withdraw the U-bolt, clamp brackets and rubbers from the bulkhead.
56 The remaining procedure is identical to that given in Chapter 11, Section 22, paragraphs 13 to 16 inclusive, except that the rack should be centralised as described in paragraph 49 of this Section prior to connecting the flexible joint. The rack clamp nuts should be tightened to a torque wrench setting of 17 to

19 lbf ft (2.3 to 2.6 kgf m) and the lower flexible joint pinch bolt to 17 to 20 lbf ft (2.35 to 2.77 kgf m).

Steering rack and pinion — removal and refitting (Austin Marina models)
57 The procedure is similar to that described in Chapter 11, Section 22 but instead of paragraphs 1 and 2 it is only necessary to remove the parcel tray. When refitting the rack, it should be centralised as described in paragraph 49 of this Section prior to connecting the flexible joint. The lower flexible joint pinch bolt should be tightened to a torque wrench setting of 17 to 20 lbf ft (2.35 to 2.77 kgf m).

Front suspension trim height adjustment (late Marina Mk 1, and all Marina Mk 2 and Austin Marina models).
58 The early fine adjustment bolt described in Chapter 11 was modified to the arrangement shown in Fig. 13.58 and therefore the bolt must be turned clockwise to increase the trim height or anti-clockwise to reduce it.

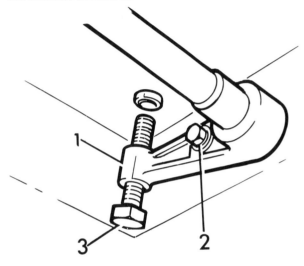

HI3437

Fig. 13.58 Front suspension trim height adjustment bolt (later type)

1 *Adjustment lever*   2 *Lockbolt*   3 *Adjuster bolt*

13 Bodywork and underframe

Door trim panel and capping — removal and refitting (Marina Mk 2 models)
1 The procedure is similar to that described in Chapter 12, Section 10 but it will be necessary to unscrew the remote door pull bezel retaining screw in order to remove the bezel. The ashtray must also be removed (when fitted), and the locking button unscrewed and removed.

Door exterior handle — removal and refitting (late Marina Mk 1 and Austin Marina models)
2 Refer to Chapter 12, Section 10 and remove the door trim pad.
3 Unscrew and remove the window glass channel retaining screw and washer, then prise the retainer from the lock rod and detach the rod from the exterior handle.
4 Prise the triangular shaped transfer lever from the lock pivot.
5 Unscrew and remove the two nuts retaining the handle and clamp to the door and withdraw both components.
6 Refitting is a reversal of the removal procedure.

Door exterior handle — removal and refitting (Marina Mk 2 models)

7 Refer to paragraph 1 of this Section, and Section 10 of Chapter 12, and remove the door trim panel.
8 Peel back the polythene covering from the interior door panel and prise off the operating link retainer to release the link; on rear door handles detach the link from the door panel clip.
9 Prise off the retainer and detach the locking link from the lock mechanism (rear doors only).
10 Prise off the retainer and detach the outside handle operating link from the lock mechanism.
11 Unscrew and remove the nuts, shakeproof washers and plain washers, from the handle retaining screw threads and withdraw the clamp and handle from the door.
12 Refitting is a reversal of the removal procedure but before reconnecting the exterior handle operating link, move the handle to the open position and check that the cranked end of the link is in line with the bush in the operating lever of the lock mechanism; screw it up or down until the alignment is correct.

Rear quarter trim pad and capping — removal and refitting (Marina Mk 1 models)

13 Remove the rear seat cushion and squab.
14 Unscrew and remove the two arm rest securing screws and withdraw the armrest.
15 Carefully unclip the trim pad and lift away from the body.
16 Undo and remove the screws securing the trim capping.
17 Carefully unclip the trim capping and lift away from the body.
18 Refitting the quarter trim pad and capping is the reverse sequence to removal.

Tailgate hinge (Estate models) — removal and refitting

19 Refer to Chapter 12, Section 19 and remove the tailgate.
20 Remove the rear interior light; note the earth wire secured beneath one fixing screw.
21 Carefully detach the rear compartment rear headlining and collect the press fasteners.
22 Detach the courtesy light switch from the right-hand hinge bracket. Disconnect the wire from the rear of the switch.
23 Using a pencil mark the position of the hinges relative to the body to act as a datum for refitting.
24 Undo and remove the four screws, spring and plain washers, that secure the hinge and torsion bar to each side of the body.
25 Lift away the hinge and torsion bar assembly.
26 Refitting the hinge and torsion bar assembly is the reverse sequence to removal.

Tailgate lock (Estate models) — removal and refitting

27 Remove the tailgate trim pad.
28 Carefully unclip the retainer and detach the operating rod from the outside handle assembly.
29 Undo and remove the three screws and spring washers securing the lock to the tailgate.
30 Lift away the tailgate lock assembly.
31 Refitting the tailgate lock assembly is the reverse sequence to removal. Lubricate all moving parts.

Tailgate lock striker plate (Estate models) — removal and refitting

32 Lift up the tailgate.
33 Using a pencil mark the position of the striker plate relative to the body to act as a datum for refitting.
34 Undo and remove the three screws, spring and plain washers securing the striker plate to the body.
35 Lift away the striker plate.
36 Refitting the striker plate is the reverse sequence to removal.

Tailgate exterior handle and lock (Estate models) — removal and refitting

37 Lift up the tailgate and remove the trim pad.

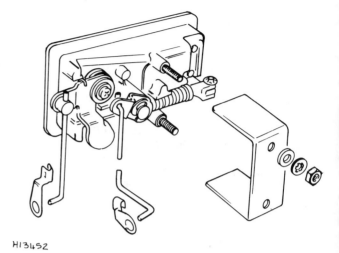

H13452

Fig. 13.59 Front door handle mechanism (Marina Mk 2 models)

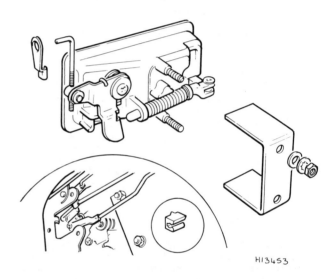

H13453

Fig. 13.60 Rear door handle mechanism (Marina Mk 2 models)

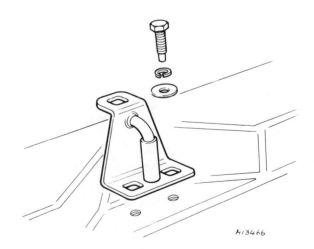

H13466

Fig. 13.61 Tailgate lock striker plate (Estate)

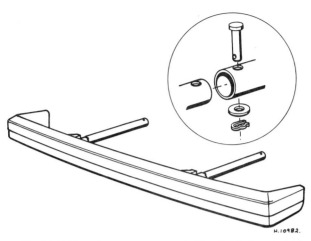

Fig. 13.62 Front bumper components (Austin Marina models)

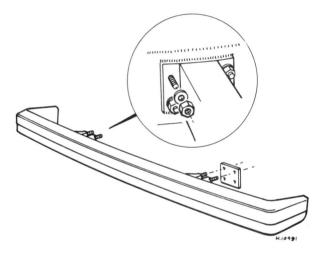

Fig. 13.63 Rear bumper components (Austin Marina models)

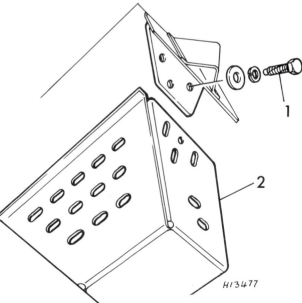

Fig. 13.64 Location of sump guard

1 Retaining bolt   2 Sump guard

38 Carefully unclip the retainer and detach the lock operating rod from the operating lever.
39 Undo and remove the nut securing the handle assembly to the tailgate.
40 Detach the operating lever assembly and remove the handle assembly and seal.
41 To remove the lock cylinder from the outside handle, first detach the retaining circlip.
42 Lift away the plain washer and coil spring and withdraw the cylinder assembly.
43 Refitting the lock cylinder and exterior handle is the reverse sequence to removal, but the following additional points should be noted:

   a) *Lubricate all moving parts.*
   b) *The handle grip should face downwards when fitted.*

Bumpers — removal and refitting (UK models)
44 Unscrew and remove the bolt, spring washer and plain washer, together with the mounting rubber from each end of the bumper.
45 Unscrew and remove the four bolts retaining the bumper support brackets to the body and on the rear bumper disconnect the electrical leads to the number plate lamp.
46 The bumper can now be withdrawn from the car and the support brackets detached by unscrewing the retaining bolts.
47 Refitting is a reversal of the removal procedure.

Bumpers — removal and refitting (Austin Marina models)
48 *Front bumper:* Extract the hairpin clips from the bottom of the shackle pins and recover the plain washers, then withdraw the shackle pins and pull the bumper and support tube assembly from the car. Make sure that the two rubber grommets in the front lower panel are not damaged or worn before refitting the bumper using the reverse procedure to removal.
49 *Rear bumper:* Unscrew and remove the eight nuts and washers securing the bumper to the body, and withdraw the bumper and spacer plates. Refitting is a reversal of the removal procedure.

Sump guard — removal and refitting
50 Undo and remove the three screws and washers securing each side of the guard to the mounting brackets.
51 Lift the sump guard away from under the front of the car.
52 Refitting the sump guard is the reverse sequence to removal.

Tailgate glass and backlight — removal and refitting
53 The procedure is identical to that given in Chapter 12, Section 21, except that where a heated backlight is fitted, it will be necessary to disconnect the supply leads.

Rear parcel tray — removal and refitting
54 Remove the rear seat squab and cushion.
55 Working inside the boot carefully push up the rear parcel tray and release it from its retaining clips.
56 Refitting the rear parcel tray is the reverse sequence to removal.

Console assembly — removal and refitting (Marina Mk 1 models)
57 Carefully remove the two inset rim panels.
58 Unscrew and remove the gearchange lever knob.
59 Slide off the handbrake lever grip.
60 Undo and remove the screws and plain washers securing the console.
61 Chock the wheels, release the handbrake and then detach the cable from the handbrake lever. The cable is retained by a split pin, washer and clevis pin.
62 Raise the handbrake lever fully and remove the centre console assembly.
63 Refitting the console assembly is the reverse sequence to removal.

Facia panel — removal and refitting (Marina Mk 2 models)

64 Disconnect the battery negative terminal.
65 Remove the steering wheel, instrument panel, parcel shelf, and glovebox with reference to this Supplement and Chapters 11 and 12.
66 Disconnect the face level vent tubes, and detach the steering column bridge bracket.
67 Carefully pull off the heater control knobs.
68 Unscrew and remove the heater control retaining screws and secure it to one side.
69 Note the position of all the switches and multi-plug connectors and then disconnect them from the facia panel.
70 Unscrew and remove the five facia panel retaining screws and the three panel retaining nuts, then press the centre of the panel downwards to release it from the retaining clip.
71 The facia panel assembly can now be removed.
72 If further dismantling is necessary unscrew the retaining screws and detach the two face level vents and glovebox hinge brackets.
73 Remove the ashtray and cigar lighter (if fitted).
74 Remove the speaker grille and prise out the radio blank.
75 Unscrew and remove the two retaining screws which secure the instrument pack support bracket to the facia panel.
76 Finally drill out the facia panel stud clip fasteners and remove the vent, glovebox, and steering column bracket fixings.
77 Refitting is a reversal of the removal procedure.

Lower facia panel — removal and refitting (Austin Marina models)

78 The procedure is similar to that described in Chapter 12, Section 24 except that there are no choke control cable operations, and in addition, it will be necessary to remove the cigar lighter.

Glovebox — removal and refitting (Marina Mk 2 models)

79 Open the lid and detach the hinge stay from the lid.
80 Unscrew and remove the upper and lower hinge bracket retaining screws and withdraw the lid.
81 Unscrew and remove the two glovebox lock striker plate retaining screws then remove the two glovebox retaining screws.
82 The glovebox can now be withdrawn from the facia panel but on GT and HL models it will be necessary to disconnect the electrical leads from the glovebox lamp and switch.
83 Refitting is a reversal of the removal procedure.

Radiator grille — removal and refitting (Austin Marina models)

84 Disconnect the battery negative terminal.
85 Disconnect the front flasher/parking lamp electrical supply leads, then unscrew and remove the two lens and lamp retaining screws.
86 Remove the front flasher/parking lamps from each side.
87 Unscrew and remove the four self tapping screws and plain washers which secure the case to the body and lift the grille and case assembly upwards and forwards away from the front of the car.
88 Unscrew and remove the four lamp adaptor bracket retaining screws and withdraw the bracket.
89 The remaining procedure is identical to that given in Chapter 12, Section 27, paragraphs 3 and 4.

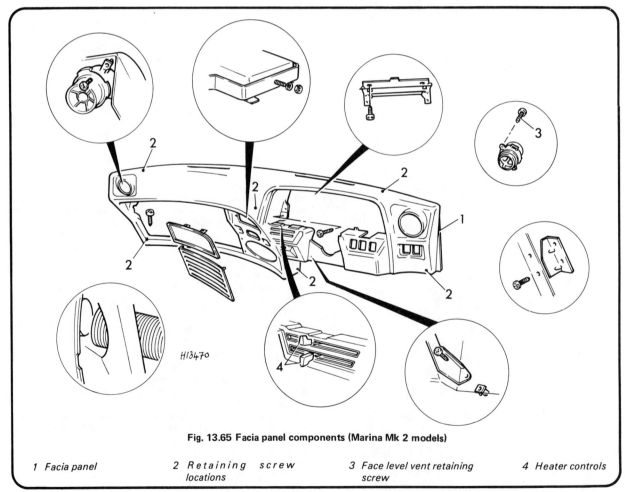

H13470

Fig. 13.65 Facia panel components (Marina Mk 2 models)

| 1 Facia panel | 2 Retaining screw locations | 3 Face level vent retaining screw | 4 Heater controls |

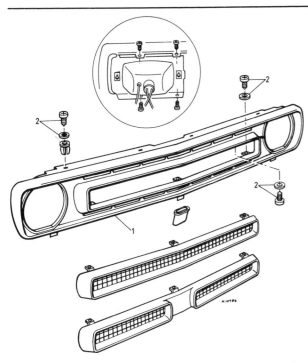

Fig. 13.66 Radiator grille components (Austin Marina models)

1 Grille   2 Retaining bolts and washers

Heater unit — removal and refitting (Marina Mk 2 models)

90 Disconnect the battery negative terminal.

91 Refer to Chapter 2 and drain the cooling system.

92 Remove the instrument panel and facia panel with reference to Chapter 12 and this Supplement.

93 Disconnect the demister and heating duct tubes from the heater and detach the fusebox from the parcel shelf.

94 Remove the parcel shelf (see Chapter 12).

95 Note the location of the heater motor supply leads and then disconnect them at their connectors.

96 On GT and HL models, remove the centre console as described in paragraphs 42 to 47 inclusive of the braking system section of this Supplement.

97 Detach the passenger side facia support stay.

98 Loosen the clips and disconnect the two water hoses from the heater.

99 Pull off the two plenum drain point caps at the front of the bulkhead.

100 Unscrew and remove the two nuts and four washers retaining the heater side brackets to the bulkhead, then remove the upper windshield panel heater retaining bolt.

101 Carefully pull the bottom of the heater rearwards and out of its location.

102 Detach the inner and outer control cables from the heater unit, withdraw the heater, and remove the insulation and seal pads.

103 Refitting follows a reversal of the removal procedure but before connecting the outer control cable clamp, hold the control levers in the 'OFF' position and slightly pull the outer cable away from the operating arm.

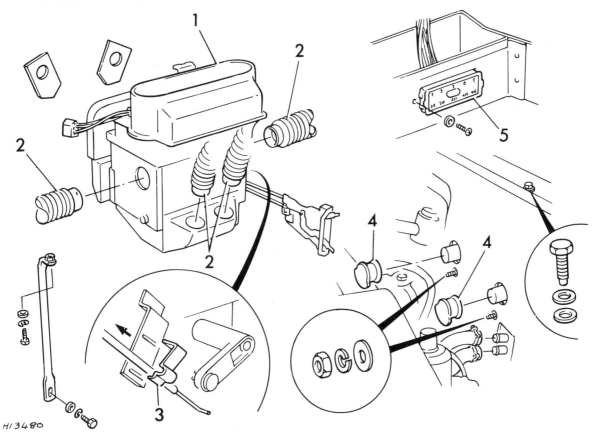

1 Heater
2 Air ducts

3 Outer control cable retaining clamp

4 Plenum drain point caps

5 Fuse box (mounted on parcel shelf)

Fig. 13.67 Heater unit components (Marina Mk 2 models)

Heater control cables — removal and refitting (Marina Mk 2 models)

104 Disconnect the battery earth terminal and then carefully pull the knobs off the heater control arms.

105 Undo and remove the control panel retaining screws and ease the control panel down and out of the facia.

106 Release the clips securing the two outer cables to the heater unit and disengage the inner cables from the levers.

107 Withdraw the heater control panel complete with cables from the facia. If necessary, release the remaining spring clips and remove the cables from the control panel.

108 Refitting is the reverse sequence to removal, bearing in mind the following points:

   a) Ensure that the forked ends of the inner cables face each other when fitted to the control unit.

   b) When reconnecting the cables to the heater levers, set the controls in the 'OFF' position and slightly pull the outer cables away from the heater levers, then refit the clips.

Windscreen demister duct — removal and refitting (Marina Mk 2 models)

109 Remove the instrument panel and facia panel with reference to Chapter 12 and this Supplement.

110 Disconnect the demister duct tubes, then unscrew and remove the demister duct nuts and washers and lift the duct from its location holes.

111 Refitting the duct is a reversal of the removal procedure.

Instrument panel — removal and refitting (Marina Mk 2 models)

112 Refer to paragraphs 201 to 207 inclusive of the electrical system section of this Supplement.

Front seat (type 1) — removal and refitting
Two-door models:

113 Undo and remove the two bolts and spring washers securing each bracket to the car floor panel.

114 Undo and remove the nuts that secure the lock down bar.

115 Lift away the front seat and lock bar.

Four-door models:

116 Undo and remove the locknut and dished washer that secures each front stud to the car floor panel.

117 Undo and remove the locknut and plain washer that secures each rear stud to the car floor panel. Note that early cars are fitted with a shaped washer.

118 Remove the front seat. Note that on later four-door cars a 1.5 inch (38.1 mm) diameter plain washer is fitted between the spacer and inside floor on the rear fixing studs only.

All models:

119 Refitting the front seat is the reverse sequence to removal. It is recommended by the manufacturers that on early four door cars the curved washer under the floor panel on the rear fixing only is discarded and a plain washer fitted. Also inside the car a 1.5 inch (38.1 mm) diameter plain washer is fitted between the spacer and the floor. The spacer should be fitted with the curved side away from the seat runner.

Front seat (type 2) — removal and refitting

The following is applicable to controlled movement type front seats.

120 Move the seat fully forwards and then, working under the car, undo and remove the two locknuts and large plain washers that secure the seat rear fixing stud.

121 Now move the seat fully rearwards and working under the car, undo and remove the two locknuts and large plain washers that secure the seat front fixing studs.

122 Lift away the front seat.

123 Refitting the front seat is the reverse sequence to removal.

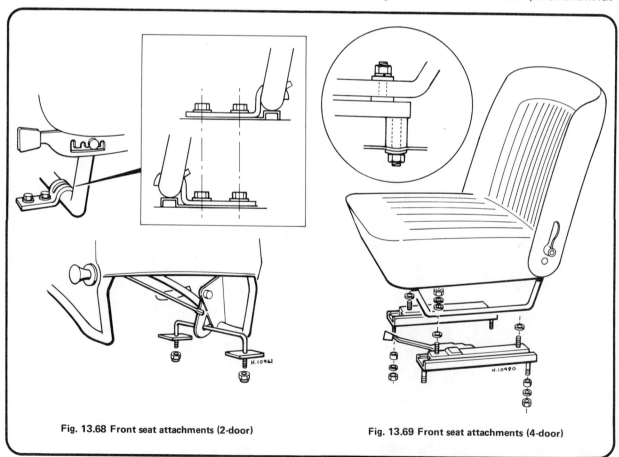

Fig. 13.68 Front seat attachments (2-door)   Fig. 13.69 Front seat attachments (4-door)

Rear seat squab and cushion (Saloon) — removal and refitting

124 Release the two cushion retaining clips and lift away the seat cushion.
125 Slacken the two screws and remove the arm rest.
126 Using a drill remove the two rivet heads securing the squab brackets. Do not pass the drill through the body as it may damage or even puncture the brake pipes.
127 Raise the squab to release the back panel from the three retaining hooks and lift away the squab.
128 Refitting the seat squab and cushion is the reverse sequence to removal. Always use pop rivets to retain the squab brackets. Do not use self-tapping screws.

Rear seat cushion (Estate) — removal and refitting

129 Pivot the cushion assembly forwards.
130 Using a pencil mark the position of the hinges on the seat to act as a datum for refitting.
131 Undo and remove the two screws, shakeproof and plain washers securing the hinges to the seat.

132 Lift the cushion from the hinges.
133 Refitting the rear seat cushion is the reverse sequence to removal.

Rear seat squab (Estate) — removal and refitting

134 Release the squab from its retaining catches and pivot the squab forwards.
135 Undo and remove the two countersunk screws securing the squab pivots to the body at each side.
136 The squab may now be lifted away.
137 Refitting the rear seat squab is the reverse sequence to removal.

Rear body side glass (Estate) — removal and refitting

138 With an assistant ready to catch the glass and rubber surround assembly, push outwards on the glass to release it from the aperture flange.
139 Carefully remove the finisher from the rubber surround.

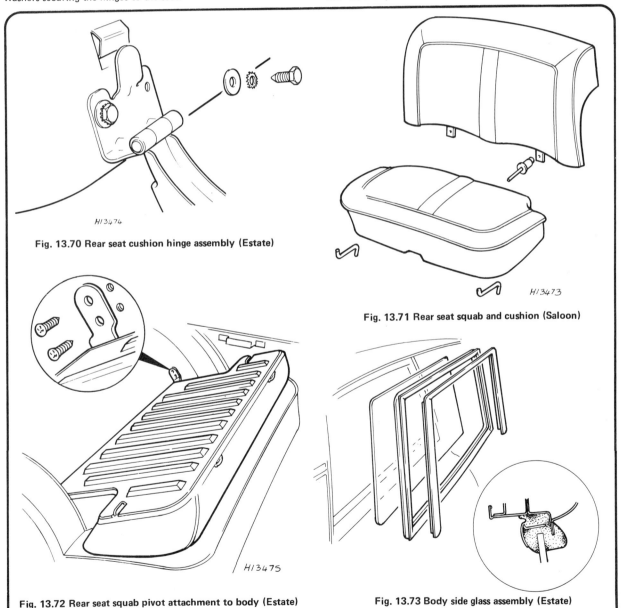

Fig. 13.70 Rear seat cushion hinge assembly (Estate)

Fig. 13.71 Rear seat squab and cushion (Saloon)

Fig. 13.72 Rear seat squab pivot attachment to body (Estate)

Fig. 13.73 Body side glass assembly (Estate)

140 Remove the rubber surround from the glass.
141 If the original glass and/or rubber surround are to be used again all traces of old sealer should be removed.
142 Refit the rubber surround to the glass.
143 Using a suitable sealer, seal the rubber surround to the glass at the outside face.
144 Lubricate the finisher channel in the rubber surround with a soapy solution or washing up liquid.
145 Fit the finisher to the rubber surround.
146 Apply some sealer to the middle groove around the outside edge of the rubber surround.
147 Apply some sealer to the outside face of the window aperture in the body.
148 Fit some cord around the locating groove in the rubber surround and with the ends inside the body, place the assembly up to the aperture.
149 Pull on the cord, whilst an assistant pushes hard on the glass. The retaining lip should now move over the aperture flange and hold the glass and surround assembly in position. Clean off any surplus sealer.

Quarter light — removal and refitting

150 With an assistant ready to catch the glass and rubber surround assembly push outwards on the glass to release it from the aperture flange.
151 Carefully remove the finisher strip from the sealing rubber.
152 Remove the rubber surround from the glass.
153 If the original glass and/or rubber surround are to be used again all traces of old sealer should be removed.
154 Inject some sealer into the glass channel of the rubber surround.
155 Fit the rubber surround to the glass.
156 Lubricate the finisher channel of the seal and its surrounding area with a soapy solution or washing up liquid.
157 Insert the end of the finisher into the seal at the centre point of the curve.

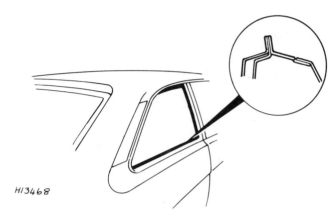

H13468

Fig. 13.74 Sealer area of quarter light assembly

158 Continue by feeding the finisher in at this point and pushing it along the rubber in its fitted position until the end of the seal slot is reached.
159 Position the remaining finisher over the seal slot and tap into place by hand until the glass corner is reached.
160 Using a soft faced hammer, strike the outside edge of the straight finisher length, aiming the blows towards the glass.
161 Apply some sealer to the outside face of the quarter-light aperture in the body.
162 Insert a cord into the body aperture flange groove of the rubber surround, and with the ends inside the body, place the assembly up to the aperture.
163 Pull on the cord whilst an assistant pushes hard on the glass. The retaining lip should now move over the aperture flange and hold the glass and surround assembly in position. Clean off any surplus sealer.

See overleaf for Wiring Diagrams

Key to wiring diagram on page 241

1 Battery
2 Starter motor
3 Starter motor solenoid
4 Starter motor (pre-engaged)
5 Fuse unit
6 In-line fuse
7 Ignition switch
8 Ignition coil
9 Ignition warning lamp
10 Distributor
11 Dynamo
12 Alternator
13 Control box (A-RB106, B-RB340)
14 Horn(s)
15 Horn switch
16 Ballast resistor (coil)
17 Lighting switch
18 Headlamp main beam
19 Main beam warning lamp
20 Dip switch
21 Headlamp dipped beam
22 Headlamp flasher switch
23 Headlamp (inner - RH)
24 Headlamp (inner - LH)
25 Sidelamp (RH)
26 Sidelamp (LH)
27 Rear lamp (RH)
28 Rear lamp (LH)
29 Number plate lamp(s)
30 Stop lamp(s)
31 Stop lamp switch
32 Indicator unit
33 Indicator switch
34 Indicator warning lamp
35 Indicator (front - RH)
36 Indicator (front - LH)
37 Indicator (rear - RH)
38 Indicator (rear — LH)
39 Indicator repeater unit
40 Indicator repeater lamp (RH)
41 Indicator repeater lamp (LH)
42 Hazard warning lamp
43 Hazard warning switch
44 Hazard warning flasher unit
45 Reversing lamp(s)
46 Reversing lamp(s) switch
47 Reversing lamp(s) and auto inhibitor switch
48 Voltage stabilizer
49 Panel lamp(s)

50 Panel lamp(s) resistor
51 Printed circuit instrument panel
52 Fuel gauge
53 Fuel gauge sender unit
54 Oil pressure warning lamp
55 Oil pressure switch
56 Water temperature gauge
57 Water temperature gauge sender unit
58 Tachometer
59 Clock
60 Split braking test switch
61 Split braking shuttle valve
62 Handbrake switch
63 Handbrake warning lamp
64 Anti-run-on valve
65 Anti-run-on valve relay
66 Mixture control warning lamp switch
67 Mixture control warning lamp switch
68 Wiper switch
69 Wiper motor
70 Screen washer motor
71 Screen washer motor switch
72 Induction heater and thermostat
73 Tailgate switch
74 Tailgate wiper motor
75 Tailgate washer motor (estate)
76 Tailgate wiper/washer switch
77 Screen wiper/washer switch
78 Rear window demist switch
79 Rear window demist unit
80 Rear window demist warning lamp
81 Heater blower motor switch
82 Heater blower motor
83 Automatic gearbox safety switch
84 Automatic gearbox quadrant lamp
85 Interior lamp switch
86 Interior lamp switch (rear)
87 Interior lamp
88 Interior lamp (rear - estate)
89 Door switch
90 Luggage compartment lamp switch
91 Luggage compartment lamp
92 Cigar lighter
93 Radio
94 Glovebox lamp
95 Glovebox lamp switch
96 Bonnet lamp
97 Bonnet switch
98 Panel lamp switch

Colour code

Black BK   Yellow YW
Blue BL   White WH
Brown BR   Light green LGR
Red RD   Orange OR
Green GR   Pink PI
Grey GY   Purple PU

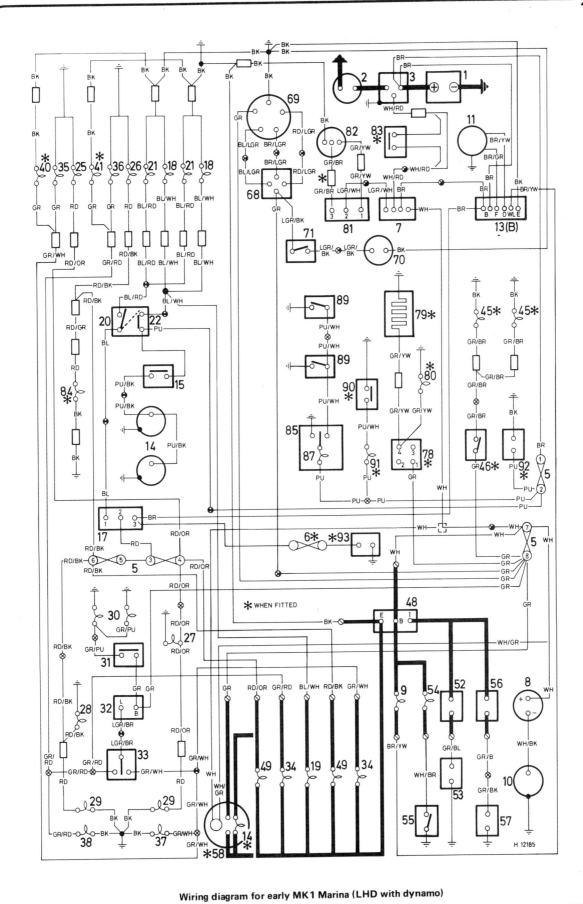

Wiring diagram for early MK1 Marina (LHD with dynamo)

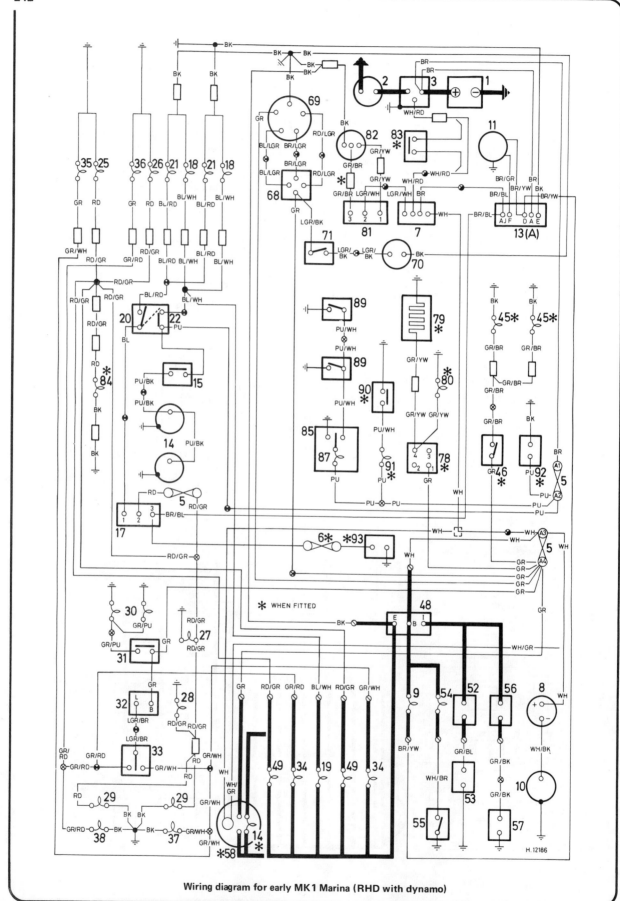

Wiring diagram for early MK1 Marina (RHD with dynamo)

Key to wiring diagram on page 242

1 Battery
2 Starter motor
3 Starter motor solenoid
4 Starter motor (pre-engaged)
5 Fuse unit
6 In-line fuse
7 Ignition switch
8 Ignition coil
9 Ignition warning lamp
10 Distributor
11 Dynamo
12 Alternator
13 Control box (A-RB106, B-RB340)
14 Horn(s)
15 Horn switch
16 Ballast resistor (coil)
17 Lighting switch
18 Headlamp main beam
19 Main beam warning lamp
20 Dip switch
21 Headlamp dipped beam
22 Headlamp flasher switch
23 Headlamp (inner - RH)
24 Headlamp (inner - LH)
25 Sidelamp (RH)
26 Sidelamp (LH)
27 Rear lamp (RH)
28 Rear lamp (LH)
29 Number plate lamp(s)
30 Stop lamp(s)
31 Stop lamp switch
32 Indicator unit
33 Indicator switch
34 Indicator warning lamp
35 Indicator (front - RH)
36 Indicator (front - LH)
37 Indicator (rear - RH)
38 Indicator (rear — LH)
39 Indicator repeater unit
40 Indicator repeater lamp (RH)
41 Indicator repeater lamp (LH)
42 Hazard warning lamp
43 Hazard warning switch
44 Hazard warning flasher unit
45 Reversing lamp(s)
46 Reversing lamp(s) switch
47 Reversing lamp(s) and auto inhibitor switch
48 Voltage stabilizer
49 Panel lamp(s)

50 Panel lamp(s) resistor
51 Printed circuit instrument panel
52 Fuel gauge
53 Fuel gauge sender unit
54 Oil pressure warning lamp
55 Oil pressure switch
56 Water temperature gauge
57 Water temperature gauge sender unit
58 Tachometer
59 Clock
60 Split braking test switch
61 Split braking shuttle valve
62 Handbrake switch
63 Handbrake warning lamp
64 Anti-run-on valve
65 Anti-run-on valve relay
66 Mixture control warning lamp switch
67 Mixture control warning lamp switch
68 Wiper switch
69 Wiper motor
70 Screen washer motor
71 Screen washer motor switch
72 Induction heater and thermostat
73 Tailgate switch
74 Tailgate wiper motor
75 Tailgate washer motor (estate)
76 Tailgate wiper/washer switch
77 Screen wiper/washer switch
78 Rear window demist switch
79 Rear window demist unit
80 Rear window demist warning lamp
81 Heater blower motor switch
82 Heater blower motor
83 Automatic gearbox safety switch
84 Automatic gearbox quadrant lamp
85 Interior lamp switch
86 Interior lamp switch (rear)
87 Interior lamp
88 Interior lamp (rear - estate)
89 Door switch
90 Luggage compartment lamp switch
91 Luggage compartment lamp
92 Cigar lighter
93 Radio
94 Glovebox lamp
95 Glovebox lamp switch
96 Bonnet lamp
97 Bonnet switch
98 Panel lamp switch

Colour code

Black BK   Yellow YW
Blue BL   White WH
Brown BR   Light green LGR
Red RD   Orange OR
Green GR   Pink PI
Grey GY   Purple PU

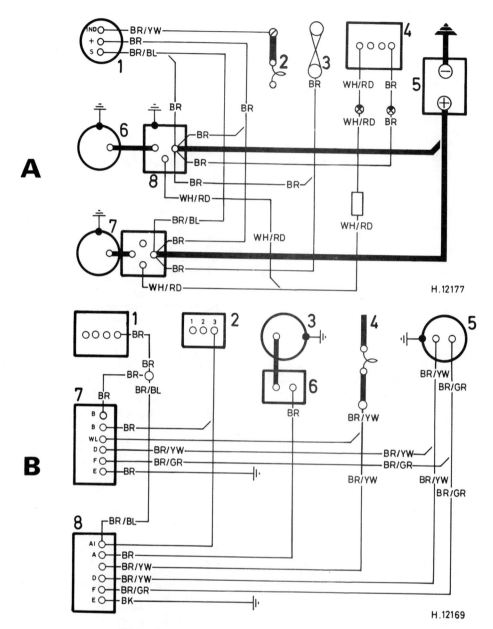

244

Wiring diagram A: Alternator with inertia or pre-engaged starter

1 Alternator
2 Ignition warning lamp
3 Fuse unit
4 Ignition switch
5 Battery
6 Inertia starter motor
7 Pre-engaged starter motor
8 Starter solenoid

Wiring diagram B: Dynamo with RB106 or RB340 regulator

1 Ignition switch
2 Lighting switch
3 Motor
4 Ignition warning lamp
5 Dynamo
6 Starter solenoid
7 Regulator RB340
8 Regulator RB106

Cable colour code

Brown BR	White WH
Blue BL	Yellow YW
Red RD	Black BK
Orange OR	Purple PU
Light green LGR	Green GR

When a cable has two colour code letters the first denotes the main colour and the second the tracer colour

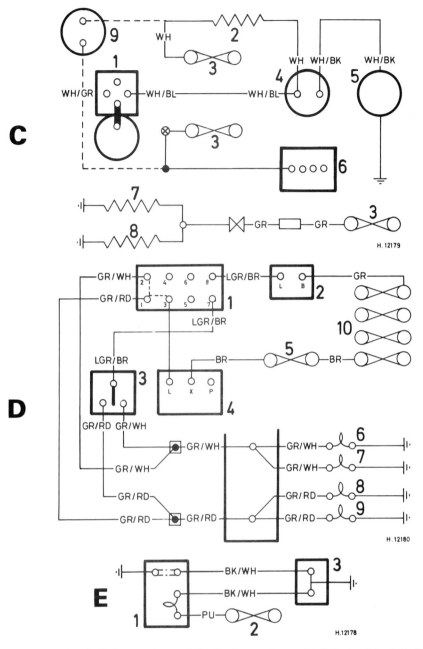

H.12179

H.12180

H.12178

Wiring diagram C: Carburetter heater, induction heater, thermostat. Ballast resistor to ignition coil

1 Starter	4 Coil	6 Ignition switch	8 Suction chamber heater
2 Ballast resistor	5 Distributor	7 Induction heater and thermostat	9 Tachometer
3 Fuse unit			

Wiring diagram D: Hazard warning circuit

1 Hazard warning switch	4 Hazard warning flasher unit	7 RH rear direction indicator	10 Fuse unit
2 Flasher unit	5 Line fuse	8 LH front direction indicator	11 Hazard warning lamp
3 Direction indicator switch	6 RH front direction indicator	9 LH rear direction indicator	

Wiring diagram E: Brake failure warning circuit

1 Split braking test switch	2 Fuse unit	3 Split braking shuttle valve

Cable colour code

Brown BR	Green GR
Blue BL	Light Green LGR
Red RD	White WH
Orange OR	Yellow YW
Purple PU	Black BK

When a cable has two colour code letters the first denotes the main colour and the second the tracer colour

Key to wiring diagram on page 247

1 Battery
2 Starter motor
3 Starter motor solenoid
4 Starter motor (pre-engaged)
5 Fuse unit
6 In-line fuse
7 Ignition switch
8 Ignition coil
9 Ignition warning lamp
10 Distributor
11 Dynamo
12 Alternator
13 Control box (A-RB106, B-RB340)
14 Horn(s)
15 Horn switch
16 Ballast resistor (coil)
17 Lighting switch
18 Headlamp main beam
19 Main beam warning lamp
20 Dip switch
21 Headlamp dipped beam
22 Headlamp flasher switch
23 Headlamp (inner - RH)
24 Headlamp (inner - LH)
25 Sidelamp (RH)
26 Sidelamp (LH)
27 Rear lamp (RH)
28 Rear lamp (LH)
29 Number plate lamp(s)
30 Stop lamp(s)
31 Stop lamp switch
32 Indicator unit
33 Indicator switch
34 Indicator warning lamp
35 Indicator (front - RH)
36 Indicator (front - LH)
37 Indicator (rear - RH)
38 Indicator (rear — LH)
39 Indicator repeater unit
40 Indicator repeater lamp (RH)
41 Indicator repeater lamp (LH)
42 Hazard warning lamp
43 Hazard warning switch
44 Hazard warning flasher unit
45 Reversing lamp(s)
46 Reversing lamp(s) switch
47 Reversing lamp(s) and auto inhibitor switch
48 Voltage stabilizer
49 Panel lamp(s)

50 Panel lamp(s) resistor
51 Printed circuit instrument panel
52 Fuel gauge
53 Fuel gauge sender unit
54 Oil pressure warning lamp
55 Oil pressure switch
56 Water temperature gauge
57 Water temperature gauge sender unit
58 Tachometer
59 Clock
60 Split braking test switch
61 Split braking shuttle valve
62 Handbrake switch
63 Handbrake warning lamp
64 Anti-run-on valve
65 Anti-run-on valve relay
66 Mixture control warning lamp switch
67 Mixture control warning lamp switch
68 Wiper switch
69 Wiper motor
70 Screen washer motor
71 Screen washer motor switch
72 Induction heater and thermostat
73 Tailgate switch
74 Tailgate wiper motor
75 Tailgate washer motor (estate)
76 Tailgate wiper/washer switch
77 Screen wiper/washer switch
78 Rear window demist switch
79 Rear window demist unit
80 Rear window demist warning lamp
81 Heater blower motor switch
82 Heater blower motor
83 Automatic gearbox safety switch
84 Automatic gearbox quadrant lamp
85 Interior lamp switch
86 Interior lamp switch (rear)
87 Interior lamp
88 Interior lamp (rear - estate)
89 Door switch
90 Luggage compartment lamp switch
91 Luggage compartment lamp
92 Cigar lighter
93 Radio
94 Glovebox lamp
95 Glovebox lamp switch
96 Bonnet lamp
97 Bonnet switch
98 Panel lamp switch

Colour code

Black BK	Yellow YW
Blue BL	White WH
Brown BR	Light green LGR
Red RD	Orange OR
Green GR	Pink PI
Grey GY	Purple PU

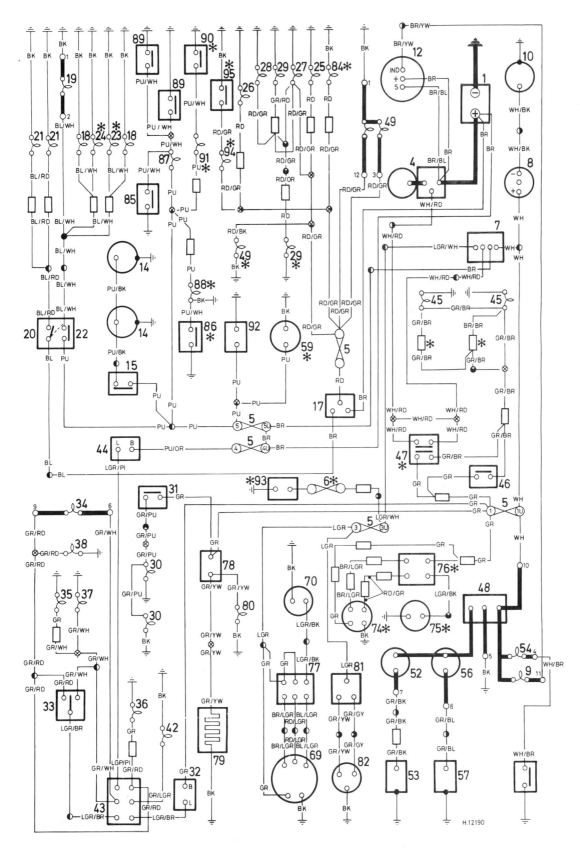

Wiring diagram for MKII Marina Saloon and Estate (RHD)

248

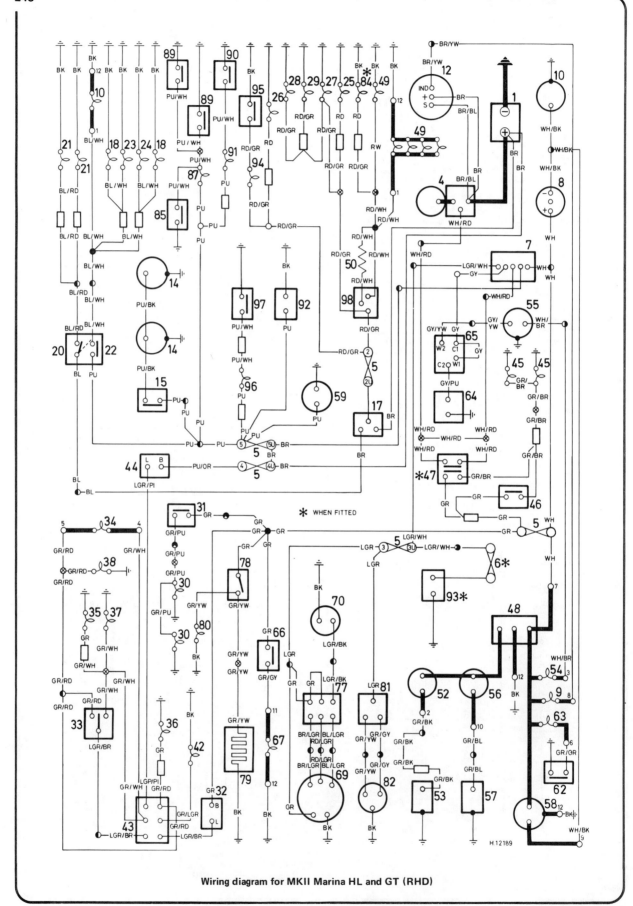

Wiring diagram for MKII Marina HL and GT (RHD)

Key to wiring diagram on page 248

1 Battery
2 Starter motor
3 Starter motor solenoid
4 Starter motor (pre-engaged)
5 Fuse unit
6 In-line fuse
7 Ignition switch
8 Ignition coil
9 Ignition warning lamp
10 Distributor
11 Dynamo
12 Alternator
13 Control box (A-RB106, B-RB340)
14 Horn(s)
15 Horn switch
16 Ballast resistor (coil)
17 Lighting switch
18 Headlamp main beam
19 Main beam warning lamp
20 Dip switch
21 Headlamp dipped beam
22 Headlamp flasher switch
23 Headlamp (inner - RH)
24 Headlamp (inner - LH)
25 Sidelamp (RH)
26 Sidelamp (LH)
27 Rear lamp (RH)
28 Rear lamp (LH)
29 Number plate lamp(s)
30 Stop lamp(s)
31 Stop lamp switch
32 Indicator unit
33 Indicator switch
34 Indicator warning lamp
35 Indicator (front - RH)
36 Indicator (front - LH)
37 Indicator (rear - RH)
38 Indicator (rear — LH)
39 Indicator repeater unit
40 Indicator repeater lamp (RH)
41 Indicator repeater lamp (LH)
42 Hazard warning lamp
43 Hazard warning switch
44 Hazard warning flasher unit
45 Reversing lamp(s)
46 Reversing lamp(s) switch
47 Reversing lamp(s) and auto inhibitor switch
48 Voltage stabilizer
49 Panel lamp(s)

50 Panel lamp(s) resistor
51 Printed circuit instrument panel
52 Fuel gauge
53 Fuel gauge sender unit
54 Oil pressure warning lamp
55 Oil pressure switch
56 Water temperature gauge
57 Water temperature gauge sender unit
58 Tachometer
59 Clock
60 Split braking test switch
61 Split braking shuttle valve
62 Handbrake switch
63 Handbrake warning lamp
64 Anti-run-on valve
65 Anti-run-on valve relay
66 Mixture control warning lamp switch
67 Mixture control warning lamp switch
68 Wiper switch
69 Wiper motor
70 Screen washer motor
71 Screen washer motor switch
72 Induction heater and thermostat
73 Tailgate switch
74 Tailgate wiper motor
75 Tailgate washer motor (estate)
76 Tailgate wiper/washer switch
77 Screen wiper/washer switch
78 Rear window demist switch
79 Rear window demist unit
80 Rear window demist warning lamp
81 Heater blower motor switch
82 Heater blower motor
83 Automatic gearbox safety switch
84 Automatic gearbox quadrant lamp
85 Interior lamp switch
86 Interior lamp switch (rear)
87 Interior lamp
88 Interior lamp (rear - estate)
89 Door switch
90 Luggage compartment lamp switch
91 Luggage compartment lamp
92 Cigar lighter
93 Radio
94 Glovebox lamp
95 Glovebox lamp switch
96 Bonnet lamp
97 Bonnet switch
98 Panel lamp switch

Colour code

Black BK	Yellow YW
Blue BL	White WH
Brown BR	Light green LGR
Red RD	Orange OR
Green GR	Pink PI
Grey GY	Purple PU

Key to wiring diagram on page 251

1 Battery
2 Starter motor
3 Starter motor solenoid
4 Starter motor (pre-engaged)
5 Fuse unit
6 In-line fuse
7 Ignition switch
8 Ignition coil
9 Ignition warning lamp
10 Distributor
11 Dynamo
12 Alternator
13 Control box (A-RB106, B-RB340)
14 Horn(s)
15 Horn switch
16 Ballast resistor (coil)
17 Lighting switch
18 Headlamp main beam
19 Main beam warning lamp
20 Dip switch
21 Headlamp dipped beam
22 Headlamp flasher switch
23 Headlamp (inner - RH)
24 Headlamp (inner - LH)
25 Sidelamp (RH)
26 Sidelamp (LH)
27 Rear lamp (RH)
28 Rear lamp (LH)
29 Number plate lamp(s)
30 Stop lamp(s)
31 Stop lamp switch
32 Indicator unit
33 Indicator switch
34 Indicator warning lamp
35 Indicator (front - RH)
36 Indicator (front - LH)
37 Indicator (rear - RH)
38 Indicator (rear — LH)
39 Indicator repeater unit
40 Indicator repeater lamp (RH)
41 Indicator repeater lamp (LH)
42 Hazard warning lamp
43 Hazard warning switch
44 Hazard warning flasher unit
45 Reversing lamp(s)
46 Reversing lamp(s) switch
47 Reversing lamp(s) and auto inhibitor switch
48 Voltage stabilizer
49 Panel lamp(s)

50 Panel lamp(s) resistor
51 Printed circuit instrument panel
52 Fuel gauge
53 Fuel gauge sender unit
54 Oil pressure warning lamp
55 Oil pressure switch
56 Water temperature gauge
57 Water temperature gauge sender unit
58 Tachometer
59 Clock
60 Split braking test switch
61 Split braking shuttle valve
62 Handbrake switch
63 Handbrake warning lamp
64 Anti-run-on valve
65 Anti-run-on valve relay
66 Mixture control warning lamp switch
67 Mixture control warning lamp switch
68 Wiper switch
69 Wiper motor
70 Screen washer motor
71 Screen washer motor switch
72 Induction heater and thermostat
73 Tailgate switch
74 Tailgate wiper motor
75 Tailgate washer motor (estate)
76 Tailgate wiper/washer switch
77 Screen wiper/washer switch
78 Rear window demist switch
79 Rear window demist unit
80 Rear window demist warning lamp
81 Heater blower motor switch
82 Heater blower motor
83 Automatic gearbox safety switch
84 Automatic gearbox quadrant lamp
85 Interior lamp switch
86 Interior lamp switch (rear)
87 Interior lamp
88 Interior lamp (rear - estate)
89 Door switch
90 Luggage compartment lamp switch
91 Luggage compartment lamp
92 Cigar lighter
93 Radio
94 Glovebox lamp
95 Glovebox lamp switch
96 Bonnet lamp
97 Bonnet switch
98 Panel lamp switch

Colour code

Black BK	Yellow YW
Blue BL	White WH
Brown BR	Light green LGR
Red RD	Orange OR
Green GR	Pink PI
Grey GY	Purple PU

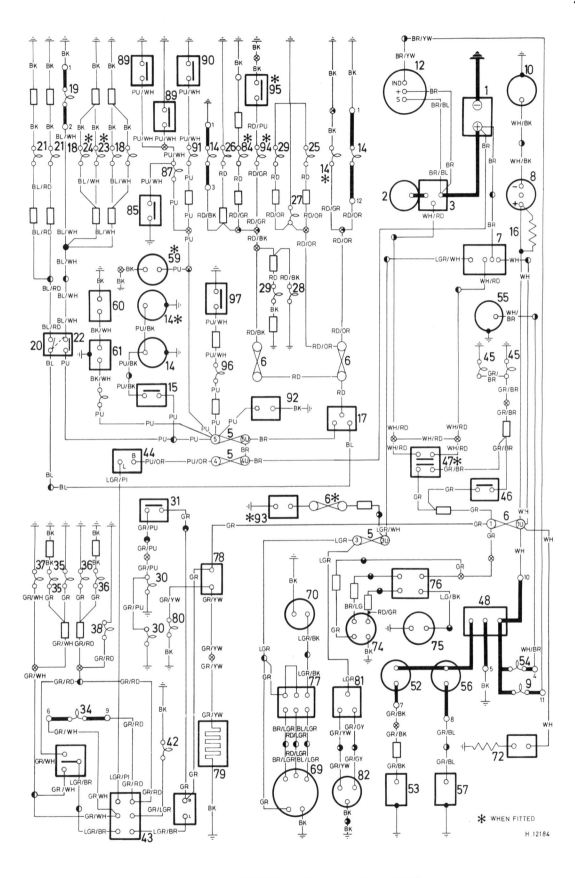

Wiring diagram for MK II Marina Saloon and Estate (LHD)

H.12184

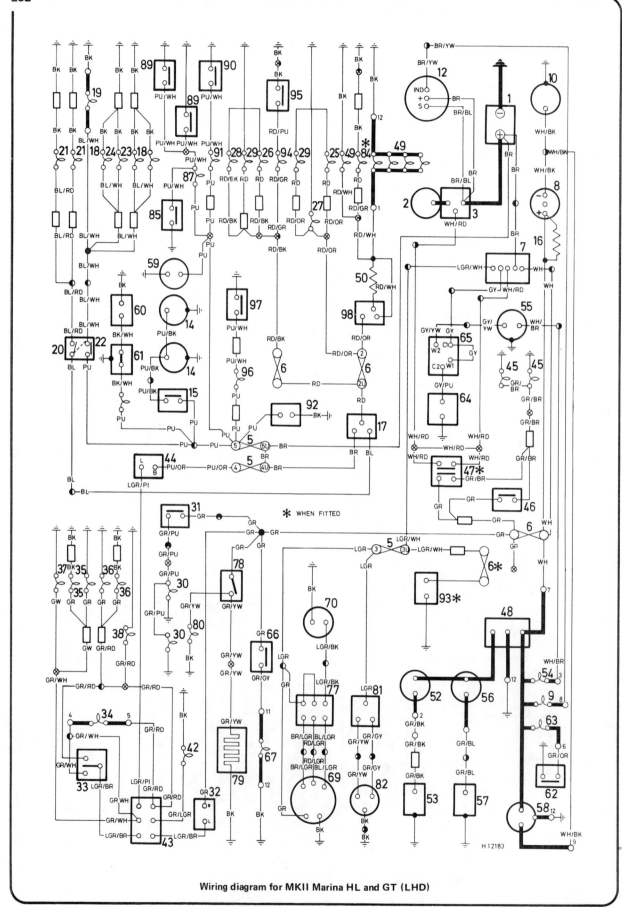

Wiring diagram for MKII Marina HL and GT (LHD)

Key to wiring diagram on page 252

1 Battery
2 Starter motor
3 Starter motor solenoid
4 Starter motor (pre-engaged)
5 Fuse unit
6 In-line fuse
7 Ignition switch
8 Ignition coil
9 Ignition warning lamp
10 Distributor
11 Dynamo
12 Alternator
13 Control box (A-RB106, B-RB340)
14 Horn(s)
15 Horn switch
16 Ballast resistor (coil)
17 Lighting switch
18 Headlamp main beam
19 Main beam warning lamp
20 Dip switch
21 Headlamp dipped beam
22 Headlamp flasher switch
23 Headlamp (inner - RH)
24 Headlamp (inner - LH)
25 Sidelamp (RH)
26 Sidelamp (LH)
27 Rear lamp (RH)
28 Rear lamp (LH)
29 Number plate lamp(s)
30 Stop lamp(s)
31 Stop lamp switch
32 Indicator unit
33 Indicator switch
34 Indicator warning lamp
35 Indicator (front - RH)
36 Indicator (front - LH)
37 Indicator (rear - RH)
38 Indicator (rear — LH)
39 Indicator repeater unit
40 Indicator repeater lamp (RH)
41 Indicator repeater lamp (LH)
42 Hazard warning lamp
43 Hazard warning switch
44 Hazard warning flasher unit
45 Reversing lamp(s)
46 Reversing lamp(s) switch
47 Reversing lamp(s) and auto inhibitor switch
48 Voltage stabilizer
49 Panel lamp(s)
50 Panel lamp(s) resistor
51 Printed circuit instrument panel
52 Fuel gauge
53 Fuel gauge sender unit
54 Oil pressure warning lamp
55 Oil pressure switch
56 Water temperature gauge
57 Water temperature gauge sender unit
58 Tachometer
59 Clock
60 Split braking test switch
61 Split braking shuttle valve
62 Handbrake switch
63 Handbrake warning lamp
64 Anti-run-on valve
65 Anti-run-on valve relay
66 Mixture control warning lamp switch
67 Mixture control warning lamp switch
68 Wiper switch
69 Wiper motor
70 Screen washer motor
71 Screen washer motor switch
72 Induction heater and thermostat
73 Tailgate switch
74 Tailgate wiper motor
75 Tailgate washer motor (estate)
76 Tailgate wiper/washer switch
77 Screen wiper/washer switch
78 Rear window demist switch
79 Rear window demist unit
80 Rear window demist warning lamp
81 Heater blower motor switch
82 Heater blower motor
83 Automatic gearbox safety switch
84 Automatic gearbox quadrant lamp
85 Interior lamp switch
86 Interior lamp switch (rear)
87 Interior lamp
88 Interior lamp (rear - estate)
89 Door switch
90 Luggage compartment lamp switch
91 Luggage compartment lamp
92 Cigar lighter
93 Radio
94 Glovebox lamp
95 Glovebox lamp switch
96 Bonnet lamp
97 Bonnet switch
98 Panel lamp switch

Colour code

Black BK — Yellow YW
Blue BL — White WH
Brown BR — Light green LGR
Red RD — Orange OR
Green GR — Pink PI
Grey GY — Purple PU

Fault diagnosis

Introduction

The car owner who does his or her own maintenance according to the recommended schedules should not have to use this section of the manual very often. Modern component reliability is such that, provided those items subject to wear or deterioration are inspected or renewed at the specified intervals, sudden failure is comparatively rare. Faults do not usually just happen as a result of sudden failure, but develop over a period of time. Major mechanical failures in particular are usually preceded by characteristic symptoms over hundreds or even thousands of miles. Those components which do occasionally fail without warning are often small and easily carried in the car.

With any fault finding, the first step is to decide where to begin investigations. Sometimes this is obvious, but on other occasions a little detective work will be necessary. The owner who makes half a dozen haphazard adjustments or replacements may be successful in curing a fault (or its symptoms), but he will be none the wiser if the fault recurs and he may well have spent more time and money than was necessary. A calm and logical approach will be found to be more satisfactory in the long run. Always take into account any warning signs or abnormalities that may have been noticed in the period preceding the fault - power loss, high or low gauge readings, unusual noises or smells, etc - and remember that failure of components such as fuses or spark plugs may only be pointers to some underlying fault.

The pages which follow here are intended to help in cases of failure to start or breakdown on the road. There is also a Fault Diagnosis Section at the end of each Chapter which should be consulted if the preliminary checks prove unfruitful. Whatever the fault, certain basic principles apply. These are as follows:

Verify the fault. This is simply a matter of being sure that you know what the symptoms are before starting work. This is particularly important if you are investigating a fault for someone else who may not have described it very accurately.

Don't overlook the obvious. For example, if the car won't start, is there petrol in the tank? (Don't take anyone else's word on this particular point, and don't trust the fuel gauge either!). If an electrical fault is indicated, look for loose or broken wires before digging out the test gear.

Cure the disease, not the symptom. Substituting a flat battery with a fully charged one will get you off the hard shoulder, but if the underlying cause is not attended to, the new battery will go the same way. Similarly, changing oil-fouled spark plugs for a new set will get you moving again, but remember that the reason for the fouling (if it wasn't simply an incorrect grade of plug) will have to be established and corrected.

Don't take anything for granted. Particularly, don't forget that a new component may itself be defective (especially if it's been rattling round in the boot for months), and don't leave components out of a fault diagnosis sequence just because they are new or recently fitted. When you do finally diagnose a difficult fault, you'll probably realise that all the evidence was there from the start.

Electrical faults

Electrical faults can be more puzzling than straightforward mechanical failures, but they are no less susceptible to logical analysis if the basic principles of operation are understood. Car electrical wiring exists in extremely unfavourable conditions - heat, vibration and chemical attack - and the first things to look for are loose or corroded connections and broken or chafed wires, especially where the wires pass through holes in the bodywork or are subject to vibration.

All metal-bodied cars in current production have one pole of the battery 'earthed', ie connected to the car bodywork, and in nearly all modern cars it is the negative (−) terminal. The various electrical components - motors, bulb holders etc - are also connected to earth, either by means of a lead or directly by their mountings. Electric current flows through the component and then back to the battery via the car bodywork. If the component mounting is loose or corroded, or if a good path back to the battery is not available, the circuit will be incomplete and malfunction will result. The engine and/or gearbox are also earthed by means of flexible metal straps to the body or subframe; if these straps are loose or missing, starter motor, generator and ignition trouble may result.

Assuming the earth return to be satisfactory, electrical faults will be due either to component malfunction or to defects in the current supply. Individual components are dealt with in Chapter 10. If supply wires are broken or cracked internally this results in an open-circuit, and the easiest way to check for this is to bypass the suspect wire temporarily with a length of wire having a crocodile clip or suitable connector at each end. Alternatively, a 12V test lamp can be used to verify the presence of supply voltage at various points along the wire and the break can be thus isolated.

If a bare portion of a live wire touches the car bodywork or other earthed metal part the electricity will take the low-resistance path thus formed back to the battery: this is known as a short-circuit. Hopefully a short-circuit will blow a fuse, but otherwise it may cause burning of the insulation (and possible further short-circuits) or even a fire. This is why it is inadvisable to bypass persistently blowing fuses with silver foil or wire.

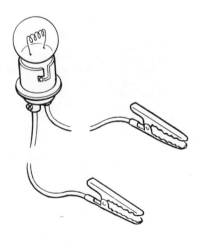

A simple test lamp is useful for investigating electrical faults

Spares and tool kit

Most cars are only supplied with sufficient tools for wheel changing; the *Maintenance and minor repair* tool kit detailed in *Tools and working facilities*, with the addition of a hammer, is probably sufficient for those repairs that most motorists would consider attempting at the roadside. In addition a few items which can be fitted without too much trouble in the event of a breakdown should be carried. Experience and available space will modify the list below, but the following may save having to call on professional assistance:

Spark plugs, clean and correctly gapped
HT lead and plug cap - long enough to reach the plug furthest from the distributor
Distributor rotor, condenser and contact breaker points
Drivebelt - emergency type may suffice
Spare fuses
Set of principal light bulbs
Tin of radiator sealer and hose bandage
Exhaust bandage
Roll of insulating tape
Length of soft iron wire
Length of electrical flex
Torch or inspection lamp (can double as test lamp)
Battery jump leads
Tow rope
Tyre valve core
Ignition waterproofing aerosol
Litre of engine oil
Sealed can of hydraulic fluid
Emergency windscreen

If spare fuel is carried, a can designed for the purpose should be used to minimise the risk of leakage and collision damage. A first aid kit and a warning triangle, whilst not at present compulsory in the UK, are obviously sensible items to carry in addition to the above.

When touring abroad it may be advisable to carry additional spares which, even if you cannot fit them yourself, could save having to wait while parts are obtained. The items below may be worth considering:

Cylinder head gasket
Alternator brushes
Spare fuel pump

One of the motoring organisations will be able to advise on availability of fuel etc in foreign countries

---

Engine will not start

Engine fails to turn when starter operated

Flat battery (recharge, use jump leads, or push start)
Battery terminals loose or corroded
Battery earth to body defective
Engine earth strap loose or broken
Starter motor (or solenoid) wiring loose or broken
Ignition/starter switch faulty
Major mechanical failure (seizure) or long disuse (piston rings rusted to bores
Starter or solenoid internal fault (see Chapter 10)

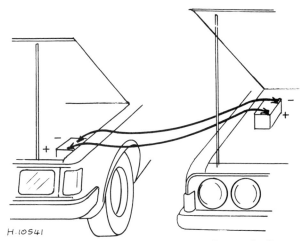

H.10541

Correct way to connect jump leads. Do not allow car bodies to touch!

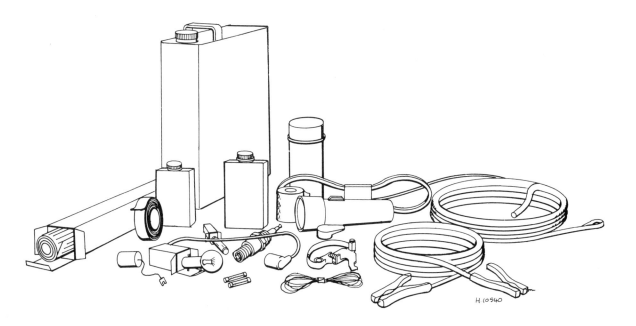

H.10540

Carrying a few spares can save you a long walk!

Starter motor turns engine slowly
    Partially discharged battery (recharge, use jump leads, or
    push start)
    Battery terminals loose or corroded
    Battery earth to body defective
    Engine earth strap loose
    Starter motor (or solenoid) wiring loose
    Starter motor internal fault (see Chapter 10)

Starter motor spins without turning engine
    Flat battery
    Starter motor pinion sticking on sleeve
    Flywheel gear teeth damaged or worn
    Starter motor mounting bolts loose

Engine turns normally but fails to start
    Damp or dirty HT leads and distributor cap (crank engine
    and check for spark)
    Dirty or incorrectly gapped contact breaker points
    No fuel in tank (check for delivery at carburettor)
    Excessive choke (hot engine) or insufficient choke (cold
    engine)
    Fouled or incorrectly gapped spark plugs (remove, clean
    and regap)
    Other ignition system fault (see Chapter 4)
    Other fuel system fault (see Chapter 3)
    Poor compression (see Chapter 1)
    Major mechanical failure

Engine fires but will not run
    Insufficient choke (cold engine) - check adjustment
    Air leaks at carburettor or inlet manifold
    Fuel starvation (see Chapter 3)
    Ballast resistor defective or other ignition fault (see Chapter
    4)

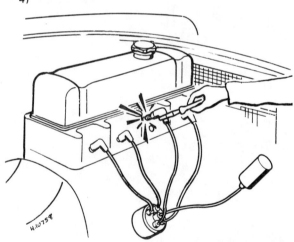

Crank engine and check for a spark. Note use of insulated pliers -
dry cloth or a rubber glove will suffice

Engine cuts out and will not restart

Engine cuts out suddenly - ignition fault
    Loose or disconnected LT wires
    Wet HT leads or distributor cap (after traversing water splash)
    Coil or condenser failure (check for spark)
    Other ignition fault (see Chapter 4)

Engine misfires before cutting out - fuel fault
    Fuel tank empty
    Fuel pump defective or filter blocked (check for delivery)
    Fuel tank filler vent blocked (suction will be evident on
    releasing cap)

    Carburettor needle valve sticking
    Carburettor jets blocked (fuel contamination)
    Other fuel system fault (see Chapter 3)

Engine cuts out - other causes
    Serious overheating
    Major mechanical failure (eg camshaft drive)

**Remove fuel pipe from carburettor and check that fuel is being
delivered**

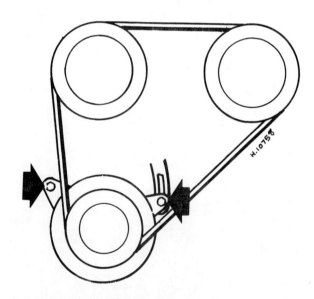

**A slack drivebelt may cause overheating and battery charging
problems. Slacken bolts (arrowed) to adjust**

Engine overheats

Ignition (no-charge) warning light illuminated
    Slack or broken drivebelt - retension or renew (Chapter 2)

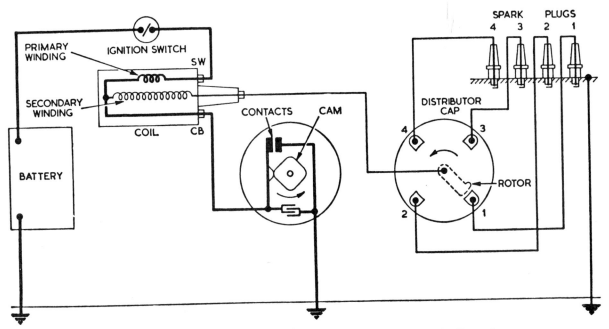

Ignition system schematic diagram. Some later models have a 6V coil and ballast resistor

Ignition warning light not illuminated

Coolant loss due to internal or external leakage (see Chapter 2)
Thermostat defective
Low oil level
Brakes binding
Radiator clogged externally or internally
Engine waterways clogged
Ignition timing incorrect or automatic advance malfunctioning
Mixture too weak

Note: *Do not add cold water to an overheated engine or damage may result*

Low engine oil pressure

Warning light illuminated with engine running

Oil level low or incorrect grade
Defective sender unit
Wire to sender unit earthed
Engine overheating
Oil filter clogged or bypass valve defective
Oil pressure relief valve defective
Oil pick-up strainer clogged
Oil pump worn or mountings loose
Worn main or big-end bearings

Note: *Low oil pressure in a high-mileage engine at tickover is not necessarily a cause for concern. Sudden pressure loss at speed is far more significant. In any event, check the warning light sender before condemning the engine.*

Engine noises

Pre-ignition (pinking) on acceleration

Incorrect grade of fuel
Ignition timing incorrect
Distributor faulty or worn
Worn or maladjusted carburettor
Excessive carbon build-up in engine

Whistling or wheezing noises

Leaking vacuum hose
Leaking carburettor or manifold gasket
Blowing head gasket

Tapping or rattling

Incorrect valve clearance
Worn valve gear
Worn timing chain
Broken piston ring (ticking noise)

Knocking or thumping

Unintentional mechanical contact (eg fan blades)
Worn fanbelt
Peripheral component fault (generator, water pump etc)
Worn big-end bearings (regular heavy knocking, perhaps less under load)
Worn main bearings (rumbling and knocking, perhaps worsening under load)
Piston slap (most noticeable when cold)

Use of English

As this book has been written in England, it uses the appropriate English component names, phrases, and spelling. Some of these differ from those used in America. Normally, these cause no difficulty, but to make sure, a glossary is printed below. In ordering spare parts remember the parts list will probably use these words:

English	American	English	American
Aerial	Antenna	Layshaft (of gearbox)	Countershaft
Accelerator	Gas pedal	Leading shoe (of brake)	Primary shoe
Alternator	Generator (AC)	Locks	Latches
Anti-roll bar	Stabiliser or sway bar	Motorway	Freeway, turnpike etc
Battery	Energizer	Number plate	License plate
Bodywork	Sheet metal	Paraffin	Kerosene
Bonnet (engine cover)	Hood	Petrol	Gasoline
Boot lid	Trunk lid	Petrol tank	Gas tank
Boot (luggage compartment)	Trunk	'Pinking'	'Pinging'
Bottom gear	1st gear	Propeller shaft	Driveshaft
Bulkhead	Firewall	Quarter light	Quarter window
Cam follower or tappet	Valve lifter or tappet	Retread	Recap
Carburettor	Carburetor	Reverse	Back-up
Catch	Latch	Rocker cover	Valve cover
Choke/venturi	Barrel	Roof rack	Car-top carrier
Circlip	Snap-ring	Saloon	Sedan
Clearance	Lash	Seized	Frozen
Crownwheel	Ring gear (of differential)	Side indicator lights	Side marker lights
Disc (brake)	Rotor/disk	Side light	Parking light
Drop arm	Pitman arm	Silencer	Muffler
Drop head coupe	Convertible	Spanner	Wrench
Dynamo	Generator (DC)	Sill panel (beneath doors)	Rocker panel
Earth (electrical)	Ground	Split cotter (for valve spring cap)	Lock (for valve spring retainer)
Engineer's blue	Prussian blue	Split pin	Cotter pin
Estate car	Station wagon	Steering arm	Spindle arm
Exhaust manifold	Header	Sump	Oil pan
Fast back (Coupe)	Hard top	Tab washer	Tang; lock
Fault finding/diagnosis	Trouble shooting	Tailgate	Liftgate
Float chamber	Float bowl	Tappet	Valve lifter
Free-play	Lash	Thrust bearing	Throw-out bearing
Freewheel	Coast	Top gear	High
Gudgeon pin	Piston pin or wrist pin	Trackrod (of steering)	Tie-rod (or connecting rod)
Gearchange	Shift	Trailing shoe (of brake)	Secondary shoe
Gearbox	Transmission	Transmission	Whole drive line
Halfshaft	Axleshaft	Tyre	Tire
Handbrake	Parking brake	Van	Panel wagon/van
Hood	Soft top	Vice	Vise
Hot spot	Heat riser	Wheel nut	Lug nut
Indicator	Turn signal	Windscreen	Windshield
Interior light	Dome lamp	Wing/mudguard	Fender

Miscellaneous points

An 'oil seal' is fitted to components lubricated by grease!

A 'damper' is a 'shock absorber', it damps out bouncing, and absorbs shocks of bump impact. Both names are correct, and both are used haphazardly.

Note that British drum brakes are different from the Bendix type that is common in America, so different descriptive names result. The shoe end furthest from the hydraulic wheel cylinder is on a pivot; interconnection between the shoes as on Bendix brakes is most uncommon. Therefore the phrase 'Primary' or 'Secondary' shoe does not apply. A shoe is said to be 'Leading' or 'Trailing'. A 'Leading' shoe is one on which a point on the drum, as it rotates forward, reaches the shoe at the end worked by the hydraulic cylinder before the anchor end. The opposite is a 'Trailing' shoe and this one has no self servo from the wrapping effect of the rotating drum.

Conversion factors

Length (distance)
Inches (in)	X	25.4	= Millimetres (mm)	X	0.0394	= Inches (in)
Feet (ft)	X	0.305	= Metres (m)	X	3.281	= Feet (ft)
Miles	X	1.609	= Kilometres (km)	X.	0.621	= Miles

Length:
- Inches (in) X 25.4 = Millimetres (mm) — X 0.0394 = Inches (in)
- Feet (ft) X 0.305 = Metres (m) — X 3.281 = Feet (ft)
- Miles X 1.609 = Kilometres (km) — X. 0.621 = Miles

Volume (capacity)
- Cubic inches (cu in; in³) X 16.387 = Cubic centimetres (cc; cm³) — X 0.061 = Cubic inches (cu in; in³)
- Imperial pints (Imp pt) X 0.568 = Litres (l) — X 1.76 = Imperial pints (Imp pt)
- Imperial quarts (Imp qt) X 1.137 = Litres (l) — X 0.88 = Imperial quarts (Imp qt)
- Imperial quarts (Imp qt) X 1.201 = US quarts (US qt) — X 0.833 = Imperial quarts (Imp qt)
- US quarts (US qt) X 0.946 = Litres (l) — X 1.057 = US quarts (US qt)
- Imperial gallons (Imp gal) X 4.546 = Litres (l) — X 0.22 = Imperial gallons (Imp gal)
- Imperial gallons (Imp gal) X 1.201 = US gallons (US gal) — X 0.833 = Imperial gallons (Imp gal)
- US gallons (US gal) X 3.785 = Litres (l) — X 0.264 = US gallons (US gal)

Mass (weight)
- Ounces (oz) X 28.35 = Grams (g) — X 0.035 = Ounces (oz)
- Pounds (lb) X 0.454 = Kilograms (kg) — X 2.205 = Pounds (lb)

Force
- Ounces-force (ozf; oz) X 0.278 = Newtons (N) — X 3.6 = Ounces-force (ozf; oz)
- Pounds-force (lbf; lb) X 4.448 = Newtons (N) — X 0.225 = Pounds-force (lbf; lb)
- Newtons (N) X 0.1 = Kilograms-force (kgf; kg) — X 9.81 = Newtons (N)

Pressure
- Pounds-force per square inch (psi; lbf/in²; lb/in²) X 0.070 = Kilograms-force per square centimetre (kgf/cm²; kg/cm²) — X 14.223 = Pounds-force per square inch (psi; lbf/in²; lb/in²)
- Pounds-force per square inch (psi; lbf/in²; lb/in²) X 0.068 = Atmospheres (atm) — X 14.696 = Pounds-force per square inch (psi; lbf/in²; lb/in²)
- Pounds-force per square inch (psi; lbf/in²; lb/in²) X 0.069 = Bars — X 14.5 = Pounds-force per square inch (psi; lbf/in²; lb/in²)
- Pounds-force per square inch (psi; lbf/in²; lb/in²) X 6.895 = Kilopascals (kPa) — X 0.145 = Pounds-force per square inch (psi; lbf/in²; lb/in²)
- Kilopascals (kPa) X 0.01 = Kilograms-force per square centimetre (kgf/cm²; kg/cm²) — X 98.1 = Kilopascals (kPa)

Torque (moment of force)
- Pounds-force inches (lbf in; lb in) X 1.152 = Kilograms-force centimetre (kgf cm; kg cm) — X 0.868 = Pounds-force inches (lbf in; lb in)
- Pounds-force inches (lbf in; lb in) X 0.113 = Newton metres (Nm) — X 8.85 = Pounds-force inches (lbf in; lb in)
- Pounds-force inches (lbf in; lb in) X 0.083 = Pounds-force feet (lbf ft; lb ft) — X 12 = Pounds-force inches (lbf in; lb in)
- Pounds-force feet (lbf ft; lb ft) X 0.138 = Kilograms-force metres (kgf m; kg m) — X 7.233 = Pounds-force feet (lbf ft; lb ft)
- Pounds-force feet (lbf ft; lb ft) X 1.356 = Newton metres (Nm) — X 0.738 = Pounds-force feet (lbf ft; lb ft)
- Newton metres (Nm) X 0.102 = Kilograms-force metres (kgf m; kg m) — X 9.804 = Newton metres (Nm)

Power
- Horsepower (hp) X 745.7 = Watts (W) — X 0.0013 = Horsepower (hp)

Velocity (speed)
- Miles per hour (miles/hr; mph) X 1.609 = Kilometres per hour (km/hr; kph) — X 0.621 = Miles per hour (miles/hr; mph)

Fuel consumption*
- Miles per gallon, Imperial (mpg) X 0.354 = Kilometres per litre (km/l) — X 2.825 = Miles per gallon, Imperial (mpg)
- Miles per gallon, US (mpg) X 0.425 = Kilometres per litre (km/l) — X 2.352 = Miles per gallon, US (mpg)

Temperature
Degrees Fahrenheit = (°C x 1.8) + 32   Degrees Celsius (Degrees Centigrade; °C) = (°F - 32) x 0.56

*It is common practice to convert from miles per gallon (mpg) to litres/100 kilometres (l/100km), where mpg (Imperial) x l/100 km = 282 and mpg (US) x l/100 km = 235

Index

A

About this manual — 2
Absorption canister (emission control system)
    general — 206
Acknowledgements — 2
Air injection system (emission control system)
    servicing — 204
Air pump drivebelt (Austin Marina models)
    adjustment — 194
Alternator
    general description — 139
    · overhaul — 218
    removal and refitting — 216
    routine maintenance — 140
    test — 218
    testing the charging circuit *in situ* — 216
Ancillary engine components
    removing — 28
Anti-freeze mixture — 59
Anti-roll bar (Marina Mk 2 models)
    removal and refitting
        front — 228
        rear — 229
Anti-run-on valve (emission control system)
    general — 207
Automatic transmission
    fault diagnosis — 110
    fluid level — 106
    fluid level (Marina Mk 2 models)
        checking — 210
    general (Marina Mk 2 models) - 210
    general description — 106
    removal and refitting — 210
    removal and replacement — 106
Axle shaft
    removal and replacement — 120

B

Battery
    charging — 139
    electrolyte replenishment — 139
    maintenance and inspection — 138
    removal and replacement — 138
Bearing (rear axle)
    removal and replacement — 120
Big-end bearing
    examination and renovation — 40
    removal — 35
Bleeding the hydraulic system
    brakes — 126
    clutch — 85
Bodywork
    body repairs
        major — 174
        minor — 174
    bonnet
        removal and refitting — 179
    bonnet lock
        removal and refitting — 179
    bonnet lock control cable
        removal and refitting — 180

    boot lid hinge
        removal and refitting — 180
    boot lid lock
        removal and refitting — 180
    boot lid tailgate
        removal and refitting — 180
    bumpers
        removal and refitting — 185
    bumpers (UK models)
        removal and refitting — 233
    door
        removal and refitting — 175
    door exterior handle
        removal and refitting — 176
    door glass
        removal and refitting — 178
    door hinge
        removal and refitting — 175
    door lock
        adjustment — 176
    door private lock
        removal and refitting — 178
    door rattles
        tracing and rectification — 175
    door remote control handle
        removal and refitting — 177
    door trim panel and capping
        removal and refitting — 176
    facia panel
        removal and refitting — 184
    front seat (type 1)
        removal and refitting — 236
    front seat (type 2)
        removal and refitting — 236
    general description — 173
    glovebox
        removal and refitting — 185
    heater fan and motor
        removal and refitting — 186
    heater matrix
        removal and refitting — 187
    heater unit
        removal and refitting — 186
    instrument panel
        removal and refitting — 187
    lower facia panel
        removal and refitting — 185
    maintenance
        body and chassis — 173
        upholstery and carpets — 174
    panel tray
        removal and refitting — 184
    radiator grille
        removal and refitting — 185
    rear window
        removal and refitting — 181
    repair sequence (colour) — 182, 183
    windscreen
        removal and refitting — 181
    windscreen demister duct
        removal and refitting — 187
Bodywork (Austin Marina and Mk 1 models)
    bumpers
        removal and refitting — 233

console assembly
  removal and refitting — 233
door exterior handle
  removal and refitting — 231
lower facia panel
  removal and refitting — 234
radiator grille
  removal and refitting — 234
rear quarter trim pad and capping
  removal and refitting — 232
Bodywork (Estate models)
tailgate exterior handle and lock
  removal and refitting — 232
tailgate glass and backlight
  removal and refitting — 233
tailgate hinge
  removal and refitting — 232
tailgate lock
  removal and refitting — 232
tailgate lock striker plate
  removal and refitting — 232
rear seat cushion
  removal and refitting — 237
rear seat squab
  removal and refitting — 237
rear body side glass
  removal and refitting — 237
Bodywork (Marina Mk 2 models)
door exterior handle
  removal and refitting — 232
door trim panel and capping
  removal and refitting — 231
facia panel
  removal and refitting — 234
glovebox
  removal and refitting — 234
heater control cables
  removal and refitting — 236
heater unit
  removal and refitting — 235
instrument panel
  removal and refitting — 236
windscreen demister duct
  removal and refitting — 236
Braking system
bleeding
  dual brake system — 212
  hydraulic system — 126
brake pedal assembly
  removal and refitting — 132
brake pressure warning switch (early type)
  centralisation — 216
brake servo unit
  air filter renewal — 134
  description — 132
  removal and refitting — 134
fault diagnosis — 136
flexible hose
  inspection, removal and refitting — 216
front brake disc
  removal and refitting — 127
front disc brake caliper
  overhaul — 130
  removal and refitting — 127
front disc brake caliper pad
  removal and refitting — 126
general description — 125, 212
handbrake cable
  adjustment — 132
  removal and refitting — 132
handbrake lever assembly
  removal and refitting — 132
hydraulic pipes and hoses

general — 216
master cylinder
  dismantling and reassembly — 129
  removal and refitting — 128
pressure differential warning actuator valve (early type)
  removal, overhaul and refitting — 214
pressure differential warning actuator valve (self-reset type)
  removal, overhaul and refitting — 215
rear drum backplate
  removal and refitting — 128
rear drum brake
  adjustment (manual adjusters) — 126
rear drum brake shoes
  inspection, removal and refitting — 128
rear drum brake wheel cylinder
  overhaul — 130
  removal and refitting — 130
tandem brake master cylinder
  removal and refitting — 212
tandem brake master cylinder (early type)
  dismantling and reassembly — 212
tandem brake master cylinder (later type)
  dismantling and reassembly — 213
torque wrench settings — 125
Braking system (Marina Mk 2 models)
brake pedal assembly
  removal and refitting — 214
brake servo unit
  removal and refitting — 214
handbrake cable
  removal and refitting — 214
handbrake lever assembly
  removal and refitting — 214
Bumpstop
removal and refitting — 164
Buying spare parts — 5

C

Camshaft
bearings
  examination and renovation — 42
examination and renovation — 42
removal — 34
replacement — 48
Carburettor
description — 64
dismantling and reassembly — 66
examination and repair — 66
fault diagnosis — 74
float chamber flooding — 68
float chamber fuel level adjustment — 68
float needle sticking — 68
general description — 61
hot air intake
  general — 204
jet centring — 68
needle replacement — 68
piston sticking — 66
tuning — 198
water or dirt in carburettor — 68
Carburettor (single)
adjustment and tuning — 69
removal and replacement — 64
Carburettor (single SU)
adjustment and tuning — 196
Carburettor (SU HIF6)
dismantling, inspection and reassembly — 199
general description and tuning (early Austin Marina models) —198
heater
  general — 201

Carburettor (twin)
  adjustment and tuning — 69
  linkage adjustment — 70
  removal and replacement — 66
Carburettor (twin SU)
  adjustment and tuning — 197
Carburettor (Zenith 175CD5T)
  dismantling, inspection and reassembly — 202
  general description and tuning (later Austin Marina models)
                                                         — 202
Carpets
  maintenance — 174
Centre bearing
  removal and replacement — 116
Centre console (Marina Mk 2 GT and HL models)
  removal and refitting — 214
Chassis
  maintenance — 173
Choke cable
  removal and refitting — 71
Choke cable (Marina Mk 2 models)
  removal and refitting — 197
Clutch
  bleeding — 85
  fault diagnosis and cure — 89
  flexible hose
    removal and replacement — 87
  general description — 84
  inspection — 86
  judder — 90
  master cylinder
    dismantling, examination and reassembly — 87
    removal and refitting — 87
  pedal
    removal and replacement — 85
  pedal (Marina Mk 2 models)
    removal and refitting — 210
  release bearing assembly
    removal, overhaul and refitting — 89
  removal and replacement — 85
  slave cylinder
    dismantling, examination and reassembly — 88
    removal and replacement — 88
  slip — 89
  spin — 89
  squeal — 89
Colour
  repair sequence — 182, 183
  spark plugs — 81
Compression test — 207
Condenser
  removal, testing and replacement — 77
Condenser (Marina Mk 2 and Austin Marina models)
  removal and refitting — 208
Connecting rod
  removal — 35
  to crankshaft reassembly — 48
Console assembly (Marina Mk 1 models)
  removal and refitting — 233
Contact breaker points
  adjustment — 76
  removal and replacement — 77
Contact breaker points (Marina Mk 2 and Austin Marina models)
  adjustment — 208
  removal and refitting — 208
Control box (RB 106/2)
  cut-out adjustment — 220
  cut-out and regulator contacts maintenance — 220
  general description — 220
  voltage regulator adjustment — 220
Control box (RB 340)
  cut-out adjustment — 221
  cut-out and regulator contacts maintenance — 221

  general description — 220
  regulator adjustment — 221
Cooling system
  draining — 56
  fault diagnosis — 60
  filling — 56
  flushing — 56
  general description — 55
  specifications — 55
Cooling system (Austin Marina models)
  air pump
    adjustment — 194
  fan belt
    removal and refitting — 194
  radiator
    removal and refitting — 194
  thermostat
    removal and refitting — 194
  water pump
    removal and refitting — 196
Crankcase emission control
  general — 204
Crankshaft
  examination and renovation — 40
  removal — 39
  replacement — 44
  specifications — 13
  torque wrench settings — 17
Cylinder bores
  examination and renovation — 40
  decarbonisation — 44
Cylinder head
  decarbonisation — 44
  removal
    engine in car — 30
    engine on bench — 33
  replacement — 51

D

Decarbonisation
  cylinder bore — 44
  cylinder head — 44
Differential assembly
  removal and replacement — 121
Differential unit
  dismantling, inspection, reassembly and adjustment — 121
Disc brakes see **Braking system**
Dismantling the engine — 28
Direction indicator
  switch
    removal and replacement — 148
Distributor
  dismantling — 78
  fault diagnosis — 83
  inspection and repair — 78
  lubrication — 77
  reassembly — 78
  removal and replacement — 78
  specifications — 74
  torque wrench settings — 76
Distributor (Marina Mk 2 and Austin Marina models)
  removal and refitting — 208
Distributor (43D4 and 45D4)
  dismantling — 208
  inspection and repair — 209
  reassembly — 209
Distributor drive
  removal — 35
  replacement — 52
Doors
  exterior handle

removal and refitting — 176
glass
  removal and refitting — 178
hinges
  removal and refitting — 175
lock
  adjustment — 176
private lock
  removal and refitting — 178
rattles
  tracing and rectification — 175
remote control handle
  removal and refitting — 177
removal and refitting — 175
trim panel and capping
  removal and refitting — 176
Doors (late Marina Mk 1 and Austin Marina models)
exterior handle
  removal and refitting — 231
Doors (Marina Mk 2 models)
exterior handle
  removal and refitting — 232
trim panel and capping
  removal and refitting — 231
Down shift cable
adjustment — 109
Draining
cooling system — 56
Drive cable tubes
removal and replacement — 145
Drum backplate (rear)
removal and refitting — 128
Drum brakes (rear) *see* **Braking system**
Dynamo
dismantling and inspection — 219
removal and refitting — 219
repair and reassembly — 220
testing in position — 218

E

Electrical faults — 254
Electrical system
alternator
  general description — 139
  overhaul — 218
  removal and refitting — 216
  routine maintenance — 140
  test — 218
  testing the charging circuit *in situ* — 216
drive cable tubes
  removal and replacement — 145
fault diagnosis — 142
flasher unit and circuit
  fault tracing and rectification — 144
front flasher bulbs
  removal and replacement — 146
fuses — 151
gauge units
  removal and replacement — 150
handbrake warning light switch
  removal and refitting — 226
headlight
  beam adjustment — 146
headlight dip/flasher
  removal and replacement — 148
headlight units
  removal and replacement — 146
horn
  fault tracing and rectification — 146
horn direction indicator switch

removal and replacement — 148
ignition switch
  removal and replacement — 148
instrument operation
  testing — 151
instrument panel printed circuit
  removal and replacement — 150
lighting switch
  removal and replacement — 149
long range driving lamps
  removal and refitting — 225
number plate light bulbs
  removal and replacement — 146
panel illumination lamp bulbs
  removal and replacement — 146
rear flasher bulb
  removal and replacement — 146
reversing lamp (flush fitting type)
  removal and refitting — 224
reversing lamp (protruding type)
  removal and refitting — 224
side flasher bulbs
  removal and replacement — 146
specifications — 137
speedometer
  removal and replacement — 151
starter switch
  removal and replacement — 148
steering lock switch
  removal and replacement — 148
stop bulbs
  removal and replacement — 146
stop light switch
  removal and replacement — 149
voltage stabilizer
  removal and replacement — 151
wheelboxes
  removal and replacement — 145
windscreen wiper arms
  removal and replacement — 144
windscreen wiper blades
  changing wiping arc — 144
windscreen wiper mechanism
  fault diagnosis and rectification — 144
windscreen wiper motor
  dismantling, inspection and reassembly — 145
  removal and replacement — 145
Electrical system (Austin Marina models)
front flasher repeat lamp bulb
  removal — 223
headlamp relay
  removal and refitting — 227
seat belt buzzer and timer module
  removal and refitting — 227
seat switch
  removal and refitting — 227
starter circuit relay
  removal and refitting — 227
Electrical system (Estate)
flasher lamp
  removal and refitting — 223
rack tubes
  removal and refitting — 226
rear number plate lamp
  removal and refitting — 224
roof lamp
  removal and refitting — 225
stop lamp
  removal and refitting — 223
tail lamp
  removal and refitting — 223
tailgate wiper motor
  removal and refitting — 226

wheelbox
removal and refitting — 226
Electrical system (Marina Mk 2 models)
gauge units
removal and refitting — 226
heater fan switch
removal and refitting — 226
instrument panel printed circuit
removal and refitting — 226
lighting switch
removal and refitting — 225
reverse lamp bulb
renewal — 223
speedometer
removal and refitting — 226
tachometer
removal and refitting — 226
wiper/washer switch
removal and refitting — 225
Electrical system (Saloon)
roof lamp
removal and refitting — 225
Emission control systems
absorption canister
general — 206
air injection system
servicing — 204
anti-run-on valve
general — 207
exhaust port air injection
general — 204
fault diagnosis and routine maintenance — 208
fuel line filter
general — 206
Engine
backplate
refitting — 49
compression test — 207
dismantling
general — 28
examination and renovation
general — 40
fault diagnosis — 54
fault diagnosis
engine cuts out and will not restart — 256
engine noises — 257
engine overheats — 256
engine will not start — 255
low engine oil pressure — 257
general description — 20
initial start-up after overhaul or major repair — 53
major operations
engine in place — 20
engine removed — 20
methods of engine removal — 20
reassembly
general — 44
removal
less gearbox — 26
through engine compartment — 28
with gearbox (from underside) — 22
removing ancillary engine components — 28
replacement — 53
separating the engine from gearbox — 28
specifications — 13
torque wrench settings — 17
Engine (Austin Marina models)
removal and repair procedure — 194
Engine (Marina Mk 2 models)
changes — 194
Exhaust emission regulations (Austin Marina models) — 198
Exhaust port air injection (emission control system)
general — 204

Expansion tank — 59
Eyebolt bush
removal and refitting — 162

F

Facia panel
removal and refitting — 184
Facia panel (Marina Mk 2 models)
removal and refitting — 234
Fan belt
adjustment — 58
removal and replacement — 58
Fan belt (Austin Marina models)
removal and refitting — 194
Fault diagnosis/finding
automatic transmission — 110
braking system — 136
carburation — 74
clutch — 89
cooling system — 60
electrical faults — 254
electrical system — 151
emission control system — 208
engine — 54
engine
cuts out and will not restart — 256
noises — 257
overheats — 256
will not start — 83, 255
flasher unit and circuit — 144
ignition system — 83
low engine oil pressure — 257
manual gearbox — 105
spares and tool kit — 255
steering — 172
Filters
air — 8
oil
removal and replacement — 39
Flasher bulbs
side and front
removal and replacement — 146
stop, tail and rear
removal and replacement — 146
Flasher repeater lamp bulb (Austin Marina models)
front bulb renewal — 223
Flasher unit and circuit
fault tracing and rectification — 144
Flywheel
refitting — 50
removal — 37
starter ring gear
examination and renovation — 44
Front disc brakes *see* **Braking system**
Front hub bearings
adjustment — 158
removal and refitting — 158
Front seats
removal and refitting (type 1) — 236
removal and refitting (type 2) — 236
Front shock absorber
removal and refitting — 160
Front shock absorber (Marina Mk 2 models)
removal and refitting — 228
Front suspension trim height
adjustment — 171
Front suspension trim height (later Marina Mk 1 and all Marina Mk 2 and Austin Marina models)
adjustment — 231
Front wheel alignment — 171
Fuel line filter (emission control system)

general — 206
Fuel pump
dismantling, inspection and reassembly — 62
general description — 61
removal and replacement — 62
testing — 64
Fuel pump (Austin Marina models)
removal and refitting — 196
Fuel tank
cleaning — 72
removal and refitting — 72
sender unit
removal and refitting — 72
Fuel tank (Marina Mk 2 models)
removal and refitting — 197
Fuses — 151

G

Gauge units
removal and replacement — 150
Gauge units (Marina Mk 2 models)
removal and refitting — 226
Gearbox (automatic)
down shift cable
adjustment — 109
fault diagnosis — 110
fluid level — 106
general description — 106
removal and refitting — 210
removal and replacement — 106
selector linkage
adjustment — 110
starter inhibitor/reverse light switch
check and adjustment — 109
removal and refitting — 212
torque converter
removal and replacement — 108
Gearbox (Marina Mk 2 models, automatic)
fluid level checking — 210
general — 210
Gearbox (manual)
dismantling — 95
examination and renovation — 95
fault diagnosis — 105
general description — 92
input shaft
dismantling and reassembly — 97
mainshaft
dismantling and reassembly — 97
reassembly — 100
removal and refitting — 210
removal and replacement — 92
specifications — 91
torque wrench settings — 92
Gearbox (Marina Mk 2 models, manual)
dismantling and reassembly — 210
Glovebox
removal and refitting — 185
Glovebox (Marina Mk 2 models)
removal and refitting — 234
Gudgeon pin
removal — 36

H

Handbrake
cable
adjustment — 132
removal and refitting — 132
lever assembly

removal and refitting — 132
warning light switch
removal and refitting — 226
Handbrake (Marina Mk 2 models)
cable
removal and refitting — 214
lever assembly
removal and refitting — 214
Headlights
beam
adjustment — 146
dip/flasher switch
removal and replacement — 148
units
removal and replacement — 146
Heater
fan
removal and refitting — 186
fan switch
removal and replacement — 149
matrix
removal and refitting — 187
motor
removal and refitting — 186
unit
removal and refitting — 186
Heater (Marina Mk 2 models)
control cables
removal and refitting — 236
fan switch
removal and refitting — 226
unit
removal and refitting — 235
High tension leads — 82
Horns
fault tracing and rectification — 146
Hub bearings (front)
adjustment — 158
removal and refitting — 159
Hydraulic pipes and hoses
general — 216
Hydraulic system
bleeding
brakes — 126
clutch — 85

I

Ignition switch
removal and replacement — 148
Ignition system
condenser
removal, testing and replacement — 77
contact breaker points
adjustment — 76
removal and replacement — 77
distributor
dismantling — 78
inspection and repair — 78
lubrication — 77
reassembly — 78
removal and replacement — 78
distributor (43D4 and 45D4)
dismantling — 208
inspection — 209
repair — 209
fault diagnosis — 83
general description — 73
ignition
timing — 78
spark plugs and leads — 82
specification — 74

torque wrench settings — 76
Ignition system (Marina Mk 2 and Austin Marina models)
  condenser
    removal and refitting — 208
  contact breaker points
    adjustment — 208
    removal and refitting — 208
  distributor
    removal and refitting — 208
  ignition
    timing — 210
Input shaft
  dismantling and reassembly — 97
Instrument operation
  testing — 151

L

Leads (plugs) — 82
Lighting switch
  removal and replacement — 149
Locks
  bonnet
    removal and refitting — 179
  bonnet control cable
    removal and refitting — 180
  bonnet lid
    removal and refitting — 180
  door
    adjustment — 176
  private door
    removal and refitting — 178
Long range driving lamps
  removal and refitting — 225
Lower facia panel
  removal and refitting — 185
Lower facia panel (Austin Marina models)
  removal and refitting — 234
Lower suspension arm
  removal and refitting — 159
Lower suspension arm (Marina Mk 2 models)
  removal and refitting — 228
Lower swivel pin link
  removal and refitting — 160
Lower swivel pin link (Marina Mk 2 models)
  removal and refitting — 228
Lubrication
  approved list — 11
Lubrication system
  description — 39

M

Main bearings
  examination and renovation — 40
  removal — 39
Mainshaft
  dismantling and reassembly — 97
Maintenance
  body and chassis — 173
  locks and hinges — 175
  routine — 8
  upholstery and carpets — 174
Major operations
  with engine in place — 20
  with engine removed — 20
Master cylinder
  braking system
    dismantling and reassembly — 129
    removal and refitting — 128
  clutch

dismantling, examination and reassembly — 87
  removal and refitting — 87
Methods of engine removal   20

N

Number plate light bulbs
  removal and replacement — 146

O

Oil filter
  removal and replacement — 39
Oil pressure relief valve
  removal and replacement — 40
Oil pressure relief valve and switch
  replacement — 50
Oil pump
  examination and renovation — 44
  removal and dismantling — 40
  replacement — 48

P

Panel illumination lamp bulbs
  removal and replacement — 148
Panel tray
  removal and refitting — 184
Parcel tray (rear)
  removal and refitting — 233
Pinion oil seal
  removal and replacement — 120
Pistons
  examination — 42
  reassembly — 46
  removal — 35
  replacement — 48
Piston rings
  examination and renovation — 42
  removal — 37
  replacement — 46
Pressure differential warning actuator valve (early type)
  removal, overhaul and refitting — 214
Pressure differential warning actuator valve (self-reset type)
  removal, overhaul and refitting — 215
Propeller shaft
  front
    removal and replacement — 113
  rear
    removal and replacement — 113

Q

Quarter light
  removal and refitting — 238

R

Radiator
  anti-freeze — 59
  draining — 56
  filling — 56
  flushing — 56
  grille
    removal and refitting — 185
  inspection and cleaning — 56
  removal and refitting — 56, 194
Radiator (Austin Marina models)
  grille

removal and refitting — 234
removal and refitting — 194
Rear axle
  bearing and oil seal
    removal and replacement — 120
  differential assembly
    removal and replacement — 121
  differential unit
    dismantling, inspection, reassembly and adjustment — 121
  general description — 117
  removal and replacement — 119
  specifications — 117
  torque wrench settings — 117
Rear axle (Marina Mk 2 models)
  removal and replacement — 212
Rear body side glass (Estate)
  removal and refitting — 237
Rear flasher bulbs
  removal and replacement — 146
Rear hub assembly
  removal and refitting — 163, 229
Rear number plate lamp (Estate)
  removal and refitting — 224
Rear parcel tray
  removal and refitting — 233
Rear quarter trim pad and capping (Marina Mk 1 models)
  removal and refitting — 232
Rear road spring
  removal and refitting — 163
  shackles
    removal and refitting — 164
Rear seat (Estate)
  cushion
    removal and refitting — 237
  squab
    removal and refitting — 237
Rear seat (Saloon)
  cushion
    removal and refitting — 237
  squab
    removal and refitting — 237
Rear shock absorber
  removal and refitting — 164
Rear window
  removal and refitting — 181
Recommended lubricants and fluids — 10
Reverse lamp bulb (Marina Mk 2 models)
  renewal — 223
Reverse light switch
  check and adjustment — 109
Reversing lamp (flush fitting type)
  removal and refitting — 224
Reversing lamp (protruding type)
  removal and refitting — 224
Rocker assembly
  dismantling — 33
Rocker arm valve
  adjustment — 51
Rockers and rocker shaft
  examination and renovation — 43
  shaft
    reassembly — 51
Roof lamp (Estate)
  removal and refitting — 225
Roof lamp (Saloon)
  removal and refitting — 225
Routine maintenance — 8

S

Safety first! — 6
Seats

front (type 1)
  removal and refitting — 236
front (type 2)
  removal and refitting — 236
rear (Estate) cushion and squab
  removal and refitting — 237
rear (Saloon) squab and cushion
  removal and refitting — 237
Seat belt buzzer and timer module (Austin Marina models)
  removal and refitting — 227
Seat switch (Austin Marina models)
  removal and refitting — 227
Selector linkage
  adjustment — 110
Separating the engine from the gearbox — 28
Shock absorbers
  front
    removal and refitting — 160
  rear
    removal and refitting — 164
Shock absorber (Marina and Mk 2 models)
  removal and refitting — 228
Side flasher bulbs
  removal and replacement — 146
Sliding joint
  dismantling, overhaul and reassembly — 116
Spark plugs
  colour chart — 81
  fault diagnosis — 83
  specifications — 74
  torque wrench settings — 76
Specifications (technical)
  automatic transmission — 91, 92
  braking system — 125, 192
  carburation — 61, 190
  clutch — 84, 192
  cooling system — 55, 190
  electrical system — 137, 192
  engine — 13, 190
  gearbox — 19, 192
  ignition system — 75, 191
  lubrication — 10, 190
  propeller shaft and universal joints — 113
  rear axle — 117, 192
  steering — 155, 193
  suspension — 155, 193
Speedometer
  removal and replacement — 151
Speedometer (Marina Mk 2 models)
  removal and refitting — 226
Springs
  rear road
    removal and refitting — 163
  rear road spring shackles
    removal and refitting — 164
Starter circuit relay (Austin Marina models)
  removal and refitting — 227
Starter inhibitor/reverse light switch
  check and adjustment — 109
  removal and refitting — 212
Starter motor
  general description — 141
  solenoid
    removal and replacement — 143
Starter motor (M35J)
  dismantling and reassembly — 222
  testing, removal and refitting — 221
Starter motor (M35J PE) pre-engaged type
  dismantling and reassembly — 223
  testing, removal and refitting — 223
Starter motor (M418G)
  dismantling and reassembly — 142

removal and replacement — 141
testing on engine — 141
Starter motor (2M100 PE) pre-engaged type
dismantling and reassembly — 143
removal and replacement — 143
testing on engine — 143
Steering
column lock and ignition starter switch housing
removal and refitting — 167
column top bush
removal and refitting — 165
column universal joint couplings
removal and refitting — 168
fault diagnosis — 172
lock switch
removal and replacement — 148
rack and pinion
dismantling, overhaul and reassembly — 168
removal and refitting — 168
torque wrench settings — 156
upper steering column
removal and refitting — 168
wheel
removal and refitting — 165
Steering (Austin Marina models)
column lock and ignition starter switch
removal and refitting — 230
column universal joint coupling
removal and refitting — 231
upper steering column
removal and refitting — 231
Steering (Later Marina Mk 1 models)
column universal joint coupling
removal and refitting — 231
upper steering column
removal and refitting — 231
Steering (Marina Mk 2)
column lock and ignition starter switch
removal and refitting — 230
rack and pinion
removal and refitting — 231
upper steering column
removal and refitting — 231
wheel
removal and refitting — 229
Stop light switch
removal and replacement — 149
Stop/flasher bulbs
removal and replacement — 146
Stop/flasher lamp (Estate)
removal and refitting — 223
Sump
refitting — 49
removal — 35
Supplement: Revisions and information on later models
Bodywork and underframe — 231 to 238
Braking system — 212 to 216
Clutch — 210
Cooling system — 194 to 196
Electrical system — 216 to 227
Engine — 194
Fuel system and carburation — 196 to 208
Gearbox and automatic transmission — 210 to 212
Ignition system — 208 to 210
Introduction — 189
Rear axle — 212
Specifications — 190 to 194
Suspension and steering — 228 to 231
Wiring diagrams — 240 to 253
Suspension
fault diagnosis — 172
front suspension trim height
adjustment — 171

general description — 156, 228
lower suspension arm
removal and refitting — 159
tie rod
removal and refitting — 163
torsion bar
removal and refitting — 162
Suspension (Marina Mk 2 models)
general description — 228
lower suspension arm
removal and refitting — 228
torsion bar
removal and refitting — 228
Swivel pin
balljoint
removal and refitting — 160
lower swivel pin link
removal and refitting — 160
removal and refitting — 160
Swivel pin (Marina Mk 2 models)
balljoint
removal and refitting — 228
lower swivel pin link
removal and refitting — 228
removal and refitting — 228

T

Tachometer (Marina Mk 2 models)
removal and refitting — 226
Tail/flasher bulbs
removal and replacement — 146
Tail/flasher lamp (Estate)
removal and refitting — 223
Tailgate
glass and backlight
removal and refitting — 233
removal and refitting — 180
Tailgate (Estate)
exterior handle and lock
removal and refitting — 232
hinge
removal and refitting — 232
lock
removal and refitting — 232
lock striker plate
removal and refitting — 232
Tandem brake master cylinder
removal and refitting — 212
Tandem brake master cylinder (early type)
dismantling and reassembly — 212
Tandem brake master cylinder (later type) — 213
Tappets
examination and renovation — 44
replacement — 51
Temperature gauge thermal transmitter — 59
Thermostat
removal, testing and replacement — 56
Thermostat (Austin Marina models)
removal and refitting — 194
Throttle
cable
removal and refitting — 70
pedal
removal and refitting — 72
Throttle (Marina Mk 2 models)
pedal
removal and refitting — 197
Timing chain
examination and renovation — 43
removal — 33
tensioner

removal and dismantling — 40
replacement — 48
Timing cover
removal — 33
replacement — 48
Timing gears
examination and renovation — 43
removal — 33
replacement — 48
Timing tensioner
removal — 33
Tools and working facilities — 11
Torque converter
removal and replacement — 108
Torsion bar
removal and refitting — 162

U

Universal joints
dismantling — 116
inspection and repair — 113
renewal — 116

V

Valve guides
examination and renovation — 44
removal — 33
Valve and seats
examination and renovation — 42
Valve and spring
reassembly — 50

Voltage stabilizer
removal and replacement — 151

W

Water pump
dismantling and overhaul — 58
refitting — 50
removal and refitting — 56
Water pump (Austin Marina models)
removal and refitting — 196
Wheel alignment — 171
Windows
rear
removal and refitting — 181
Windscreen
demister duct
removal and refitting — 187
removal and refitting — 181
wiper arms
removal and replacement — 144
wiper blades
changing wiping arc — 144
wiper mechanism
fault diagnosis and rectification — 144
wiper motor
dismantling, inspection and reassembly — 145
removal and replacement — 145
Windscreen (Marina Mk 2 models)
demister duct
removal and refitting — 236
Wiper/washer switch (Marina Mk 2 models)
removal and refitting — 225
Wiring diagrams — 153, 240 to 253

Printed by
Haynes Publishing Group
Sparkford Yeovil Somerset
England